THE DAYS OF VENGEANCE

*But when you see Jerusalem surrounded by armies,
then know that her desolation is at hand. Then let those
who are in Judea flee to the mountains, and let those who
are in the midst of the city depart, and let not those who are
in the country enter the city; because these are the Days of
Vengeance, in order that all things which are written may
be fulfilled.*

Luke 21:20-22

THE DAYS OF VENGEANCE

An Exposition of the Book of Revelation

David Chilton

Dominion Press
Tyler, Texas

The Days of Vengeance
An Exposition of the Book of Revelation
by David Chilton

Copyright © 2006, 2011 by Sharon North
Printed June 2022
Originally published © 1987 by Dominion Press

Published in the United States by
Dominion Press
P.O. Box 2778
Dallas, GA 30132

Dominion Press books are available free of charge at www.GaryNorth.com/freebooks

Cover design by Luis Lovelace

Printed in the United States of America

Library of Congress Catalog Card No. 86-050798

David H. Chilton, 1951–1997
The Days of Vengeance: An Exposition of the Book of Revelation

ISBN 0-930462-02-2
1. Eschatology. 2. Millennialism. 3. Postmillennialism
4. Dominion Theology

To my father and mother

TABLE OF CONTENTS

FOREWORD

Readers of the Book of Revelation are either mesmerized or mystified by it. The mesmerized come up with such startling interpretations that the mystified often conclude that sober-minded Christians should leave the book well alone.

David Chilton's commentary ought to be studied by both types of reader. He shows that Revelation is a book, like every other book of the New Testament, addressed primarily to the first-century church and easily understood by them, because they were thoroughly familiar with Old Testament imagery. He shows that once we grasp these idioms, Revelation is not difficult for us to understand either.

Revelation remains, though, a challenging and relevant book for us, not because it gives an outline of world history with special reference to our era, but because it shows us that Christ is in control of world history, and how we should live and pray and worship. In vivid powerful imagery it teaches us what it means to believe in God's sovereignty and justice. May this valuable commentary prompt us to pray with John and the universal church in heaven and on earth, 'Even so come, Lord Jesus!'

Gordon Wenham
The College of St.
Paul and St. Mary
Cheltenham, England

AUTHOR'S PREFACE

From the very beginning, cranks and crackpots have attempted to use Revelation to advocate some new twist on the Chicken Little Doctrine: *The Sky Is Falling!* But, as I hope to show in this exposition, St. John's Apocalypse teaches instead that Christians will overcome all opposition through the work of Jesus Christ. My study has convinced me that a true understanding of this prophecy must be based on the proper application of five crucial interpretive keys:

1. *Revelation is the most "Biblical" book in the Bible.* St. John quotes hundreds of passages from the Old Testament, often with subtle allusions to little-known religious rituals of the Hebrew people. In order to understand Revelation, we need to know our Bibles backward and forward. One reason why this commentary is so large is that I have tried to explain this extensive Biblical background, commenting on numerous portions of Scripture that shed light on St. John's prophecy. I have also reprinted, as Appendix A, Philip Carrington's excellent survey of the Levitical symbolism in Revelation.

2. *Revelation has a system of symbolism.* Almost everyone recognizes that St. John wrote his message in symbols. But the meaning of those symbols is not up for grabs. There is a systematic structure in Biblical symbolism. In order to understand Revelation properly, we must become familiar with the "language" in which it is written. Among other goals, this commentary seeks to bring the Church at least a few steps closer to a truly Biblical Theology of Revelation.

3. *Revelation is a prophecy about imminent events* — events that were about to break loose on the world of the first century. Revelation is not about nuclear warfare, space travel, or the end

of the world. Again and again it specifically warns that "the time is near!" St. John wrote his book as a prophecy of the approaching destruction of Jerusalem in A.D. 70, showing that Jesus Christ had brought the New Covenant and the New Creation. Revelation cannot be understood unless this fundamental fact is taken seriously.

4. *Revelation is a worship service.* St. John did not write a textbook on prophecy. Instead, he recorded a heavenly worship service in progress. One of his major concerns, in fact, is that the worship of God is central to everything in life. It is the most important thing we do. For this reason I have devoted special attention throughout this commentary to the very considerable liturgical aspects of Revelation, and their implications for our worship services today.

5. *Revelation is a book about dominion.* Revelation is not a book about how terrible the Antichrist is, or how powerful the devil is. It is, as the very first verse says, *The Revelation of Jesus Christ.* It tells us about His lordship over all; it tells us about our salvation and victory in the New Covenant, God's "wonderful plan for our life"; it tells us that the kingdom of the world has become the Kingdom of our God, and of His Christ; and it tells us that He and His people shall reign forever and ever.

I have many people to thank for making this book possible. First and foremost, I am grateful to Dr. Gary North, without whose patience and considerable financial investment it simply could not have been written. The week I moved to Tyler, Gary took me along on one of his periodic book-buying sprees at a large used bookstore in Dallas. As I helped him haul hundreds of carefully chosen volumes to the checkstand (I bought a few books, too — a couple every hour or so, just to keep my hand in the game), Gary asked me what long-term project I'd like to work on, along with my other duties at the Institute for Christian Economics. "How about a medium-sized, popular-style, introductory-level, easy-to-read book on Revelation?" I suggested. "I think I could knock something like that out in about three months." That was, almost to the day, 3 years and six months ago — or, as Gary might be tempted to mutter under his breath: A time, times, and half a time. At last, the tribulation has ended.

The book, of course, has vastly outgrown its projected size and scope. No small part of that is due to the Rev. James B.

Jordan and the Rev. Ray Sutton, pastors of Westminster Presbyterian Church in Tyler, Texas, who have greatly influenced my understanding of the Bible's literary and symbolic connections and liturgical structures. The Rev. Ned Rutland, of Westminster Presbyterian Church in Opelousas, Louisiana, read an early version of some chapters and, with consummate tact and graciousness, steered me in a more Biblical direction. James M. Peters, Tyler's resident historian of antiquities and computer whiz, was a rich treasury of information on the ancient world.

There are others who contributed in various ways to the production of this volume. ICE's patient and cheerful secretaries, Mrs. Maureen Peters and Mrs. Lynn Dwelle, assisted me with many technical details and secured out-of-print books; they have developed the virtue of "going the extra mile" into a high art. Typesetter David Thoburn, a true artist, labored long hours in works of supererogation, solving unusual problems and ensuring the high quality and readability of the book. He has abundantly confirmed my conviction of his superior craftsmanship. His assistant, Mrs. Sharon Nelson, was a valuable mediator, making sure our computers remained on speaking terms. The indexes were prepared by Mitch Wright and Vern Crisler.

One of the most outstanding Bible scholars of our day is the British theologian Gordon J. Wenham, of the College of St. Paul and St. Mary, whose knowledgable and well-written commentaries have made a significant mark throughout the evangelical world. My first contact with Dr. Wenham was last year, when, with no advance warning, I sent him a copy of my book *Paradise Restored*. To my great surprise and delight, he wrote back to express his appreciation. This encouraged me (though not without a degree of fear and trembling) to solicit his comments on the uncorrected proofs of the present work. Dr. Wenham graciously took valuable time to read it, to offer suggestions, and to write the Foreword. I am grateful for his kindness. Naturally, he cannot be held responsible for the numerous shortcomings of this book.

The latter point should perhaps be emphasized. This commentary makes no claim whatsoever to be the "last word" on the subject; indeed, if my eschatology is correct, the Church has many more years left to write many more words! I am greatly indebted to the important contributions of many other commentators — especially Philip Carrington, Austin Farrer, J. Massyngberde Ford, Meredith G. Kline, J. Stuart Russell, Moses Stuart, Henry Barclay Swete, and Milton S. Terry — and I hope I have done justice to them in building on their foundation. Yet I am painfully aware that the task of commenting on St. John's magnificent prophecy far exceeds my abilities. Where I have failed adequately to set forth the message of the Revelation, I beg the indulgence of my brothers and sisters in Christ, and earnestly desire their comments and corrections. Letters may be addressed to me at P.O. Box 2314, Placerville, CA 95667.

My beloved wife, Darlene, has always been my greatest source of encouragement. Our children (Nathan David, Jacob Israel, and Abigail Aviva) endured our collective "exile to Patmos" with true Johannine grace (mixed, perhaps, with occasional rumblings of Boanergean thunder as well!); and if their bedtime stories were somehow filled with more than the usual quota of cherubs, dragons, flying horses, and flaming swords, they never complained.

Finally, I am grateful to my parents, the Rev. and Mrs. Harold B. Chilton. I was immeasurably blessed to grow up in a home where the Word of God is so highly honored, so faithfully taught, so truly lived. The environment they structured was constantly flooded with musical grandeur and richness, as the atmosphere was charged with rousing theological discussion, all in the context of caring for the needy, sheltering the homeless, feeding the hungry, and bringing to all the precious message of the Gospel. From the steaming jungles and rice paddies of the Philippines to the shaded lawns of Southern California, they set before me a remarkable and unforgettable example of what it means to be bondservants of the Lord. Some of my earliest memories are of seeing my parents' faith tested beyond what seemed the limits of human endurance; and when God had tried them, they came forth as gold. Holding forth the Testimony of Jesus, suffering the loss of all things in order to win Christ, they are what St. John has exhorted us all to be: faithful witnesses. This book is dedicated to them.

David Chilton
Tyler, Texas
May 8, 1986
Ascension Day

PUBLISHER'S PREFACE

Gary North

In the first edition of *The Days of Vengeance* (1987), I included a Publisher's Preface. This is no longer appropriate, because my wife now owns the rights to this book and also David Chilton's other books on eschatology, *Paradise Restored* (1985) and *The Great Tribulation* (1987). Yet I decided that this reprint deserves a new Preface. Two decades have made a difference.[1]

This Preface includes some of what I wrote in late 1986, but it deletes my predictions about the impact that this book would have. Most of those predictions have turned out to be accurate. The book has gone through several printings. In 1996, Steve Gregg was assigned the task by Nelson Reference, Thomas Nelson's scholarly book division, of compiling a book of parallel commentaries on the Book of Revelation. Each major Protestant eschatological system was to be represented. He wrote to my wife to seek permission to include long extracts of *Days of Vengeance*. She gave permission. The book is titled, *Revelation: Four Views*. It was published in 1997. After you finish reading *Days of Vengeance*, I think you will understand why Mr. Gregg wanted David Chilton in his compilation.

So, issues that matter today are not always those that seemed to matter in 1986. Back then, I was deliberately positioning this book as a classic-to-be. Today, it has achieved classic status. It

---

1. Anyone who wants to read my original Preface can do so by going to my Web site: **www.freebooks.com**. There, all of the theological books and articles that I either wrote or published are available free of charge. You can read them on-screen or print them out.

achieved this almost immediately after its publication. Here, I attempt to show the reader why it is a classic.

What matters greatly to me may not matter much to you. So, let us get to three issues that I sincerely hope matter to you.

Ask Yourself Three Crucial Questions

First, have ever wondered why Christians in the United States are clearly in the majority, and always have been, yet they have so little cultural influence?

Here are three good reasons: (1) They have no plan; (2) they have little or no personal incentive; (3) they see no long-run hope of success.

In contrast are the anti-Christians, who either dominate American culture or plan to replace those who do. For example, throughout most of the twentieth century, American Communists made long-term plans for a political revolution, and they attempted to implement these plans. The evolutionists who control the media have plans to retain control. Yet the Christians have no plans. Why not?

Here is one reason: They are so utterly pessimistic about the cultural future of Christianity that they see no reason to commit resources – especially time – to long-term programs of cultural capture and transformation. They are not like their cultural opponents, who have been optimistic about their prospects for retaining control over American culture or transforming it.

Yet opinions can change. After the bureaucratic Communist leaders of the Soviet Union finally lost faith in the future of Soviet Communism – no later than the 1980 Moscow Olympics, when they saw how wealthy non-Russians attendees were – they eventually surrendered the entire Communist empire in just three days: August 19–21, 1991. However, they did not surrender to Christians, who had no interest in gaining influence and the accompanying responsibility. The Communists surrendered to other humanists. Once again, Christians sat on the sidelines, just watching events. They did not take the lead.

Second, let me ask you another question. What about you? Are you tired of sitting in the back of humanism's bus?

Third, let me ask you one final question. Do you think God has predestinated Christians to sit in the back of humanism's bus – or Islam's – until the end of time? If your answer is "no," you have bought the right book.

David Chilton, more than anyone else in the twentieth century, called Christians back to faith in the future of Christianity. He provided biblical reasons for believing that God has promised victory to His people – not just in heaven, not just after the long-delayed any-moment Rapture, but in history.

Who Was David Chilton, and What Did He Accomplish?

In 1997, David Chilton died of heart failure at a young age: 45. He was a gifted writer. I say this on the basis of considerable experience. I have supported myself by writing ever since 1967. From 1974 until 1992, I was an editor of other people's books and articles.[2] I have only encountered one author in my career whose work needed no editing: David Chilton. I regard him as the most skilled Bible expositor of my generation, if we consider all three factors: grammar (textual exposition), logic (theology), and rhetoric (style).[3]

With his first book on eschatology, *Paradise Restored* (1985),[4] he launched an eschatological revival. "Revolution" would be too strong a word, for his viewpoint is an old one, and it was widely held in early America. Overnight, *Paradise Restored* began to influence religious leaders, especially in two segments of

---

2. I edited *The Journal of Christian Reconstruction* from its inception in 1974 through 1981.

3. Amazingly, he did not like to write. His password for his Corvus external hard disk drive (1986 technology) was *suffer*. He wrote *Power in the Blood* (1987), a book on AIDS, published by the soon-defunct publishing house Wolgemuth & Hyatt. He never wrote another book.

4. David Chilton, *Paradise Restored: A Biblical Theology of Dominion* (Ft. Worth: Dominion Press, 1985). This is available free of charge on **www.free-books.com**.

American Christianity: Pentecostal-charismatic and Calvinistic. It changed the minds of people who had believed all their adult lives that the biblical case for cultural victory was long dead – a relic of the nineteenth century.

Then came *The Days of Vengeance*, a verse-by-verse exposition of the most difficult book in the Bible.[5] What was generalized in *Paradise Restored* is supported here with chapter and verse – indeed, lots and lots of chapters and verses.

His third book, *The Great Tribulation* (1987),[6] is a short paperback extension of what is in *Days of Vengeance*.

Days of Vengeance is not just another boring commentary on the Book of Revelation, which nobody is likely to read. It is not a book to be put on a shelf, unread, to gather dust. Yet even if it were only that, its publication would have been a major event in 1987, because the publication of any conservative, Bible-believing commentary on the Book of Revelation is a major event. William Hendriksen's amillennial commentary, *More Than Conquerors*, was published in 1939, and is less than half the size of this one, and not in the same league in terms of Biblical scholarship. Yet it remains in print and is regarded by amillennialists as definitive, or close to it. John Walvoord's dispensational *Revelation of Jesus Christ* (1966) is only half the size of Chilton's, yet it remains in print. Despite all the fascination with biblical prophecy in the twentieth century, full-length commentaries on this most prophetic of biblical books were rare.

Commentaries on Revelation have always have been rare. Few commentators have dared to explain the book. John Calvin taught through all the books of the Bible, save one: Revelation. Martin Luther wrote something in the range of a hundred volumes of material, but he did not write a commentary on Revelation. Moses Stuart wrote a great one in the mid-nineteenth century,

---

6. Ft. Worth, Texas: Dominion Press, 1987. It is available free of charge on **www.freebooks.com**.

5. The possible exception is Ezekiel, on which the Book of Revelation depends heavily.

but it is forgotten today. The Book of Revelation has resisted almost all previous attempts to unlock its secret of secrets. Then David Chilton discovered this secret, the long-lost key that "unlocks the code."

This long-ignored key is the Old Testament.

The Old Testament Background

"Very funny," you may be saying to yourself. All right, I will admit it: It is funny – funny peculiar, not funny ha, ha. What Chilton does in this book is to go back again and again to the Old Testament in order to make sense of the Apostle John's frame of reference. This exegetical technique works. It is the only technique that does work for the Book of Revelation!

Those people who never worked personally with Chilton cannot readily appreciate his detailed knowledge of the Bible, especially the Old Testament. I used him dozens of times as my personal concordance. He worked in the office next to mine. I would yell to him: "Hey, David, do you know where I can find the passage about. . . ?" I would relate a smattering of a Bible story, or some disjointed verse that was rattling around in my memory, and he would almost instantly tell me the chapter. He might or might not get the exact verse; usually, he was within three or four verses. That was always close enough. Rare was the occasion when he could not think of it; even then he would putter around in his extensive personal library until he found it. It never took him long.

In this book, he took his remarkable memory of the Old Testament, and he fused it with an interpretive technique developed by James Jordan in his book, *Judges: God's War Against Humanism* (1985).[7] In that book, Jordan worked with dozens of Old Testament symbols that he had sifted from the historical narratives and the descriptions of the Tabernacle

---

7. Tyler, Texas: Geneva Ministries, 1985. This is available for free on **www. freebooks.com**.

and Temple. Then he applied these symbols and models to other parallel Bible stories, including the New Testament's account of the life of Christ and the early church. Chilton successfully applied this same Biblical hermeneutic (principle of interpretation) to the Book of Revelation in many creative ways. He was not the first expositor to do this, as his footnotes and appendixes reveal, but he was unquestionably the best at it that the Christian church has yet produced with respect to the Book of Revelation. These Old Testament background stories and symbols make sense of the difficult passages in Revelation. Chilton makes clear the many connections between Old and New Testament symbolic language and historical references. This is why his commentary is so easy to read, despite the magnitude of what he has accomplished academically.

The Missing Piece: The Covenant Structure

There was a missing piece in the puzzle, however, and this kept the book in Chilton's computer for an extra year, at least. That missing piece was identified in the fall of 1985 by Pastor Ray Sutton. Sutton had been seriously burned in a kitchen accident, and his mobility had been drastically reduced. This gave him time to work on a manuscript on the symbolism of the sacraments. After he had completed the first draft, a crucial connection occurred to him. The connection was supplied by Westminster Seminary Professor Meredith G. Kline.

Years earlier, he had read Professor Kline's studies on the ancient suzerainty (kingly) treaties of the ancient Near East.[8] Pagan kings would establish covenants with their vassals. Kline had pointed out that these treaties paralleled the structure of the Book of Deuteronomy. They had five points: (1) an identification of the king; (2) the historical events that led to the establishment of the covenant; (3) stipulations (terms) of the covenant; (4) a warning

---

8. Meredith G. Kline, *Treaty of the Great King* (Grand Rapids: Eerdmans, 1963); reprinted in part in his later book, *The Structure of Biblical Authority* (Grand Rapids: Eerdmans, 1972).

of judgment against anyone who disobeyed, but a promise of blessing to those who did obey; and (5) a system of reconfirming the treaty at the death of the king or the vassal.

Kline had developed a few of the implications of this covenant scheme. Sutton developed a great many more. These remarkable, path-breaking discoveries can be found in his book, *That You May Prosper.*[9] This book has almost nothing to do with his original manuscript on the sacraments, which he abandoned. After I read Sutton's new manuscript, I recognized the five-point model in the two-part structure of the Ten Commandments (5-5), just before I had finished my economic commentary on the Ten Commandments.[10] It also governs the structure of Exodus, Leviticus, and Deuteronomy. This insight later helped me to structure my commentaries on all three books of the Pentateuch.

Sutton presented his discovery in a series of Wednesday night Bible studies. The first night that Chilton heard one of them, he was stunned. He came up to Sutton after the message and told him that this was clearly the key to Revelation's structure. He had been trying to work with a four-point model, and he had be come thoroughly stuck. Chilton went back to work, and within a few weeks he had restructured the manuscript. Within a few months, he had finished it, after three and a half years. (Time, times, and half a time.)

The Days of Vengeance is especially concerned with Revelation's covenant structure and the historical focus of its judgment passages. If, as Chilton argues so brilliantly, these passages of imminent doom and gloom relate to the fall of Jerusalem in 70 A.D., then there is no legitimate way to build a case for a Great Tribulation that lies ahead of us. It is long behind us. Thus, the Book of Revelation cannot legitimately be used to buttress the

---

9. Ray R. Sutton, *That You May Prosper: Dominion By Covenant* (Tyler, Texas: Institute for Christian Economics, 1897).Second edition: 1992.This is available free on **www.freebooks.com**.

10. Gary North, *The Sinai Strategy: Economics and the Ten Commandments* (Tyler, Texas: Institute for Christian Economics, 1986), Preface. This is available for free on **www.freebooks.com**.

case for eschatological pessimism. A lot of readers will reject his thesis at this point. The ones who are serious about the Bible will finish reading it before they reject his thesis.

This leads to a conclusion: Fear of the Great Tribulation is illegitimate. In the past, this fear has been a major disincentive for Christians to sacrifice both time and treasure in order to build up the comprehensive kingdom of God on earth and in history. When Christians at long last abandon this fear, they can begin to challenge the Establishment that dominates Western culture.

But if there is no Great Tribulation ahead of us, then what of the any-moment Rapture – a word that does not appear in the Bible? Could it be that the passages used by expositors to support the Rapture doctrine actually apply to the final judgment? If so, then there is an answer to a question that baffles all dispensational theologians: Why did Christ deny in the parable of the wheat and the tares that the two would ever be separated prior to the final judgment (Matt. 13)?[11]

Pessimism and Paralysis

The vast majority of Christians through the ages have believed that things will get progressively worse in almost every area of life until Jesus returns with His angels. Premillennialists believe that He will then establish an earthly visible kingdom, with Christ in charge and bodily present. Amillennialists do not believe in any earthly visible kingdom of God prior to the final judgment. They believe that only the church and Christian schools and Christian families will visibly represent God's kingdom on earth. The world will fall increasingly under the domination of Satan.[12] Both

---

11. Gary North, *Priorities and Dominion: An Economic Commentary on Matthew*, 2nd electronic edition (Harrisonburg, Virginia: Dominion Educational Ministries, Inc., [2000] 2003), ch. 29. This is available for free here: **www.garynorth. com**, *Capitalism and the Bible*.

12. Gary North, *Millennialism and Social Theory* (Tyler, Texas: Institute for Christian Economics, 1990), chaps 4, 5. This is available for free on **www.free-books.com**.

eschatologies teach the cultural defeat of Christ's church prior to His physical return in power. Both deny that the *kingdom of God* means the *civilization of God*. For both groups, all civilizations will be God-hating in the church era.

A practical problem results from such an outlook. When the predictable defeats in life come, Christians have a theological incentive to shrug their shoulders, and say to themselves, "That's life. That's the way God prophesied it would be. Things are getting worse." They read the dreary headlines of the daily newspaper or on the Web, and they think to themselves, "Jesus' return is just around the corner . . . and just in time!" The inner strength that people need to rebound from life's normal external defeats is sapped by a theology that preaches inevitable earthly defeat for the church of Jesus Christ. People think to themselves: "If even God's holy church cannot triumph, then how can *I* expect to triumph?" Christians therefore become the psychological victims of pessimistic headlines. They begin with a false assumption: the inevitable defeat in history of Christ's church by Satan's earthly forces, despite the fact that Satan was mortally wounded at Calvary. Satan is not "alive and well on Planet Earth." He is alive, but he is not well. To argue otherwise is to argue for the historical impotence and cultural irrelevance of Christ's work on Calvary. This line of reasoning leads to an unpleasant yet inevitable conclusion, namely, that Christ's bodily resurrection is irrelevant to history and culture, and so is his ascension to the right hand of God. So, in addition, is the sending of the Holy Spirit at Pentecost. Despite all of this, we are assured by pessimillennialists,[13] Satan will triumph in history representatively during the entire era of the institutional church. Why representatively? Because Satan is not omnipresent, unlike God. He rules representatively through fallen angels that are not trustworthy and human beings who also are not trustworthy. Yet his utterly untrustworthy army will defeat Christ's people in history.

---

13. The term was coined by Dr. Francis Nigel Lee.

Even though neither Satan nor Christ rules physically on earth, Christians believe that Christ's representatives are doomed to failure in their attempts to displace Satan's representatives until Christ returns bodily to give them victory. They do not believe this verse: "And I say also unto thee, That thou art Peter, and upon this rock I will build my church; and the gates of hell shall not prevail against it" (Matt. 16:18). Instead, they think of the church as defensively besieged by Satan's offensive army. They have things backwards. This is because they have eschatology backwards.

Although pessimistic eschatologies have been popular with American Protestants ever since the 1870's, there has always been an alternative theology, a theology of dominion. This was the reigning faith of the New England Puritans in the first generation (1630–1660), when they began to subdue the wilderness. It was also a widely shared faith in the era of the American Revolution. Jonathan Edwards held it. But it began to fade under the onslaught of Darwinian evolutionary thought in the second half of the nineteenth century. It almost completely disappeared after World War I, but it is rapidly returning today. David Chilton's books on eschatology were the primary manifestos in this revival of theological optimism.

In the years that followed the publication of *Days of Vengeance*, the Institute for Christian Economics published three of Kenneth Gentry's books, *The Beast of Revelation* (1989), *Before Jerusalem Fell: Dating the Book of Revelation* (1989), and *The Greatness of the Great Commission* (1990). Then ICE published Gentry's definitive exposition of postmillennialism, *He Shall Have Dominion* (1992).[14] American Vision published Gary DeMar's *Last Days Madness* (1999),[15] a comprehensive critique of popular dispensationalism's end-times prophecies.

---

14. All of these are available for free on **www.freebooks.com**.

15. Gary DeMar, *Last Days Madness: Obsession of the Modern Church*, 4th ed. (Powder Springs, GA: American Vision, 1999).

Producing New Leaders: Key to Victory

Because pessimillennialism cannot offer students long-term hope in the long-term positive effects on earth of their life's work, both of the pessimillennial movements have defaulted culturally. This withdrawal from cultural commitment culminated during the fateful years, 1965–70. In that brief period, radicals and counter-culturalists challenged the entire American Establishment. Some called for revolution. Others followed Dr. Timothy Leary's recommendation: "Tune in, turn on, drop out." I ask: When the world went through that psychological, cultural, and intellectual revolution, where were the concrete and specific Christian answers to the pressing problems of that turbulent era? Nothing of substance came from traditional seminaries. It was as if their faculty members believed that the world would never advance beyond the dominant issues of 1952. Even back in 1952, seminary professors were mostly whispering. The leaders of traditional Christianity lost their opportunity to capture the best minds of a generation. They were perceived as being muddled and confused. There was a reason for this. They were muddled and confused.

In the 1970's, only two groups within the Christian community came before the Christian public and announced: "We have the biblical answers."[16] They were at opposite ends of the political spectrum: the liberation theologians on the Left

---

16. Francis Schaeffer had been announcing since 1965 that humanist civilization is an empty shell, and that it has no earthly future. He repeated over and over that Christianity has the questions that humanism cannot answer. The problem was that as a Calvinistic premillennialist, he did not believe that any specifically Christian answers would ever be implemented before Christ's second coming. He did not devote much space in his books to providing specifically Christian answers to the Christian questions that he raised to challenge humanist civilization. He asked excellent cultural questions; he offered few specifically Christian answers. There were reasons for this: Gary North and David Chilton, "Apologetics and Strategy," *Christianity and Civilization*, 3 (1983), pp. 107–16. This journal is available on **www. freebooks.com**.

and the Christian Reconstructionists on the Right.[17] The battle between these groups intensified in the 1980's. Chilton's book, *Productive Christians in an Age of Guilt-Manipulators* (1981),[18] was the most important single document from the Right in this theological confrontation. But from the confused middle, there were no clear-cut biblical answers to either of these two positions.

The future of pessimillennialism is being eroded by its own success. As the world's social crises intensify, and as it becomes apparent that traditional conservative Protestantism still has no effective, specific, uniquely biblical, workable answers to the social crises of our day, a drastic and presently unanticipated shift of Christian opinion probably will take place – an event analogous to the collapse of a dam. There will be a revolution in the way that millions of conservative Christians think. Then there will be a revolution in what they do. As I wrote in December, 1986,

> The liberation theologians will not win this battle for the minds of Christians. There will be a religious backlash against the Left on a scale not seen in the West since the Bolshevik Revolution, and perhaps not since the French Revolution.

That prediction was fulfilled within five years. In a remarkable three-day revolution, the Soviet Union collapsed. That incredible

---

17. In the highly restricted circles of amillennial Calvinism, a short-lived movement of North American Dutch scholars appeared, 1965–75, the "cosmonomic idea" school, also known as the neoDooyeweerdians, named after the Dutch legal scholar and philosopher, Herman Dooyeweerd. They made little impression outside of the North American Dutch community, and by 1980 had faded into obscurity. Their precursors in the early 1960's had been more conservative, but after 1965, too many of them became ideological fellow travellers of the liberation theologians. They could not compete with the harder-core radicalism represented by *Sojourners* and *The Other Side*, and they faded.

18. David Chilton, *Productive Christians in an Age of Guilt-Manipulators: A Biblical Response to Ronald J. Sider* (Tyler, Texas: Institute for Christian Economics, 1981). This book went through three different editions. It was the best-selling book that the ICE published. It is available on **www.freebooks.com**.

series of events can be dated: August 19–21, 1991. The bureaucrats of the Russian Communist empire simply surrendered. Nothing like this had ever taken place in recorded history.[19]

Within weeks, Marxism became a joke on college campuses around the world. Discount book bins began filling up with books with titles such as *What Marx Really Meant*. After 1991, nobody cared what Marx had meant. Marxism had committed the worst of all sins in the world of humanism. It had become passé.

Liberation theology by 1992 was as dead as Marxism, which meant room-temperature dead. Liberation theology went down with Marxism's doomed ship. Orbis Books ceased to be relevant. Liberation theologians had bet on the wrong horse in the biggest match race of the twentieth century. It was winner take all. They took nothing. They did not make it to the lifeboats in time.

Today, Christian leadership in the future will come from the Christian school movement. A generation of Christians is now being trained to call into question the worldview of humanism. For example, there is the immensely successful weekly publication for Christian day schools, *God's World News*. Where did that idea come from? From David Chilton, who recommended such a publication in a newsletter published by ICE, *The Biblical Educator* (Sept. 1980).[20] The founders of *God's World News* took him seriously. The profits generated by *God's World News* then financed the creation of *World Magazine*.

The most important institutional strategy that the existing leadership of any movement must adopt is a program of convincing the movement's future leaders that the movement has the

---

19. The Russian Communist Party's money immediately disappeared. There has never been an accounting of where these billions of dollars worth of assets went. Soon, the factories were in the hands of the Party members as corporations. What happened in 1991 is simple to explain: the Communist Empire was privatized in the single greatest theft in modern history. It turned out that Karl Marx was right: money talks. The mode of production – capitalism – bought off the Communist leaders. They got rich – capitalist rich – overnight. The Russian and Eastern European citizens lost their Marxist chains.

20. This is on-line at **www.freebooks.com**.

vision, the program, and the first principles to defeat all enemies. To be convincing, this strategy requires evidence for such superiority. Such evidence is presently lacking within traditional pessimillennial groups. They begin with the presupposition that God has not given His church the vision, program, and first principles to defeat God's enemies, even with Christ's victory over Satan at Calvary as the foundation of the Church's ministry. The fact that God sent the Holy Spirit to lead His people into all truth does not impress the pessimillennialists. They think the truth which the Spirit has brought is this: "God's people will not win in history." Yet the Book of Job teaches a different story. But pessimillennialists regard the optimism of the Old Testament as a huge theological mistake. They think the Old Testament authors did not understand the inspiring truth of the New Testament, namely, that Christ's bodily resurrection and ascension have guaranteed historical defeat for His church.

Go figure.

Rival Claimants

The Christian evangelical Left – represented by Sojourners, Evangelicals for Social Action, and The Other Side – still operates. These organizations have very little influence in Bible-believing churches. Their main spokesman in the late 1970's and early 1980's was historian Ronald J. Sider. But Sider never recovered intellectually from Chilton's *Productive Christians in an Age of Guilt-Manipulators*. In the same issue of *Christianity Today* (April 28, 1997) in which Chilton's obituary appeared, Sider admitted that he was no longer advocating the same radical analysis and agenda that he had proposed in the 1977 edition of *Rich Christians in an Age of Hunger*. The 1997 edition adopted almost a dozen of Chilton's proposed recommendations.[21]

---

21. Gary North, "The Economic Re-education of Ronald J. Sider" (1997), reprinted in Gary North, *Inheritance and Dominion: An Economic Commentary on Deuteronomy*, 2nd electronic edition (Harrisonburg, Virginia: Dominion Educational Ministries, Inc., [1999] 2003), Appendix F.

Yet Sider never mentioned Chilton's book in any of his four revisions. His influence has waned.

The main spokesman for the evangelical Left in the late 1980s and 1990s was Tony Campolo, a sociologist. He is a very effective speaker. He wrote a lot of books that offered little exegesis of biblical texts. His career suffered a dramatic decline when President Clinton was caught in the Monica Lewinsky scandal. Campolo had been one of Clinton's spiritual counsellors. Articles in the *New York Times* and the liberal *Christian Century* undermined his reputation, both in the political Left and the evangelical Left.[22]

This leaves Jim Wallis of Sojourners. He has yet to provide textual/exegetical support for his constant calls for more State welfare to the poor. He is a full-time political activist. He is in no sense a theorist or theologian. (I provide a critique of his *Sojourner* editorials, one by one, on my Web site, **www.garynorth. com**: *Questions for Jim Wallis*.)

Today, radical Islam seems to be the only consistent worldview that is giving Christianity a serious challenge for the hearts of men – though not their minds. Islam is non-philosophical. But Islam is an old, old enemy of Christianity. It offers nothing new. It is also ill-equipped to survive in the modernism of a high-technology, consumerist world. By the time it can impose its law by majoritarian force in Western Europe or anywhere outside the economically backward ex-Soviet "stans" and the Middle East, high-tech entertainment will have eroded Islam's appeal for its teenage children. Islam is about to face what Christianity faced after 1660: the humanist world order. It is not prepared for this.

Christianity went through the humanist wringer from about 1660 until the 1970's. Ever since the late 1970's, there has been

---

22. Laurie Goodstein, "Clinton Selects Clerics to Give Him Guidance," *New York Times* (Sept. 15, 1998). **www.snipurl.com/mszs** "Clergy respond to Clinton affair," *Christian Century* (Oct. 7, 1998). **www.snipurl.com/mszi** Campolo's version of all this appears in an article published by the liberal establishment think-tank, the Brooking Institution: "Errant Evangelical? A Presidential Counselor in the Line of Fire," *Brookings Review* (Spring 1999), pp. 33–35. **www.snipurl.com/mszq**

a reversal in the United States. Christian activism has become acceptable to millions of fundamentalists, who for decades avoided politics and academic confrontation like the plague. They got involved in politics, and you do not get involved in politics in order to lose. They have become *operational* eschatological optimists – optimillennialists, in other words. This was one reason why Chilton's books had an audience in the 1980's. The allure of dispensationalism was fading. Those leaders in American fundamentalism who told their followers they had an obligation to get involved politically simply ceased preaching about Bible prophecy and the imminent Rapture. At the same time, humanism visibly went in defensive mode. It had lost its old self-confidence. Christianity is now on the upswing around the world: sub-Sahara Africa, Latin America, and China.[23]

When Christians in Third World countries come to exercise social and political authority because of their greater productivity, they will face this question: "What are we supposed to do now, in God's name?" Pessimillennialists have no explicitly biblical answers, for their eschatology has taught that there will never come a time when Christians will be called upon to exercise civil and social leadership. Pessimillennialists have therefore never had any incentive to develop comprehensive practical materials based in the Bible. Their social theology is the theology of the rescue mission. Chilton's was not.

Traditional Pessimillennialism

Here, I cover three viewpoints: traditional dispensationalism, historic premillennialism, and amillennialism. There are three main variants of dispensationalism: pre-tribulation Rapture (majority view), mid-tribulation Rapture, and post-tribulation Rapture. There is also a new variant called progressive dispensationalism. It was proposed over two decades ago by younger faculty members

---

23. Philip Jenkins, *The Next Christendom: The Coming of Global Christianity* (New York: Oxford University Press, 2002). A summary appears here: Jenkins, "The Next Christianity," *The Atlantic Monthly* (Oct. 2002).

at Dallas Theological Seminary. I have yet to see a detailed exposition of the position. I have waited two decades. But I am patient. Maybe it will appear someday.

Dispensationalism

Most people do not understand that there has not been a major dispensational commentary on the Book of Revelation since John Walvoord's *The Revelation of Jesus Christ*, published in 1966 by Moody Press and then reprinted repeatedly.

Even more significantly, there had not been a major dispensational commentary on Revelation before Walvoord's book. Understand, Walvoord's commentary appeared 87 years after W. E. B.'s *Jesus Is Coming*, the book that launched dispensationalism's popular phase in the United States. It appeared over half a century after the *Scofield Reference Bible* (1909). In short, the exegesis that supposedly proves the case for dispensationalism came at the tail end of the dispensational movement's history. The dispensationalists in 1987 could point to only a handful of books with titles such as *Lectures on Revelation* or *Notes on Revelation*. In short, bits and pieces on Revelation, but nothing definitive – not after over a century of premillennial dispensationalism. The bibliography in Walvoord's book lists a small number of explicitly dispensational commentaries on this book of the Bible, above all others, that we would expect the dispensationalists to have mastered, verse by verse.

Chilton's book was published in 1987. In early 1988, I decided to launch a newsletter, *Dispensationalism in Transition*. Why? Because I recognized what should have been obvious: 1988 was the 40th anniversary of the establishment of the State of Israel. The so-called "generation of the fig tree" had run out of time. The Rapture should have taken place seven years earlier, in 1981. I knew that the theologians at dispensational seminaries would have problems explaining this development.

In 1988, Dallas Theological Seminary allowed Lewis Sperry Chafer's *Systematic Theology* to be published by another publisher after 40 years. It was during this period that faculty members began promoting progressive dispensationalism. What this is, exactly, they did not say, nor have they ever said. There is still no systematic theology that describes it or defends it. Nevertheless, the old theology was quietly abandoned at Dallas by most of the faculty members under age fifty.

There was a brief flare-up of the old-time religion with Saddam Hussein's invasion of Kuwait. John Walvoord revised an old paperback book, *Armageddon, Oil, and the Middle East Crisis* (1973). The 1991 re-write sold 1.5 million copies, but was forgotten by 1992, just as the first version was forgotten by 1974. The first edition was written in the year of the OPEC oil crisis. The second was published just as the six-month build-up for the Gulf War was in its final stages. Both books were newspaper headline books. They sank into oblivion as soon as the headlines changed. This happens to every pop dispensational paperback book. But there is always another one at the printers.

Today, the traditional dispensational movement is being carried by the *Left Behind* novels. A theological movement that is sustained by novels rather than by theological treatises is in its final stages. The novels are not sustained by a theology that their author is willing to defend in public debate. Gary DeMar has had a standing challenge to debate Tim LaHaye publicly for two decades, long before the first novel appeared. Rev. LaHaye has wisely and prudently declined the offer. DeMar wrote a book proving his theological points against *Left Behind*. It was published by a major Christian book publishing house.[24] Rev. LaHaye wisely and prudently declined to respond in print. And so it goes, decade after decade. But the steady decline of the independent Bible Church movement is obvious today. Bible churches have become Fellowship Bible churches, which do not mention dispensational theology except as an occasional after-

---

24. Gary DeMar, *End Times Fiction: A Biblical Consideration of the **Left Behind** Theology* (Nashville: Thomas Nelson Sons, 2001).

thought. Upbeat music is their thing, not eschatology. Traditional dispensationalism is being left behind.

Whatever we conclude about the history of dispensationalism, its wide popularity had very little to do with any systematic exposition of the book that dispensationalists assert is the most prophecy-filled book in the Bible. In fact, the average dispensationalist probably does not own, has not read, and has never heard of a single dispensational commentary on the Book of Revelation. It is doubtful that his pastor knows of one, either, other than Walvoord's, which is about half the size of Chilton's and four decades old.

My point is this: It is important to get the foundations laid early if you intend to reconstruct civilization. This is what the dispensationalists has not done, 1830 to today. There are no books that present a case for dispensational social theory. Dispensationalists have never intended to change culture or civilization. They have intended only to escape from what they regarded as modern civilization's more unsavory features, things such as liquor, cigarettes, movies, and social dancing. (I have often said that if anti-abortionists were to spread the rumor that the local abortionist gives a glass of beer to each woman to calm her nerves after an abortion, half the fundamentalists in town would be on the picket lines in front of his office within a week.)

Historic Premillennialism

Historic premillennialism teaches that Jesus will return after the Great Tribulation to set up an earthly kingdom. There will not be a Rapture to begin this earthly reign, which will not be uniquely associated with Jews, Israel, or a rebuilt temple.

There isn't any historic (non-dispensational) premillennialism, institutionally speaking. Historic premillennialists are scattered in churches that are dominated either by dispensational premillennialists or amillennialists. Covenant Theological Seminary does exist, but its graduates get swallowed up ecclesiastically in churches that are eschatologically neutral officially, meaning churches run by amillennialists. Historic premillennialism has not been a separate theological force for over a century.

Amillennialism

Protestant amillennialists, who are primarily members of Dutch or Lutheran churches, or churches influenced by Continental European theology, have a far stronger academic tradition behind them. It stretches back to Augustine.[25] They teach that there is an inescapable process of victory of Satan's kingdom over Christ's as history progresses. Sometimes this process accelerates. Occasionally, it suffers a reversal. But there is no escape from the victory culturally of covenant-breakers.[26]

Amillennial churches are not noted for their evangelism programs. These churches are not out in the theological arena, challenging humanists or anyone else. Members see their churches as holding actions, as defensive fortresses, or as ports in the cultural storm. These churches are simply not on the offensive. Its members do not expect to achieve anything culturally. They also do not expect to see a wave of converts.

Yet this is a popular eschatological position. It conveys the same message as premillennialism: Because God has foreordained cultural defeat for His church, there is no reason for Christians to spend time and money on long-term projects of Christian civilization-building. The amillennialist agrees with the conclusion of the fundamentalist radio preacher of the 1950's, J. Vernon McGee: "You don't polish brass on a sinking ship." Postmillennialism teaches that the ship is not sinking. This creates areas of responsibility for Christians, which include navigation theory, leadership skills, capital investing, and a will-

---

25. Chilton draws from these amillennial traditions in explaining Biblical imagery. Nevertheless, Chilton has demonstrated that this imagery can be understood far better within a framework of historical Christian progress than within a framework that presumes increasing historical defeat at the hands of covenant-breakers.

26. The most explicit amillennial theologian is David Engelsma of the tiny Dutch denomination, the Protestant Reformed Church.

ingness to take over the helm whenever God makes this opportunity available. This is why postmillennialism is unpopular.
Christians want to avoid additional responsibility.

Conclusion

The fundamental message of Biblical eschatology is victory,
in time and on earth in the era of the church – comprehensive
victory, not simply a psychologically internal, "smile on our faces,
joy in our hearts" sort of victory. In short, the Christian is supposed to make effective use of the covenant-breakers' scholarly
contributions or medical contributions or cultural contributions,
but he must not thereby become dependent on their underlying eschatological presuppositions. He must beat something with something better. He cannot legitimately expect to beat something with
nothing. This is Chilton's position. It is not a popular position.

I knew in 1986 that there would be critics of this book. To
head off some of this criticism, I called attention to the book's
Foreword, written by Professor Gordon Wenham. At the time,
there was probably no more respected Bible-believing Old Testament commentator in the English-speaking world. His commentary on Leviticus sets a high intellectual standard. If Gordon
Wenham says that *The Days of Vengeance* is worth considering,
then to fail to consider it would be a major tactical error on the
part of the pessimillennialists. As I wrote in late 1986,

> I will go further than Wenham does. This book is a land-
> mark effort, the finest commentary on Revelation in the
> history of the Church. It has set the standard for: (1) its
> level of scholarship, (2) its innovative insights per page,
> and (3) its readability. This unique combination – almost
> unheard of in academic circles – leaves the intellectual
> opposition nearly defenseless.

I also wrote that the critics would be unable to challenge this
book academically. I think my prediction was correct.

Read it and see why.

INTRODUCTION

Author and Date

Although the author's identity has been much debated, there is really no reason to doubt that he was the same St. John who wrote the Fourth Gospel, as the virtually unanimous testimony of the early Church affirms. He identifies himself simply as "John" (1:1, 4, 9; 21:2; 22:8), apparently assuming that he will be recognized by his first-century audience on the basis of his name alone; and he writes in an authoritative, "apostolic" style, not to individuals merely, but to the Church. Taking into account the Church's highly organized government, which existed from its inception, it is unlikely that any but a recognized apostle could have written in this manner.[1] In addition, there are numerous points of resemblance between the Revelation and the Gospel of John. Even a cursory glance reveals several expressions (e.g. *Lamb of God, Word*, and *witness*) which are common only to the Gospel of John and the Revelation; no other New Testament writer uses these terms in the same way.[2] Austin Farrer[3] draws attention to a number of stylistic similarities between the Gospel

---

1. Contrast this with the tone of St. Clement's letter to the Corinthians. As J. B. Lightfoot says in his edition of *The Apostolic Fathers* (Vol. I, p. 352): "Authority indeed is claimed for the utterances of the letter in no faltering tone, but it is the authority of the brotherhood declaring the mind of Christ by the Spirit, not the authority of one man, whether bishop or pope." Cited in John A. T. Robinson, *Redating the New Testament* (Philadelphia: The Westminster Press, 1976), p. 328.

2. See William Hendriksen, *More Than Conquerors: An Interpretation of the Book of Revelation* (Grand Rapids: Baker Book House, 1939), pp. 17ff., for a list of such similarities. For example, he cites John 7:37 and Rev. 22:17; John 10:18 and Rev. 2:27; John 20:12 and Rev. 3:4; John 1:1 and Rev. 19:13; John 1:29 and Rev. 5:6.

3. Austin Farrer, *The Revelation of St. John the Divine* (Oxford: At the Clarendon Press, 1964), pp. 41ff.

1

and Revelation: Both books are arranged in series of "sevens";[4] both are structured in terms of the Biblical/heavenly liturgy and festive calendar; and both books use numbers in a symbolic sense that transcends their literal significance (this is obvious in Revelation; cf. John 2:6, 19-20; 5:2, 5; 6:7, 9, 13; 8:57; 13:38; 19:14, 23; 21:11, 14, 15-17).

There are several Biblical indications that St. John was a priest, and even came from the high priest's family.[5] His name was probably common in that family (cf. Acts 4:6; contrast Luke 1:61). St. John himself tells us of his close relationship to the high priest: On account of this he was able, on an extremely sensitive occasion, to gain access into the high priest's Court, using his influence with the guard to achieve entry for St. Peter as well (John 18:15-16). Moreover, numerous references in both the Gospel and Revelation reveal their author's unusual familiarity with the details of Temple services. As Alfred Edersheim observed, "the other New Testament writers refer to them in their narratives, or else explain their types, in such language as any well-informed worshipper at Jerusalem might have employed. But John writes not like an ordinary Israelite. He has eyes and ears for details which others would have left unnoticed. . . .

"Indeed, the Apocalypse, as a whole, may be likened to the Temple services in its mingling of prophetic services with worship and praise. But it is specially remarkable, that the Temple-references with which the Book of Revelation abounds are generally to *minutiae*, which a writer who had not been as familiar with such details, as only personal contact and engagement with them could have rendered him, would scarcely have even noticed, certainly not employed as part of his imagery. They come in naturally, spontaneously, and so unexpectedly, that the reader is oc-

---

4. One minor example of this in John is 1:9-2:11, which follows a seven-day structure patterned after the creation week; see David Chilton, *Paradise Restored: A Biblical Theology of Dominion* (Ft. Worth, TX: Dominion Press, 1985), pp. 62f.

5. This is, to some extent, substantiated in the tradition recorded in Eusebius that as Bishop of Ephesus St. John "was a priest, and wore the sacerdotal plate"—i.e., the *petalon*, insignia of the high priest worn on the forehead (*Ecclesiastical History*, v.xxiv). It is likely, of course, that St. John and the other "ministers of the New Covenant" wore a distinctive "uniform" corresponding to their official status, and it is possible that their garments and "badge of office" were similar to those worn by the Israelite priesthood.

casionally in danger of overlooking them altogether; and in language such as a professional man would employ, which would come to him from the previous exercise of his calling. Indeed, some of the most striking of these references could not have been understood at all without the professional treatises of the Rabbis on the Temple and its services. Only the studied minuteness of Rabbinical descriptions, derived from the tradition of eye-witnesses, does not leave the same impression as the unstudied illustrations of St. John."[6]

"It seems highly improbable that a book so full of liturgical allusions as the Book of Revelation—and these, many of them, not to great or important points, but to *minutiae*—could have been written by any other than a priest, and one who had at one time been in actual service in the Temple itself, and thus become so intimately conversant with its details, that they came to him naturally, as part of the imagery he employed."[7]

In this connection Edersheim brings up a point that is more important for our interpretation than the issue of Revelation's human authorship (for ultimately [see 1:1] it is *Jesus Christ's* Revelation). St. John's intimate acquaintance with the minute details of Temple worship suggests that "the Book of Revelation and the Fourth Gospel must have been written before the Temple services had actually ceased."[8] Although some scholars have uncritically accepted the statement of St. Irenaeus (A.D. 120-202) that the prophecy appeared "toward the end of Domitian's reign" (i.e., around A.D. 96),[9] there is considerable room for doubt about his precise meaning (he may have meant that the Apostle John *himself* "was seen" by others).[10] The language of St. Irenaeus is somewhat ambiguous; and, regardless of what he was talking about, he could have been mistaken.[11] (St. Irenaeus, incidentally, is the *only* source for this late dating of Revelation;

---

6. Alfred Edersheim, *The Temple: Its Ministry and Services as They Were at the Time of Christ* (Grand Rapids: William B. Eerdmans Publishing Co., 1980), pp. 141f.

7. Ibid., p. 142.

8. Ibid., p. 141.

9. St. Irenaeus, *Against Heresies*, v.xxx.3; quoted by Eusebius in his *Ecclesiastical History*, iii.xviii.2-3; v.viii.6.

10. See Arthur Stapylton Barnes, *Christianity at Rome in the Apostolic Age* (London: Methuen Publishers, 1938), pp. 167ff.

11. See the discussion in John A. T. Robinson, *Redating the New Testament* (Philadelphia: The Westminster Press, 1976), pp. 221ff.

all other "sources" are simply quoting from him. It is thus rather disingenuous for commentators to claim, as Swete does, that "Early Christian tradition is almost unanimous in assigning the Apocalypse to the last years of Domitian.")[12] Certainly, there are other early writers whose statements indicate that St. John wrote the Revelation much earlier, under Nero's persecution.[13]

A good deal of the modern presumption in favor of a Domitianic date is based on the belief that a great, sustained period of persecution and slaughter of Christians was carried on under his rule. This belief, as cherished as it is, does not seem to be based on any hard evidence at all. While there is no doubt that Domitian was a cruel and wicked tyrant (I come to bury a myth about Caesar, not to praise him), until the fifth century there is no mention in any historian of a supposedly widespread persecution of Christians by his government. It is true that he did temporarily banish some Christians; but these were eventually recalled. Robinson remarks: "When this limited and selective purge, in which no Christian was for certain put to death, is compared with the massacre of Christians under Nero in what two early and entirely independent witnesses speak of as 'immense multitudes,'[14] it is astonishing that commentators should have been led by Irenaeus, who himself does not even mention a persecution, to prefer a Domitianic context for the book of Revelation."[15]

Our safest course, therefore, must be to study the Revelation itself to see what internal evidence it presents regarding its date. As we will see throughout the commentary, the Book of Revelation is primarily a prophecy of the destruction of Jerusalem by the Romans. This fact alone places St. John's authorship somewhere before September of A.D. 70. Further, as we shall see, St. John speaks of Nero Caesar as still on the throne—and Nero died in June 68.

---

12. H. B. Swete, *Commentary on Revelation* (Grand Rapids: Kregel Publications, [1911] 1977), p. xcix.

13. See the detailed discussion in Moses Stuart, *Commentary on the Apocalypse* (Andover: Allen, Morrill and Wardwell, 1845), Vol. I, pp. 263-84; see also James M. MacDonald, *The Life and Writings of St. John* (London: Hodder and Stoughton, 1877), pp. 151-77.

14. Robinson has in mind the statements of the Christian pastor St. Clement (*1 Clement* 6) and the heathen historian Tacitus (*Annals* xv.44).

15. Robinson, p. 233; cf. pp. 236ff.

More important than any of this, however, we have *a priori* teaching from Scripture itself that all special revelation ended by A.D. 70. The angel Gabriel told Daniel that the "seventy weeks" were to end with the destruction of Jerusalem (Dan. 9:24-27); and that period would also serve to "seal up the vision and prophecy" (Dan. 9:24). In other words, special revelation would stop — be "sealed up" — by the time Jerusalem was destroyed. The Canon of Holy Scripture was entirely completed before Jerusalem fell.[16] St. Athanasius interpreted Gabriel's words in the same way: "When did prophet and vision cease from Israel? Was it not when Christ came, the Holy One of holies? It is, in fact, a sign and notable proof of the coming of the Word that Jerusalem no longer stands, neither is prophet raised up nor vision revealed among them. And it is natural that it should be so, for when He that was signified had come, what need was there any longer of any to signify Him? And when the Truth had come, what further need was there of the shadow? On His account only they prophesied continually, until such time as Essential Righteousness had come, Who was made the Ransom for the sins of all. For the same reason Jerusalem stood until the same time, in order that there men might premediate the types before the Truth was known. So, of course, once the Holy One of holies had come, both vision and prophecy were sealed. And the kingdom of Jerusalem ceased at the same time, because kings were to be anointed among them only until the Holy of holies had been anointed. . . .

"The plain fact is, as I say, that there is no longer any king or prophet nor Jerusalem nor sacrifice nor vision among them; yet the whole earth is filled with the knowledge of God,[17] and the Gentiles, forsaking atheism, are now taking refuge with the God

---

16. While he does not base his case on theological considerations, this is J. A. T. Robinson's thesis in *Redating the New Testament*. He arrives at this conclusion through a careful study of both the internal and external evidence regarding each New Testament book. Support from archeological findings for an early New Testament is presented in David Estrada and William White Jr., *The First New Testament* (Nashville: Thomas Nelson, 1978). See also Ernest L. Martin, *The Original Bible Restored* (Pasadena: Foundation for Biblical Research, 1984), for his interesting thesis that the New Testament was canonized by St. Peter and St. John.

17. St. Athanasius, the "patron saint of postmillennialism," thus applies the "millennial" promise of Isaiah 11:9 to the triumphs of the New Covenant era.

of Abraham through the Word, our Lord Jesus Christ."[18]

The death, resurrection, and ascension of Christ marked the end of the Old Covenant and the beginning of the New; the apostles were commissioned to deliver Christ's message in the form of the New Testament; and when they were finished, God sent the Edomites and the Roman armies to destroy utterly the last remaining symbols of the Old Covenant: the Temple and the Holy City. This fact alone is sufficient to establish the writing of the Revelation as taking place before A.D. 70. The book itself gives abundant testimony regarding its date; but, even more, the nature of the New Testament as God's Final Word tells us this. Christ's death at the hands of the apostate children of Israel sealed their fate: The Kingdom would be taken from them (Matt. 21:33-43). While wrath built up "to the utmost" (1 Thess. 2:16), God stayed His hand of judgment until the writing of the New Covenant document was accomplished. With that done, He dramatically terminated the kingdom of Israel, wiping out the persecuting generation (Matt. 23:34-36; 24:34; Luke 11:49-51). Jerusalem's destruction was the last blast of the trumpet, signalling that the "mystery of God" was finished (Rev. 10:7). There would be no further canonical writings once Israel was gone.

Destination

From his exile on the island of Patmos, St. John addressed the Revelation to the churches in seven major cities of Asia Minor. These seven cities, connected by a semicircular road that ran through the interior of the province, served as postal stations for their districts. "So a messenger from Patmos landed at Ephesus, traveled north through Smyrna to Pergamum, and thence southeast through the other four cities, leaving a copy of the book in each for secondary circulation in its district. The number 'seven' is of course constantly used in the symbolism of the book of Revelation, but this fact should not be allowed to

---

18. St. Athanasius, *On the Incarnation*, Sister Penelope Lawson, Trans. (New York: Macmillan Publishing Co., 1946), pp. 61ff. Rousas John Rushdoony makes the same point in his exposition of Dan. 9:24: "'Vision and prophet' will be sealed up or ended, the New Testament revelation of Christ summing up and concluding the Scriptures." *Thy Kingdom Come: Studies in Daniel and Revelation* (Tyler, TX: Thoburn Press, [1970] 1978), p. 66.

obscure the circumstance that the book is addressed to seven actual churches in cities ideally placed to serve as the distribution points."[19]

Asia Minor was a significant destination for two reasons: First, after the fall of Jerusalem the province of Asia would become the most influential center of Christianity in the Roman Empire: "The province of Asia emerged as the area where Christianity was strongest, with Ephesus as its radial point."[20] Second, Asia was the center of the cult of Caesar-worship. "Inscription after inscription testifies to the loyalty of the cities towards the Empire. At Ephesus, at Smyrna, at Pergamum, and indeed throughout the province the Church was confronted by an imperialism which was popular and patriotic, and bore the character of a religion. Nowhere was the Caesar-cult more popular than in Asia."[21]

After Julius Caesar died (29 B.C.), a temple honoring him as *divus* (god) was built in Ephesus. The Caesars who followed him didn't wait for death to provide such honors, and, beginning with Octavian, they asserted their own divinity, displaying their titles of deity in temples and on coins, particularly in the cities of Asia. Octavian changed his name to *Augustus*, a title of supreme majesty, dignity and reverence. He was called *the Son of God*, and as the divine-human mediator between heaven and earth he offered sacrifices to the gods. He was widely proclaimed as the Savior of the world, and the inscriptions on his coins were quite frankly messianic — their message declaring, as Stauffer has written, that "salvation is to be found in none other save Augustus, and there is no other name given to men in which they can be saved."[22]

This pose was common to all the Caesars. Caesar was God; Caesar was Savior; Caesar was the only Lord. And they claimed not only the titles but the rights of deity as well. They taxed and

---

19. C. J. Hemer, "Seven Cities of Asia Minor," in R. K. Harrison, ed., *Major Cities of the Biblical World* (Nashville: Thomas Nelson Publishers, 1985), p. 235.
20. W. H. C. Frend, *The Rise of Christianity* (Philadelphia: Fortress Press, 1984), p. 127.
21. H. B. Swete, *Commentary on Revelation* (Grand Rapids: Kregel Publications, [1911] 1977), p. lxxxix.
22. Ethelbert Stauffer, *Christ and the Caesars* (Philadelphia: Westminster Press, 1955), p. 88.

confiscated property at will, took citizens' wives (and husbands) for their own pleasure, caused food shortages, exercised the power of life and death over their subjects, and generally attempted to rule every aspect of reality throughout the Empire. The philosophy of the Caesars can be summed up in one phrase which was used increasingly as the age progressed: *Caesar is Lord!*

This was the main issue between Rome and the Christians: Who is Lord? Francis Schaeffer points out: "Let us not forget why the Christians were killed. They were *not* killed because they worshiped Jesus. . . . Nobody cared who worshiped whom so long as the worshiper did not disrupt the unity of the state, centered in the formal worship of Caesar. The reason the Christians were killed was because they were rebels. . . . They worshiped Jesus as God and they worshiped the infinite-personal God only. The Caesars would not tolerate this worshiping of the one God *only*. It was counted as treason."[23]

For Rome, the goal of any true morality and piety was the subordination of all things to the State; the religious, pious man was the one who recognized, at every point in life, the centrality of Rome. "The function of Roman religion was pragmatic, to serve as social cement and to buttress the state."[24] Thus, observes R. J. Rushdoony, "the framework for the religious and familial acts of piety was Rome itself, the central and most sacred community. Rome strictly controlled all rights of corporation, assembly, religious meetings, clubs, and street gatherings, and it brooked no possible rivalry to its centrality. . . . The state alone could organize; short of conspiracy, the citizens could not. On this ground alone, the highly organized Christian Church was an offense and an affront to the state, and an illegal organization readily suspected of conspiracy."[25]

The witness of the apostles and the early Church was nothing less than a declaration of war against the pretensions of the Roman State. St. John asserted that Jesus is the *only-begotten* Son of God (John 3:16); that He is, in fact, "the true God and

---

23. Francis A. Schaeffer, *How Shall We Then Live?* (Old Tappan, NJ: Fleming H. Revell, 1976), p. 24.
24. Rousas John Rushdoony, *The One and the Many: Studies in the Philosophy of Order and Ultimacy* (Tyler, TX: Thoburn Press, [1971] 1978), p. 92.
25. Ibid., pp. 92f.

eternal life" (1 John 5:20-21). The Apostle Peter declared, shortly after Pentecost: "Salvation is found in no one else, for there is no other name under heaven given to men by which we must be saved" (Acts 4:12). "The conflict of Christianity with Rome was thus political from the Roman perspective, although religious from the Christian perspective. The Christians were never asked to worship Rome's pagan gods; they were merely asked to recognize the religious primacy of the state. As Francis Legge observed, 'The officials of the Roman Empire in time of persecution sought to force the Christians to sacrifice, not to any heathen gods, but to the Genius of the Emperor and the Fortune of the City of Rome; and at all times the Christians' refusal was looked upon not as a religious but as a political offense. . . .' The issue, then, was this: should the emperor's law, state law, govern both the state and the church, or were both state and church, emperor and bishop alike, under God's law? Who represented true and ultimate order, God or Rome, eternity or time? The Roman answer was Rome and time, and hence Christianity constituted a treasonable faith and a menace to political order."[26]

The charge brought by the Jewish prosecution in one first-century trial of Christians was that "they are all defying Caesar's decrees, saying that there is another king, one called Jesus" (Acts 17:7). This was the fundamental accusation against all the Christians of the Empire. The captain of police pleaded with the aged Bishop of Smyrna, St. Polycarp, to renounce this extreme position: "What harm is there in saying *Caesar is Lord*?" St. Polycarp refused, and was burned at the stake. Thousands suffered martyrdom on just this issue. For them, Jesus was not "God" in some upper-story, irrelevant sense; He was the only God, complete Sovereign in every area. No aspect of reality could be exempt from His demands. Nothing was neutral. The Church confronted Rome with the inflexible claim of Christ's imperial authority: Jesus is the only-begotten Son; Jesus is God; Jesus is King; Jesus is Savior; Jesus is Lord. Here were two Empires, both attempting absolute world domination; and they were implacably at war.[27]

---

26. Ibid., p. 93. Rushdoony cites Francis Legge, *Forerunners and Rivals of Christianity: From 330 B.C. to 330 A.D.* (New Hyde Park, NY: University Books, [1915], 1964), vol. I, pp. xxivf.

27. Cf. Swete, p. lxxxi.

It was necessary for the churches of Asia to recognize this fully, with all its implications. Faith in Jesus Christ requires absolute submission to His Lordship, at every point, with no compromise. The confession of Christ meant conflict with statism, particularly in the provinces where official worship of Caesar was required for the transaction of everyday affairs. Failure to acknowledge the claims of the State would result in economic hardship and ruin, and often imprisonment, torture, and death.

Some Christians attempted to compromise by drawing an unbiblical distinction between heart and conduct, as if one could have faith without works. But Christ's Kingdom is universal: Jesus is Lord of all. To acknowledge Him truly as Lord, we must serve Him everywhere. This was the primary message of the Revelation to the Christians in Asia, and one they desperately needed to hear. They lived in the very heart of Satan's throne, the seat of Emperor-worship; St. John wrote to remind them of their true King, of their position with Him as kings and priests, and of the necessity to persevere in terms of His sovereign Word.

Revelation and the Covenant

The Book of Revelation is part of the Bible. At first glance this may not seem to be a brilliant insight, but it is a point that is both crucially important and almost universally neglected in the actual practice of exposition. For as soon as we recognize that Revelation is a Biblical document, we are forced to ask a central question: What sort of book is the Bible? And the answer is this: *The Bible is a book* (The Book) *about the Covenant*. The Bible is not an Encyclopedia of Religious Knowledge. Nor is it a collection of Moral Tales, or a series of personal-psychology studies of Great Heroes of Long Ago. The Bible is God's written revelation of Himself, the story of His coming to us in the Mediator, the Lord Jesus Christ; and it is the story of the Church's relationship to Him through the Covenant He has established with her.

The Covenant is the meaning of Biblical history (Biblical history is not primarily adventure stories). The Covenant is the meaning of Biblical law (the Bible is not primarily a political treatise about how to set up a Christian Republic). And the Covenant is the meaning of Biblical prophecy as well (thus,

Biblical prophecy is not "prediction" in the occult sense of Nostradamus, Edgar Cayce, and Jean Dixon). To a man, the prophets were God's legal emissaries to Israel and the nations, acting as prosecuting attorneys bringing what has become known among recent scholars as the "Covenant Lawsuit."

That Biblical prophecy is not simply "prediction" is indicated, for example, by God's statement through Jeremiah:

> At one moment I might speak concerning a nation or concerning a kingdom to uproot, to pull down, or to destroy it; if that nation against which I have spoken turns from its evil, I will relent concerning the calamity I planned to bring on it.
>
> Or at another moment I might speak concerning a nation or concerning a kingdom to build up or to plant it; if it does evil in My sight by not obeying My voice, then I will repent of the good with which I had promised to bless it. (Jer. 18:7-10)

The purpose of prophecy is not "prediction," but evaluation of man's ethical response to God's Word of command and promise. This is why Jonah's prophecy about Nineveh did not "come true": Nineveh repented of its wickedness, and the calamity was averted. Like the other Biblical writings, the Book of Revelation is a prophecy, with a specific covenantal orientation and reference. When the covenantal context of the prophecy is ignored, the message St. John sought to communicate is lost, and Revelation becomes nothing more than a vehicle for advancing the alleged expositor's eschatological theories.

Let us consider a minor example: Revelation 9:16 tells us of a great army of horsemen, numbering "myriads of myriads." In some Greek texts, this reads *two myriads of myriads*, and is sometimes translated *200 million*. All sorts of fanciful and contrived explanations have been proposed for this. Perhaps the most well-known theory of recent times is Hal Lindsey's opinion that "these 200 million troops are Red Chinese soldiers accompanied by other Eastern allies. It's possible that the industrial might of Japan will be united with Red China. For the first time in history there will be a full invasion of the West by the Orient."[28] Such fortunetelling may or may not be accurate

---

28. Hal Lindsey, *There's a New World Coming* (Eugene, OR: Harvest House Publishers, 1973), p. 140.

regarding a coming Chinese invasion, but it tells us absolutely nothing about the Bible. To help put Lindsey's view into historical perspective, we will compare it to that of J. L. Martin, a 19th-century preacher who, while sharing Lindsey's basic presuppositions about the nature and purpose of prophecy, reached the different, and amusing, conclusion that St. John's "200 million" represented "the fighting force of the whole world" of 1870. Note Martin's shrewdly scientific, Lindsey-like reasoning:

> We have a few more than one billion inhabitants on the earth. . . . But of that billion about five hundred millions (one-half) are females, leaving an average population of male inhabitants of about five hundred millions; and of that number about one-half are minors, leaving about two hundred and fifty millions of adult males on the earth at a time. But of that number of adult males about one-fifth are superannuated — too old to fight. These are statistical facts. This leaves exactly John's two hundred millions of fighting men on earth. And when we prove a matter mathematically, we think it is pretty well done.[29]

But Martin is just hitting his stride. He continues with his exposition, taking up the terrifying description of the soldiers in 9:17-19: "The riders had breastplates of fire and of hyacinth and of brimstone; and the heads of the horses are like the heads of lions; and out of their mouths proceed fire and smoke and brimstone. A third of mankind was killed by these three plagues, by the fire and the smoke and the brimstone, which proceeded out of their mouths. For the power of the horses is in their mouths and in their tails; for their tails are like serpents and have heads; and with them they do harm." Whereas modern apocalyptists view this in terms of lasers and missile launchers, Martin had a different explanation — one which was in keeping with the state of military art in his day, when Buffalo Bill was fighting Sioux Indians as chief of scouts for General Sheridan's Fifth Cavalry:

> John is pointing to the modern mode of fighting on horseback, with the rider leaning forward, which, to his sight, and to the sight of one looking on at a distance, would appear as the

---

29. J. L. Martin, *The Voice of the Seven Thunders: or, Lectures on the Apocalypse* (Bedford, IN: James M. Mathes, Publisher, sixth ed., 1873), pp. 149f.

great mane of the lion; the man leaning on his horse's neck. He would, in fighting with firearms, have to lean forward to discharge his piece, lest he might shoot down his own horse that he was riding. In John's day the posture was very different. . . . Now, I want to ask my friendly hearers if it is not as literally fulfilled before our eyes as anything can be? Are not all nations engaged in this mode of warfare? Do they not kill men with fire and smoke and brimstone? . . . Do you not know that this is just ignited gunpowder? . . .

Could an uninspired man, in the last of the first century, have told of this matter?[30]

Unless we see the Book of Revelation as a Covenant document — i.e., if we insist on reading it primarily as either a prediction of twentieth-century nuclear weapons or a polemic against first-century Rome — its continuity with the rest of the Bible will be lost. It becomes an eschatological appendix, a view of "last things" that ultimately has little to do with the message, purpose, and concerns of the Bible. Once we understand Revelation's character as a Covenant Lawsuit, however, it ceases to be a "strange," "weird" book; it is no longer incomprehensible, or decipherable only with the complete *New York Times Index*. In its major themes at least, it becomes as accessible to us as Isaiah and Amos. The Book of Revelation must be seen from the outset in its character as Biblical *revelation*. The grasp of this single point can mean a "quantum leap" for interpretation; for, as Geerhardus Vos made clear in his pathbreaking studies of Biblical Theology, "revelation is connected throughout with the fate of Israel."[31]

The Covenant Lawsuit

God's relationship with Israel was always defined in terms of the Covenant, the marriage bond by which He joined her to Himself as His special people. This Covenant was a legal arrangement, a binding "contract" imposed on Israel by her King, stipulating mutual obligations and promises. Meredith Kline has

---

30. Ibid., pp. 151f.
31. Richard B. Gaffin Jr., ed., *Redemptive History and Biblical Interpretation: The Shorter Writings of Geerhardus Vos* (Phillipsburg, NJ: Presbyterian and Reformed Publishing Co., 1980), p. 10.

shown that the structure of the Biblical Covenant bears striking similarities to the established form for peace treaties in the ancient Near East.[32] This is how it worked: After a war, the victorious king would make a covenant with his defeated foe, making certain promises and guaranteeing protection on condition that the vassal-king and all under his authority would obey their new lord. Both lord and vassal would swear an oath, and they would thenceforth be united in covenant.

As Kline explains, the standard treaty-form in the ancient world was structured in five parts, all of which appear in the Biblical covenants:

1. Preamble (identifying the lordship of the Great King, stressing both his transcendence [greatness and power] and his immanence [nearness and presence]);

2. Historical Prologue (surveying the lord's previous relationship to the vassal, especially emphasizing the blessings bestowed);

3. Ethical Stipulations (expounding the vassal's obligations, his "guide to citizenship" in the covenant);

4. Sanctions (outlining the blessings for obedience and curses for disobedience);

5. Succession Arrangements (dealing with the continuity of the covenant relationship over future generations).

One of the best examples of a document written in this treaty-form is the Book of Deuteronomy, which Kline examines in detail in his *Treaty of the Great King*. (Recently, Kline's analysis has been considerably augmented in the more theologically oriented work of Ray R. Sutton, *That You May Prosper*.)[33] Kline's exposition shows how Deuteronomy naturally divides into the five covenantal sections:

---

32. Meredith G. Kline, *Treaty of the Great King: The Covenant Structure of Deuteronomy* (Grand Rapids: William B. Eerdmans Publishing Co., 1963); idem., *The Structure of Biblical Authority* (Grand Rapids: William B. Eerdmans Publishing Co., second ed., 1975).

33. Ray R. Sutton, *That You May Prosper: Dominion by Covenant* (Tyler, TX: Institute for Christian Economics, 1987).

14

Deuteronomy
1. Preamble (1:1-5)
2. Historical Prologue (1:6-4:49)
3. Ethical Stipulations (5:1-26:19)
4. Sanctions (27:1-30:20)
5. Succession Arrangements (31:1-34:12)

If a vassal kingdom violated the terms of the covenant, the lord would send messengers to the vassal, warning the offenders of coming judgment, in which the curse-sanctions of the covenant would be enforced. This turns out to be the function of the Biblical prophets, as I mentioned above: They were prosecuting attorneys, bringing God's message of Covenant Lawsuit to the offending nations of Israel and Judah. And the structure of the lawsuit was always patterned after the original structure of the covenant. In other words, just as the Biblical covenants themselves follow the standard five-part treaty structure, the Biblical prophecies follow the treaty form as well.[34] For example, the prophecy of Hosea is ordered according to the following outline:

Hosea
1. Preamble (1)
2. Historical Prologue (2-3)
3. Ethical Stipulations (4-7)
4. Sanctions (8-9)
5. Succession Arrangements (10-14)

Like many other Biblical prophecies, the Book of Revelation is a prophecy of Covenant wrath against apostate Israel, which irrevocably turned away from the Covenant in her rejection of Christ. And, like many other Biblical prophecies, the Book of Revelation is written in the form of the Covenant Lawsuit, with five parts, conforming to the treaty structure of the Covenant. This thesis will be demonstrated in the commentary; by way of introduction, however, it will be helpful to glance at some of the major points that lead to this conclusion. (Also, I have provided

---

34. Incidentally, the point is not that Scripture is modeled after pagan treaties; rather, as Sutton argues, the pagan treaty-forms were ultimately derived from God's Covenant.

an Introduction to each of the five parts of Revelation, correlating the message of each section with the appropriate passage in the Book of Deuteronomy.)

In order to grasp the five-part structure of Revelation, we must first consider how St. John's prophecy is related to the message of Leviticus 26. Like Deuteronomy 28, Leviticus 26 sets forth the sanctions of the Covenant: If Israel obeys God, she will be blessed in every area of life (Lev. 26:1-13; Deut. 28:1-14); if she disobeys, however, she will be visited with the Curse, spelled out in horrifying detail (Lev. 26:14-39; Deut. 28:15-68). (These curses were most fully poured out in the progressive desolation of Israel during the Last Days, culminating in the Great Tribulation of A.D. 67-70, as punishment for her apostasy and rejection of her True Husband, the Lord Jesus Christ.)[35] One of the striking features of the Leviticus passage is that the curses are arranged in a special pattern: Four times in this chapter God says, "I will punish you seven times for your sins" (Lev. 26:18, 21, 24, 28). The number *seven*, as we will see abundantly throughout Revelation, is a Biblical number for completeness or fullness (taken from the seven-day pattern laid down at the creation in Genesis 1).[36] The number *four* is used in Scripture in connection with the earth, especially the Land of Israel; thus four rivers flowed out of Eden to water the whole earth (Gen. 2:10); the Land, like the Altar, is pictured as having four corners (Isa. 11:12; cf. Ex. 27:1-2), from which the four winds blow (Jer. 49:36); the camp of Israel was arranged in four groups around the sides of the Tabernacle (Num. 2); and so on (see your concordance and Bible dictionary). So by speaking of four sevenfold judgments in Leviticus 26, God is saying that a full, complete judgment will come upon the Land of Israel for its sins. This theme is taken up by the prophets in their warnings to Israel:

---

35. The Biblical expression *Last Days* properly refers to the period from the Advent of Christ until the destruction of Jerusalem in A.D. 70, the "last days" of Israel during the transition period from the Old Covenant to the New Covenant (Heb. 1:1-2; 8:13; James 5:1-9; 1 Pet. 1:20; 1 John 2:18). See David Chilton, *Paradise Restored*, pp. 77-122, 237-90; cf. my series of studies on this subject, published in the *Geneva Review*, P.O. Box 131300, Tyler, TX 75713.

36. The number seven alone is used fifty-four times in Revelation; and there are many examples (more than I have attempted to count) of words and phrases mentioned seven times, or clustered together in groups of sevens.

And I shall appoint over them four kinds of doom, declares the LORD: the sword to slay, the dogs to drag off, and the birds of the sky and the beasts of the earth to devour and destroy. (Jer. 15:3)

Thus says the Lord GOD: I shall send My four evil judgments against Jerusalem: sword, famine, wild beasts, and plague to cut off man and beast from it! (Ezek. 14:21)

The imagery of a sevenfold judgment coming four times is most fully developed in the Book of Revelation, which is explicitly divided into four sets of seven: the Letters to the Seven Churches, the opening of the Seven Seals, the sounding of the Seven Trumpets, and the outpouring of the Seven Chalices.[37] In thus following the formal structure of the covenantal curse in Leviticus, St. John underscores the nature of his prophecy as a declaration of covenant wrath against Jerusalem.

The four judgments are preceded by an introductory vision, which serves to highlight the transcendence and immanence of the Lord—precisely the function of the Preamble in the covenantal treaties. As we read through the four series of judgments, we find that they also conform to the treaty outline: The Seven Letters survey the history of the covenant; the Seven Seals have to do with the specific stipulations set forth in the corresponding section of the covenantal treaty; the Seven Trumpets invoke the covenant sanctions; and the angels of the Seven Chalices are involved in both the disinheritance of Israel and the Church's succession in the New Covenant. Thus:

Revelation
1. Preamble: Vision of the Son of Man (1)
2. Historical Prologue: The Seven Letters (2-3)
3. Ethical Stipulations: The Seven Seals (4-7)
4. Sanctions: The Seven Trumpets (8-14)
5. Succession Arrangements: The Seven Chalices (15-22)

St. John has thus combined the four-part Curse outline of Leviticus 26 with the familiar five-part outline of the Covenant

---

37. Most commentaries, it is true, seek to find seven or more sets of seven, but in doing so they are not adhering to St. John's formal outline. Certainly, there is nothing wrong with attempting to discover the many subtle structures of the book; but we must at least *begin* with the author's explicit arrangement before making refinements.

Lawsuit. The intersection of a fourfold and fivefold curse is related to another dimension of Biblical imagery, relating to the laws of multiple restitution. Exodus 22:1 commands: "If a man steals an ox or a sheep, and slaughters it or sells it, he shall pay five oxen for the ox and four sheep for the sheep." James B. Jordan explains the symbolic aspects of this case law: "These are the animals which particularly symbolize humanity in the sacrificial system. They are, thus, repeatedly set forth as preeminent analogies for men (cf. e.g., Lev. 22:27, with Lev. 12).

"We should note here that the verb used in Exodus 22:1, 'slaughter,' is used almost always with reference to men. Ralph H. Alexander comments, 'The central meaning of the root occurs only three times (Gen. 43:16; Ex. 22:1; 1 Sam. 25:11). The root is predominantly used metaphorically, portraying the Lord's judgment upon Israel and upon Babylon as a slaughter.'[38] This again points to a basic symbolic meaning of this law."[39]

Jordan goes on to show that in Scripture the ox primarily represents the office-bearer in Israel, while the sheep represents the ordinary citizen, and especially the poor man. Fourfold restitution is thus required for the crime of oppressing the poor, and fivefold restitution is required for the penalty of rebellion against authority.[40] The Covenant Lawsuit is structured in terms of the penalty of fivefold restitution, since the rebels against the covenant are revolting against their divinely ordained authority; and St. John brings the lawsuit against Israel because she has rebelled against Jesus Christ, her Lord and High Priest (Heb. 2:17; 7:22-8:6).

But Christ was also a sheep, the sacrificial Lamb of God (John 1:29; Rev. 5:6, 9). He was wrongfully sold (Matt. 26:14-15), and was treated "like a lamb that is led to *slaughter*" (Isa. 53:7). Moreover, the early Christians were largely poor, and were persecuted, oppressed, and slaughtered by the wealthy and powerful of apostate Israel (Matt. 5:10-12; Luke 6:20-26; James 5:1-6). Unbelieving Israel thus brought upon herself all the penalties and curses of the covenant, including fourfold and fivefold as

---

38. R. Laird Harris, Gleason Archer, and Bruce Waltke, eds., *Theological Wordbook of the Old Testament* (Chicago: Moody Press, 1980), p. 341.

39. James B. Jordan, *The Law of the Covenant: An Exposition of Exodus 21-23* (Tyler, TX: Institute for Christian Economics, 1984), p. 266.

40. Ibid., pp. 266-71.

well as double restitution (Rev. 18:6). (It is also worth repeating what Ralph Alexander said about the word *slaughter* in Exodus 22:1: "The root is predominantly used metaphorically, portraying the Lord's judgment upon Israel and upon Babylon as a slaughter." As we will see, St. John brings these ideas together, metaphorically calling the apostate Jerusalem of his day *Babylon the Great*.) The Great Tribulation, culminating in the holocaust of A.D. 70, was the restitution demanded for its theft and slaughter of the Old Testament prophets, of the New Testament martyrs, and of the Lord Jesus Christ (Matt. 21:33-45; 23:29-38; 1 Thess. 2:14-16); and these motifs are built into the very structure of Revelation, the final Covenant Lawsuit.

All this is further emphasized by St. John's use of the prophetic Lawsuit terminology: the accusation of harlotry. Throughout Scripture, Israel is regarded as God's Wife; the covenant is a marriage bond, and she is expected to be faithful to it. Her apostasy from God is called adultery, and she is identified as a harlot. There are numerous examples of this in the prophets:

How the faithful city has become a harlot,
She who was full of justice!
Righteousness once lodged in her,
But now murderers. (Isa. 1:21)

For long ago I broke your yoke
And tore off your bonds;
But you said: I will not serve!
For on every high hill
And under every green tree
You have lain down as a harlot. (Jer. 2:20)

Your fame went forth among the nations on account of your beauty, for it was perfect because of My splendor which I bestowed on you, declares the Lord GOD. But you trusted in your beauty and played the harlot because of your fame, and you poured out your harlotries on every passerby who might be willing. (Ezek. 16:14-15)

Do not rejoice, O Israel, with exultation like the nations!
For you have played the harlot, forsaking your God.
You have loved harlots' earnings on every threshing floor.
(Hos. 9:1)

Throughout Scripture, it is Israel whom the prophets characteristically condemn as a harlot.[41] Accordingly, when St. John brings lawsuit against Israel for her rejection of Christ, the greatest apostasy of all time (cf. Matt. 21:33-45), he appropriately calls her "the Great Harlot . . . the Mother of the harlots and of the abominations of the Land" (Rev. 17:1, 5).

There are other indications within the structure of Revelation that it is a Covenant Lawsuit against Israel. The four sevenfold judgments are arranged in general conformity to the order of Jesus' prophecy against Jerusalem in Matthew 24.[42] Thus the Seven Letters (Rev. 2-3) deal with false apostles, persecution, lawlessness, love grown cold, and the duty of perseverance (cf. Matt. 24:3-5, 9-13); the Seven Seals (Rev. 4-7) are concerned with wars, famines, and earthquakes (cf. Matt. 24:6-8); the Seven Trumpets (Rev. 8-14) tell of the Church's witness to the world, her flight into the wilderness, the Great Tribulation, and the False Prophet (cf. Matt. 24:14-27); and the Seven Chalices (Rev. 15-22) describe the darkening of the Beast's kingdom, the destruction of the Harlot, the gathering of eagles over Jerusalem's corpse, and the gathering of the Church into the Kingdom (cf. Matt. 24:28-31).

Revelation, Ezekiel, and the Lectionary

But there is at least one other factor that has greatly influenced the outline of the Revelation. It is constructed with strict adherence to one of the most famous Covenant Lawsuits of all time: the prophecy of Ezekiel. Revelation's dependence upon the language and imagery of Ezekiel has long been recognized;[43] one scholar has found in Revelation no less than 130 separate references to Ezekiel.[44] But St. John does more than merely

---

41. The figurative image of harlotry is consistently used for apostasy from the covenant. There are, in fact, only two cases in all of Scripture in which the term is applied to other nations. In both cases (Tyre, Isa. 23:15-17; and Nineveh, Nah. 3:4), they were nations that had been in covenant with God through Israel.
42. See J. P. M. Sweet, *Revelation* (Philadelphia: The Westminster Press, 1979), pp. 52-54.
43. See, e.g., Ferrell Jenkins, *The Old Testament in the Book of Revelation* (Grand Rapids: Baker Book House, [1972] 1976), pp. 54ff.
44. Albert Vanhoye, "L'utilisation du Livre d'Ezechiel dans l'Apocalypse," *Biblica* 43 (1962), pp. 436-76 (see esp. pp. 473-76).

make literary allusions to Ezekiel. He follows him, step by step — so much so that Philip Carrington could say, with only mild hyperbole: "The Revelation is a Christian rewriting of Ezekiel. Its fundamental structure is the same. Its interpretation depends upon Ezekiel. The first half of both books leads up to the destruction of the earthly Jerusalem; in the second they describe a new and holy Jerusalem. There is one significant difference. Ezekiel's lament over Tyre is transformed into a lament over Jerusalem, the reason being that St. John wishes to transfer to Jerusalem the note of *irrevocable* doom found in the lament over Tyre. Here lies the real difference in the messages of the two books. Jerusalem, like Tyre, is to go forever."[45] Consider the more obvious parallels:[46]

1. The Throne-Vision (Rev. 4/Ezek. 1)
2. The Book (Rev. 5/Ezek. 2-3)
3. The Four Plagues (Rev. 6:1-8/Ezek. 5)
4. The Slain under the Altar (Rev. 6:9-11/Ezek. 6)
5. The Wrath of God (Rev. 6:12-17/Ezek. 7)
6. The Seal on the Saint's Foreheads (Rev. 7/Ezek. 9)
7. The Coals from the Altar (Rev. 8/Ezek. 10)
8. No More Delay (Rev. 10:1-7/Ezek. 12)
9. The Eating of the Book (Rev. 10:8-11/Ezek. 2)
10. The Measuring of the Temple (Rev. 11:1-2/Ezek. 40-43)
11. Jerusalem and Sodom (Rev. 11:8/Ezek. 16)
12. The Cup of Wrath (Rev. 14/Ezek. 23)
13. The Vine of the Land (Rev. 14:18-20/Ezek. 15)
14. The Great Harlot (Rev. 17-18/Ezek. 16, 23)
15. The Lament over the City (Rev. 18/Ezek. 27)
16. The Scavengers' Feast (Rev. 19/Ezek. 39)
17. The First Resurrection (Rev. 20:4-6/Ezek. 37)
18. The Battle with Gog and Magog (Rev. 20:7-9/Ezek. 38-39)
19. The New Jerusalem (Rev. 21/Ezek. 40-48)
20. The River of Life (Rev. 22/Ezek. 47)

As M. D. Goulder points out, the closeness of the two books' structure — the step-by-step "pegging" of Revelation with

---

45. Philip Carrington, *The Meaning of the Revelation* (London: SPCK, 1931), p. 65.

46. This list is based on Carrington (p. 64) and on M. D. Goulder, "The Apocalypse as an Annual Cycle of Prophecies," *New Testament Studies* 27, No. 3 (April 1981), pp. 342-67.

Ezekiel—implies something more than a merely literary relationship. "Level pegging is not usually a feature of literary borrowing: the Chronicler's work, for example, is far from pegging level with Samuel-Kings, with his massive expansion of the Temple material, and his excision of the northern traditions. Level pegging is a feature rather of lectionary use, as when the Church sets (set) Genesis to be read alongside Romans, or Deuteronomy alongside Acts. . . . Furthermore, it is plain that John expected his prophecies to be read aloud in worship, for he says, 'Blessed is he who reads the words of the prophecy, and blessed are those who hear' (1:3)—RSV correctly glosses 'reads aloud.' Indeed, the very fact that he repeatedly calls his book 'the prophecy' aligns it with the OT prophecies, which were familiar from their public reading in worship."[47] In other words, the Book of Revelation was intended from the beginning as a series of readings in worship throughout the Church Year, to be read in tandem with the prophecy of Ezekiel (as well as other Old Testament readings). As Austin Farrer wrote in his first study of Revelation, St. John "certainly did not think it was going to be read once to the congregations and then used to wrap up fish, like a pastoral letter."[48]

Goulder's thesis on Revelation is supported by the findings in his recent work on the Gospels, *The Evangelists' Calendar,* which has revolutionized New Testament studies by setting the Gospels in their proper liturgical context.[49] As Goulder shows, the Gospels were originally written, not as "books," but as serial readings in worship, to accompany the readings in the synagogues (the first New Testament churches). In fact, he argues, "Luke developed his Gospel in preaching to his congregation, as a series of fulfillments of the O.T.; and this development in liturgical series explains the basic structure of his Gospel, which has been a riddle so long."[50]

---

47. M. D. Goulder, "The Apocalypse as an Annual Cycle of Prophecies," p. 350.
48. Austin Farrer, *A Rebirth of Images: The Making of St. John's Apocalypse* (Gloucester, MA: Peter Smith, [1949] 1970), p. 22.
49. M. D. Goulder, *The Evangelists' Calendar: A Lectionary Explanation of the Development of Scripture* (London: SPCK, 1978).
50. Ibid., p. 7. Goulder suggests that the Book of Revelation was written in the same way, as St. John's meditations on the lectionary readings in his church.

The structures of both Ezekiel and Revelation lend themselves readily to serialized lectionary usage, as Goulder observes: "In the division of the Apocalypse and of Ezekiel into prophecies or visions, units for the successive Sundays, the interpreter has little discretion; a happy feature, since we are looking for clear, uncontroversial dividing lines. Most commentaries divide the Apocalypse into about fifty units, and they do not diverge greatly. Ezekiel is divided in the Bible into forty-eight chapters, many of which are self-evidently single prophecies standing on their own. Further, the length of Ezekiel's chapters is on the whole level. The book covers a little over 53 pages of text in the RV, and many chapters are about two columns (a page) long. Some of the divisions are perhaps questionable. For example, Ezekiel's call extends beyond the very brief ch. 2 to a clear end at 3:15, and the short ch. 9 could be taken with 8; whereas there are some enormous chapters, 16, 23, and 40, which are more than four columns in length, and which subdivide naturally. But one encouraging feature will have become obvious to the reader already: both books divide into about fifty units, and the Jewish(-Christian) year consists of fifty or fifty-one sabbaths/Sundays. So we have what looks like material for an annual cycle of Ezekiel inspiring a year's cycle of visions, which could then be read in the Asian churches alongside Ezekiel, and expounded in sermons in its light."[51] Goulder goes on to provide a lengthy table showing consecutive readings through Ezekiel and Revelation, set out alongside the Christian year from Easter to Easter; the correlations are amazing.[52]

The Paschal (Easter) emphasis of Revelation was also brought out in a study by Massey Shepherd, almost twenty years before Goulder wrote.[53] Shepherd demonstrated another striking aspect of the architecture of Revelation, showing that St. John's prophecy is laid out according to the structure of the

---

51. M. D. Goulder, "The Apocalypse as an Annual Cycle of Prophecies," pp. 350f.

52. Ibid., pp. 353-54. James B. Jordan has written a very helpful series of studies on "Christianity and the Calendar," published over a three-year period in *The Geneva Papers* (first series), available from Geneva Ministries, P.O. Box 131300, Tyler, TX 75713. See esp. No. 27 (January 1984): "Is the Church Year Desirable?"

53. Massey H. Shepherd Jr., *The Paschal Liturgy and the Apocalypse* (Richmond: John Knox Press, 1960).

early Church's worship—in fact, that both his Gospel and the Revelation "give their testimony from the vantage point of experience of the Paschal liturgy of the Asian churches."[54]

The lectionary nature of Revelation helps explain the wealth of liturgical material in the prophecy. Revelation is not, of course, a manual about how to "do" a worship service; rather, it *is* a worship service, a liturgy conducted in heaven as a model for those on earth (and incidentally instructing us that the Throne-room of God is the only proper vantage point for viewing the earthly conflict between the Seed of the Woman and the seed of the Serpent): "The worship of the Church has traditionally, quite consciously, been patterned after the divine and eternal realities revealed in [Revelation]. The prayer of the Church and its mystical celebration are one with the prayer and celebration of the kingdom of heaven. Thus, in Church, with the angels and saints, through Christ the Word and the Lamb, inspired by the Holy Spirit, the faithful believers of the assembly of the saved offer perpetual adoration to God the Father Almighty."[55]

The failure to recognize the significance of Revelation for Christian worship has greatly impoverished many modern churches. To take only one example: How many sermons have been preached on Revelation 3:20 — "Behold, I stand at the door and knock; if anyone hears My voice and opens the door, I will come in to him, and will dine with him, and he with Me" — without recognizing the very obvious sacramental reference? *Of course* Jesus is speaking about the Lord's Supper, inviting us to dine with Him; why didn't we see it before? The reason has much to do with a puritanical notion of worship that comes, not from the Bible, but from pagan philosophers.

Dom Gregory Dix, in his massive study of Christian worship, hit it right on the head: Liturgical puritanism is *not* "Protestant"; it is not even Christian. It is, instead, "a general theory about worship, not specifically protestant nor indeed confined to Christians of any kind. It is the working theory upon which all Mohammedan worship is based. It was put as well as any-

---

54. Ibid., p. 82.
55. Thomas Hopko, *The Orthodox Faith*, Vol. 4: *The Bible and Church History* (Orthodox Church in America, 1973), pp. 64f.; cited in George Cronk, *The Message of the Bible: An Orthodox Christian Perspective* (Crestwood, NY: St. Vladimir's Seminary Press, 1982), p. 259.

body by the Roman poet Persius or the pagan philosopher Seneca in the first century, and they are only elaborating a thesis from Greek philosophical authors going back to the seventh century B.C. Briefly, the puritan theory is that worship is a purely *mental* activity, to be exercised by a strictly psychological 'attention' to a subjective emotional or spiritual experience. . . . Over against this puritan theory of worship stands another — the 'ceremonious' conception of worship, whose foundation principle is that worship as such is not a purely intellectual and affective exercise, but one in which the whole man — body as well as soul, his aesthetic and volitional as well as his intellectual powers — must take full part. It regards worship as an 'act' just as much as an 'experience.' "[56] It is this "ceremonious" view of worship that is taught by the Bible, from Genesis to Revelation. Since all the action of Revelation is seen from the viewpoint of a worship service, this commentary will assume that the prophecy's liturgical structure is basic to its proper interpretation.

The Nature of Revelation: Apocalyptic?

The Book of Revelation is often treated as an example of the "apocalyptic" genre of writings which flourished among the Jews between 200 B.C. and A.D. 100. There is no basis for this opinion whatsoever, and it is unfortunate that the word *apocalyptic* is used at all to describe this literature. (The writers of "apocalyptic" themselves never used the term in this sense; rather, scholars have stolen the term from St. John, who called his book "The *Apocalypse* of Jesus Christ.") There are, in fact, many major differences between the "apocalyptic" writings and the Book of Revelation.

The "apocalyptists" expressed themselves in unexplained and unintelligible symbols, and generally had no intention of making themselves really understood. Their writings abound in pessimism: no real progress is possible, nor will there be any victory for God and His people in history. We cannot even see God acting in history. All we know is that the world is getting worse and worse. The best we can do is hope for the End — soon.[57] Ferrell

---

56. Dom Gregory Dix, *The Shape of the Liturgy* (New York: The Seabury Press, [1945] 1983), p. 312.

57. See Leon Morris, *Apocalyptic* (Grand Rapids: William B. Eerdmans Publishing Co., 1972).

Jenkins writes: "To them the forces of evil apparently had control in the present age and God would act only in the End Time."[58] (This should have a familiar ring.) Feeling impotent in the face of inexorable evil, the apocalyptist "could accordingly indulge in the wildest speculation. . . . he had written off this world and its activities, so there was no question of his trying seriously to provide workable solutions to its problems."[59] The practical result was that the apocalyptists rarely concerned themselves with ethical behavior: "In the last resort their interest is in eschatology, not ethics."[60]

St. John's approach in the Revelation is vastly different. His symbols are not obscure ravings hatched from a fevered imagination; they are rooted firmly in the Old Testament (and the reason for their *seeming* obscurity is that very fact: We have trouble understanding them only because we don't know our Bibles). In contrast to the apocalyptists, who had given up on history, "John presents history as the scene of divine redemption."[61] Leon Morris describes St. John's worldview: "For him history is the sphere in which God has wrought out redemption. The really critical thing in the history of mankind has already taken place, and it took place here, on this earth, in the affairs of men. The Lamb 'as it had been slain' dominates the entire book. John sees Christ as victorious and as having won the victory through His death, an event in history. His people share in His triumph, but they have conquered Satan 'by the blood of the Lamb and by the word of their testimony' (Rev. 12:11). The pessimism which defers God's saving activity until the End is absent. Though John depicts evil realistically, his book is fundamentally optimistic."[62]

The apocalyptists said: *The world is coming to an end: Give up!* The Biblical prophets said: *The world is coming to a beginning: Get to work!*

Thus, the Book of Revelation is not an apocalyptic tract; it

---

58. Ferrell Jenkins, *The Old Testament in the Book of Revelation* (Grand Rapids: Baker Book House, 1976), p. 41. Jenkins' book is an excellent brief introduction to the Biblical background and symbolism of the Revelation.
59. Morris, p. 71.
60. Ibid., p. 60.
61. Jenkins, p. 41.
62. Morris, p. 79.

is, instead, as St. John himself reminds us repeatedly, a *prophecy* (1:3; 10:11; 22:7, 10, 18-19), completely in keeping with the writings of the other Biblical prophets. And—again in stark contrast to the apocalyptists—if there was one major concern among the Biblical prophets, it was ethical conduct. No Biblical writer ever revealed the future merely for the sake of satisfying curiosity: The goal was always to direct God's people toward right action in the present. The overwhelming majority of Biblical prophecy had nothing to do with the common misconception of "prophecy" as foretelling the future. The prophets told of the future only in order to stimulate godly living. As Benjamin Warfield wrote: "We must try to keep fresh in our minds the great principle that all prophecy is ethical in its purpose, and that this ethical end controls not only what shall be revealed in general, but also the details of it, and the very form which it takes."[63]

The fact that many who study the prophetic writings today are interested in finding possible references to space travel and nuclear weapons, rather than in discovering God's commandments for living, is a sickening tribute to a shallow and immature faith. "The testimony of *Jesus* is the spirit of prophecy" (Rev. 19:10); to ignore Jesus in favor of atomic blasts is a perversion of Scripture, a blasphemous twisting of God's holy Word. From beginning to end, St. John is intensely interested in the ethical conduct of his readers:

> Blessed is he who reads and those who hear the words of the prophecy, and keep the things that are written in it. (1:3)
>
> Blessed is he who stays awake and keeps his garments. (16:15)
>
> Blessed is he who keeps the words of the prophecy of this book. (22:7)
>
> Blessed are those who do His commandments. (22:14)

The Symbolism of Revelation

Prophecy has often been called "history written in advance."[64]

---

63. Benjamin B. Warfield, "The Prophecies of St. Paul," in *Biblical and Theological Studies* (Philadelphia: The Presbyterian and Reformed Publishing Co., 1968), p. 470.

64. One of the greatest popularizers of this view was the rationalistic Christian apologist Joseph Butler, who claimed that "prophecy is nothing but the history of events before they come to pass." *The Analogy of Religion, Natural*

As we have already seen, however, prophecy is primarily a message from God's emissaries within the framework of the Covenant, addressed in terms of the stipulations and sanctions set forth in Biblical law. It is not simply "prediction." Certainly, the prophets did predict future events in history, but not in the form of historical writing. Instead, the prophets used symbols and figures borrowed from history, from the surrounding culture, and from creation. Most errors in interpreting the prophets stem from the neglect of this principle. I once heard a pastor deliver a very earnest and thrilling lecture on space stations and interplanetary voyages, using Revelation 21:10 as his text. Only in the modern age of space travel, he observed, could the prophecy of the New Jerusalem be fulfilled. It was, on the whole, a very enjoyable speech, and a marvelous demonstration of the pastor's wealth of learning in the field of science fiction; but the enchanted audience left the meeting at least as ignorant of Scripture as they had been when it began.

The Bible is *literature*: It is divinely-inspired and inerrant literature, but it is literature all the same. This means that we must *read* it as literature. Some parts are meant to be literally understood, and they are written accordingly — as history, or theological propositions, or whatever. But one would not expect to read the Psalms or the Song of Solomon by the same literary standards used for the Book of Romans. It would be like reading Hamlet's soliloquy "literally": "*The slings and arrows* of outrageous fortune . . . to *take arms* against a *sea of troubles*. . . ." We cannot understand what the Bible really (literally) means unless we appreciate its use of literary styles. Would we understand the Twenty-third Psalm properly if we were to take it "literally"? Would it not, instead, look somewhat silly? In fact, if taken literally, it would not be *true*: for I daresay that the Lord *doesn't* make every Christian to lie down in literal, green pastures. But we don't usually make such crude mistakes in reading Biblical poetry. We know it is written in a style that often makes use of symbolic imagery. But we must realize that the same is true of the prophets: They, also, spoke in figures and symbols, drawing on a rich heritage of Biblical images that began in the Garden of

---

and Revealed, to the Constitution and Course of Nature (Oxford: At the University Press, [1736] 1835), p. 310.

Eden.[65]

Indeed, Paradise is where prophecy began. It is worth noting that the very first promise of the coming Redeemer was stated in highly symbolic terms. God said to the Serpent:

> I will put enmity
> Between you and the woman
> And between your seed and her Seed;
> He shall crush your head,
> And you shall strike His heel. (Gen. 3:15)

Obviously, this is not simply "history written in advance." It is a symbolic statement, very much of a piece with the evocative, poetic language used throughout the Bible, and especially in Revelation. In fact, St. John plainly tells us in his opening sentence that the Revelation is written in *signs*, in symbols. He did not intend it to be read like a newspaper or a stock market analysis. He expected his audience to respond to his prophecy in terms of the Bible's own system of symbolism.

I repeat: *the Bible's own system of symbolism*. The meaning of a symbol is not whatever we choose to make it; nor did St. John create the images of the Book of Revelation out of his own imagination. He presents Christ to his readers as a Lion and a Lamb, not because he thinks those are pretty pictures, but because of the connotations of lions and lambs already established in the Bible. The Book of Revelation thus tells us from the outset that its standard of interpretation is the Bible itself. The book is crammed with allusions to the Old Testament. Merrill Tenney says: "It is filled with references to events and characters of the Old Testament, and a great deal of its phraseology is taken directly from the Old Testament books. Oddly enough, there is not one direct citation in Revelation from the Old Testament with a statement that it is quoted from a given passage; but a count of the significant allusions which are traceable both by verbal resemblance and by contextual connection to the Hebrew canon number three hundred and forty-eight. Of these approximately ninety-five are repeated, so that the actual number of different Old Testament passages that are mentioned are nearly

---

65. See Chilton, *Paradise Restored*, pp. 15-63.

two hundred and fifty, or an average of more than ten for each chapter in Revelation."⁶⁶ Tenney's count of 348 clear Old Testament references breaks down as follows: 57 from the Pentateuch, 235 from the Prophets, and 56 more from the historical and poetical books.⁶⁷

Tenney admits that his figures are conservative; one might even say hidebound. Nevertheless, even using his figures, it is obvious that the Book of Revelation depends on the Old Testament much more than does any other New Testament book. This fact alone should warn us that we cannot begin to fathom its meaning apart from a solid grasp of the Bible as a whole. The early churches had such an understanding. The Gospel had been preached first to the Jews and Gentile proselytes; often churches had been formed by worshipers at synagogues, and this was true even of the churches of Asia Minor (Acts 2:9; 13:14; 14:1; 16:4; 17:1-4, 10-12, 17; 18:4, 8, 19, 24-28; 19:1-10, 17). Moreover, it is clear from Galatians 2:9 that the Apostle John's ministry was to Jews in particular. Therefore, the first readers of the Revelation were steeped in the Old Testament to a degree that most of us today are not. The symbolism of the Revelation is saturated with Biblical allusions which were commonly understood by the early Church. Even in those rare congregations that did not have some Hebrew members, the Scriptures used in teaching and worship were primarily from the Old Testament. The early Christians possessed the authoritative and infallible key to the meaning of St. John's prophecies. Our modern failure to appreciate this crucial fact is the main cause of our inability to understand what he was talking about.

For instance, let's take a much-abused symbol from Revelation and apply this principle. In Rev. 7, 9, 14 and 22, St. John sees God's people sealed on their foreheads with His name; and in Rev. 13 he writes of the worshipers of the Beast, who are designated on their right hands and foreheads with *his* mark. Many fanciful interpretations have been made regarding these marks —ranging from tattoos and amusement-park validations to credit cards and Social Security numbers—and all without the

---

66. Merrill C. Tenney, *Interpreting Revelation* (Grand Rapids: William B. Eerdmans Publishing Co., 1957), p. 101.
67. Ibid, p. 104.

slightest notice of the clear Biblical allusions. But what would the first readers of these passages have thought? The symbols would have made them think immediately of several Biblical references: the "mark" of sweat on Adam's forehead, signifying God's Curse on his disobedience (Gen. 3:19); the forehead of the High Priest, marked with gold letters proclaiming that he was now *HOLY TO THE LORD* (Ex. 28:36); Deuteronomy 6:6-8 and Ezekiel 9:4-6, in which the servants of God are "marked" on the hand and forehead with the law of God, and thus receive blessing and protection in His name. The followers of the Beast, on the other hand, receive his mark of ownership: submission to ungodly, statist, antichristian law. The mark in Revelation is not meant to be taken literally. It is an allusion to an Old Testament symbol that spoke of a man's total obedience to God, and it stands as a warning that our god — whether it be the true God or the self-deified State — demands complete obedience to his lordship.

That will be the principle of interpretation followed in this commentary. The Revelation is a *revelation*: It was meant to be understood. Benjamin Warfield wrote: "John's Apocalypse need not be other than easy: all its symbols are either obvious natural ones, or else have their roots planted in the Old Testament poets and prophets and the figurative language of Jesus and his apostles. No one who knows his Bible need despair of reading this book with profit. Above all, he who can understand our Lord's great discourse concerning the last things (Matt. 24), cannot fail to understand the Apocalypse, which is founded on that discourse and scarcely advances beyond it."[68]

The Primacy of Symbolism

How important is symbolism in the Bible? The great Dutch theologian Herman Bavinck deals with the subject extensively in his book *The Doctrine of God*.[69] Speaking of the Bible's "symbolic" names for God, he says: "Scripture does not merely contain a few anthropomorphisms; on the contrary, *all* Scripture is anthropomorphic. . . . Hence, all the names with which God

---

68. Benjamin B. Warfield, "The Apocalypse," in *Selected Shorter Writings of Benjamin B. Warfield* (Nutley, NJ: Presbyterian and Reformed Publishing Co., 1973), vol. II, pp. 652f.

69. Herman Bavinck, *The Doctrine of God*, William Hendriksen, trans. (Edinburgh: The Banner of Truth Trust, [1951] 1977).

names himself and by means of which he allows us to address him are derived from earthly and human relations."[70] "In order to give us an idea of the majesty and exalted character of God names are derived from every kind of creature, living and lifeless, organic and inorganic."[71] In fact, "it is altogether impossible to say anything about God apart from the use of anthropomorphisms. We do not see God as he is in himself. We behold him in his works. We name him according to the manner in which he has revealed himself in his works. To see God face to face is for us impossible, at least here on earth. . . . Whosoever, therefore, objects to anthropomorphisms, thereby in principle denies the possibility of a revelation of God in his creatures."[72] "For man there are only two alternatives: absolute silence with reference to God, or speaking about him in a human way; either agnosticism, i.e., theoretical atheism, or anthropomorphism."[73]

Symbolism is thus inescapable: "Therefore, though we call God by names derived from the creature, God himself first established these names for the creature. Indeed, although we first apply to the creature the names which designate God because of the fact that we know the creature before we know God; *essentially* they apply first of all to God, then to the creature. All virtues pertain first to God, then to the creature: God possesses these virtues 'in essence,' the creature 'through participation.' As the temple was made 'according to the pattern shown to Moses in the mount,' Heb. 8:5, even so every creature was first conceived and afterward (in time) created. 'Every fatherhood' is named from 'the Father' who created all things — Eph. 3:15; cf. Matt. 23:9."[74]

Bavinck is making two very significant points: First, *all creation is primarily symbolic*. All creatures reflect the glory of God, and are images of some aspect or other of His nature. God's personality is imprinted on everything He has made. The *central* value of anything is that it is a symbol of God. All other values and relationships are secondary. And, since man is God's primary symbol, being His very "image" (both individually and

---

70. Ibid., p. 86.
71. Ibid., p. 88.
72. Ibid., p. 91.
73. Ibid., p. 92.
74. Ibid., p. 94.

corporately), everything is symbolic of man as well; thus everything reveals God and man.[75]

Second, *symbolism is analogical, not realistic*. In this the imagery used in the Bible contrasts markedly with the imagery of paganism. For example, the Bible speaks of the marriage covenant as analogous to the covenant between God and His people (2 Cor. 11:2; Eph. 5:22-33; Rev. 19:7-9; 21:9-11). The Church has always seen the Song of Solomon as, in part, an analogy of her own romance with the heavenly Bridegroom. But this is far from implying that sex is a sacrament; nor is this a doctrine of salvation through marriage. The symbolism is analogical, not metaphysical. We do not have a sexual relationship with God. There is a one-and-many complex of images involved in the Biblical picture. The theology of the Bible is analogical, not realistic. In Biblical salvation, man becomes remade in the image of God by a judicial sentence and an ethical transformation — not by a metaphysical participation in the divine essence.[76]

This means that Biblical symbolism is not a "code." It is not given in a flat "this-means-that" style: "Biblical symbols are fluid, not stereotyped."[77] A Biblical symbol is a collectivity, referring to several ideas at once. Biblical symbolism, like poetry, is evocative language, used when discursive, specific language is insufficient. The Bible uses evocative imagery to call up to our minds various associations which have been established by the Bible's own literary art.

---

75. For an extended discussion of the primary significance of symbolism, see James B. Jordan, "Symbolism: A Manifesto," in *The Sociology of the Church* (Tyler, TX: Geneva Ministries, 1986).

76. Thus, we should not be frightened when we find the Bible using certain symbols that are also used in pagan religions — for example, the Biblical references to stars or to the constellations of the Zodiac. (By the way, "Zodiac" is not an occult word; it simply refers to the apparent path of the sun across the heavens, passing "through" the twelve major constellations, the way God intended that it should.) Some forms of paganism teach that water is inhabited by spirits, and that (with the proper incantations) its application can confer magical powers. Christians do not believe this. Should we therefore (in order not to be confused with pagans) abandon the use of baptism? Or, should we give up the doctrine of the Virgin Birth, on the grounds that mythological gods have impregnated earthly maidens? Such examples can be multiplied many times over. Paganism, being a perversion of the truth, has a myriad of doctrines which bear a certain superficial similarity to Christianity. This does not mean that we should be afraid of symbolism; it means, instead, that we should reclaim the stolen symbols for the Lord Jesus Christ.

77. Rousas J. Rushdoony, *Thy Kingdom Come*, p. 174.

Austin Farrer pointed out a distinction we must always keep in mind—the difference between *sense* and *referent*. While the sense of a symbol remains the same (the words "white house" always mean "white house"), it can have numerous referents (*The* White House in Washington, D.C.; the white house across the street; the green house that belongs to Fred White; etc.). "St. John's images do not mean anything you like; their sense can be determined. But they still have an astonishing multiplicity of reference. Otherwise, why write in images rather than in cold factual prose? It has been said that the purpose of scientific statement is the elimination of ambiguity, and the purpose of symbol the inclusion of it. We write in symbol when we wish our words to present, rather than analyze or prove, their subject-matter. (Not every subject-matter; some can be more directly presented without symbol.) Symbol endeavours, as it were, to *be* that of which it speaks, and imitates reality by the multiplicity of its significance. Exact statement isolates a single aspect of fact: a theologian, for example, endeavours to isolate the relation in which the atoning death of Christ stands to the idea of forensic justice. But we who believe that the atoning death took place, must see in it a fact related to everything human or divine, with as many significances as there are things to which it can be variously related. The mere physical appearance of that death, to one who stood by then, would by no means express what the Christian thinks it, in itself, to be; it took many years for the Cross to gather round itself the force of a symbol in its own right. St. John writes 'a Lamb standing as slaughtered' and significances of indefinite scope and variety awake in the scripture-reading mind. There is a current and exceedingly stupid doctrine that symbol evokes emotion, and exact prose states reality. Nothing could be further from the truth: exact prose abstracts from reality, symbol presents it. And for that very reason, symbols have some of the many-sidedness of wild nature."[78]

78. Austin Farrer, *A Rebirth of Images*, pp. 19f. For those readers who truly wish to pursue the serious study of Scripture, I suggest the following as an absolutely necessary first step: Pack all your books on hermeneutics in a trunk until you have read Laurence Perrine, *Sound and Sense: An Introduction to Poetry* (New York: Harcourt Brace Jovanovich, sixth ed., 1982), and John Ciardi and Miller Williams, *How Does a Poem Mean* (Boston: Houghton Mifflin Co., second ed., 1975). More courageous souls may wish to continue further with two books by Northrop Frye: *Anatomy of Criticism* (Princeton: Princeton University Press, 1957) and (with caution) *The Great Code: The Bible and Literature* (New York: Harcourt Brace Jovanovich, 1982).

For example, the symbolic number 666 (Rev. 13:18) clearly refers to Nero Caesar; but if St. John had merely intended that his readers should understand "Nero Caesar," he would have written "Nero Caesar," not "666."[79] He used the number 666 because of an already established system of Biblical imagery that allowed him to say a great many things about Nero simply by using that number. As Philip Carrington says: "Many people 'interpret' the Revelation . . . as if each detail of each vision had a definable meaning which could be explained in so many words. These commentators are rationalizers, deficient in the mystical sense. Symbolism is a way of suggesting the truth about those great spiritual realities which exclude exact definition or complete systematization; that is why it is so much employed in worship. . . . The symbol is much richer in meaning than any meaning we can draw from it. The same is true of the parables and symbolic teaching of Jesus. The same is true of the sacraments and symbolic acts of the church, or even of society. Many logical systems can be made up to explain the 'meaning' of shaking hands or making the sign of the cross; but because of their simplicity and universality these actions mean more than words can explain."[80]

Further, "the prophets in general use a great deal of hyperbole and picturesque exaggeration in the manner of Oriental poetry. *As the days of a tree shall be the days of my people* (Isa. 65:22). *Yet destroyed I the Amorite whose height was like the height of the cedars* (Amos 2:9): statements which mean respectively 'very old' and 'very tall.' It goes right back to primitive poetry: *The mountains skipped like rams. . . . The earth trembled and shook* (Ps. 114). Poets, even Western poets, will always continue to use it. It includes the use of huge figures; a reign of forty years means a good long reign, and a kingdom of a thousand years means a good long kingdom. The poetry of Jesus has it to a superlative degree; camels are swallowed or passed

---

79. The idea that he wrote it in "code" because he was afraid of being arrested for treason is obviously false: The prophets were not timid men; and anyway, the Book of Revelation is "treasonous" long before St. John gets around to talking about Nero. Christians could be killed for saying simply what St. John says in Chapter 1—that Jesus Christ is "the Ruler of the kings of the earth."

80. Philip Carrington, *The Meaning of the Revelation*, pp. 84f.

through needles' eyes; mountains are thrown into the depths of the sea; a man gets a tree-trunk stuck in his eye.

"People without sufficient imagination to understand this and to enjoy it ought to steer clear of the Apocalypse. Just as a witness has to understand 'the nature of an oath,' so a commentator ought to understand the nature of a poem, or even of a joke. Many who are deficient in a sense of poetry and a sense of humor have tried their hands on the Apocalypse, and made a mess of it."[81]

Interpretive Maximalism

James Jordan once observed that most conservative evangelicals unintentionally pursue a "liberal" approach toward Scripture in their sermons and commentaries. Liberals have held for years that the Bible is not revelation itself; rather, they maintain, it is a [flawed] *record* of revelation. While conservative evangelicals profess to believe that the Bible itself is revelation (and as such is inspired, authoritative, and inerrant), their expository methods deny this. In practice, conservatives themselves often treat the Bible as only a "record" of revelation. Evangelical commentaries tend not to deal with the actual text of the Bible, treating only of the *events* related in the text and paying scant attention to the wording and literary achitecture of God's revelation. (Ironically, since liberals don't believe the events really happened, they sometimes tend to pay closer attention to the text itself. That's all they've got left.)

The mark of a good Bible teacher is that he is constantly asking: *Why* is the story told in this particular way? Why is this particular word or phrase repeated several times? (How many times?) What does this story have in common with other stories? How is it different? Why does the text draw our attention to seemingly unimportant details? How do the minor incidents fit into the argument of the book as a whole? What literary devices (metaphor, satire, drama, comedy, allegory, poetry, etc.) does the author use? Why does the book sometimes depart from a strict chronological account (e.g., placing some stories "out of order")? How are these stories related to the larger Story that the Bible tells? What does this story tell us about Jesus

---

81. Ibid., pp. 136f.

Christ? What does this story have to do with our salvation? Why did God bother to give us this particular information?

In his inaugural address as Professor of Biblical Theology in Princeton Theological Seminary in 1894, Geerhardus Vos spoke of the advantages of the Biblical-Theology approach to the study of Scripture; among these, he said, is "the new life and freshness which it gives to the old truth, showing it in all its historic vividness and reality with the dew of the morning of revelation upon its opening leaves. It is certainly not without significance that God has embodied the contents of revelation, not in a dogmatic system, but in a book of history, the parallel to which in dramatic interest and simple eloquence is nowhere to be found. It is this that makes the Scriptures speak and appeal to and touch the hearts and lead the minds of men captive to the truth everywhere. No one will be able to handle the Word of God more effectually than he to whom the treasure-chambers of its historic meaning have been opened up."[82]

One of the most important discoveries that can be made by any Bible teacher is an understanding of the basic imagery laid down in the early chapters of Genesis — light and darkness, water and land, sky and clouds, mountains and gardens, beasts and dragons, gold and jewels, trees and thorns, cherubs and flaming swords — all of which form a grand and glorious Story, the *true* "fairy tale," one which can be grasped and delighted in even by very young children.[83] *Everything* in Scripture is "symbolic." Jordan calls this "interpretive maximalism," an approach that harmonizes with the interpretive method used by the Church Fathers, as opposed to the "minimalism" that has characterized fundamentalist-evangelical commentaries since the rise of rationalism.[84]

A good example of this is Jordan's discussion of Judges 9:53: "But a certain *woman* threw an *upper millstone* on Abimelech's

---

82. Geerhardus Vos, "The Idea of Biblical Theology," in Richard B. Gaffin, ed., *Redemptive History and Biblical Interpretation: The Shorter Writings of Geerhardus Vos* (Presbyterian and Reformed, 1980), p. 23.

83. A good introduction to the literary motifs of Scripture is Leland Ryken's *How to Read the Bible as Literature* (Grand Rapids: Zondervan, 1984).

84. James B. Jordan, *Judges: God's War Against Humanism* (Tyler, TX: Geneva Ministries, 1985), p. xii.

head, crushing his *skull.*" (Note: The text does not simply say that "Abimelech got killed." The details are there for a reason.) It is important, for symbolic reasons, that a *woman* crushed the tyrant's *head* (see, e.g., Gen. 3:15; cf. Jud. 5:24-27); that he was destroyed by a *stone* (cf. Deut. 13:10; Jud. 9:5; 1 Sam. 17:49; Dan. 2:34; Matt. 21:44); and that it was a *millstone*, an implement of work to overcome tyranny (cf. Zech. 1:18-21).[85]

But are there any controls on the "maximalist"? How does he evade the accusation that he is merely being speculative, interpreting the text according to his personal prejudice or the whim of the moment? Of course, the charge that an interpreter is being "speculative" can be, as often as not, little more than a smokescreen to disguise the accuser's ignorance of what the interpreter is talking about. The appropriate question, therefore, is whether or not the interpreter is proceeding in his investigations along *Biblical* lines of thought. Does this mean that he must stick to the so-called "plain sense" of the text? It might be answered that one man's "plain sense" is another man's "speculation." A hyper-literalist would object to any level of symbolism at all. (For example, one popular preacher actually does teach, on the basis of the "plain sense" of Revelation 12, that there is a real, live, fire-breathing, seven-headed dragon flying around in outer space!) The more usual, run-of-the-mill literalist rejects all symbolism not explicitly explained as such in Scripture. But neither of these positions is countenanced by the Bible. God has given us principles of interpreting His Word, and He expects us to use them. Our goal in Bible teaching is, to put it plainly, *Bible teaching*, according to the Bible's own standards of exegesis — whether or not those fit everyone's notions of "plainness."

There are at least two things that can keep an interpreter on a Biblical track, avoiding the pitfalls of willy-nilly speculation. First, he must be faithful to the *system of doctrine* taught in the Bible. Reading the Bible with theological eyes, in terms of systematic and historical theology, is an effective check on unbridled speculation. Second, the interpreter must keep in mind that the symbols in the Bible are not isolated; rather, they are part of a *system of symbolism* given in the Bible, an architecture of im-

---

85. Ibid., pp. 175f.

ages in which all the parts fit together. If we honestly and carefully read the Bible theologically and with respect to the Bible's own literary structure, we will not go very far astray.[86]

The Contemporary Focus of Revelation

The purpose of the Revelation was to reveal Christ as Lord to a suffering Church. Because they were being persecuted, the early Christians could be tempted to fear that the world was getting out of hand—that Jesus, who had claimed "all authority . . . in heaven and on earth" (Matt. 28:18), was not really in control at all. The apostles often warned against this man-centered error, reminding the people that God's sovereignty is over all of history (including our particular tribulations). This was the basis for some of the most beautiful passages of comfort in the New Testament (e.g. Rom. 8:28-39; 2 Cor. 1:3-7; 4:7-15).

St. John's primary concern in writing the Book of Revelation was just this very thing: to strengthen the Christian community in the faith of Jesus Christ's Lordship, to make them aware that the persecutions they suffered were integrally involved in the great war of history. The Lord of glory had ascended to His throne, and the ungodly rulers were now resisting His authority by persecuting His brethren. The suffering of Christians was *not* a sign that Jesus had abandoned this world to the devil; rather, it revealed that He was King. If Jesus' Lordship were historically meaningless, the ungodly would have had no reason whatsoever to trouble the Christians. But instead, they persecuted Jesus' followers, showing their unwilling recognition of His supremacy over their rule. The Book of Revelation presents Jesus seated on a white horse as "King of kings and Lord of lords" (19:16), doing battle with the nations, judging and making war in righteous-

---

86. For more on Biblical interpretation, see Geerhardus Vos, *Biblical Theology: Old and New Testaments* (Grand Rapids: Eerdmans, 1948); Meredith G. Kline, *Images of the Spirit* (Grand Rapids: Baker Book House, 1980); Vern S. Poythress, *The Stained-Glass Kaleidoscope: Using Perspectives in Theology* (privately printed syllabus, Westminster Theological Seminary, Philadelphia, 1985); Richard L. Pratt, Jr., "Pictures, Windows, and Mirrors in Old Testament Exegesis," *Westminster Theological Journal* 45 (1983), pp. 156-67. James B. Jordan's three lectures on "How to Interpret Prophecy" are an excellent introduction to the understanding of Biblical symbolism. The three tapes are available from Geneva Ministries, P.O. Box 131300, Tyler, TX 75713.

ness. The persecuted Christians were not at all forsaken by God. In reality they were on the front lines of the conflict of the ages, a conflict in which Jesus Christ had already won the decisive battle. Since His resurrection, all of history has been a "mopping up" operation, wherein the implications of His work are gradually being implemented throughout the world. St. John is realistic: The battles will not be easy, nor will Christians emerge unscathed. The war will often be bloody, and much of the blood will be our own. But Jesus is King, Jesus is Lord, and (as Luther says) "He must win the battle." The Son of God goes forth to war, conquering and to conquer, until He has put all enemies under His feet.

The subject of the Revelation thus was *contemporary*; that is, it was written to and for Christians who were living at the time it was first delivered. We are wrong to interpret it futuristically, as if its message were primarily intended for a time 2000 years after St. John wrote it. (It is interesting — but not surprising — that those who interpret the book "futuristically" always seem to focus on their own era as the subject of the prophecies. Convinced of their own importance, they are unable to think of themselves as living at any other time than the climax of history.) Of course, the events St. John foretold *were* "in the future" to St. John and his readers; but they occurred soon after he wrote of them. To interpret the book otherwise is to contradict both the scope of the work as a whole, and the particular passages which indicate its subject. For us, the great majority of the Revelation is *history*: It has already happened.

The greatest enemy of the early Church was apostate Israel, which used the power of the pagan Roman Empire to try to stamp out Christianity, just as it had used Rome in the crucifixion of the Lord Himself. St. John's message in Revelation was that this great obstacle to the Church's victory over the world would soon be judged and destroyed. His message was contemporary, not futuristic.

Some will complain that this interpretation makes the Revelation "irrelevant" for our age. A more wrong-headed idea is scarcely imaginable. Are the books of Romans and Ephesians "irrelevant" just because they were written to believers in the first century? Should 1 Corinthians and Galatians be dismissed because they dealt with first-century problems? Is not *all* Scripture profitable for believers in every age (2 Tim. 3:16-17)? Actually, it is the futurists who have made the Revelation irrelevant — for on the futurist hypothesis the book has been inapplicable from the time it was written until the twentieth century! Only if we see the Revelation in terms of its contemporary relevance is it anything but a dead letter. From the outset, St. John stated that his book was intended for "the seven churches which are in Asia" (1:4), and we must assume that he meant what he said. He clearly expected that even the most difficult symbols in the prophecy could be understood by his first-century readers (13:18). Not once did he imply that his book was written with the twentieth century in mind, and that Christians would be wasting their time attempting to decipher it until the *Scofield Reference Bible* would become a best-selling novel. The primary relevance of the Book of Revelation was for its first-century readers. It still has relevance for us today as we understand its message and apply its principles to our lives and our culture. Jesus Christ still demands of us what He demanded of the early Church: absolute faithfulness to Him.

The contemporary nature of the Revelation will be defended throughout the commentary, but we may consider several lines of evidence here. First, there is the general tone of the book, which is taken up with the martyrs (see, e.g., 6:9; 7:14; 12:11).[87] The subject is clearly the present situation of the churches: The Revelation was written to a suffering Church in order to comfort believers during their time of testing (which took place, as we have seen, under Nero, not Domitian). J. Stuart Russell's remarks on this point are particularly apt: "Was a book sent by an apostle to the churches of Asia Minor, with a benediction on its readers, a mere unintelligible jargon, an inexplicable enigma, to them? That can hardly be. Yet if the book were meant to unveil the secrets of distant times, must it not of necessity have been unintelligible to its first readers — and not only unintelligible, but even irrelevant and useless? If it spake, as some would have us believe, of Huns and Goths and Saracens, of medieval emperors and popes, of the Protestant Reformation and the French Revolution, what possible interest or meaning could it have for the Christian churches of Ephesus, and Smyrna, and Philadelphia, and Laodicea? Especially when we consider the actual circum-

---

87. See Louis Bouyer, *The Spirituality of the New Testament and the Fathers*, trans. Mary P. Ryan (Minneapolis: The Seabury Press, 1963), pp. 120f.

stances of those early Christians — many of them enduring cruel sufferings and grievous persecutions, and all of them eagerly looking for an approaching hour of deliverance which was now close at hand — what purpose could it have answered to send them a document which they were urged to read and ponder, which was yet mainly occupied with historical events so distant as to be beyond the range of their sympathies, and so obscure that even at this day the shrewdest critics are hardly agreed on any one point?

"Is it conceivable that an apostle would mock the suffering and persecuted Christians of his time with dark parables about distant ages? If this book were really intended to minister faith and comfort to the very persons to whom it was sent, it must unquestionably deal with matters in which they were practically and personally interested. And does not this very obvious consideration suggest the true key to the Apocalypse? *Must it not of necessity refer to matters of contemporary history?* The only tenable, the only reasonable, hypothesis is that it was intended to be understood by its original readers; but this is as much as to say that it must be occupied with the events and transactions of their own day, and these comprised within a comparatively brief space of time."[88]

Second, St. John writes that the book concerns "the things which must shortly take place" (1:1), and warns that "the time is near" (1:3). In case we might miss it, he says again, at the close of the book, that "the Lord, the God of the spirits of the prophets, sent His angel to show to His bond-servants the things which must shortly take place" (22:6). Given the fact that one important proof of a true prophet lay in the fact that his predictions came true (Deut. 18:21-22), St. John's first-century readers had every reason to expect his book to have immediate significance. The words *shortly* and *near* simply cannot be made to mean anything but what they say. Some will object to this on the basis of 2 Peter 3:8, that "one day is with the Lord as a thousand years, and a thousand years as one day." But the context there is entirely different: Peter is exhorting his first-century readers to have patience with respect to God's promises, assuring them

---

88. J. Stuart Russell, *The Parousia: A Critical Inquiry into the New Testament Doctrine of Our Lord's Second Coming* (Grand Rapids: Baker Book House, [1887] 1983), p. 366.

that God's faithfulness to His holy Word will not wear out or diminish.

The Book of Revelation is not about the Second Coming of Christ. It is about the destruction of Israel and Christ's victory over His enemies in the establishment of the New Covenant Temple. In fact, as we shall see, the word *coming* as used in the Book of Revelation never refers to the Second Coming. Revelation prophesies the judgment of God on apostate Israel; and while it does briefly point to events beyond its immediate concerns, that is done merely as a "wrap-up," to show that the ungodly will never prevail against Christ's Kingdom. But the main focus of Revelation is upon events which were soon to take place.

Third, St. John identifies certain situations as contemporary: In 13:18, he clearly encourages his contemporary readers to calculate the "number of the Beast" and decipher its meaning; in 17:10, one of the seven kings is currently on the throne; and St. John tells us that the great Harlot "*is* [present tense] the Great City, which *reigns* [present tense] over the kings of the earth" (17:18). Again, the Revelation was meant to be understood in terms of its contemporary significance. A futuristic interpretation is completely opposed to the way St. John himself interprets his own prophecy.

Fourth, we should notice carefully the words of the angel in 22:10: "Do not seal up the words of the prophecy of this book, for the time is near." Again, of course, we are told explicitly that the prophecy is contemporary in nature; but there is more. The angel's statement is in contrast to the command Daniel received at the end of his book: "Conceal the words and *seal up the book* until the time of the end" (Dan. 12:4). Daniel was specifically ordered to seal up his prophecy, because it referred to "the end," in the distant future. But St. John is told *not* to seal up his prophecy, because the time of which it speaks is *near*.

Thus, the focus of the Book of Revelation is upon the contemporary situation of St. John and his first-century readers. It was written to show those early Christians that Jesus is Lord, "ruler over the kings of the earth" (Rev. 1:5). It shows that Jesus is the key to world history — that nothing can occur apart from His sovereign will, that He will be glorified in all things, and that His enemies will lick the dust. The Christians of that day were tempted to compromise with the statism and false religions of their day, and they needed this message of Christ's absolute dominion over all, that they might be strengthened in the warfare to which they were called.

And we need this message also. We too are subjected daily to the threats and seductions of Christ's enemies. We too are asked — even by fellow Christians — to compromise with modern Beasts and Harlots in order to save ourselves (or our jobs or property or tax exemptions). And we too are faced with a choice: surrender to Jesus Christ or surrender to Satan. The Revelation speaks powerfully today, and its message to us is the same as it was to the early Church: that "there is not a square inch of ground in heaven or on earth or under the earth in which there is peace between Christ and Satan";[89] that our Lord demands universal submission to His rule; and that He has predestined His people to victorious conquest and dominion over all things in His name. We must make no compromise and give no quarter in the great battle of history. We are commanded to win.

A Note on the Text

I do not profess to be a textual critic. Nevertheless, in order to produce a detailed commentary, it was necessary to decide one way or another about which New Testament textual tradition to follow. The translation in this commentary is based largely on the recommendations of Hodges and Farstad in their "Majority Text" *Greek New Testament*.[90] The basic arguments for the Majority Text position have been presented in the works of Jakob van Bruggen,[91] Wilbur N. Pickering,[92] Harry A. Sturz,[93] and

---

89. Cornelius Van Til, *Essays on Christian Education* (Nutley, NJ: Presbyterian and Reformed Publishing Co., 1977), p. 27.

90. Zane C. Hodges and Arthur L. Farstad, *The Greek New Testament According to the Majority Text* (Nashville: Thomas Nelson Publishers, 1982). That is to say, where the evidence presented by Hodges and Farstad seems unequivocal, I have followed it; where it is less clear, I have felt free to disagree.

91. Jakob van Bruggen, *The Ancient Text of the New Testament* (Winnipeg: Premier Printing Ltd., 1976); idem, *The Future of the Bible* (Nashville: Thomas Nelson Publishers, 1978).

92. Wilbur N. Pickering, *The Identity of the New Testament Text* (Nashville: Thomas Nelson Publishers, 1977).

93. Harry A. Sturz, *The Byzantine Text-Type in New Testament Textual Criticism* (Nashville: Thomas Nelson Publishers, 1984). Sturz takes a much

others;[94] they do not need to be rehearsed here. I do wish to stress, however, that the issue is not really one of *majority* (i.e., simply counting manuscripts) but catholicity: The point of the "Majority Text" is that it is the Catholic Text, the New Testament used by the universal Church of all ages[95] — in contrast to the so-called "critical text" of most modern translations, representing a tiny, variant tradition produced in Egypt.

Overview of Revelation

The following outline is simply a more detailed version of the covenantal structure mentioned above. The Revelation is so complex that one is tempted to indulge in endless structural analyses (some will be noted as we proceed through the commentary). There is one further point that should not be missed at the outset, however. Overlaying the whole book is the theme of the Bridegroom and the Bride, and the prophecy is divided right in the middle between these two motifs. Thus:

I. The Bridegroom, Chapters 1-11: This section begins (1:9-20) and ends (10:1-7) with visions of the Son of Man, clothed in glory.

II. The Bride, Chapters 12-22: This section begins (12:1-2) and ends (21:9-27) with visions of the Church, clothed in glory.

---

more moderate position than do Hodges, Pickering, and the other defenders of the Majority Text. His valuable study demonstrates that the so-called "Byzantine" (i.e. Majority Text) readings are both early and independent. Thus, while he does not believe that the Byzantine text is "primary," he shows that it cannot be regarded as "secondary" either.

94. Cf. David Otis Fuller, ed., *Which Bible?* (Grand Rapids: International Publishers, fifth ed., 1975); *True or False? The Westcott-Hort Textual Theory Examined* (Grand Rapids: International Publishers, 1973); *Counterfeit or Genuine? — Mark 16? John 8?* (Grand Rapids: International Publishers, 1975); Edward F. Hills, *The King James Version Defended!* (Des Moines: Christian Research Press, 1956, 1973). It is important to note, however, that the position of the Majority-Text advocates is not quite the same as that of the defenders of the King James Version (or of the Textus Receptus). The argument of this latter group is that the true text has been providentially preserved in the Textus Receptus readings, even in those cases (e.g., 1 John 5:7; Rev. 22:19) where the actual Greek manuscript evidence is either slim or nonexistent. It is interesting that (in contrast to the rest of the New Testament) the Majority Text readings for the Book of Revelation are more often in agreement with the "critical text" than with the Textus Receptus.

95. For this reason, it is most unfortunate that Hodges and Farstad chose to ignore the readings of the traditional lectionaries in collating their edition (*The Greek New Testament According to the Majority Text*, p. xviii).

Outline of Revelation

I. Preamble: St. John's Vision of the Son of Man (1:1-20)

II. Historical Prologue: Letters to the Seven Churches (2:1-3:22)
   A. Ephesus (2:1-7)
   B. Smyrna (2:8-11)
   C. Pergamum (2:12-17)
   D. Thyatira (2:18-29)
   E. Sardis (3:1-6)
   F. Philadelphia (3:7-13)
   G. Laodicea (3:14-22)

III. Stipulations: The Seven Seals (4:1-7:17)
   A. The Throne (4:1-11)
   B. The Sealed Book (5:1-5)
   C. The Lamb Standing as Slain (5:6-14)
   D. The First Four Seals: Horsemen (6:1-8)
   E. The Fifth Seal: Martyrs (6:9-11)
   F. The Sixth Seal: De-Creation (6:12-17)
   G. The 144,000 Sealed (7:1-8)
   H. The Innumerable Multitude (7:9-17)

IV. Sanctions: The Seven Trumpets (8:1-14:20)
   A. The Seventh Seal: The Incense Altar (8:1-5)
   B. The First Four Trumpets (8:6-13)
   C. The Fifth Trumpet: Locusts from the Abyss (9:1-12)
   D. The Sixth Trumpet: The Army of Myriads (9:13-21)
   E. The Angel of the Oath (10:1-7)
   F. The Little Book (10:8-11)
   G. The Two Witnesses (11:1-14)
   H. The Seventh Trumpet: The Kingdom Comes (11:15-19)
   I. The Woman, the Seed, and the Dragon (12:1-6)
   J. Michael and the Dragon (12:7-12)
   K. The Flight of the Woman (12:13-17)
   L. The Beast from the Sea (13:1-10)
   M. The Beast from the Land (13:11-18)
   N. The Lamb and the 144,000 on Mount Zion (14:1-5)
   O. The Gospel and the Poisoned Cups (14:6-13)
   P. The Harvest and the Vintage of the Land (14:14-20)

V. Succession Arrangements: The Seven Chalices (15:1-22:21)
   A. The Song of Victory (15:1-4)
   B. The Sanctuary is Opened (15:5-8)
   C. The First Four Chalices: God's Creation Takes Vengeance (16:1-9)
   D. The Last Three Chalices: It Is Finished! (16:10-21)

46

E. Babylon: The Great Harlot (17:1-5)
F. Babylon: The Mystery Explained (17:6-18)
G. Babylon Is Fallen! (18:1-8)
H. Reactions to Babylon's Fall (18:9-20)
I. Babylon Is Thrown Down (18:20-24)
J. The Marriage Supper of the Lamb (19:1-10)
K. The Rider on the White Horse (19:11-16)
L. The Feast of the Scavengers (19:17-18)
M. The Destruction of the Beasts (19:19-21)
N. The Binding of Satan (20:1-3)
O. The First Resurrection and the Last Battle (20:4-10)
P. The Final Judgment (20:11-15)
Q. The New Creation (21:1-8)
R. The New Jerusalem (21:9-27)
S. The River of Life (22:1-5)
T. Come, Lord Jesus! (22:6-21)

Part One

PREAMBLE: THE SON OF MAN
(Revelation 1)

Introduction

The Preamble in Deuteronomy (1:1-5) begins: "These are the words. . . ."[1] The text then identifies the speaker as Moses, who as mediator of the Covenant has been "commanded" to give and expound God's "law" to Israel. "Yahweh is, therefore, the Suzerain who gives the covenant and Moses is his vicegerent and the covenant mediator. This section thus corresponds to the preamble of the extra-biblical treaties, which also identified the speaker, the one who by the covenant was declaring his lordship and claiming the vassal's obedience."[2] The Preamble in Revelation begins with a similar expression: "The Revelation of Jesus Christ, which God gave Him to show to His servants, the things that must shortly take place; and He sent and signified it by His angel to His servant John, who bore witness to the Word of God and to the Testimony of Jesus Christ, even to all that he saw" (1:1-2).

The purpose of the covenantal Preamble is thus to proclaim the lordship of the Great King, declaring his *transcendence and immanence* and making it clear from the outset that his will is to be obeyed by the vassals, his servants. Biblical treaties set forth God's transcendence and immanence by referring to one or more of three activities: creation, redemption, and revelation. It is the latter two that are especially emphasized in Revelation's

---

1. The Hebrew title of Deuteronomy is simply: *The Words*.
2. Meredith G. Kline, *Treaty of the Great King* (Grand Rapids: William B. Eerdmans Publishing Co., 1963), p. 30.

49

Preamble. We have already noted the stress on divine revelation in the opening sentence, and this is underscored in the following verses. The churches are to "hear the words of the prophecy, and keep the things that are written in it," and the Lord pronounces a special blessing upon those who obey (1:3); St. John again speaks of himself as one who has borne witness to "the Word of God and the Testimony of Jesus" (1:9); further, he tells of the revelation that came to him in terms of the standard and familiar patterns of covenantal revelation throughout Biblical history: "I was in the Spirit on the Lord's Day, and I heard behind me a loud Voice like the sound of a trumpet, saying: Write in a book what you see. . . ." (1:10-11; see below).

Redemption is also stressed in this passage: "Jesus Christ, the faithful Witness, the Firstborn from the dead, and the Ruler of the kings of the earth . . . who loves us and released us from our sins by His blood . . . has made us to be a Kingdom, priests to His God and Father; to Him be the glory and dominion forever and ever. Amen" (1:5-6). Moreover, Christ is specifically stated to be the Redeemer, the Son of Man, who "comes with the clouds" in His glorious Ascension to the Father and coming judgment upon Israel to receive worldwide dominion, glory, and a Kingdom; who will be seen by "those who pierced him," and mourned over by "all the tribes of the Land" (1:7; cf. Dan. 7:13-14; Zech. 12:10-14; Matt. 24:30; John 19:37; Eph. 1:20-22). St. John's vision of Christ develops the idea of His redemptive work: He is clothed as the High Priest (1:13), revealed as the incarnate Glory of God (1:14-15), the Creator and Sustainer of the world, whose powerful Word goes forth to conquer the nations (1:16); who died, and rose again from the dead, and who is alive forevermore (1:17-18).

1

KING OF KINGS

Title and Benediction (1:1-3)

1 The Revelation of Jesus Christ, which God gave Him to show His servants the things that must shortly take place; and He sent and signified it by His angel to His servant John;
2 who bore witness to the Word of God and to the Witness of Jesus Christ, even to all that he saw.
3 Blessed is he who reads and those who hear the words of the prophecy, and keep the things that are written in it; for the time is near.

1 St. John makes it clear from the outset that his book is a **revelation,** an unveiling or disclosure of God's purposes. It is not intended to be mysterious or enigmatic; it is, emphatically, *a revealing* of its subject. Specifically, it is **the Revelation of Jesus Christ, which God gave Him** — in other words, a revelation mediated by our Lord Himself (cf. Heb. 1:2), about **the things that must shortly take place.** The Revelation, therefore, is not concerned with either the scope of world history or the end of the world, but with events that were in the near future to St. John and his readers. As we shall see throughout the commentary, the Book of Revelation is a "covenant lawsuit," prophesying the outpouring of God's wrath on Jerusalem. It is a prophecy of the period known in Scripture as "the Last Days," meaning the last days of the covenantal nation of Israel, the forty-year "generation" (Matt. 24:34) between the Ascension of Christ (A.D. 30) and the Fall of Jerusalem to the Romans (A.D. 70).[1] It foretells

---

1. See David Chilton, *Paradise Restored: A Biblical Theology of Dominion* (Ft. Worth, TX: Dominion Press, 1985), pp. 112, 115-22. I have explained this in much greater detail in a series of articles on the Last Days, published in *The Geneva Review,* P.O. Box 131300, Tyler, TX 75713.

events that St. John expected his readers to see very soon.

This clearly militates against any "futurist" interpretation of the book. The futurists would have it that St. John was warning the Christians of his day mostly about things they would never see — meaning that the Book of Revelation has been irrelevant for 1900 years! To claim that the book has relevance only for our generation is egocentric; and it is contrary to the testimony of the book itself. It must be stressed that the Greek expression for our English word **shortly** plainly means *soon*, and those who first read the phrase would not have understood it to mean anything else (cf. Luke 18:8; Acts 12:7; 22:18; 25:4; Rom. 16:20; Rev. 22:6). A futurist interpretation is refuted in the very first verse of Revelation.

Before we go any further, we should also note that St. John's opening statement presupposes the Biblical philosophy of history: God is Lord of all, He has an all-embracing plan for His creation, and He rules every atom of reality according to His plan. After all, how does God know the future? The Bible does not indicate that God has some sort of crystal ball with which He can perceive future events. Think about it. There is really no such thing as "the future," in the sense of something "out there" that can be divined with the proper equipment. To say that something is in the future is simply to say that it does not yet exist. How then does God know the future? The Bible gives only one answer: God knows the future because He planned it:

> The LORD has established His throne in the heavens, and His Kingdom rules over all. (Ps. 103:19)

> Our God is in the heavens; He does whatever He pleases. (Ps. 115:3)

> And all the inhabitants of the earth are accounted as nothing, but He does according to His will in the host of heaven and among the inhabitants of earth; and no one can hold back His hand, or say to Him: What have You done? (Dan. 4:35)

> We have obtained an inheritance, having been predestined according to His purpose who works all things after the counsel of His will. (Eph. 1:11)

Thus, even though "the future" does not yet exist, it is absolutely certain and secure, because the all-powerful Lord of the universe has infallibly planned it. He "gives life to the dead and calls into being that which does not exist" (Rom. 4:17). God knows all things exhaustively because He planned all things exhaustively.

Arthur Pink wrote: "The Lord God omnipotent reigneth. His government is exercised over inanimate matter, over the brute beasts, over the children of men, over angels good and evil, and over Satan himself. No revolving of a world, no shining of a star, no storm, no movement of a creature, no actions of men, no errands of angels, no deeds of the Devil — *nothing in all the vast universe can come to pass otherwise than God has eternally purposed.* Here is a foundation for faith. Here is a resting place for the intellect. Here is an anchor for the soul, both sure and steadfast. It is not blind fate, unbridled evil, man or Devil, but the Lord Almighty who is ruling the world, ruling it according to His own good pleasure and for His own eternal glory."[2]

Now St. John says that these things regarding the future were **signified**, or "*sign*-ified," to him by the angel. The use of this word tells us that the prophecy is not simply to be taken as "history written in advance." It is a book of *signs*, symbolic representations of the approaching events. The symbols are not to be understood in a literal manner. We can see this by St. John's use of the same term in his Gospel (12:33; 18:32; 21:19). In each case, it is used of Christ "signifying" a future event by a more or less symbolic indication, rather than by a prosaic, literal description. And this is generally the form of the prophecies in the Revelation. It is a book of symbols from beginning to end. As G. R. Beasley-Murray well said, "The prophet wishes to make clear that he does not provide photographs of heaven."[3] This does not mean the symbols are unintelligible; the interpretation is not what any individual chooses to make it. Nor, on the other hand, are the symbols written in some sort of code, so that all we need is a dictionary or grammar of symbolism to "translate" the symbols into English. The only way to understand St. John's system of symbolism is to become familiar with the Bible itself.

---

2. Arthur Pink, *The Sovereignty of God* (London: The Banner of Truth Trust, [1928] 1968), pp. 43f.

3. G. R. Beasley-Murray, *The Book of Revelation* (Grand Rapids: William B. Eerdmans Publishing Co., [1974] 1981), p. 51.

2-3   An important relationship is set up here. Verse 1 showed us Jesus Christ giving the Revelation to St. John; now St. John states that he himself **bore witness to the Word of God and to the Witness of Jesus Christ.** Thus we see that Jesus is the pre-eminent Witness-Bearer, testifying to His **servants;** and we see also that St. John bears witness of Christ's Witness, testifies of Christ's Testimony. He can do this because he is one of Christ's servants, and has become like his Master. In giving testimony, St. John is conformed to the image of Christ. These two patterns — Christ and His servants bearing dual witness, and Christ's servants bearing His image — are carried on throughout the book, and will inform our understanding of such passages as 11:4-12.

Because this dual testimony (the Book of Revelation) is the very Word of God, a blessing — the first of the prophecy's seven "beatitudes" (1:3; 14:13; 16:15; 19:9; 20:6; 22:7; 22:14) — is pronounced upon those who are faithful to its message. Let us note the specific form of the blessing, for it offers another important pointer to the book's content: **Blessed is he who reads and those who hear.** St. John has written this prophecy, not merely (or primarily) for individual edification, but for the Church in its official gathering for worship. From the beginning, the Book of Revelation is placed in a liturgical setting, in which a Reader reads out the prophecy to the congregation. The Greek word for **reads** is often used in the New Testament for this liturgical activity (Luke 4:16; Acts 13:27; 15:21; 2 Cor. 3:15; Eph. 3:4; Col. 4:16; 1 Thess. 5:27; 1 Tim. 4:13). The Book of Revelation, as we shall see, is greatly concerned with liturgy; indeed, worship is a central theme of the prophecy. By showing us how God's will is done in heavenly worship, St. John reveals how the Church is to perform His will on earth.

From the liturgy of special worship we go out into the world, to serve God in the liturgy of life. We respond to Truth ("Amen") in special worship, and then respond further in general worship, throughout our whole life. St. John's benediction is thus not only for the one who reads and those who hear, but for those who **keep** its message. The goal of the book is not merely to inform us about "prophetic" events. The goal of apostolic instruction is always ethical: It is written to produce "love from a pure heart and a good conscience and a sincere faith"

(1 Tim. 1:5). The Revelation gives us commandments to keep; and, in particular, the first-century readers were to heed and obey its instruction, for the crisis was upon them. **The time is near,** St. John warns, again emphasizing the contemporary relevance of his prophecy. He repeats this warning at the end of the book (22:6-7, 10). The ancient world would soon be in an uproar as kingdoms shook and crumbled to their foundations, and the Christians needed the Revelation as a stable guide during the period of dramatic change which was to come. The end of the world was approaching—not the destruction of the physical universe, but the passing away of the old world-order, the governing of the world around the central sanctuary in Jerusalem. God had established a new nation, a new priesthood, a new humanity worshiping in a new sanctuary. God's House was nearing completion, and the old, provisional dwelling, like scaffolding, was about to be torn away.

Greeting and Doxology (1:4-8)

4 John to the seven churches in Asia: Grace to you and peace from Him who is, and who was, and who is to come, and from the seven Spirits who are before His Throne,

5 and from Jesus Christ, who is the faithful Witness, the First-born from the dead, and the Ruler of the kings of the earth. To Him who loves us and released us from our sins by His blood,

6 and has made us to be a Kingdom and priests to His God and Father; to Him be the glory and the dominion forever and ever. Amen.

7 Behold, He is coming with the Clouds, and every eye will see Him, even those who pierced Him; and all the tribes of the Land will mourn over Him. Even so, amen.

8 I am the Alpha and the Omega, says the Lord God, who is and who was and who is to come, the Almighty.

4-6 St. John addresses his prophecy **to the seven churches in Asia.** It is obvious from the descriptions that follow (chapters 2-3) that he definitely has these actual churches in mind. The notion propagated by C. I. Scofield and others that these represent "seven phases of the *spiritual* history of the church"[4] is a

---

4. *The Scofield Reference Bible* (Oxford University Press, 1909), note on

mere fiction, with no objective evidence; and it is quite arbitrarily and selectively applied. There are at least three fallacious presuppositions held by those who advocate this doctrine.

First, the "seven ages" doctrine presupposes that the Book of Revelation covers all of Church history, from beginning to end. In defending his view, Scofield says: "It is incredible that in a prophecy covering the church period there should be no such foreview."[5] Very true, perhaps; but who says the Book of Revelation does cover Church history? St. John certainly doesn't. His only claim is that the prophecy covers "the things that must *shortly* take place" (1:1), and that the time of which it speaks is *near* (1:3). Thus, the most basic presupposition of the "seven ages" view is utterly false.

The second presupposition holds that the Church will end in defeat and apostasy: The Laodicean, lukewarm, practically apostate church, about which Christ has nothing good to say (3:14-22), is supposed to symbolize the Church of Jesus Christ at the end of the age. (A corollary of this view is that the "Last Days" spoken of in Scripture, in which apostasy is rampant, are the actual last days of earth's history.) The fact that the Church ends in victory and triumph is, of course, what the present commentary is intended to demonstrate; thus no more need be said here. But it is important to note that the notion of end-time apostasy is a *presupposition* of the "seven ages" view; and those who hold it are assuming what they purport to prove.

The third presupposition, of course, is that *we* are living in the last age of the Church (again, we should note that these people are too often unable to think of themselves as living at any time other than the climax of history). This presupposition is erroneous. The prophecies of the glorious condition of the Church, to be fulfilled before the return of Christ, are far from their accomplishment. We probably have thousands of years to go before the End. We are still in the early Church! And, while it is fashionable for modern Christian intellectuals to speak of

---

Revelation 1:20; this notion has also been popularized in the notes of such "study Bibles" as the *Thompson Chain-Reference Bible: New International Version* (Indianapolis: B. B. Kirkbride Bible Co.; Grand Rapids: The Zondervan Corporation, 1983), "Outline Studies of the Bible," No. 4308j ("The Seven Churches of Asia"), p. 1602.

5. Ibid.

our civilization as "post-Christian," we should turn that around and make it Biblically accurate: Our culture is not post-Christian — our culture is still largely *pre*-Christian![6]

Although, therefore, we may not say that the seven churches represent seven ages in Church history, there is an important point to be observed here. The fact that *seven* churches are mentioned in a book packed with numerical symbols should not be overlooked. *Seven* is the number in Scripture that indicates *qualitative fullness*, the essential nature of a thing (as *ten* indicates "manyness," a fullness of *quantity*); here it represents the fact that the Revelation is intended for the whole Church in every age. The messages to the churches of Asia are to be applied to all, just as St. Paul's letters to the Romans and the Philippians have worldwide significance. But in our application of these letters, we must be careful not to rip them out of their historical context.[7]

St. John uses the characteristic blessing of the apostles: **grace** (the favor of God bestowed upon those who, apart from Christ, deserve wrath) and **peace** (the state of permanent reconciliation with God through Christ's atonement). These blessings, he says, are **from** each member of the Godhead: the Father, the Holy Spirit, and the Son. Each of the Three participates fully and equally in extending grace and peace to the elect. The Father chose us from before the foundation of the world, and sent His Son to redeem us; the Son, in our place, lived a perfect life in obedience to the Law and paid the full penalty for our sins; and the Spirit applies the work of Father and Son through regeneration and sanctification. The fitting summary of all God has done for us is contained in these words: **grace and peace.**

---

6. Cf. Loraine Boettner, *The Millennium* (Philadelphia: The Presbyterian and Reformed Publishing Co., 1957), pp. 38-47, 63-66; Benjamin B. Warfield, "Are There Few That Be Saved?" in *Biblical and Theological Studies* (Philadelphia: The Presbyterian and Reformed Publishing Co., 1968), pp. 334-350. Warfield cites William Temple: "The earth will in all probability be habitable for myriads of years yet. If Christianity is the final religion, the church is still in its infancy. Two thousand years are as two days. The appeal to the 'primitive church' is misleading; we are the 'primitive church' "; and James Adderly: "But we must remember that Christianity is a very young religion, and that we are only at the beginning of Christian history even now" (pp. 347f.).

7. It so happens, however, that there is a sense in which St. John intended his descriptions of these seven churches to be legitimately related to seven "ages" of the Church; see the introduction to Part II, below.

The Persons of the Trinity are named here in *liturgical* (as distinguished from *theological*) order. Michael Wilcock's explanation is very helpful: "John's vision is going to take him into the heavenly sanctuary, of which the Jewish Tabernacle was a copy and shadow (Heb. 8:5); and perhaps the unusual order of the Trinity here (Father, Spirit, Son) corresponds to the plan of the earthly sanctuary, where the ark in the Holy of Holies represents the throne of God, the seven-branched lampstand in the Holy Place before it represents the Spirit,[8] and in the courtyard before that stands the altar, with its priest and sacrifice both representing, of course, the redeeming work of Christ."[9]

The greeting is a clear expression of the Trinitarian faith — later hammered out in creedal form at the councils of Nicea (A.D. 325) and Constantinople (381), but certainly explicit in the teaching of the Bible.[10] The doctrine of the Trinity is that there is one God (one Person) who is three distinct Persons — Father, Son, and Holy Spirit — and that each of those Persons is Himself God. There are not three Gods — only One. Yet those three Persons are not different ways or modes of God making Himself known to us, nor are they to be confused with one another; they are three *distinct* Persons. Cornelius Van Til states it about as clearly as anyone has: "The Father, the Son, and the Holy Ghost are each a personality and together constitute the exhaustively personal God. There is an eternal, internal self-conscious interaction between the three persons of the Godhead. They are co-substantial. Each is as much God as are the other two. The Son and the Spirit do not derive their being from the Father. The diversity and the unity in the Godhead are therefore equally ultimate; they are exhaustively correlative to one another and not correlative to anything else."[11]

---

8. Wilcock's footnote: "Compare 1:4 with 4:5, 5:6, and Zech. 4:1-5, 10b: lamps = eyes = spirits. The symbolism of the lamps in 1:12, 20 is not so very different; here it is the Spirit, there the earthly dwelling-place of the Spirit (1 Cor. 3:16), which is being depicted."

9. Michael Wilcock, *I Saw Heaven Opened: The Message of Revelation* (Downers Grove, IL: InterVarsity Press, 1975), p. 34.

10. One of the most helpful works on the meaning of the creeds, including their sociological implications, is Rousas John Rushdoony's *The Foundations of Social Order: Studies in the Creeds and Councils of the Early Church* (Tyler, TX: Thoburn Press, [1968] 1978); see also Gerald Bray, *Creeds, Councils, and Christ* (Downers Grove, IL: InterVarsity Press, 1984).

11. Cornelius Van Til, *Apologetics* (class syllabus, Westminster Theological Seminary, Philadelphia, 1959), p. 8.

What this means is that God is not "basically" one, with the individual Persons being derived from the oneness; nor is God "basically" three, with the unity of the Persons being secondary. Neither God's oneness nor His "threeness" is prior to the other; both are basic. God is One, and God is Three. There are three distinct, individual Persons, each of whom is God. But there is only One God.[12] To put it in more philosophical language, God's unity (oneness) and diversity (threeness, individuality) are equally ultimate. God is basically One and basically Three at the same time.[13]

First, St. John describes the Father: **Him who is, and who was, and who is to come.** Philip Carrington has caught the spirit of this expression, which is atrocious Greek but excellent theology: **the Being and the Was and the Coming.**[14] God is eternal and unchangeable (Mal. 3:6); as the early Christians faced what seemed to them an uncertain future, they had to keep before them the absolute certainty of God's eternal rule. God is not at the mercy of an environment; He is not defined by any external conditions; all things exist in terms of His inerrant Word. Threatened, opposed, and persecuted by those in power, they were nevertheless to rejoice in the knowledge of their eternal God who "is to come," who is coming continually in judgment against His adversaries. God's **coming** refers not simply to the end of the world but to His unceasing rule over history. He comes again and again to deliver His people and to judge the

---

12. Contrast this with the all-too-common Sunday School "illustrations" of the Trinity—such as an egg, the sun, a pie, or water. These are generally more misleading than helpful. In fact, their ultimate implications are heretical. They end up either dividing God into three "parts"—like an egg's shell, white, and yolk—or showing God as one substance taking on three different forms, like water (solid, liquid and gas).

13. On the radical impact of the doctrine of the Trinity in every area of life, see R. J. Rushdoony, *Foundations of Social Order* and *The One and the Many* (Tyler, TX: Thoburn Press, 1978).

14. Philip Carrington, *The Meaning of the Revelation* (London: SPCK, 1931), p. 74. In effect, the whole phrase is one proper noun, and indeclinable. The grammatical problem arises from St. John's attempt to render into Greek the theological nuances contained in the Hebrew of Exodus 3:14: *I AM WHO I AM.* St. John is not afraid to massacre the Greek language in order to get across a point, as in John 16:13, where he "incorrectly" uses a masculine pronoun in order to emphasize the Personality of the Holy Spirit (*Spirit* in Greek is neuter, but St. John wanted to stress that He is truly a He and not an It).

wicked.[15]

Second, St. John speaks of the Holy Spirit as **the seven Spirits who are before His Throne**. Although some have tried to see this as a reference to seven angels, it is inconceivable that *grace and peace* can originate **from** anyone but God. The Person spoken of here is clearly on a par with the Father and the Son. The picture of the Holy Spirit here (as also in 3:1; 4:5; 5:6) is based on Zechariah 4, in which the prophet sees the Church as a lampstand with seven lamps, supplied without human agency by an unceasing flow of oil through "seven spouts to the seven lamps" (v. 2) – the interpretation of which is, as God tells Zechariah: "Not by might, nor by power, but by My Spirit" (v. 6). The Holy Spirit's filling and empowering work in the Church is thus described in terms of the number *seven,* symbolizing fullness and completeness. So it is here in Revelation: "To the *seven churches* . . . grace and peace be unto you . . . from the *seven* Spirits." And the Spirit's work in the Church takes place in terms of God's dominion and majesty, **before His Throne**. This is, in fact, a marked emphasis in the Book of Revelation: The word *Throne* occurs here forty-six times (the New Testament book that comes closest to matching that number is the Gospel of Matthew, where it is used only five times). The Revelation is a book, above all, about *rule*: it reveals Jesus Christ as the Lord of history, restoring His people to dominion through the power of the Holy Spirit.

The word *Throne* is used particularly in Scripture to refer to God's official court, where He receives *official worship* from His people on the Sabbath.[16] The entire vision of the Revelation was seen on *the Lord's Day* (1:10) – the Christian day of corporate,

---

15. There are several good discussions of the various meanings of *Coming* in Scripture. See Oswald T. Allis, *Prophecy and the Church* (Grand Rapids: Baker Book House, 1945, 1947), pp. 175-91; Loraine Boettner, *The Millennium*, pp. 252-62; Roderick Campbell, *Israel and the New Covenant* (Tyler, TX: Geneva Ministries, [1954] 1983), pp. 68-80; David Chilton, *Paradise Restored*, pp. 67-75, 97-105; Geerhardus Vos, *The Pauline Eschatology* (Grand Rapids: Baker Book House, 1930), pp. 70-93.

16. See, for example, 1 Chron. 28:2; Ps. 132:7-8, 13-14; Isa. 11:10. Cf. Meredith G. Kline, *Images of the Spirit* (Grand Rapids: Baker Book House, 1980), pp. 20f., 39ff., 46, 111ff. As Geerhardus Vos observed, the significance of the Tabernacle in the Old Testament is that "it is the palace of the King in which the people render Him homage" (*Biblical Theology: Old and New Testaments* [Grand Rapids: William B. Eerdmans Publishing Co., 1948], p. 168).

official worship; and all the action in the book centers on the worship around the Throne of God. St. John wants us to see that the public, official worship of the Sovereign Lord is central to history—history both as a whole and in its constituent parts (i.e., your life and mine). The Spirit communicates grace and peace to the churches, in the special sense, through public worship. We can go so far as to say this: We cannot have continuing fellowship with God, and receive blessings from Him, apart from the public worship of the Church, the "place" of access to the Throne. The Spirit works in individuals, yes—but He does not work apart from the Church. His corporate and individual workings may be distinguished, but they cannot be separated. The notion that we can have fellowship with God, yet separate ourselves from the Church and from the corporate worship of the Body of Christ, is an altogether pagan idea, utterly foreign to Holy Scripture. The Church, *as the Church*, receives grace and peace from the sevenfold Spirit; and He is *continually* before the Throne, the special sphere of His ministry.

"Our lives are congested and noisy. It is easy to think of the Church and the sacraments as competing for our attention with the other world of daily life, leading us off into some other life —secret, rarified, and remote. We might do better to think of that practical daily world as something incomprehensible and unmanageable unless and until we can approach it sacramentally through Christ. Nature and the world are otherwise beyond our grasp; time also, time that carries all things away in a meaningless flux, causing men to despair unless they see in it the pattern of God's action, reflected in the liturgical year, the necessary road to the New Jerusalem."[17]

The third member of the Godhead (in this liturgical order) is Jesus Christ, spoken of by St. John under three designations: **the faithful Witness, the Firstborn from the dead, and the Ruler of the kings of the earth.** R. J. Rushdoony has forcefully pointed out how the term **Witness** (in Greek, *martyr*), has acquired connotations foreign to the word's original meaning: "In the Bible, the witness is one who works to enforce the law and assist in its execution, even to the enforcement of the death pen-

---

17. Alexander Schmemann, *Church, World, Mission: Reflections on Orthodoxy in the West* (Crestwood, NY: St. Vladimir's Seminary Press, 1979), p. 226.

alty. 'Martyr' has now come to mean the exact reverse, i.e., one who is executed rather than an executioner, one who is persecuted rather than one who is central to prosecution. The result is a serious misreading of Scripture. . . . The significance of Jesus Christ as 'the faithful and true witness' is that He not only witnesses against those who are at war against God, but He also executes them. . . . Jesus Christ therefore witnesses against every man and nation that establishes its life on any other premise than the sovereign and triune God and His infallible and absolute law-word."[18]

The theme of Christ as the preeminent Witness is important in Revelation, as we noted above on v. 2. By way of supplementing Rushdoony's analysis, we may observe that a central aspect of Christ's witness-bearing was His death at the hands of false witnesses. Those in this book who bear witness in His image will also do so at the cost of their lives (6:9; 12:11). The modern connotation of the word *martyr* is thus not so far-fetched and unbiblical as it might appear at first glance; but it is necessary, as Rushdoony has shown, to recall the basic meaning of the term.

Jesus is also **the Firstborn from the dead.** By His resurrection from the dead, He has attained supremacy, having "first place in everything" (Col. 1:18). As Peter said on the Day of Pentecost: "This Jesus God raised up again, to which we are all witnesses. Therefore having been exalted to the right hand of God, and having received from the Father the promise of the Holy Spirit, He has poured forth this which you both see and hear. For it was not David who ascended into heaven, but he himself says: The Lord said to my Lord, Sit at My right hand, until I make Thine enemies a footstool for Thy feet. Therefore let all the house of Israel know for certain that God has made Him both Lord and Christ—this Jesus whom you crucified" (Acts 2:32-36). God fulfilled the promise He had made long before: "I will make Him My Firstborn, the highest of the kings of the earth" (Ps. 89:27).

St. John obviously had this passage from the Psalms in mind, for the next designation he gives to our Lord is **the Ruler of the kings of the earth.** Christ's priority and sovereignty are

---

18. Rousas John Rushdoony, *The Institutes of Biblical Law* (Nutley, NJ: The Craig Press, 1973), pp. 573f.

above all. He is not "only" the Savior, waiting for a future cataclysmic event before He can become King; He is the universal King now, in this age — sitting at His Father's right hand while all His enemies are being put under His feet. This process of taking dominion over all the earth in terms of His rightful title is going on at this moment, and has been ever since He rose from the dead. As Firstborn (and only-begotten!), Christ possesses the crown rights of all creation: "*All* authority in heaven and earth has been given to Me," He claimed (Matt. 28:18). All nations have been granted to Him as His inheritance, and the kings of earth are under court order to submit to Him (Ps. 2:8-12). Commenting on Christ's title **Ruler of the kings of the earth**, William Symington wrote: "The persons who are here supposed to be subject to Christ, are kings, civil rulers, supreme and subordinate, all in civil authority, whether in the legislative, judicial, or executive branches of government. Of such Jesus Christ is Prince; — ὁ ἄρχων, ruler, lord, chief, the first in power, authority, and dominion."[19]

This, in fact, is precisely the reason for the persecution of Christians by the State. Jesus Christ by the Gospel has asserted His absolute sovereignty and dominion over the rulers and nations of earth. They have a choice: Either submit to His government and law, accepting His non-negotiable terms of surrender and peace, or be smashed to bits by the rod of His anger. Such an audacious, uncompromising position is an affront to the dignity of any self-respecting humanist — much more so to rulers who are accustomed to thinking of themselves as gods walking on earth. Perhaps this Christ can be allowed a place in the pantheon, along with the rest of us gods; but for His followers to proclaim Him as Lord of all, whose law is binding upon all men, whose statutes call into judgment the legislation and decrees of the nations — this is too much; it is inexcusable, and cannot be allowed.

It would have been much easier on the early Christians, of course, if they had preached the popular retreatist doctrine that

---

19. William Symington, *Messiah the Prince: or, The Mediatorial Dominion of Jesus Christ* (Philadelphia: The Christian Statesman Publishing Co., [1839] 1884), p. 208.

Jesus is Lord of the "heart," that He is concerned with "spiritual" (meaning non-earthly) conquests, but isn't the least bit interested in political questions; that He is content to be "Lord" in the realm of the spirit, while Caesar is Lord everywhere else (i.e., where we feel it really matters). Such a doctrine would have been no threat whatsoever to the gods of Rome. In fact, Caesar couldn't ask for a more cooperative religion! Toothless, impotent Christianity is a gold mine for statism: It keeps men's attention focused on the clouds while the State picks their pockets and steals their children.

But the early Church was not aware of this escapist teaching. Instead, it taught the *Biblical* doctrine of Christ's Lordship — that He is Lord of all, "Ruler of the kings of the earth." It was this that guaranteed their persecution, torture, and death at the hands of the State. And it was also this that guaranteed their ultimate victory. Because Jesus *is* universal Lord, all opposition to His rule is doomed to failure, and will be crushed. Because Christ is King of kings, Christians are assured of two things: warfare to the death against all would-be-gods; and the complete triumph of the Christian faith over all its enemies.

For this reason, St. John breaks into a doxology of praise to Jesus Christ, **who loves us and freed us from our sins by** the ransom-price of **His blood, and has made us to be a Kingdom and priests to His God and Father; to Him be the glory and the dominion forever and ever.** Not only have we been redeemed from our slavery, but we have been constituted as a Kingdom of priests. The Kingdom has begun: Christians are now ruling with Christ (Eph. 1:20-22; 2:6; Col. 1:13), and our dominion will increase across the world (Rev. 5:9-10). We are a victorious, conquering priesthood, bringing all areas of life under His rule.

7-8 Verse 7 announces the theme of the book, which is not the Second Coming of Christ, but rather the Coming of Christ in judgment upon Israel, in order to establish the Church as the new Kingdom. **He is coming with the Clouds,** St. John proclaims, using one of the most familiar Biblical images for judgment (cf. Gen. 15:17; Ex. 13:21-22; 14:19-20, 24; 19:9, 16-19; Ps. 18:8-14; 104:3; Isa. 19:1; Ezek. 32:7-8; Matt. 24:30; Mark 14:62; Acts 2:19). This is the Glory-Cloud, God's heavenly chariot by which He makes His glorious presence known.[20] The Cloud is a revelation of His Throne, as He comes to protect His people and destroy the wicked. One of the most striking descriptions of God's "coming in the clouds" is in Nahum's prophecy against Nineveh (Nah. 1:2-8):

> The LORD is a jealous and avenging God;
> The LORD takes vengeance and is filled with wrath.
> The LORD takes vengeance on His foes
> And maintains His wrath against His enemies.
> The LORD is slow to anger and great in power;
> He will not leave the guilty unpunished.
> His way is in the whirlwind and the storm,
> And clouds are the dust of His feet.
> He rebukes the sea and dries it up;
> He makes all the rivers run dry.
> Bashan and Carmel wither
> And the blossoms of Lebanon fade.
> The mountains quake before Him
> And the hills melt away.
> The earth trembles at His presence,
> The world and all who live in it.
> Who can withstand His indignation?
> Who can endure His fierce anger?
> His wrath is poured out like fire;
> The rocks are shattered before Him.
> The LORD is good,
> A refuge in times of trouble.
> He cares for those who trust in Him,
> But with an overwhelming flood
> He will make an end of Nineveh;
> He will pursue His foes into darkness.

His coming in the clouds thus brings judgment and deliverance in history; there is no reason, in either the overall Biblical usage of this term or its immediate context here, to suppose that the literal end of the physical world is meant (although the sense can certainly be applied to the Last Day as well). St. John is speaking of the fact, stressed throughout the "last days" period

---

20. See Chilton, *Paradise Restored*, pp. 57ff., 97ff.; cf. Kline, *Images of the Spirit*.

by the apostles, that a crisis was quickly approaching: As He had promised, Christ would come against the present generation "in the clouds," in wrathful judgment against apostate Israel (Matt. 23-25). **And every eye will see Him, even those who pierced Him** (the Gentiles, John 19:34, 37): The crucifiers would **see Him** coming in judgment—that is, they would *experience* and *understand* that His Coming would mean wrath on the Land (cf. the use of the word *see* in Mark 1:44; Luke 17:22; John 3:36; Rom. 15:21). The Lord had used the same terminology of His Coming against Jerusalem at the end of that generation (Matt. 24:30), and He even warned the high priest: "You shall see the Son of Man sitting at the right hand of Power, and coming on the clouds of heaven" (Matt. 26:64). In other words, the apostates of that evil generation would understand the meaning of Christ's Ascension, the definitive Coming of the Son of Man, the Second Adam (Dan. 7:13). In the destruction of their city, their civilization, their Temple, their entire world-order, they would understand that Christ had ascended to His Throne as Lord of heaven and earth. They would see that the Son of Man had come to the Father.

Jesus had said also that "all the tribes of the Land will mourn" on the day of His Coming (Matt. 24:30), that "weeping shall be there and the gnashing of teeth" (Matt. 24:51). St. John repeats this as part of the theme of his prophecy: **all the tribes of the Land** [the Jews] **will mourn over Him.** Both Jesus and St. John thus reinterpreted this expression, borrowed from Zechariah 12:10-14, where it occurs in an original context of Israel's mourning in repentance. But Israel had gone beyond the point of no return; their mourning would not be that of repentance, but sheer agony and terror.

Yet this does not negate the promises in Zechariah. Indeed, through Christ's judgment on Israel, by means of her excommunication, the world will be saved; and, through the salvation of the world, Israel herself will turn again to the Lord and be saved (Rom. 11:11-12, 15, 23-24). Because Christ comes in the clouds, in history, judging men and nations, the earth is redeemed. He comes not simply for judgment, but for judgment unto salvation. "When Your judgments come upon the earth, the people of the world learn righteousness" (Isa. 26:9). From the beginning, the ultimate purpose of the coming of Christ has been redemptive: "For God did not send His Son into the world to condemn the world, but to save the world through Him" (John 3:17). Christ "comes in the Clouds" in historical judgments so that the world may know **the Lord God** as the eternal and unchangeable Source and Goal of all history (Rom. 11:36), **the Alpha and the Omega,** the A and Z (cf. Isa. 44:6), **who is and who was and who is to come,** the eternal Origin and Consummation of all things. **Almighty** is the usual translation of the Greek word *Pantokratōr,* which means *the One who has all power and rules over everything,* the New Testament equivalent of the Old Testament expression *Lord of Hosts,* the "Captain of the Armies" (meaning the armies of Israel, or the star/angel armies of heaven, or the armies of the heathen nations, whom God used to pour out His wrath on His disobedient people). Christ was about to demonstrate to Israel and to the world that He had ascended to the Throne as Supreme Ruler.

Jesus Christ, Transcendent and Immanent (1:9-16)

9 I, John, your brother and companion in the Tribulation and Kingdom and perseverance which are in Christ Jesus, was on the island of Patmos because of the Word of God and the Testimony of Jesus.

10 I came to be in the Spirit on the Lord's Day, and I heard behind me a loud Voice like a trumpet,

11 saying: Write in a book what you see and send it to the seven churches: to Ephesus, Smyrna, Pergamum, Thyatira, Sardis, Philadelphia and Laodicea.

12 And I turned to see the Voice that was speaking to me. And when I turned I saw seven golden lampstands;

13 and in the middle of the seven lampstands one like a Son of Man, clothed in a robe reaching to His feet and with a golden sash around His chest.

14 And His head and His hair were white like wool, as white as snow, and His eyes were like blazing fire.

15 His feet were like bronze glowing in a furnace, and His Voice was like the sound of rushing waters.

16 In His right hand he held seven stars, and out of His mouth came a sharp two-edged sword; and His face was like the sun shining in its strength.

9 In this remarkable verse we have a concise summary of St.

John's worldview, his fundamental outlook on what life is all about. It stands in stark contrast to the views of modern American evangelical and dispensational theology, which holds that (1) there is no **tribulation** for the Christian, (2) Christ does not have a **Kingdom** in this age, and (3) the Christian is not required or expected to **persevere**! But for St. John and his readers, the Christian life did involve these things. Of course, tribulation is not the whole story of the Christian life; nor does the Church suffer identically in all times and places. As the Gospel takes hold of the world, as Christians take dominion, tribulation is lessened. But it is absolute folly (and wickedness) for Christians to suppose that they are somehow immune from all suffering. Jesus had warned his disciples that tribulation, suffering, and persecution would come (John 15:18-20; 16:33; 17:14-15).

More particularly, however, St. John is thinking about a special period of hardship; not just tribulation in general, but **the Tribulation**, the subject of much apostolic writing as the age of the Last Days progressed to its climax (1 Thess. 1:6; 3:4; 2 Thess. 1:4-10; 1 Tim. 4:1-3; 2 Tim. 3:1-12). During this period of political upheaval and social disruption, apostasy and persecution broke out with a vengeance, as Jesus had foretold (Matt. 24:4-13). Christians suffered greatly; yet they had the certain knowledge that the Tribulation was but the prelude to the firm establishment of Christ's rule over the earth. St. Paul and St. Barnabus had encouraged other Asian Christians to continue in the faith, reminding them that "through many tribulations we must enter the Kingdom of God" (Acts 14:22). What gave their suffering meaning was that it was **in Christ Jesus**, in union with His suffering; as St. Paul wrote, "I rejoice in my sufferings for your sake, and I fill up what is lacking of the tribulations of Christ in my flesh, on behalf of His Body, the Church" (Col. 1:24).

Thus St. John's worldview does not involve only tribulation. He is also **in the Kingdom . . . in Christ Jesus**. As we saw above (v. 5-6), the New Testament doctrine, based on such Old Testament passages as Daniel 2:31-45 and 7:13-14, is that the Kingdom has arrived in the First Coming of Jesus Christ. Since His Ascension to the Throne, He has been reigning "far above all rule and authority and power and dominion, and every name that is named, not only in this age, but also in the one to come.

And He put all things in subjection under His feet" (Eph.
1:21-22; cf. Mark 1:14-15; Matt. 16:28; 28:18; Acts 2:29-36; Col.
1:13). If all things are now in subjection under His feet, what
more could be added to His dominion? Of course, the "rulers
and authorities" still have got to be put down; that is what much
of St. John's prophecy is about. But in principle, and definitively, the Kingdom has arrived. This means that we do not have
to wait for some future redemptive or eschatological event before we can effectively take dominion over the earth. The dominion of God's people throughout the world will simply be the
result of a progressive outworking of what Christ Himself has
already accomplished. St. John wanted his readers to understand that they were in both the Great Tribulation *and* the Kingdom—that, in fact, they were in the Tribulation precisely because the Kingdom had come (Dan. 7:13-14). They were in a
war, fighting for the Kingdom's victory (Dan. 7:21-22), and thus
they needed the third element in St. John's worldview: **perseverance in Christ Jesus**. Perseverance is an important word in the
message of the Revelation, and St. John uses it seven times (1:9;
2:2, 3, 19; 3:10; 13:10; 14:12).

Here, too, there is a radical contrast with much of modern
dispensationalism. Because the diluted version of Christianity
currently fashionable in contemporary America rejects the concepts of the Kingship and Lordship of Christ,[21] it also rejects the
Biblical teaching on perseverance—and the predictable result is
that comparatively few converts of modern evangelicalism are
able to stick with even *that* minimally-demanding faith![22] The
popular doctrine of "eternal security" is only a half-truth, at
best: it gives people an unbiblical basis for assurance (e.g., the

---

21. For a recent example of this position, see Norman Geisler, "A Premillennial View of Law and Government," *Bibliotheca Sacra* (July-September
1985), pp. 250-66. Writing against the postmillennialism of R. J. Rushdoony
and other "reconstructionists," Geisler actually says: "Postmillenarians work
to make a Christian America. Premillenarians work for a truly free America"
(p. 260). The choice is clear: Shall we choose Christianity? Or shall we choose
freedom instead? Geisler must be commended for having stated the matter
with such precision; technically speaking, however, he is not the first to have
posed the dilemma in this way. He stands in an ancient tradition (Gen. 3:1-5).
22. See Walter Chantry, *Today's Gospel: Authentic or Synthetic?* (Edinburgh: The Banner of Truth Trust, 1970), and Arend J. ten Pas, *The Lordship
of Christ* (Vallecito, CA: Ross House Books, 1978).

fact that they walked down the aisle during a revival meeting, etc.), rather than the kind of assurance given in Scripture — assurance that is related to perseverance (cf. 1 John 2:3-4). The Bible teaches not simply that we are preserved, but that we also persevere to the end (see John 10:28-29; Rom. 8:35-39; 2 Cor. 13:5; Phil. 1:6; 2:12-13; Col. 1:21-23; 2 Pet. 1:10).

St. John tells the suffering but reigning and persevering Christians of Asia that he is their **brother and companion** in all these things, even now in exile **on the island of Patmos.** This was a punishment for his apostolic activity, but the language in which he expresses it is interesting: **Because of the Word of God and the Testimony of Jesus Christ.** St. John does not say that he is imprisoned on a rock in the sea on account of his own testimony about Christ, but on account of God's Word and Jesus' Testimony. He suffers because God has spoken, because Jesus has testified. Christ the faithful Witness has borne the Testimony against the would-be gods of this age, and they have fought back by imprisoning the apostle. This is why **the Tribulation and Kingdom and perseverance** in which these believers share are all **in Christ Jesus:** His Testimony has determined the course of history.

10   When St. John says he **came to be in the Spirit,** he does not mean that he felt good. The expression has nothing to do with his personal, subjective attitude or frame of mind; but it does refer to a definite experience. This is technical prophetic language (Matt. 22:43; cf. Num. 11:25; 2 Sam. 23:2; Ezek. 2:2; 3:24; 2 Pet. 1:21), and refers to the fact that the author is an inspired apostle, receiving revelation, as he is admitted to the heavenly council-chamber.[23]

St. John tells us that this vision was seen **on the Lord's Day.** The origin of this important term goes all the way back to the first Sabbath, when God rested from creation (Gen. 2:2-3). The term *rest* in Scripture often refers to God being seated on His throne as Judge, receiving worship from His creatures (1 Chron. 28:2; Ps. 132:7-8, 13-14; Isa. 11:10; 66:1). This original Sabbath was the prototype of the "Day of the Lord" in Scripture, the

---

23. See the discussion of the prophet in Meredith G. Kline, *Images of the Spirit,* pp. 57-96; esp. pp. 93f.

Day of Judgment. The weekly Sabbath in Israel was a re-enactment (and pre-enactment) of the first and final *Day of the Lord*,[24] in which the people gathered together for judgment, execution, the judicial declaration of forgiveness, and the proclamation of the King's Word. For us too, this is the meaning of the Lord's Day, when we come before God's throne to be forgiven and restored, to hear His Word, and to commune with Him (thus, in a *general* sense—and not exactly the special sense in which St. John uses it here—*all* Christians are "in the Spirit" on the Lord's Day: In worship, we are all caught up to the Throneroom of God.)[25] The Lord's Day is the Day of the Lord in action.

One of the most basic Biblical images for the Judgment is the Glory-Cloud, and this theophany is generally associated with three other images: the *Spirit*, the *Day* (or *light*, since the light of day was originally "cloned" from the light of the Cloud[26]), and the *Voice* (often sounding like a trumpet; cf. Ex. 19:16-19). In fact, these three are mentioned right at the beginning in the Garden, when Adam and Eve "heard the *Voice* of the LORD God traversing the Garden as the *Spirit* of the *Day*," as the text literally reads (Gen. 3:8).[27] What Adam and Eve heard on that awful day of judgment was not a gentle, cool breeze wafting through the eucalyptus leaves—they heard the explosive thunderclaps of the God of heaven and earth blasting through the Garden. It was terrifying, and that is why they attempted to hide. Repeating this theme, St. John tells us: "I was in the **Spirit** on the Lord's **Day**, and I heard behind me a loud **Voice** like a trumpet." St. John was going to be caught up into the Glory-Cloud to receive revelation, and his readers were expected to understand this imagery.

11-15 The Voice of God instructs St. John to **write in a book** the Revelation and **send it to the seven churches** of Asia. He turns **to see the Voice**—and sees the Lord Jesus Christ. This minor detail establishes a pattern that is repeated throughout the book—John *hears* first, and then he *sees*. At the end of the

---

24. See Chilton, *Paradise Restored*, pp. 133ff.
25. See Kline, *Images of the Spirit*, pp. 97-131.
26. Ibid., pp. 106ff.
27. For a full exegesis of this text, see ibid., pp. 97-131; cf. Chilton, *Paradise Restored,* pp. 58, 134ff.

prophecy (22:8) he tells us: "I, John, am the one who *heard* and *saw* these things. And when I *heard* and *saw*. . . ." This pattern is not always followed in the book, but it happens often enough that we should be aware of St. John's use of it — for it is occasionally important in understanding how to interpret the symbols (cf. 5:5-6): The verbal revelation is necessary in order to understand the visual revelation.

St. John suddenly finds himself in the Holy Place, for he sees **seven golden lampstands; and in the middle of the seven lampstands one like a Son of Man.** The imagery here is clearly taken from the Tabernacle, but with a significant difference: in the earthly Holy Place, there was one lampstand, with seven lamps; here, St. John sees seven lampstands, connected to each other in the Person who stands in their midst. The symbolism involved here will be discussed under verse 20; the important thing to note at present is simply the picture conveyed by this imagery: Jesus Christ is the one Lampstand, uniting the seven lamps — each of which turns out to be itself a lampstand; Christ is surrounded by light. As St. Germanus, the eighth-century Archbishop of Constantinople, put it at the outset of his work on the Liturgy: "The Church is an earthly heaven in which the super-celestial God dwells and walks about."[28]

The description of Christ in verses 13-16 involves a blend of Old Testament images: the Glory-Cloud, the Angel of the Lord, the Ancient of Days, and the Son of Man. Our understanding will be heightened if we read this description in conjunction with the following passages from Daniel:

I kept looking
Until thrones were set up,
And the Ancient of Days took His seat;
His vesture was like white snow,
And the hair of His head like pure wool.
His throne was ablaze with flames,
Its wheels were a burning fire.
A river of fire was flowing
And coming out from before Him;
Thousands upon thousands were attending Him,

---

28. St. Germanus of Constantinople, *On the Divine Liturgy*, Paul Meyendorff, trans. (Crestwood, NY: St. Vladimir's Seminary Press, 1984), p. 57.

And myriads upon myriads were standing before Him;
The court sat,
And the books were opened. (Dan. 7:9-10)

I kept looking in the night visions,
And behold, with the Clouds of heaven
One like a Son of Man was coming,
And He came up to the Ancient of Days
And was presented before Him.
And to Him was given dominion,
Glory and a Kingdom,
That all the peoples, nations, and men of every language
Might serve Him.
His dominion is an everlasting dominion
Which will not pass away;
And His Kingdom is one
Which will not be destroyed. (Dan. 7:13-14)

I lifted my eyes and looked, and behold, there was a certain
man dressed in linen, whose waist was girded with a belt of pure
gold of Uphaz. His body also was like beryl, His face like lightning, His eyes were like flaming torches, His arms and feet like
the gleam of polished bronze, and the sound of His words like
the sound of a multitude. Now, I, Daniel, alone saw the vision,
while the men who were with me did not see the vision; nevertheless, a great dread fell on them, and they ran away to hide themselves. So I was left alone and saw this great vision; yet no
strength was left in me, for my natural color turned to a deathly
pallor, and I retained no strength. But I heard the sound of His
words; and as soon as I heard the sound of His words, I fell into
a deep sleep on my face, with my face to the ground. Then behold, a hand touched me and set me trembling on my hands and
knees. And He said to me, "O Daniel, man of high esteem, understand the words that I am about to tell you and stand upright,
for I have now been sent to you." And when He had spoken this
word to me, I stood up trembling. (Dan. 10:5-11)[29]

These and other passages are combined to form the picture
of Christ in St. John's introductory vision. The **robe reaching to
His feet** and the **golden sash around His chest**[30] (cf. Ex. 28:4;

---

29. Cf. the discussion of this text in relation to Rev. 12:7-9 below.
30. According to Josephus, the priest wore the sash around his chest when he
was at rest and "not about any laborious service" (*Antiquities of the Jews*, iii.vii.2).

29:5; 39:27-29; Lev. 16:4) are reminders of the official dress of the High Priest, whose clothing was a representation of the Glory-Spirit, a symbol of the radiant image of God. "Contributing to the impression of radiance was the flame-colored linen material prescribed for the ephod, with its band and breastpiece, and for the bottom of the robe of the ephod—a shimmering blend of bright reds and blues with the metallic glint of threads of gold. Highlighting the fiery effect were the rings and the braided chains of gold, the radiant golden crown of the mitre, and the gleam of precious stones set in gold on the shoulder straps of the ephod and the breastpiece. Artist could scarcely do more with an earthly palette in a cold medium to produce the effect of fiery light."[31]

Fiery light: that is exactly the impression given by the vision of Christ here. The whiteness of His head and hair (like the Ancient of Days in Dan. 7),[32] the flaming fire from His eyes (like the throne of Dan. 7 and the eyes of the Son of Man in Dan. 10), and His feet **like bronze glowing in a furnace** (the term for *bronze* may refer to an alloy of gold and silver; cf. Mal. 3:2-3) —all these combine to make the point of Christ's appearance in a flashing, brilliant blaze of glory: **And His face was like the sun shining in its strength** (v. 16). Compare with this Jesus Ben Sirach's striking description of the glory of the High Priest:

> How splendid he was with the people thronging around him,
> when he emerged from the curtained shrine,
> like the morning star among the clouds,
> like the moon at the full,
> like the sun shining on the Temple of the Most High,
> like the rainbow gleaming against brilliant clouds,
> like roses in the days of spring,
> like lilies by a freshet of water,
> like a sprig of frankincense in summertime,
> like fire and incense in the censer
> like a vessel of beaten gold
> encrusted with every kind of precious stone,
> like an olive tree loaded with fruit,
> like a cypress soaring to the clouds;

---

31. Kline, *Images of the Spirit*, p. 43.
32. Note that *white* hair is glorious, in contrast to the "perpetual youth" culture of our age.

when he put on his splendid vestments,
    and clothed himself in glorious perfection,
when he went up to the holy altar,
    and filled the sanctuary precincts with his grandeur;
when he received the portions from the hands of the priests,
    himself standing by the altar hearth,
surrounded by a crowd of his brothers,
    like a youthful cedar of Lebanon
as though surrounded by the trunks of palm trees.
(Ecclesiasticus 50:5-12, Jerusalem Bible)

Completing the glorious picture of Christ is the statement that **His Voice was like the sound of rushing waters**. St. John is identifying the voice of Christ with the sound of the Cloud — a sound which, throughout Scripture, resembles numerous earthly phenomena: wind, thunder, trumpets, armies, chariots, and waterfalls;[33] or perhaps we should say that all these earthly phenomena were created to resemble various facets of the Cloud.[34] The conclusion should be obvious: The resurrected, transfigured Jesus is the incarnate Glory of God.

16   In His right hand He held seven stars; St. John goes on more fully to interpret this in verse 20, but we should consider first the immediate impression this sight would give to St. John and his readers. The **seven stars** make up the open cluster of stars known as the Pleiades, poetically thought of in the ancient world as being bound together on a chain, like a necklace. The Pleiades, forming part of the constellation Taurus, are mentioned in Job 9:5-9; 38:31-33; and Amos 5:8. The sun is with Taurus in Spring (Easter), and the Pleiades are thus a fitting symbol in connection with the coming of Christ: He holds the stars that announce the rebirth and flowering of the world. The other Biblical references make it clear that the One who holds the seven stars is the almighty Creator and Sustainer of the universe.

But there is another dimension to this imagery. The symbolic use of the seven stars was quite well known in the first century,

---

33. See Chilton, *Paradise Restored*, p. 58; cf. Ex. 19:16, 19; Ezek. 1:24.
34. See Herman Bavinck, *The Doctrine of God* (London: The Banner of Truth Trust, [1951] 1977), pp. 88ff.

for the seven stars appeared regularly on the Emperor's coins as symbols of his supreme political sovereignty. At least some early readers of the Revelation must have gasped in amazement at St. John's audacity in stating that the seven stars were in *Christ's* hand. The Roman emperors had appropriated to themselves a symbol of dominion that the Bible reserves for God alone — and, St. John is saying, Jesus Christ has come to take it back. The seven stars, and with them all things in creation, belong to Him. Dominion resides in the right hand of the Lord Jesus Christ.

Naturally there will be opposition to all this. But St. John makes it clear that Christ is on the offensive, coming forth to do battle in the cause of His crown rights: **out of His mouth came a sharp two-edged sword**, His Word that works to save and to destroy. The image here is taken from the prophecy of Isaiah: "He will strike the Land with the rod of His mouth, and with the breath of His lips He will slay the wicked" (Isa. 11:4). It is used again in Revelation to show Christ's attitude toward heretics: "I will make war against them with the sword of my mouth" (2:16); and yet again to show the Word of God conquering the nations (19:11-16). Not only is Christ in conflict with the nations, but He declares that He will be completely victorious over them, subduing them by His bare Word, the sharp and powerful two-edged sword that comes from His mouth (Heb. 4:12).

St. John's Commission (1:17-20)

17 And when I saw Him, I fell at His feet as a dead man. And He laid His right hand upon me, saying, Do not be afraid; I am the first and the last,

18 and the living One; and I was dead, and behold, I am alive forevermore, amen; and I have the keys of Death and of Hades.

19 Write therefore the things you have seen, and what they are, and what things shall take place after these things.

20 As for the mystery of the seven stars that you saw in My right hand, and the seven golden lampstands: the seven stars are the angels of the seven churches, and the seven lampstands are the seven churches.

17-18   When he saw the Angel of the Lord, Daniel says, "I fell into a deep sleep with my face to the ground. Then behold, a

hand touched me and set me trembling on my hands and knees.
. . . And when He had spoken this word to me, I stood up
trembling" (Dan. 10:9-11). St. John's reaction to the sight of the
glorified Lord is much the same; yet Christ tells him not to fear.
While fear is a proper first reaction, it must be replaced. Ultimately, the awesome majesty of God is not a reason for terror in
the Christian; rather, it is the ground of our confidence and stability. The presence of Christ is, very properly, the occasion for
unbelievers to faint away and hide, out of sheer fright (cf.
6:15-17); but our Lord comes to St. John (as to us) in love, and
sets him on his feet. The presence and activity of God in the
Cloud was to the Egyptians a terrifying omen of their destruction; but, for the covenant people, He was the Comforter and
Savior. The same contrast is set out in Habakkuk 3:10-13:

> The mountains saw You and quaked.
> Torrents of water swept by;
> The deep uttered its voice,
> And lifted high its hands.
> Sun and moon stood still in the heavens;
> They went away at the light of Your arrows,
> At the radiance of Your gleaming spear.
> In wrath You strode through the earth
> And in anger You threshed the nations.
> You went forth to deliver Your people,
> For the salvation of Your anointed one.
> You crushed the head of the house of evil,
> You laid him open from thigh to neck.

Jesus is God, **the First and the Last**, as the LORD says of
Himself in Isa. 44:6: "I am the First and I am the Last, and there
is no God besides Me" (cf. Isa. 48:12). Appropriating another
Old Testament title for God, Jesus declares that He is **the living
One** (cf. Deut. 5:26; Josh. 3:10; Ps. 42:2; Jer. 10:10): He is self-
existent, independent, the All-Controller—and He, "having
been raised from the dead, is never to die again; death is no
longer master over Him" (Rom. 6:9). St. John can be resurrected in verse 17 because of the truth of verse 18, that Christ is
alive forevermore. As the Risen Lord, Christ has **the keys of**

Death and of Hades.[35] The Empire claimed to have all authority, to possess the power over life and death, and over the grave; Jesus declares instead that He — and not the State, nor the emperor, nor Satan, nor the ruler of the synagogue — has command over all reality. He is the Lord of life and death, of all history, and of eternity; and it is in terms of this complete dominion that He commissions St. John to write this book which so clearly and unequivocally sets forth the truth of His eternal and comprehensive government.

19 St. John's commission was interrupted by his falling into a dead faint; now that he has been "resurrected," he is again commanded: **Write therefore**[36] **the things you have seen, and what they are, and what things are about to take place after these things.** Some interpreters read this as a threefold outline of the whole book: St. John writes about what he has seen (the vision of Christ), then about the present (the churches, in chapters 2-3), and finally about the future (chapters 4-22). Such a division is quite arbitrary, however; the Revelation (like all other Biblical prophecies) weaves past, present, and future together throughout the entire book.

A more likely meaning of this statement is that St. John is to write what he has **seen** — the vision of Christ among the lampstands holding the stars — **and what they are,** i.e., what they *signify* or *correspond to.* The word *are* (Greek *eisin*) is most often used in Revelation in this sense (1:20; 4:5; 5:6, 8; 7:13-14; 11:4; 14:4; 16:14; 17:9, 10, 12, 15). Thus verse 20 goes on to do just that, explaining the symbolism of "the things you have seen" (the stars and lampstands). St. John is then commissioned to write **the things that are about to happen,** or (as he told us in

---

35. Adam originally held the Key of Death and Hades, for he was the Priest of Eden, with the priestly responsibility of guarding the Gate of Paradise (Gen. 2:15; see Meredith G. Kline, *Kingdom Prologue* (privately published syllabus, 1981), Vol. I, pp. 127ff. When he abdicated that responsibility, he himself was turned out into death, away from the Tree of Life, and the cherubim took his place as guardians, holding the flaming sword (the key). By the Resurrection, Jesus Christ as the Second Adam returned to Paradise as Priest, the guardian of Eden's Gate, to cast the Serpent into Death and Hades (cf. Rev. 20:1-3).

36. The *therefore* shows the connection with St. John's original commission in v. 11.

verse 1) "the things that must shortly take place." It appears that
the phrasing is intended to provide a parallel to the description
of the One "who was and who is and who is coming": Thus "the
process of temporal history reflects the eternal nature of God."[37]

We might pause at this point to consider an error that is
common among those who adopt a preterist interpretation of
Revelation. The two facts of St. John's symbolic style and his
clearly anti-statist content have led some to believe that the politically sensitive message determined the use of symbolism — that
St. John wrote the Revelation in a secret code in order to hide
his message from the imperial bureaucrats. This is the view of
James Kallas (who, incidentally, also holds that John wrote in
the time of the emperor Domitian, rather than Nero):

> He writes in deliberately disguised language. He resorts to
> imagery the Romans will not understand. He cannot write in a
> literal and obvious way. He cannot say in clear and unambig-
> uous terms what lies closest to his heart. What would happen if
> he wrote what he believed, that Domitian was a blasphemous
> son of the devil himself? What would happen if he cried out that
> the Roman empire, in its demand that men bow down and wor-
> ship Caesar, was a diabolical scheme of Satan himself designed
> to win men away from Jesus? The letter would never be deliv-
> ered. It would never clear the censors.
>
> And thus he must camouflage and conceal his true meaning.
> He must resort to non-literal symbolism, to obscure and appar-
> ently meaningless references which his Roman censors would see
> merely as the senile musings of a mad old man.[38]

There may be some truth to this, as a tangential slant on the
use of the number 666 in 13:18 in reference to Nero (not Domitian) — a "code" that the Romans would be unable to decipher
correctly. But even without that reference, the Book of Revelation is a clearly treasonous document, and any State bureaucrat
would have been able to figure that out. Consider what we have
seen already in St. John's description of Jesus Christ: The mere
assertion that He is Ruler of the kings of the earth is an assault

---

37. Philip Carrington, *The Meaning of the Revelation*, p. 95.
38. James Kallas, *Revelation: God and Satan in the Apocalypse* (Minneapolis: Augsburg Publishing House, 1973), pp. 58f.

on the emperor's autonomy. The very first chapter of Revelation is actionable, and the symbolism does not obscure that fact in the slightest. The reason for the use of symbolism is that the Revelation is a *prophecy*, and symbolism is prophetic language. We must remember too that the Roman government knew very well who St. John was. He was not "a mad old man" who had been exiled for mere "senile musings." He was an Apostle of the Lord Jesus Christ, under the imperial ban *on account of the Word of God and the Testimony of Jesus* (1:9).

20   Jesus explains to St. John **the mystery of the seven stars** and of **the seven golden lampstands.** Here, too, it is important to stress that these are not code-names. Biblical symbolism doesn't work that way. Instead, Biblical symbolism sets things in relationship to each other; it builds associations in our minds, and asks us to see objects from this perspective. These statements about the stars and lampstands are not "definitions," but state different ways of looking at the angels and the churches. Michael Wilcock's comments help us understand this use of symbolism: "A very cursory study of the New Testament use of the word 'mystery' shows that it does not there carry its usual modern sense of 'puzzle.' It is indeed something hidden, but not in such a way that you can follow a series of clues and eventually find it out; rather, it is a truth which you either know or do not know, depending on whether or not it has been revealed to you."[39] Thus, when Christ identifies these things with each other, He is not saying "that one is a symbol while the other is what the symbol 'really' means. He is saying that here are two things which correspond to each other, being *equally real from different points of view.*"[40] In other words, "we have, not an explanation of a symbolic term by a real one, but a statement that these two terms, which are equally real, are simply interchangeable. . . . John is not giving explanations, but equivalents. He is not concerned to tell us that 'lampstands,' which we do not understand, means 'church,' which we do. He is rather concerned to tell us things *about* the lampstands and the bride and the city and the church, the twenty-four elders and the 144,000 and the numberless multitude; their meaning we

---

39. Wilcock, *I Saw Heaven Opened*, p. 153.
40. Ibid., p. 154.

should know already from the rest of Scripture, and he merely reminds us in passing that all of these correspond to one another and are different descriptions of the same thing."[41]

The seven stars thus "correspond" to **the angels of the seven churches.**[42] Angels and stars are often linked up in the Bible (cf. Jud. 5:20; Job 38:7; Isa. 14:13; Jude 13; Rev. 8:10-12; 9:1; 12:4), and here the "angels" of the churches are associated with the constellation of the Pleiades (see comments on v. 16). In addition —and this is one of those things that, as Wilcock pointed out above, "we should know already from the rest of Scripture"— both angels and stars are associated with government and rule (cf. Gen. 37:9; Jud. 5:20; Dan. 8:9-11; 10:13, 20-21). Now, when the Lord speaks to the seven churches in Chapters 2-3, He addresses the **angel** of each church; clearly, Christ holds the angels of the churches responsible for the life and conduct of their respective churches. Then, in the later portions of the prophecy, we see *seven angels* pouring out judgments upon the rebellious earth (cf. Rev. 8-9, 16). These all are *correspondences:* The seven stars, the constellation of resurrection and dominion, are the angels, which correspond to the government of the Church.

A further aspect of the Bible's angel-imagery which supports this interpretation concerns the relationship between angels and prophets. The chief mark of the Biblical prophet was that he had stood in the presence of God and the angels during the sessions of the heavenly Council (cf. Isa. 6:1-8; Ezek. 1-3, 10), thereby becoming its authoritative spokesman to God's people (cf. Jer. 15:19). The essential difference between the true prophet and the false prophet was that the true prophet had been taken up by the Spirit into the Cloud to take part in this assembly:

> Thus says the LORD of hosts:
> Do not listen to the words of the prophets who are prophesying
>   to you.
> They are leading you into futility;
> They speak a vision of their own imagination,

---

41. Ibid., p. 156.

42. An interesting aspect of the conceptual background of all this is the reference in the apocryphal book of Tobit to "the seven holy angels, who present the prayers of the saints, and who go in and out before the glory of the Holy One" (12:15; cf. 1 Enoch 20:1-7).

Not from the mouth of the LORD. . . .
But who has stood in the Council of the LORD,
That he should see and hear His Word?
Who has given heed to His Word and listened? . . .
I did not send these prophets,
But they ran.
I did not speak to them,
But they prophesied.
But if they had stood in My Council,
Then they would have announced My words to My people,
And would have turned them back from their evil way
And from the evil of their deeds. (Jer. 23:16-22)

The prophets not only observed the deliberations of the heavenly Council (cf. 1 Kings 22:19-22); they actually participated in them. Indeed, the LORD did nothing without consulting His prophets (Amos 3:7). This is why the characteristic activity of the Biblical prophet is intercession and mediation (cf. Gen. 18:16-33; 20:7, the first occurrence of the word *prophet* in Scripture). As members of the Council the prophets have freedom of speech with God, and are able to argue with Him, often persuading Him to change His mind (cf. Ex. 32:7-14; Amos 7:1-6). They are His friends, and so He speaks openly with them (Gen. 18:17; Ex. 33:11; 2 Chron. 20:7; Isa. 41:8; John 15:15). As images of fully redeemed Man, the prophets shared in God's glory, exercising dominion over the nations (cf. Jer. 1:10; 28:8), having been transfigured ethically (cf. Isa. 6:5-8) and physically (cf. Ex. 34:29). They thus resembled the angels of heaven, and so it is not surprising that the term *angel* (Heb. *mal'āk̲*, Greek *angelos*) is used to describe the Biblical prophet (cf. 2 Chron. 36:15-16; Hag. 1:13; Mal. 3:1; Matt. 11:10; 24:31; Luke 7:24; 9:52). In fact, the archetypical Prophet in Scripture is the Angel of the LORD.[43]

There is therefore abundant Biblical precedent for the prophetic rulers of the churches to be referred to as **the angels of the churches**. It is likely that each angel represents a single pastor or bishop; but St. John could be referring to the stars/angels simply as personifications of the *government* of each

---

43. The most comprehensive study of the prophetic order and its relationship to the angelic Council is in Kline, *Images of the Spirit*, pp. 57-96. See also George Vandervelde, "The Gift of Prophecy and the Prophetic Church" (Toronto: Institute for Christian Studies, 1984).

church as a whole. And the Lord of heaven and earth is holding them in His **right hand**. (This is the same hand that Christ used to resurrect St. John in v. 17; St. John is thus an "angel.") In a more general sense, what is true of the angels is true of the Church as a whole: St. Paul urged the Philippians to prove themselves to be "blameless and innocent, children of God above reproach in the midst of a crooked and perverse generation, among whom you shine as lights [*luminaries, stars*] in the world" (Phil. 2:15).

The seven lampstands are (correspond to) **the seven churches**; and the seven churches are, as we have noted already, both the particular churches referred to *and* the fullness of the whole Church in every age. In terms of the symbolism of the number *seven* as it relates to the Church, the comment of Victorinus (a bishop martyred in A.D. 304) regarding the Apostle Paul is interesting: "In the whole world Paul taught that all the churches are arranged by sevens, that they are called seven, and that the Catholic Church is one. And first of all, indeed, that he himself also might maintain the type of seven churches, he did not exceed that number. But he wrote to the Romans, to the Corinthians, to the Galatians, to the Ephesians, to the Thessalonians, to the Philippians, to the Colossians; afterwards he wrote to individual persons, so as not to exceed the number of seven churches."[44]

The one lampstand (a stylized tree) of the old Tabernacle is now Christ (the Tree of Life) with His seven lampstands. Before, in the Old Testament, the Church had a centralized, national character; and the unity of the particular congregations of Israel was focused geographically, in Jerusalem. But that is no longer the case. The Church, the New Israel, has been geographically and nationally decentralized—or, better, *multi*centralized: The Church is still a *seven*—still a unity—but what holds it together is not a special, holy piece of real estate; the unity of the Church is centered on Jesus Christ. The Church is no longer tied to one place, for it has been sent into all the world

---

44. Victorinus, *Commentary on the Apocalypse of the Blessed John*, in Alexander Roberts and James Donaldson, eds., *The Ante-Nicene Fathers* (Grand Rapids: Eerdmans, [1886] 1970), vol. VII, p. 345.

to take dominion in the name of the universal King.[45] There is no longer any special space on earth that is holy; rather, the whole world has become "holy space," for Jesus Christ has redeemed it. And in recapturing the world, He has recreated the Church in His image. For just as Christ is seen here in a blaze of glorious light, so the Church which He carries and upholds is characterized by light (cf. the description of the Church in 21:9-22:5). The lightbearing churches, whose very governments glisten with starlike brilliance, shine upon the world with the light of Jesus Christ, with the result that men will see their good works and glorify their Father who is in heaven.

---

45. According to Exodus 18 and Deuteronomy 1, the eldership was arranged hierarchically, with "rulers of thousands, rulers of hundreds, rulers of fifties, and rulers of tens." This was the Biblical basis for the hierarchical organization of the early church, the bishop of the city corresponding to the "ruler over thousands" (see James B. Jordan, "Biblical Church Government, Part 3: Concilar Hierarchy—Elders and Bishops," *Presbyterian Heritage*, No. 9 [January 1986], P.O. Box 131300, Tyler, TX 75713). A central headquarters (a "vatican") may therefore be useful for Church government, although it is not necessary (there is a distinction between what may be *good* for the *well-being* [bene esse] or the *fulness of being [plene esse]* of the Church, and what is *necessary* for the *being [esse]* of the Church). The best available historical study of the rise of the episcopate is J. B. Lightfoot, *The Christian Ministry*, Philip Edgcumbe Hughes, ed. (Wilton, CT: Morehouse-Barlow Co., 1983).

Part Two

HISTORICAL PROLOGUE: THE LETTERS TO THE SEVEN CHURCHES
(Revelation 2-3)

Introduction

The second part of the covenantal treaty structure (cf. Deut. 1:6-4:49)[1] is the Prologue, which recounts the history of the Great King's relationship with the vassal, reminding him of his lord's authority and covenant faithfulness, listing the benefits that have been provided, enumerating the vassal's transgressions of the law, commanding the vassal to repent and renew his obedience, and promising future rewards. An important aspect of the Prologue is the *covenant grant,*[2] the command to take possession over the land, conquering it in the name of the Great King (cf. Deut. 2:24-25, 31; 3:18-22; 4:1, 14, 37-40).[3]

The Seven Messages to the churches correspond to the Covenant Prologue in several ways. Their structure follows the same general pattern: Christ's lordship over the Church, the individual church's record of faithfulness or disobedience, warnings of punishment, and promises of blessings in response to obedience. Moreover, in each case the church is given a *covenant grant,* a commission to *conquer,* to *overcome* and exercise dominion under Christ's lordship (2:7, 11, 17, 26-29; 3:5, 12, 21).

In addition, each message itself recapitulates the entire five-part covenant structure. Consider the first message, to the church in Ephesus (2:1-7):

---

1. See Meredith G. Kline, *Treaty of the Great King: The Covenant Structure of Deuteronomy* (Grand Rapids: William B. Eerdmans Publishing Co., 1963), pp. 52-61.
2. See Ray R. Sutton, *That You May Prosper: Dominion by Covenant,* (Tyler, TX: Institute for Christian Economics, 1987).
3. Kline, *Treaty of the Great King,* pp. 56ff.

85

1. *Preamble*: "The One who holds the seven stars in His right hand, the One who walks among the seven golden lampstands" (2:1)

2. *Historical Prologue*: "I know your deeds. . . ." (2:2-4).

3. *Ethical Stipulations*: "Remember therefore from where you have fallen, and repent, and do the deeds you did at first" (2:5a).

4. *Sanctions*: "Or else I am coming to you, and will remove your lampstand out of its place—unless you repent" (2:5b).

5. *Succession Arrangements*: ". . . To him who overcomes, I will grant to eat of the Tree of Life, which is in the Paradise of My God" (2:6-7).

Recapitulation of Covenantal History

We discussed under 1:4 the view (strangely common among modern "literalists"!) that the seven churches symbolically represent "seven ages of Church history"; and, while on several counts that interpretation is patently erroneous, there is another sense in which these seven churches are related to seven periods of Church history—*Old Testament* Church history. For the imagery used to describe the seven churches of Asia progresses chronologically from the Garden of Eden to the situation in the first century A.D.:

1. *Ephesus* (2:1-7). The language of Paradise is evident throughout the passage. Christ announces Himself as the Creator, the One who holds the seven stars; and as the One who walks among the lampstands to evaluate them, as God walked through the Garden in judgment (Gen. 3:8). The "angel" of Ephesus is commended for properly guarding the church against her enemies, as Adam had been commanded to guard the Garden and his wife from their Enemy (Gen. 2:15). But the angel, like Adam, has "fallen," having left his first love. Christ therefore threatens to come to him in judgment and remove his lampstand out of its place, as He had banished Adam and Eve from the Garden (cf. Gen. 3:24). Nevertheless, Eden's gate is open to those who gain victory over the Tempter: "To him who overcomes, I will grant to eat of the Tree of Life, which is in the Paradise of My God."

2. *Smyrna* (2:8-11). The situation of the Patriarchs (Abraham, Isaac, Jacob, and Joseph) and of the children of Israel in

Egypt appears to be reflected in the words of this message. Christ describes Himself as He "who was dead, and has come to life," a redemptive act foreshadowed in the lives of Isaac (Gen. 22:1-14; Heb. 11:17-19) and Joseph (Gen. 37:18-36; 39:20- 41:45; 45:4-8; 50:20), as well as in the salvation of Israel from the house of bondage. The Smyrnaeans' condition of seeming poverty and actual riches is analogous to the experience of all the patriarchs, who "lived as aliens in the land of promise" (Heb. 11:9). False "Jews" are persecuting the true heirs of the promises, just as Ishmael persecuted Isaac (Gen. 21:9; cf. Gal. 4:22-31). The danger of imprisonment at the instigation of a slanderer is paralleled in the life of Joseph (Gen. 39:13-20), as is the blessing of the crown of life for the faithful (Gen. 41:40- 44); Aaron too, as the glorious image of Man fully redeemed, wore a crown of life (Ex. 28:36-38). The "tribulation of ten days" followed by victory reflects the story of Israel's endurance through the ten plagues before its deliverance.

3. *Pergamum* (2:12-17). The imagery in this section is taken from the sojourn of Israel in the wilderness, the abode' of demons (Lev. 16:10; 17:7; Deut. 8:15; Matt. 4:1; 12:43); the Christians of Pergamum also had to dwell "where Satan's throne is . . . where Satan dwells." The enemies of the church are described as "Balaam" and "Balak," the false prophet and evil king who tried to destroy the Israelites by tempting them to idolatry and fornication (Num. 25:1-3; 31:16). Like the Angel of the LORD and Phineas the priest, Christ threatens to make war against the Balaamites with the sword (cf. Num. 22:31; 24:7-8). To those who overcome, He promises a share in the "hidden manna" from the Ark of the Covenant (Heb. 9:4), and a white stone with a "new name" inscribed on it, the emblem of the redeemed covenant people worn by the High Priest (Ex. 28:9-12).

4. *Thyatira* (2:18-29). St. John now turns to imagery from the period of the Israelite monarchy and the Davidic covenant. Christ announces Himself as "the Son of God," the greater David (cf. Ps. 2:7; 89:19-37; Jer. 30:9; Ezek. 34:23-24; 37:24-28; Hos. 3:5; Acts 2:24-36; 13:22-23). He rebukes the angel of Thyatira, whose toleration of his "wife, Jezebel," is leading to the apostasy of God's people (cf. 1 Kings 16:29-34; 21:25-26). She and those who commit adultery with her (cf. 2 Kings 9:22) are threatened with "tribulation," like the three and one-half

years of tribulation visited upon Israel in Jezebel's day (1 Kings 17:1; James 5:17); she and her offspring will be killed (cf. 2 Kings 9:22-37). But he who overcomes will be granted, like David, "authority over the nations" (cf. 2 Sam. 7:19; 8:1-14; Ps. 18:37-50; 89:27-29). The concluding promise alludes to David's Messianic psalm of dominion: "And he shall rule them with a rod of iron; like the vessels of a potter they shall be broken to pieces, as I also have received from My Father" (cf. Ps. 2:9).

5. *Sardis* (3:1-6). The imagery of this section comes from the later prophetic period (cf. the references to the Spirit and the "seven stars," speaking of the prophetic witness) leading up to the end of the monarchy, when the disobedient covenant people were defeated and taken into captivity. The description of the church's reputation for "life" when it is really "dead," the exhortations to "wake up" and to "strengthen the things that remain," the acknowledgement that there are "a few people" who have remained faithful, all are reminiscent of prophetic language about the Remnant in a time of apostasy (Isa. 1:5-23; 6:9-13; 65:8-16; Jer. 7:1-7; 8:11-12; Ezek. 37:1-14), as is the warning of imminent judgment (Isa. 1:24-31; 2:12-21; 26:20-21; Jer. 4:5-31; 7:12-15; 11:9-13; Mic. 1:2-7; Zeph. 1).

6. *Philadelphia* (3:7-13). The Return from the Exile under Ezra and Nehemiah is reflected in this message, which speaks in the imagery of the synagogue and the rebuilding of Jerusalem and the Temple (cf. the prophecies of Haggai, Zechariah, and Malachi). The Philadelphians, like the returning Jews, have "a little power." The reference to "the synagogue of Satan, who say that they are Jews, and are not" recalls the conflicts with "false Jews" in Ezra 4 and Nehemiah 4, 6, and 13. The warning of a coming "hour of testing . . . which is about to come on the whole world, to test those who dwell upon the Land" reminds us of the tribulation suffered under Antiochus Epiphanes (cf. Dan. 8 and 11). But Christ promises the overcomer that he will be made "a pillar in the Temple" and share in the blessings of the "New Jerusalem."

7. *Laodicea* (3:14-22). The period of the Last Days (A.D. 30-70) provides the motifs for the seventh and last message. The "lukewarm" church, boasting of its wealth and self-sufficiency yet blind to its actual poverty and nakedness, is a fitting image of the Pharisaical Judaism of the first century (Luke 18:9-14; cf.

Rev. 18:7). Warned that she is about to be spewed out of the Land (the curse of Lev. 18:24-28; cf. Luke 21:24), Israel is urged to repent and accept Christ, offered in the Eucharistic meal. Those who overcome are granted the characteristic blessing of the age brought in by the New Covenant: dominion with Christ (cf. Eph. 1:20-22; 2:6; Rev. 1:6).

The Structure of Revelation Foreshadowed

Finally, the messages to the seven churches also contain a miniature outline of the entire prophecy. As we have noted, the four sections of Revelation following the Preamble (Chapter 1) are structured in terms of the four sevenfold curses of the Covenant, set forth in Leviticus 26:18, 21, 24, 28. These four sets of judgments in Revelation may be summarized as follows:

1. *Judgment on the False Apostles* (2-3). Heretical teachers propagating false doctrines are exposed, condemned, and excommunicated by St. John and those who are faithful to the true Apostolic tradition.

2. *Judgment on the False Israel* (4-7). Apostate Israel, which is persecuting the saints, is condemned and punished; the believing Remnant is protected from judgment, inherits the blessings of the Covenant, and fills the earth with fruit.

3. *Judgment on the Evil King and False Prophet* (8-14). The Beast and the False Prophet wage war against the Church and are defeated by the True King and His army of faithful witnesses.

4. *Judgment on the Royal Harlot* (15-22). Babylon, the False Bride, is condemned and burned, and the True Bride celebrates the Marriage Supper of the Lamb.

This is the same general pattern we find in the first four messages themselves:

1. Ephesus: *Judgment on the False Apostles* (2:1-7). The conflicts of all seven churches are evident in the struggles of this church against the Nicolaitans, "those who call themselves apostles but are not."

2. Smyrna: *Judgment on the False Israel* (2:8-11). The Smyrnaeans are suffering from the opposition of "those who say they are Jews and are not, but are a synagogue of Satan."

89

3. Pergamum: *Judgment on the Evil King and False Prophet* (2:12-17). This church is experiencing persecution and temptation from the first-century counterparts of "Balak," the evil king of Moab, and the false prophet "Balaam."

4. Thyatira: *Judgment on the Royal Harlot* (2:18-29). The leader of the heretics, who entices God's servants into idolatry and fornication, is named after Jezebel, the adulterous queen of ancient Israel.

The cycle now begins over again, so that these first four messages are "recapitulated" in the last three, but with attention to different details. To understand this, we must start from the first message again. St. John's descriptions of Christ in the preamble to each message are drawn from those in the vision of the Son of Man in Chapter 1. But his order is chiastic (that is, he takes up each point in reverse order). Thus:

The Vision of the Son of Man
A. His *eyes* were *like a flame of fire*, and His *feet* were *like burnished bronze* (1:14-15).
   B. Out of His mouth came a *sharp two-edged sword* (1:16).
      C. I am *the First and the Last*, and the Living One; and I *was dead*, and behold, I am alive forevermore, *Amen*; and I have *the keys* of death and of Hades (1:17-18).
         D. The mystery of *the seven stars* that you saw in My *right hand*, and *the seven golden lampstands* (1:20).
The Letters to the Seven Churches
         D. *Ephesus* The One who holds *the seven stars* in His *right hand*, the One who walks among *the seven golden lampstands* (2:1).
      C. *Smyrna* *The First and the Last*, who was *dead*, and has come to life (2:8).
   B. *Pergamum* The One who has the *sharp two-edged sword* (2:12).
A. *Thyatira* The Son of God, who has *eyes like a flame of fire*, and His *feet* are *like burnished bronze* (2:18).
         D. *Sardis* He who has the seven Spirits of God, and *the seven stars* (3:1).
      C. *Philadelphia* He who is holy, who is true, who has *the key* of David, who opens and no one will shut, and who shuts and no one will open (3:7).
      C. *Laodicea* The *Amen*, the faithful and true Witness, the

Beginning of the creation of God (3:14).[4]

The repetition of the overall pattern is reinforced by other points of similarity. The parallel between Smyrna and Philadelphia can be seen also in that both deal with the "synagogue of Satan"; and the association of the "seven lampstands" of Ephesus with the "seven Spirits of God" of Sardis is accounted for in the following chapter, during St. John's vision of the heavenly Throne: "And there were seven lamps of fire burning before the Throne, which are the seven Spirits of God" (4:5).

---

4. We would have expected St. John to pattern the Laodicean Preamble after B (or perhaps even A) rather than C; for some reason, he chose not to make the structure symmetrical.

THE SPIRIT SPEAKS TO
THE CHURCH: OVERCOME!

Ephesus: Judgment on the False Apostles (2:1-7)

1 To the angel of the church in Ephesus write: The One who holds the seven stars in His right hand, the One who walks in the middle of the seven golden lampstands, says this:

2 I know your deeds and your toil and your perseverance, and that you cannot endure evil men — that you have tested those who call themselves apostles but are not, and have found them to be false.

3 And you have perseverance, and have endured hardships for My name, and have not grown weary.

4 But I have this against you: You have left your first love.

5 Remember therefore from where you have fallen, and repent and do the deeds you did at first; or else I am coming to you quickly, and will remove your lampstand out of its place — unless you repent.

6 Yet this you do have: You hate the deeds of the Nicolaitans, which I also hate.

7 He who has an ear, let him hear what the Spirit says to the churches. To him who overcomes, I will grant to eat of the Tree of Life, which is in the Paradise of My God.

1 The city of Ephesus was the most important city in Asia Minor, both in politics and trade. It was an important cultural center as well, boasting such attractions as art, science, witchcraft, idolatry, gladiators, and persecution. Main Street ran from the harbor to the theater, and on the way the visitor would pass the gymnasium and public baths, the public library, and the public brothel. Its temple to Artemis (or Diana — the goddess of fertility and "nature in the wild") was one of the Seven Wonders of the ancient world. St. Luke tells us another interesting fact about the city, one that has important bearing on the Seven

Messages as a whole: Ephesus was a hotbed of *Jewish* occultism and magical arts (Acts 19:13-15, 18-19). Throughout the world of the first century, apostate Judaism was accommodating itself to numerous pagan ideologies and heathen practices, developing early strains of what later came to be known as Gnosticism — various hybrids of occult wisdom, rabbinical lore, mystery religion, and either asceticism or licentiousness (or both), all stirred up together with a few bits and pieces of Christian doctrine.[1] This mongrelized religious quackery was undoubtedly a primary spawning ground for the heresies that afflicted the churches of Asia Minor.

Yet, despite all the multiform depravity within Ephesus (cf. Eph. 4:17-19; 5:3-12) the Lord Jesus Christ had established His Church there (Acts 19); and in this message He assures the angel of the congregation that He **holds the seven stars in His right hand**, upholding and protecting the rulers whom He has ordained: "He fills them with light and influence," says Matthew Henry's *Commentary*; "He supports them, or else they would soon be falling stars."[2] He also **walks in the middle of the lampstands**, the churches, guarding and examining them, and connecting them to one another through their unity in Him. "I will put My dwelling place among you, and I will not abhor you. I will walk among you and be your God, and you will be my people" (Lev. 26:11-12).

2-3   The church in Ephesus was well known for its **toil** and hard work for the faith, and its **perseverance** in the face of opposition and apostasy, having **endured hardships** for the name of Christ. This was a church that did not know the meaning of compromise, willing to take a strong stand for orthodoxy, regardless of the cost. (It is noteworthy that, of all Paul's letters to the churches, *Ephesians* alone does not mention a single doctrinal issue that needed apostolic correction.) The rulers of the

---

1. See Elizabeth Schüssler Fiorenza, *The Book of Revelation: Justice and Judgment* (Philadelphia: Fortress Press, 1985), pp. 114-32. For an example of the sort of insane literature this movement produced, see James M. Robinson, ed., *The Nag Hammadi Library* (San Francisco: Harper & Row, Publishers, 1977).

2. Matthew Henry, *Commentary on the Whole Bible* (New York: Fleming H. Revell Co., n.d.), vol. VI, p. 1123.

church were not afraid to discipline **evil men**. They knew the importance of heresy trials and excommunications, and it seems that this church had had a good share of both: Its rulers had **tested** the false "apostles," and had convicted them. The elders of Ephesus heeded well the exhortation Paul had given them (Acts 20:28-31): "Guard yourselves and all the flock of which the Holy Spirit has made you overseers. Be shepherds of the Church of God, which He bought with His own blood. I know that after I leave, savage wolves will come in among you and will not spare the flock. Even from your own number men will arise and distort the truth in order to draw away disciples after them. So be on your guard!"

Forty years later, this church was still renowned for its orthodoxy, as St. Ignatius (martyred A.D. 107) observed in his letter to the Ephesians: "You all live according to truth, and no heresy has a home among you: indeed, you do not so much as listen to anyone, if he speaks of anything except concerning Jesus Christ in truth. . . . I have learned that certain persons passed through you bringing evil doctrine; and you did not allow them to sow seeds among you, for you stopped up your ears, so that you might not receive the seed sown by them. . . . You are arrayed from head to foot in the commandments of Jesus Christ."[3]

There are several striking parallels in these verses: Christ tells the church, "I know . . . your **toil** [literally, **weariness**] and your **perseverance**, and that you cannot **endure** evil men. . . . And you have **perseverance** and have **endured** for My sake, and have not grown **weary**."

4-6 Yet the Lord rebukes the angel: **I have this against you: You have left your first love.** The church's desire for sound doctrine had become perverted into a hardening-up against their brothers in Christ, so that they lacked love. It is important to note that even the most rigorous concern for orthodoxy does not automatically mean an absence of love. It is only a perversion of orthodoxy that results in hardness toward brethren. Christ does not criticize the Ephesians for being "too orthodox," but for leaving, forsaking the love which they had at first. The

---

3. St. Ignatius, *Ephesians* vi, ix.

question of "doctrine *versus* love" is, Biblically speaking, a non-issue. In fact, it is a specifically pagan issue, seeking to put asunder what God has joined together. Christians are required to be both orthodox and loving, and a lack of either will eventually result in the judgment of God.

Remember therefore from where you have fallen: The Ephesians had once had a harmonious combination of love and doctrinal orthodoxy, and Christ calls them to **repent,** to change their minds about their actions **and do the deeds you did at first.** Love is not simply a state of mind or an attitude; love is action in terms of God's law: "By this we know that we love the children of God, when we love God and keep His commandments. For this is the love of God, that we keep His commandments; and His commandments are not burdensome" (1 John 5:2-3; cf. Rom. 13:8-10). Christ's antidote for the Bride's spiritual malaise is not simply an exhortation to change her attitude as such. Instead, He commands her to change her actions, to perform the works that had characterized her romance with the Bridegroom at the beginning. Repentant actions will nourish and cultivate a repentant attitude.

If they do not repent, however, Christ warns: **I am coming to you** in judgment—a warning stated three more times in these letters (2:16; 3:3, 11). As we have seen before (1:7), the **Coming** of Christ does not simply refer to a cataclysm at the end of history, but rather refers to His comings in history. In fact, He warns, He will come **quickly,** a term emphasized by its seven occurrences in Revelation (2:5, 16; 3:11; 11:14; 22:7, 12, 20). The Lord is not threatening the church at Ephesus with His Second Coming; He is saying that He will come against *them*: **I will remove your lampstand out of its place.** Their influence will be taken away, and, indeed, they will cease to be a church at all. For lack of love, the entire congregation is in danger of excommunication. If the elders of a church fail to discipline and disciple the church toward love as well as doctrinal orthodoxy, Jesus Christ Himself will step in and administer judgment—and at that point it may very well be too late for repentance.

It is likely that St. John was using an important "current event" in the life of Ephesus as a partial basis for this imagery. The coastline was continually changing because of the sediment brought down by the nearby river Cayster; sand and pebbles progressively filled up the harbor, threatening to turn it into a marsh. The city was in danger of being, in effect, **moved out of its place**, completely cut off from the sea. Two centuries before, a massive engineering project had dredged the harbor, at the cost of much **toil, perseverance**, and **hardship**. By the middle of the first century, however, the harbor was again filling with silt. It became apparent that if Ephesus was to retain her influence as a seaport, the citizens would have to **repent** of their negligence and **do the first works** again. In A.D. 64, the city finally began dredging the harbor, and Ephesus remained in its place for years to come. (Over later centuries, the silting was allowed to go on unimpeded. Now, the sea is six miles away from the ruins of Ephesus, and what was once the harbor of Ephesus is now a grassy, windswept plain.)[4]

But a return to love does not imply any lessening of theological standards (in a real sense, it means a heightening and enforcing of a full-orbed theological standard). True love for Christ and His people requires the hatred of evil, and the Lord commends them for their steadfastness in this: **Yet this you do have: You hate the deeds of the Nicolaitans, which I also hate.** According to the second-century bishop St. Irenaeus, "the Nicolaitans are the followers of that Nicolas who was one of the seven first ordained to the diaconate by the apostles [Acts 6:5]. They lead lives of unrestrained indulgence . . . teaching that it is a matter of indifference to practice adultery, and to eat things sacrificed to idols."[5] If St. Irenaeus is correct here—his viewpoint is certainly debatable[6]—the deacon Nicolas (in Greek, *Nikolaos*) had apostatized and become a "false apostle," seeking to lead others into heresy and compromise with paganism.

One thing is obvious: St. John is calling the heretical faction

---

4. William J. McKnight, *The Apocalypse: A Reappearance*, Vol. I: *John to the Seven Churches* (Boston: Hamilton Brothers, Publishers, 1927), pp. 81ff.; C. J. Hemer, "Seven Cities of Asia Minor," in R. K. Harrison, ed., *Major Cities of the Biblical World* (Nashville: Thomas Nelson Publishers, 1985), p. 236.

5. St. Irenaeus, *Against Heresies*, i.xxvi.3; in Alexander Roberts and James Donaldson, eds., *The Ante-Nicene Fathers* (Grand Rapids: Eerdmans, [1885], 1973), p. 352.

6. It is debatable on two counts: first, the question of whether the "Nicolas" of Ephesus was really the deacon of Jerusalem; second, whether the "fornication" and idolatrous feasting (v. 14, 20) are to be taken literally.

in Ephesus after someone named Nikolaos (even if we allow that St. Irenaeus was confused about his identity). His reason appears to be based on linguistic considerations, for in Greek *Nikolaos* means *Conqueror of the people*. Interestingly, in the third of the seven messages St. John mentions a group of heretics in Pergamum, whom he calls followers of "Balaam" (2:14). In Hebrew, *Balaam* means *Conqueror of the people*. St. John is making a play on words, linking the "Nicolaitans" of Ephesus with the "Balaamites" of Pergamum; in fact, he clearly tells us in 2:14-15 that their doctrines are the same. Just as *Nikolaos* and *Balaam* are linguistic equivalents of one another (cf. the same technique in 9:11), they are theological equivalents as well. The "Nicolaitans" and the "Balaamites" are participants in the same heretical cult.

This conclusion is strengthened by a further connection. When we compare the actual teachings of the Nicolaitan/Balaamite heresy with those of the "Jezebel" faction in the church of Thyatira, mentioned in the fourth message (2:20), we find that their doctrines are identical to each other. There thus seems to be one particular heresy that is the focus of these messages to the churches during the Last Days, a heresy seeking to seduce God's people into idolatry and fornication. As St. Paul had foretold, wolves had arisen from within the Christian community attempting to devour the sheep, and it was the duty of the pastors/angels to be on guard against them, and to put them out of the Church. Jesus Christ declares that He **hates** the deeds of the Nicolaitans; His people are to show forth His image in loving what He loves and hating what He hates (cf. Ps. 139:19-22).

7   As in each of these messages, the letter to the church at Ephesus concludes by exhorting them to **hear what the Spirit says to the churches**. Although the messages are different, in terms of the needs of each congregation, the Spirit is really issuing one basic command: **Overcome!** The Greek verb is *nikaō*, the same as the root of *Nicolaitan*; Christ is charging His church with the responsibility of overcoming those who seek to overcome her. One side or the other will be the victor in this battle. Satan's opposition to the churches will appear in various forms, and different churches (and different ages of the Church) will have different issues to face, different enemies to overcome. But

no matter what are the particular problems facing it, each church is under divine mandate to conquer and completely overwhelm its opposition. The duty of overcoming is not something reserved for a select few "super-Christians" who have "dedicated" themselves to God over and above the usual requirements for Christians. All Christians are overcomers: *Whatever is born of God overcomes the world; and this is the victory that has overcome the world — our faith* (1 John 5:4). The Christians spoken of in Revelation overcame the devil "because of the blood of the Lamb and because of the Word of their testimony" (12:11). The question is not one of victory or defeat. The question is victory or treason.

The Christian overcomes; and to him Christ grants the privilege **to eat of the Tree of Life, which is in the Paradise of My God**. This is not only an otherworldly hope. Although the full consummation of this promise is brought in at the end of history, it is a present and increasing possession of the people of God, as they obey their Lord and take dominion over the earth. For the Tree of Life is Jesus Christ Himself, and to partake of the Tree is to possess the blessings and benefits of salvation.[7] In Christ, the overcoming Christian has *Paradise Restored*, in this life and forever.

Smyrna: Judgment on the False Israel (2:8-11)

8 And to the angel of the church in Smyrna write: The First and the Last, who was dead, and has come to life, says this:

9 I know your works and your tribulation and your poverty (but you are rich), and the blasphemy by those who say they are Jews and are not, but are a synagogue of Satan.

10 Do not fear what you are about to suffer. Behold, the devil is about to cast some of you into prison, that you may be tested, and you will have tribulation ten days. Be faithful unto death, and I will give you the crown of life.

---

7. The Cross has long been used in Christian art as a symbol for the Tree of Life. There is strong evidence, however, that Christ was actually crucified on a living tree (with his wrists nailed to the crosspiece he carried and his feet nailed to the trunk; cf. Acts 5:30; 10:39; 13:29; Gal. 3:13; 1 Pet. 2:24). The symbol of the Cross is simply a stylized tree, and was often pictured in ancient churches and tombs with branches and leaves growing out of it. See Ernest L. Martin's fascinating and informative work, *The Place of Christ's Crucifixion: Its Discovery and Significance* (Pasadena: Foundation for Biblical Research, 1984), pp. 75-94.

11 He who has an ear, let him hear what the Spirit says to the churches. He who overcomes shall not be hurt by the second death.

8   There were two characteristics of Smyrna that meant severe problems for the church there. First, the people of the city were strongly devoted to the Emperor cult; and, second, Smyrna had a large population of Jews who were hostile to the Christian faith. To this faithful church, suffering mightily under the persecutions of these unbelievers, Jesus Christ announces Himself as **the First and the Last**, a name for God taken from Isaiah 44:6 and 48:12. It is obvious from the contexts of those verses that the expression identifies God as the supreme Lord and Determiner of history, the Planner and Controller of all reality. The Biblical doctrine of predestination, when rightly understood, should not be a source of fear for the Christian; rather, it is a source of comfort and assurance.

The opposite of the doctrine of predestination is not freedom, but meaninglessness; if the smallest details of our lives are not part of the Plan of God, if they are not *created facts* with a divinely determined significance, then they can have no meaning at all. They cannot be "working together for good." But the Christian who understands the truth of God's sovereignty is assured thereby that nothing in his life is without meaning and purpose — that God has ordained all things for His glory and for our ultimate good. This means that even our sufferings are part of a consistent Plan; that when we are opposed, we need not fear that God has abandoned us. We can be secure in the knowledge that, since we have been "called according to His purpose" (Rom. 8:28), all things in our life are a necessary aspect of that purpose. Martin Luther said: "It is, then, fundamentally necessary and wholesome for Christians to know that God foreknows nothing contingently, but that He foresees, purposes, and does all things according to His own immutable, eternal and infallible will. . . . For the Christian's chief and only comfort in adversity lies in knowing that God does not lie, but brings all things to pass immutably, and that His will cannot be resisted, altered or impeded."[8]

---

8. Martin Luther, *The Bondage of the Will*, J. I. Packer and O. R. Johnston, trans. (Old Tappan, NJ: Fleming H. Revell Co., 1957), pp. 80, 84.

Not only is Christ the First and the Last, but He **was dead, and has come to life**: He is completely victorious over death and the grave as the "first fruits" of all those who die in the Lord (1 Cor. 15:20-22), guaranteeing our resurrection as well, so that even "death is swallowed up in victory" (1 Cor. 15:54). Regardless of the force and cruelty of their persecutors, the Christians in Smyrna cannot be defeated, either in this life or the next.

9-10 But it was not easy to be a Christian in Smyrna. Certainly, they didn't get "raptured" out of their **tribulation**; and this often meant **poverty** as well, because of their stand for the faith. Perhaps they were subjected to confiscation of their property (cf. Heb. 10:34) or vandalism; it is also likely that they were the objects of an economic boycott on account of their refusal to align themselves with either the pagan State-worshipers or the apostate Jews (cf. 13:16-17). Yet in their poverty, they were **rich** in the most basic and ultimate sense: regarded by the world "as poor, yet making many rich; as having nothing, yet possessing all things" (2 Cor. 6:10). **I know** all about what you are enduring, their Lord assures them; He identifies with them in their sufferings, so much so that "in all their afflictions He is afflicted" (Isa. 63:9; cf. v. 2-3). As the Puritan theologian John Owen observed, all our persecutions "are His in the first place, ours only by participation" (cf. Col. 1:24).[9]

And he knows all about the **blasphemy** of their persecutors as well — **those who say they are Jews and are not**. Here the Lord is explicit about the identity of the opposition faced by the early Church: Those who are otherwise known as Nicolaitans, the followers of the false apostles Balaam and Jezebel, are defined here as those who claim to be Jews, children of Abraham, but in reality are children of the devil. These are the Israelites who have rejected Christ and thus rejected the God of Abraham, Isaac, and Jacob. A popular myth holds that non-Christian Jews are true believers in the God of the Old Testament, and that they only need to "add" the New Testament to their otherwise adequate religion. But the New Testament itself is adamant on this point: Non-Christian Jews are not believers in God, but

---

9. John Owen, *Works*, 16 vols., William H. Goold, ed. (Edinburgh: The Banner of Truth Trust, [1850-53] 1965-68), Vol. 2, p. 145.

are covenant-breaking apostates. As Jesus said to those Jews who rejected Him: "If you are Abraham's children, do the deeds of Abraham. But as it is, you are seeking to kill Me. . . . You are doing the deeds of your father. . . . If God were your Father, you would love Me. . . . You are of your father the devil, and you want to do the deeds of your father. He was a murderer from the beginning, and does not stand in the truth, because there is no truth in him. Whenever he speaks the Lie, he speaks from his own nature; for he is a liar, and the father of it" (John 8:39-44). The truth is that there is no such thing as an "orthodox" Jew, unless he is a Christian; for if Jews believed the Old Testament, they would believe in Christ. If a man does not believe in Christ, he does not believe Moses either (John 5:46).

St. Paul wrote: "He is not a Jew who is one outwardly; neither is circumcision that which is outward in the flesh. But he is a Jew who is one inwardly; and circumcision is that which is of the heart, by the Spirit, not by the letter; and his praise is not from men, but from God" (Rom. 2:28-29). For this reason, St. Paul was bold enough to use this language in warning the churches against the seductions of the apostate Jews: "Beware of the dogs, beware of the evil workers, beware of the false circumcision; for we are the true circumcision, who worship in the Spirit of God and glory in Christ Jesus and put no confidence in the flesh" (Phil. 3:2-3). The expression translated *true circumcision* is, in the Greek, simply *circumcision*, meaning *a cutting around*; the *false circumcision* is literally *concision*, meaning *a cutting in pieces*. The Jews' circumcision, the covenant sign in which they trusted, was in reality an emblem of their own spiritual mutilation and destruction, the sign that through their own rebellion they had inherited the covenant curses. The cutting away of the foreskin was always a mark of damnation. To the righteous, the ritual application of God's wrath signified that they would not undergo its terrible reality; to the disobedient, however, it was a foretaste of things to come, a certain sign of the utter destruction that lay ahead.

Who then is the true Jew? Who belongs to the true Israel? According to the clear teaching of the New Testament, the person (regardless of his ethnic heritage) who has been clothed with Jesus Christ is the inheritor of the promises to Abraham, and possesses the blessings of the Covenant (Rom. 11:11-24; Gal.

3:7-9, 26-29). But a congregation of apostates and persecutors is nothing more, our Lord says, than **a synagogue of Satan**. **Satan** means *Accuser*, and early Christian history is rife with examples of Satanic false witness by the Jews against the Christian Church (Acts 6:9-15; 13:10; 14:2-5; 17:5-8; 18:6, 12-13; 19:9; 21:27-36; 24:1-9; 25:2-3, 7). This point is underscored by the statement that some of them would be cast into prison by **the devil** (meaning *the Slanderer*).

Because the One who knows their sufferings is also the First and the Last, the All-Controller, He can give authoritative comfort: **Do not fear what you are about to suffer.** Some of the Smyrnaean Christians would soon be **cast into prison** at the instigation of the Jews; but Christ assures them that this too is a part of the great cosmic conflict between Christ and Satan. The persecutions inflicted upon them by the Jews allied with the Roman Empire have their origin in **the devil**, in his hostility to the followers of Jesus Christ, in his frantic attempts to retain the shreds of his tattered kingdom. He is desperately waging a losing battle against the relentlessly marching hordes of a nation of kings and priests who are predestined to victory.

And thus behind even the devil's attempts to overthrow us is the absolute decree of God. Satan inspired the Chaldeans to steal Job's flocks, and yet Job's righteous response was: "The LORD gave, and the LORD has taken away. Blessed be the name of the LORD" (Job 1:21).[10] So the divinely ordained purpose for the devil's wicked activity is **that you may be tested**: as Samuel Rutherford wrote, "the devil is but God's master fencer, to teach us to handle our weapons."[11] The trials of Christians are not ordained ultimately by Satan, but by God; and the outcome is not destruction, but purity (cf. Job 23:10; 1 Pet. 4:12-19). The **tribulation** of the church at Smyrna would be fierce, but relatively short in duration: **ten days**. Daniel and his three friends had been tested for ten days, but they passed the test, and were promoted to high privilege (Dan. 1:11-21). Similarly, the Jewish persecution of the church in Smyrna would be allowed to continue for only a short while longer, and then the church would be free:

---

10. See John Calvin's comments on this passage in his *Institutes of the Christian Religion*, ii.iv.2.

11. *The Letters of Samuel Rutherford*, Frank E. Gaebelein, ed. (Chicago: Moody Press, 1951), p. 219.

Ten days of tribulation in exchange for one thousand years of victory (20:4-6). Even so, the time of testing was to cost the lives of many in the church, and they are exhorted to **be faithful until death**, in order to win **the crown of life**. This is not a blessing reserved for some unusually consecrated class of Christians, for all Christians are to be faithful until death. The Bible simply does not know of any other kind of Christian. "If we endure, we shall also reign with Him; if we deny Him, He also will deny us" (2 Tim. 2:12). "You will be hated by all on account of My name," Jesus said; "but it is the one who has endured to the end who will be saved" (Matt. 10:22). The crown of life is salvation itself.

11 The faithful Christian who **overcomes** opposition and temptation **shall not be hurt by the Second Death**. The fact that this was originally said to a first-century church helps us understand the meaning of another passage in this book. Revelation 20:6 states that those who are not hurt by the "Second Death" are the same as those who partake of "the First Resurrection," and that they are priests and kings with Christ—a blessing St. John has already affirmed to be a present reality (1:6). Necessarily, therefore, the First Resurrection cannot refer to the physical resurrection at the end of the world (1 Cor. 15:22-28). Rather, it must refer to what St. Paul clearly taught in his epistle to the Ephesians: "And *you were dead* in your trespasses and sins. . . . But God, being rich in mercy, . . . even when *we were dead* in our transgressions, made us alive together with Christ (by grace you have been saved), *and raised us up with Him*" (Eph. 2:1, 4-6). The Christian, in every age, is a partaker in the First Resurrection to new life in Christ, having been cleansed from his (first) death in Adam.[12] He "has eternal life, and does not come into judgment, but has passed out of death into life" (John 5:24).

Pergamum: Judgment on the False Prophet and Godless King (2:12-17)

12 And to the angel of the church in Pergamum write: The One who has the sharp two-edged sword says this:

---

12. Of course, there will also be a second resurrection (a physical one) at the end of history, but that is not mentioned in Rev. 20:6. See John 5:24-29, where Christ discusses both resurrections.

13 I know your works, and where you dwell, where Satan's throne is; and you hold fast My name, and did not deny My faith, even in the days of Antipas, My faithful witness, who was killed among you, where Satan dwells.

14 But I have a few things against you, because you have there some who hold the teaching of Balaam, who kept teaching Balak to put a stumbling block before the sons of Israel, to eat things sacrificed to idols, and to commit fornication.

15 Thus you also have some who in the same way hold the teaching of the Nicolaitans.

16 Repent therefore; or else I am coming to you quickly, and I will make war against them with the sword of My mouth.

17 He who has an ear, let him hear what the Spirit says to the churches. To him who overcomes, to him I will give of the hidden manna, and I will give him a white stone, and a new name written on the stone which no one knows but he who receives it.

12 Pergamum was another important Asian city, and played host to a number of popular false cults, the most prominent being those of Zeus, Dionysos, Asklepios (the serpent-god who was officially designated *Savior*), and, most importantly, Caesar-worship. Pergamum boasted magnificent temples to the Caesars and to Rome, and "of all the seven cities, Pergamum was the one in which the church was most liable to clash with the imperial cult."[13]

To this major center of deified statism, Christ announces Himself as **the One who has the sharp two-edged sword.** Rome claimed for itself the position of Creator and Definer of all: The Empire's power over life and death was absolute and final. But, whereas Rome asserted that its right of execution was original, the message of Christianity was that all power and authority outside the triune God was derivative—the various rulers and authorities are *created*, and receive their dominion from God (Rom. 13:1-4). It is Jesus Christ who wields all power in heaven and on earth (Matt. 28:18), and the ultimate power of the sword belongs to Him. As the Sovereign Lord and Ruler of the kings of earth (1:5), He has laid down the law to the nations. If the

---

13. Robert H. Mounce, *The Book of Revelation* (Grand Rapids: Eerdmans, 1977), p. 96.

rulers do not apply and enforce His commands throughout their divinely-ordained jurisdiction, He will bring his sharp sword down upon their necks.[14]

13 The believers of Pergamum are living **where Satan's throne is** (cf. comments at 1:4 on the centrality of the throne-theme in Revelation). Robert H. Mounce notes several of the suggestions as to the meaning of this expression (none of which must necessarily exclude the others): "Frequent mention is made of the great throne-like altar to Zeus which overlooked the city from the citadel. . . . Others take the phrase in reference to the cult of Asklepios, who was designated Savior and whose symbol was the serpent (this would obviously remind Christians of Satan; cf. 12:9; 20:2). . . . As the traveler approached Pergamum by the ancient road from the south, the actual shape of the city-hill would appear as a giant throne towering above the plain. The expression is best understood, however, in connection with the prominence of Pergamum as the official cult center of emperor worship in Asia. . . . It was here that Satan had established his official seat or chair of state. As Rome had become the center of Satan's activity in the West (cf. 13:2; 16:10), so Pergamum had become his 'throne' in the East."[15]

While this last designation — the throne as the seat of emperor-worship and deified statism — is a central aspect of the text's meaning, there is a much more basic dimension that is generally overlooked. **Satan** has already been identified in these messages as united to the synagogue, the unbelieving Jewish community that has abandoned the covenant in favor of a mythical religion. The foremost enemy of the Church, throughout the New Testament, is apostate Judaism, whose representatives were continually haling Christians before the Roman magistrate (Acts 4:24-28; 12:1-3; 13:8; 14:5; 17:5-8; 18:12-13; 21:11; 24:1-9; 25:2-3,

---

14. That this is true for all nations, and not just Old Testament Israel, can be seen by reading (for example) Psalm 2 and Daniel 4. Comprehensive discussions of God's law as it relates to nations and rulers are contained in James B. Jordan, *The Law of the Covenant: An Exposition of Exodus 21-23* (Tyler, TX: Institute for Christian Economics, 1984); Rousas John Rushdoony, *The Institutes of Biblical Law* (Nutley, NJ: The Craig Press, 1973); and Greg L. Bahnsen, *Theonomy in Christian Ethics* (Phillipsburg, NJ: Presbyterian and Reformed Publishing Co., second ed., 1984).

15. Mounce, pp. 96f.

9, 24). As St. John will reveal in Chapters 12-13, Satan is the moving force behind the Jewish/Roman attempt to destroy the Church.

The close relationship in Pergamum between organized Judaism and the imperial officials, combined with Christianity's opposition to statism and the worship of the creature, made it only natural that persecution and martyrdom would begin here, if anywhere in Asia. And on this account, Christ regards the church at Pergamum as faithful: They **hold fast** to His **name** — confessing Him alone as Savior, Mediator and Lord, proclaiming that His identity as the link between heaven and earth was absolutely unique. They **did not deny** the **faith**, even when bitter persecution came **in the days of Antipas . . . who was killed among you, where Satan dwells.** No one now knows who this Antipas was, but it is enough that Christ singles him out for special acknowledgment: **My faithful witness,** He calls him. By his very name — *Against All* — Antipas personifies the steadfastness of the Pergamene church in resisting persecution.

14-16 Yet not all in the church were of the faithful character of Antipas; moreover, a threat that posed a danger to the integrity of the faith, even greater than the danger of persecution, is the sly, insidious working of heresy. St. John draws on the history of the Church in the wilderness to illustrate his point: **You have there some who hold the teaching of Balaam,** whose name means, like Nikolaos, *Conqueror* (or *Destroyer*) *of the people.* When it was discovered that the people of God could not be defeated in open warfare (see Num. 22-24), the false prophet Balaam suggested another plan to Balak, the evil King of Moab. The only way to destroy Israel was through *corruption.* Thus Balaam **kept teaching Balak** (cf. Num. 31:16) **to put a stumbling block before the sons of Israel, to eat things sacrificed to idols, and to commit fornication** (cf. Num. 25).[16] **Thus you also have some who in the same way** — i.e., in imitation of Balaam — **hold the teaching of the Nicolaitans:** In other words, those who hold the teaching of Balaam and those who hold the teaching of the Nicolaitans (cf. 2:6) comprise the same group. The church in Pergamum was standing steadfastly for the faith when it came

---

16. Josephus provides an expanded version of the story in his *Antiquities of the Jews*, iv.vi.6.

to outright persecution by an ungodly state—yet they were falling prey to other forms of compromise with Satan.

What exactly was the Nicolaitan doctrine? St. John describes it in terms of the doctrine of Balaam, using his ancient error as a symbol of the contemporary heresy. Like Balaam, the false apostles attempt to destroy Christians by corrupting them, by enticing them **to eat things sacrificed to idols, and to commit fornication.** Both of these practices were commonplace in the pagan religious atmosphere of the day, and St. John's language seems to be drawn from the Jerusalem Council's instructions to Gentile converts:

> For it seemed good to the Holy Spirit and to us to lay upon you no greater burden than these essentials: that you abstain from *things sacrificed to idols* and from blood and from things strangled and from *fornication*; if you keep yourselves free from such things, you will do well (Acts 15:28-29).[17]

In disobedience to the true apostolic Council, the false Nicolaitan apostles advocated antinomianism—the teaching that, perhaps through the sacrifice of Christ, Christians were "freed from the law," in a sense completely opposed to the Biblical teaching of sanctification. It was no longer a sin, in their account, to commit idolatry and fornication; the believer was not under obligation to obey the law, but can live as he pleases (although they probably claimed, as antinomians do today, the "leading of the Spirit" as justification for their abominable practices).

There is, however, an important aspect of the imagery involved here that we should not overlook: The false apostles are seeking to seduce the Christians into *idolatrous eating and for-*

---

17. "Writing to Corinth some fifteen years after the council St. Paul had occasion to argue with Christians who regarded the eating of things sacrificed to idols as a thing indifferent; and though he does not take his stand on the Jerusalem decree, he opposes the practice on the ground that it gave offense to weak brethren (1 Cor. 8:4, 9-10), and also because of the connection which he regarded as existing between idol-worship and unclean spirits (1 Cor. 10:20: *The things that the Gentiles sacrifice, they sacrifice to demons, and not to God; and I do not want you to become sharers in demons*); to partake of the 'table of unclean spirits' (1 Cor. 10:21) was inconsistent with participation in the Eucharist." Henry Barclay Swete, *Commentary on Revelation* (Grand Rapids: Kregel Publications, [1911] 1977), pp. 37f.

nication, and this is analogous to the serpent's seduction of Eve. Her eating of the forbidden tree was, in essence, idolatry; it is also spoken of by St. Paul in terms of fornication (2 Cor. 11:2-3). But those who overcome the Nicolaitan enticements, St. John says, will be granted access to the Tree of Life (2:7). Those who refuse to eat Balaam's food will eat manna from heaven, and will be included in the number of those whose names are written on the stone (2:17).

If the church is to be blessed, however, the false teaching must not be permitted. Christ, speaking to the rulers of the church, orders them to **repent**. The offenders must be recognized in their true character as heretical apostates, who will cause the downfall of the church if they are not excommunicated. The church that fails to discipline its members will be destroyed — even an otherwise faithful and exemplary church such as that at Pergamum. The Lord threatens that if they do not repent, **I am coming to you quickly, and I will make war against them with the sword of my mouth**; the Angel of the Lord had met Balaam with a drawn sword (Num. 22:31), and a sword was used to kill him (Num. 31:8). As we have observed already (see on 1:7 and 2:5), this warning of Christ's Coming is not a statement about the Second Coming of Christ at the end of history, but rather refers to a judgment within history. It is a judgment that was imminent to the church in Pergamum, especially in light of the fact that judgment was about to be unleashed upon the whole world (3:10). The same principle has been repeated again and again throughout the history of Christianity. Wherever heretics are indulged by the people or by the leadership, the church is on the verge of being destroyed by the jealous wrath of Christ.

17 The overcomer is promised three things. First, Christ will give him **of the hidden manna** (i.e., the manna hidden in the Ark, which is Christ: Ex. 16:33-34; Heb. 9:4) — a symbol taken from the supernatural gift of "angels' food" (Ps. 78:25), giving daily strength and sustenance to the people of God during the Exodus from Egypt. In essence, that is what Christ communicates to His Church at every moment. Definitively, we have been restored to Edenic provision for our needs, and that will be progressively realized in history until the final consummation and fulfillment of all of God's plans and promises for His people.

Second, the Christian is promised **a white stone**. This has been seen variously as referring to a ticket to a feast, a token of acquittal (i.e., justification), or some such reflection of a common practice of John's day. While these interpretations do not need to be excluded, of course, there is a much more satisfactory way to look at this stone in terms of Biblical revelation. There is a white stone connected in the Bible with manna, and it is called *bdellium* (cf. Ex. 16:31 with Num. 11:7).[18] Moreover, this stone is connected with the Garden of Eden, and is intended to be a reminder of it (Gen. 2:12): Salvation is a New Creation, and restores God's people to Paradise.

Third, the Christian is granted **a new name**, speaking of the new character and identity of those who belong to Christ. As always, God the Lord is the Definer, who has called us into being and wholly interpreted us in terms of his predetermined plan:

> The nations will see your righteousness,
> And all kings your glory;
> And you will be called by a new name,
> Which the mouth of the LORD will bestow. (Isa. 62:2)

The fact that the name is **written on the stone** would seem to argue against the interpretation of the white stone given above, for we are never told in Scripture of any writing of names on the bdellium. Yet this only serves to confirm the interpretation. The stone which was marked with a name in the Old Testament was the *onyx* stone. Two onyx stones were placed on the shoulders of the High Priest, and on them were engraved the names of the tribes of Israel (Ex. 28:9-12). Yet the onyx stone was not a white stone — it was black. The explanation for this seems to be that the bdellium and onyx are simply combined in this imagery (a common device in Scripture) to create a new image that still retains the older associations. The connecting link here is the bdellium: it is associated in Genesis 2:12 with *onyx*, and in Numbers 11:7 with *manna*. Together, they speak of the restoration of Eden in the blessings of salvation.

One further point about this promise should be explained.

---

18. See Chilton, *Paradise Restored*, pp. 33f.; cf. Ruth V. Wright and Robert L. Chadbourne, *Gems and Minerals of the Bible* (New Canaan, CT: Keats Publishing, 1970), pp. 16f.

No one knows the new name, Christ says, **but he who receives it.** The meaning of this expression, rooted in a Hebrew idiom, is that the name is "known" by the receiver in the sense of *owning* it. In other words, the point is not that the new name is secret, but that it is exclusive: Only the overcomer possesses the name, the divinely-ordained definition of himself as belonging to the covenant of the Lord Jesus Christ; no one else has the right to it.[19] In its particular application to the situation at Pergamum, the Nicolaitan heretic, who by his doctrine or life is a traitor to the cause of Christ, does not truly own the designation *Christian*. The name belongs only to the overcomers. They, and they alone, are granted readmittance to the Garden. They gain entrance through the sacrifice of Christ, in whom they have been redefined and renamed.

Thyatira: Judgment on the Royal Harlot (2:18-29)

18 And to the angel of the church of Thyatira write: The Son of God, who has eyes like a flame of fire, and His feet are like burnished bronze, says this:

19 I know your deeds, and your love and faith and service and perseverance, and that your deeds of late are greater than at first.

20 But I have this against you, that you tolerate your wife, Jezebel, who calls herself a prophetess, and she teaches and leads my servants astray, so that they commit fornication and eat things sacrificed to idols.

21 And I gave her time to repent; and she does not want to repent of her fornication.

22 Behold, I will cast her upon a bed, and those who commit adultery with her into great tribulation, unless they repent of her deeds.

23 And I will kill her children with death; and all the churches will know that I am He who searches the minds and hearts; and I will give to each one of you according to your deeds.

---

19. This passage should be compared to 19:12-13 and 15-16. In the chiastic arrangement given there, v. 15 explains the meaning of v. 13 (how the blood came to be on the robe); and v. 16 explains v. 12 (the name written on the Lord). There, too, the point is not that no one knows *what* His name is — for the text itself tells us His name! — but, rather, that He is the only One who *knows* it in the sense of *possessing it as His own*. (See Kline's discussion of this point in *Images of the Spirit*, p. 130.)

24 But I say to you, the rest who are in Thyatira, who do not
hold this teaching, who have not known the deep things of
Satan, as they call them — I place no other burden on you.
25 Nevertheless what you have, hold fast until I come.
26 And he who overcomes, and he who keeps My deeds until
the end, to him I will give authority over the nations.
27 And he shall rule them with a rod of iron; like the vessels of
a potter they shall be broken to pieces, as I also have received
from My Father.
28 And I will give him the morning star.
29 He who has an ear, let him hear what the Spirit says to the
churches.

18   One of the most significant things about the city of **Thyatira** was the dominance of trade guilds over the local economy.
Every imaginable manufacturing industry was strictly controlled
by the guilds: In order to work in a trade, you had to belong to
the appropriate guild. And to be a member of a guild meant also
to worship pagan gods; heathen worship was integrally connected with the guilds, which held their meetings and common
meals in pagan temples. Two central aspects of the required
pagan worship were the eating of meat sacrificed to idols, and illicit sexual relations. Any Christian who worked in a craft or
trade was thus presented with severe problems: his faithfulness
to Christ would affect his calling, his livelihood, and his ability
to feed his family.

The local god, the guardian of the city, was Tyrimnos, the
son of Zeus; and Tyrimnos-worship was mixed in Thyatira with
the worship of Caesar, who was also proclaimed the incarnate
Son of God. The conflict of Christianity and paganism in Thyatira was immediate and central — and so the first word of Christ
to this church is the proclamation that He alone is **the Son of
God** (the only place in the Revelation where this specific designation of Christ is used). The letter to this church begins with an
uncompromising challenge to paganism and statism, affirming
the definitive, absolute uniqueness of Jesus Christ.

19-20   There was much that could be commended in the
church at Thyatira. It was active in **love and faith and service
and perseverance** — in fact, its activity was increasing: **Your
deeds of late are greater than at first.** But, in spite of all good

112

works of the church, its great defect in the eyes of Christ was its doctrinal and moral laxity (the Thyatirans were thus the opposite number of the doctrinally correct Ephesians). The elders were allowing false doctrine to have a place in the church. Christ again calls the heresy by a symbolic name, as He had before (*Nikolaos* and *Balaam*); this time, the cult is identified with **Jezebel,** the wicked queen of Israel during the ninth century B.C., who led the covenant people into the idolatrous and adulterous worship of pagan gods (1 Kings 21:25-26; cf. 2 Kings 9:22, where her actions are specifically called "harlotries" and "witchcrafts"). The "Jezebel" of the Thyatiran church similarly advocated compromise with paganism. Of course, very pious-sounding terminology would have accompanied this — perhaps to the effect that, after all, there is only one God, so any worship rendered to false gods is "really" offered to the true God; or, that by joining pagans in their religious services one might be able to witness for Christianity; or, that going along with the heathen will enable Christians to survive rather than be wiped out by persecution; or perhaps that all religions have something to teach each other, and that we Christians should abandon our arrogant absolutism and seek to combine the best of our traditions with the best in the heathen traditions, thus creating a truly universal faith, one which answers the needs of *all* people and *all* cultures.

Regardless of the rationale involved, the doctrine was heresy, and was not to be tolerated. That is the precise term used here: **You tolerate** this woman, the Lord accuses them. And by tolerating her, the elders were placing the entire church in jeopardy, for **she teaches and leads My servants astray, so that they commit fornication and eat things sacrificed to idols**. This must be clearly understood: Orthodox, Biblical Christianity is intolerant. A church that tolerates evil and false doctrine is a church under judgment; God will not long tolerate her. This is not to say that Christians should be intolerant of each other's mistakes, idiosyncrasies, and differences over nonessentials. But when it comes to clear violations of Biblical law and orthodox doctrine, the government of the church is required by Scripture to put a stop to it before it destroys the church.

"Jezebel" was, figuratively if not literally, leading Christians into fornication and idolatrous communion, the effective abandonment of the Christian faith for paganism and state-worship.

Was there literally a woman leading the Judaizers in this local area? The possibility is at least indicated by the specific accusation against the angel/bishop of Thyatira: "You tolerate **your wife, Jezebel.**" It may be that the arch-heretic of Thyatira was the leading pastor's wife! On the other hand, Christ may be pointing in a more general way to the angel's failure, like Adam, properly to guard the Bride — a central function of the priestly calling. Because he had failed, she had become a Harlot.[20]

21-23   Christ had given Jezebel **time to repent . . . of her fornication,** and she had refused. We must emphasize again that this term is used in both a literal and a symbolic sense in Scripture. Apparently, Jezebel had actually encouraged God's people to commit physical fornication in connection with the religious rites of the trade guilds; on the other hand, the use of the word *fornication* has a long Biblical history as a symbol of rebellion against the true God by those who belong to him (see, e.g., Ezek. 16 and 23). We have already noted the symbolic aspects of idolatrous eating and fornication; it is important to recognize also that St. John describes the Great Harlot of Babylon, identified with apostate Judaism, with very clear references to the Biblical story of Jezebel, the Harlot Queen (17:5, 16; 19:2). This again confirms the interpretation that the doctrines of the Nicolaitans, the Balaamites, and the Jezebelites were identical, and were connected with the false Israel, the "synagogue of Satan."

"Jezebel" had to be punished, and in a play on words the Lord declares: **Behold, I will cast her into a bed!** As many of the modern translations point out, this is a *sickbed*, explained by the next clause: **and those who commit adultery with her into Great Tribulation.** With grim humor, Jesus is saying: Do you want to "get in bed" (i.e., commit fornication)? Very well — here's a deathbed for you! Let us note carefully too that this first-century judgment against the followers of Jezebel is spoken of in terms of the Great Tribulation. Every Biblical indication regarding the Great Tribulation leads to the plain conclusion that it took place during the generation after Christ's death and resurrection — just as He said it would (Matt. 24:21, 34).[21] **And I**

---

20. This is a major theme in the Book of Judges. See James B. Jordan, *Judges: God's War Against Humanism* (Tyler, TX: Geneva Ministries, 1985).
21. See Chilton, *Paradise Restored*, pp. 85ff.

will kill her children (her followers; cf. Isa. 57:3) **with death** is, to our ears, a strange way of putting it. But this is a common Hebrew means of emphasis known as a *pleonasm*, a linguistic "double witness" to the certainty of its fulfillment (cf. Gen. 2:17, "Dying thou shalt die").[22]

What happens when apostates are disciplined and judged? **All the churches will know that I am He who searches the minds and hearts.** God's character as the holy and omniscient Judge is vindicated in the churches (and in the world as well, Isa. 26:9) when He punishes those who rebel against Him. Those who truly love the Lord will heed the judgment and be spurred on to renewed obedience when they are reminded again that He renders to each of us according to our deeds.

24-25   Apparently, a central part of Jezebel's heresy involved a search into **the deep things of Satan, as they call them.** Connecting this with what we already know of her teaching, it seems that her doctrine was a proto-Gnostic teaching that Christians would attain new and greater levels of sanctification by immersion into the depths of Satanism: worshiping idols, committing fornication, entering to the fullest extent into the depravities of the heathen around them — sinning that grace might abound. The fact that such activity could be both sensually satisfying and economically profitable would not, of course, have been overlooked; but there was more to it than this. Jezebel's doctrine of sanctification through idolatry and fornication was simply a slightly Christianized version of the most ancient heresy in the world, and one which has been manifested in every culture from the beginning: *salvation through chaos.* Eve saw chaos, anarchy and revolution as the key to wisdom and the attainment of divine status; and the original Adulteress has had many followers, as R. J. Rushdoony points out: "Chaos as revitalization has a long and continuing history in Western civilization, and, with the French Revolution, it gained a new vitality as revolution and sexual chaos became the means to social regeneration. In the world of art, the creative artist came to be identified as of necessity with a social and sexual anarchist, and in popular thinking,

---

22. This underscores the fact that the human author of the Revelation was expressing his thoughts in Hebraic modes of speech. On the use of the pleonasm, see Jordan, *The Law of the Covenant*, pp. 96, 106.

order and morality came to mean monotony and devitalizing, enervating palls, whereas lawlessness means liberty and power. The middle-aged 'fling' and sexual license came into being as a grasping after renewal, and Negress prostitutes came to be used as a 'change of luck' device, an especial sin against order as a means of a recharging of luck and power. Basic to all these manifestations, from ancient Egypt through Caesar to modern man, is one common hope: destroy order to create order afresh, or, even more bluntly, destroy order to create order."[23]

But, Christ says, there are faithful Christians in Thyatira, **who do not hold this teaching,** who have not sought after forbidden knowledge in Satanic practices, despite the economic and social consequences of their refusal to compromise; **I place no other burden on you. Nevertheless what you have, hold fast until I come.** This, again, reflects the language of the Jerusalem Council's letter to the Gentile converts: "For it seemed good to the Holy Spirit and to us to lay upon you *no greater burden* than these essentials: that you abstain from things sacrificed to idols . . . and from fornication; if you keep yourselves free from such things, you will do well" (Acts 15:28-29). The faithful are to continue practicing the essentials of the faith, holding to orthodox standards of doctrine and life, until Christ comes with tribulation to judge the heretics and apostates who are illegally remaining in the Church.

26-29   The faithful Christians in Thyatira were suffering from both the heathen world outside and the compromising heretics within the church. They probably were tempted to doubt whether they would ever win in this struggle. The most prosperous and successful Christians were the ones who were the most faithless to Christ; it looked as if the orthodox were fighting a losing battle. They were so powerless by now that they were unable even to oust the apostates from the church. Yet Christ promises the angel/bishop: **He who overcomes, and he who keeps My deeds until the end, to him I will give authority over the nations. And he shall rule them with a rod of iron, as the vessels of a potter are broken to pieces, as I also have received**

---

23. R. J. Rushdoony, *The One and the Many: Studies in the Philosophy of Order and Ultimacy* (Tyler, TX: Thoburn Press, [1971] 1978), p. 105.

from My Father. This is a reference to the Father's promise to the Son, as recorded in Psalm 2:8-9:

Ask of Me, and I will surely give the nations as Thine inheritance,
And the very ends of the earth as Thy possession.
Thou shalt break them with a rod of iron,
Thou shalt shatter them like earthenware.

God the Son has been granted the rule of all the world, and all nations will come under His messianic kingship (see also Ps. 22:27-31; 46:4, 10; 65:2; 66:4; 68:31-32; 72; 86:9; 102:15-22; 138:4-5; 145:10-11). Whatever opposition is offered against His Kingdom will be crushed absolutely. And the installation of Christ as universal King, prophesied in this passage, clearly took place at Christ's *First* Coming, through His birth, life, death, resurrection, and ascension to glory (this can be confirmed by simply looking up the numerous New Testament quotations of Psalms 2 and 110, both of which are about Christ's kingship[24]).

The point of the quotation here is that the Christian overcomers, in this age, are promised a share in the messianic reign of Jesus Christ, in time and on earth. In spite of all opposition, God has set up His King over the nations (cf. Ps. 2:1-6). Those who are obedient to His commands will rule the world, reconstructing it for His glory in terms of His laws. Psalm 2 shows God laughing and sneering at the pitiful attempts of the wicked to fight against and overthrow His Kingdom. He has already given His Son "all authority in heaven and earth," and the King is with His Church until the end of the age (Matt. 28:18-20)! Is it possible that the King will be defeated? He has, in fact, warned all earthly rulers to submit to His government, or perish (Ps. 2:10-12). And the same is true of His Church. The nation that will not serve us will perish (Isa. 60:12); all the peoples of the earth will be subdued under our feet (Ps. 47:1-3) — promises made originally to Israel, but now to be fulfilled in the New Israel, the Church.

---

24. Psalms 2 and 110 are the two most quoted Psalms in the New Testament. For Psalm 2, see Matt. 3:17; 17:5; Mark 1:11; 9:7; Luke 3:22; 9:35; John 1:49; Acts 4:25-26; 13:33; Phil. 2:12; Heb. 1:2, 5; 5:5; Rev. 2:26-27; 11:18; 12:5; 19:15, 19. For Psalm 110, see Matt. 22:44; 26:64; Mark 12:36; 14:62; 16:19; Luke 20:42-43; 22:69; John 12:34; Acts 2:34-35; Rom. 8:34; 1 Cor. 15:25; Eph. 1:20; Col. 3:1; Heb. 1:3, 13; 5:6, 10; 6:20; 7:3, 17, 21; 8:1; 10:12-13; 12:2.

For the persecuted and seemingly weak church in Thyatira, this was good news. At the time, they were at the mercy of a powerful economic and political power; statism and state-worship were increasing; even their fellow Christians were being seduced by false prophets and heretics. To be a faithful Christian in Thyatira meant hardship and suffering, and not necessarily a very glorious, headline-making sort of suffering, either. Just the day-to-day grind of faithfulness to Christ's Word; just the fact of being unemployed and unemployable in the midst of a booming economy, when everyone around them could get work for the mere price of burning a little incense, eating a little meat from a pagan altar, and engaging in a little "harmless" sex between consenting adults. There was no opportunity for a great moral crusade; everyone just thought you were weird. And night after night your children would cry for food. No, this kind of martyrdom was not very glamorous at all. But those who remained faithful were promised that they would overcome, that they would rule with Christ. The situation would be reversed, the tables were about to be turned. Christ was coming, to save and to judge.

The sufferings of these Christians did not mean the end of the world, but rather the beginning. What may have seemed like the approach of a long, dark night was really the herald of Christ's triumph over the nations. The conflicts they experienced were not a sign of Christ's defeat by the world, but simply the assurance that the battle had finally been joined; and the inspired prophecy of Psalm 2 guaranteed that their Lord would be victorious, and they with Him. It was paganism, statism, and Judaism which were about to enter the darkness, as Christ turned the lights out all across apostate Israel and the Roman Empire. But for Christians the night was just ending; the redeemed and liberated universe was rushing headlong into a bright Day. Christ was about to give these overcomers **the Morning Star.**

3

THE DOMINION MANDATE

Sardis: Judgment on the Dead (3:1-6)

1 And to the angel of the church in Sardis write: He who has the seven Spirits of God, and the seven stars, says this: I know your deeds, that you have a name that you are alive, but you are dead.

2 Wake up, and strengthen the things that remain, which were about to die; for I have not found your deeds completed in the sight of My God.

3 Remember therefore what you have received and heard; and keep it, and repent. If therefore you will not wake up, I will come upon you like a thief, and you will not know at what hour I will come upon you.

4 But you have a few people in Sardis who have not soiled their garments; and they will walk with Me in white; for they are worthy.

5 He who overcomes shall thus be clothed in white garments; and I will not erase his name from the Book of Life, and I will confess his name before My Father, and before His angels.

6 He who has an ear, let him hear what the Spirit says to the churches.

1 To the bishop of the church in Sardis, Christ announces Himself as the One **who has the seven Spirits of God.** As we have seen (on 1:4) this is a term for the Holy Spirit who, as the Nicene Creed declares, "proceeds from the Father and the Son." Christ also possesses **the seven stars,** the angels of the churches (1:16, 20). The rulers of the churches are owned by Him and are at all points accountable to Him. And the elders in Sardis desperately needed to be reminded of this, for they had allowed the church to die.

I know your deeds, the Lord tells them. **You have a name**

that you are alive. The church of Sardis had a reputation for being an active congregation, "alive" for Christ. Undoubtedly it was well-known in Asia as the representative of the Christian faith in a wealthy and famous city. It was, perhaps, fashionable and popular in the community; there is no evidence that, in a period of growing persecution, the church in Sardis was coming under attack. In fact, the evidence is all the other way, indicating that the church had almost totally compromised with the surrounding culture. This busy, seemingly fruitful and growing church was, in fact, **dead.** We should note that the death of Sardis did not necessarily consist in a lack of youth activities or fellowship meetings (which is the reason why churches tend to be called "dead" today). Rather, the church had become, as Mounce correctly observes, *secularized.*[1] Its fundamental worldview was no different from that of the surrounding pagan culture. Its outlook was similar to that of those who are elsewhere in Scripture characterized as "dead in trespasses and sins" (Eph. 2:1-3). Sardis had "completely come to terms with its pagan environment."[2]

2-3   The Lord gives Sardis two admonitions. First, He says, **Wake up!** G. R. Beasley-Murray points out some interesting history about the town of Sardis which serves as an appropriate background to this statement: "Sardis was built on a mountain, and an acropolis was constructed on a spur of this mountain, which was all but impregnable. Yet twice in the city's history it had been taken unawares and captured by enemies. The parallel with the church's lack of vigilance, and its need to wake up lest it fall under judgment is striking."[3] Sardis is not quite completely dead, but these things are **about to die.** Although the Lord has not written off the entire church yet, the danger is real and immediate. The elders at Sardis must begin now to **strengthen the things that remain.**

At this point, some members of Sardis could have complained: "What are You scolding us for? We haven't done anything!"

---

1. Robert H. Mounce, *The Book of Revelation* (Grand Rapids: William B. Eerdmans Publishing Co., 1977), p. 112.
2. Ibid., p. 109.
3. G. R. Beasley-Murray, *The Book of Revelation* (Grand Rapids: William B. Eerdmans Publishing Co., [1978] 1981), p. 94.

And that was precisely the problem. Sardis had **works**; but they were **not completed**; they were unfulfilled in God's sight. In fact, Sardis may have appeared to be the most "alive" church for this very reason: As a dead church, it experienced neither theological controversy nor persecution. "Content with mediocrity, lacking both the enthusiasm to entertain a heresy and the depth of conviction which provokes intolerance, it was too innocuous to be worth persecuting."[4] Satan may have felt that Sardis was coming along rather nicely without his interference, and was better off left alone.

In His second admonition, Christ commands: **Remember therefore what you have received and heard** — the Gospel, the ministry and sacraments, and (in the case of the elders to whom this is specifically addressed) the privileges and responsibilities of officebearing in the Church of Jesus Christ. All these things they were to **keep**, to watch over and guard; and that meant that they must **repent** of their slothful attitude and conduct.

If therefore you will not repent, Christ warns, **I will come upon you like a thief, and you will not know at what hour I will come upon you.** To repeat what has been painstakingly pointed out above (see on 1:7; 2:5, 16), the threat of Christ's coming against a local church, or even against a nation or group of nations, is not the same as the Second Coming (i.e., the end of the world). Everyone is accessible to Christ the Lord at all times, and any disobedient individual, family, church, business, society, or nation is liable to have Christ come in judgment — a judgment which may include any or all the covenantal curses listed in Leviticus 26 and Deuteronomy 28. In any case, the words **upon you** indicate a local coming; the failure of commentators and preachers to understand this simple fact is the predictable result of a flat, futurist hermeneutic bordering on Biblical illiteracy.

4-6 There were **a few people in Sardis,** however, who had remained faithful to what they had received and heard, and had **not soiled their garments**; they had not become secularized and conformed to the surrounding heathen culture. Of them, Christ

---

4. G. B. Caird, *The Revelation of St. John the Divine* (New York: Harper & Row, Publishers, 1966), p.48.

says: **They will walk with Me in white; for they are worthy. He who overcomes shall thus be clothed in white garments.** The saints are seen in **white garments** seven times in the Book of Revelation (3:5, 18; 4:4; 6:11; 7:9, 13; 19:14), and it is obviously a symbol in Scripture for cleanliness and righteousness, with its ultimate origins in the sunlike brightness of the Glory-Cloud: In Christ, the saints are re-created in the image of God, and are clothed with the New Man, Jesus Christ (Gal. 3:27; Eph. 4:24; Col. 3:10). Our being clothed in the white robes of righteousness, therefore, takes place *definitively* at our baptism (Gal. 3:27), *progressively* as we work out our salvation in daily obedience to God's commandments, "putting on" the Christian graces and virtues (Col. 3:5-17), and *finally* at the Last Day (Col. 3:4; Jude 24). As with all the promises to the overcomers in Revelation, this too is simply a description of an aspect of salvation, in which all of God's elect have a share.

In this letter's second promise regarding the overcomer, Christ says: **I will not erase his name from the Book of Life.** This statement has been the source of controversy for generations. Can a true Christian fall away? Can you lose your salvation? At least three erroneous answers have been offered:

1. Those who have been truly saved by Christ's redemption can fall away and be lost forever. This is the classical Arminian position, and it is absolutely and categorically denied by Scripture. The nature of the salvation provided by Christ is eternal, and our justification in God's sight is not based on our works but on the perfect, finished righteousness and substitutionary atonement of Jesus Christ. (See John 3:16; 5:24; 6:35-40; 10:27-30; Rom. 5:8-10; 8:28-39; Eph. 1:4-14; 1 Thess. 5:23-24; 1 John 2:19).

2. All those who have "accepted Christ" will be saved; no matter what they do afterwards, they cannot be damned. This is the classic "chicken Evangelical" position, and it too is opposed by Scripture. Those who take this view are attempting to have it both ways: They don't want the predestinating God preached by the Calvinist, but they don't have the courage to affirm full Arminianism, either. They want man to be sovereign in choosing his salvation, without interference from God's decree; yet they want the door of salvation to slam shut as soon as man gets inside, so that he can't get out. But the Bible teaches that God has absolutely predestined all things and rules sovereignly over all. He has infallibly chosen all those who will be saved, extending His irresistible grace toward them; and He has determined who will be damned, withholding His grace from them (see Matt. 11:25-27; 20:16; 22:14; Mark 4:11-12; Luke 4:25-27; 17:1; 22:22; John 6:37-39, 44; 12:39-40; Acts 4:27-28; 13:48; Rom. 9:10-26; 11:2, 5-10; 1 Cor. 1:27-31; Eph. 1:4-5, 11; 1 Thess. 5:9; 2 Thess. 2:13; 2 Tim. 1:9; 2 Tim. 2:10; 1 Pet. 1:1-2; 2:8-9; Jude 4).[5]

The Bible also teaches, however, that there are those who profess Christ, and by all accounts appear to be among the elect, who will finally apostatize from the faith and inherit damnation rather than salvation. Judas is the obvious example, but he is by no means the only one. The Old Testament provides countless examples of members of the Covenant who departed from the faith, and the New Testament warns us again and again of the wrath of God against those who break His covenant (see Matt. 7:15-23; 13:20-21; 24:10-12; Mark 4:5-17; Luke 8:13; John 15:1-10; 1 Cor. 9:27; 10:1-12; 2 Thess. 2:3, 11-12; 1 Tim. 4:1-3; 2 Tim. 3:1-9; 4:3-4; Heb. 2:1-3; 3:12-14; 6:4-6; 10:26-31, 35-39; 2 Pet. 2:1-3, 20-22; 3:17). As John Murray wrote: "It is utterly wrong to say that a believer is secure quite irrespective of his subsequent life of sin and unfaithfulness. The truth is that the faith of Jesus Christ is *always respective* of the life of holiness and fidelity. And so it is never proper to think of a believer irrespective of the fruits in faith and holiness. To say that a believer is secure whatever may be the extent of his addiction to sin in his subsequent life is to abstract faith in Christ from its very definition and it ministers to that abuse which turns the grace of God into lasciviousness. The doctrine of perseverance is the doctrine that believers *persevere*; it cannot be too strongly stressed that it is the *perseverance* of the saints. And that means that the saints, those united to Christ by the effectual call of the Father and indwelt by the Holy Spirit, will persevere unto the end. If they persevere, they endure, they continue. It is not at all that they

---

5. Those readers who would like to study this further should consult the following books, all published by the Banner of Truth Trust (P.O. Box 621, Carlisle, PA 17013): Arthur Pink, *The Sovereignty of God*; John Cheeseman et al., *The Grace of God in the Gospel*; John Murray, *Redemption Accomplished and Applied*; J. Gresham Machen, *The Christian View of Man*; and R. B. Kuiper, *The Bible Tells Us So*.

will be saved irrespective of their perseverance or their continuance, but that they will assuredly persevere. Consequently the security that is theirs is inseparable from their perseverance. Is this not what Jesus said? 'He that endureth to the end, the same shall be saved.' "[6]

3. Everyone in the world is written in the Book of Life, but unbelievers are erased from it after they have passed the age of accountability. This idea is so ridiculous that the Bible doesn't even take the time to refute it directly (although the passages already listed demonstrate that it is pure poppycock, to put it nicely). Where in Scripture is there a shred of evidence for an "age of accountability"? Where does the Bible give any support whatsoever to the following little gem from a well-known Christian scholar?

> Since Christ died for the sin inherent in every person conceived, a child who dies before becoming a deliberate and conscious sinner does not need to be "saved" from sin, since he has never sinned, and since Christ has made propitiation for his innate sin.[7]

There are at least five theological errors in that one sentence, but let's zero in on the main point: the notion that children are basically sinless, or without "deliberate" sin, when they are born, and remain in that condition until they reach the mystical "age of accountability." In the first place, *the true age of accountability is reached at the moment of conception: All men, at all times, are accountable to God* (see Ps. 51:5; Rom. 3:23). Second, *all men are under the sentence of condemnation already; apart from the saving grace of God, they are condemned from the moment they exist* (see John 3:18, 36; Rom. 5:12-19).[8] Why else do babies *die* (Rom. 6:23)? Third, *infants are deliberate sinners*: "Even from birth the wicked go astray; from

---

6. John Murray, *Redemption Accomplished and Applied* (Grand Rapids: William B. Eerdmans Publishing Co., 1955), pp. 154f.
7. Out of sincere respect for this God-fearing author, who has rendered the Church valuable service, I shall omit his name.
8. This is the doctrine of the *imputation* of Adam's sin (which should be distinguished from the doctrine of *innate* sin; but most evangelicals, including preachers and commentators, don't seem to know the difference). A helpful exposition of this is in John Murray, *The Imputation of Adam's Sin* (Nutley, NJ: Presbyterian and Reformed, [1959] 1977).

the womb they are wayward and speak lies" (Ps. 58:3; cf. Ps. 53:2-3; Rom. 3:10-12, 23; Eph. 2:1-3). Now, either the "age of accountability" doctrine is in error, or the Bible is wrong. Which are we to believe? The fact is that the idea of the essential sin-lessness of infants is a pagan notion, unsupported by the Bible. It is merely antichristian sentimentalism, which refuses to hear the Word of God and attempts to replace it with the word of man — or, more likely, with the word of effeminate poets scribbling mushy greeting cards. It is right on the same level with the sentiment that every time a fairy blows its wee nose a baby is born.

To conclude this point: The threat stated by Jesus Christ here is very real. Those who are in the Book of Life — i.e., who are bap-tized Church members professing Christ, and are thus counted as, and treated as, Christians — must remain faithful to Christ. If they apostatize into heresy, immorality, or simply the "seculariza-tion" that plagued Sardis, they will be erased, written out of the record of the redeemed. But the Christian who overcomes these temptations, thus demonstrating that Christ has truly purchased him for His own, is in no danger — his name will never be erased.

The final promise to the overcomer reinforces the idea: **I will confess his name before My Father, and before His angels.** This echoes Jesus' statements in the Gospels: "Everyone therefore who shall confess Me before men, I will also confess him before My Father who is in heaven. But whoever shall deny Me before men, I will also deny him before My Father who is in heaven" (Matt. 10:32-33; cf. Mark 8:38; Luke 12:8-9). Many of the Christians in Sardis were denying Christ before their commun-ity, as they endeavored to be praised of men rather than of God. At the Last Judgment they would hear these words from the Son of God: *I never knew you; depart from Me, you who prac-tice lawlessness* (Matt. 7:23). But those who overcame these temptations would be joyfully acknowledged by Christ as His own. This message is as important and needed today as it was 2000 years ago. Do we have ears to **hear what the Spirit says to the churches?**

Philadelphia: Judgment on the Synagogue of Satan (3:7-13)

7 And to the angel of the church in Philadelphia write: He who is holy, who is true, who has the key of David, who opens and no one will shut, and who shuts and no one opens, says this:

8 I know your deeds. Behold, I have put before you an open door which no one can shut, because you have a little power, and have kept My Word, and have not denied My name.

9 Behold, I will cause those of the synagogue of Satan, who say that they are Jews, and are not, but lie—behold, I will make them to come and bow down at your feet, and to know that I have loved you.

10 Because you have kept the word of My perseverance, I also will keep you from the hour of testing, that hour which is about to come upon the whole world, to test those who dwell upon the Land.

11 I am coming quickly; hold fast what you have, in order that no one take your crown.

12 He who overcomes, I will make him a pillar in the Temple of My God, and he will not go out from it anymore; and I will write upon him the name of My God, and the name of the City of My God, the new Jerusalem, which comes down out of heaven from My God, and My new name.

13 He who has an ear, let him hear what the Spirit says to the churches.

7 Like the church in Smyrna, the church in Philadelphia had been especially persecuted by the apostate Jews. Christ begins his message to the elders by declaring Himself as the One who is holy, an established Biblical term for God (cf. Isa. 40:25), and who is true, in contrast to the lying leaders of the Jews, who had rejected the truth. Jesus Christ also has the key of David: He opens and no one will shut, and He shuts and no one opens. This is an allusion to Isaiah 22:15-25, in which God accuses a royal steward of falsehood, of betraying his trust. God declares: "I will depose you from your office, and I will pull you down from your station" (v. 19; cf. Gen. 3:22-24). Moreover, God would replace the false steward with a faithful one (cf. 1 Sam. 13:13-14):

> And I will clothe him with your tunic,
> And tie your sash securely about him.
> I will entrust him with your authority,
> And he will become a father to the inhabitants of Jerusalem
>   and to the house of Judah.
> Then I will set the key of the house of David on his shoulder:
> When he opens no one will shut,
> When he shuts no one will open. (Isa. 22:21-22)

Christ is thus announcing that the officers of apostate Israel are false stewards: they have been thrown out of office, removed from all rightful authority, and replaced by the One who is holy and true. The keepers of the door at the synagogue had excommunicated the Christians, declaring them to be apostates. In reality, Christ says, it is you of the synagogue who are the apostates; it is you who have been cast out of the Covenant; and I have taken your place as the True Steward, the Pastor and Overseer of the Covenant (cf. 1 Pet. 2:25).

8-9 And so the Lord can comfort these suffering Christians who, on account of their faithful following of Christ, have suffered wrongful excommunication from the Covenant. **I know your deeds**, He assures them. You have been shut out of the door by the keyholders, but you must remember that I am the One who has the key, and **behold, I have put before you a door which no one can shut.** The Lord of the Covenant Himself has admitted them to fellowship, and has cast out those who pretend to hold the keys; the faithful Christians have nothing to fear. The church of Philadelphia has only **a little power**—it is not prominent, stylish, or outwardly prosperous, in contrast to the impressive, apparently "alive," compromising church at Sardis. Yet they have been faithful with what they have been given (cf. Luke 19:26): **You . . . have kept My Word, and have not denied my name.**

Therefore, **I will cause those of the synagogue of Satan, who say that they are Jews, and are not, but lie**—**behold, I will make them to come and bow down at your feet, and to know that I have loved you.** Again the apostate Jews are revealed in their true identity: the synagogue of Satan (cf. 2:9). Again, there is no such thing as "orthodox" Judaism; there is no such thing as a genuine belief in the Old Testament that is consistent with a rejection of Jesus Christ as Lord and God. Those who do not believe in Christ do not believe the Old Testament either. The god of Judaism is the devil. The Jew will not be recognized by God as one of His chosen people until he abandons his demonic religion and returns to the faith of his fathers—the faith which embraces Jesus Christ and His Gospel. When Christ-rejecting Jews claim to follow in the footsteps of Abraham, Jesus says, they **lie.** And, although they currently have the upper hand in

Philadelphia, their domination of the true covenant people will not last long. Christ Himself will force them **to come and bow down** at the Christians' feet. In this statement is an ironic reference to Isaiah 60:14, where God gives this promise to the covenant people, who had been persecuted by the heathen:

> The sons of those who afflicted you will come bowing to you,
> And all those who despised you will bow themselves at the
>   soles of your feet;
> And they will call you the City of the LORD,
> The Zion of the Holy One of Israel.

Those who falsely claim to be Jews are really in the position of the persecuting heathen; and they will be forced to acknowledge the covenantal status of the Church as the inheritor of the promises to Abraham and Moses. For the Church is the true Israel, and in coming into the Church, these believers "have come to Mount Zion and to the city of the living God" (Heb. 12:22). Apostate Israel has been pruned out of the tree of life of the covenant people, while believers in Christ from all nations have been grafted in (Rom. 11:7-24). The only hope for those outside the covenant line, regardless of their ethnic or religious heritage, is to recognize Christ as the only Savior and Lord, submitting themselves to Him. Unless and until the Jews become grafted into the covenant line by God's grace, they will remain outside the people of God, and will perish with the heathen. The Bible does hold out the promise that the descendants of Abraham will return to the faith of Jesus Christ (Rom. 11:12, 15, 23-32).[9] But until they do, Scripture classes them with the heathen (with one major difference, however: the condemnation of the apostate Jew is much more severe than that of the unenlightened pagan; see Rom. 2:1-29).

10-11 Because the persecuted Christians of Philadelphia had **kept the word of perseverance**, their Lord promises in return to **keep** them **from the hour of testing**. Note well: Christ is not promising to rapture them or to take them away, but to **keep** them. In other words, He is promising to preserve them in trial,

---

9. See David Chilton, *Paradise Restored: A Biblical Theology of Dominion* (Ft. Worth, TX: Dominion Press, 1985), pp. 125ff.

to keep them from falling (Jude 24). Although this is one of the verses that dispensationalists have claimed for support of the "pre-tribulation rapture" theory, on close examination it actually reveals itself to be nothing of the sort. In fact, it says nothing about the end of the world or the Second Coming at all: The "hour of testing" spoken of here is identified as **that hour which is about to come upon the whole world, to test those who dwell upon the Land**. It is speaking of the period of tribulation which, in the experience of the first-century readers, was **about to come**. Does it make sense that Christ would promise the church in Philadelphia protection from something that would happen thousands of years later? "Be of good cheer, you faithful, suffering Christians of first-century Asia Minor: I won't let those Soviet missiles and Killer Bees of the 20th century get you!" When the Philadelphian Christians were worried about more practical, immediate concerns — official persecution, religious discrimination, social ostracism, and economic boycotts — what did they care about Hal Lindsey's lucrative horror stories? By twisting such passages as these to suit their passing fancies, certain modern dispensationalists have added to the Word of God, and detracted from its message; and they thus come under the curses of Revelation 22:18-19.

No, the promised hour of testing was in the immediate future, as Scripture universally testifies; a mere **hour** of trial, to be replaced by a thousand years of rule (20:4-6). St. John uses the expression **those who dwell on the Land** twelve times in Revelation (once for each of the twelve tribes) to refer to *apostate Israel* (3:10; 6:10; 8:13; 11:10 [twice]; 13:8, 12, 14 [twice]; 14:6; 17:2, 8). In the Greek Old Testament (the version used by the early Church), it is a common prophetic expression for *rebellious, idolatrous Israel about to be destroyed and driven from the Land* (Jer. 1:14; 10:18; Ezek. 7:7; 36:17; Hos. 4:1, 3; Joel 1:2, 14; 2:1; Zeph. 1:18), based on its original usage in the historical books of the Bible for *rebellious, idolatrous pagans about to be destroyed and driven from the Land* (Num. 32:17; 33:52, 55; Josh. 7:9; 9:24; Judg. 1:32; 2 Sam. 5:6; 1 Chron. 11:4; 22:18; Neh. 9:24); Israel has become a nation of pagans, and is about to be destroyed, exiled, and supplanted by a new nation, the Church. The entire Roman world itself would be thrown into massive convulsions, part of which would involve the persecution of Christians by a crazed, self-deified emperor, with the aid of the Jews. Days were coming in which the devil—in both his Roman and Jewish manifestations—would attempt to destroy Christianity once and for all. The end result would be the destruction of Israel and Rome instead, but in the meantime there were hard times in store for the Christians, and many enticements to turn from the faith. Christ is here promising His faithful followers that they will be protected and enabled to persevere in the coming hour of trial. So again He reminds them: **I am coming quickly**—the promised judgment is not far off. Therefore, **hold fast what you have, in order that no one take your crown.** Christ has opened the door for the Church, granting it the privilege of royal fellowship with God as His priests and kings; and they must endure for His sake, while His coming Kingdom shakes the nations of earth and routs His enemies from their strongholds.

12-13   Again the promise to the overcomer involves a symbolic designation of salvation. First, Christ says, **I will make him a pillar in the Temple of My God.** This is related to the complex imagery of the Tabernacle and the Temple, whose architectural structures corresponded to the garments of the priests.[10] The two side-posts of the Tabernacle (the pillars of the Temple) are called *shoulders*, while the headdress of the priest, inscribed with the name of God, corresponded to the *lintel* which overarched the pillars.[11] Just as the two temple pillars were named *He shall establish* and *In Him is strength* (1 Ki. 7:21), so the shoulder-pieces of the high priest's ephod were inscribed with the names of the sons of Israel (Ex. 28:9-12). All this is brought together in Revelation, where the faithful overcomer is conceived of as a pillar in God's Temple. **And he will not go out from it anymore:** The people of God are characterized by stability and permanence (cf. Jer. 1:18; 1 Tim. 3:15). We have been redeemed from our wanderings.

Continuing this imagery, Christ says: **I will write upon him**

---

10. Meredith G. Kline has devoted an entire chapter to this subject. See "A Priestly Model of the Image of God," in *Images of the Spirit* (Grand Rapids: Baker Book House, 1980), pp. 35-56.

11. Ibid., pp. 40., 44f., 54f.; cf. Ex. 27:14-15; 1 Kings 6:8; 7:15, 21, 39; 2 Kings 11:11; 2 Chron. 3:17; Ezek. 40:18, 40ff.; 41:2, 26; 46:19; 47:1-2.

the name of My God, and the name of the City of My God, . . . and My new name. All this speaks of the full restoration of God's people to the image of God, as we see in the final chapter of Revelation: "And they shall see His face, and His name shall be in their foreheads" (Rev. 22:4). One of the basic blessings of the covenant is contained in the familiar benediction: "The LORD make His face shine upon you" (Num. 6:25); to see the shining of God's face means to partake of salvation and to reflect the glory of God as His image-bearer (see Ex. 34:29-35; Num. 12:6-8; Ps. 80:3, 7, 19; 2 Cor. 3:7-18; 4:6; 1 John 3:2). Similarly, as we have already seen, the name of God inscribed on the forehead symbolizes the restoration of redeemed man to the ethical and physical glory which belongs to the image of God (cf. Gen. 3:19; Ex. 28:36-38; Deut. 6:4-9; and contrast 2 Chron. 26:19).

The picture is completed as the Christian is declared to be a citizen of **the new Jerusalem, which comes down out of heaven from My God**. The old Jerusalem, which had apostatized from the faith of Abraham, was under judgment, about to be destroyed; the old Temple, which God had abandoned, had become a sanctuary for demons, and was soon to be so completely demolished that not one stone would lie upon another (Matt. 24:1-2). But now the Church of Christ is declared to be the city of God, the new Jerusalem, whose origin was not on earth but in heaven. The citizens of the old Jerusalem were to be scattered to the ends of the earth (Luke 21:24), while the Christian's relationship to God is so intimate that he could be described as a very pillar in the Temple, the dwelling-place of God—a pillar, moreover, that could not be moved from its place, for the Christian **will not go out from it anymore**. The children of the old Jerusalem were, like their mother, enslaved; while "the Jerusalem above is free; she is our mother" (Gal. 4:26). Jesus had said: "Many shall come from east and west, and shall recline at the table with Abraham, and Isaac, and Jacob, in the kingdom of heaven; but the sons of the kingdom shall be cast out into the outer darkness; in that place there shall be weeping and gnashing of teeth" (Matt. 8:11-12). And this was true of the overcoming Christians in Philadelphia. Although persecuted and discriminated against by the false Israel, as Isaac had been by Ishmael (Gen. 21:8-14; Gal. 4:22-31), they would see the false

131

sons disinherited and cast out, while they through Christ received the blessings of their father Abraham, and inherited the world (Rom. 4:13; Gal. 3:29).

Laodicea: Judgment on the Lukewarm (3:14-22)

14 And to the angel of the church in Laodicea write: The Amen, the faithful and true Witness, the Beginning of the creation of God, says this:

15 I know your deeds, that you are neither cold nor hot; I would that you were cold or hot.

16 So because you are lukewarm, and neither hot nor cold, I will spit you out of my mouth.

17 Because you say: I am rich, and have become wealthy, and have need of nothing; and you do not know that you are wretched and miserable and poor and blind and naked.

18 I advise you to buy from Me gold refined by fire, that you may become rich, and white garments, that you may clothe yourself, and that the shame of your nakedness may not be revealed; and eye salve to anoint your eyes, that you may see.

19 Those whom I love, I reprove and discipline; be zealous therefore, and repent.

20 Behold, I stand at the door and knock; if anyone hears My voice and opens the door, I will come in to him, and will dine with him, and he with Me.

21 He who overcomes, I will grant to him to sit down with Me on My throne, as I also overcame and sat down with My Father on His throne.

22 He who has an ear, let him hear what the Spirit says to the churches.

14   The wealthiest city in the region, Laodicea was another important center of emperor-worship. In His message to the elders of this church, Christ identifies Himself in three ways. First, Jesus says, He is **the Amen.** This is a familiar word to all Christians: We repeat it at the close of our creeds, hymns, and prayers.[12] It is generally understood to mean *So be it;* but its ac-

---

12. Unfortunately, many fundamentalists and evangelicals use the term nowadays to mean *I feel good.* Such usage, implicitly (though certainly not intentionally) bordering on blasphemy, is only one symptom of the subjective, man-centered attitude toward life which has become common during the past two centuries.

tual force, in terms of the theology of the Bible, is much stronger. It is really an oath: to say *Amen* means to call down upon oneself the curses of the Covenant (cf. Num. 5:21-22; Deut. 27:15-26; Neh. 5:12-13). As our "Yes and Amen" Jesus Christ is the guarantee of the covenantal promises, by His perfect obedience, atoning sacrifice, and continuing intercession in the court of heaven (2 Cor. 1:20; Gal. 3:13; Heb. 7:22-28; 9:24-28; 10:10-14). Thus, our *Amen* in liturgical response to God's Word is both an oath and a recognition that our salvation is wholly dependent not upon our keeping of the Covenant but upon the perfect covenantkeeping of Jesus Christ, who placed Himself under the Covenant stipulations and curses in our place.

Second, this means that Jesus is also **the faithful and true Witness**, on whose Word we may eternally depend. "He is a *faithful* Witness because his witness is true; and he is a *true* Witness because in him is the complete realization of all the qualifications which constitute any one really and truly a witness."[13] And it is as this infallible and fully authoritative Witness that Christ bears convicting testimony against the church of Laodicea.

Third, Jesus says, He is **the Beginning of the creation of God**: He is the *archē*, both the Origin and the Ruler of all creation, as Paul also wrote in a letter he specifically intended the Laodicean church to read (see Col. 4:16):

> And He is the image of the invisible God, the Firstborn of all creation. For by Him all things were created, both in the heavens and on earth, visible and invisible, whether thrones or dominions or rulers or authorities — all things have been created by Him and for Him. And He is before all things, and in Him all things hold together. He is also the head of the Body, the Church; and He is the Beginning, the Firstborn from the dead; so that He Himself might come to have first place in everything. (Col. 1:15-18)

Thus the One who speaks to Laodicea is the Amen, the great Guarantor of the Covenant, the infallible Witness who is Truth Himself, with all the authority possessed by the Creator and King of the universe. And He has come to bear testimony against His church.

---

13. A. Plummer in *The Pulpit Commentary: The Revelation of St. John the Divine* (London: Funk and Wagnalls Company, n.d.), p. 115.

15-16 Laodicea was **lukewarm, and neither hot nor cold.** This has often been interpreted as if **hot** meant *godly enthusiasm* and **cold** meant *ungodly antagonism*; but there is another explanation which suits the historical and geographical context better. Laodicea was situated between two other important cities, Colossae and Hieropolis. Colossae, wedged into a narrow valley in the shadow of towering mountains, was watered by icy streams which tumbled down from the heights. In contrast, Hieropolis was famous for its hot mineral springs which flowed out of the city and across a high plain until it cascaded down a cliff which faced Laodicea. By the time the water reached the valley floor, it was lukewarm, putrid, and nauseating. At Colossae, therefore, one could be refreshed with clear, cold, invigorating drinking water; at Hieropolis, one could be healed by bathing in its hot, mineral-laden pools. But at Laodicea, the waters were neither **hot** (for health) nor **cold** (for drinking).[14]

In other words, the basic accusation against Laodicea is that it is ineffectual, good for nothing. The Laodicean church brings neither a cure for illness nor a drink to soothe dry lips and parched throats. The sort of Christianity represented by Laodicea is worthless. The church provided "neither refreshment for the spiritually weary, nor healing for the spiritually sick. It was totally ineffective, and thus distasteful to its Lord."[15] Thus, says Mounce, "the church is not being called to task for its spiritual temperature but for the barrenness of its works."[16] This explains Christ's statement: **I would that you were cold or hot.** He is not saying that outright apostasy is preferable to middle-of-the-roadism; rather, He is wishing that the Laodicean Christians would have an influence upon their society.

> The Hippopotamus's day
> Is passed in sleep; at night he hunts;
> God works in a mysterious way —
> The Church can sleep and feed at once.[17]

---

14. C. J. Hemer, "Seven Cities of Asia Minor," in R. K. Harrison, ed., *Major Cities of the Biblical World* (Nashville: Thomas Nelson Publishers, 1985), pp. 246ff.
15. M. J. S. Rudwick and E. M. B. Green, "The Laodicean Lukewarmness," in *Expository Times*, Vol. 69 (1957-58), p. 178; cited in Mounce, p. 125.
16. Mounce, pp. 125f.
17. From T. S. Eliot, "The Hippopotamus," *Collected Poems 1909-1962* (New York: Harcourt Brace Jovanovich, 1963), p. 42.

The Christian's calling is not to blend in with a pagan environment but to convert it, reform it, reconstruct it in terms of the whole counsel of God as mandated in His Word. To cite but one example of a modern Laodiceanism, consider the many Bible-believing, evangelical churches — which would shudder at the suggestion that they are "worldly" or "liberal" — which continue on in their complacent lifestyle, organizing encounter groups and summer camps, completely oblivious to the murder of over 4000 unborn infants every day. Often, these churches are afraid of making "political" statements on the grounds that they might lose their tax exemptions. But whatever the excuse, such a church is disobedient to the Word of God. If a church is not transforming its society, if it is not Christianizing the culture, what good is it? "If the salt has become tasteless, how will it be made salty again? It is good for nothing anymore, except to be thrown out and trampled under foot by men" (Matt. 5:13).

So because you are lukewarm . . . I will spit you out of my mouth. This is an echo of Leviticus 18:24-28:

> Do not defile yourselves by any of these things; for by all these the nations which I am casting out before you have become defiled. For the land has become defiled, therefore I have visited its punishment upon it, so the land has spewed out its inhabitants. But as for you, you are to keep My statutes and My judgments, and shall not do any of these abominations, neither the native, nor the alien who sojourns among you (for the men of the land who have been before you have done all these abominations, and the land has become defiled); so that the land may not spew you out, should you defile it, as it has spewed out the nation which has been before you.

The Laodicean lukewarmness is an abomination to the Lord. Because it is such a failure in making an impression upon the world (and thus conforming to heathen standards — or not making a fuss about those standards, which amounts to the same thing) the church is in danger of being cut off from Christ, its very leadership threatened with wholesale excommunication.

17-18 The city of Laodicea was proud of its three outstanding characteristics: Its great wealth and financial independence as an important banking center; its textile industry, which produced "a very fine quality of world-famous black, glossy wool";[18] and its scientific community, renowned not only for its prestigious medical school, but also for an eyesalve (called "Phrygian Powder") which had been well-known since the days of Aristotle. Using these facts to illustrate the problems in the church, Christ cites the general attitude of the Laodicean Christians: **You say: I am rich, and have become wealthy, and have need of nothing.** In reality, despite the church's wealth and undoubted social standing, it was ineffectual, accomplishing nothing for the kingdom of God. It is not a sin for a church (or an individual) to be rich — in fact, God wants us to acquire wealth (Deut. 8:18). What is sinful is the failure to use our resources for the spread of the kingdom. When a relatively poor church such as that at Smyrna (see Rev. 2:9) was having a rich effect upon its community, there was no excuse for Laodicea's impotence. Her problem was not wealth, but disobedience: **You do not know that you are wretched and miserable and poor and blind and naked.**

Yet, in grace, Christ makes an offer of mercy: **I advise you to buy from Me gold refined by fire, that you may become rich; and white garments, that you may clothe yourself, and that the shame of your nakedness may not be revealed; and eyesalve to anoint your eyes, that you may see.** The symbolism here should be obvious. True faith and genuine works of obedience are spoken of in Scripture in terms of jewelry, and especially **gold** (1 Pet. 1:7; 1 Cor. 3:12-15); **nakedness** is symptomatic of disobedience (Gen. 3:7), whereas being **clothed** in **white robes** is a symbol of righteousness, with regard to both justification and sanctification (Gen. 3:21; Matt. 22:11; Rev. 19:8); and **blindness** is a symbol for man's impotence and fallenness (Lev. 21:18; Deut. 29:4; Matt. 13:13-15; 16:3; 2 Cor. 4:3-4; 1 John 2:11) apart from God's restoration of him to true sight — the godly, mature ability to judge righteous judgment (Luke 4:18; Acts 26:18; 1 Cor. 2:14-15).

19-20   But Laodicea is not yet to be cast off by the Lord. Harsh as His words are, He still professes His **love** for His Bride. That, in fact, is the source of His anger: Because I love you, He

---

18. Charles F. Pfeiffer and Howard F. Vos, *The Wycliffe Historical Geography of Bible Lands* (Chicago: Moody Press, 1967), p. 377.

declares, **I reprove and discipline**. A characteristic of those who
are true sons of God, and not bastards (cf. Heb. 12:5-11) is their
response to rebuke and discipline. All Christians need reproof
and correction at times, and some more than others; what is important is whether or not we heed the warning, and mend our
ways. As far as Laodicea has fallen, it can still be restored if it
renews its obedience and becomes faithful to God's Word: **Be
zealous therefore, and repent!**

At this point Jesus speaks some of the most beautiful words
in all the Bible, in what is perhaps the most well-known New
Testament verse aside from John 3:16. **Behold, I stand at the
door and knock; if anyone hears My voice and opens the door, I
will come in to him, and will dine with him, and he with Me**.
Several Reformed commentators have pointed out the widespread abuse of this passage by modern evangelicals, who rip
the verse from its context as a message to the elders of a church,
and turn it into a watered-down, Arminian request from a weak
and helpless deity who is at the mercy of man. We must remember that Christ is speaking here as the Amen, the faithful and
true Witness, the Creator and Sovereign Lord of all. He is not
making a feeble plea, as if He did not rule history and predestine
its most minute details; He is the King of Kings, who makes war
on His enemies and damns them to everlasting flames. Nor is he
speaking to people in general, for He is directing His message to
His Church; nor, again, is he simply speaking to Christians as
individuals, but to Christians *as members of the Church*. This
verse cannot be made to serve the purposes of Arminian, subjective individualism without violently wrenching it from its
covenantal and textual context.[19]

Nevertheless, there is a distortion on the other side that is
just as serious. It will not do merely to point out the failures of
Arminians to deal satisfactorily with this text, for Calvinists
have traditionally been at fault here as well. Reformed worship
tends to be overly intellectual, centered around *preaching*. In
the name of being centered around the *Word*, it is actually often

---

19. Of course, the Lord offers Himself to people outside the Kingdom as
well: Even the dogs are given crumbs from the children's table (Matt.
15:21-28); and the king in Christ's parable (Luke 14:23) sent his servants out to
compel the Gentiles to come in. But Christ's offer of salvation is never made
outside the context of the Covenant, the Kingdom, and the Church.

centered around the *intellect*. Reformed rationalism has thus produced its equal and opposite reaction in Arminian revivalism, irrationalism, and anti-intellectualism. People have fled the barren, overly intellectual emphasis of Reformed worship and have run into the anti-theology heresies of what is unfortunately known as evangelicalism (which has, indeed, precious little of the original *evangel*).[20]

What is the answer? We must take seriously the Biblical doctrine of the Real Presence of Christ in the sacrament of the Eucharist. We must return to the Biblical pattern of worship centered on *Jesus Christ*, which means the weekly celebration of the Lord's Supper, as well as instruction about its true meaning and efficacy.[21] We must abandon the rank platonism which informs our bare, intellectualized worship, and return to a truly corporate, liturgical worship characterized by artistic beauty and musical excellence.[22]

For it should be obvious that in this verse He is extending to the Church an offer of renewed communion with Himself. The very heart and center of our fellowship with Christ is at His table (i.e., our earthly table which He has made His). The most basic, and most profound, offer of salvation is Christ's offer to dine with us. In Holy Communion we are genuinely having dinner with Jesus, lifted up into His heavenly presence; and, moreover, we are feasting on Him:

> Truly, truly, I say to you, unless you eat the flesh of the Son

---

20. See James B. Jordan's essay "Holistic Evangelism" in his *Sociology of the Church* (Tyler, TX: Geneva Ministries, 1986).

21. See Geddes MacGregor, *Corpus Christi: The Nature of the Church According to the Reformed Tradition* (Philadelphia: The Westminster Press, 1958); and Ronald S. Wallace, *Calvin's Doctrine of the Word and Sacrament* (Tyler, TX: Geneva Ministries, [1953] 1982).

22. One of the most helpful books on worship from a Reformed perspective is Richard Paquier, *Dynamics of Worship: Foundations and Uses of Liturgy* (Philadelphia: Fortress Press, 1967). For viewpoints from other traditions see Louis Bouyer, *Liturgical Piety* (University of Notre Dame Press, 1955); Josef A. Jungmann, S.J., *The Early Liturgy to the Time of Gregory the Great* (University of Notre Dame Press, 1959); Alexander Schmemann, *Introduction to Liturgical Theology* (Crestwood, NY: St. Vladimir's Seminary Press, 1966); Luther D. Reed, *The Lutheran Liturgy* (Philadelphia: Muhlenberg Press, 1947); Massey H. Shepherd Jr., *The Worship of the Church* (Greenwich, CT: The Seabury Press, 1952); and Cheslyn Jones *et al.*, eds., *The Study of Liturgy* (New York: Oxford University Press, 1978).

of Man and drink His blood, you have no life in yourselves. He who eats My flesh and drinks My blood has eternal life, and I will raise him up on the last day. For My flesh is true food, and My blood is true drink. He who eats My flesh and drinks My blood abides in Me, and I in Him. As the living Father sent Me, and I live because of the Father, so he who eats Me, he also shall live because of Me. (John 6:53-57)

21-22 The final promise to the overcomer is a promise of dominion with Christ: **I will grant to him to sit down with Me on My Throne, as I also overcame and sat down with My Father on His Throne.** Is this only a future hope? Assuredly not. The privilege of ruling with Christ belongs to all Christians, in time and on earth, although the dominion is progressive through history until the final consummation. But Christ has entered upon His Kingdom already (Col. 1:13); He has disarmed Satan and the demons already (Col. 2:15); and we are kings and priests with Him already (Rev. 1:6); and just as He conquered, so we are to go forth, conquering in His name. He reigns now (Acts 2:29-36), above all creation (Eph. 1:20-22), with all power in heaven and in earth (Matt. 28:18-20), and is engaged *now* in putting all enemies under His feet (1 Cor. 15:25), until His kingdom becomes a great mountain, filling the whole earth (Dan. 2:35, 45).

We have thus been faced again and again in these messages to the churches with the fundamental command of Revelation, that which St. John admonished us to keep (1:3): *Overcome! Conquer!* Even aside from the fact that the prophecy is not about the twentieth century, we will miss its point if we concentrate on persecutions or emperor-worship in the same way that the Hal Lindseys of this age concentrate on oil embargoes, common markets and hydrogen bombs: the basic message is about none of these, but rather about the duty of the Church to conquer the world. R. J. Rushdoony has well said: "The purpose of this vision is to give comfort and assurance of victory to the Church, not to confirm their fears or the threats of the enemy. To read Revelation as other than the triumph of the kingdom of God in time and eternity is to deny the very essence of its meaning."[23]

---

23. Rousas John Rushdoony, *Thy Kingdom Come: Studies in Daniel and Revelation* (Tyler, TX: Thoburn Press, [1970] 1978), p. 90.

The great failure of what is commonly known as "amillennialism" is its unwillingness to come to terms with these dominical implications of the mediatorial reign of Jesus Christ. The New Testament writers constantly urge God's people to "overcome" in the light of Christ's definitive victory. Having been recreated in His image, according to His likeness (Eph. 4:24; Col. 3:10), and becoming more and more conformed to His image (Rom. 8:29-30), we are kings with Him now, in this age. He has given us legal title to all things (cf. Rom. 8:32; 1 Cor. 3:21-22), and on this basis we are to exercise dominion under His lordship in every area of life. Amillennialists, however, while professing to believe in the existence of Christ's present Kingdom, often characteristically deny its practical relevance to this world. For example, Dr. Meredith G. Kline's brilliant study *Images of the Spirit* has an excellent chapter on "A Prophetic Model of the Image of God," in which he shows how the restoration of God's image to the Church through Christ means that "all the Lord's people are prophets" (cf. Num. 11:29; Acts 2:17-18).[24] Kline also has a superb chapter on "A Priestly Model of the Image of God," a fascinating exposition of the priesthood of all believers in the image of Christ, our definitive High Priest.[25] But Christ is Prophet, Priest, and *King* — yet, significantly, Kline neglected to write an essay on "A Kingly Model of the Image of God." But if Christians image Christ in His role of Prophet and Priest, they are kings as well, in the image of the King. That is precisely the burden of the verses under discussion: The Lord Jesus Christ shares His conquest and enthronement with His people. Because He overcame and sat down with the Father on His Throne, He now summons us to enjoy regal dominion with Him, inheriting all things.

---

24. Kline, *Images of the Spirit*, pp. 57-96.
25. Ibid., pp. 35-56.

Part Three

ETHICAL STIPULATIONS:
THE SEVEN SEALS
(Revelation 4-7)

Introduction

The third section of the covenantal treaty (cf. Deut. 5:1-26:19)[1] declared the way of Covenant life required of the vassals, the laws of citizenship in the Kingdom. As St. Paul declared, all men "live and move and exist" in God (Acts 17:28); He is the Foundation of our very being. This means that our relationship to Him is at the center of our existence, of our actions and thinking in every area of life. And central to this relationship is His Sanctuary, where His subjects come to worship Him before His Throne. Thus the major concern of the Stipulations section is the thorough consecration of the people to God, with special importance placed on the establishment of one central Sanctuary:

> You shall seek the LORD at the place which the LORD your God shall choose from all your tribes to establish His name there for His dwelling, and there you shall come. (Deut. 12:5; cf. all of ch. 12)

As Meredith Kline observes, "The centralization requirement must . . . be understood in terms of Deuteronomy's nature as a suzerainty treaty. Such treaties prohibited the vassal to engage in any independent diplomacy with a foreign power other than the covenant suzerain. In particular, the vassal must not pay tribute to any other lord."[2] The centrality of the Sanc-

---

1. See Meredith G. Kline, *Treaty of the Great King: The Covenant Structure of Deuteronomy* (Grand Rapids: William B. Eerdmans Publishing Co., 1963), pp. 62-120.
2. Ibid., p. 80.

tuary helped to underscore the fact that it was an image of the Sanctuary in heaven (Ex. 25:9, 40; 26:30; Num. 8:4; Acts 7:44; Heb. 8:5; 9:23).

This is also the emphasis of the Stipulations section of Revelation. The passage opens with St. John's ascension to God's Throneroom, and this provides the central vantage point for the prophecy as a whole: All things are seen in relation to the Throne. The judgments that are bound on earth were first bound in heaven.[3]

Obviously, an important aspect of the Stipulations section in Deuteronomy is the Law itself, the sign of God's covenantal lordship. Moses takes great care repeatedly to remind Israel of the Covenant at Sinai, with the Ten Commandments engraved on the tablets of stone (Deut. 5, 9-10). Similarly, this section of Revelation (ch. 5) deals with a Covenant document that, like the original stone tablets, is written on both front and back.

The laws of the Covenant decreed a program of conquest over the ungodly nations of Canaan: Israel defeated its enemies through the application of the Covenant. The holy war simply carried out the death sentence declared in the courtroom; it was fundamentally an ethical, judicial action, bringing the death penalty against the wicked.[4] The program of conquest, based on the law of God, thus issued from the central Sanctuary. (It is interesting that as this program is spelled out in Deuteronomy 7, Moses speaks symbolically of "seven nations" to be destroyed.)[5] Of course, the law provides not only for the judgment of the Canaanites, but also for Israelites who apostatize from the Covenant: Those who repudiate God's authority and follow after other gods are to be put to death, a judgment that, like the others, proceeds ultimately from the altar in the central Sanctuary (Deut. 13:1-18; 17:1-13).[6]

As Deuteronomy 20 makes clear, this Sanctuary-judicial

---

3. Cf. Matt. 18:18, which literally reads: "Truly I say to you, whatever you shall bind on earth *shall have been* bound in heaven; and whatever you loose on earth *shall have been* loosed in heaven." In delivering righteous judgments, ministers on earth are manifesting the Judgment of heaven.

4. See Ray R. Sutton, *That You May Prosper: Dominion by Covenant* (Tyler, TX: Institute for Christian Economics, 1987).

5. Cf. Kline, p. 68.

6. Ibid., pp. 84ff., 94ff.

aspect is central even to the warfare waged against foreign nations, beyond the borders of the theocracy: Battles were consecrated by the priest to the glory of God and His covenantal Kingdom (v. 1-4). A war of this kind was always preceded by an offer of peace; if the offer were refused, all the men of the city would be put to the sword. Kline explains the typology: "In Israel's offer of peace (v. 10) and in the submission of the Gentile city as a covenant tributary to Yahweh (v. 11) there was imaged the saving mission of God's people in the world (cf. Zech. 9:7b, 10b; Luke 10:5-16). The judgment of those who refuse to make their peace with God through Christ was exhibited in the siege, conquest, and punishment of the unsubmissive city (v. 13)."[7]

We find all this in Revelation as well—with the difference that, as a Covenant Lawsuit against apostate Israel, the judgments once decreed against the ungodly Gentiles are now unleashed on the lawless Covenant people, who had rejected Christ's offer of peace. As the book of the Covenant is opened, the cherubic creatures carrying the altar cry out: "Come!"—and four horsemen ride out to conquer the Land, bringing destruction and death in fulfillment of the covenantal curses, applying the just and holy judgment of the Sanctuary in heaven.

Another major subject of the Stipulations section in Deuteronomy is the requirement to appear at the sacred feasts, involving three annual pilgrimages to the central Sanctuary: for the feasts of Passover/Unleavened Bread (16:1-8), Pentecost [Weeks] (16:9-12), and Tabernacles [Booths] (16:13-15).[8] The same order is followed in this section of Revelation. Chapter 5 contains imagery from Passover, where we see worshipers in the sanctuary giving thanks for "the Lamb that was slain." Chapter 6 takes up the theme of Pentecost (the anniversary of the giving of the Law at Sinai): The lawbook of the Covenant is unsealed, bringing a series of judgments patterned after Habakkuk 3, a synagogue reading for Pentecost.[9] Then chapter 7 brings us into a vision of the eschatological Feast of Tabernacles,[10] in which

---

7. Ibid., p. 106.
8. Ibid., pp. 91-94.
9. M. D. Goulder, *The Evangelists' Calendar: A Lectionary Explanation for the Development of Scripture* (London: SPCK, 1978), p. 177.
10. See David Chilton, *Paradise Restored: A Biblical Theology of Dominion* (Ft. Worth, TX: Dominion Press, 1985), pp. 44ff., 60.

the countless multitudes redeemed from every nation stand before the Throne with palm branches in their hands (cf. Lev. 23:39-43), praising God as their Redeemer-King (cf. Deut. 26:1-19)[11] and receiving the fullness of blessing foreshadowed in this feast: "And He who sits on the Throne shall spread His Tabernacle over them. They shall hunger no more, neither thirst any more; neither shall the sun beat down on them, nor any heat; for the Lamb in the center of the Throne shall be their Shepherd, and shall guide them to the springs of the water of life; and God shall wipe away every tear from their eyes" (Rev. 7:15-17).

---

11. See Kline, pp. 118ff.

4

THE THRONE ABOVE THE SEA

The Pattern for Worship (4:1-11)

1 After these things I looked, and behold, a door standing open in heaven, and the first Voice which I had heard, like the sound of a trumpet speaking with me, said: Come up here, and I will show you what must take place after these things.

2 Immediately I was in the Spirit; and behold, a Throne was standing in heaven, and One sitting

3 like a jasper stone and a sardius in appearance; and there was a rainbow around the Throne, like an emerald in appearance.

4 And around the Throne were twenty-four thrones; and upon the thrones I saw twenty-four elders sitting, clothed in white garments, and golden crowns on their heads.

5 And from the Throne proceed flashes of lightning and voices and peals of thunder. And there were seven lamps of fire burning before His Throne, which are the seven Spirits of God;

6 and before the Throne there was, as it were, a sea of glass like crystal; and in the middle of the Throne and around it were four living creatures full of eyes in front and behind.

7 And the first creature was like a Lion, and the second creature was like a Bull, and the third creature had a face like that of a Man, and the fourth creature was like a flying Eagle.

8 And the four living creatures, each one of them having six wings, are full of eyes around and within; and they have no rest day and night, saying:

Holy, holy, holy, is the Lord God, the Almighty, who was and who is and who is to come.

9 And when the living creatures give glory and honor and thanks to Him who sits on the Throne, to Him who lives forever and ever,

10 the twenty-four elders will fall down before Him who sits on the Throne, and will worship Him who lives forever and ever, and will cast their crowns before the Throne, saying:

11   Worthy art Thou, our Lord and God, the Holy One, to receive glory and honor and power; for Thou didst create all things, and because of Thy will they existed, and were created.

1   This verse is used by advocates of Dispensationalism to support their "Rapture Theory," the notion that the Church will be snatched away from this world before a coming Tribulation; indeed, this verse seems to be *the* main proof-text for a pre-Tribulation rapture. St. John's "rapture" into heaven is regarded as a sign that the whole Church will disappear before the plagues recorded in the following chapters are poured out. Part of the rationale for this understanding is that the **Voice** John heard was **like the sound of a trumpet,** and St. Paul says that a trumpet will sound at the "rapture" (1 Thess. 4:16). Some advocates of this position seem oblivious to the fact that God uses a trumpet on numerous occasions. In fact, as we have seen in the first chapter, the connection between God's *Voice* and the sound of a *trumpet* occurs throughout Scripture, beginning with the judgment in the Garden of Eden. For that matter, St. John heard the voice like a trumpet in the first vision (Rev. 1:10). (Does this indicate a possible "double rapture"?)[1]

The Dispensationalist school of interpretation also appeals to the fact that, after the Voice has said **Come up here,** "The word 'church' does not again occur in the Revelation till all is fulfilled."[2] This singular observation is set forth as abundant proof that the Book of Revelation does not speak of the "Church"[3] from this point until the Second Coming (generally

---

1. But wait! Chapters 8-11 record the soundings of no less than *seven* more trumpets—could there be nine raptures?

2. *The Scofield Reference Bible* (New York: Oxford University Press, [1909] 1945), note on Rev. 4:1; cf. Hal Lindsey, *There's a New World Coming: A Prophetic Odyssey* (Eugene, OR: Harvest House Publishers, 1973), pp. 74ff.

3. The Dispensationalist use of the word Church is very different from its use in historical, orthodox theology. See O. T. Allis, *Prophecy and the Church* (Grand Rapids: Baker Book House, 1945, 1947), pp. 54-110; L. Berkhof, *Systematic Theology* (Grand Rapids: William B. Eerdmans Publishing Co., fourth revised ed., 1949), pp. 562-78; and Roderick Campbell, *Israel and the New Covenant* (Tyler, TX: Geneva Ministries, [1954] 1983).

placed in 19:11), which in turn proves that the Church has been raptured and is absent, in heaven, away from all the excitement — all because the *word* "Church" is missing! On the basis of such a curious principle of interpretation we could say with assurance that Revelation doesn't tell us anything about Jesus either until chapter 12, because the name "Jesus" does not occur until then (thus "the Lion of the tribe of Judah" and "the Lamb that was slain" [5:5-6] must be terms for someone else).[4] Of course, this method of interpretation involves even more problems for the Dispensationalist: for *the word "Church" never again appears in the entire Book of Revelation at all!* This interpretation of the words **Come up here** does not, therefore, support the pretribulation *rapture* of the Church; it possibly even teaches the pretribulation *annihilation* of the Church. After the last verse in Revelation 3, the Church simply disappears, and is never heard from again.

Obviously, this is not true. The Church is known by numerous names and descriptions throughout the Bible,[5] and the mere fact that the single *term* "Church" does not appear is no indication that the *concept* of the Church is not present. Those who see in this verse some "rapture" of the Church are importing it into the text. The only one "raptured" is St. John himself. The fact is that St. John only uses the word *Church* with reference to particular congregations — *not* for the whole body of Christ.

Nevertheless, we must also recognize that St. John does ascend to a worship service on the Lord's Day; and this is a clear image of the *weekly* ascension of the Church into heaven every Lord's Day where she joins in the communion of saints and angels "in festal array" (Heb. 12:22-23) for the heavenly liturgy. The Church acts out St. John's experience every Sunday at the *Sursum Corda*, when the officiant (reflecting Christ's **Come up here!**) cries out, *Lift up your hearts!* and the congregation sings

---

4. This principle can be fruitfully applied elsewhere in Scripture as well. For example, the word *love* does not appear anywhere in the Book of Ruth; thus her story turns out not to be, after all, one of the greatest romances in the Bible, for Boaz and Ruth did not love each other. Again, the word *God* does not appear in the book of Esther; on these principles, He must not have been involved with those events, and the book must not tell us anything about Him. In addition, the first fifteen chapters of Paul's letter to the Romans doesn't concern the Church, for the word *Church* doesn't appear there either!

5. Paul Minear lists ninety-six of them in the New Testament alone: *Images of the Church in the New Testament* (Philadelphia: The Westminster Press, 1960), pp. 222ff., 268f.

in response, *We lift them up to the Lord!* We noted in an earlier chapter the comment of St. Germanus that "the Church is an earthly heaven"; the Patriarch continued: "The souls of Christians are called together to assemble with the prophets, apostles, and hierarchs in order to recline with Abraham, Isaac, and Jacob at the mystical banquet of the Kingdom of Christ. Thereby having come into the unity of faith and communion of the Spirit through the dispensation of the One who died for us and is sitting at the right hand of the Father, we are no longer on earth but standing by the royal Throne of God in heaven, where Christ is, just as He Himself says: 'Righteous Father, sanctify in Your name those whom You gave me, so that where I am, they may be with Me' (cf. John 17)."[6] John Calvin agreed: "In order that pious souls may duly apprehend Christ in the Supper, they must be raised up to heaven. . . . And for the same reason it was established of old that before consecration the people should be told in a loud voice to lift up their hearts."[7]

We have already seen (on 1:10) that the expression **in the Spirit** (v. 2) is technical prophetic language, referring not to St. John's subjective feelings but to his objective experience as an inspired receiver of divine revelation. Being "in the Spirit" was the special privilege of the Biblical prophets. Summarizing his extensive research on this point, Meredith Kline writes: "Adam's creation as image-reflector of the glory of the Creator-Spirit was recapitulated in the history of the prophets. The critical event in the formation of a prophet was a transforming encounter with the Glory-Spirit from which the prophet emerged as a man reflecting the divine Glory. . . . To be caught up in the Spirit was to be received into the divine assembly, the heavenly reality within the theophanic Glory-Spirit. The hallmark of the true prophet was that he had stood before the Lord of Glory in the midst of this deliberative council of angels."[8]

But, with the coming of the New Covenant, what was once the special prerogative of the prophetic class within the Cove-

---

6. St. Germanus of Constantinople, *On the Divine Liturgy*, trans. Paul Meyendorff (Crestwood, NY: St. Vladimir's Seminary Press, 1984), p. 101.

7. John Calvin, *Institutes of the Christian Religion,* 4:17:36 (Philadelphia: The Westminster Press, 1960), Ford Lewis Battles trans., p. 1412.

8. Meredith G. Kline, *Images of the Spirit* (Grand Rapids: Baker Book House, 1980), pp. 57f.

nant community has become the privilege of all. The desire of Moses — "Would that all the LORD's people were prophets, that the LORD would put His Spirit on them!" (Num. 11:29) — has been fulfilled in the Pentecostal outpouring of the Holy Spirit (Acts 2:17-21). Just as Moses (the prophet *par excellence* of the Old Covenant) was uniquely privileged to speak with God face to face (Num. 12:6-8), partaking of His glory (Ex. 34:33-35), so now "we *all*, with unveiled face beholding as in a mirror the glory of the Lord, are being transformed into the same image from glory to glory, just as from the Lord, the Spirit" (2 Cor. 3:18). Every believer has received the prophetic anointing (1 John 2:20, 27); and every week we ascend in the Spirit into the heavenly assembly.[9]

In part, therefore, the "Rapture Theory" is based on a misunderstanding of the Christian doctrine of the Ascension of the Church. The *definitive* Ascension took place *positionally* with Jesus Christ, in whom we are seated in the heavenlies (Eph. 1:20; 2:6); the *progressive* (experiential) Ascension takes place *liturgically* with Jesus Christ every week, in the celebration of the Eucharist (Heb. 12:22-24); and the *final* (culminative) Ascension takes place *eschatologically* with Christ a) spiritually, at death (Rev. 20:4), and b) bodily, at the end of history (1 Cor. 15:50-55; 1 Thess. 4:17).[10]

2-3 In order to receive the revelation, St. John is caught up to **heaven**, where he sees **a Throne** and **One sitting:** John is going to view the coming events from the true vantage point, the Chariot-Throne of God in the Glory-Cloud. God is the Determiner of all things, and a right understanding of the world must begin from a right understanding of the centrality of His Throne. "In the infinite wisdom of the Lord of all the earth, each event falls with exact precision into its proper place in the unfolding of His eternal plan; nothing, however small, however strange, occurs without His ordering, or without its peculiar fitness for its place in the working out of His purpose; and the end

---

9. See George Vandervelde's paper, "The Gift of Prophecy and the Prophetic Church" (Toronto: Institute for Christian Studies, 1984).

10. On this definitive-progressive-final pattern, see David Chilton, *Paradise Restored: A Biblical Theology of Dominion* (Ft. Worth, TX: Dominion Press, 1985), pp. 24, 42, 73, 136, 146-57, 206, 209, 223.

of all shall be the manifestation of His glory, and the accumulation of His praise."[11]

And He who was sitting was like a jasper stone and a sardius in appearance: God is seen as in a blaze of unapproachable light (cf. 1 Tim. 6:16), for St. John has been caught up into the heavenly holy of holies, the inner Sanctuary of the cosmic Temple in the Cloud of glory. Underscoring this is the fact that John sees **a rainbow around the Throne, like an emerald in appearance.** It is worth noting that these three stones, **jasper** (perhaps an opal or a diamond),[12] **sardius** (a reddish stone), and **emerald**, represented three of the twelve tribes of Israel on the breastplate of the high priest (Ex. 28:17-19, LXX); they are also mentioned among the jewelry that littered the ground in the Garden of Eden (Ezek. 28:13, LXX). Compare John's vision with that of the prophet Ezekiel:

> . . . there was something resembling a Throne, like lapis lazuli in appearance; and on that which resembled a Throne, high up, was a figure with the appearance of a man. Then I noticed from the appearance of His loins and upward something like glowing metal that looked like fire all around within it, and from the appearance of His loins and downward I saw something like fire; and there was a radiance around Him. As the appearance of the rainbow in the clouds on a rainy day, so was the appearance of the surrounding radiance. Such was the appearance of the likeness of the glory of the LORD. (Ezek. 1:26-28)

St. John is thus in the true Temple, the heavenly archetype that formed the pattern for Moses' construction of the Tabernacle (Ex. 25:40; Heb. 8:1-2, 5; 9:23-24). He sees the Throne, corresponding to the Mercy-Seat; the Seven Lamps, corresponding to the Seven-Branched Lamp; the Four Living Creatures, corresponding to the Cherubim; the Sea of Glass, corresponding to the Bronze "Sea"; and the Twenty-Four Elders, cor-

---

11. Benjamin B. Warfield, "Predestination," in *Biblical and Theological Studies* (Nutley, NJ: Presbyterian and Reformed Publishing Co., 1968), p. 285.

12. "In antiquity the name was not limited to the variety of quartz now called jasper, but could designate any opaque precious stone." William F. Arndt and F. Wilbur Gingrich, *A Greek-English Lexicon of the New Testament and Other Early Christian Literature* (Chicago: The University of Chicago Press, 1957), p. 369.

responding to the Twenty-Four Courses of Priests. (See Appendix A for a more full account of the Levitical symbolism here and throughout Revelation.)

4 Around the Throne St. John sees **twenty-four thrones**, on which are seated **twenty-four elders**. Who are these elders? In a well-known essay, the great New Testament scholar Ned Stonehouse, of Westminster Seminary, defended the view that these elders are "celestial beings of a rank superior to the angels in general, like the cherubim and seraphim of the Old Testament if they are not to be identified specifically with them."[13] Despite Stonehouse's masterful defense of his position, it rests on an assumption about the text that is certainly incorrect, and thus his interpretation is seriously astray. (More on this textual issue, and Stonehouse's opinion, will be covered below, in the discussion of 5:9).

On the other hand, there are cogent reasons for understanding these elders as representatives of the Church in heaven (or, as St. John progressively unfolds throughout his prophecy, the earthly Church that worships in heaven). First, the mere name **elders** would indicate that these beings represent the Church, rather than a class of angels. Nowhere else in the Bible is the term *elder* given to anyone but men, and from earliest times it has stood for those who have rule and representation within the Church (see Ex. 12:21; 17:5-6; 18:12; 24:9-11; Num. 11:16-17; 1 Tim. 3:1-7; Tit. 1:5-9; Heb. 13:17; James 5:14-15). Thus, the elders in Revelation would appear, at face value, to be representatives of God's people, the senate sitting in council around their bishop.

This consideration is reinforced by a second observation about these elders: They are seen sitting on **thrones**. We have already been told in this prophecy that Christians are reigning with Christ (1:6), that they wear crowns (2:10; 3:11), that they have been granted kingly authority with Him over the nations (2:26-27), that apostates will be forced to bow before them (3:9), and that they are seated with Christ on His Throne (3:21). Now, in chapter 4, we see elders seated on thrones; is this not a

---

13. Ned B. Stonehouse, "The Elders and the Living-Beings in the Apocalypse," in *Paul Before the Areopagus, and Other New Testament Studies* (Grand Rapids: William B. Eerdmans Publishing Co., 1957), p. 90.

continuation of the teachings already presented?

Third, we should consider the symbolism of the number **twenty-four.** In general, since twenty-four is a multiple of twelve, there is again a *prima facie* reason to assume that this number has something to do with the Church. *Twelve* is a number Biblically associated with the people of God: Israel was divided into twelve tribes; and even the administration of the New Covenant Church is spoken of in terms of "twelve tribes," because the Church is the New Israel (see Matt. 19:28; Mark 3:14-19; Acts 1:15-26; cf. James 1:1). St. John uses the word *elder* twelve times in Revelation (4:4, 10; 5:5, 6, 7, 11, 14; 7:11, 13; 11:16; 14:3; 19:4). The number *twenty-four* is thus a "double portion" of *twelve.* Multiples of twelve are also built into the symbolic structure of the New Jerusalem, as we read in the final vision of the prophecy (21:12-14):

> It had a great and high wall, with twelve gates, and at the gates twelve angels; and names were written on them, which are those of the twelve tribes of the sons of Israel. . . .
> And the wall of the city had twelve foundation stones, and on them were the twelve names of the twelve apostles of the Lamb.

But the picture of the twenty-four elders is based on something much more specific than the mere notion of multiplying twelve. In the worship of the Old Covenant there were **twenty-four** divisions of priests (1 Chron. 24) and twenty-four divisions of singers in the Temple (1 Chron. 25). Thus, the picture of twenty-four leaders of worship was not a new idea to those who first read the Revelation: It had been a feature of the worship of God's people for over a thousand years.[14] In fact, St. John has brought together two images that support our general conclusion: (1) The elders sit on thrones—they are *kings*; (2) The elders are twenty-four in number—they are *priests.* What St. John sees is simply the Presbytery of Heaven: the representative assembly

---

14. See Alfred Edersheim, *The Temple: Its Ministry and Services as They Were at the Time of Jesus Christ* (Grand Rapids: William B. Eerdmans Publishing Co., 1980), pp. 75, 86ff. Ezekiel saw twenty-five men serving in the Temple: the representatives of the twenty-four courses of the priesthood, plus the High Priest (Ezek. 8:16).

of the Royal Priesthood, the Church.[15]

That these elders are both priests and kings shows that the Aaronic priesthood of the Old Covenant has been superseded and transcended; the New Covenant priesthood, with Jesus Christ as High Priest, is a Melchizedekal priesthood. Thus St. John tells us that these priest-elders are wearing **crowns**, for the crown of the high priest has been given to all. The two independent testimonies from the second century that St. James in Jerusalem and St. John at Ephesus wore the golden crown of the high priest have generally been discounted by modern scholars;[16] but these traditions may reflect the actual practice of the early Church.

This brings us to another point that should be mentioned before we move on. We have already noted (see on 3:20) several problems caused by the rationalistic tendencies of those groups that grew out of the Reformation. Unfortunately, it became common in those same groups to dispense with the elders' robe of office. Though the concern was for "spirituality," the actual effects were to platonize doctrine and worship, and to democratize government and ministry — further steps on the long, dusty road toward Reformed barrenness. As Richard Paquier reminds us, "Color is a teacher through sight, and it creates moods. We misunderstand human nature and the place of perception in our inner life when we downgrade this psychological factor in the worship of the Church."[17] God has created us this way, and the continuing validity of official robes follows properly from the patterns laid down in the Old Testament: The official character of the elder is emphasized by the use of official robes, in the same way that the judges in our culture still wear robes — a practice, incidentally, that grew out of the practice of the Church.

Paquier continues: "It is natural, therefore, that the man

---

15. A further argument for this interpretation will be developed in the discussion of 5:9. We will see that the song of the elders recorded there states clearly that they are among the redeemed — a group that does not include angels (Heb. 2:16). The elders, therefore, must be taken in the usual sense as meaning the representatives of the Church.

16. See Dom Gregory Dix, *The Shape of the Liturgy* (New York: The Seabury Press, [1945] 1982), p. 313; W. H. C. Frend, *The Rise of Christianity* (Philadelphia: Fortress Press, 1984), p. 127.

17. Richard Paquier, *Dynamics of Worship: Foundations and Uses of Liturgy* (Philadelphia: Fortress Press, 1967), p. 143.

who officiates in the worship of the Church be clothed in a manner corresponding to the task assigned to him and expressing visibly what he does. Moreover, whoever leads in the act of worship does not perform as a private party but as a minister of the Church; he is the representative of the community and the spokesman of the Lord. Hence, an especially prescribed vestment, a sort of ecclesiastical 'uniform,' is useful for reminding both the faithful and himself that in this act he is not Mr. So-and-So, but a minister of the Church in the midst of a multitude of others. What was not any less indispensable in ancient times, when the sense of community and of the objectivity of cultic action prevailed, has become in our time a very useful aid, and indeed truly necessary, since individualism and subjectivity have become so deeply rooted in the piety of the Reformed churches."[18]

5-8   St. John describes the heavenly court in terms of the familiar acoustic and visual effects which accompany the Glory-Cloud, as at Sinai (Ex. 19:16-19): **From the Throne proceed flashes of lightning and voices and peals of thunder.** Again, as in 1:4-5, the imagery is shown to be the heavenly original of the Tabernacle structure (Heb. 8:5; 9:23): Like the Lampstand with its seven lamps burning within the Holy Place, there are **seven lamps of fire burning before His Throne,** the seven lamps imaging **the seven Spirits of God,** the Holy Spirit in His sevenfold fulness of activity. Here, again, is the combination of the three aspects of the Glory-Cloud imagery: the *Voice* (v. 1), the radiant *Glory* (v. 3), and the *Spirit* (v. 5).

Then **before the Throne** St. John sees, **as it were, a sea of glass like crystal.** This is another point at which this vision in-

---

18. Ibid., p. 138. As it turned out, some of those Reformation churches that retained the robe chose the black academic gown, perhaps partly in reaction against what were perceived as the excesses of the Roman Church, and in order to emphasize the teaching function of the minister. But, as Paquier points out, "there is not a single reference to black robes in the Bible, whereas white robes and vestments are mentioned many times, either actually or symbolically.

"Indeed, if there is one color that suggests itself as an adequate expression of the Gospel and the evangelical divine service, certainly it is white. In the Bible the color white is the divine color *par excellence* because it symbolizes the holiness and perfection of God (Ps. 104:2; Dan. 7:9; Rev. 1:14; 19:11; 20:11)" (ibid., pp. 139f.).

tersects with that recorded in Ezekiel 1. But the Throne is seen from two different perspectives. Whereas St. John is standing in the heavenly court itself, looking *down* upon the "sea" of glass (which corresponds, in regard to Tabernacle furniture, to the Laver, also called the "sea": Ex. 30:17-21; 1 Kings 7:23-26), Ezekiel is standing at the *bottom* of the Glory-Cloud, looking *up* through its cone, and the "sea" at its top appears as a blue *firmament*[19] above him:

> And as I looked, behold, a storm wind was coming from the north, a great Cloud with fire flashing forth continually and a bright light around it, and in its midst something like glowing metal in the midst of the fire. And within it there were figures resembling four living beings. . . . Now over the heads of the living beings there was something like a firmament, like the awesome gleam of crystal, extended over their heads. . . . And above the expanse that was over their heads there was something resembling a Throne. . . . (Ezek. 1:4-5, 22, 26)

Another similarity to Ezekiel's vision is that St. John sees **four living creatures** standing **in the middle of the Throne and around it,** supporting the Chariot-Throne in its flight (cf. Ps. 18:10), as do the four cherubim in Ezekiel (note that they are both "in the middle" and "around" the Throne; cf. the close connection between the Throne and the living creatures in 5:6). These creatures (not "beasts," as in the King James rendering) are **full of eyes in front and behind,** and appear in the forms of a **Lion,** a **Bull,** a **Man,** and an **Eagle.** A detailed comparison of these verses with Ezekiel 1 and 10 will reveal many interesting parallels as well as differences between the accounts (reference should also be made to the vision of the six-winged seraphim in Isaiah 6:1-4). That there are **four** of them indicates some relationship to the altar-shaped earth (compare the Biblical ideas of four corners of the earth, four winds, four directions, the four rivers from Eden that watered the whole earth, and so on). Michael Wilcock explains: "The cherubs of the Bible are very far from being chubby infants with wings and dimples. They are awesome creatures, visible indications of the presence of God.

---

19. To Moses and the elders of Israel, the firmament-sea appeared as a sapphire-colored (blue) *pavement* (Ex. 24:10).

So when we are told (Ps. 18:10) that the Lord travels both on a cherub and on the wings of the wind, we may begin to see a link between the four living creatures of 4:6 and the four winds of 7:1. We might call these cherub-creatures 'nature,' so long as we remember what nature really is — an immense construction throbbing with the ceaseless activity of God. . . . Perhaps their faces (4:7; Ezek. 1:10) represent his majesty, his strength, his wisdom, and his loftiness, and their numberless eyes his ceaseless watchfulness over every part of his creation. It is appropriate then that there should be four of them, corresponding to the points of the compass and the corners of the earth, and standing for God's world, as the twenty-four elders stand for the Church."[20]

While John Calvin would have agreed with Wilcock, his remarks on the significance of the four faces of the cherubim are even more radical: "By these heads all living creatures were represented to us. . . . These animals comprehend within themselves all parts of the universe by that figure of speech by which a part represents the whole. Meanwhile since angels are living creatures we must observe in what sense God attributes to angels themselves the head of a lion, an eagle, and a man: for this seems but little in accord with their nature. But he could not better express the inseparable connection which exists in the motion of angels and all creatures. . . . We are to understand, therefore, that while men move about and discharge their duties, they apply themselves in different directions to the object of their pursuit, and so also do wild beasts; yet there are angelic motions underneath, so that neither men nor animals move themselves, but their whole vigor depends on a secret inspiration."[21]

As Calvin says a few pages later, with more force, "*all creatures are animated by angelic motion.*"[22] This goes directly

---

20. Michael Wilcock, *I Saw Heaven Opened: The Message of Revelation* (Downers Grove, IL: InterVarsity Press, 1975), p. 64.

21. John Calvin, *Commentaries on the First Twenty Chapters of the Book of the Prophet Ezekiel* (Grand Rapids: Baker Book House, 1979), Vol. 1, pp. 334f.

22. Ibid., p. 340; cf. pp. 65-74, 333-340. Calvin was attacked by his own translator for making these and like statements (see Vol. 1, pp. xxvf.; Vol. 2, pp. 421f., 448-55, 466-68, 473f.) Nevertheless, these thoughts are very carefully worked out in the course of his exposition, and this commentary, which Calvin did not live to finish, represents his mature thought on the subject. It is one of the most fascinating volumes I have ever read, and is a rich storehouse of valuable insights.

counter to humanistic notions of "nature" and "natural law," but it is the Biblical teaching. The reason it sounds strange to us is that our worldview has been permeated by a philosophy that has much in common with ancient Baalism. James B. Jordan has written: "The details of the Baal cult are not of much importance to us now. It is the underlying philosophy of Baalism which is regnant in American education and life today, and which is taught in the science departments of almost all Christian colleges today, and not just in science departments either. Scripture teaches that God sustains life directly, not indirectly. There is no such thing as Nature. God has not given any inherent power of development to the universe as such. God created the universe and all life by immediate *actions*, not by mediate *processes*. When God withdraws His Breath (which is the Holy Spirit, the Lord and Giver of life), death follows immediately (Gen. 7:22). The idea that God wound up the universe and then let it run its course, so that there is such a thing as Nature which has an intrinsic power, is Deism, not Christianity. Theistic evolution is Deism, not Christianity. To the extent to which the processes of Nature replace the acts of God in any system, to that extent the system has become Baalistic."[23]

"Because of the influence of neo-Baalism (secular humanism) in our modern culture, we tend to think that God, when He made the world, installed certain 'natural laws' or processes that work automatically and impersonally. This is a Deistic, not a Christian, view of the world. What we call natural or physical law is actually a rough approximate generalization about the ordinary activity of God in governing His creation. Matter, space, and time are created by God, and are ruled directly and actively by Him. His rule is called 'law.' God almost always causes things to be done the same way, according to covenant regularities (the Christian equivalent of natural laws), which covenant regularities were established in Genesis 8:22. Science and technology are possible because God does not change the rules, so man can confidently explore the world and learn to work it. Such confidence, though, is always a form of faith, faith either in Nature (Baal) and natural law, or faith in God and in the trustworthi-

---

23. James B. Jordan, *Judges: God's War Against Humanism* (Tyler, TX: Geneva Ministries, 1985), pp. 37f.

ness of His commitment to maintain covenant regularities."[24]

There is another aspect of the symbolism connected with the four living creatures that should be mentioned: their correspondence to the signs of the Zodiac. The Biblical writers were familiar with the same system of constellations as that which we know today, except that the name of the Eagle seems to have been usually substituted for that of the Scorpion. The reason for this may be that the ancient association between the Scorpion and the Serpent (cf. Luke 10:17-19) led Biblical writers to substitute the Eagle in its place; some scholars, however, have argued that "in Abraham's day Scorpio was figured as an Eagle," according to the Chaldean system then in vogue.[25] The faces of the cherubim, in both Ezekiel and Revelation, are the middle signs in the four quarters of the Zodiac: the **Lion** is Leo; the **Bull** is Taurus; the **Man** is Aquarius, the Waterer; and the **Eagle**, as we have seen, is "Scorpio." St. John lists them here in counterclockwise order, backward around the Zodiac (probably because he is viewing them fron above, in heaven, rather than from below, on earth); but when he uses them in the structure of his prophecy itself, he lists them in the direct order of the seasons.[26] After the Preamble (chapter 1), the Revelation is divided into four quarters, each "ruled" by one of these creatures. The first quarter (Chapters 2-3) was ruled by Taurus; thus the emphasis on the Seven Stars, on the shoulder of the Bull. The second quarter (Chapters 4-7) is ruled by the figure of "the Lion of the Tribe of Judah," who has conquered to open the sealed Book. The Eagle flies in midheaven with cries of woe throughout the third quarter (Chapters 8-14). And the fourth quarter (Chapters 15-22) is governed by the Man, Aquarius the "Water-Pourer" (cf. the pouring out of the Chalices of wrath, and the River of Life flowing out from the Throne).

There is nothing occult about any of this. Indeed, the Bible strongly condemns all forms of occultism (the desire for esoteric or autonomous wisdom), including astrological occultism

24. Ibid., p. 102. See also John Calvin, *Commentaries on the Last Four Books of Moses* (Grand Rapids: Baker Book House, 1979), Vol. 1, pp. 385-87; *Commentary on a Harmony of the Evangelists* (Grand Rapids: Baker Book House, 1979), Vol. 1, pp. 213-15.

25. Richard Hinckley Allen, *Star Names: Their Lore and Meaning* (New York: Dover Publications, [1899] 1963), p. 57; cf. p. 362.

26. Incidentally, the term *Zodiac* is not an occult word; it simply means *circle*, and refers to the apparent path of the sun through the heavens. The twelve major constellations are the groups of stars arranged along the sun's path.

(Deut. 18:9-13; 2 Kings 23:3-5; Isa. 8:19-20; 44:24-25; 47:8-15).[27] But this does not mean that the constellations themselves are evil, any more than pagan sun-worship prohibits us from seeing the sun as a symbol of Christ (Ps. 19:4-6; Mal. 4:2; Luke 1:78; Eph. 5:14). On the contrary: The constellations were created by God and manifest His glory (Ps. 19:1-6). They are not simply random groups of stars (nothing in God's universe is random, in the ultimate sense); rather, they have been specifically placed there by God (Job 9:7-9; 26:13; 38:31-33; Amos 5:8).[28] The arrangement of the twelve tribes of Israel around the Tabernacle (Num. 2) corresponded to the order of the Zodiac;[29] and, like the cherubim, four of the tribes represented the middle signs of each quarter: Judah was the Lion, Reuben the Man, Ephraim the Bull, and Dan the Eagle.[30] The reason for the correspondences between Israel and the stars is explained by Gordon J. Wenham: "Scripture frequently refers to the celestial bodies as God's heavenly host (e.g. Deut. 4:19), while the armies of Israel are his earthly hosts (e.g. Josh. 5:14 and throughout Num. 1). The earthly tabernacle was a replica of God's heavenly dwelling (Ex. 25:9, 40). Both were attended by the armies of the LORD. Finally, Genesis 37:9 compares Jacob and his sons (the ancestors of the twelve tribes) to the sun, moon, and stars."[31] The most

---

27. The best Christian refutation of the astrological delusion is in St. Augustine's *City of God*, Book V, chapters 1-11.

28. For a study of the relationship of the constellations to the Biblical message, see Joseph A. Seiss, *The Gospel in the Stars* (Grand Rapids: Kregel Publications, [1882] 1972).

29. Or, as good Augustinians, we can say that the Zodiac corresponds to the order of the twelve tribes!

30. See Ernest L. Martin, *The Birth of Christ Recalculated* (Pasadena, CA: Foundation for Biblical Research, second ed., 1980), pp. 167ff.; cf. J. A. Thompson, *Numbers*, in D. Guthrie and J. A. Motyer, eds., *The New Bible Commentary* (Grand Rapids: William B. Eerdmans Publishing Co., third ed., 1970), p. 173.

31. Gordon J. Wenham, *Numbers: An Introduction and Commentary* (Downers Grove, IL: Inter-Varsity Press, 1981), p. 65. Wenham is not referring to the Zodiacal constellations, but to something even more astonishing: the fact that the census figures of the tribes of Israel correspond to the synodic periods of the planets! As Wenham points out, the census numbers "affirm the sacred character of Israel. They remind us that God's promises to Abraham have been fulfilled, and that the holy people of God is called to struggle for him on earth as the stars fight for him in the heavenly places" (ibid.). Wenham's information is based on M. Barnouin, "Les recensements du Livre des Nombres et l'astronomie babylonienne," *Vetus Testamentum* 27, 1977, pp.

famous example of astronomical symbolism in the Bible, of course, is that the birth of the Messiah Himself was announced to the Magi by the stars (Matt. 2:2), as had been foretold (Num. 24:17; Isa. 60:1-3).[32]

St. John next describes the worship carried on by the four living creatures, using a choral section to interpret for us the meaning of the symbols in his vision of the Throne — a device he repeats throughout the book. He draws our attention to the living creatures' **six wings**, in order to associate them with the seraphim of Isaiah's vision:

> In the year of King Uzziah's death, I saw the LORD sitting on a Throne, lofty and exalted, with the train of His robe filling the Temple. Seraphim stood above Him, each having six wings; with two he covered his face, and with two he covered his feet, and with two he flew. And one called to another and said:
> Holy, Holy, Holy, is the LORD of hosts,
> The whole earth is full of His glory. (Isa. 6:1-3)

Similarly, the living creatures in the Revelation have it as their chief end to glorify God and to enjoy Him forever, praising Him — apparently antiphonally, as Isaiah's seraphim did — for His holiness, His almighty power, and His eternity: **Holy, Holy, Holy, is the Lord God, the Almighty, who was and who is and who is to come.** This too has its counterpart in the standard Christian liturgy, in which the *Sanctus* follows the *Sursum Corda*:

> *Officiant*: Therefore with Angels and Archangels, and with all the company of heaven, we laud and magnify Thy glorious Name; evermore praising Thee and saying,
> *All*: HOLY, HOLY, HOLY, Lord God of Sabaoth; Heaven and earth are full of Thy glory; Hosanna in the highest!

9-11   But the heavenly praise does not end with the song of the living creatures; for **when** they **give glory and honor and thanks** to God, **the twenty-four elders** join in with antiphonal (or responsive) praise themselves. They **will fall down before**

280-303. This paper is available in English translation from Geneva Ministries, P.O. Box 131300, Tyler, TX 75713.
32. See Martin, *The Birth of Christ Recalculated*, pp. 4-25.

Him . . . and will worship Him . . . and will cast their crowns before the Throne, acknowledging that their authority and dominion derive from Him. They go on to praise Him for His works in creation and history: **Worthy art Thou, our Lord and God, to receive glory and honor and power; for Thou didst create all things, and because of Thy will they existed, and were created.**

To appreciate the full import of this forthright affirmation of the doctrine of creation, let us contrast it with a statement issued a few years ago by the officers of one of the largest churches in the United States:

IN THE BEGINNING – CHOICE

In the beginning God created choice. Before God made anything – earth, sky, or man – he had already made up his mind that man was to have a choice. Not limited choice like what color socks to wear today. God gave man complete power of selection, so complete that man could choose – or reject – God. God placed himself in a rather risky position when he armed man with such a tool. He gave man a weapon to use against God.

Can you imagine something you've made saying, "I don't want you, not even for a friend." God gave man that very option, even though he knew what man's choice would be. God knew that his creation would turn away from him, hate him. But he also realized there is no better way to prove love than by risking the alternative of rejection. Genuine love requires decision, because genuine love cannot be demanded, ordered, or even regulated. It must be voluntary.

This tells us something about God. God doesn't do things just for kicks. He must have felt, in some sense, a need of being loved. Do you think it is fair to conclude that God "needs" us? I think so. But he never downgrades the caliber of his love by trying to force us to love him. . . .[33]

Speaking charitably, this is blasphemous nonsense. The only honest thing about it is its lack of Bible references. There are many objectionable points we could consider, but the main one for our purposes is the issue of God's sovereignty and independence. Did God *need* to create? Is God lonely? Does He stand in need of His creation? Let the Scriptures speak:

---

33. Leaflet published c. 1978 by a church in Santa Ana, California, advertising its Saturday Night Concerts.

All the nations are as nothing before Him; they are regarded by Him as less than nothing and meaningless. (Isa. 40:17)

I am God, and there is no other; I am God, and there is no one like Me, declaring the end from the beginning, and from ancient times things which have not been done, saying, My purpose will be established, and I will accomplish all My good pleasure. (Isa. 46:9-10)

The God who made the world and all things in it, since He is Lord of heaven and earth, does not dwell in temples made with hands; neither is He served by human hands, as though He needed anything, since He Himself gives to all life and breath and all things. (Acts 17:24-25)[34]

In their divinely sanctioned worship, the elders have proclaimed the truth: The creation exists, not because God needed to create, or is dependent upon His creation in any way, but simply because it was His *will* to create; it *pleased* Him to do so. God is sovereign, utterly independent from the creation. The Scriptural distinction between the Creator and the creature is absolute.

The heavenly worship service here shows us what God wants in earthly worship. First, *worship must be corporate*. Biblical worship is not individualistic, quietistic, or solely internal. This is not to say that there is no place for private worship; but it does mean that the Biblical emphasis on corporate worship is a far cry from the bastardized "worship" of many evangelicals, who see individual worship as having a priority over corporate worship, and who even conceive of corporate worship as simply an aggregation of individual worshipers.[35] Another forgotten aspect of the need for corporate worship is the fact that the so-called "worship services" in modern churches are, in reality, either lecture halls or three-ring circus entertainments. In both cases there are star performers, and there are spectators — but the

---

34. One further point should receive at least a notice in a footnote: Is it true, as the pamphlet alleges, that "genuine love cannot be demanded, ordered, or even regulated"? See Deut. 6:5-6; Matt. 22:37-40; Eph. 5:25; 1 John 4:19.

35. One example of this from the Reformed camp, among many that could be cited, is B. M. Palmer, *The Theology of Prayer* (Sprinkle Publications, [1894] 1980). This lengthy (352 pp.) work, which purports to provide "a full articulation of prayer in the system of grace," is wholly concerned with individual devotions alone; it does not mention corporate prayer even once.

Church, *as the Church*, is not worshiping corporately. In contrast, the pattern of Biblical worship is the corporate worship service, with full participation among the united members of the congregation, demonstrating a harmony of unity and diversity.

Second, *worship must be responsorial.* We will see more of this as we proceed through the Book of Revelation—which is about worship as much as anything else—but this has already been the case with the passage we have just studied. The elders and the four living creatures are shown singing musical responses back and forth, carrying on a dialogue. And, in the worship of the Church on earth, that is what we do (or should do) also. We respond liturgically to the reading of Scripture, to the prayers, to the singing of Psalms and hymns, to the teaching, and to the Sacraments. For this is what we see in heavenly worship, and our worship should be structured as far as possible in imitation of the heavenly pattern, according to the prayer Christ taught us: "Thy will be done on earth as it is in heaven" (Matt. 6:10).

Third, *worship must be orderly.* The elders and the living creatures do not interrupt each other or attempt to upstage one another. While worship should be *corporate*, involving the entire Church, it must not be *chaotic*. A basic standard for worship is laid down in 1 Cor. 14:40: "Let everything be done decently and in order." Charismatics tend to have certain correct instincts—that worship should include the whole congregation —but their actual practice tends toward confusion and disorder, with everyone *individually* "worshiping" all at once. The solution, recognized in both Old and New Testaments, and by the Church throughout history, is to provide a common liturgy, with formal prayers and responses, so that the people may intelligently worship together in a manner that is both corporate and orderly.

Biblical public worship is very different from private or family worship; it is radically different from a mere Bible study group, as important as that may be. The Sunday worship of the Church is qualitatively unique: It is God's people coming into the palace for a formal ceremony before the Throne, an official audience with the King. We come to confess our faith and allegiance, to take solemn oaths, to receive forgiveness, to offer up prayers, to be instructed by God's officers, to eat at His table,

163

and to render thanksgiving for all His benefits; and we are to respond to all of this with music and singing. All of this is *corporate*, and that necessarily means *liturgy*. This may mean certain complex and involved changes in our habits and patterns of worship. But God should have nothing less than the best. He is the King, and worship means serving Him.

5

CHRISTUS VICTOR

The Lamb and the Book (5:1-14)

1 And I saw in the right hand of Him who sat on the Throne a Book written on the front and on the back, sealed up with seven seals.

2 And I saw a strong angel proclaiming with a loud voice, Who is worthy to open the Book and to break its seals?

3 And no one in heaven, or on the earth, or under the earth, was able to open the Book, or to look into it.

4 And I began to weep greatly, because no one was found worthy to open the Book, or to look into it;

5 and one of the elders says to me, Stop weeping; behold, the Lion from the tribe of Judah, the Root of David, has conquered so as to open the Book and its seven seals.

6 And I saw in the middle of the Throne and of the four living creatures, and in the middle of the elders, a Lamb standing, as if slain, having seven horns and seven eyes, which are the seven Spirits of God, sent out into all the earth.

7 And He came, and He took it out of the right hand of Him who sat on the Throne.

8 And when He had taken the Book, the four living creatures and the twenty-four elders fell down before the Lamb, having each one a harp, and golden bowls full of incense, which are the prayers of the saints.

9 And they sing a New Song, saying:
Worthy art Thou to take the Book, and to break its seals; for Thou wast slain, and didst purchase us for God with Thy blood out of every tribe and tongue and people and nation.

10 And Thou hast made them to be kings and priests to our God; and they will reign upon the earth.

11 And I looked, and I heard as it were the voice of many

165

angels around the Throne and the living creatures and the
elders; and the number of them was myriads of myriads,
and thousands of thousands,

12 saying with a loud voice:
Worthy is the Lamb that was slain to receive power
and riches and wisdom and might and honor and glory
and blessing.

13 And every created thing which is in heaven and on the earth
and under the earth and on the sea, and all things in them, I
heard saying:
To Him who sits on the Throne, and to the Lamb, be
blessing and honor and glory and dominion forever
and ever. Amen.

14 And the four living creatures kept saying, Amen. And the
elders fell down and worshiped.

1-4 St. John sees the One sitting on the Throne holding **a
Book . . . sealed with seven seals.** As Theodor Zahn observed,
the seven seals indicate that this document is a testament. While
this is not the entire explanation, it is important for a proper understanding of the Book. Zahn wrote: "The word *biblion* [book]
itself permits of many interpretations, but for the readers of
that time it was designated by the seven seals on its back beyond
possibility of mistake. Just as in Germany before the introduction of money-orders everybody knew that a letter sealed with
five seals contained money, so the most simple member of the
Asiatic churches knew that a *biblion* made fast with seven seals
was a testament. When a testator dies the testament is brought
forward, and when possible opened in the presence of the seven
witnesses who sealed it; i.e., it was unsealed, read aloud, and executed. . . . The document with seven seals is the symbol of the
promise of a future kingdom. The disposition long ago occurred
and was documented and sealed, but it was not yet carried out."[1]

The Book was also **written on the front and on the back.**
Any Christian reader[2] would immediately have understood the

---

1. Theodor Zahn, *Introduction to the New Testament*, Vol. III, pp. 393f.;
quoted in G. R. Beasley-Murray, *The Book of Revelation* (Grand Rapids:
William B. Eerdmans Publishing Co., revised ed., 1978), p. 121.

2. In saying this, I am assuming that the average Christian of the first century had more sense than the average commentator of the twentieth. There is
hardly a single commentary that even gives the Ten Commandments a passing
glance in this connection.

significance of this description, for it is based on the description of the Ten Commandments. The two tablets of the Testimony, which were *duplicate copies,*[3] were inscribed on both front and back (Ex. 32:15). An analogue of this is found in the suzerainty treaties of the Ancient Near East: A victorious king (the suzerain) would impose a treaty/covenant upon the conquered king (the vassal) and all those under the vassal's authority. Two copies of the treaty were drawn up (as in modern contracts), and each party would place his copy of the contract in the house of his god, as a legal document testifying to the transaction. In the case of Israel, of course, the LORD was both Suzerain and God; so both copies of the Covenant were placed in the Tabernacle (Ex. 25:16, 21; 40:20; Deut. 10:2).

Meredith Kline explains: "The purpose of Israel's copy of the covenant was that of a documentary witness (Deut. 31:26). It was witness to and against Israel, reminding of obligations sworn to and rebuking for obligations violated, declaring the hope of covenant beatitude and pronouncing the doom of the covenant curses. The public proclamation of it was designed to teach the fear of the Lord to all Israel, especially to the children (Deut. 31:13; cf. Ps. 78:5ff.). . . . Considered in relation to the divine oath and promise, Yahweh's duplicate table of the covenant served a purpose analogous to that of the rainbow in his covenant with Noah (Gen. 9:13-16). Beholding this table, he remembered his oath to his servants and faithfully brought to pass the promised blessing."[4]

We have seen that St. John has organized this prophecy in terms of the established covenant structure. More than this, much of the specific information in Revelation has indicated that the idea of covenant is central to its message. The book presents itself from the outset as part of the Canon, primarily written to be read in the liturgy (1:3). Tabernacle imagery is used in the opening Doxology (1:4-5), and the Church is declared to be constituted as the new Kingdom of priests, as Israel had been

---

3. See Meredith G. Kline, *Treaty of the Great King: The Covenant Structure of Deuteronomy* (Grand Rapids: William B. Eerdmans Publishing Co., 1963), pp. 13ff.; idem, *The Structure of Biblical Authority* (Grand Rapids: William B. Eerdmans Publishing Co., second ed., 1975), pp. 113ff.

4. Kline, *Treaty of the Great King,* pp. 21, 24; *The Structure of Biblical Authority,* pp. 123f., 127.

at Sinai (1:6). The theme of the book, stated in 1:7, is Christ's coming in the Glory-Cloud; then, almost immediately, St. John uses three words that almost always occur in connection with covenant-making activity: *Spirit, Day*, and *Voice* (1:10). The following vision of Christ as the glorious High Priest (1:12-20) combines many images from the Old Testament – the Cloud, the Day of the LORD, the Angel of the LORD, the Creator and universal Sovereign, the Son of Man/Second Adam, the Conqueror of the nations, the Possessor of the Church – all of which are concerned with the prophecies of the coming of the New Covenant. The vision is followed by Christ's own message to the churches, styled as a recounting of the history of the Covenant (Chapters 2-3). Then, in Chapter 4, St. John sees the Throne, supported by the Cherubim and surrounded by the royal priesthood, all singing God's praises to the accompaniment of Sinai-like lightning and voices and thunder. We should not be surprised to find this magnificent array of covenant-making imagery culminating in the vision of a testament/treaty document, written on front and back, in the hand of Him who sits on the Throne. The Book is nothing less than the Testament of the resurrected and ascended Christ: the New Covenant.

But the coming of the New Covenant implies the passing away of the Old Covenant, and the judgment of apostate Israel. As we saw in the Introduction, the Biblical prophets spoke in terms of the covenantal treaty structure, acting as prosecuting attorneys on behalf of the divine Suzerain, bringing covenant lawsuit against Israel. The imagery of the document inscribed on both sides is used in the prophecy of Ezekiel, on which St. John has modeled his prophecy. Ezekiel tells of receiving a scroll containing a list of judgments against Israel:

> Then He said to me, "Son of man, I am sending you to the sons of Israel, to a rebellious people who have rebelled against Me; they and their fathers have transgressed against Me to this very day. . . ." Then I looked, and behold, a hand was extended to me; and lo, a Book was in it. When He had spread it out before me, it was written on the front and back; and written on it were lamentations, mourning and woe. (Ezek. 2:3-10)

As St. John sees the opening of the New Covenant, therefore, he will also see the curses of the Old Covenant fulfilled on the apostate Covenant people. This conclusion becomes clearer as we look at the overall movement of the prophecy. The Seven Seals of the Book are broken in order to reveal the Book's contents; but the breaking of the Seventh Seal initiates the sounding of the Seven Trumpets (8:1-2). The final vision of the Trumpets-section closes with a horrifying scene of a great Vintage, in which human "grapes of wrath" are trampled and the whole Land is flooded with a torrent of blood (14:19-20). This leads directly into the final section of Revelation, in which St. John sees the blood from the Winepress being poured out from the Seven Chalices of wrath (16:1-21). It would seem, therefore, that we are meant to understand the Seven Chalices as the content of the Seventh Trumpet, "the last Woe" to fall upon the Land (cf. 8:13; 9:12; 11:14-15; 12:12). All of these—Seals, Trumpets, and Chalices—are the contents of the seven-sealed Book, the New Covenant.

But there is a crisis: **No one** in all of creation—**in heaven, or on the earth, or under the earth**—is **able** (or, as St. John explains, **worthy) to open the Book, or to look into it.** No one can fulfill the conditions required of the Mediator of the New Covenant. All previous mediators—Adam, Moses, David, and the rest—had ultimately proved inadequate for the task. No one could take away sin and death; for all have sinned, and continually fall short of the Glory of God (Rom. 3:23). The sacrifice of animals could not really take away sins, for such a thing is *impossible* (Heb. 10:4); and the high priest who offered up the sacrifices was a sinner himself, "beset with weakness" (Heb. 5:1-3; 7:27) and having to be replaced after his death (7:23). No one could be found to guarantee a better covenant. With the prophetic yearning and sadness of the Old Covenant Church, St. John **began to weep greatly.** The New Covenant had been offered by the One sitting on the Throne, but no one was worthy to act on behalf of both God and man to ratify the Covenant. The seven-sealed Book would remain locked.

5-7 St. John is comforted by **one of the elders,** who says (as it reads literally): **Stop weeping; behold, He has conquered!** The Church thus preaches the Gospel to St. John; and it seems as if the elder is so excited about his message that he blurts out the climax before he even explains *who* has conquered. He goes on to describe Christ the Conqueror: **the Lion from the tribe of**

Judah, the strong and powerful fulfillment of Jacob's ancient prophecy to his fourth son:

> You are a lion's cub, O Judah;
> You return from the prey, my son.
> Like a lion he crouches and lies down,
> Like a lioness — who dares to rouse him?
> The scepter will not depart from Judah,
> Nor the ruler's staff from between his feet,
> Until He comes to whom it belongs,
> And the obedience of the nations is His. (Gen. 49:9-10)

It was David, the conquering Lion of Judah of the Old Covenant, to whom God revealed both the plan of the Temple (1 Chron. 28:11-19) and the plan of the everlasting covenant, the "Charter for Humanity" by which the coming Priest-King would bring the blessing of Abraham to all nations (2 Sam. 7:18-29; 23:2-5; 1 Chron. 17:16-27; Ps. 16; 110; Acts 2:25-36).[5] At last David's greater Son came and conquered, establishing everlasting dominion and opening the Covenant. Embodying and fulfilling all its promises, He is the One "to whom it belongs."

Christ is also called **the Root of David** — a strange expression, to our way of thinking. We can more easily understand Isaiah's term: "a shoot from the stem of Jesse" (Isa. 11:1). As a descendant of Jesse and David, Jesus could be called a "branch" (Jer. 23:5; Zech. 3:8); but how could He be called the **Root**? Our perplexity originates in our non-Biblical views of how history works. We are accustomed to thinking of history as if it were a cosmic Rube Goldberg machine: Trip a lever at one end, and a series of domino-like thingamajigs and whatsits bang into each other, at long last producing a whatchamacallit at the far end of the machine. By pure cause and effect, each event causes other events, in direct chronological succession.

Now, this is true — but it is not the whole truth. In fact, taken alone and autonomously, it is not true at all, for such a thesis is evolutionary in its assumptions, rather than Biblical. History is

---

5. See Walter C. Kaiser Jr., "The Blessing of David: The Charter for Humanity," in John H. Skilton ed., *The Law and the Prophets: Old Testament Studies Prepared in Honor of Oswald Thompson Allis* (Presbyterian and Reformed Publishing Co., 1974), pp. 298-318.

CHRISTUS VICTOR 5:5-7

not simply a matter of the past causing the future; it is also true that *the future causes the past*, as R. J. Rushdoony explains: "The movement of time, according to the Bible, is from eternity, since it is created by God and moves out of and in terms of His eternal decree. . . . Because time is predestined, and because its beginning and end are already established, time does not develop in evolutionary fashion from past to present to future. Instead, it unfolds from future to present to past."[6]

A simple illustration might help us understand this. Let us say someone finds you packing a sack lunch on a warm Saturday morning, and asks the reason for it. You answer, "Because I'm going to have a picnic at the park today." What has happened? In a sense, *the future*—the planned picnic—*has determined the past*. Because you wanted a picnic at the park, you *then* planned a lunch. Logically, the picnic preceded, and caused, the making of the lunch, even though it followed it chronologically. In the same way, God desired to glorify Himself in Jesus Christ; therefore He created Jesse and David, and all the other ancestors of Christ's human nature, in order to bring His Son into the world. The **Root** of David's very existence was the Son of David, Jesus Christ. The "effect" determined the "cause"![7]

The Lord Jesus Christ is thus presented in the most radical way possible as the Center of all history, the divine Root as well as the Branch, the Beginning and the End, Alpha and Omega. And it is as the conquering Lion and the determining Root that He has prevailed **so as to open the Book and its seven seals**.

St. John turns to see the One who is described in this way— and, instead of seeing a Lion or a Root, he sees **a Lamb standing** before **the Throne**. This is the pattern we first noticed at 1:11, in which John first *hears,* then *sees.* Obviously, the One St. John heard about in verse 5 is identical with the One he now beholds in verse 6. The Lion is the Lamb.

---

6. Rousas John Rushdoony, *The Biblical Philosophy of History* (Nutley, NJ: Presbyterian and Reformed Publishing Co., 1969), p. 11; cf. Rushdoony, *The One and the Many*, p. 145; St. Augustine, *The City of God*, Bk. XII, Chap. 13-15; Nathan R. Wood, *The Secret of the Universe* (Grand Rapids: William B. Eerdmans Publishing Co., [1936] 1955), pp. 43-45.

7. One of the clearest statements of this idea is in Gordon H. Clark, *Biblical Predestination* (Nutley, NJ: Presbyterian and Reformed Publishing Co., 1969), esp. pp. 18-30.

In what sense is Jesus Christ a Lamb? The passage is not referring to Jesus in His Nature — He is not "lamblike" in the sense of being gentle, sweet, or mild, as some would falsely understand this text.[8] Christ is called a Lamb, not in view of His Person (which pop-theology degrades to the modern concept of "personality" anyway), but in view of His *work*. He is the Lamb that was **slain**, "who takes away the sin of the world" (John 1:29). Thus, the center of history is *the finished, sacrificial work of Christ*. The foundation for His mediatorial kingship (Christ as the Lion) is His mediatorial atonement (Christ as the Lamb). It is because of His sacrifice that He has been exalted to the place of supreme rule and authority. Christ has attained victory through His sacrificial suffering and death on our behalf.

St. John emphasizes this by his specific language: **a Lamb standing, as if slain.** Philip Carrington suggests that the Greek word *standing* (*hestēkos*) is "a rough Greek translation of the Hebrew Tamid, which means 'standing' or 'continual,' and refers to the daily burnt-offering in the Temple. It is the regular technical term, and forms the title of the section of the Mishnah which deals with that sacrifice. The Lamb of the Tamid is an intelligible expression, which might well have been turned into the *Arnion Hestēkos* of the Greek. The Greek word *Hestēkos* does not mean 'continual,' but only 'standing' in the literal sense; but it might be a rough equivalent like *Christos* (smeared), which stands for Messiah. *Arnion Hestēkos* might thus be 'baboo' Greek for Lamb of the Sacrifice.

"The word *Arnion* has also aroused discussion. Our Lord is called Lamb of God in the fourth gospel (1:29), just as he is here called Lamb of the Tamid; but the two words are different, *Arnion* here and *Amnos* in the gospel. It is possible that while *Amnos* is the more common and natural word for Lamb, *Arnion Hestēkos* might be a technical term of the Jewish Temple. . . ."[9]

St. John continues the symbolic imagery: Christ the Lamb has **seven horns.** The horn in Scripture is an understandable symbol for strength and power (cf. Ps. 75:10); more than this,

8. Hal Lindsey speaks in this connection of Christ's "lamblike meekness and gentleness" in *There's a New World Coming: A Prophetic Odyssey* (Eugene, OR: Harvest House Publishers, 1973), p. 94.

9. Philip Carrington, *The Meaning of The Revelation* (London: SPCK, 1931), pp. 119f.

however, the thinking of the Biblically literate reader would have been jogged into recalling the seven rams' horns that were used to herald the judgment of God on His enemies and the victory and salvation of the covenant people in the historic battle of Jericho (Josh. 6:2-5). In the same way, the great Sacrificial Lamb, to whom all other sacrifices pointed, now provides power and strength and victory for His people in their war for dominion over the earth. It is the definitive victory of Christ that guarantees the Church's progressive victories and ultimate dominion of all the territory assigned to her — which, in this age, is not merely Palestine but the entire world (Matt. 28:18-20).

The Lamb also has **seven eyes, which are the seven Spirits of God sent out into all the earth** (cf. Zech. 6:5). In order to understand this, we have to go back to Genesis 1, where we find the first mention of the **Spirit**: hovering over the **earth**, brooding over it, forming and filling it, calling forth life. As the creation progresses, the Spirit performs **seven** acts of *seeing* — the sevenfold Spirit's **eyes**, if you will. Seven times we are told that "God *saw* that it was good" (Gen. 1:4, 10, 12, 18, 21, 25, 31). As God was creating His world, He was also judging it, assessing and approving it, until the final, climactic judgment was made as the prelude to the beginning of the seventh day.[10] Here in Revelation Christ is presented as the Center of history, the Overcomer who receives the New Covenant for men; and, as such, He is seen to be both Creator and Judge, with fullness of knowledge through His immeasurable possession of the seeing and discerning Spirit (Jn. 3:34). Even in the beginning, when the Spirit went forth to fashion the earth and to assess it, He "proceeded from the Father *and the Son*." Christ's understanding of creation and history originates not from history itself but from the fact that He is both the Creator and Redeemer of the world. Thus, on the basis of His Person, His work, and His exalted position as Savior and World-Ruler, Jesus Christ ascended to heaven, stepped forward to the Throne of His Father, and **took** the **Book out of the right hand of Him who sat upon the Throne**. This is how the prophet Daniel described it:

---

10. See Meredith G. Kline, *Images of the Spirit* (Grand Rapids: Baker Book House, 1980), pp. 107ff.

I kept looking in the night visions,
And behold, with the clouds of heaven
One like a Son of Man was coming,
And He came up to the Ancient of Days
And was presented before Him.
And to Him was given dominion,
Glory and a Kingdom,
That all the peoples, nations, and men of every language
Might serve Him.
His dominion is an everlasting dominion
Which will not pass away;
And His Kingdom is one
Which will not be destroyed. (Dan. 7:13-14)

The central message of the Bible is salvation through Jesus Christ, the Mediator of the New Covenant. Apart from His work, through which He acquired and eternally possesses the Covenant, there is no hope for mankind. He has overwhelmingly conquered so as to open the Treaty of the Great King; and through Him we too are more than conquerors.

8-10   At this, the company of saints and angels in heaven burst forth into praise: **The four living creatures and the twenty-four elders fell down before the Lamb,** prostrating themselves in adoration as they prepare to worship Him in song, **having each one a harp.** Another important aspect of the scene involves the **golden bowls full of incense, which are** (i.e., which represent, or set forth symbolically) **the prayers of the saints** (cf. Ps. 141:2; Luke 1:10). Geerhardus Vos explained: "The symbolism lies partly in that the smoke is, as it were, the refined quintessence of the offering, partly in the ascending manner of the same. That the altar of incense has its place nearest to the curtain before the 'holy of holies' signifies the religious specificness of prayer as coming nearest to the heart of God. The offering was of a perpetual character. The notion of the grateful smell of the burning incense in the nostrils of Jehovah is somewhat removed from our own taste of religious imagery, but should not on that account be overlooked, since it is not in the slightest degree felt to be inappropriate by the Hebrew sense of religion."[11]

---

11. Geerhardus Vos, *Biblical Theology: Old and New Testaments* (Grand Rapids: William B. Eerdmans Publishing Co., 1948), p. 168.

The living creatures and the elders then sing **a New Song**, and again a choral section is used to explain the symbols. Indeed, our interpretation is confirmed by the expression St. John uses here. The **New Song** is mentioned seven times in the Old Testament (Ps. 33:3; 40:3; 96:1; 98:1; 144:9; 149:1; Isa. 42:10), always in reference to God's redemptive/creative acts in history. The New Song celebrates the making of the Covenant and foretells the coming of Christ to bring salvation to the nations and universal victory to the godly:

O sing to the Lord a New Song,
For He has done wonderful things,
His right hand and His holy arm have gained the victory for Him.
The Lord has made known His salvation:
He has revealed his righteousness in the sight of the nations.
He has remembered His lovingkindness and His faithfulness to
　the house of Israel;
All the ends of the earth have seen the salvation of our God.
(Ps. 98:1-3)

Sing to the Lord a New Song,
Sing His praise from the end of the earth! . . .
Let them give glory to the Lord,
And declare His praise in the coastlands.
The Lord will go forth like a warrior,
He will arouse His zeal like a man of war.
He will utter a shout, yes, He will raise a war cry.
He will prevail against His enemies. (Isa. 42:10-13)

Each time a new stage in redemptive history is reached in the Bible (such as the Exodus, the founding of the theocratic kingdom, etc.), there is a corresponding period of canonical revelation; as Geerhardus Vos said, "Revelation follows events."[12] More specifically, the appearance of canonical Scripture attends God's victorious redemption of His people, as Meredith G. Kline points out with regard to "the birth of the Bible": "In the midst of a fallen world and in the face of Satanic hostility manifested in various historical guises, an elect people of God could not attain to kingdom status apart from redemptive judgments delivering them from the power of the adversary. Only when the

---

12. Ibid., p. 203.

175

Lord God had accomplished this soteric triumph would the way be prepared for him to promulgate his kingdom-treaty, setting his commandments among his elect people and ordering their kingdom existence under the dominion of his sovereign will. . . .

"Covenantal revelation was already addressed to Abraham, Isaac, and Jacob, with their households, offering them the kingdom in promise. But Scripture required for its appearance more than merely the promise of a kingdom. It was necessary that the promise and oath given to the patriarchs be fulfilled; the chosen people must actually attain to nationhood. Not until God had created the kingdom-community of Israel brought forth from Pharaoh's tyranny to the Sinai assembly could he issue canonical covenant of the biblical type. The appearance of canonical Scripture thus had to await the exodus victory of Yahweh. That victory signalized the fulness of time for the birth of God's treaty Word.

"The scheduling of the nativity of the written Word at precisely that historical juncture points us to the peculiar quality of canonical Scripture. Originating as it does in consequence of an awesome display of Yahweh's power in salvation and judgment, in accordance with prophetic promises given to the patriarchs, Scripture from the outset bears the character of a word of triumphal fulfillment. It is the incontestable declaration that the name of Israel's God is Yahweh, mighty Lord of the covenant. Although the Mosaic kingdom established at Sinai was itself still only provisional and promissory in relation to the Messianic realities of the New Testament age, yet unmistakably the Old Testament Word of God which heralded the Israelite kingdom was for the pre-Messianic stage of redemptive history a word of promises manifestly fulfilled and of Yahweh's triumphant kingship decisively and dramatically displayed. From its first emergence in the sequel of victory, therefore, canonical Scripture confronts men as a divine word of triumph."[13]

What Sinai showed in provisional form, Calvary and Olivet revealed definitively: the victorious redemption of God's elect people in the New Covenant, when the Lion of the Tribe of

---

13. Meredith G. Kline, *The Structure of Biblical Authority* (Grand Rapids: William B. Eerdmans Publishing Co., second ed., 1975), pp. 77ff.

Judah conquered so as to open the Book. And because Jesus Christ obtained the New Covenant for His people, He commissioned the writing of the canonical Scriptures of the New Testament as the decisive and dramatic display of His triumphant kingship, His "divine word of triumph."

Along with the new written revelation, this new and final stage of redemptive history brought by the New Covenant called for **a New Song**, a new liturgical response by God's worshiping assembly. Just as the previous epochs in covenantal history evoked a New Song,[14] the definitive establishment of the new nation with its new kingdom-treaty necessitated a new worship, one that would be a true fulfillment of the old, a transcending of all that it foreshadowed. The new wine of the New Covenant could not be contained in the wineskins of the Old; the new redemption required for its full and proper expression the New Song of the Christian liturgy. This is exactly what the New Song proclaims as its basis:

> Kingdom-Treaty: **Worthy art Thou to take the Book, and to break its seals.**
>
> Redemption: **For Thou wast slain, and didst purchase us for God with Thy blood.**
>
> Nationhood: **Thou hast made them to be a Kingdom and priests to our God.**
>
> Dominion: **And they will reign on the earth.**

One aspect of the Song has raised a serious interpretive issue: As we noted at 4:4, Ned Stonehouse (with a host of others) held that **the twenty-four elders** are a class of angels. The basis for Stonehouse's opinion boils down to the fact that one Greek New Testament manuscript contains a textual variation which, he claimed, indicates this. Whereas most manuscripts read that Christ purchased **us**, the variant reading preferred by Stonehouse says that Christ purchased *men*. The difference, obviously, would be that the singers in the first case are definitely

---

14. Songs produced by the Exodus redemption include those recorded in Ex. 15, Deut. 32, and Ps. 90; the new organization of the theocratic kingdom under a human ruler, and the events leading to the establishment of the Temple, resulted in the Psalter (the definitive collection of "new songs" under the Old Covenant).

177

identified as among the redeemed, while the singers in the second reading are not necessarily including themselves among those purchased by Christ's blood.

Unfortunately for Stonehouse's interpretation, there are two facts which, at the outset, argue against it. In the first place, even if all the manuscripts contained Stonehouse's preferred reading, it would not prove his case; Stonehouse was simply making an assumption that *may* (but does not necessarily) follow from his premise. (After all, any believer could still pray for "the Church" or "God's people" without excluding himself; the mere fact that the elders thank God for redeeming "men" would not necessarily mean that they are not redeemed themselves.)

Secondly, however, of the hundreds of manuscripts containing the Book of Revelation, only *one* carries this extremely dubious reading. The variant is not found in any "family" of manuscripts, and certainly not in anything that could be called a manuscript "tradition"; it occurs in only one solitary manuscript. To base an interpretation on such a shaky foundation is, to say the least, an exceedingly subjective and precarious method of Bible study.

Without a doubt, the traditional reading (**"us"**) is the true one. But saying this seems to raise two further problems: (1) The four living creatures, who do not seem to represent the Church, are said to be singing this song; (2) the song shifts to the third person between verses 9 and 10. In verse 9 we read: "Thou didst purchase **us**"; and in verse 10 we read: "Thou hast made **them** to be kings . . . and **they** will reign." Actually, these two problems solve each other. It is apparently an example of what we have already seen in this book, and what will become more familiar as we progress through it: *antiphonal praise*. This pattern of choral responses continues in this chapter (cf. v. 11-14). A probable outline of this portion of the heavenly liturgy would be as follows:

Elders and Living Creatures: **Worthy art Thou to take the Book and to break its seals.**

Elders: **For Thou wast slain, and didst purchase us for God with Thy blood out of every tribe and tongue and people and nation.**

Living Creatures: **And Thou hast made them to be kings and**

178

priests to our God; and they will reign upon the earth.[15]

Christ has purchased His people out of the nations, not only to redeem them from sin, but to enable them to fulfill God's original Dominion Mandate for man. As the Second Adam, Christ sets His New Creation the task Adam forfeited—this time, however, on the unshakeable foundation of His death, resurrection, and ascension. Salvation has a purpose, a saving *to* as well as a saving *from*. Christ has **made** His people **to be kings and priests to our God**, and has guaranteed their destiny: **They will reign upon the earth**. This shows us the direction of history: The redeemed of the Lord, already a nation of kingly priests, are moving toward the complete dominion God had planned as His original program for man. In Adam it had been lost; Jesus Christ, the Second Adam, has redeemed us and restored us to our royal priesthood, so that we will reign **upon the earth**. Through the work of Christ the definitive victory over Satan has been won. We are promised increasing victories, and increasing rule and dominion, as we bring the Gospel and law of the great King to fruition throughout the world.

11-14 In response to the praise of the four living creatures and the twenty-four elders, the entire choir of **angels**, composing **myriads of myriads,**[16] **and thousands of thousands**, joins in **with a loud voice**, proclaiming that **the Lamb that was slain** is, on the basis of His Person and work, **worthy** to inherit all things (the seven enumerated items indicating fullness) in heaven and earth: **power and riches and wisdom and might and honor and glory and blessing**. And, as if in joyful answer to this great declaration of Christ's universal inheritance, the whole (fourfold) creation responds with praise, as a climax to this section of the liturgy. **Every created thing that is a) in heaven and b) on the earth and c) under the earth and d) in the sea, and all things in them**—all of created reality becomes part of the cosmic chorus,

---

15. This outline is also suggested by Moses Stuart, *A Commentary on the Apocalypse*, 2 vols. (Andover: Allen, Morrill and Wardwell, 1845), Vol. 2, p. 134.

16. Literally, a *myriad* is 10,000; but it is often, especially in the plural, used in a more vague sense to mean "a very large number." *Myriads of myriads* obviously means simply "countless thousands."

singing: **To Him who sits on the Throne, and to the Lamb, be a) blessing and b) honor and c) glory and d) dominion forever and ever.** One day, all of creation will acknowledge Christ as Lord (Phil. 2:10-11); in principle, however, this is already established by the sacrifice and victory of the Lamb. Again, St. John has revealed to us the goal of history as the universal recognition of Christ's Lordship and the eternal glory of God through Jesus Christ.

The Church in St. John's day was about to experience a time of severe testing and persecution. Already they were seeing what, in a sane age, could scarcely be imagined: a union between Israel and the antichristian Beast of Rome. These Christians needed to understand history as something not ruled by chance or evil men or even the devil, but ruled instead from God's Throne by Jesus Christ. They needed to see that Christ was reigning *now,* that He had already wrested the world from Satan's grasp, and that even now all things in heaven and earth were bound to acknowledge Him as King. They needed to see themselves in the true light: Not as forgotten troops in a lonely outpost fighting a losing battle, but as kings and priests already, waging war and overcoming, predestined to victory, with the absolute assurance of conquest and dominion with the High King over the earth. They needed the Biblical philosophy of history: that all of history, created and controlled by God's personal and total government, is moving inexorably toward the universal dominion of the Lord Jesus Christ. The new and final age of history has arrived; the New Covenant has come. Behold, He has conquered!

6

IN THE PATH OF THE WHITE HORSE

St. John brings us now to the breaking of the Seven Seals of the Book (six of the Seals are broken in Chapter 6; the Seventh Seal is broken in 8:1, and is connected to the Seven Trumpets). We have seen that the Book represents the treaty document of the New Covenant, the opening of which will result in the destruction of apostate Israel (see on 5:1-4). What then does the breaking of the Seals represent? Some have thought this to signify a chronological reading through the Book, and that the events depicted are in a straight, historical order. This is unlikely for two reasons. First, the Seals seem to be on the *outside edge* of the Book (which is in the form of a scroll): one cannot really begin to read the Book until all the Seals are broken. The Seventh Seal, consisting of a call to action by the blowing of the Seven Trumpets, actually opens the Book so that we may read its contents.

Second, a careful reading of the events shown by each Seal reveals that they are not listed in chronological order. For example, in the Fifth Seal—after all the havoc wreaked by the Four Horsemen—the martyrs calling for judgment are told to wait. But the judgment is immediately poured out in the Sixth Seal, the entire creation "unseam'd from the nave to the chaps." Yet, after all this, God commands the angels to withhold judgment until the servants of God are protected (7:3). Obviously, the Seals are not meant to represent a progressive chronology. It is more likely that they reveal the main ideas of the Book's contents, the major themes of the judgments that came upon Israel during the Last Days, from A.D. 30-70.

R. H. Charles pointed out the close structural similarity between the Six Seals of this chapter and the events of the so-called

Little Apocalypse recorded in the Synoptic Gospels. As his outline (adapted below) demonstrates, "they present practically the same material."[1]

Revelation 6
1. War (v. 1-2)
2. International strife (v. 3-4)
3. Famine (v. 5-6)
4. Pestilence (v. 7-8)
5. Persecution (v. 9-11)
6. Earthquake; De-creation (v. 12-17)

Matthew 24
1. Wars (v. 6)
2. International strife (v. 7a)
3. Famines (v. 7b)
4. Earthquakes (v. 7c)
5. Persecutions (v. 9-13)
6. De-creation (v. 15-31)

Mark 13
1. Wars (v. 7)
2. International strife (v. 8a)
3. Earthquakes (v. 8b)
4. Famines (v. 8c)
5. Persecutions (v. 9-13)
6. De-creation (v. 14-27)

Luke 21
1. Wars (v. 9)
2. International strife (v. 10)
3. Earthquakes (v. 11a)
4. Plagues and famines (v. 11b)
5. Persecution (v. 12-19)
6. De-creation (v. 20-27)

This is very perceptive of Charles, and of the many commentators who have followed his lead. What is astonishing is that they should fail to see St. John's purpose in presenting "the same material" as the Synoptic writers: to prophesy the events leading up to the destruction of Jerusalem. While all readily ad-

---

1. R. H. Charles, *A Critical and Exegetical Commentary on the Revelation of St. John*, 2 vols. (Edinburgh: T. & T. Clark, 1920), Vol. 1, p. 158.

mit that the *Little Apocalypse* is a prophecy against Israel (see Matt. 23:29-39; 24:1-2, 15-16, 34; Mark 13:2, 14, 30; Luke 21:5-6, 20-24, 32), few seem able to make the obvious connection: The *Big Apocalypse* is a prophecy against Israel as well!

The Four Horsemen (6:1-8)

1 And I saw that the Lamb broke one of the Seven Seals, and I heard one of the four living creatures saying as with a voice of thunder: Come!

2 And I looked, and behold, a white horse, and He who sat on it had a Bow; and a crown was given to Him; and He went out conquering, and to conquer.

3 And when He broke the Second Seal, I heard the second living creature saying: Come!

4 And another, a blood-red horse, went out; and to him who sat on it, it was granted to take peace from the Land, and that men should slay one another; and a great sword was given to him.

5 And when He broke the Third Seal, I heard the third living creature saying: Come! And I looked, and behold, a black horse; and he who sat on it had a pair of scales in his hand.

6 And I heard a Voice in the center of the four living creatures saying: A quart of wheat for a denarius, and three quarts of barley for a denarius; and do not harm the oil and the wine.

7 And when He broke the Fourth Seal, I heard the voice of the fourth living creature saying: Come!

8 And I looked, and behold, a green horse; and he who sat on it had the name Death; and Hades was following with him. And authority was given to him over a fourth of the Land, to kill with sword and with famine and with death and by the wild beasts of the Land.

The central Old Testament passage behind the imagery of the "Four Horsemen of the Apocalypse" is Zechariah 6:1-7, which pictures the Four Winds as God's chariots driven by His agents, who go back and forth patrolling the earth. Following and imitating the action of the Spirit (see 5:6), they are God's means of controlling history (see below at 7:1, where the Four Winds are identified with, and controlled by, angels; cf. also Ps. 18:10, where the "wings of the wind" are connected with "cherubs"). Biblical symbolism views the earth (and especially the Land of Israel) as God's four-cornered altar, and thus often represents wide-sweeping, national judgments in a fourfold manner. The Horsemen, therefore, show us God's means of controlling and bringing judgment upon the disobedient nation of Israel.

Milton Terry's comments are helpful: "The true interpretation of these first four seals is that which recognizes them as a symbolic representation of the 'wars, famines, pestilences, and earthquakes' which Jesus declared would be 'the beginning of sorrows' in the desolation of Jerusalem (Matt. 24:6-7; Luke 21:10-11, 20). The attempt to identify each separate figure with one specific event misses both the spirit and method of apocalyptic symbolism. The aim is to give a fourfold and most impressive picture of that terrible war on Jerusalem which was destined to avenge the righteous blood of prophets and apostles (Matt. 23:35-37), and to involve a 'great tribulation,' the like of which had never been before (Matt. 24:21). Like the four successive but closely connected swarms of locusts in Joel 1:4; like the four riders on different colored horses in Zechariah 1:8, 18, and the four chariots drawn by as many different colored horses in Zechariah 6:1-8, these four sore judgments of Jehovah move forth at the command of the four living creatures by the Throne to execute the will of Him who declared the 'scribes, Pharisees, and hypocrites' of His time to be 'serpents and offspring of vipers,' and assured them that 'all these things should come upon this generation' (Matt. 23:33, 36). The writings of Josephus abundantly show how fearfully all these things were fulfilled in the bloody war of Rome against Jerusalem."[2]

Just as important as Zechariah in the background of this passage is the Prayer of Habakkuk (Hab. 3), the traditional synagogue reading for the second day of Pentecost,[3] in which the prophet relates a vision of God coming in judgment, shining like the sun, flashing with lightning (Hab. 3:3-4; cf. Rev. 1:16; 4:5), bringing pestilence and plague (Hab. 3:5; Rev. 6:8), shattering the mountains and collapsing the hills (Hab. 3:6, 10; Rev. 6:14), riding on horses against His enemies (Hab. 3:8, 15; Rev. 6:2,

2. Milton Terry, *Biblical Apocalyptics: A Study of the Most Notable Revelations of God and of Christ in the Canonical Scriptures* (New York: Eaton and Mains, 1898), pp. 329f.

3. M. D. Goulder, *The Evangelists' Calendar: A Lectionary Explanation for the Development of Scripture* (London: SPCK, 1978), p. 177.

4-5, 8), armed with a Bow (Hab. 3:9, 11; Rev. 6:2), extinguishing sun and moon (Hab. 3:11; Rev. 6:12-13) and trampling the nations in His fury (Hab. 3:12; Rev. 6:15). Habakkuk clearly interprets his imagery as a prophecy of the military invasion of Judah by the Chaldeans, God's heathen instruments of divine wrath (Hab. 3:16; cf. 1:5-17). Under similar imagery, St. John portrays Israel's destruction at the hands of the invading Edomite and Roman armies.

1-2 The Book-visions begin, as the Messages did, with Christ holding a cluster of seven in His hand. As **the Lamb** breaks each of the first four **Seals,** St. John hears **one of the four living creatures saying as with a voice of thunder: Come!** This is not spoken as a direction to St. John to "come and see."[4] It is, rather, that each of the living creatures calls forth one of the Four Horsemen. The four corners of the earth, as it were, standing around the altar, are calling for God's righteous judgments to come and destroy the wicked — just as the apostolic Church's characteristic cry for judgment and salvation was *Maranatha! O Lord, Come!* — and bring *Anathema!*[5]

As the first living creature calls, St. John sees **a white horse,** its rider armed for battle, carrying **a Bow.** The Rider is *already victorious*, for **a crown was given to Him** (St. John generally uses the impersonal passive throughout the prophecy to indicate that something is done by God; cf. 6:2, 4, 8, 11; 7:2, 4; 8:2, 3, etc.). Having achieved victory, He rides on to further victories: **He went out conquering, and to conquer.** Amazingly, the run-of-the-mill Dispensational interpretation claims that this rider on the white horse is the Antichrist.[6] Showing where his faith

---

4. Contrary to the reading in the King James Version, which is not supported by most manuscripts.

5. 1 Cor. 16:22 (cf. Rev. 6:10); according to the *Didache* (Ch. 10), *Maranatha* was repeated at the end of the Eucharistic liturgy. If John A. T. Robinson's hypothesis is correct (that the *Didache* was written in A.D. 40-60), this represents the closing prayer of every worship service for decades prior to the Fall of Jerusalem. See his *Redating the New Testament* (Philadelphia: The Westminster Press, 1976), pp. 324-27, 352.

6. This is not true of all Dispensationalists. Among the dissenters on this point I am happy to note Henry Morris, *The Revelation Record* (Wheaton, IL: Tyndale House, 1983), p. 112, and Zane C. Hodges, "The First Horseman of the Apocalypse," *Bibliotheca Sacra* 119 (1962), pp. 324ff.

lies, Hal Lindsey goes all the way and declares that the Antichrist is "the only person who could accomplish all of these feats."[7]

But there are several points about this Rider that demonstrate conclusively that He can be none other than the Lord Jesus Christ. First, He is riding a white horse, as Jesus does in 19:11-16. Second, He carries a Bow. As we have seen, the passage from Habakkuk that forms the basis for Revelation 6 shows the Lord as the Warrior-King carrying a Bow (Hab. 3:9, 11). St. John is also appealing here to Psalm 45, one of the great prophecies of Christ's victory over His enemies, in which the psalmist joyously calls to Him as He rides forth conquering, and to conquer:

> Gird Thy sword on Thy thigh, O Mighty One,
> In Thy splendor and Thy majesty!
> And in Thy majesty ride on victoriously,
> For the cause of truth and meekness and righteousness;
> Let Thy right hand teach Thee awesome things.
> Thine arrows are sharp;
> The peoples fall under Thee;
> Thine arrows are in the heart of the King's enemies.
> (Ps. 45:3-5)

We should ask a rather obvious question at this point — so obvious that we are apt to miss it altogether: *Where did Christ get the Bow?* The answer (as is usually the case) begins in Genesis. When God made the covenant with Noah, He declared that He was no longer at war with the earth, because of the "soothing aroma" of the sacrifice (Gen. 8:20-21); and as evidence of this He unstrung His Bow and hung it up "in the Cloud" for all to see (Gen. 9:13-17). Later, when Ezekiel was "raptured" up to the Throneroom at the top of the Glory-Cloud, he saw the Bow hanging above the Throne (Ezek. 1:26-28); and it was still there when St. John ascended to heaven (Rev. 4:3). But when the Lamb stepped forward to receive the Book from His Father's hand, He also reached up and took down the Bow, to use it in judgment against the apostates of

---

7. *There's a New World Coming: A Prophetic Odyssey* (Eugene, OR: Harvest House Publishers, 1973), p. 103.

Israel. For those who "go on sinning willfully after receiving the knowledge of the truth, there no longer remains a sacrifice for sins, but a certain terrifying expectation of judgment, and the fury of a fire that will consume the adversaries. Anyone who has set aside the Law of Moses dies without mercy on the testimony of two or three witnesses. How much severer punishment do you think he will deserve who has trampled under foot the Son of God, and has regarded as unclean the blood of the covenant by which he was sanctified, and has insulted the Spirit of Grace? For we know Him who said: 'Vengeance is Mine, I will repay.' And again: 'The Lord will judge His people.' It is a terrifying thing to fall into the hands of the living God" (Heb. 10:26-31). It was thus necessary that the first Rider should be seen carrying the Bow of God's vengeance, to signify the unleashing of the Curse upon Israel's ground; for these apostates, the Noachic covenant is undone.

St. John's first readers would immediately have understood his reference to this Rider with the Bow as speaking of Jesus Christ, on the basis of what we have already seen. But, third, there is the fact that the Rider is given a **crown**, and this too agrees with what we know about Christ from Revelation (14:14; 19:11-13).[8] The fourth and final point, however, should render this interpretation completely secure: the Rider goes out **conquering**.[9] This is the very same word in the Greek as was used in the letters to the seven churches for *overcoming* or *conquering* (see Rev. 2:7, 11, 17, 26; 3:5, 12, 21). Consider how the Revelation has used this word up to this point:

> He who *conquers*, I will grant to him to sit down with Me on My Throne, as I also *conquered* and sat down with My Father on His Throne. (3:21)

> The Lion that is from the tribe of Judah, the Root of David, has *conquered* so as to open the Book. (5:5)

> And I looked, and behold, a white horse; and He who sat upon it had a Bow; and a crown was given to Him; and He went out *conquering*, and to *conquer*. (6:2)

---

8. This word for *crown* (*stephanos*) is used seven times in Revelation with reference to Christ and His people (2:10; 3:11; 4:4, 10; 6:2; 12:1; 14:14).

9. Cf. St. Irenaeus, *Against Heresies*, iv.xxi.3.

It is Christ who is the Conqueror *par excellence.* All events in history are at His command, and it is entirely appropriate that He should be the One represented here as the leader of the judgments of God. He is the Center of history, and it is He who brings judgments upon the Land. His opening of the New Covenant guaranteed the fall of Israel; as He conquered to open the Book, so He rode out in victory to implement the meaning of the Book in history. He rode forth at His Resurrection and Ascension as the already victorious King, conquering and to conquer, extending the applications of His once-for-all, definitive victory throughout the earth. And we should take special notice of the awful judgments following in His train. The Horsemen represent the forces God always uses in breaking disobedient nations, and now they are turned against His covenant people. The same holds true, of course, for all men and nations. All attempts to find peace and safety apart from Jesus Christ are doomed to failure. The nation that will not submit will be crushed by His armies, by the historical forces that are constantly at His absolute disposal.

There are differences between this vision of Christ and that in Revelation 19. The primary reason for this is that in Chapter 19, Christ is seen with a sword proceeding out of His mouth, and the vision symbolizes His conquest of the nations after A.D. 70 with the Gospel. But that is not in view during the breaking of the seals. Here, Christ is coming against His enemies in judgment. He is coming, not to save, not to heal, but to destroy. The awful and terrifying riders who follow Him are not messengers of hope but of wrath. Israel is doomed.

3-4   The Lamb breaks **the Second Seal,** and St. John hears **the second living creature saying: Come!** In answer to the call, a rider on **a blood-red horse** comes forth, who is **granted** by God the power **to take peace from the Land, and that men should slay one another; and a great sword** is **given to him.** This second rider, standing for *war,* shows how utterly depraved man is. God does not have to incite men to fight against each other; He simply orders His angels to take away the conditions of peace. In a sinful world, why are there not more wars than there are? Why is there not more bloodshed? It is because there are *restraints on man's wickedness,* on man's freedom to work out the consistent implications of his hatred and rebellion. But if God removes the restraints, man's ethical degeneracy is revealed in all its ugliness. John Calvin wrote: "The mind of man has been so completely estranged from God's righteousness that it conceives, desires, and undertakes, only that which is impious, perverted, foul, impure, and infamous. The heart is so steeped in the poison of sin, that it can breathe out nothing but a loathsome stench. But if some men occasionally make a show of good, their minds nevertheless ever remain enveloped in hypocrisy and deceitful craft, and their hearts bound by inner depravity."[10]

All this was abundantly fulfilled in Israel and the surrounding nations during the Last Days, when the Land was filled with murderers, revolutionaries, and terrorists of every description; when "every city was divided into two armies encamped against one another, and the preservation of the one party was in the destruction of the other; so the day-time was spent in the shedding of blood, and the night in fear. . . . It was then common to see cities filled with dead bodies, still lying unburied, and those of old men, mixed with infants, all dead, and scattered about together; women also lay amongst them, without any covering for their nakedness; you might then see the whole province full of inexpressible calamities, while dread of still more barbarous practices which were threatened, was everywhere greater than what had been already perpetrated."[11]

5-6 Following on the heels of war is the third angelic rider, on **a black horse,** holding **a pair of scales in his hand,** a symbol of famine from the prophecy of Ezekiel, in which the starving inhabitants of Jerusalem were forced to weigh their food carefully (Ezek. 4:10). This Horseman brings *economic hardship,* a situation described as completely chaotic. A voice from **the center of the living creatures** — i.e., from God's Throne — says: **A quart of wheat for a denarius, and three quarts of barley for a denarius; and do not harm the oil and the wine.** This curse thus

---

10. John Calvin, *Institutes of the Christian Religion,* ii.v.19, Ford Lewis Battles, trans. (Philadelphia: The Westminster Press, 1960), p. 340.

11. Flavius Josephus, *The Jewish War,* ii.xviii.2; to gain an accurate (and thus horrifying) picture of how closely the prophecies in Revelation and the Synoptic Gospels parallel the events of Israel's Last Days, leading up to Titus's siege of Jerusalem, it is necessary to read Books ii-iv of Josephus' history.

means a shortage of the necessary staples—a measure of wheat rising to more than 1000% of its former price, consuming an entire day's wages,[12] so that a man's entire labor is spent in obtaining food. This is God's curse on men whenever they rebel: The land itself spews them out (Lev. 18:24-28; Isa. 24). The Curse devours productivity in every area, and the ungodly culture perishes through starvation, disease, and oppression (Deut. 28:15-34). This is how God controls the wicked: They must spend so much time just surviving that they are unable to exercise ungodly dominion over the earth. In the long run, this is the history of every culture that departs from God's Word.[13]

Josephus describes the frantic search for food during the final siege: "As the famine grew worse, the frenzy of the insurgents kept pace with it, and every day both these horrors burned more fiercely. For, since nowhere was grain to be seen, men would break into houses, and if they found some they mistreated the occupants for having denied their possession of it; if they found none, they tortured them as if they had concealed it more carefully. Proof whether they had food or not was provided by the physical appearance of the wretches; those still in good condition were deemed to be well provided with food, while those who were already wasting away were passed over, for it seemed pointless to kill persons who would soon die of starvation. Many secretly bartered their possessions for a single measure of wheat if they happened to be rich, barley if they were poor. Then they shut themselves up in the darkest corners of their houses; in the extremity of hunger some even ate their grain underground, while others baked it, guided by necessity and fear. Nowhere was a table laid—the food was snatched half-cooked from the fire and torn into pieces."[14]

On the other hand, however, in this specific curse on Jerusalem the luxuries of oil and wine are unaffected by the general price rise; the black Horseman is forbidden to touch them. The **scales** are the sign of Libra, spanning September and October;

---

12. Robert H. Mounce, *The Book of Revelation* (Grand Rapids: William B. Eerdmans Publishing Co., 1977), p. 155.

13. See David Chilton, *Productive Christians in an Age of Guilt-Manipulators: A Biblical Response to Ronald J. Sider* (Tyler, TX: Institute for Christian Economics, third ed., 1985), pp. 92ff.

14. Josephus, *The Jewish War*, v.x.2.

Farrer surmises that if the grain harvest failed in April and May, "men might begin to tighten their belts in October. They would then be just finishing the fruit-gathering, and might observe the irony of nature, that grapes and olives had gone unscathed; of the traditional triad corn, wine, and oil, corn, at a pinch, will keep you alive without the other two, but not they without the corn."[15] In all likelihood, another dimension of this expression's import is that God's messengers of destruction are kept from harming the righteous: Scripture often speaks of God's blessings upon the righteous in terms of **oil and wine** (cf. Ps. 104:15); and, of course, oil and wine are used in the rites of the Church (James 5:14-15; 1 Cor. 11:25). This would then parallel those other passages in which the godly are protected from destruction (cf. 7:3).

7-8   Finally, **the Fourth Seal** is broken, and **the fourth living creature** calls up the last Horseman of judgment, who rides **a green horse**—the green color[16] connoting a sickly pallor, a presage of death. Thus the fourth rider, with a much broader and more comprehensive commission, is named **Death**; and he is followed by **Hades** (the grave)—both having been set loose by the Son of Man, who unlocked them with His key (1:18). **And authority was given to him** to bring four plagues upon the four-cornered Land: **to kill with sword and with famine and with death and by the wild beasts of the Land**. This is simply a summary of all the covenantal curses in Leviticus 26 and Deuteronomy 28. Moreover, it parallels God's listing of His four basic categories of curses with which He punishes ungodly and disobedient nations—"My four severe judgments against Jerusalem: sword, famine, wild beasts, and plague to cut off man and beast from it!" (Ezek. 14:21; cf. Ezek. 5:17). At this preliminary stage, however—and in keeping with the "fourness" of the passage as a whole—Death and the grave are given authority to swallow up only **a fourth of the Land**. The Trumpet-judgments

---

15. Austin Farrer, *The Revelation of St. John the Divine* (Oxford: At the Clarendon Press, 1964), p. 100. J. Massyngberde Ford mentions an order by Titus during the siege of Jerusalem that olive groves and vineyards were not to be disturbed (*Revelation: Introduction, Translation, and Commentary* [Garden City, NY: Doubleday and Co., 1975], p. 107).

16. The Greek word is *chloros*, and simply means *green*; it is used two more times in Revelation (8:7; 9:4), and once in Mark (6:39). Translators have usually rendered it as *pale*, apparently under the firm conviction that, since there is no such thing as a green horse, St. John could not possibly have seen one.

will take a third of the Land (cf. 8:7-12), and the Chalice-judgments will devastate it all.

Perhaps the most significant obstacle to a correct interpretation of this passage has been that commentators and preachers have been afraid and unable to see that it is *God* who is bringing forth these judgments upon the Land — that they are called forth from the Throne, and that the messengers of judgment are the very angels of God. Especially vicious and harmful is any interpretation which seems to pit the Son of God against the court of heaven, so that the curses recorded here are seen as somehow beneath His character. But it is Jesus, the Lamb, who breaks the seals of judgment, and it is Jesus, the King of kings, who rides out in conquest, leading the angelic armies against the nations, to destroy those who rebel against His universal rule.

It was crucial for the early Christians to understand this, for these judgments were even then breaking loose upon their world. In every age, Christians must face the world with confidence, with the unshakable conviction that *all* events in history are predestined, originating from the Throne of God. When we see the world convulsed with wars, famines, plagues and natural disasters, we must say, with the Psalmist, "Come, behold the works of the LORD, who has wrought desolations in the earth" (Ps. 46:8). Ultimately, the Christian's attitude toward God's judgments upon a wicked world is the same as that of the four living creatures around the Throne, who joyfully call out to God's messengers of judgment: *"Come!"* We too, in our prayers, are to plead with God to bring down His wrath on the ungodly, to manifest His righteousness in the earth. Faced with these awesome revelations of judgment, what is our proper response? We are told, in 22:17: The Spirit and the Bride say, *"Come!"*

The Martyrs Avenged (6:9-17)

9 And when He broke the Fifth Seal, I saw underneath the altar the souls of those who had been slain because of the Word of God, and because of the Testimony which they had maintained;

10 and they cried out with a loud voice, saying: How long, O Lord, holy and true, dost Thou not judge and avenge our blood on those who dwell on the Land?

11 And there was given to each of them a white robe; and they were told that they should rest for a little while longer, until

the number of their fellow servants and their brethren who were to be killed even as they had been, should be completed also.

12 And I looked when He broke the Sixth Seal, and there was a great earthquake; and the sun became black as sackcloth made of hair, and the whole moon became like blood;

13 and the stars of the heaven fell to the earth, as a fig tree casts its unripe figs when shaken by a great wind.

14 And the heaven vanished like a scroll when it is rolled up; and every mountain and island were moved out of their places.

15 And the kings of the earth and the great men and the commanders and the rich and the strong and every slave and free man, hid themselves in the caves and among the rocks of the mountains;

16 and they said to the mountains and to the rocks: Fall on us and hide us from the presence of Him who sits on the Throne, and from the wrath of the Lamb;

17 for the great Day of His wrath has come; and who is able to stand?

9-10 For the first-century readers of this book, the tribulations depicted in it were becoming all too real: Each church would soon know the anguish of having some of its most forthright and able leaders imprisoned and executed **because of the Word of God, and because of the Testimony which they had maintained.** For many Christians, all across the empire, the coming months and years would involve great distress, as families would be separated and loved ones killed. When tragedy strikes, we are tempted to ask: Does God care? This question is especially intense when the pain is caused by vicious enemies of the faith bent on destroying God's people, and the injustice of the suffering becomes apparent. If Christians were truly the servants of the King, when would He act? When would He come to punish the apostates who had first used the power of the Roman State to crucify the Lord, and now were using that same power to kill and crucify the "prophets and wise men and scribes" (Matt. 23:34) whom Christ had sent?

Thus the breaking of **the Fifth Seal** reveals a scene in heaven, where **the souls of those who had been slain** are **underneath,** or around the base of, **the altar.** The image is taken from the Old

Testament sacrifices, in which the **blood** of the slain victim would stream down the sides of the altar and form into a pool around its base ("the *soul* [Heb. *nephesh*] of the flesh is in the *blood*," Lev. 17:11).[17] The blood of the martyrs has been poured out (cf. 2 Tim. 4:6), and as it fills the trench below the altar it cries out from the ground **with a loud voice, saying, How long, O Lord, holy and true, dost Thou not judge and avenge our blood upon those who dwell on the Land?** The Church in heaven agrees with the cherubim in calling forth God's judgments: **How long?** is a standard phrase throughout Scripture for invoking divine justice for the oppressed (cf. Ps. 6:3; 13:1-2; 35:17; 74:10; 79:5; 80:4; 89:46; 90:13; 94:3-4; Hab. 1:2; 2:6). The particular background for its use here, however, is again in the prophecy of Zechariah (1:12): After the Four Horsemen have patrolled through the earth, the angel asks, "O LORD of Hosts, how long wilt Thou have no compassion for Jerusalem?" St. John reverses this. After his Four Horsemen have been sent on their mission, he shows the martyrs asking how long God will continue to put up with Jerusalem. St. John's readers would not have failed to notice another subtle point: If the martyrs' blood is flowing around the base of the altar, it must be the priests of Jerusalem who have spilled it. The officers of the Covenant have slain the righteous. As Jesus and the apostles testified, Jerusalem was *the* murderer of the prophets (Matt. 23:34-37; Luke 13:33; Acts 7:51-52). The connection with "the blood of Abel" crying out from the ground near the altar (Gen. 4:10) is another indication that this passage as a whole refers to judgment upon Jerusalem (cf. Matt. 23:35-37). Like Cain, the "older brothers" of the Old Covenant envied and murdered their righteous "younger brothers" of the New Covenant (cf. 1 John 3:11-12). And so the blood of the righteous cries out: The saints pray that Christ's prophecy of "the days of vengeance" (Luke 21:22) will be fulfilled.

That this blunt cry for vengeance strikes us as strange just shows how far our pietistic age has degenerated from the Biblical worldview. If our churches were more acquainted with the foundational hymnbook of the Church, the Psalms, instead

---

17. See Rousas John Rushdoony, *Thy Kingdom Come: Studies in Daniel and Revelation* (Tyler, TX: Thoburn Press, [1970] 1978), p. 145.

of the sugary, syrupy, sweetness-and-light choruses that charac-
terize modern evangelical hymnals, we would understand this
much easier. But we have fallen under a pagan delusion that it is
somehow "unchristian" to pray for God's wrath to be poured out
upon the enemies and persecutors of the Church. Yet that is what
we see God's people doing, with God's approval, in both Testaments of the Holy Scriptures.[18] It is, in fact, a characteristic of
the godly man that he despises the reprobate (Ps. 15:4). The spirit
expressed in the imprecatory prayers of Scripture is a necessary
aspect of the Christian's attitude (cf. 2 Tim. 4:14). Much of the
impotence of the churches today is directly attributable to the
fact that they have become emasculated and effeminate. Such
churches, unable even to confront evil — much less "overcome" it
— will eventually be captured and dominated by their enemies.

11   The righteous and faithful saints in heaven are recognized
as kings and priests of God, and thus there is **given to each of
them a white robe**, symbolizing God's acknowledgment of their
purity before Him, a symbol of the victory of the overcomers
(cf. 3:4-5). The whiteness of the robe is part of a pattern already
set up in Revelation (the Seven Letters) in which the last three
items in a sevenfold structure match the first four items. Thus:

First Seal: White horse	*Fifth Seal:*	White robes
Second Seal: Red horse	*Sixth Seal:*	Moon like blood
Third Seal: Black horse		Sun black
Fourth Seal: Green horse	*Seventh Seal:*	Green grass burned

In answer to the saints' plea for vengeance, God answers **that
they should rest for a little while longer, until the number of
their fellow servants and their brethren who were to be killed
even as they had been, should be completed also.** The full number of martyrs has not yet been completed; the full iniquity of
their persecutors has not yet been reached (cf. Gen. 15:16), although it is fast approaching the doom of God's "wrath to the

---

18. See, e.g., Ps. 5, 7, 35, 58, 59, 68, 69, 73, 79, 83, 109, 137, 140. The common
term for these and other passages is *Imprecatory Psalms*; such an expression can
be misleading, however, since *most* of the Psalms have imprecatory sections
(*curses*) in them (cf. Ps. 1:4-6; 3:7; 6:8-10; 34:16; 37:12-15; 54:7; 104:35;
139:19-22), and *all* the Psalms are implicitly imprecatory, in that the blessings of
the righteous are mentioned with the corollary assumed: The wicked are cursed.

uttermost" being poured out upon them (1 Thess. 2:14-16). We must remember that the primary application of this has to do with apostate Israel—those who dwell on the Land—which (in cooperation with the Roman authorities) was murdering the saints. The martyrs are instructed to wait a little while, and God's judgment will assuredly strike, bringing the promised "Great Tribulation" upon covenant-breaking Israel.

12-14 As the Sixth Seal is broken, we are more clearly brought into the closing events of the Last Days. The Lamb reveals the next great aspect of His covenantal judgments, in a symbol often used in Biblical prophecy: *de-creation*. Just as the salvation of God's people is spoken of in terms of creation (cf. 2 Cor. 4:6; 5:17; Eph. 2:10; 4:24; Col. 3:10),[19] so God's judgments (and the revelation of His presence as Judge over a sinful world) are spoken of in terms of de-creation, the collapse of the universe—God ripping apart and dissolving the fabric of creation.[20] Thus St. John uses the fundamental structures of creation in describing the fall of Israel:

1. Earth
2. Sun
3. Moon
4. Stars
5. Firmament
6. Land
7. Man

These seven judgments are detailed in terms of the familiar prophetic imagery of the Old Testament. First, destabilization: **a giant earthquake** (cf. Ex. 19:18; Ps. 18:7, 15; 60:2; Isa. 13:13-14; 24:19-20; Nah. 1:5). Second, the eclipse and mourning of Israel: **The sun became black as sackcloth made of hair** (Ex. 10:21-23; Job 9:7; Isa. 5:30; 24:23; Ezek. 32:7; Joel 2:10, 31; 3:15; Amos 8:9; Mic. 3:6). Third, the continued image of an eclipse, with the idea of *defilement* added: **The whole moon became like blood** (Job 25:5; Isa. 13:10; 24:23; Ezek. 32:7; Joel 2:10, 31). The fourth judgment affects the stars, which are images of govern-

---

19. See David Chilton, *Paradise Restored: A Biblical Theology of Dominion* (Ft. Worth, TX: Dominion Press, 1985), pp. 22ff.
20. See ibid., pp. 98ff., 133ff.

ment (Gen. 1:16); they are also clocks (Gen. 1:14), and their fall shows that *Israel's time has run out:* **The stars fell to the earth, as a fig tree casts its unripe figs when shaken by a great wind** (Job 9:7; Eccl. 12:2; Isa. 13:10; 34:4; Ezek. 32:8; Dan. 8:10; Joel 2:10; 3:15); the **great wind,** of course, was brought by the Four Horsemen, who in Zechariah's original imagery were the Four Winds (Zech. 6:5), and who will be reintroduced to St. John in that form in 7:1; and the **fig tree** is Israel herself (Matt. 21:19; 24:32-34; Luke 21:29-32). Fifth, Israel now simply disappears: **The heaven vanished like a scroll when it is rolled up**[21] (Isa. 34:4; 51:6; Ps. 102:25-26; on the symbolism of Israel as "heaven," see Isa. 51:15-16; Jer. 4:23-31; cf. Heb 12:26-27). Sixth, the Gentile powers are shaken as well: **Every mountain and island were moved out of their places** (Job 9:5-6; 14:18-19; 28:9-11; Isa. 41:5, 15-16; Ezek. 38:20; Nah. 1:4-8; Zeph. 2:11).[22] God's "old creation," Israel, is thus to be de-created, as the Kingdom is transferred to the Church, the New Creation (cf. 2 Pet. 3:7-14). Because the rulers in God's Vineyard have killed His Son, they too will be killed (Matt. 21:33-45). The Vineyard itself will be broken down, destroyed, and laid waste (Isa. 5:1-7). In God's righteous destruction of Israel, He will shake even heaven and earth (Matt. 24:29-30; Heb. 12:26-28) in order to deliver His Kingdom over to His new nation, the Church.

15-17   Old Testament prophetic imagery is still in view as St. John here describes the apostates under judgment. This is the seventh phase of de-creation: the destruction of men. But this

---

21. Referring to the Biblical imagery (cf. Gen. 1:7) of a "solid" sky, Ford explains: "Heaven's having been 'wrenched apart like a scroll that is rolled up' leads to an image not of a papyrus or leather roll but rather a scroll like the two copper ones found in Qumran. The idea of noise is conveyed more dramatically if the reader is meant to picture a metal scroll suddenly snapping shut." J. Massyngberde Ford, *Revelation: Introduction, Translation, and Commentary* (Garden City, NY: Doubleday and Co., 1975), p. 100.

22. In contrast to popular interpretations of the texts which speak of faith moving mountains (Matt. 17:20; 21:21; Mark 11:23), it should be noted that this expression occurs in passages which speak of the coming judgment upon, and fall of, apostate Jerusalem. Jerusalem is often called "the mountain" in Scripture (e.g. Dan. 9:16); thus the saints at the altar (6:9-11) are pictured as crying out, in faith, for this great mountain to fall down. Jerusalem's destruction is accordingly portrayed, in part, as a burning mountain being cast into the sea (8:8; cf. Zech. 14:4).

seventh item in the list opens up to reveal another "seven" within it (just as the Seventh Seal and Seventh Trumpet each contains the next set of seven judgments), for seven classes of men are named here, showing that the destruction is total, affecting small and great alike: **the kings of the earth and the great men and the commanders and the rich and the strong and every slave and free man.** None will be able to escape, regardless of either privileged status or insignificance. The whole Land has rejected Christ, and the whole Land is being excommunicated. Again, the parallels show that the judgment upon Israel is intended by this prophecy (cf. Isa. 2 and 24-27), although other nations ("the kings of the earth") will be affected as well.

As the earth is de-created, and the mediating natural revelation is removed — placing sinners face-to-face with the bare revelation of the holy and righteous God — the men of Israel attempt to flee and to seek protection in anything that might seem to offer refuge. Flight underground and into caves is a sign of being under a curse (cf. Gen. 19:30-38). Thus they **hid themselves** (cf. Gen. 3:8) **in the caves and among the rocks of the mountains** (the *lex talionis* for their mistreatment of the righteous: Heb. 11:38; cf. Jud. 7:25),[23] **and they said to the mountains and to the rocks: Fall on us and hide us from the presence of Him who sits on the Throne, and from the wrath of the Lamb; for the great day of His wrath has come;**[24] **and** (Nah. 1:6; Mal. 3:2) **who is able to stand?** The interpretation given here is again confirmed: This passage is not speaking of the End of the World, but of *the End of Israel in* A.D. 70. The origin of the symbolism used here is in the prophecy of Hosea against Israel:

> Ephraim will be seized with shame,
> And Israel will be ashamed of its own counsel.
> Samaria will be cut off with her king,
> Like a stick on the surface of the water.

---

23. See James B. Jordan, *Judges: God's War Against Humanism* (Tyler, TX: Geneva Ministries, 1985), pp. 114, 140.

24. G. B. Caird attains the breathtaking *ne plus ultra* of absurd commentary with his astounding assertion that "the wrath of God in the Revelation, as elsewhere in the Old and New Testaments, represents not the personal attitude of God towards sinners, but an impersonal process of retribution working itself out in the course of history." *A Commentary on the Revelation of St. John the Divine* (New York: Harper and Row, 1966), p. 91.

Also, the high places of Aven, the sin of Israel, will be destroyed;
Thorn and thistle will grow on their altars.
Then they will say to the mountains: Cover us!
And to the hills: Fall on us! (Hos. 10:6-8)

Jesus cited this text on His way to the crucifixion, stating
that it would be fulfilled upon idolatrous Israel within the life-
times of those who were then present:

> And there were following Him a great multitude of the peo-
> ple, and of women who were mourning and lamenting Him. But
> Jesus turning to them said, Daughters of Jerusalem, stop weep-
> ing for Me, but *weep for yourselves and for your children.* For
> behold, the days are coming when they will say: Blessed are the
> barren, and the wombs that never bore, and the breasts that
> never nursed. Then they will begin to say to the mountains: Fall
> on us! and to the hills: Cover us! (Luke 23:27-30)

As the churches in Asia Minor were first reading this vision,
the prophesied judgments were already taking place; the final
End was fast approaching. The generation that had rejected the
Landlord's Son (cf. Matt. 21:33-45) would soon be screaming
these very words. The crucified and resurrected Lord was coming to destroy the apostates. This was to be the great Day of the
outpoured wrath of the Lamb, whom they had slain.

7

THE TRUE ISRAEL

The two visions of this chapter (v. 1-8 and v. 9-17) are still part of the Sixth Seal, providing a resolution of the problem of Israel's fall. Yet they also form an interlude or intermission, a period of delay between the sixth and seventh seals that serves to heighten the sense of waiting complained of by the saints in 6:10, since this section is in part the divine answer to their prayer (cf. the delay between the sixth and seventh trumpets, 10:1-11:14). Before the Fall of Jerusalem, Christianity was still largely identified with Israel, and the futures of the two were interconnected. The Christians were not separatists; they regarded themselves as the true heirs of Abraham and Moses, their religion as the fulfillment of all the promises to the fathers. For the Church to exist completely separate from the Israelite nationality and from the Holy Land was virtually unimaginable. Thus, if God's wrath were to be unleashed upon Israel with all the undiluted fury portrayed in the Sixth Seal, bringing the decreation of heaven and earth and the annihilation of mankind, what would become of the Church? What about the faithful who find themselves in the midst of a collapsing civilization? Would the believing remnant be destroyed in the coming conflagration along with the enemies of the faith?

The answer given in these visions is that "God has not destined us for wrath, but for obtaining salvation through our Lord Jesus Christ" (1 Thess. 5:9): The Church will be preserved. In terms of the coming judgment on Israel, in fact, the Lord had given explicit instructions about how to escape from the Tribulation (see Matt. 24:15-25; Mark 13:14-23; Luke 21:20-24). The Christians living in Jerusalem obeyed the prophetic warning, and were preserved, as Marcellus Kik pointed out in his study of Matthew 24: "One of the most remarkable things about the siege of Jerusalem was the miraculous escape of the Christians. It has been estimated that over a million Jews lost their lives in that terrible siege, but not one of them was a Christian. This our Lord indicated in verse 13: 'But he that shall endure to the end, the same shall be saved.' That the 'end' spoken of was not the termination of a Christian's life but rather the end of Jerusalem is evident from the context. Immediately after this verse Christ goes on to relate the exact time of the end. Christians who would live to the end would be saved from the terrible tribulation. Christ indicates also the time for the Christian to flee from the city so that he could be saved during its destruction. This is verified in a parallel passage (Luke 21:18): 'But there shall not an hair of your head perish.' In other words, during the desolation of Jerusalem, Christians would be unharmed, although in the period previous to this some would lose their lives through persecution."[1]

The 144,000 Sealed (7:1-8)

1 And after this I saw four angels standing at the four corners of the Land, holding back the Four Winds of the earth, so that no wind should blow on the Land or on the sea or on any tree.

2 And I saw another angel ascending from the rising of the sun, having the Seal of the living God; and he cried out with a loud Voice to the four angels to whom it was granted to harm the Land and the sea,

3 saying: Do not harm the Land or the sea or the trees, until we have sealed the bond-servants of our God on their foreheads.

4 And I heard the number of those who were sealed, one hundred and forty-four thousand sealed from every tribe of the sons of Israel:

5 From the tribe of Judah, twelve thousand were sealed, from the tribe of Reuben twelve thousand, from the tribe of Gad twelve thousand,

---

1. J. Marcellus Kik, *An Eschatology of Victory* (Nutley, NJ: The Presbyterian and Reformed Publishing Company, 1971), pp. 96f.

6 from the tribe of Asher twelve thousand, from the tribe of Naphtali twelve thousand, from the tribe of Manasseh twelve thousand,

7 from the tribe of Simeon twelve thousand, from the tribe of Levi twelve thousand, from the tribe of Issachar twelve thousand,

8 from the tribe of Zebulun twelve thousand, from the tribe of Joseph twelve thousand, from the tribe of Benjamin, twelve thousand were sealed.

1-3 St. John sees **four angels standing at the four corners of the Land,** divine messengers **to whom it was granted to harm the Land and the sea;** yet here they are **holding back the Four Winds of the earth, so that no wind should blow on the Land or on the sea or on any tree.** While *Land* and *sea* are in the genitive case, *tree* is in the accusative, indicating that St. John wishes to draw special attention to it. Throughout the Bible, trees are images of men (Jud. 9:8-15). In particular, they are symbols for the righteous (Ex. 15:17; Ps. 1:3; 92:12-14; Isa. 61:3; Jer. 17:5-8).[2]

The wind in Scripture is used in connection with the coming of God and the action of His angels in either blessing or curse (cf. Gen. 8:1; 41:27; Ex. 10:13, 19; 14:21; 15:10; Num. 11:31; Ps. 18:10; 104:3-4; 107:25; 135:7; 147:18; 148:8; John 3:8; Acts 2:2). In this case, the angel is speaking of the sirocco, the hot desert blast that scorches vegetation as a figure of God's burning judgment of the ungodly (cf. 16:9, and contrast 7:16):

Though he flourishes among the reeds,
An east wind shall come,
The wind of the LORD coming up from the wilderness;
And his fountain will become dry,
And his spring will be dried up;
It will plunder his treasury of every precious article.
Samaria will be held guilty,
For she has rebelled against her God.
They will fall by the sword,
Their little ones will be dashed in pieces,

---

2. See James B. Jordan's forthcoming studies, *Food and Faith* and *Trees and Thorns*.

And their pregnant women will be ripped open.
(Hos. 13:15-16)

As we have seen,[3] the association of angels with "nature" is not "mere" imagery. God through His angels really does control weather patterns, and He uses weather as an agency of blessing and judgment. From the very first verse, the Bible is written in terms of what Gary North calls *cosmic personalism*: "God did not create a self-sustaining universe which is now left to operate in terms of autonomous laws of nature. The universe is not a giant mechanism, like a clock, which God wound up at the beginning of time. Ours is not a mechanistic world, nor is it an autonomous biological entity, growing according to some genetic code of the cosmos. Ours is a world which is actively sustained by God on a full-time basis (Job 38-41). All creation is inescapably *personal* and *theocentric*. 'For the invisible things of him from the creation of the world are clearly seen, being understood by the things that are made, even his eternal power and Godhead . . .' (Rom. 1:20).

"If the universe is inescapably personal, then there can be no phenomenon or event in the creation which is independent from God. No phenomenon can be said to exist apart from God's all-inclusive plan for the ages. There is no uninterpreted 'brute factuality.' Nothing in the universe is *autonomous*. . . . Nothing in the creation generates its own conditions of existence, including the law structure under which something operates or is operated upon. Every fact in the universe, from beginning to end, is exhaustively interpreted by God in terms of His being, plan, and power."[4]

The four angels are restraining the judgment in obedience to the command of **another angel**, whom St. John sees **ascending from the rising of the sun**, whence God's actions in history traditionally came (cf. Isa. 41:1-4, 25; 46:11; Ezek. 43:1-3). This angel comes as the representative of Christ, the Sunrise from on high

---

3. See comments on 4:5-8, above.
4. *The Dominion Covenant: Genesis* (Tyler, TX: Institute for Christian Economics, 1982), pp. 1-2; cf. pp. 2-11, 425-54; see also Rousas John Rushdoony, *The Mythology of Science* (Nutley, NJ: The Craig Press, 1967).

who has visited us (Luke 1:78), the Sun of righteousness who has risen with healing in His wings (Mal. 4:2; cf. Eph. 5:14; 2 Pet. 1:19). He possesses the Spirit without measure (John 3:34), **the Seal of the living God** with which He marks out the people of His own possession, and by His order the judgments on the Land are not fully poured out **until we** – Christ and His messengers – **have sealed the servants of our God on their foreheads**: The Seal of the Spirit (Eph. 1:13; 4:30) is applied to the righteous before the Seals of wrath are applied to the wicked; Pentecost precedes Holocaust.

The seal in the Biblical world signified a grant of authority and power, a guarantee of protection, and a mark of ownership (cf. 2 Cor. 1:21-22; 2 Tim. 2:19). The primary Old Testament background for St. John's imagery is Ezekiel 9:1-7, which shows God commissioning executioners to destroy everyone in the city of Jerusalem; the first to be slain are the elders at the Temple. First, however, He commands another angel to "go through the midst of the city, even through the midst of Jerusalem, and put a mark on the foreheads of the men who sigh and groan over all the abominations that are being committed in its midst" (v. 4). The godly are marked for protection, in order that the apostates in Jerusalem may be destroyed.

The mark on the forehead is thus a symbol of man restored to fellowship with God. One striking example of this was the High Priest, whose forehead was marked with gold letters proclaiming that he was *HOLY TO THE LORD* (Ex. 28:36). Further, in Deuteronomy 6:6-8, all God's people are sealed in the forehead and the hand with the law of God, just as they are characterized in life by faithful obedience in thought and action to every word of God.

The protective "mark" in Ezekiel 9 is literally *tav*, the last letter of the Hebrew alphabet. The ancient Hebrew form of the *tav* was +, a cross – a fact that was not lost on the early Church, which saw it as "a quasi-prophetic reference to the sign of the cross as used by Christians, and it is possible that the use of that sign in baptism may have originated in this passage."[5] Tertullian

---

5. E. H. Plumptre, *The Pulpit Commentary: Ezekiel* (London: Funk and Wagnalls Co., n.d.), Vol. 1, pp. 162f.

believed that God had given Ezekiel "the very form of the cross, which He predicted would be the sign on our foreheads in the true Catholic Jerusalem."[6] Holy Baptism, the Seal of the Spirit (2 Cor. 1:21-22; Gal. 3:27; Eph. 1:13-14; 4:30; cf. Rom. 4:11), marks these believers as the covenant-keeping **bond-servants of our God**, who will be preserved from God's wrath as the ungodly are destroyed. "The purpose of the sealing was to preserve the true Israel of God as a holy seed. It was not designed to save them from tribulation, but to preserve them in the midst of the great tribulation about to come and to glorify them thereby. Though the old Israel be cast off, a new and holy Israel is to be chosen and sealed with the Spirit of the living God."[7]

4-8   The number of those who were sealed is read to St. John: **one hundred and forty-four thousand sealed from every tribe of the sons of Israel**, with **twelve thousand** from each of the twelve tribes. The number 144,000 is obviously symbolic: *twelve* (the number of Israel) squared, then multiplied by *1000* (*ten* and its multiples symbolizing *many;* cf. Deut. 1:11; 7:9; Ps. 50:10; 68:17; 84:10; 90:4). St. John pictures for us the ideal Israel, Israel as it was meant to be, in all its perfection, symmetry, and completeness; the holy Army of God, mustered for battle according to her thousands (cf. 1 Chron. 4-7). The "thousand" was the basic military division in the camp of Israel (Num. 10:2-4, 35-36; 31:1-5, 48-54; 2 Sam. 18:1; 1 Chron. 12:20; 13:1; 15:25; 26:26; 27:1; 28:1; 29:6; 2 Chron. 1:2; 17:14-19; Ps. 68:17). This is the significance of Micah's famous prophecy of the Nativity: Even though Bethlehem is too small to be counted "among the thousands of Judah," too insignificant to be considered seriously in the nation's military strategy, yet "from you One will go forth for Me to be Ruler in Israel," the King who

---

6. Tertullian, *Against Marcion*, iii.22, in Alexander Roberts and James Donaldson, eds., *The Ante-Nicene Fathers* (Grand Rapids: William B. Eerdmans Publishing Co., 1973), Vol. III, pp. 340f. On the legitimacy of the sign of the cross as a symbolic action, see James B. Jordan, *The Sociology of the Church: Essays in Reconstruction* (Tyler, TX: Geneva Ministries, 1986), pp. 207ff.

7. Milton Terry, *Biblical Apocalyptics: A Study of the Most Notable Revelations of God and of Christ in the Canonical Scriptures* (New York: Eaton and Mains, 1898), p. 336.

will establish God's justice and peace to the ends of the earth (Mic. 5:1-15). It is in terms of this Biblical imagery that St. John hears the names of the tribes shouted out: He is listening to the military roll-call of the Lord's Hosts. In this case, each of the twelve tribes is able to field twelve full divisions, a numerically perfect army of **144,000** soldiers of the Lord.

St. John's vision of an Israelite army is thus, in Milton Terry's words, "an apocalyptic picture of that 'holy seed' of which Isaiah speaks in Isaiah 6:13 — that surviving remnant which was destined to remain like the stump of a fallen oak after cities had been laid waste and the whole land had become a desolation — that 'remnant of Jacob,' which was to be preserved from the 'consumption determined in the midst of all the land' (Isa. 10:21-23). It is the same 'remnant according to the election of grace' of which Paul speaks in Romans 9:27-28; 11:5. God will not destroy Jerusalem and make the once holy places desolate until He first chooses and seals a select number as the beginning of a new Israel. The first Christian Church was formed out of chosen servants of God from 'the twelve tribes of the dispersion' (James 1:1), and the end of the Jewish age was not to come until by the ministry of Jewish Christian apostles and prophets the gospel of the kingdom had been preached in the whole world for a testimony unto all the nations (Matt. 24:14)."[8]

St. John comforts his readers: Judgment will assuredly be poured out upon the apostates of the Old Covenant, but the Church herself is not in danger. Indeed, the true Covenant people are safe, whole, and entire. Even though God is about to destroy Jerusalem, annihilating every last vestige of the Old Covenant world-order and system of worship, Israel endures. The Covenant promises to Abraham, Isaac, and Jacob are not jeopardized in the slightest. In fact, the outpouring of God's wrath in the destruction of Jerusalem will only serve to reveal the true Israel in greater glory than ever before. Jerusalem is sacked and burned, its inhabitants killed and scattered; but *Israel* — all of her people, in all of her tribes — is sealed and saved. "Judgment thus is not only the other side of the coin to salvation, but it is also an act of grace and mercy to the people of

---

8. *Ibid.*, pp. 341f.

God. However devastating the fall of Jerusalem was to the faithful remnant, without that fall no remnant would have remained."[9]

The Order of the Twelve Tribes in Revelation

[I have set this out as a separate section because it will undoubtedly be the most wearying part of the book to read. The reader who tires easily should give it a brief glance and move on. While I have tried to simplify the discussion as much as possible, I fear it still looks exceedingly complex. All this would be much easier if we knew our Bibles as well as the children in the first-century synagogues: If we knew by heart the names of Jacob's sons and their mothers, and the twenty or so different orders in which they are listed in the Old Testament (and the reasons for each variation), we would almost immediately understand what St. John has done with his list, and why.

Some remarks by Austin Farrer are especially pertinent here: "The purpose of symbols is that they should be immediately understood, the purpose of expounding them is to restore and build up such an understanding. This is a task of some delicacy. The author had not with his conscious mind thought out every sense, every interconnection of his imagery. They had worked in his thinking, they had not themselves been thought. If we endeavor to expose them, we shall appear to over-intellectualize the process of his mind, to represent an imaginative birth as a speculative construction. Such a representation not merely misrepresents, it also destroys belief, for no one can believe in the process when it is thus represented. No mind, we realize, could *think* with such complexity, without destroying the life of the product of thought. Yet, if we do not thus intellectualize, we cannot expound at all; it is a necessary distortion of method, and must be patiently endured by the reader. Let it be said once for all that the convention of intellectualization is not to be taken literally. We make no

---

9. Rousas John Rushdoony, *Salvation and Godly Rule* (Vallecito, CA: Ross House Books, 1983), p. 141.

pretence of distinguishing between what was discursively thought and what intuitively conceived in a mind which penetrated its images with intelligence and rooted its intellective acts in imagination. . . .

"The reader who perseveres through the analyses which follow may naturally ask, 'How much of all this did the congregations of the Seven Churches comprehend, when the apocalyptic pastoral of their archbishop was read out to them?' The answer is, no doubt, that of the schematic analysis to which we resort they understood nothing, because they were listening to the Apocalypse of St. John, and not to the lucubrations of the present writer. They were men of his own generation, they constantly heard the Old Testament in their assemblies, and were trained by the preacher (who might be St. John himself) to interpret it by certain conventions. And so, without intellectual analysis, they would receive the symbols simply for what they were. They would understand what they would understand, and that would be as much as they had time to digest."][10]

Scholars have long puzzled over the order of the tribes in St. John's list. Obviously, Judah is named first because that is the tribe of Jesus Christ; other than that, many have supposed that the list is either haphazard (given the Biblical writers' — especially St. John's — extreme attention to detail, this is highly unlikely), or else permanently locked in mystery (this is just sheer arrogance; we should always remember that, if we can't answer a question, someone probably will come along in the next hundred years or so who will). As usual, however, Austin Farrer's explanation has the most to offer. Pointing out that the names of the twelve tribes are written on the gates of the four-cornered New Jerusalem (21:12), he proposes that the order of the tribes corresponds to the order in which the gates are listed: *east, north, south, west.* As we can see in the first diagram (which, like the maps of the ancient world, is oriented toward the east),[11]

---

10. Austin Farrer, *A Rebirth of Images: The Making of St. John's Apocalypse* (Gloucester, MA: Peter Smith, [1949] 1970), pp. 20f.

11. *Orient* means *east*; thus, if you are truly "oriented," you are "easted" already, placed so that you are facing the right direction (which is usually, but not always, east).

St. John begins at the eastern corner with **Judah** (because the sealing angel comes from the east, v. 2), goes through **Reuben** and **Gad** to **Asher** at the north corner, then down the northwest side with **Naphtali** and **Manasseh**; starting over again (we'll see why in a moment), he lists **Simeon** and **Levi** on the southeast side to **Issachar** at the south, then turns round the corner and goes through **Zebulun** and **Joseph**, ending with **Benjamin** at the western corner.

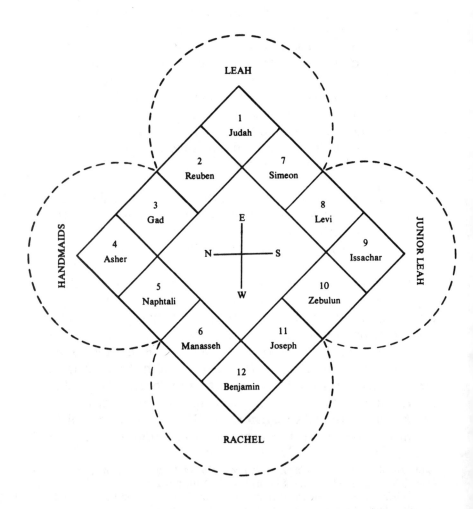

Why did St. John arrange the list of tribes in this manner? The most likely answer (Farrer's) is found in Genesis and Ezekiel. The twelve tribes descended from the twelve sons of Jacob, whom he sired through his wives Leah and Rachel, and their respective handmaids, Zilpah and Bilhah (legally, the handmaids' children belonged to Leah and Rachel; see Gen. 29:31-30:24 and 35:16-18). The list of Jacob's sons is as follows:

LEAH: Reuben   Gad (from Zilpah)
        Simeon   Asher (from Zilpah)
        Levi   Issachar
        Judah   Zebulun

RACHEL: Dan (from Bilhah)   Joseph
         Naphtali (from Bilhah)   Benjamin

When the prophet Ezekiel set forth his vision of the ideal Jerusalem, he too showed twelve gates, one for each tribe (Ezek. 48:30-35).

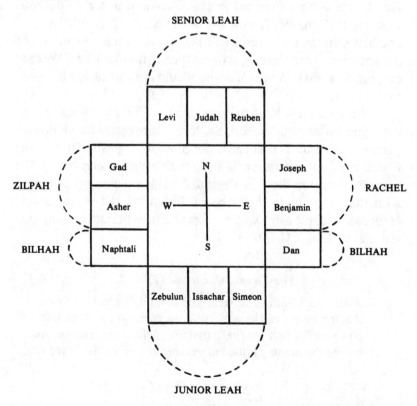

211

At first glance, it does not seem to have much in common with St. John's; yet once we view them together, they appear very close indeed. Ezekiel's list is arranged very symmetrically. Ezekiel has divided Leah's sons into two major groups of three ("senior" and "junior"), balancing each other on north and south. Rachel's two sons on the east are set across from Zilpah's two sons on the west; and below each pair is one of Bilhah's sons. Ezekiel has also brought Judah (the royal tribe) into the top row of three by having him change places with Simeon.

Farrer explains St. John's revision of Ezekiel: "He makes a genuine three for Rachel, by substituting Manasseh's name for Dan's. In fact, the tribe of Joseph had become two tribes, Ephraim and Manasseh. Since Ephraim was Joseph's principal heir, Joseph covers Ephraim; Manasseh is added. A by-product of this improvement is the disappearance from the list of Dan, one of the Twelve. Perhaps it will not have displeased St. John; let Dan be the Judas of the patriarchs. Dan had, in fact, a dubious reputation (Gen. 49:17; Lev. 24:10-11; 1 Kings 12:28-30; Jer. 4:15 and 8:16). In the end (Rev. 21:12-14), St. John puts the names of the apostles round the city, pairing them with the tribes. We cannot suppose that Iscariot's name would stand there, any more than Dan's.

"Then, as to the artificial promotion of Judah: instead of exchanging Judah and Simeon, St. John simply puts Judah up two places. The result is that Levi, not Simeon, is pushed out of the first three. The alteration is presumably deliberate, for in the new dispensation Levi is degraded. The priesthood is united with the kingship in the tribe of Judah, as the writer to the Hebrews so copiously explains; Levi has no special standing (see especially Heb. 7:11-14)."[12]

The Great Multitude (7:9-17)

9 After these things I looked, and behold, a great multitude, that no one could count, from every nation and all tribes and peoples and tongues, standing before the Throne and before the Lamb, clothed in white robes, and palm branches

---

12. Austin Farrer, *The Revelation of St. John the Divine*, p. 108.

were in their hands;

10 and they cry out with a loud voice, saying:
> Salvation to our God who sits on the Throne, and to
> the Lamb!

11 And all the angels were standing around the Throne and
around the elders and the four living creatures; and they fell
on their faces before the Throne and worshiped God,

12 saying:
> Amen! Blessing and glory and wisdom and thanksgiv-
> ing and honor and power and might, be to our God
> forever and ever! Amen!

13 And one of the elders answered, saying to me, These who
are clothed in the white robes, who are they, and from where
have they come?

14 And I said to him, My lord, you know. And he said to me,
These are the ones who come out of the Great Tribulation,
and they have washed their robes and made them white in
the blood of the Lamb.

15 For this reason, they are before the Throne of God; and they
serve Him day and night in His Temple; and He who sits on
the Throne shall spread His Tabernacle over them.

16 They shall hunger no more, neither thirst anymore; neither
shall the sun beat down on them, nor any heat;

17 for the Lamb in the center of the Throne shall be their Shepherd, and shall guide them to the springs of the Water of
Life; and God shall wipe every tear from their eyes.

9   We have already noticed a literary device that St. John
uses to display his images from various angles: *hearing*, then
seeing. For example, in 1:10-13, St. John *hears* a Voice, then
turns to *see* the Lord; in 5:5-6, he *hears* of the Lion of Judah,
then *sees* the Lamb; in 6:1-8, he *hears* a living creature say
"Come!"—and then *sees* the object of the creature's command.
The same pattern occurs here in this chapter: St. John tells us, **I
heard the number of those who were sealed** (v. 4); then, **after
these things**—after hearing the number of the redeemed—**I
looked, and behold, a great multitude** (v. 9). This pattern, and
the fact that the blessings ascribed to both groups are blessings
that belong to the Church, indicate that these two groups are, to
some extent, two different aspects of the one, universal Church.

213

So, from one standpoint, God's people are definitely numbered; none of the elect are missing, and the Church is perfectly symmetrical and whole. From another standpoint, the Church is innumerable, a great host **that no one could count**. Seen from one perspective, the Church is the new, the *true*, Israel of God: the sons of Jacob gathered into all their tribes, full and complete. From another, equally true perspective, the Church is the whole world: a great multitude redeemed **from every nation and all tribes and peoples and tongues.**

In other words, the 144,000 are the Remnant of Israel; yet the fulfillment of the promises to Israel takes place through the salvation of the world, by bringing the Gentiles in to share the blessings of Abraham (Gal. 3:8). The number of the Remnant is filled by the multitudes of the saved from all nations, just as the New Jerusalem — whose dimensions are measured in twelves and whose gates are inscribed with the names of the twelve tribes — is filled with the glory and honor of the nations of the world (21:12-27). Farrer says: "By the contrast between the numbered tribes and the innumerable host, St. John gives expression to two antithetical themes, both equally traditional. God knows the number of His elect; those who inherit the blessing of Abraham are as numberless as the stars (Gen. 15:5). Yet St. John cannot mean either that the number of Gentile saints is unknown to God, or that the number of righteous Israelites can be counted by men. What he tells us is, that his ear receives a number resulting from an angelic census; and that his eye is presented with a multitude he cannot count, as was Abraham's when called upon to look at the stars. The vision of the white-robed host, purified by martyrdom, must in any case reflect Daniel 11:35. The theme is continued in Daniel 12:1-3, where the same persons are described as 'registered in the book' and as 'like the stars'; it is easy to conclude 'numbered, therefore, yet uncountable.' "[13]

In St. John's vision, therefore, the sealed Remnant of Israel is the holy seed, the "first fruits" (14:4) of the new Church, destined to expand into an innumerable multitude gathered in worship before the Throne in heaven. The nucleus of Israel becomes the Church, redeemed from every nation in fulfillment of the

---

13. Ibid., p. 110.

Abrahamic promise (Gen. 15:5; 22:17-18); and thus the Church becomes the whole world. The salvation of Israel alone had never been God's intention; He sent his Son "that the world should be saved through Him" (John 3:16-17). As the Father said to the Son, in planning the Covenant of Redemption:

> It is too small a thing that You should be My Servant
> To raise up the tribes of Jacob,
> And to restore the preserved ones of Israel;
> I will also make of You a Light to the nations
> So that My salvation may reach to the end of the earth.
> (Isa. 49:6)

The actual number of the saved, far from being limited to mere tens of thousands, is in reality **a multitude that no one could count**, so vast that it cannot be comprehended. For the fact is that *Christ came to save the world*. Traditionally— although Calvinists have been technically correct in declaring that the full benefits of the atonement were intended only for the elect—both Calvinists and Arminians have tended to miss the point of John 3:16. That point has been beautifully summarized by Benjamin Warfield: "You must not fancy, then, that God sits helplessly by while the world, which He has created for Himself, hurtles hopelessly to destruction, and He is able only to snatch with difficulty here and there a brand from the universal burning. The world does not govern Him in a single one of its acts: He governs it and leads it steadily onward to the end which, from the beginning, or ever a beam of it had been laid, He had determined for it. . . . Through all the years one increasing purpose runs, one *increasing* purpose: the kingdoms of the earth become ever more and more the Kingdom of our God and His Christ. The process may be slow; the progress may appear to our impatient eyes to lag. But it is God who is building: and under His hands the structure rises as steadily as it does slowly, and in due time the capstone shall be set into its place, and to our astonished eyes shall be revealed nothing less than a saved world."[14]

---

14. Benjamin B. Warfield, from a sermon on John 3:16 entitled "God's Immeasurable Love," in *Biblical and Theological Studies* (Philadelphia: Presbyterian and Reformed Publishing Co., 1968), pp. 518f.

Unfortunately, many have failed to appreciate fully the implications of this passage. For more than a century, Christianity has been plagued by an altogether unwarranted defeatism: We have believed in the depravity of man more than in the sovereignty of God. We have more faith in an unregenerate creature's power to resist God's Word, than in the power of the almighty Creator to turn a man's heart according to His will. Such an impotent attitude has not always characterized God's people. Charles Spurgeon encouraged a gathering of missionaries with these words: "I myself believe that King Jesus will reign, and the idols be utterly abolished; but I expect the same power which turned the world upside down once will still continue to do it. The Holy Ghost would never suffer the imputation to rest upon His holy name that He was not able to convert the world."[15]

Because of the Resurrection and Ascension of Christ, this is the age of the triumph of the Gospel. The plain indications of Scripture are that the tendency of the nations, over time, will be toward conversion. The saved will vastly outnumber the lost. Throughout the Book of Revelation, as in the rest of the Bible, we find Satan continually defeated before the great army of the elect. Even when Satan appears to be dominant, he knows that "he has only a short time" (12:12). The period of Satan's seeming triumph is counted in days and months (12:6; 13:5), and even then it is nothing more than a mad, futile scramble for fleeting power; in marked contrast, the period of the saints' dominion is measured in *years* – a thousand of them – and from first (1:6) to last (20:4-6) they are designated as *kings*. Jesus is Victor! He has come to save the world, to redeem the nations, and He will not be disappointed: "He will see His offspring, He will prolong His days, and the good pleasure of the LORD will prosper in His hand" (Isa. 53:10).

St. John sees the redeemed world of victorious saints **standing before the Throne and before the Lamb** in worship. They are **clothed in white robes,** symbolizing righteousness, with **palm branches in their hands,** as the well-known symbol of the restoration of God's people to Paradise. This is also reminiscent of the Feast of Tabernacles, initiated during the Exodus: It is no

---

15. Quoted in Iain Murray, *The Puritan Hope: Revival and the Interpretation of Prophecy* (London: The Banner of Truth Trust, 1971), p. 258.

accident that the word *tabernacle* occurs in this passage (see on v. 15 below).[16] R. J. Rushdoony shows how extensive the Exodus imagery is in the symbolism of Revelation: "Jesus is both the true Moses (the Song of Moses is cited in Rev. 15:2ff.), and the greater Joshua. He is the deliverer of God's people. Simeon at the temple declared that his eyes had seen God's salvation, having seen the infant saviour (Luke 2:30; cf. Isa. 52:10), for he was one of those 'who were looking for the redemption of Jerusalem' (Luke 2:38), i.e., its deliverance from captivity, from spiritual Egypt. Pharaoah's killing of the infants is paralleled by Herod's murderous order (Ex. 1:16; 2:15; 4:19; Matt. 2:16). The infant Christ is called the true Israel called out of Egypt (Matt. 2:14f.; cf. Ex. 4:22; Hos. 11:1). Israel's 40 years of temptation in the wilderness, and its failure, is matched by Christ's 40 days of temptation in the wilderness, ending in victory; Jesus resisted by quoting Moses. Jesus sent out 12 disciples, to be the new Israel of God, the new heads of a new nation or people. Jesus also sent out 70 (Luke 10:1ff.), even as Moses gathered 70, to whom God gave the Spirit (Num. 11:16ff.). We are given parallels to the conquest of Canaan, and the destruction of its cities by the fire of judgment (Matt. 10:15; 11:20ff.; Luke 10:12ff.; Deut. 9:1ff.; Matt. 24). The old Jerusalem now has the role of Canaan and is to be destroyed (Matt. 24). The whole world is the new Canaan, to be judged and conquered: 'Go ye into all the world. . . .' Both Exodus and Revelation conclude with the Tabernacle, the first with the type, the second with the reality."[17]

There are other parallels here as well. The Feast of Dedication (Hanukkah) commemorated the cleansing of the Temple by Judas Maccabaeus in 164/165 B.C., after its defilement by Antiochus IV Epiphanes, when the Jews rejoiced "with thanksgiving, and branches of palm trees, and with harps, and cymbals, and with viols, and hymns, and songs: because there was destroyed a great enemy out of Israel" (1 Mac. 13:51). Jesus attended this feast (John 10:22), and on Palm Sunday He imitated Judas Maccabaeus's action by cleansing the Temple of its defilement by the

---

16. See David Chilton, *Paradise Restored: A Biblical Theology of Dominion* (Ft. Worth, TX: Dominion Press, 1985), pp. 44-46, 60.

17. Rousas John Rushdoony, *Thy Kingdom Come: Studies in Daniel and Revelation* (Tyler, TX: Thoburn Press, [1970] 1978), pp. 149f.

moneychangers (Matt. 21:12-13; Mark 11:15-17; Luke 19:45-46; cf. John 2:13-16).

In paralleling the cleansing of the Temple, the scene of the redeemed multitude in Revelation also reverses the image; for, unlike the great multitude that greeted Jesus with palm branches (Matt. 21:8), but possessed only leaves and no fruit (Matt. 21:19), the multitude of Revelation 7 is Christ's new nation, bearing fruit and inheriting the Kingdom (Matt. 21:43). That St. John intends us to see such a parallel is clear from the fact that the word translated **palm** (*phoinix*) occurs only two times in the New Testament—here, and in the story of Palm Sunday in the Gospel of John (12:13).

10 Joining in the heavenly liturgy, the innumerable multitude shouts: **Salvation** (i.e., **Hosanna!** cf. John 12:13) **unto our God who sits on the Throne, and to the Lamb!**—ascribing to God and to the Lamb what Rome claimed for the Caesars. Mark Antony said of Julius Caesar that his "only work was to save where anyone needed to be saved";[18] and now Nero was on the throne, whom Seneca (speaking as "Apollo") had praised as the divine Savior of the world:

> He is like me in much, in form and appearance, in his poetry and singing and playing. And as the red of morning drives away dark night, as neither haze nor mist endure before the sun's rays, as everything becomes bright when my chariot appears, so it is when Nero ascends the throne. His golden locks, his fair countenance, shine like the sun as it breaks through the clouds. Strife, injustice and envy collapse before him. He restores to the world the golden age.[19]

In direct contradiction to the State-worshiping blasphemies of Rome and Israel, the Church declares that salvation is the province of God and His Son alone. In every age, this has been a basic issue. Who is the Owner and Determiner of reality? Whose word is law? Is the State the provider of salvation? For

---

18. Ethelbert Stauffer, *Christ and the Caesars* (Philadelphia: The Westminster Press, 1955), p. 52.

19. Ibid., p. 139. Nero eventually repaid Seneca for a lifetime of servile idolatry by ordering him to commit suicide.

us, as for the early Church, there is no safe middle ground between faith and apostasy.

11-12 The **angels** too are seen here in this heavenly worship service, encircling the congregation around the Throne and giving a sevenfold blessing to God in praise — a blessing both preceded and ended with an oath: **Amen! Blessing and glory and wisdom and thanksgiving and honor and power and might, be to our God forever and ever! Amen!** As in many other Biblical descriptions of worship, the position of the worshipers is noted here: **They fell on their faces before the Throne.** Official, public worship in Scripture never shows the participants sitting at prayer; public prayer is always performed in the reverential positions of standing or bowing down. The modern, nominalistic platonist, thinking himself to be more spiritually-minded than Biblical characters (even angels!), would respond that the bodily position is irrelevant, so long as the proper attitude is filling the heart. But this overlooks the fact that Scripture connects the attitude of the heart with the attitude of the body. In *public* worship, at the very least, our churches should follow the Biblical pattern of physical reverence in prayer.

When rationalistic Protestants abandoned the use of the kneeling rail in worship, they contributed to the outbreaks of individualistic pietism that have brought so much ruin to the Church. *Man needs liturgy and symbolism.* God created us that way. When the Church denies man this aspect of his God-given nature, he will seek to fulfill it by inadequate or sinful substitutes. A return to Biblically based liturgy is not a cure-all; but it will prove to be a corrective to the shallow, frenetic, and misplaced "spirituality" that has been the legacy of centuries of liturgical poverty.

13-14 **One of the elders** now challenges St. John to tell him the identity of this great multitude from every nation. St. John confesses his inability, and the elder explains: **These are the ones who come out of the Great Tribulation.** While this text may and should be used to comfort Christians going through any period of suffering and persecution, its primary reference is to "the hour of testing, that hour which is about to come upon the whole world, to test those who dwell upon the Land" (3:10), the

"Great Tribulation" of which Jesus warned as He spoke to His disciples on the Mount of Olives (Matt. 24:21; Mark 13:19)—a tribulation that He stated would take place during the then-existing generation (Matt. 24:34; Mark 13:30; Luke 21:32); the greatest tribulation that ever was, or ever will be (Matt. 24:21; Mark 13:19).

The point, for the first-century Christians reading it, was that the Tribulation they were about to suffer would not destroy them. In facing persecution they were to see themselves, first, as "the Israel of God" (Gal. 6:16), sealed and protected; and second, as an innumerable, victorious multitude. As God saw them, they were not scattered, isolated groups of poor and persecuted individuals accused as criminals by a merciless, demonic power-State; they were, rather, a vast throng of conquerors, who had **washed their robes and made them white in the blood of the Lamb,** standing before God's Throne and robed in the righteousness of Jesus Christ. St. John is probably drawing on the ordination-investiture ritual after the rigorous examination for the priesthood. First, the prospective priest was examined as to his geneology. "If he failed to satisfy the court about his perfect legitimacy, the candidate was dressed and veiled in black, and permanently removed. If he passed that ordeal, inquiry was next made as to any physical defects, of which Maimonides enumerates a hundred and forty that permanently, and twenty-two which temporarily disqualified for the exercise of priestly office. . . . Those who had stood the twofold test were dressed in white raiment, and their names permanently inscribed."[20] The white robes of these priests thus correspond to the white robe of their High Priest; and just as His robe is said to be "dipped in blood," so theirs are **washed and made white in the blood of the Lamb.**

In striking contrast to what some Christian groups in recent years have been taught, the early Church did not expect to be miraculously preserved from all hardship in this life. They knew that they would be called upon to suffer persecution (2 Tim. 3:12) and tribulation (John 16:33; Acts 14:22; Rom. 5:3; 8:35;

---

20. Alfred Edersheim, *The Temple: Its Ministry and Services as They Were at the Time of Jesus Christ* (Grand Rapids: William B. Eerdmans Publishing Co., 1980), p. 95; cf. Rev. 3:5.

Rev. 1:9). The Apostle Peter had already written to prepare the Church for the Great Tribulation: "Beloved, do not be surprised at the fiery ordeal among you, which comes upon you for your testing, as though some strange thing were happening to you; but to the degree that you share the sufferings of Christ, keep on rejoicing; so that also at the revelation of His glory, you may rejoice with exultation" (1 Pet. 4:12-13). In a secondary sense, this is certainly applicable to Christians everywhere who suffer in tribulation. We are not to see salvation as a magic formula for trouble-avoidance. As the white-robed army of Christ, we are more than conquerors. Our calling is to endure and to overcome.

In his influential study of the expansion of the early Church, Adolf Harnack wrote: "The remarkable thing is that although Christians were by no means numerous till after the middle of the second century, they recognized that Christianity formed the central point of humanity as the field of political history as well as its determining factor. Such a self-consciousness is perfectly intelligible in the case of Judaism, for the Jews were really a large nation and had a great history behind them. But it is truly amazing that a tiny set of people should confront the entire strength of the Roman empire, that it should see in the persecution of the Christians the chief role of that empire, and that it should make the world's history culminate in such a conflict. The only explanation of this lies in the fact that the Church simply took the place of Israel, and consequently felt herself to be a *people*; this implied that she was also a political factor, and indeed the factor which ranked as decisive alongside of the state and by which in the end the state was to be overcome."[21]

15-17 The elder continues his explanation: **For this reason** — because of their redemption and union with the Lamb through His blood, **they are before the Throne of God** in worship. Imitating the cherubim (4:8), these white-robed priests **serve Him day and night in His Temple** (cf. 1 Chron. 9:33; 23:30; Ps. 134:1). They thus receive the most characteristic blessing of the Covenant, the Shadow of the Almighty: **He who sits**

---

21. Adolf Harnack, *The Mission and Expansion of Christianity in the First Three Centuries*, James Moffatt, trans. (Gloucester, MA: Peter Smith, [1908] 1972), pp. 257f.

on the Throne shall spread His Tabernacle over them. This is referring to shade provided by the Glory-Cloud, which hovered over both the earth at its creation (Gen. 1:2) and Israel in the wilderness (Deut. 32:10-11).[22] Filled with "many thousands of angels" (Ps. 68:17; cf. 2 Kings 6:17), the Cloud provided a winged shelter, "a refuge from the storm, a shade from the heat" (Isa. 25:4; cf. Ps. 17:8; 36:7; 57:1; 61:4; 63:7; 91:1-13; 121:5-6). All this was summarized in a prophecy of the coming New Covenant Church: "When the LORD has washed away the filth of the daughters of Zion, and purged the blood of Jerusalem from her midst by the Spirit of judgment and the Spirit of burning, then the LORD will create over the whole area of Mount Zion and over her assemblies a Cloud by day, even smoke, and the brightness of a flaming fire by night; for over all the glory will be a canopy" (Isa. 4:4-5; cf. 51:16).

This Cloud/canopy of God's presence is also called a *covering* (2 Sam. 22:12; Ps. 18:11; Lam. 3:44; Ps. 91:4), the same word used to describe the position of the carved cherubim that hovered over the Ark of the Covenant (Ex. 25:20). This term is also the word translated *booths* or *tabernacles* in Leviticus 23:33-43, where God commands His people to erect booths of leafy branches to dwell in during the Feast of Tabernacles. As the Restoration prophets saw, this feast was an acted-out prophecy of the conversion of all nations, the filling out of the Covenant people with the entire world. On the last day of the Feast of Tabernacles, God spoke through Haggai: "I will shake all the nations; and they will come with the wealth of all nations; and I will fill this House [the Temple] with glory" (Hag. 2:7). Zechariah too prophesied of the meaning of this feast in terms of the conversion of the nations and the sanctification of every area of life (Zech. 14:16-21).

In the Last Days, during the celebration of the same feast, Jesus Christ again set forth its meaning: the outpouring of the Spirit upon the restored believer, so that the Church becomes a means of restoration to the entire world. The promise of the Feast of Tabernacles was about to be fulfilled, after the glorious Ascension of the Son to the Throne: "Now on the last day, the

---

22. See Meredith G. Kline, *Images of the Spirit* (Grand Rapids: Baker Book House, 1980), pp. 13ff.; cf. Chilton, *Paradise Restored*, pp. 58ff.

great day of the feast, Jesus stood and cried out, saying, 'If any man is thirsty, let him come to Me and drink. He who believes in Me, as the Scripture has said, out of his belly shall flow rivers of living water.' But this He spoke of the Spirit, whom those who believed in Him were to receive; for the Spirit was not yet given, because Jesus was not yet glorified" (John 7:37-39).

St. John's vision of the redeemed world reveals the inescapable outcome of Christ's Ascension, the consummation of Paradise: **They shall hunger no more, neither thirst anymore; neither shall the sun beat down on them, nor any heat; for the Lamb in the center of the Throne shall be their Shepherd, and shall guide them to the springs of the Water of Life; and God shall wipe away every tear from their eyes.** We noted earlier the Father's words to the Son from Isaiah 49, giving the promise of the salvation of the world as well as Israel. The passage continues:

> I will keep You and give You for a covenant of the people,
> To restore the land, to make them inherit the desolate heritages;
> Saying to those who are bound: Go forth!
> To those who are in darkness: Show yourselves!
> Along the roads they will feed,
> And their pasture will be on all bare heights.
> They will not hunger or thirst,
> Neither will the scorching heat or sun strike them down;
> For He who has compassion on them will lead them,
> And will guide them to springs of water.
> And I will make all My mountains a road,
> And My highways will be raised up.
> Behold, these shall come from afar,
> And lo, these will come from the north and from the west,
> And these from the land of Sinim [China].
> Shout for joy, O heavens! And rejoice, O earth!
> For the LORD has comforted His people,
> And will have compassion on His afflicted. (Isa. 49:8-13)

The churches of the first century were on the brink of the greatest Tribulation of all time. Many would lose their lives, their families, their possessions. But St. John writes to tell the churches that the Tribulation is not a death, but a Birth (cf. Matt. 24:8), the prelude to the establishment of the worldwide Kingdom of Christ. He shows them the scene on the other side:

the inevitable victory celebration.

In Nero's Circus Maximus, the scene of his bloody and revolting slaughters of Christians — by wild beasts, by crucifixion, by fire and sword — there stood a great stone obelisk, silent witness to the valiant conduct of those brave saints who endured tribulation and counted all things as loss for the sake of Christ. The bestial Nero and his henchmen have long since passed from the scene to their eternal reward, but the Obelisk still stands, now in the center of the great square in front of St. Peter's Basilica. Chiseled on its base are these words, taken from the overcoming martyrs' hymn of triumph:

CHRISTUS VINCIT

CHRISTUS REGNAT

CHRISTUS IMPERAT

— which is, being interpreted: Christ is conquering; Christ is reigning; Christ rules over all.

Part Four

COVENANT SANCTIONS:
THE SEVEN TRUMPETS
(Revelation 8-14)

Introduction

The fourth section of the standard treaty document dealt with the sanctions (curses and blessings) of the covenant (cf. Deut. 27:1-30:20).[1] In Deuteronomy, these sanctions are set forth in the context of a ratification ceremony, in which the Covenant between God and the people is renewed. Moses instructed the people to divide into two groups, six tribes on Mount Gerizim (the symbol of blessing) and six at an altar built on Mount Ebal (the symbol of cursing). The congregation was to take a solemn oath, repeating *Amen* as the Levites repeated the curses of the Covenant, calling down those curses upon themselves if they should ever forsake the law (Deut. 27:1-26). Moses made it clear that this Covenant oath involved not only the people who swore to it, with their wives, children, and servants, but also with the generations to come (Deut. 29:10-15).

Deuteronomy 28 is practically the paradigmatic blessing/curse section of the entire Bible. The blessings for obedience are listed in verses 1-14, and the curses for disobedience are enumerated (in more detail) in verses 15-68. *The Jewish War* by Josephus reads almost like a commentary on this passage, for the Great Tribulation culminating in the Fall of Jerusalem in A.D. 70 and the subsequent scattering of the Jews throughout the earth was the definitive fulfillment of its curses. When the

---

1. See Meredith G. Kline, *Treaty of the Great King: The Covenant Structure of Deuteronomy* (Grand Rapids: William B. Eerdmans Publishing Co., 1963), pp. 121-34; cf. Ray R. Sutton, *That You May Prosper: Dominion By Covenant* (Tyler, TX: Institute for Christian Economics, 1987).

225

Jewish mob was screaming for Jesus to be crucified, they invoked the woes of this chapter: "All the people answered and said, 'His blood be on us and on our children!' " (Matt. 27:25). When the days of vengeance finally came to that generation, they were cursed in every aspect of life (Deut. 28:15-19); smitten with pestilence of every sort (Deut. 28:20-26); visited with plague, violence, and oppression (Deut. 28:27-37); struck by poor harvests, economic reversals, and the loss of their children (Deut. 28:38-48); beseiged by enemies and starved into cannibalistic practices (Deut. 28:49-57); enslaved and scattered throughout the nations of the world, living in fear and despair night and day (Deut. 28:58-68).

Moses warned that the Land of Israel would become a desolation if the people forsook the Covenant; like Sodom and Gomorrah, a monument to the judgment of God. "Now the generation to come, your sons who rise up after you and the foreigner who comes from a distant land, when they see the plagues of the Land and the diseases with which the LORD has afflicted it, will say, 'All its land is brimstone and salt, a burning waste, unsown and unproductive, and no grass grows in it, like the overthrow of Sodom and Gomorrah, Admah and Zeboiim, which the LORD overthrew in His anger and in His wrath.'

"And all the nations shall say, 'Why has the LORD done thus to this Land? Why this great outburst of anger?' Then men shall say, 'Because they forsook the Covenant of the LORD, the God of their fathers, which He made with them when He brought them out of the land of Egypt. And they went and served other gods and worshiped them, gods whom they have not known and whom He had not alloted to them. Therefore, the anger of the LORD burned against that Land, to bring upon it every curse that is written in this book; and the LORD uprooted them from their Land in anger and in fury and in great wrath, and cast them into another land, as it is this day' " (Deut. 29:22-28).

The Seven Trumpets of Revelation announce that this judgment is about to be poured out upon Israel for her rejection of Christ. Throughout this section flies the Eagle-cherub with his cry of Woe, a reminder of the conquering nation warned of in Deuteronomy 28:49. The Eagle is a Biblical symbol of both Covenant blessing (cf. Ex. 19:4; Deut. 32:11) and Covenant curse (cf.

226

Jer. 4:13; Hab. 1:8). Like the opening of Hosea's Sanctions/ Covenant Ratification section (Hos. 8:1), the Eagle in Revelation is connected with the blowing of Trumpets signalling disaster; yet the Eagle brings salvation as well to the faithful of the covenant (cf. Rev. 12:14).

As in Deuteronomy, this section of Revelation shows us two mountains: the Mount of Cursing in Chapter 8, which is ignited with coals from the altar and thrown into the Abyss; and the Mount of Blessing in Chapter 14, Mount Zion, where the Lamb meets with His army of 144,000, the Remnant from the Land of Israel. Deuteronomy 30:1-10 promises an ultimate restoration of the people, when God would truly circumcise their hearts, and when He would again abundantly bless them in every area of life. Kline comments: "As the development of this theme in the prophets shows, the renewal and restoration which Moses foretells is that accomplished by Christ in the New Covenant. The prophecy is not narrowly concerned with ethnic Jews but with the covenant community, here concretely denoted in its Old Testament identity as Israel. Within the sphere of the New Covenant, however, the wall of ethnic distinctions disappears. Accordingly, the Old Testament figure used here of exiled Israelites being regathered to Yahweh in Jerusalem (v. 3b, 4; cf. 28:64) finds its chief fulfillment in the universal New Testament gathering of sinners out of the human race, exiled from Paradise, back to the Lord Christ enthroned in the heavenly Jerusalem."[2]

Thus, the central image of this section of Revelation is a Covenant ratification ceremony (Chapter 10), in which the Angel of the Covenant stands on the Sea and on the Land, lifting His right hand to heaven, swearing an oath and proclaiming the coming of the New Covenant, the inauguration of a new administration of the world under "the Lord and His Christ; and He will reign forever and ever" (Rev. 11:15).

---

2. Kline, pp. 132f.

8

LITURGY AND HISTORY

The Book is Opened (8:1-5)

1 And when He broke the Seventh Seal, there was silence in heaven for about half an hour.

2 And I saw the seven angels who stand before God; and Seven Trumpets were given to them.

3 And another angel came and stood at the altar, holding a golden censer; and much incense was given to him, that he might add it to the prayers of all the saints upon the golden altar which was before the throne.

4 And the smoke of the incense, with the prayers of the saints, went up before God out of the angel's hand.

5 And the angel took the censer; and he filled it with the fire of the altar and threw it onto the Land; and there followed peals of thunder and voices and flashes of lightning and an earthquake.

1-2 Finally, **the Seventh Seal** is broken, opening up to reveal the **seven trumpets** that herald the doom of Jerusalem, the once-holy City which has become paganized and which, like its precursor Jericho, will fall by the blast of seven trumpets (cf. Josh. 6:4-5). But first, in this grand heavenly liturgy which makes up the Book of Revelation, there is **silence in heaven for about half an hour.** Milton Terry comments: "Perhaps the idea of this *silence* was suggested by the cessation of singers and trumpets when King Hezekiah and those with him bowed themselves in reverent worship (2 Chron. 29:28-29), and the *half hour* may have some reference to the offering of incense described in verses 3 and 4, for that would be about the length of time necessary for a priest to enter the temple and offer incense and return (comp.

Lev. 16:13-14; Luke 1:10, 21)."[1]

Alfred Edersheim's description of this Temple ceremony helps us understand the setting reflected here: "Slowly the incensing priest and his assistants ascended the steps to the Holy Place, preceded by the two priests who had formerly dressed the altar and the candlestick, and who now removed the vessels they had left behind, and, worshipping, withdrew. Next, one of the assistants reverently spread the coals on the golden altar; the other arranged the incense; and then the chief officiating priest was left alone within the Holy Place, to await the signal of the president before burning the incense. It was probably while thus expectant that the angel Gabriel appeared to Zacharias [Luke 1:8-11]. As the president gave the word of command, which marked that 'the time of incense had come,' 'the whole multitude of the people without' withdrew from the inner court, and fell down before the Lord, spreading their hands[2] in silent prayer.

"It is this most solemn period, when throughout the vast Temple buildings deep silence rested on the worshipping multitude, while within the sanctuary itself the priest laid the incense on the golden altar, and the cloud of 'odours' [5:8] rose up before the Lord, which serves as the image of heavenly things in this description."[3]

Following this awe-filled silence, **the seven angels who stand before God**[4] are given **Seven Trumpets** (the Temple liturgy used seven trumpets: 1 Chron. 15:24; Neh. 12:41). St. John seems to assume that we will recognize these seven angels; and well we should, for we have met them already. The letters of Revelation 2-3 were written to "the seven angels" of the churches, and it is they who are represented here (granting, of course, that these

---

1. Milton S. Terry, *Biblical Apocalyptics: A Study of the Most Notable Revelations of God and of Christ in the Canonical Scriptures* (New York: Eaton and Mains, 1898), pp. 343f. See also Alfred Edersheim, *The Temple: Its Ministry and Services as They Were at the Time of Jesus Christ* (Grand Rapids: William B. Eerdmans, 1980), pp. 167f.

2. Edersheim notes here that "the practice of folding the hands together in prayer dates from the fifth century of our era, and is of purely Saxon origin."

3. Alfred Edersheim, *The Temple*, p. 167.

4. Tobit 12:15 speaks of "the seven holy angels, which present the prayers of the saints, and which go in and out before the glory of the Holy One."

figures are not necessarily "identical" to the angels of the churches). They are clearly meant to be related to each other, as we can see when we step back from the text (and our preconceived ideas) and allow the whole picture to present itself to us. When we do this, we see the Revelation structured in sevens, and in recurring patterns of sevens. One of those recurring patterns is that of **seven angels** (chapters 1-3, 8-11, 14, 15-16). Just as earthly worship is patterned after heavenly worship (Heb. 8:5; 9:23-24), so is the government of the Church (Matt. 16:19; 18:18; John 20:23); moreover, according to Scripture, there are numerous correspondences between human and angelic activities (cf. 21:17). Angels are present in the worship services of the Church (1 Cor. 11:10; Eph. 3:10) – or, more precisely, on the Lord's Day *we* are gathered in worship around the Throne of God, in the heavenly court.

Thus we are shown in the Book of Revelation that the government of the earthly Church corresponds to heavenly, angelic government, just as our official worship corresponds to that which is conducted around the heavenly Throne by the angels. Moreover, the judgments that fall down upon the Land are brought through the actions of the seven angels (again, we cannot divorce the human angels from their heavenly counterparts). The officers of the Church are commissioned and empowered to bring God's blessings and curses into fruition in the earth. Church officers are the divinely appointed managers of world history. The implications of this fact, as we shall see, are quite literally earth-shaking.

3-5 St. John sees **another angel** standing at the heavenly **altar** of incense, **holding a golden censer.** A large amount of **incense,** symbolic of **the prayers of all the saints** (cf. comments on 5:8), is given to the angel **that he might add it** to the prayers of God's people, assuring that the prayers will be received as a sweet-smelling offering to the Lord. Then **the smoke of the incense, with the prayers of the saints,** ascends **before God out of the angel's hand,** as the minister offers up the petitions of his congregation.

What happens next is amazing: The angel fills the censer with coals of fire from the incense altar and casts the fire onto the earth in judgment; and this is followed by **peals of thunder**

and voices and flashes of lightning and an earthquake. These phenomena, of course, should be familiar to us as the normal accompaniments of the Glory-Cloud: "So it came about on the third day, when it was morning, that there were thunder and lightning flashes and a thick cloud upon the mountain and a very loud trumpet sound. . . . Now Mount Sinai was all in smoke because the LORD descended upon it in fire; and its smoke ascended like the smoke of a furnace, and the whole mountain quaked violently" (Ex. 19:16, 18).

The irony of this passage becomes obvious when we keep in mind that it is a prophecy against apostate Israel. In the worship of the Old Testament, the fire on the altar of burnt offering originated in heaven, coming down upon the altar when the Tabernacle and the Temple were made ready (Lev. 9:24; 2 Chron. 7:1). This fire, started by God, was kept burning by the priests, and was carried from place to place so that it could be used to start other holy fires (Lev. 16:12-13; cf. Num. 16:46-50; Gen. 22:6). Now, when God's people were commanded to destroy an apostate city, Moses further ordered : "You shall gather all its booty into the middle of its open square and burn all its booty with fire *as a whole burnt offering* to the LORD your God" (Deut. 13:16; Jud. 20:40; cf. Gen. 19:28). The only acceptable way to burn a city as a whole burnt sacrifice was with God's fire — *fire from the altar.*[5] Thus, when a city was to be destroyed, the priest would take fire from God's altar and use it to ignite the heap of booty which served as kindling, so offering up the entire city as a sacrifice. It is this practice of putting a city "under the ban," so that nothing survives the conflagration (Deut. 13:12-18), that the Book of Revelation uses to describe God's judgment against *Jerusalem.*[6]

God rains down His judgments upon the earth in specific response to the liturgical worship of His people. As part of the formal, official worship service in heaven, the angel of the altar offers up the prayers of the corporate people of God; and God responds to the petitions, acting into history on behalf of the

---

5. To offer a sacrifice with "strange fire" (i.e., man-made fire, not from the altar) was punished with death: Lev. 10:1-4.

6. For an in-depth study of this whole subject, see James B. Jordan, *Sabbath-Breaking and the Death Penalty: A Theological Investigation* (Tyler, TX: Geneva Ministries, 1986), esp. chaps. 3-5.

saints. The intimate connection between liturgy and history is an inescapable fact, one which we cannot afford to ignore. This is not to suggest that the world is in danger of lapsing into "non-being" when the Church's worship is defective. In fact, God will use historical forces (even the heathen) to chastise the Church when she fails to live up to her high calling as the Kingdom of priests. The point here is that the official worship of the covenantal community is cosmically significant. Church history is the key to world history: When the worshiping assembly calls upon the Lord of the Covenant, the world experiences His judgments. History is managed and directed from the altar of incense, which has received the prayers of the Church.[7]

In my distress I called upon the LORD,
And cried to my God for help;
He heard my voice out of His Temple,
And my cry for help before Him came into His ears.
Then the earth shook and quaked;
And the foundations of the mountains were trembling
And were shaken, because He was angry.
Smoke went up out of His nostrils,
And fire from His mouth devoured;
Coals were kindled by it.
He bowed the heavens also, and came down
With thick darkness under His feet.
And He rode upon a cherub and flew;
And He sped upon the wings of the wind.
He made darkness His hiding place, His canopy around Him,
Darkness of waters, thick clouds of the skies.
From the brightness before Him passed His thick clouds,
Hailstones and coals of fire.
The LORD also thundered in the heavens,
And the Most High uttered His voice,
Hailstones and coals of fire.
And He sent out His arrows, and scattered them,
And lightning flashes in abundance, and routed them.
Then the channels of waters appeared,
And the foundations of the world were laid bare
At Thy rebuke, O LORD,
At the blast of the breath of Thy nostrils. (Psalm 18:6-15)

---

7. The symbolic use of incense is therefore appropriate (but of course not binding) in the liturgy of the New Covenant.

Several areas of the symbolic significance of **trumpets** are in view in this passage. First, trumpets were used in the Old Testament liturgy for ceremonial processions, particularly as an escort for the Ark of the Covenant; the obvious, prime example of this is the march around Jericho before it fell (Josh. 6; cf. 1 Chron. 15:24; Neh. 12:41). As G. B. Caird says, "John must have had this story in mind when he wrote; for he tells us that with the blowing of the seventh trumpet the ark appeared (11:19), and also that one of the consequences of the trumpet blasts was that a tenth of the great city fell (11:13)."[8]

Second, trumpets were blown to proclaim the rule of a new king (1 Kings 1:34, 39; cf. Ps. 47:5): "John's seventh trumpet is the signal for the heavenly choir to sing their coronation anthem, praising God because He has assumed the sovereignty and begun to reign (11:15)."[9]

Third, the trumpet sounded an alarm, warning Israel of approaching judgment and urging national repentance (Isa. 58:1; Jer. 4:5-8; 6:1, 17; Ezek. 33:1-6; Joel 2:1, 15). "John too believed that the purpose of the trumpet blasts and the disasters they heralded was to call men to repentance, even if that purpose was not achieved. 'The rest of mankind who survived these plagues still did not renounce the gods of their own making' (9:20; cf. Amos 4:6-11)."[10]

Fourth, Moses was instructed to use two silver trumpets both "for summoning the congregation" to worship and "for having the camps set out" in battle against the enemy (Num. 10:1-9). It is significant that these two purposes, warfare and worship, are mentioned in the same breath. Gordon Wenham observes that "like the arrangement of the camp with the tabernacle at the middle, and the ordering of the tribes in battle formation, the silver trumpets declare that Israel is the army of the King of kings preparing for a holy war of conquest."[11] The irony in Revelation, of course, is that God is now ordering the trumpets of holy war blown against Israel herself.

---

8. G. B. Caird, *The Revelation of St. John the Divine* (New York: Harper & Row, Publishers, 1966), p. 108.

9. Ibid.

10. Ibid., p. 109.

11. Gordon J. Wenham, *Numbers: An Introduction and Commentary* (Downers Grove, IL: Inter-Varsity Press, 1981), p. 102.

Fifth, trumpets were also blown at the feasts and on the first day of every month (Num. 10:10), with special emphasis on Tishri 1, the civil New Year's Day (in the ecclesiastical year, the first day of the seventh month); this Day of Trumpets was the special liturgical acknowledgement of the Day of the Lord (Lev. 23:24-25; Num. 29:1-6). Of course, the most basic background to all this is the Glory-Cloud, which is accompanied by angelic trumpet blasts announcing the sovereignty and judgment of the Lord (Ex. 19:16); the earthly liturgy of God's people was a recapitulation of the heavenly liturgy, another indication that God's redeemed people had been restored to His image. (This was the reason for the method Gideon's army used to rout the Midianites, in Judges 7:15-22: By surrounding the enemy with lights, shouting, and the blowing of trumpets, the Israelites were an earthly reflection of God's heavenly army in the Cloud, coming in vengeance upon God's enemies.) The Biblical symbolism would have been very familiar to St. John's first-century readers, and "in any case John himself has told them clearly enough that the trumpets were an escort for the ark, a proclamation of the divine sovereignty, and a summons to general repentance; and by placing them in the hands of the Angels of the Presence he has indicated their close association with worship."[12]

As J. Massyngberde Ford notes,[13] there are four striking "reversals" in the text:

1. From the Throne and altar, the "mercy seat," comes wrath;
2. Incense, the "soothing aroma to the LORD" (Lev. 1:13), becomes an agent of death (cf. 2 Cor. 2:14-16);
3. The trumpets, which called Israel to worship, now become heralds of her destruction;
4. The heavenly liturgy itself, appointed for Israel's sanctification, becomes the means of her overthrow and dissolution.

The First Trumpet (8:6-7)

6 And the seven angels who had the Seven Trumpets prepared themselves to sound them.

---

12. Caird, p. 111.
13. J. Massyngberde Ford, *Revelation: Introduction, Translation, and Commentary* (Garden City, NY: Doubleday & Co., 1975), pp. 135f.

7 And the first sounded, and there came hail and fire, mixed
with blood, and they were thrown onto the Land; and a
third of the Land was burned up, and a third of the trees
were burned up, and all the green grass was burned up.

6-7   Not only reminding us of the fall of Jericho, the judgments brought about by the sounding of these trumpets also are
reminiscent of the plagues that came upon Egypt prior to the
Exodus. Together, they are represented as destroying one third
of the Land. Obviously, since the judgment is neither total nor
final, it cannot be the end of the physical world. Nevertheless,
the devastation is tremendous, and does work to bring about the
end of the Jewish nation, the subject of these terrible prophecies. Israel has become a nation of Egyptians and Canaanites,
and worse: a land of covenant apostates. All the curses of the
Law are about to be poured out upon those who had once been
the people of God (Matt. 23:35-36). The first four trumpets apparently refer to the series of disasters that devastated Israel in
the Last Days, and primarily the events leading up to the outbreak of war.

As the Seal-judgments were counted in fourths, the Trumpet-
judgments are counted in thirds. The First Trumpet sounds, and
a *triple* curse (hail, fire, blood) is thrown down, affecting a *third*
of the Land; *three* objects in particular are singled out. St. John
sees **hail and fire, mixed with blood, and they were thrown onto
the Land**. The blood of the slain witnesses is mixed with the fire
from the altar, bringing wrath down upon the persecutors. The
result of this curse, which has some similarities to the seventh
Egyptian plague (Ex. 9:22-26), is the burning of **a third of the
Land** and **a third of the trees**, and **all the green grass** (i.e., all the
grass on a third of the Land; cf. 9:4). If the trees and grass represent the elect remnant (as they seem to in 7:3 and 9:4), this indicates that they are not exempt from physical suffering and death
as God's wrath is visited upon the wicked. Nevertheless, (1) the
Church cannot be completely destroyed in any judgment (Matt.
16:18), and (2) unlike the wicked, the Christian's ultimate destiny
is not wrath but life and salvation (Rom. 2:7-9; 1 Thess. 5:9).

To those pagans who scoffed that God had failed to rescue
Christians from their enemies, St. Augustine replied: "The
whole family of God, most high and most true, has therefore a

consolation of its own—a consolation which cannot deceive, and which has in it a surer hope than the tottering and falling affairs of life can afford. They will not refuse the discipline of this temporal life, in which they are schooled for life eternal; nor will they lament their experience of it, for the good things of life they use as pilgrims who are not detained by them, and its ills either prove or improve them.

"As for those who insult over them in their trials, and when ills befall them say, 'Where is thy God?' [Ps. 42:10] we may ask them where their gods are when they suffer the very calamities for the sake of avoiding which they worship their gods, or maintain they ought to be worshipped; for the family of Christ is furnished with its reply: Our God is everywhere present, wholly everywhere; not confined to any place. He can be present unperceived, and be absent without moving; when He exposes us to adversities, it is either to prove our perfections or correct our imperfections; and in return for our patient endurance of the sufferings of time, He reserves for us an everlasting reward. But who are you, that we should deign to speak with you even about your own gods, much less about our God, who is 'to be feared above all gods? For all the gods of the nations are idols; but the LORD made the heavens' [Ps. 96:4-5]."[14]

The wicked, on the other hand, have only wrath and anguish, tribulation and distress ahead of them (Rom. 2:8-9). Literally, the vegetation of Judea, and especially of Jerusalem, would be destroyed in the Roman scorched-earth methods of warfare: "The countryside, like the city, was a pitiful sight, for where once there had been a multitude of trees and parks, there was now an utter wilderness stripped bare of timber; and no stranger who had seen the old Judea and the glorious suburbs of her capital, and now beheld utter desolation, could refrain from tears or suppress a groan at so terrible a change. The war had blotted out every trace of beauty, and no one who had known it in the past and came upon it suddenly would have recognized the place, for though he was already there, he would still have been looking for the city."[15] Yet this was only the beginning; many more sorrows—and much worse—lay ahead (cf. 16:21).

---

14. St. Augustine, *The City of God*, i.29 (Marcus Dods, trans.; New York: The Modern Library, 1950, pp. 34f.).
15. Josephus, *The Jewish War*, vi.i.1.

The Second Trumpet (8:8-9)

8 And the second angel sounded, and something like a great
mountain burning with fire was thrown into the sea; and a
third of the sea became blood;

9 and a third of the creatures that were in the sea and had life,
died; and a third of the ships were destroyed.

8-9   With the trumpet blast of **the second angel,** we see a parallel to the first plague on Egypt, in which the Nile was turned to
blood and the fish **died** (Ex. 7:17-21). The cause of this calamity
was that **a great mountain burning with fire was cast into the
sea.** The meaning of this becomes clear when we remember that
the nation of Israel was God's "Holy Mountain," the "mountain
of God's inheritance" (Ex. 15:17). As the redeemed people of
God, they had been brought back to Eden, and the repeated use
of mountain-imagery throughout their history (including the
fact that Mount Zion was the accepted symbol of the nation)
demonstrates this vividly. But now, as apostates, Israel had become a "destroying mountain," against whom God's wrath had
turned. God is now speaking of *Jerusalem* in the same language
He once used to speak of *Babylon*, a fact that will become central to the imagery of this book:

> Behold, I am against you, O destroying mountain,
> Destroyer of the whole earth, declares the LORD,
> And I will stretch out My hand against you,
> And roll you down from the crags
> And I will make you a burnt out mountain. . . .
> The sea has come up over Babylon;
> She has been engulfed with its tumultuous waves.
> (Jer. 51:25, 42)

Connect this with the fact that Jesus, in the middle of a
lengthy series of discourses and parables about the destruction
of Jerusalem (Matt. 20-25), cursed an unfruitful fig tree, as a
symbol of judgment upon Israel. He then told his disciples,
"Truly I say to you, if you have faith, and do not doubt, you
shall not only do what was done to the fig tree, but even if you
say to *this mountain*, 'Be taken up and cast into the sea,' it shall
happen. And all things you ask in prayer, believing, you shall
receive" (Matt. 21:21-22). Was Jesus being flippant? Did He

really expect His disciples to go around praying about moving literal mountains? Of course not. More importantly, Jesus was not changing the subject. He was still giving them a lesson about the fall of Israel. What was the lesson? Jesus was instructing His disciples to pray imprecatory prayers, beseeching God to destroy Israel, to wither the fig tree, to cast the apostate mountain into the sea.[16]

And that is exactly what happened. The persecuted Church, under oppression from the apostate Jews, began praying for God's vengeance upon Israel (6:9-11), calling for the mountain of Israel to "be taken up and cast into the sea." Their offerings were received at God's heavenly altar, and in response God directed His angels to throw down His judgments to the Land (8:3-5). Israel was destroyed. We should note that St. John is writing this before the destruction, for the instruction and encouragement of the saints, so that they will continue to pray in faith. As he had told them in the beginning, "Blessed is he who reads and those who hear the words of the prophecy, and *keep* the things that are written in it; for the time is near" (1:3).

The Third Trumpet (8:10-11)

10 And the third angel sounded, and a great star fell from heaven, burning like a torch, and it fell on a third of the rivers and on the springs of waters;
11 and the name of the star is called Wormwood; and a third of the waters became wormwood; and many men died from the waters, because they were made bitter.

10-11 Like the preceding symbol, the vision of the Third Trumpet combines Biblical imagery from the fall of both Egypt and Babylon. The effect of this plague — the waters being **made bitter** — is similar to the first plague on Egypt, in which the water became bitter because of the multitude of dead and decaying fish (Ex. 7:21). The bitterness of the waters is caused by **a great star** that **fell from heaven, burning like a torch.** This parallels Isaiah's prophecy of the fall of Babylon, spoken in terms of the

---

16. According to William Telford, *this mountain* was a standard expression among the Jewish people for the Temple Mount, "the mountain *par excellence*"; see *The Barren Temple and the Withered Tree* (Department of Biblical Studies, University of Sheffield, 1980), p. 119.

239

original Fall from Paradise:

> How you have fallen from heaven,
> O star of the morning, son of the dawn!
> You have been cut down to the earth,
> You who have weakened the nations!
> But you said in your heart,
> I will ascend to heaven,
> I will raise my throne above the stars of God,
> And I will sit on the mount of assembly,
> In the recesses of the north.
> I will ascend above the heights of the clouds;
> I will make myself like the Most High.
> Nevertheless you will be thrust down to Sheol,
> To the recesses of the pit. (Isa. 14:12-15)

The **name** of this fallen star is **Wormwood**, a term used in the Law and the Prophets to warn Israel of its destruction as a punishment for apostasy (Deut. 29:18; Jer. 9:15; 23:15; Lam. 3:15, 19; Amos 5:7). Again, by combining these Old Testament allusions, St. John makes his point: Israel is apostate, and has become an Egypt; Jerusalem has become a Babylon; and the covenant-breakers will be destroyed, as surely as Egypt and Babylon were destroyed.

The Fourth Trumpet (8:12-13)

12 And the fourth angel sounded, and a third of the sun and a third of the moon and a third of the stars were smitten, so that a third of them might be darkened and the day might not shine for a third of it, and the night in the same way.
13 And I looked, and I heard an Eagle flying in midheaven, saying with a loud voice, Woe; Woe; Woe to those who dwell on the Land, because of the remaining blasts of the Trumpet of the three angels who are about to sound!

12 Like the ninth Egyptian plague of "thick darkness" (Ex. 10:21-23), the curse brought by **the fourth angel** strikes the light-bearers, the **sun, moon**, and **stars, so that a third of them might be darkened**. The imagery here was long used in the prophets to depict the fall of nations and national rulers (cf. Isa. 13:9-11, 19; 24:19-23; 34:4-5; Ezek. 32:7-8, 11-12; Joel 2:10, 28-32; Acts 2:16-21). In fulfillment of this, Farrar observes, "ruler after ruler, chieftain after chieftain of the Roman Empire and the Jewish nation was assassinated and ruined. Gaius, Claudius, Nero, Galba, Otho, Vitellius, all died by murder or suicide; Herod the Great, Herod Antipas, Herod Agrippa, and most of the Herodian Princes, together with not a few of the leading High Priests of Jerusalem, perished in disgrace, or in exile, or by violent hands. All these were quenched suns and darkened stars."[17]

13 The flying Eagle-cherub (4:7) rules the Trumpets section of the Revelation (cf. Hos. 8:1), and it is appropriate that St. John now sees **an Eagle flying in midheaven**, warning of wrath to come. The Eagle, like many other covenantal symbols, has a dual nature. On one side, he signifies the salvation God provided for Israel:

> For the LORD's portion is His people;
> Jacob is the allotment of His inheritance.
> He found him in a desert land,
> And in the howling waste of a wilderness;
> He encircled him, He cared for him,
> He guarded him as the pupil of His eye.
> Like an Eagle that stirs up its nest,
> That hovers over its young,
> He spread His wings and caught them,
> He carried them on His pinions. (Deut. 32:9-11; cf. Ex. 19:4)

But the Eagle is also a fearsome bird of prey, associated with blood and death and rotting flesh:

> His young ones also suck up blood;
> And where the slain are, there is he. (Job 39:30)

The prophetic warnings of Israel's destruction are often couched in terms of eagles descending upon carrion (Deut. 28:49; Jer. 4:13; Lam. 4:19; Hos. 8:1; Hab. 1:8; Matt. 24:28). Indeed, a basic aspect of the covenantal curse is that of being devoured by the birds of the air (Gen. 15:9-12; Deut. 28:26, 49; Prov. 30:17; Jer. 7:33-34; 16:3-4; 19:7; 34:18-20; Ezek. 39:17-20;

---

17. F. W. Farrar, *The Early Days of Christianity* (Chicago: Belford, Clarke and Co., Publishers, 1882), p. 519.

Rev. 19:17-18). The Eagle-cherub will reappear in this section of Revelation as an image of salvation (12:14), and at the end will be replaced by (or seen again as) an angel **flying in midheaven** proclaiming the *Gospel* **to those who dwell on the Land** (14:6), for his mission is ultimately redemptive in its scope. But the salvation of the world will come about through Israel's fall (Rom. 11:11-15, 25). So the Eagle begins his message with wrath, proclaiming three **Woes** that are to come upon **those who dwell on the Land.**

Like the original plagues on Egypt, the curses are becoming intensified, and more precise in their application. St. John is building up to a crescendo, using the three woes of the Eagle (corresponding to the fifth, sixth, and seventh **blasts of the Trumpet;** cf. 9:12; 11:14-15) to dramatize the increasing disasters being visited upon the Land of Israel. After many delays and much longsuffering by the jealous and holy Lord of Hosts, the awful sanctions of the Law are finally unleashed against the Covenant-breakers, so that Jesus Christ may inherit the kingdoms of the world and bring them into His Temple (11:15-19; 21:22-27).

9

ALL HELL BREAKS LOOSE

The Fifth Trumpet (9:1-12)

1 And the fifth angel sounded, and I saw a star from heaven which had fallen to the earth; and the key of the well of the Abyss was given to him.

2 And he opened the well of the Abyss; and smoke went up out of the well, like the smoke of a burning furnace; and the sun and the air were darkened by the smoke of the well.

3 And out of the smoke came forth locusts upon the earth; and power was given them, as the scorpions of the earth have power.

4 And they were told that they should not hurt the grass of the earth, nor any green thing, nor any tree, but only the men who do not have the seal of God on their foreheads.

5 And they were not permitted to kill anyone, but that they should be tormented for five months; and their torment was like the torment of a scorpion when it stings a man.

6 And in those days men will seek death and will not find it; and they will long to die and death shall flee from them.

7 And the appearance of the locusts was like horses prepared for battle; and on their heads, as it were, crowns like gold, and their faces were like the faces of men.

8 And they had hair like the hair of women, and their teeth were like the teeth of lions.

9 And they had breastplates like breastplates of iron; and the sound of their wings was like the sound of chariots, of many horses rushing to battle.

10 And they have tails like scorpions, and stings; and in their tails is their power to hurt men for five months.

11 They have as king over them, the angel of the Abyss; his name in Hebrew is Abaddon, and in the Greek he has the name Apollyon.

12 The first Woe is past; behold, two Woes are still coming after these things.

1-6   With the first Woe, the plagues become more intense. While this curse is similar to the great swarms of **locusts** which came upon Egypt in the eighth plague (Ex. 10:12-15), these "locusts" are different: they are *demons* from **the Abyss**, the bottomless pit, spoken of seven times in Revelation (9:1, 2, 11; 11:7; 17:8; 20:1, 3). The Septuagint first uses the term in Genesis 1:2, speaking of the original deep-and-darkness which the Spirit creatively overshadowed (and metaphorically "overcame"; cf. John 1:5). The Abyss is the farthest extreme from heaven (Gen. 49:25; Deut. 33:13) and from the high mountains (Ps. 36:6). It is used in Scripture as a reference to the deepest parts of the sea (Job 28:14; 38:16; Ps. 33:7) and to subterranean rivers and vaults of water (Deut. 8:7; Job 38:16), whence the waters of the Flood came (Gen. 7:11; 8:2; Prov. 3:20; 8:24), and which nourished the kingdom of Assyria (Ezek. 31:4, 15). The Red Sea crossing of the covenant people is repeatedly likened to a passage through the Abyss (Ps. 77:16; 106:9; Isa. 44:27; 51:10; 63:13). The prophet Ezekiel threatened Tyre with a great desolation of the land, in which God would bring up the Abyss to cover the city with a new Flood, bringing its people down to the pit in the lower parts of the earth (Ezek. 26:19-21), and Jonah spoke of the Abyss in terms of excommunication from God's presence, a banishment from the Temple (Jon. 2:2-6). The domain of the Dragon (Job 41:31; Ps. 148:7; Rev. 11:7; 17:8), the prison of the demons (Luke 8:31; Rev. 20:1-3; cf. 2 Pet. 2:4; Jude 6), and the realm of the dead (Rom. 10:7) are all called by the name *Abyss*. St. John is thus warning his readers that hell is about to break loose upon the Land of Israel; as with Tyre of old, the Abyss is being dredged up to cover the Land with its unclean spirits. Apostate Israel is to be cast out of God's presence, excommunicated from the Temple, and filled with demons. One of the central messages of Revelation is that the Church tabernacles in heaven; the corollary of this is that the false church tabernacles in hell.

Why does the locust plague last for **five months**? This figure is, first of all, a reference to the period of five months, from May through September, when locusts normally appeared. (The unusual feature is that *these* locusts *remain* for the entire period, engaging in constant torment of the population.) Second, this may refer in part to the actions of Gessius Florus, the procurator of Judea, who for a five-month period (beginning in May of 66 with the slaughter of 3,600 peaceful citizens) terrorized the Jews, deliberately seeking to incite them to rebellion. He was successful: Josephus dates the beginning of the Jewish War from this occasion.[1] Third, the use of the term *five* is associated in Scripture with power, and specifically with military organization — the arrangement of the Israelite militia in a five-squad platoon formation (Ex. 13:18; Num. 32:17; Josh. 1:14; 4:12; Jud. 7:11; cf. 2 Kings 1:9ff.).[2] By God's direction, Israel was to be attacked by a demonic army from the Abyss.

During the ministry of Christ, Satan had **fallen to the earth like a star from heaven** (cf. 12:4, 9, 12); **and the key of the well of the Abyss was given to him. And he opened the well of the Abyss.** What all this means is exactly what Jesus prophesied during His earthly ministry: the Land which had received the benefits of His work and then rejected Him, would become glutted with demons from the Abyss. We should note here that the key is *given* to Satan, for it is God who sends the demons as a scourge upon His rebellious people.

> The men of Nineveh shall stand up with this generation at the judgment, and shall condemn it because they repented at the preaching of Jonah; and behold, something greater than Jonah is here. The Queen of the South shall rise up with this generation at the judgment and shall condemn it, because she came from the ends of the earth to hear the wisdom of Solomon; and behold, something greater than Solomon is here.
>
> Now when the unclean spirit goes out of a man, it passes through waterless places, seeking rest, and does not find it. Then it says, "I will return to my house from which I came"; and when it comes, it finds it unoccupied, swept, and put in order. Then it goes, and takes along with it seven other spirits more wicked than itself, and they go in and live there; and the last state of that man becomes worse than the first. *That is the way it will also be with this evil generation.* (Matt. 12:41-45)

---

1. Flavius Josephus, *The Jewish War*, ii.xiv.9-xix.9.
2. The Hebrew word in these texts is usually translated *harnessed, armed*, or *in martial array*, but the literal rendering is simply *five in a rank* (that is, five squads of ten men in each squad). See James B. Jordan, *The Law of the Covenant: An Exposition of Exodus 21-23* (Tyler, TX: Institute for Christian Economics, 1984), pp. 264f.; idem, *Judges: God's War Against Humanism* (Tyler, TX: Geneva Ministries, 1985), p. 17.

Because of Israel's rejection of the King of kings, the blessings they had received would turn into curses. Jerusalem had been "swept clean" by Christ's ministry; now it would become "a dwelling place of demons and a prison of every unclean spirit, and a prison of every unclean and hateful bird" (18:2). The entire generation became increasingly demon-possessed; their progressive national insanity is apparent as one reads through the New Testament, and its horrifying final stages are depicted in the pages of Josephus' *The Jewish War*: the loss of all ability to reason, the frenzied mobs attacking one another, the deluded multitudes following after the most transparently false prophets, the crazed and desperate chase after food, the mass murders, executions, and suicides, the fathers slaughtering their own families and the mothers eating their own children. Satan and the host of hell simply swarmed throughout the land of Israel and consumed the apostates.

The vegetation of the earth is specifically exempted from the destruction caused by the "locusts." This is a curse on disobedient *men*. Only the Christians are immune to the **scorpion**-like sting of the demons (cf. Mk. 6:7; Lk. 10:17-19; Acts 26:18); the unbaptized Israelites, **who do not have the seal of God on their foreheads** (see on 7:3-8), are attacked and tormented by the demonic powers. And the immediate purpose God has in unleashing this curse is not death, but merely **torment**, misery and suffering, as the nation of Israel was put through a series of demoniac convulsions. St. John repeats what he has told us in 6:16, that **in those days men will seek death and will not find it; and they will long to die and death shall flee from them.** Jesus had specifically prophesied this longing for death among the final generation, the generation of Jews which crucified Him (Lk. 23:27-30). As the Wisdom of God had said long before: "He who sins against Me wrongs his own soul; all those who hate Me love death" (Prov. 8:36).

7-12   The description of the demon-locusts bears many similarities to the invading heathen armies mentioned in the prophets (Jer. 51:27; Joel 1:6; 2:4-10; cf. Lev. 17:7 and 2 Chron. 11:15, where the Hebrew word for *demon* is *hairy one*). This passage may also refer, in part, to the Satanic gangs of murderous Zealots that preyed on the citizens of Jerusalem. As Josephus tells us, the people had more to fear from the Zealots than from the Romans: "With their insatiable hunger for loot, they ransacked the houses of the wealthy, murdered men and violated women for sport; they drank their spoils with blood, and from mere satiety they shamelessly gave themselves up to effeminate practices, plaiting their hair and putting on women's clothes, drenching themselves with perfumes and painting their eyelids to make themselves attractive. They copied not merely the dress, but also the passions of women, devising in their excess of licentiousness unlawful pleasures in which they wallowed as in a brothel. Thus they entirely polluted the city with their foul practices. Yet though they wore women's faces, their hands were murderous. They would approach with mincing steps, then suddenly become fighting men, and, whipping out their swords from under their dyed cloaks, they would run through every passerby."[3]

One particularly interesting point about the description of the demon army is St. John's statement that **the sound of their wings was like the sound of chariots, of many horses rushing to battle.** That is the same sound made by the wings of the angels in the Glory-Cloud (Ezek. 1:24; 3:13; 2 Kings 7:5-7); the difference here is that the noise is made by *fallen* angels.

St. John goes on to identify the **king** of the demons, **the angel of the Abyss,** giving his name in both Hebrew **(Abaddon)** and Greek **(Apollyon)** — one of many indications of the essentially Hebraic character of the Revelation.[4] The words mean *Destruction* and *Destroyer*; **Abaddon** is used in the Old Testament for the realm of the dead, the "place of destruction" (Job 26:6; 28:22; 31:12; Ps. 88:11; Prov. 15:11; 27:20). St. John thus presents Satan as the very personification of death itself (cf. 1 Cor. 10:10; Heb. 2:14). Clearly, for Satan's entire host of destroyers to be let loose upon the Jewish nation was a hell on earth indeed. And yet St. John tells us that this outbreak of demons in the land is only **the first Woe.** Even this is not the worst, for **two Woes** (i.e., the sixth and seventh trumpets) **are still coming after these things.**

---

3. Flavius Josephus, *The Jewish War*, iv.ix.10.

4. For a lengthy discussion of St. John's grammar, with particular attention to the Hebraic style, see R. H. Charles, *A Critical and Exegetical Commentary on the Revelation of St. John*, 2 vols. (Edinburgh: T. & T. Clark, 1920), Vol. 1, pp. cxvii-clix. Charles's summary of the reason for St. John's unique style is that *"while he writes in Greek, he thinks in Hebrew"* (p. cxliii).

The Sixth Trumpet (9:13-21)

13 And the sixth angel sounded, and I heard a voice from the four horns of the golden altar which is before God,

14 one saying to the sixth angel who had the trumpet: Release the four angels who are bound at the great river Euphrates.

15 And the four angels, who had been prepared for the hour and day and month and year, were released, so that they might kill a third of mankind.

16 And the number of the armies of the horsemen was myriads of myriads; I heard the number of them.

17 And this is how I saw in the vision the horses and those who sat on them: They had breastplates of fire and of hyacinth and of brimstone; and the heads of the horses are like the heads of lions; and out of their mouths proceed fire and smoke and brimstone.

18 A third of mankind was killed by these three plagues, by the fire and the smoke and the brimstone, which proceeded out of their mouths.

19 For the power of the horses is in their mouths and in their tails; for their tails are like serpents and have heads; and with them they do harm.

20 And the rest of the men, who were not killed by these plagues, did not repent of the works of their hands, so as not to worship demons, and the idols of gold and of silver and of brass and of stone and of wood, which can neither see nor hear nor walk;

21 and they did not repent of their murders nor of their sorceries nor of their fornication nor of their thefts.

13 Again we are reminded that the desolations wrought by God in the earth are on behalf of His people (Ps. 46), in response to their official, covenantal worship: the command to **the sixth angel** is issued by **a voice from the four horns of the golden altar** (i.e., the incense altar) **which is before God.** The mention of this point is obviously intended to encourage God's people in worship and prayer, assuring them that God's actions in history proceed from his altar, where He has received their prayers. St. John states that the voice came from **the four horns** (hornlike projections at each corner of the altar), referring to an important aspect of the Old Testament liturgy: the purification offering. This offering referred to the pollution and defilement of *a place* through sin. If the place defiled by sin is not purified, death will result. In his excellent study of the Levitical system, Gordon Wenham tells us that "the purification offering dealt with the pollution caused by sin. If sin polluted the land, it defiled particularly the house where God dwelt. The seriousness of pollution depended on the seriousness of the sin, which in turn related to the status of the sinner. If a private citizen sinned, his action polluted the sanctuary only to a limited extent. Therefore the blood of the purification offering was only smeared on the horns of the altar of burnt sacrifice. If, however, the whole nation sinned or the holiest member of the nation, the high priest, sinned, this was more serious. The blood had to be taken inside the tabernacle and sprinkled on the veil and the altar of incense."[5]

The sins of the nation were atoned for by offering a sacrifice on the brazen altar, then taking the blood and smearing it on the horns of the golden altar of incense (Lev. 4:13-21). In this way the altar was purified, so that the incense could be offered with the assurance that God would hear their prayers. The first-century readers of Revelation would have recognized the significance of this: God's command to His angels, in response to the prayers of His people, is spoken from the **horns** of the golden altar. Their sins have been covered, and do not stand in the way of free access to God.

One further point should be observed. The prayers of the Church at the altar of incense are imprecatory prayers against the nation of Israel. The "Israel" that has rejected Christ is polluted and defiled (cf. Lev. 18:24-30), and its prayers will not be heard by God, for it has rejected the one atonement for sin. The unclean land of Israel will therefore be judged in terms of the curses of Leviticus 26, a chapter which repeatedly threatens a sevenfold judgment upon the nation if it becomes polluted by sin (Lev. 26:18, 21, 24, 28; we have seen that this is the source for the repeated sevenfold judgments in the Book of Revelation). But the Church of Jesus Christ is the new Israel, the holy nation, the true people of God, who possess "confidence to enter the holy place by the blood of Jesus" (Heb. 10:19). Again, the first-century Church is assured by St. John that her prayers will be heard and answered by God. He will take vengeance upon

---

5. Gordon J. Wenham, *The Book of Leviticus* (Grand Rapids: William B. Eerdmans Publishing Co., 1979), p. 96.

her persecutors, for the earth is both blessed and judged by the liturgical actions and judicial decrees of the Church.

God's readiness to hear and willingness to grant His people's prayers are continually proclaimed throughout Scripture (Ps. 9:10; 10:17-18; 18:3; 34:15-17; 37:4-5; 50:14-15; 145:18-19). God has given us numerous examples of imprecatory prayers, showing repeatedly that one aspect of a godly man's attitude is hatred for God's enemies and fervent prayer for their downfall and destruction (Ps. 5:10; 10:15; 35:1-8, 22-26; 59:12-13; 68:1-4; 69:22-28; 83; 94; 109; 137:8-9; 139:19-24; 140:6-11). Why then do we not see the overthrow of the wicked in our own time? An important part of the answer is the unwillingness of the modern Church to pray Biblically; and God has assured us: *You do not have because you do not ask* (James 4:2). But the first-century Church, praying faithfully and fervently for the destruction of apostate Israel, had been heard at God's heavenly altar. His angels were commissioned to strike.

14-16 The **sixth angel** is commissioned to **release the four angels** who had been **bound at the great river Euphrates**; they then bring against Israel an army consisting of **myriads of myriads**. The Euphrates River formed the boundary between Israel and the fearsome, pagan forces which God used as a scourge against His rebellious people. "It was the northern frontier of Palestine [cf. Gen. 15:18; Deut. 11:24; Josh. 1:4], across which Assyrian, Babylonian, and Persian invaders had come to impose their pagan sovereignty on the people of God. All the scriptural warnings about a foe from the north, therefore, find their echo in John's bloodcurdling vision" (cf. Jer. 6:1, 22; 10:22; 13:20; 25:9, 26; 46:20, 24; 47:2; Ezek. 26:7; 38:6, 15; 39:2).[6] It should be remembered too that the *north* (the original location of Eden)[7] was the area of God's throne (Isa. 14:13); and both the Glory-Cloud and God's agents of vengeance are seen coming from the north, i.e., from the Euphrates (cf. Ezek. 1:4; Isa. 14:31; Jer. 1:14-15). Thus, this great army from the north is *God's* army, and under His control and direction, although it is plainly

---

6. G. B. Caird, p. 122.
7. See David Chilton, *Paradise Restored: A Biblical Theology of Dominion* (Ft. Worth, TX: Dominion Press, 1985), pp. 29f.

demonic and pagan in character (on the binding of fallen angels, cf. 2 Pet. 2:4; Jude 6). God is completely sovereign, and uses both demons and the heathen to accomplish His holy purposes (1 Kings 22:20-22; Job 1:12-21; of course, He then punishes the heathen for their wicked motives and goals which led them to fulfill His decree: cf. Isa. 10:5-14). The angels bound at the Euphrates **had been prepared for the hour and day and month and year,** their role in history utterly predestined and certain.

St. John hears the **number** of the horsemen: **myriads of myriads.** We noted in the Introduction to this volume some of the more fanciful interpretations of this expression (see pp. 11-13). If we keep our imaginations harnessed to Scripture, however, we will observe that it is taken from Psalm 68:17, which reads: "The chariots of God are *double myriads, thousands of thousands.*" Mounce correctly observes that "attempts to reduce this expression to arithmetic miss the point. A 'double myriad of myriads' is an indefinite number of incalculable immensity."[8] The term simply means *many thousands,* and indicates a vast host that is to be thought of in connection with the Lord's angelic army of thousands upon thousands of chariots.

17-19 Avoiding the dazzling technological speculations advanced by some commentators, we will note simply that while the *number* of the army is meant to remind us of God's army, the *characteristics* of the horses — **the fire and the smoke and the brimstone which proceeded out of their mouths** — remind us of the Dragon, the fire-breathing Leviathan (Job 41:18-21). "The picture is meant to be inconceivable, horrifying, and even revolting. For these creatures are not of the earth. Fire and sulphur belong to hell (19:20; 21:8), just as the smoke is characteristic of the pit (9:2). Only monsters from beneath belch out such things."[9] Thus, to sum up the idea: An innumerable army is advancing upon Jerusalem from the Euphrates, the origin of Israel's traditional enemies; it is a fierce, hostile, demonic force sent by God in answer to His people's prayers for vengeance. In short, this army is the fulfillment of all the warnings in the law

---

8. Robert H. Mounce, *The Book of Revelation* (Grand Rapids: William B. Eerdmans Publishing Co., 1977), p. 201.

9. G. R. Beasley-Murray, *The Book of Revelation* (Grand Rapids: William B. Eerdmans Publishing Co., [1974] 1981), pp. 165f.

and the prophets of an avenging horde sent to punish the Cove-nant-breakers. The horrors described in Deuteronomy 28 were to be visited upon this evil generation (see especially verses 49-68). Moses had declared: *You shall be driven mad by the sight of what you see* (Deut. 28:34).

As it actually worked out in history, the Jewish rebellion in reaction to the "locust plague" of Gessius Florus during the summer of 66 provoked Cestius' invasion of Palestine in the fall, with large numbers of mounted troops from the regions near the Euphrates[10] (although the main point of St. John's ref-erence is the symbolic significance of the river in Biblical history and prophecy). After ravaging the countryside, his forces arriv-ed at the gates of Jerusalem in the month of Tishri—the month that begins with the Day of Trumpets. The army surrounded the city: "For five days the Romans pressed their attacks on all sides but made no progress; on the sixth, Cestius led a large force of picked men with the archers to an assault on the north side of the Temple. The Jews from the roof of the portico resisted the attack and repeatedly drove back those who reached the wall, but at length, overwhelmed by the hail of missiles, gave way. The front rank of the Romans then planted their bucklers against the wall and on those the second row rested theirs and so on, till they formed a protective covering known as 'the tortoise,' from which the missiles glanced off harmlessly, while the soldiers undermined the wall and prepared to set fire to the gate of the Temple Mount.

"Utter panic now seized the insurgents, and many now began to run from the city, believing that it would fall any minute. The people thereupon took heart again, and the more the wretches[11] gave ground, the nearer did the former advance to open the gates and welcome Cestius as a benefactor."[12] Then, at the very moment when complete victory was within his grasp, Cestius suddenly and inexplicably withdrew his forces. En-couraged, the Jews pursued the retreating soldiers and attacked

---

10. See Josephus, *The Jewish War*, ii.xviii.9-xix.7; cf. J. Massyngberde Ford, *Revelation: Introduction, Translation, and Commentary* (Garden City, NY: Doubleday and Co., 1975), p. 154.

11. The Zealots, who were holding the city in defiance against Rome and against the wishes of the more prosperous and pacifistic among the Jews.

12. Josephus, *The Jewish War*, ii.xix.5-6.

them, inflicting heavy casualties. Gaalya Cornfeld comments that "Cestius' failure transformed the revolt against Rome into a real war. A success so unexpected and sensational had naturally strengthened the hands of the war-party. The majority of the opponents to the revolt found themselves in a minority and tended to ally themselves with the winning Zealots, even though they did not believe that victory was possible. Nevertheless, although they did not proclaim themselves openly, they thought it more advisable to give the appearance of approval for fear of losing control over the people as a whole. Thus, the high-priestly circles and moderates, although notorious in their allegiance to the side of peace, decided to assume the direction of the war which was now considered inevitable. . . . The respite gained by the Jews after Cestius' retreat to Syria was exploited to organize a national defense force."[13]

20-21 Yet the rest of the men, who were not killed by these plagues, did not repent . . . so as not to worship demons and the idols. The Jews had so completely given themselves over to apostasy that neither God's goodness nor His wrath could turn them from their error. Instead, as Josephus reports, even up to the very end — after the famine, the mass murders, the cannibalism, the crucifixion of their fellow Jews at the rate of 500 per day — the Jews went on heeding the insane ravings of false prophets who assured them of deliverance and victory: "Thus were the miserable people beguiled by these charlatans and false messengers of God, while they disregarded and disbelieved the unmistakable portents that foreshadowed the coming desolation; but, as though thunderstruck, blind, senseless, paid no heed to the clear warnings of God."[14]

What "clear warnings" had God given them? Apart from the apostolic preaching, which was all they really needed (cf. Luke 16:27-31), God had sent miraculous signs and wonders to testify of the coming judgment; Jesus had warned that, preceding the Fall of Jerusalem, "there will be terrors and great signs from heaven" (Luke 21:11). This was especially true during the festival

---

13. Gaalya Cornfeld, ed., *Josephus: The Jewish War* (Grand Rapids: Zondervan Publishing House, 1982), p. 201.
14. Josephus, *The Jewish War*, vi.v.3.

seasons of the year 66, as Josephus reports: "While the people were assembling for the Feast of Unleavened Bread, on the eighth of the month Xanthicus [Nisan], at the ninth hour of the night [3:00 A.M.] so bright a light shone round the altar and Temple that it looked like broad daylight; and this lasted for half an hour. The inexperienced regarded it as a good omen, but it was immediately interpreted by the sacred scribes in conformity with subsequent events."[15]

During the same feast another shocking event took place: "The east gate of the inner sanctuary was a very massive gate made of brass and so heavy that it could scarcely be moved every evening by twenty men; it was fastened by iron-bound bars and secured by bolts that were sunk very deep into a threshold that was fashioned from a single stone block; yet this gate was seen to open of its own accord at the sixth hour of the night [midnight]. The Temple guards ran and reported the news to the captain and he came up and by strenuous efforts managed to close it.[16] To the uninitiated this also appeared to be the best of omens as they had assumed that God had opened to them the gate of happiness. But wiser people realized that the security of the Temple was breaking down of its own accord and that the opening of the gates was a present to the enemy; and they interpreted this in their own minds as a portent of the coming desolation."[17] (A similar event, incidentally, happened in A.D. 30, when Christ was crucified and the Temple's outer veil—24 feet wide and over 80 feet high!—ripped from top to bottom [Matt. 27:50-54; Mark 15:37-39; Luke 23:44-47]: The Talmud records that in A.D. 30 the gates of the Temple opened by themselves, apparently due to the collapse of the overhead lintel, a stone weighing about 30 tons.)[18]

Those who were unable to attend the regular Feast of Passover were required to celebrate it a month later (Num. 9:9-13).

---

15. Ibid.
16. Presumably with the help of the two hundred gatekeepers who were on duty at the time.
17. Josephus, vi.v.3.
18. *Yoma* 39b; cf. Alfred Edersheim, *The Life and Times of Jesus the Messiah*, 2 vols. (McLean, VA: MacDonald Publishing Co, n.d.), Vol. 2, pp. 610f.; Ernest L. Martin, *The Place of Christ's Crucifixion* (Pasadena: Foundation for Biblical Research, 1984), pp. 9-14.

Josephus reports a third great wonder that happened at the end of this Second Passover in 66: "A supernatural apparition was seen, too amazing to be believed. What I am now to relate would, I imagine, be dismissed as imaginary, had this not been vouched for by eyewitnesses, then followed by subsequent disasters that deserved to be thus signalized. For before sunset chariots were seen in the air over the whole country, and armed battalions speeding through the clouds and encircling the cities."[19]

A fourth sign occurred inside the Temple on the next great feast day, and was witnessed by the twenty-four priests who were on duty: "At the feast called Pentecost, when the priests had entered the inner courts of the Temple by night to perform their usual ministrations, they declared that they were aware, first, of a violent commotion and din, then of a voice as of a host crying, 'We are departing hence!'"[20]

There was a fifth sign in the heavens that year: "A star that looked like a sword stood over the city and a comet that continued for a whole year."[21] It was obvious, as Josephus says, that Jerusalem was "no longer the dwelling place of God."[22] Appealing four years later to the Jewish revolutionaries to surrender, he declared: "I believe that the Deity has fled from the holy places and stands now on the side of those with whom you are at war. Why, when an honorable man will fly from a wanton home and abhor its inmates, do you think that God still remains with this household in its iniquity—God who sees each hidden thing and hears what is wrapped in silence?"[23] Yet Israel did not repent of her wickedness. Blind to her own evils and to the increasing judgments coming upon her, she remained steadfast in her apostasy, continuing to reject the Lord and cleaving instead to her false gods.

---

19. Josephus, *The Jewish War*, vi.v.3.
20. Ibid.; cf. the summary of these events by the Roman historian Tacitus: "In the sky appeared a vision of armies in conflict, of glittering armour. A sudden lightning flash from the clouds lit up the Temple. The doors of the holy place abruptly opened, a superhuman voice was heard to declare that the gods were leaving it, and in the same instant came the rushing tumult of their departure" (*Histories*, v.13).
21. Ibid.
22. Ibid., v.i.3.
23. Ibid., v.ix.4; cf. the discussion of these and related events of the Last Days in Ernest L. Martin, *The Original Bible Restored* (Pasadena: Foundation for Biblical Research, 1984), pp. 154-60.

Did the Jews really **worship demons** and **idols**? We have already noted (see on 2:9 and 3:9) the Satanic character of Judaism, which is not Old Testament religion, but is rather a false cult claiming Biblical authorization (just as Mormonism, the Unification Church, and other cults claim to be Biblical). As Herbert Schlossberg points out, "Idolatry in its larger meaning is properly understood as any substitution of what is created for the creator."[24] By rejecting Jesus Christ, the Jews had inescapably involved themselves in idolatry; they had departed from the faith of Abraham and served gods of their own making. Moreover, as we shall see, the Jewish idolatry was not some vague, undefined, apostate "theism." Forsaking Christ, the Jews actually became worshipers of Caesar.

Josephus bears eloquent testimony to this, writing repeatedly of God's wrath against the apostasy of the Jewish nation as the cause of their woes: "These men, therefore, trampled upon all the laws of man, and laughed at the laws of God; and as for the oracles of the prophets, they ridiculed them as the tricks of jugglers; yet did these prophets foretell many things concerning the rewards of virtue, and punishments of vice, which when these zealots violated, they occasioned the fulfilling of those very prophecies belonging to their own country."[25]

"Neither did any other city ever suffer such miseries, nor did any age ever breed a generation more fruitful in wickedness than this was, from the beginning of the world."[26]

"I suppose that had the Romans made any longer delay in coming against these villains, the city would either have been swallowed up by the ground opening upon them, or been overflowed by water, or else been destroyed by such thunder as the country of Sodom perished by, for it had brought forth a generation of men much more atheistical than were those that suffered such punishments; for by their madness it was that all the people came to be destroyed."[27]

"When the city was encircled and they could no longer gather herbs, some persons were driven to such terrible distress

---

24. Herbert Schlossberg, *Idols for Destruction: Christian Faith and Its Confrontation with American Society* (Nashville: Thomas Nelson Publishers, 1983), p. 6.
25. Josephus, *The Jewish War*, iv.vi.3.
26. Ibid., v.x.5.
27. Ibid., v.xiii.6.

that they searched the common sewers and old dunghills of cattle, and ate the dung they found there; and what they once could
not even look at they now used for food. When the Romans
barely heard this, their compassion was aroused; yet the rebels,
who saw it also, did not repent, but allowed the same distress to
come upon themselves; for they were blinded by that fate which
was already coming upon the city, and upon themselves also."[28]

Israel's **idols** are said to be **of gold and of silver and of brass
and of stone and of wood**, a standard Biblical accounting of the
materials used in the construction of false gods (cf. Ps. 115:4;
135:15; Isa. 37:19). The Bible consistently ridicules men's idols as
the works of their hands, mere stocks and stones **which can
neither see nor hear nor walk**. This is an echo of the Psalmist's
mockery of heathen idols:

> They have mouths, but they cannot speak;
> They have eyes, but they cannot see;
> They have ears, but they cannot hear;
> They have noses, but they cannot smell;
> They have hands, but they cannot feel;
> They have feet, but they cannot walk;
> They cannot make a noise with their throat.

Then comes the punchline:

> Those who make them will become like them,
> Everyone who trusts in them. (Ps. 115:5-8; cf. 135:16-18)

Schlossberg comments: "When a civilization turns idolatrous, its people are profoundly changed by that experience. In
a kind of reverse sanctification, the idolater is transformed into
the likeness of the object of his worship. Israel 'went after
worthlessness, and became worthless' (Jer. 2:5)."[29] As the
prophet Hosea thundered, Israel's idolaters "became as detestable as that which they loved" (Hos. 9:10).

St. John's description of Israel's idolatry is in line with the
usual prophetic stance; but his accusation is an even more direct
reference to Daniel's condemnation of *Babylon*, specifically

---

28. Ibid., v.xiii.7.
29. Schlossberg, p. 295.

regarding its *worship of false gods with the holy utensils from the Temple*. Daniel said to king Belshazzar: "You have exalted yourself against the Lord of heaven; and they have brought the vessels of His House before you, and you and your nobles, your wives and your concubines have been drinking wine from them; and you have praised the gods of silver and gold, of bronze, iron, wood, and stone, which do not see, hear, or understand. But the God in whose hand are your life-breath and your ways, you have not glorified" (Dan. 5:23).

St. John's implication is clear: Israel has become a Babylon, committing sacrilege by worshiping false gods with the Temple treasures; like Babylon, she has been "weighed in the balance and found wanting"; like Babylon, she will be conquered and her kingdom will be possessed by the heathen (cf. Dan. 5:25-31).

Finally, St. John summarizes Israel's crimes, all stemming from her idolatry (cf. Rom. 1:18-32): This led to her **murders** of Christ and the saints (Acts 2:23, 36; 3:14-15; 4:26; 7:51-52, 58-60); her **sorceries** (Acts 8:9, 11; 13:6-11; 19:13-15; cf. Rev. 18:23; 21:8; 22:15); her **fornication**, a word St. John uses twelve times with reference to Israel's apostasy (2:14; 2:20; 2:21; 9:21; 14:8; 17:2 [twice]; 17:4; 18:3 [twice]; 18:9; 19:2); and her **thefts**, a crime often associated in the Bible with apostasy and the resultant oppression and persecution of the righteous (cf. Isa. 61:8; Jer. 7:9-10; Ezek. 22:29; Hos. 4:1-2; Mark 11:17; Rom. 2:21; James 5:1-6).

Throughout the Last Days, until the coming of the Romans, the trumpets had blown, warning Israel to repent. But the alarm was not heeded, and the Jews became hardened in their impenitence. The retreat of Cestius was of course taken to mean that Christ's prophecies of Jerusalem's destruction were false: The armies from the Euphrates had come and surrounded Jerusalem (cf. Luke 21:20), but the threatened "desolation" had not come to pass. Instead, the Romans had fled, dragging their tails between their legs. Increasingly confident of divine blessing, the Jews recklessly plunged ahead into greater acts of rebellion, unaware that even greater forces beyond the Euphrates were being readied for battle. This time, there would be no retreat. Judea would be turned into a desert, the Israelites would be slaughtered and enslaved, and the Temple would be razed to the ground, without a stone left upon another.

10

THE FAITHFUL WITNESS

The Witness to the New Creation (10:1-7)

1 And I saw another strong Angel coming down out of heaven, clothed with a cloud; and the rainbow was on His head, and His face was like the sun, and His legs like pillars of fire;

2 and He had in His hand a little book that was open. And He placed His right foot on the Sea and His left on the Land;

3 and He cried out with a loud voice, as when a Lion roars; and when He had cried out, the seven peals of thunder uttered their voices.

4 And when the seven peals of thunder had spoken, I was about to write; and I heard a Voice from heaven saying: Seal up the things that the seven peals of thunder have spoken, and do not write them.

5 And the Angel whom I saw standing on the Sea and on the Land lifted up His right hand to heaven,

6 and swore by Him who lives forever and ever, who created heaven and the things in it, and the earth and the things in it, and the sea and the things in it, that there shall be delay no longer,

7 but in the days of the voice of the seventh angel, when he is about to sound, then the Mystery of God is accomplished, as He preached the Gospel to His servants the prophets.

1 The **strong Angel** can be none other than Jesus Christ Himself, the "Angel of the LORD" who appeared in the Old Testament. This will be clear enough if the description of this Angel is compared with that of Christ in 1:14-16, and of God on His throne in Ezekiel 1:25-28. There are, however, further indications of the divine identity of this strong Angel.

First, the Angel is seen **clothed with a cloud** — an expression

259

that should call to mind the Glory-Cloud. And while the Cloud is filled with innumerable angels (Deut. 33:2; Ps. 68:17), there is only One who could be said to be **clothed** with it. Compare Psalm 104:1-3:

> O LORD my God, Thou art very great;
> Thou art clothed with splendor and majesty,
> Covering Thyself with light as with a cloak,
> Stretching out heaven like a tent curtain —
> The One who lays the beams of His upper chambers in the waters;
> Who makes the clouds His chariot;
> Who walks upon the wings of the wind. . . .

The basic reference for this, of course, is the fact that God was indeed "clothed with the Cloud" in the Tabernacle (cf. Ex. 40:34-38; Lev. 16:2). This could not be said of any created angel. To be clothed with the Cloud is to be clothed with the entire court of heaven; it is, in fact, the created angels who form the Cloud. Jesus Christ is wearing the host of heaven (cf. Gen. 28:12; Jn. 1:51).

Second, the Angel had **the rainbow upon His head**. We have seen the rainbow already in 4:3, around the throne of God; and Ezekiel says of the One whom he saw enthroned that "there was a radiance around Him. As the appearance of the rainbow in the clouds on a rainy day, so was the appearance of the surrounding radiance. Such was the appearance of the likeness of the glory of the LORD" (Ezek. 1:27-28).

Third, the Angel's **face was like the sun**. This fits the description of Christ in 1:16, and in Matthew 17:2, the account of Christ's transfiguration (cf. Ezek. 1:4, 7, 27; Acts 26:13; 2 Cor. 4:6). He is "the Sun of righteousness" (Mal. 4:2), "the Sunrise from on high" (Lk. 1:78; cf. Ps. 84:11; 2 Pet. 1:16-19). In particular, the imagery of the sun and sunrise — as we have already noted with the words *day* and *light* — is often used to describe the glory of God shining in judgment (cf. Ps. 19:4-6; Ezek. 43:2; Zech. 14:7; Mal. 4:1-3; Rom. 13:12); and the "flaming fire" of judgment is spoken of by Paul as Christ's "face" and "glory" (2 Thess 1:7-9).[1] This is especially appropriate here, since Christ

---

1. Cf. Meredith G. Kline, *Images of the Spirit* (Grand Rapids: Baker Book House, 1980), pp. 108, 121.

has come to St. John to announce the annihilation of Jerusalem.

Fourth, His **legs** were **like pillars of fire**. This refers to some of the most complex imagery in all the Bible. Obviously, the phrase is intended to remind us of "the pillar of fire and cloud" —the Glory-Cloud of the Exodus (Ex. 14:24). As we have seen, it is the Lord who "wears" the Cloud (Deut. 31:15), and the Cloud is also identified as the Angel of the LORD (Ex. 32:34; 33:2; Num. 20:16). It appears that the dual aspect of the Cloud (the smoke and the fire) symbolically represented God's legs. Thus, the LORD *walked* before the people in the Cloud (Ex. 13:21-22; 14:19, 24; 23:20, 23); He came in the Cloud and *stood* before them (Ex. 33:9-10; Num. 12:5; Hag. 2:5). In terms of this imagery, the Bride describes the Bridegroom's legs as "pillars" (Cant. 5:15). We should also note that the dual nature of the pillar, representing the legs of God, was incorporated into the architecture of the Temple (1 Kings 7:15-22; 2 Chron. 3:15-17); thus "the ark of the covenant located beneath the enthroned Glory is accordingly called God's footstool (Isa. 60:13)."[2] The significance of all this, and its relationship to the passage as a whole, will become apparent below. Enough has been seen, however, to demonstrate beyond reasonable doubt that this rainbow-haloed, Cloud-clothed Angel **coming down out of heaven** is (or represents) the Lord Jesus Christ.

2-3 The Angel, holding **a little book,**[3] then **placed His right foot on the Sea and His left on the Land**. H. B. Swete comments: "The Angel's posture denotes both his colossal size and his mission to the world: 'sea and land' is an O.T. formula for the totality of terrestrial things (Ex. 20:4,11; Ps. 69:34)."[4] We might modify this point with the observation that in the Bible, and especially in the Book of Revelation, "Sea and Land" seems to represent *the Gentile nations* contrasted with *the Land of*

---

2. Ibid., p. 19; cf. 1 Chron. 28:2; Ps. 99:5; 132:7. In the larger, cosmic Temple ("the heavens and the earth"), the earth is called God's footstool (Isa. 66:1), and thus the earth is said to have pillars (1 Sam. 2:8; Job 38:4-6; Ps. 75:3; 104:5; Isa. 51:13, 16; 54:11), and sockets to hold the pillars (Job 38:6; the same word is used for the pillar sockets in the tabernacle, in Num. 3:36-37; 4:31-32).

3. The meaning of the little scroll will be discussed below, in connection with v. 8-11.

4. Henry Barclay Swete, *Commentary on Revelation* (Grand Rapids: Kregel Publications, 3rd ed., [1911] 1977), p. 127.

Israel (2 Sam. 22:4-5; Ps. 65:7-8; Isa. 5:30; 17:12-13; 57:20; Jer. 6:23; Lk. 21:25; Rev. 13:1, 11). Thus, this picture does contain a cosmic, worldwide import; but its meaning, as we shall see further on, is tied up with the fact that Christ is standing on Israel and the nations (cf. v. 5-7).

And He cried out with a loud Voice, as when a Lion[5] **roars;** by now, of course, we are familiar with the great Voice coming from the Cloud; as Kline says, the Voice "is characteristically loud, arrestingly loud. It is likened to the crescendo of ocean and storm, the rumbling roar of earthquake. It is the noise of war, the trumpeting of signal horns and the din of battle. It is the thunder of the storm-chariot of the warrior-Lord, coming in judgments that convulse creation and confound the kings of the nations."[6] In worshipful response to His Voice, **the seven peals of thunder uttered their voices.** This sevenfold thunder is itself identified with the Voice in Psalm 29, where some of its phenomenal effects are noted: It shatters cedars in pieces, rocks whole nations with earthquakes, shoots forth mighty bolts of lightning, cracks open the very bowels of the earth, causes animals to calve, and topples the trees, stripping entire forests bare. This adds a dimension to our understanding of the nature of the Voice that issues from the Cloud: It consists of the heavenly antiphony in which the angelic chorus answers the declarations of the Sovereign Lord.

4 Of course, everyone wants to know: What did the seven thunders *say*? An astounding amount of scholarly ink has been wasted on the solution of this problem. But, in this life at least, we can never know the answer. St. John **was about to write** down what the thunders had spoken, when he **heard a Voice from heaven saying: Seal up the things that the seven thunders have spoken, and do not write them.** The message was intended for St. John's ears only. It was not intended for the Church at large. But what is important here is that God wanted St. John to record the fact that he was not supposed to reveal whatever the seven thunders said. God wanted the Church to know that there

---

5. Here is yet another identification of the Angel with Christ: He is the Lion who "has overcome so as to open the Book" (Rev. 5:5).
6. Kline, p. 101.

are some things (many things, actually) that God has no intention of telling us beforehand.

This serves well as a rebuke to the tendency of most sermons and commentaries on this book—that of a curious searching into those things that God has not seen fit to reveal. "The secret things belong to the LORD our God, but the things revealed belong to us and to our sons forever, that we may observe all the words of this law" (Deut. 29:29). In other words, "Man has been given the law, which he must obey. He has been told what the consequences of obedience and disobedience are. More than that, man does not need to know."[7] R. J. Rushdoony writes: "Man is more often prompted by curiosity than by obedience. . . . For every question a pastor receives about the details of God's law, he normally receives several which express little more than a curiosity about God, the life to come, and other things which are aspects of 'the secret things which belong to God.'. . . As against curiosity and a probing about 'secret things,' we are plainly commanded to obey God's law and to recognize that the law gives us a knowledge of the future which is legitimate."[8]

In the final chapter of the book St. John is commanded: "*Do not seal up* the words of the prophecy of this book, for the time is near" (22:10); the message of the Book of Revelation as a whole is contemporary in nature, referring to events about to take place. In contrast, however, the message of the Seven Thunders points us to the far distant future: Daniel was told to "conceal these words and seal up the book until the time of the end" (Dan. 12:4), for the reason that the time of its fulfillment was *not* at hand. Similarly, when St. John is instructed to **seal up** the words spoken by the Thunders, it is another indication that the purpose of Revelation is not "futuristic"; the prophecy refers to the time of the establishment of the New Covenant, and points beyond itself to a "time of the end" that was still very distant to St. John and his readers. We are thus taught two things: First, the Book of Revelation is a contemporary prophecy, concerned almost entirely with the redemptive-eschatological events of the first century; second, the events of the first century were

7. Rousas John Rushdoony, *Salvation and Godly Rule* (Vallecito, CA: Ross House Books, 1983), p. 388.
8. Ibid.

not exhaustive of eschatology. Contrary to the theories of those interpreters who would style themselves as "consistent preterists," the Fall of Jerusalem did not constitute the Second Coming of Christ, the end of the world, and the final resurrection. There is more to come.[9]

5-7 St. John now shows us Christ's purpose in revealing Himself in this way: The Angel **lifted up His right hand to heaven** (the proper stance for a witness in a court of law: Gen. 14:22; Ex. 6:8; Deut. 32:40; Ezek. 20:5-6; Dan. 12:7) **and swore an oath**. Some commentators have taken this fact as their basis for holding that this Angel is *not* Christ, apparently regarding swearing as somehow below His dignity or out of character. One wonders, in response, about the soundness of these commentators' views regarding the doctrines of the Trinity and Christ's deity. For, assuredly, the Lord God swears oaths throughout Holy Scripture (cf. Gen. 22:16; Isa. 45:23; Jer. 49:13; Amos 6:8), and in fact our salvation is based on God's faithfulness to His covenant oath, the ground of the Christian's assurance and hope (Heb. 6:13-20).

We must observe carefully that Christ is presented here in the position of a *witness*, as St. John has informed us on two occasions already (1:5; 3:14). This is the point at which the various details of the vision converge. We have noted some of the significance of His legs appearing like pillars of fire (v. 1), and this must be further developed. For, in the first place, pillars are used in Biblical symbolism and ritual as *witnesses* (cf. Gen. 31:45, 52; Deut. 27:1-8; Josh. 8:30-35; 22:26-28, 34; 24:26-27). Similarly, the two stone tablets containing the Ten Commandments served as witnesses (Deut. 31:26), legal documents of testimony to the covenant stipulations. Thus the law is called *the Testimony* (Ex. 16:34; 25:16, 21-22; 32:15; 34:29; Lev. 16:13;

---

9. See, e.g., Max R. King, *The Spirit of Prophecy* (n.p., 1971). While King's work has a great deal of value for the discerning student, its ultimate thesis — that there is no future Coming of Christ or Final Judgment — is heretical. Historic, orthodox Christianity everywhere, with one voice, has always taught that Christ "shall come again, with glory, to judge both the living and the dead" (*Nicene Creed*). This is a non-negotiable article of the Christian faith. Cf. David Chilton, *Paradise Restored: A Biblical Theology of Dominion* (Ft. Worth, TX: Dominion Press, 1985), pp. 138-48.

24:3; Num. 1:50, 53; 4:5; Josh. 4:16; 2 Kings 11:12).[10] When God stood in the dual pillar of cloud/fire before Israel at the "tent of testimony" (Num. 9:15; 10:11), He was identifying Himself as the Witness to the Covenant (cf. 1 Sam. 12:5; Jer. 29:23; 42:5; Mic. 1:2; Mal. 2:14).

The Angel-Witness swears **that there shall be delay[11] no longer, but in the days of the seventh angel, when he is about to sound, then the Mystery of God is accomplished.** The word **Mystery** does not mean something "mysterious" in our modern sense, but rather "something formerly concealed and now unveiled."[12] It is *revelation*: knowledge that God formerly withheld, but has now "revealed to His holy apostles and prophets in the Spirit" (Eph. 3:5), a mystery "that has been hidden from the past ages and generations, but has now been manifested to His saints" (Col. 1:26). This "Mystery" is a major aspect of the letters to the Ephesians and Colossians: *the union of believing Jews and Gentiles in one Church, without distinction*; "that the Gentiles are fellow heirs and fellow members of the body, and fellow partakers of the promise in Jesus Christ through the Gospel" (Eph. 3:6). Gentiles, who had been strangers and aliens from the commonwealth of Israel and from the covenantal promises, are now, through the work of Christ, full sons of Abraham, heirs of the Covenant, on an equal and indistinguishable standing with believing Jews (Eph. 2:11-22; Gal. 3). They form one "new man," one Church, one Body of Christ, in the one New Covenant. And this one covenantal Kingdom, the fulfillment of the Old Testament promises, will have universal dominion: All nations will now flow to the Mountain of the Lord, as the kingdoms of the world become the one Kingdom of Christ (11:15). The **Mystery of God**, the universalization of the Kingdom of God, is to be **accomplished — as He preached the Gos-**

---

10. Meredith G. Kline, *The Structure of Biblical Authority* (Grand Rapids: William B. Eerdmans Publishing Co., 1975), pp. 113-30. The law required two witnesses (Deut. 17:6; 19:15), and, as we have noted in the Introduction, the two tablets were duplicate copies of the covenant.

11. "The sense here is not an abolition of time and its replacement by timelessness, but 'no more time' from the words of the angel until the completion of the divine purpose." James Barr, *Biblical Words for Time* (Naperville, IL: Alec R. Allenson Inc., rev. ed. 1969), p. 80.

12. F. F. Bruce, *Commentary on the Epistle to the Colossians* (Grand Rapids: William B. Eerdmans Publishing Co., 1957), p. 218.

pel[13] to His servants the prophets. The Mystery is simply the revelation of the message of the Gospel.

This is why the Angel stands as witness **on the Sea and on the Land** (cf. v. 2), a fact that is repeated for emphasis in verse 5. The Angel takes the oath with His pillar-legs planted on Israel and the nations, proclaiming the New Covenant which will unite the two into one new nation in Christ. Moreover, He swears *in the name of the Creator*: **by Him who lives forever and ever, who created heaven and the things in it, and the earth and the things in it, and the sea and the things in it** (cf. Ex. 20:11; Ps. 146:6; Neh. 9:6). The Angel swears in this manner because He is standing as divine Witness to the New Creation. The details of the passage remind us of two other "New Creation" events: the covenant with Noah (the rainbow) and the covenant at Sinai (the pillar of fire). Both of these recalled how "the Spirit at the beginning overarched creation as a divine witness to the Covenant of Creation, as a sign that creation existed under the aegis of his covenant lordship. Here is the background for the later use of the rainbow as a sign of God's covenant with the earth."[14] "At the ratification of the old covenant at Sinai, this cloud-pillar form of theophany represented God standing as witness to his covenant with Israel. Once again at the ratification of the new covenant at Pentecost, it was God the Spirit, appearing in phenomena that are to be seen as a New Testament version of the Glory-fire, who provided the confirmatory divine testimony."[15]

Thus, we have seen several Biblical ideas joining together at this point to form a consistent pattern: *covenant, oath, creation, testimony*, and *witness*. The Spirit, appearing as the original cloudy pillar of fire, was present at the original creation, and then at the later re-creation events in the history of redemption: the Flood, the Exodus, the erection of the Tabernacle and the Temple, and the Day of Pentecost. The coming of the Spirit at Pentecost was prophetically described by Joel in terms of the Glory-Cloud: "I will display wonders in heaven and on earth:

---

13. "Preached the Gospel," rather than "declared" or "preached," is the literal translation of the Greek text.

14. Kline, *Images of the Spirit*, pp. 19f.

15. Meredith G. Kline, *Kingdom Prologue*, Volume I (privately published syllabus, 1981), p. 28. Kline also points out (pp. 5f.) that the words *oath* and *covenant* are often used interchangeably (cf. Deut. 29:12; Ezek. 16:8).

blood, fire, and pillars of smoke" (Joel 2:30); and the Apostle Peter, quoting Joel's statement, declared that the Pentecost event was the fulfillment of the ancient prophecy (Acts 2:16-21).[16]

The various creation-events thus interpret and are re-interpreted by each other. That the covenants were made in terms of the creation shows them to be provisional re-creations which point to the final New Creation in Christ (2 Cor. 5:17; Eph. 4:24). And that the creation accounts use covenantal language and settings (witness-pillar, oath, and testimony) shows it to have been a covenant (i.e., if *covenants* are *re-creations*, then the *creation* was *covenantal*).[17]

Another motif common to creation and covenant is the sabbatical form in which both are structured.[18] The entire book of Revelation is, as we have previously noted, structured in sevens, revealing its nature as a record of a covenant-making process; and here we see "the Mystery of God" declared to be completed with the sounding of the Seventh Trumpet. The Sabbath "is a day of divine action featuring divine judgment with the penetration of the darkness by the light of the theophanic glory, it is a day of creating heaven and earth and consummating a temple of God made in the likeness of the Glory, it is a day of the revelation of the sovereign glory of the covenant Lord. Taken together, the seven days are the fulness of time of creation, the sevenfold fulness of the day of the Lord. In redemptive re-creation, the day of the Lord, wherein the old passes away and all is created anew, is again a fulness of time, in which, as Paul declares, all the mystery of God comes finally into eschatological realization" (see Gal. 4:4; Eph. 1:9-10; cf. Matt. 13:11-17; Mk. 1:15; Col. 1:15-20; Rev. 10:7).[19]

Revelation 10 thus serves to introduce us to the first great climax of the prophecy: the announcement of the destruction of Jerusalem. And through its use of multi-layered Biblical imagery it declares the fall of Jerusalem to be an inescapable aspect of the great and final Covenant-making event. The sounding of

---

16. No other construction may legitimately be placed upon the apostle's words. The coming of the Spirit was *the* fulfillment of Joel 2:28-32. "The Last Days" had *arrived*. See Chilton, *Paradise Restored*, pp. 115-22.

17. See Kline, *Kingdom Prologue*, Vol. I, pp. 33f.

18. Ibid., p. 33.

19. Kline, *Images of the Spirit*, pp. 114f.

the seventh angel will be the irrefutable sign that the promised New Creation, the New Covenant, is an accomplished fact. The great Mystery of God — the completion and filling of His new and final Temple — will have been revealed to the world (11:15-19).

The Bittersweet Book (10:8-11)

8 And the Voice which I had heard from heaven, I heard again speaking with me, saying: Go, take the book that is open in the hand of the Angel who stands on the Sea and on the Land.

9 And I went to the Angel, telling Him to give me the little book. And He said to me: Take it, and eat it; and it will make your stomach bitter, but in your mouth it will be sweet as honey.

10 And I took the little book out of the Angel's hand and ate it, and it was in my mouth sweet as honey; and when I had eaten it, my stomach was made bitter.

11 And they said to me: You must prophesy again concerning many peoples and nations and tongues and peoples.

8-10   The instructions to **take** and **eat** the book held by the Angel are based on a similar incident in the life of Ezekiel, who was commanded to eat a scroll symbolizing the prophetic denunciation of the "rebellious house" of Israel (2:8-10; 3:1-3). This reference enables us to identify the book given to St. John as his commission, based on the New Covenant, to prophesy "lamentations, mourning and woe" against apostate Israel. The book is thus, essentially, the Book of Revelation itself. As with Ezekiel, the Covenant Lawsuit tasted to St. John as **sweet as honey** (cf. Ezek. 3:3), but his **stomach was made bitter** (cf. Ezek. 3:14). This should not be difficult to understand. St. John was called to prophesy about the victory of the Church and of the kingdom of God. A necessary corollary to the triumph of the righteous is the destruction of the wicked. The pattern holds throughout Scripture in the history of salvation: The same judgments that deliver us also destroy God's enemies. "Salvation and judgment are two aspects of the same event."[20] Old Israel had turned from the true God to worship idols and demons; she had become a harlot and a persecutor of the saints, and had to be

---

20. See R. J. Rushdoony, *Salvation and Godly Rule,* pp. 19ff., 140f.

destroyed. And while St. John could rejoice in the victory of the Church over her enemies, it would still be a wrenching experience to see the once-holy city levelled to rubble, the Temple torn down and burned to ashes, and hundreds of thousands of his relativies and countrymen starved and tortured, murdered, or sold into slavery. All the prophets experienced this same emotional wrenching — which did not usually involve a rebellion against their calling (Jonah is a notable exception), but rather a deeply rooted recognition of the two-edged nature of prophecy, of the fact that the same "Day of the Lord" would bring both immeasurable blessing and unspeakable woe (cf. Amos 5:18-20). It should be noted further, however, that a vast chasm separates the prophets from many of their interpreters in our own day. For while modern theologians will affect a weepy attitude over the sufferings of "humanity" in general, or in the abstract, the prophets suffered from no such humanitarian impulses.[21] The prophets grieved over the disobedient children of the Covenant. The bitterness St. John will experience is not over the fate of the Roman Empire. He grieves for Israel, considered as the Covenant people. They are about to be disinherited and executed, never to be restored as the Covenant nation.[22] The divorce of old Israel is necessary in God's plan of redemption, and St. John both welcomes it and proclaims it with vigorous joy. Yet there is legitimate sorrow for the lost sheep of the house of Israel.

11   In the Old Testament background of the Book of Revela-

---

21. For an incisive analysis of humanitarianism, see Herbert Schlossberg, *Idols for Destruction: Christian Faith and Its Confrontation with American Society* (Nashville: Thomas Nelson Publishers, 1983), pp. 39-87.

22. That Israel will someday repent and turn to Christ is, to me, indisputable (Rom. 11; cf. Chilton, *Paradise Restored,* pp. 125-31). That is not at issue here. The point remains, however, that in order to be restored to the Covenant, Jews must join the Church of Jesus Christ along with everyone else. Israel will never have a covenantal identity distinct from the Church. For more in-depth discussions of the place of Israel in prophecy, see (in ascending levels of complexity) Iain Murray, *The Puritan Hope: Revival and the Interpretation of Prophecy* (Edinburgh: The Banner of Truth Trust, 1971); John Murray, *The Epistle to the Romans,* 2 vols. (Grand Rapids: William B. Eerdmans Publishing Co., [1959, 1965] 1968), Vol. 2, pp. 65-108; Willem A. VanGemeren, "Israel as the Hermeneutical Crux in the Interpretation of Prophecy" (I), *Westminster Theological Journal* 45 (1983), pp. 132-44; idem, "Israel as the Hermeneutical Crux in the Interpretation of Prophecy" (II), *Westminster Theological Journal* 46 (1984), pp. 254-297.

tion, the Angel of the Lord is identified as the original Prophet (cf. Ex. 23:20-23; Deut. 18:15-19).[23] As such, He raised up and commissioned other prophets in His image, reproducing Himself in them (Ex. 3:2ff.; 33:14; 34:5ff.; 29-35; 2 Ki. 1:3, 15; 1 Chron. 21:18). For this reason, the prophets are often called **angels** (messengers), expressing their re-creation in the image of the divine Prophet-Angel (2 Chron. 36:15-16; Hag. 1:13; Mal. 3:1).[24] The same pattern is continued here: the Angel-Prophet, who proclaims His message while straddling the inhabited earth, commissions St. John to **prophesy again concerning many peoples and nations and tongues and kings**. St. John's prophecy regarding the destruction of Israel and the establishing of the New Covenant will encompass the nations of the world. Christ has announced the Gospel, the message of the universal sway of the Kingdom, to "His servants the prophets" (v.7), and now His servant John is to extend the proclamation of that Gospel to all nations. Christ has redeemed men from every nation (7:9). The mighty Roman Empire itself is ultimately an instrument of God's will (17:16-17), eventually to be crushed and cast away when its usefulness has ceased (19:17-21; cf. Dan. 2:44). "The kingdoms of the world are but the scaffolding for God's spiritual temple, to be thrown down when their purpose is accomplished."[25]

---

23. See Kline's discussion of this in *Images of the Spirit*, pp. 75-81, 91-95.
24. Ibid., pp. 57ff.
25. Thomas V. Moore, *A Commentary on Haggai and Malachi* (London: The Banner of Truth Trust, [1856] 1968), p. 80.

11

THE END OF THE BEGINNING

The Two Witnesses Against Jerusalem (11:1-14)

1 And there was given me a reed like a staff; and someone said: Rise and measure the Temple of God, and the altar, and those who worship in it.

2 And cast out the court that is outside the Temple, and do not measure it; for it has been given to the nations; and they will tread under foot the Holy City for forty-two months.

3 And I will grant authority to My two Witnesses, and they will prophesy for twelve hundred and sixty days, clothed in sackcloth.

4 These are the two olive trees and the two lampstands that stand before the Lord of the earth.

5 And if anyone desires to harm them, fire proceeds out of their mouth and devours their enemies; and if anyone would desire to harm them, in this manner he must be killed.

6 These have the power to shut up the sky, in order that rain may not fall during the days of their prophesying; and they have power over the waters to turn them into blood, and to smite the earth with every plague, as often as they desire.

7 And when they have finished their testimony, the Beast that comes up out of the Abyss will make war with them, and overcome them and kill them.

8 And their dead bodies will lie in the street of the Great City which Spiritually is called Sodom and Egypt, where also their Lord was crucified.

9 And those from the peoples and tribes and tongues and nations will look at their dead bodies for three and a half days, and will not permit their dead bodies to be laid in a tomb.

10 And those who dwell on the Land will rejoice over them and make merry; and they will send gifts to one another, because these two prophets tormented those who dwell on the Land.

11 And after the three and a half days the breath of life from God came into them, and they stood on their feet; and great fear fell upon those who were beholding them.

12 And they heard a loud voice from heaven saying to them: Come up here. And they went up into heaven in the Cloud, and their enemies beheld them.

13 And in that Day there was a great earthquake, and a tenth of the City fell; and seven thousand people were killed in the earthquake, and the rest were terrified and gave glory to the God of heaven.

14 The Second Woe is past; the Third Woe, behold, is coming quickly.

1-2   St. John is commanded to **measure the Temple of God** (literally, **the inner sanctuary** of the Temple, **the holy place), and the altar, and those who worship in it.** The imagery is taken from Ezekiel 40-43, where the angelic priest measures the ideal Temple, the New Covenant people of God, the Church (cf. Mark 14:58; John 2:19; 1 Cor. 3:16; Eph. 2:19-22; 1 Tim. 3:15; Heb. 3:6; 1 Pet. 2:5; Rev. 3:12). R. J. McKelvey explains how the idea of the Temple is interpreted in the Letter to the Hebrews: "According to the writer to the Hebrews the sanctuary in heaven is the pattern (*typos*), *i.e.,* the original (cf. Ex. 25:8f.), and the one on earth used by Jewry is a 'copy and shadow' (Heb. 8:5, RSV). The heavenly sanctuary is therefore the true sanctuary (Heb. 9:24). It belongs to the people of the new covenant (Heb. 6:19-20). Moreover, the fact that Christ our High Priest is in this sanctuary means that we, although still on earth, already participate in its worship (10:19ff., 12:22ff.). What is this Temple? The writer supplies a clue when he says that the heavenly sanctuary was cleansed (9:23), *i.e.* made fit for use (cf. Num. 7:1). The assembly of the firstborn (Heb. 12:23), that is to say, the Church triumphant, is the heavenly Temple."[1]

That this is St. John's meaning as well should be clear from what we have already seen, for much of the action in this book has either taken place in, or originated from, the inner sanctuary. Moreover, **those who worship** at the incense altar in the Holy Place are *priests* (Ex. 28:43; 29:44): St. John has told us

---

1. R. J. McKelvey, "Temple," in J. D. Douglas, ed., *The New Bible Dictionary* (William B. Eerdmans Publishing Co., [1962] 1965), p. 1249.

that we are a kingdom of priests (1:6; 5:10; cf. Matt. 27:51; Heb. 10:19-20), and he has shown us God's people offering up their prayers on the altar of incense (5:8; 6:9-10; 8:3-4).

St. John is to **measure** the inner court, the Church, but he is to **cast out the court that is outside the Temple**, and is specifically commanded: **Do not measure it.** Measuring is a symbolic action used in Scripture to "divide between the holy and the profane" and thus to indicate divine protection from destruction (see Ezek. 22:26; 40-43; Zech. 2:1-5; cf. Jer. 10:16; 51:19; Rev. 21:15-16). "Throughout Scripture the priests are those who measure out the dimensions of the temple of God, the man with the measuring rod of Ezekiel 40ff. being but the most prominent example. Such measuring, like witness-bearing, entails *seeing*, and is the precondition of *judging*, as we have seen these in God's covenant actions in Genesis 1. The priestly aspect of measuring and witnessing can be seen in that it correlates to guarding, because it sets up and establishes boundaries, and bears witness regarding whether or not those boundaries have been observed. We might say that the kingly function has to do with filling, and the priestly with separating, the former with cultivation and the latter with jealousy, propriety, and protection."[2]

Between the Sixth and Seventh Seals, the 144,000 saints of the True Israel were protected from the coming judgment (7:1-8). That action is paralleled here by St. John's measuring of the inner court between the sixth and seventh Trumpets, now protecting the True Temple from the outpouring of God's wrath. The outer court (the "court of the Gentiles") accordingly represents apostate Israel (cf. Isa. 1:12), which is to be cut off from the number of the faithful Covenant people, God's dwellingplace. St. John, as an authoritative priest of the New Covenant, is commanded to **cast out** (excommunicate) the unbelievers. This verb (*ekballō*) is generally used in the Gospels for casting out evil spirits (cf. Mark 1:34, 39; 3:15; 6:13); it is also used for Christ's ejection of the moneychangers from the Temple (Matt. 21:12; Mark 11:15; John 2:15). Jesus warned that unbelieving Israel as a whole would be cast out from the Church, while be-

---

2. James B. Jordan, "Rebellion, Tyranny, and Dominion in the Book of Genesis," in Gary North, ed., *Tactics of Christian Resistance*, Christianity and Civilization No. 3 (Tyler, TX: Geneva Ministries, 1983), p. 42.

lieving Gentiles would stream into the Kingdom and receive the blessings promised to the Seed of Abraham:

> Strive to enter by the narrow door; for many, I tell you, will seek to enter and will not be able, once the head of the house gets up and shuts the door, and you begin to stand outside and knock on the door, saying, "Lord, open up to us!"
> And He will answer and say to you, "I do not know where you are from."
> Then you will begin to say, "We ate and drank in Your presence, and You taught in our streets!"
> And He will say, "I tell you, I do not know where you are from! Depart from Me, all you evildoers!"
> There will be weeping and gnashing of teeth there when you see Abraham and Isaac and Jacob and all the prophets in the Kingdom of God, but yourselves being cast out [*ekballō*]. And they will come from east and west, and from north and south, and will recline at the Table in the Kingdom of God. (Luke 13:24-29; cf. Matt. 8:11-12)

Unbelieving Israel has been excluded from the protective measuring, **for it has been given to the nations; and they will tread under foot the holy city for forty-two months** (see Luke 21:24). God guarantees His protection to the Church, but Jerusalem has been delivered up to destruction. **Forty-two months** (which equals *1,260 days* and *three and a half years*) is taken from Daniel 7:25, where it symbolizes a limited period during which the wicked are triumphant; it also speaks of a period of wrath and judgment due to apostasy, a reminder of the three and a half years of drought between Elijah's first appearance and the defeat of Baal on Mount Carmel (1 Kings 17-18; cf. James 5:17). Whereas *seven* is used to represent wholeness and completion, *three and a half* appears to be a *broken* seven: sadness, death, and destruction (cf. Dan. 9:24; 12:7; Rev. 12:6, 14; 13:5). The periods of time mentioned in the Trumpets section are arranged chiastically, another indication of their symbolic nature:

> A. 11:2 — forty-two months
>   B. 11:3 — twelve hundred and sixty days
>   C. 11:9 — three and a half days
>   C. 11:11 — three and a half days
>   B. 12:6 — twelve hundred and sixty days
> A. 13:5 — forty-two months

This kind of imagery is used throughout the Bible.[3] In his Gospel, St. Matthew deliberately goes out of his way to draw our attention to the number **forty-two**, arranging his list of Christ's ancestors to add up to it: "Therefore all the generations from Abraham to David are fourteen generations; and from David to the deportation to Babylon are fourteen generations; and from the deportation to Babylon to Christ are fourteen generations" (Matt. 1:17)[4] – all adding up to forty-two, the number of waiting between promise and fulfillment, from bondage to redemption. But now, in the Revelation, the time has been shortened: The Church does not need to wait forty-two generations any longer, but only **forty-two months**. The message of these verses, therefore, is that the Church will be saved through the coming Tribulation, during which Jerusalem is to be destroyed by an invasion of Gentiles. The end of this period will mean the full establishment of the Kingdom. The passage thus parallels the Olivet Discourse (Matt. 24, Mark 13, Luke 21), where Jesus prophesies the destruction of Jerusalem, culminating in the Roman invasion of A.D. 70.[5]

---

3. For example, Daniel was told: "From the time that the regular sacrifice is abolished, and the abomination of desolation is set up, there will be 1,290 days. How blessed is he who keeps waiting and attains to the 1,335 days!" (Dan. 12:11-12). These numbers are based on the 430-year period of oppression in Egypt (Ex. 12:40) and the 45 years from bondage to the conquest of the Land (Josh. 14:6-10); the symbols indicate that the coming period of oppression, compared to that in Egypt, will be brief (*days* as opposed to *years*), but *three times* as intense (3 × 430 = 1,290). Those who persevere in faith, however, will attain to the 1,335th day of victory and dominion.

4. St. Matthew probably chose to divide the genealogy into three groups of fourteen to highlight the name of David, which has a numerical value of 14 in Hebrew. David is the central figure in Christ's genealogy, and Christ is presented throughout Scripture as the greater David (cf. Acts 2:25-36). In order to arrive at this symmetrical arrangement, however, St. Matthew leaves out three generations between Joram and Uzziah in v. 8 (Ahaziah, Joash, and Amaziah; cf. 2 Kings 8:25; 11:21; 14:1), and counts Jeconiah twice in v. 11-12. Now, St. Matthew was not stupid: He could add figures correctly (he had been a tax collector!); moreover, he knew that the actual genealogies were available to his readers. But he wrote his Gospel to provide a Christology, not chronology. His list is written to expound the "forty-two-ness" of the period leading up to Christ's advent, and the "fourteen-ness" of Christ Himself – all revealing the Savior as "the son of David, the son of Abraham" (1:1).

5. Interestingly, the Roman siege of Jerusalem under Vespasian and Titus did last a literal three and a half years, from 67 to 70. But the main point of the term is its symbolic significance, which is based on its use in the prophets. As in many other cases, God obviously brought about the historical events in a way that harmonizes with the Biblical symbolism He authored.

3-4   But before Jerusalem is destroyed, St. John hears further testimony of its guilt, a summary of the apostate history of the City, focusing on its perennial persecution of the prophets. God tells St. John that He has ordained **two Witnesses** to **prophesy for twelve hundred and sixty days,** the number of days in an idealized forty-two months (of thirty days each). This number, therefore, is related (but not identical) to the forty-two months, and continues to express the essential "forty-two-ness" of the period preceding the full establishment of the Kingdom.[6] The Witnesses are **clothed in sackcloth,** the traditional dress of the prophets from Elijah through John the Baptizer, symbolizing their mourning over national apostasy (2 Kings 1:8; Isa. 20:2; Jon. 3:6; Zech. 13:4; Matt. 3:4; Mark 1:6). Biblical law required two witnesses (Num. 35:30; Deut. 17:6; 19:15; Matt. 18:16; cf. Ex. 7:15-25; 8-11; Luke 10:1); the idea is a pervasive theme throughout Biblical prophecy and symbolism. A preliminary conclusion about the two Witnesses, therefore, is that they represent the line of prophets, culminating in John the Baptizer, who bore witness against Jerusalem during the history of Israel.

The two Witnesses are identified as **the two olive trees and the two lampstands that stand before the Lord of the earth.** At this point the imagery becomes much more complex. St. John returns again to Zechariah's prophecy of the lampstand (Zech. 4:1-5; cf. Rev. 1:4, 13, 20; 4:5). The seven lamps on the lampstand are connected to two olive trees (cf. Ps. 52:8; Jer. 11:16), from which flow an unceasing supply of oil, symbolizing the Holy Spirit's filling and empowering work in the leaders of His covenant people. The meaning of the symbol is summarized in Zechariah 4:6: "Not by might nor by power, but by My Spirit, says the LORD of hosts." The same passage in Zechariah also speaks of two Witnesses, two *sons of oil* ("anointed ones"), who lead God's people: Joshua the *priest* and Zerubbabel the *king* (Zech. 3-4; cf. Ezra 3, 5-6; Hag. 1-2). In brief, then, Zechariah tells us of an olive tree/lampstand complex representing the officers of the covenant: two Witness-figures who belong to the royal house and the priesthood. The Book of Revelation freely connects all of these, speaking of two shining lampstands which

---

6. For some interesting aspects of the number 1,260 and its relationship to the number of the Beast (666), see comments on 13:18.

are two oil-filled olive trees, which are also two Witnesses, a king and a priest—all representing the Spirit-inspired prophetic testimony of the Kingdom of priests (Ex. 19:6). (A major aspect of St. John's message, as we have seen, is that the New Covenant Church comes into the full inheritance of the promises as the true Kingdom of priests, the royal priesthood in which "all the LORD's people are prophets.") That these Witnesses are members of the Old Covenant rather than the New is shown, among other indications, by their wearing of sackcloth—the dress characteristic of Old Covenant privation rather than New Covenant fullness.

5-6 St. John now speaks of the two Witnesses in terms of the two great witnesses of the Old Testament, Moses and Elijah —the Law and the Prophets. **If anyone desires to harm them, fire proceeds from their mouth and devours their enemies.** In Numbers 16:35, fire came down from heaven at Moses' word and consumed the false worshipers who had rebelled against him; and, similarly, fire fell from heaven and consumed Elijah's enemies when he spoke the word (2 Ki. 1:9-12). This becomes a standard symbol for the power of the prophetic Word, as if fire actually proceeds from the mouths of God's Witnesses. As the Lord said to Jeremiah, "Behold, I am making My words in your mouth fire, and this people wood, and it shall consume them" (Jer. 5:14).

Extending the imagery, St. John says that the Witnesses **have the power to shut up the sky, in order that rain may not fall during the days of their prophesying,** i.e., for the twelve hundred and sixty days (three and a half years)—the same duration of the drought caused by Elijah in 1 Kings 17 (see Luke 4:25; James 5:17). Like Moses (Ex. 7-13), the Witnesses **have power over the waters to turn them into blood, and to smite the earth with every plague, as often as they desire.**

Both of these prophetic figures pointed beyond themselves to the Greater Prophet, Jesus Christ. The very last message of the Old Testament mentions them together in a prophecy of Christ's Advent: "Remember the law of Moses My servant. . . . Behold, I am going to send you Elijah the prophet. . . ." (Mal. 4:4-5). Malachi goes on to declare that Elijah's ministry would be recapitulated in the life of John the Baptizer (Mal. 4:5-6; cf.

277

Matt. 11:14; 17:10-13; Luke 1:15-17). But John, like Elijah, was only a Forerunner, preparing the way for One coming after him, the Firstborn, who would have a double — nay, measureless — portion of the Spirit (cf. Deut. 21:17; 2 Kings 2:9; John 3:27-34). And, like Moses, John was succeeded by a Joshua, Jesus the Conqueror, who would bring the covenant people into their promised inheritance. The two Witnesses, therefore, summarize all the witnesses of the Old Covenant, culminating in the witness of John.

7 Now the scene changes: The Witnesses are — to all appearances — defeated and destroyed. **When they have finished their testimony, the Beast that comes up out of the Abyss will make war with them, and overcome and kill them.** This is the first mention of **the Beast** in this book, but St. John certainly seems to expect his readers to understand his reference. Indeed, the Beast theme is a familiar one in Biblical history. In the beginning we are told of how Adam and Eve refused to become "gods" through submission to God,[7] and sought autonomous and ulti-

---

7. The Christian doctrine of *deification* (cf. Ps. 82:6; John 10:34-36; Rom. 8:29-30; Eph. 4:13, 24; Heb. 2:10-13; 12:9-10; 2 Pet. 1:4; 1 John 3:2) is generally known in the Western churches by the terms *sanctification* and *glorification*, referring to man's full inheritance of the image of God. This doctrine (which has absolutely nothing in common with pagan realistic theories of the continuity of being, humanistic notions about man's "spark of divinity," or Mormon polytheistic fables regarding human evolution into godhood) is universal throughout the writings of the Church Fathers; see, e.g., Georgios I. Mantzaridis, *The Deification of Man: St. Gregory Palamas and the Orthodox Tradition*, Liadain Sherrard, trans. (Crestwood, NY: St. Vladimir's Seminary Press, 1984). St. Athanasius wrote: "The Word is not of things created, but rather is Himself their Creator. For therefore He assumed a created human body, that, having renewed it as its Creator, He might deify it in Himself, and thus bring us all into the Kingdom of heaven through our likeness to Him. For man would not have been deified if joined to a creature, or unless the Son were very God; nor would man have been brought into the Father's presence, unless He had been His natural and true Word who had put on the body. And as we would not have been delivered from sin and the curse, had not the flesh that the Word assumed been by nature human (for we should have had nothing in common with what is alien to us); so too humanity would not have been deified, if the Word who became flesh had not been by nature derived from the Father and true and proper to Him. For therefore the union was of this kind, that He might unite what is man by nature to Him who naturally belonged to the Godhead, that his salvation and deification might be sure" (*Orations Against the Arians*, ii.70). He put it more succinctly in a famous statement from his classic work *On the Incarnation of the Word of God* (54): "The Word was made man in order that we might be made gods."

mate godhood instead. By submitting to a beast (the Serpent) they themselves became "beasts" instead of gods, with the Beast's mark of rebellion displayed on their foreheads (Gen. 3:19); even in redemption they remained clothed with the skins of beasts (Gen. 3:21).[8] A later picture of the Fall is displayed in the fall of Nebuchadnezzar, who was, like Adam, "the king of kings, to whom the God of heaven has given the kingdom, the power, the strength, and the glory" (Dan. 2:37). Yet, through pride, through seeking autonomous godhood, he was judged: "And he was driven away from mankind and began eating grass like cattle, and his body was drenched with the dew of heaven, until his hair had grown like eagles' feathers and his nails like birds' claws" (Dan. 4:33). Man's rebellion against God is also imaged by the beasts' rebellion against man; thus the wicked persecutors of Christ at the crucifixion are called "dogs" and "bulls of Bashan," and are likened to "a ravening and roaring lion" (Ps. 22:12-13, 16).

Another image of the "beastliness" of rebellion was contained in the Old Covenant sacrificial/dietary requirements against "unclean" animals, as James Jordan observes: "All unclean animals *resemble the serpent* in three ways. They eat 'dirt' (rotting carrion, manure, garbage). They move in contact with 'dirt' (crawling on their bellies, fleshy pads of their feet in touch with the ground, no scales to keep their skin from contact with their watery environment). They revolt against human dominion, killing men or other beasts. Under the symbolism of the Old Covenant, such Satanic beasts represent the Satanic nations (Lev. 20:22-26), for animals are 'images' of men.[9] To eat Satanic animals, under the Old Covenant, was to 'eat' the Satanic lifestyle, to 'eat' death and rebellion."[10]

The enemy of God and the Church is thus always **Beast**, in

---

8. Representing the restored image of God, the priests were clothed in vegetables (linen) rather than in animals (wool); they were forbidden to wear the skins of beasts, because they produced *sweat* (Ezek. 44:17-18; cf. Gen. 3:19). On "judicial godhood" and the clothing of Adam and Eve with skins, see James B. Jordan, "Rebellion, Tyranny, and Dominion in the Book of Genesis," in Gary North, ed., *Christianity and Civilization* 3 (1983): *Tactics of Christian Resistance*, pp. 43-47.

9. Cf. Prov. 6:6; 26:11; 30:15, 19, 24-31; Dan. 5:21; Ex. 13:2, 13.

10. James B. Jordan, *The Law of the Covenant: An Exposition of Exodus 21-23* (Tyler, TX: Institute for Christian Economics, 1984), p. 122.

its various historical manifestations. The prophets often spoke of pagan states as terrifying beasts that warred against the Covenant people (Ps. 87:4; 89:10; Isa. 51:9; Dan. 7:3-8, 16-25). All this will be gathered together in St. John's description of Rome and apostate Israel in Revelation 13. Yet we must remember that these persecuting powers were but the immediate manifestations of the agelong enemy of the Church—the Dragon, who is formally introduced in 12:3,[11] but who was well-known to any Biblically literate person in St. John's audience. The Christians already knew the ultimate identity of the Beast who arises from **the Abyss**. It is Leviathan, the Dragon, the Serpent of old, who comes out of his prison in the sea again and again to plague the people of God. The Abyss, the dark, raging Deep, is where Satan and his evil spirits are kept imprisoned except for periodic releases in order to torment men when they commit apostasy.[12] (Note that the legion of evil spirits in the Gadarene demoniac pleaded to be kept out of the Abyss; with divine deception, Jesus sent them into the herd of swine, and the swine rushed headlong into the sea: Luke 8:31-33). The persecution of the Covenant people is never a merely "political" contest, regardless of how evil states attempt to color their wicked actions. It always originates in the pit of hell.

Throughout the history of redemption, the Beast **made war** against the Church, particularly against its prophetic witnesses. The final example of this in the Old Covenant period is the war of Herod against John the Forerunner, whom he **overcame and killed** (Mark 6:14-29); and the culmination of this war against the prophets was the murder of Christ, the final Prophet, of whom all the other prophets were images, and whose testimony they bore. Christ was crucified by the collaboration of Roman and Jewish authorities, and this partnership in persecution continued throughout the history of the early Church (see Acts 17:5-8; 1 Thess. 2:14-17).[13]

---

11. Closely related to the Biblical doctrine of the Beast is the Bible's "dinosaur theology"; for this, see my comments on 12:3.

12. See above on 9:1-6.

13. The Beast's attempt to erase the testimony of God's witnesses eventually led to its attack on the land of Israel, the birthplace of the Church; Titus supposed that he could destroy Christianity by destroying the Temple in A.D. 70 (see on 17:14). The central religious motive behind the Roman war against the Jews was its deeply rooted hatred for the Christian Church.

8-10   The **dead bodies** of the Old Covenant Witnesses, "from righteous Abel to Zechariah" (Matt. 23:35) lie metaphorically **in the street of the Great City which Spiritually** [i.e., *by the revelation of the Holy Spirit*] **is called Sodom and Egypt**. This City is, of course, Jerusalem; St. John explains that it is **where also their Lord was crucified** (on Israel as Sodom, see Deut. 29:22-28; 32:32; Isa. 1:10, 21; 3:9; Jer. 23:14; Ezek. 16:46). Commentators are generally unable to find Bible references comparing Israel (or Jerusalem) to Egypt, but this is the old problem of not being able to see the forest for the trees. For the proof is contained in the whole message of the New Testament. Jesus is constantly regarded as the new Moses (Acts 3:20-23; Heb. 3-4), the new Israel (Matt. 2:15), the new Temple (John 1:14; 2:19-21), and in fact a living recapitulation/transcendence of the entire history of the Exodus (cf. 1 Cor. 10:1-4).[14] On the Mount of Transfiguration (Luke 9:31), He spoke with *Moses and Elijah* (another link with this passage), calling His coming death and resurrection in Jerusalem an *"Exodus"* (the Greek word is *exodon*). Following from all this is the language of Revelation itself, which speaks of the Egyptian plagues being poured out upon Israel (8:6-12; 16:2-12). The war of the Witnesses with apostate Israel and the pagan states is described in the same terms as the original Exodus from Egypt (cf. also the Cloud and the pillar of fire in 10:1). Jerusalem, the once-holy, now apostate city, has become pagan and perverse, an oppressor of the true Covenant people, joining with the Beast in attacking and killing them. It is Jerusalem that is guilty of the blood of the Old Covenant Witnesses; she is, *par excellence*, the killer of prophets (Matt. 21:33-43; 23:34-38). In fact, said Jesus, "it cannot be that a prophet should perish outside of Jerusalem" (Luke 13:33).

With the death of the Witnesses, their voice of condemnation is silenced; and now **those from the peoples and tribes and tongues and nations** regard the Church itself as dead, openly displaying their contempt for God's people, whose **dead bodies** lie unburied **in the street**, under an apparent curse, for they **will**

---

14. The evidence is far too extensive to repeat here, but see Meredith G. Kline, *The Structure of Biblical Authority* (Eerdmans, 2nd ed., 1975), pp. 183-95; see also Robert D. Brinsmead, *The Pattern of Redemptive History* (Fallbrook, CA: Verdict Publications, 1979), pp. 23-33.

not permit their dead bodies to be laid in a tomb (cf. 1 Kings 13:20-22; Jer. 8:1-2; 14:16; 16:3-4). The desire for insertion into the Promised Land in death was a central concern to the faithful Witnesses of the Old Covenant, as a pledge of their future resurrection (Gen. 23; 47:29-31; 49:28-33; 50:1-14, 24-26; Ex. 13:19; Josh. 24:32; 1 Sam. 31:7-13; Acts 7:15-16; Heb. 11:22). The oppression of the Kingdom of priests by the heathen was often expressed in these terms:

> O God, the nations have invaded Thine inheritance;
> They have defiled Thy holy Temple;
> They have laid Jerusalem in ruins.
> They have given the dead bodies of Thy servants for food to the
>   birds of the heavens,
> The flesh of Thy godly ones to the beasts of the earth.
> They have poured out their blood like water round about
>   Jerusalem;
> And there was no one to bury them. (Ps. 79:1-3)

The irony, however, is that it is now **those who dwell on the Land** — the Jews themselves (cf. 3:10) — who join with the heathen nations in oppressing the righteous. The apostates of Israel **rejoice and make merry; and they will send gifts to one another, because these two prophets tormented those who dwell on the Land** (cf. Herod's party, during which John was imprisoned and then beheaded: Matt. 14:3-12). The price of the world's peace was the annihilation of the prophetic Witness; Israel and the heathen world united in their evil gloating at the destruction of the prophets, whose faithful double witness had **tormented** the disobedient with conviction of sin, driving them to commit murder (cf. Gen. 4:3-8; 1 John 3:11-12; Acts 7:54-60). Natural enemies were reconciled to each other through their joint participation in the murder of the prophets. This was especially true in their murder of Christ: "Now Herod and Pilate became friends with one another that very day; for before they had been at enmity with each other" (Luke 23:12). At Christ's death all manner of people rejoiced and mocked: the rulers, the priests, the competing religious factions, the Roman soldiers, the servants, the criminals; all joined in celebrating His death (cf. Matt. 27:27-31, 39-44; Mark 15:29-32; Luke 22:63-65; 23:8-12, 35-39); all sided with the Beast against the Lamb (John

19:15). The attempt to destroy the Witnesses seemed to be successful, not only in silencing individual prophets, but in abolishing the Testimony of the Covenant itself. The progressive war against the Word reached its climax with the murder of Christ; this was the ultimate crime that brought on Jerusalem's destruction. Moses had instructed the people of Israel about the coming Prophet, warning them that they would be cursed if they refused to listen to Him (Deut. 18:15-19); the martyr Stephen quoted this prophecy (Acts 7:37), and concluded:

> You men who are stiff-necked and uncircumcised in heart and ears are always resisting the Holy Spirit; you are doing just as your fathers did. Which one of the prophets did your fathers not persecute? And they killed those who had previously announced the coming of the Righteous One, whose betrayers and murderers you have now become! (Acts 7:51-52)

For now, the persecutors are victorious, and rejoice for **three and a half days.** This is no more a literal period than the previous figures of 42 months and 1,260 days. As we have noted, "three and a half" represents a broken seven, a period of sadness and oppression. In each section of Revelation, St. John's figures harmonize with each other: The Seal-judgments are in *fourths,* the Trumpet-judgments are in *thirds,* and the numbers in chapters 11-13 correspond to *three and a half* (42 months and 1,260 days both equal three and a half years). St. John's poetic symmetry continues this symbolism: The days during which the righteous are oppressed, their bodies abused, are a *three-and-a-half,* a time of grief when the wicked are triumphant. Yet the evil time is brief, being limited to a mere three and a half **days.** Thus several lines of imagery converge here; and St. John has kept the period in general agreement with the three days of Christ's descent into hell. In His death, the entire Covenant community and its Testimony lie dead in the streets of Jerusalem, under the Curse.

11-12   After the three and a half days, the Witnesses are resurrected: **The breath of life from God entered into them** in the New Creation (cf. Gen. 2:7; Ezek. 37:1-14; John 20:22) **and they stood on their feet** (cf. Acts 7:55), causing terror and consternation to their enemies. **Great fear came upon those who were**

283

beholding them (cf. Acts 2:43; 5:5; 19:17; contrast John 7:13; 12:42; 19:38; 20:19), and with good reason: Through the resurrection of Christ, the Church and her Testimony became unstoppable. In union with Christ in His Ascension to glory (Eph. 2:6), **they went up to heaven in the Cloud, and their enemies beheld them.**[15] The Witnesses did not survive the persecutions; they died. But in Christ's resurrection they rose to power and dominion that existed not by might, nor by power, but by God's Spirit, the very breath of life from God. "We are not the lords of history and do not control its outcome, but we have assurance that there is a lord of history and he controls its outcome. We need a theological interpretation of disaster, one that recognizes that God acts in such events as captivities, defeats, and crucifixions. The Bible can be interpreted as a string of God's triumphs disguised as disasters."[16]

St. John draws an important parallel here that should not be missed, for it is close to the heart of the passage's meaning. The ascension of the Witnesses is described in the same language as that of St. John's own ascension:

4:1   After these things I looked, and behold, a door standing open in heaven, and the first Voice which I had heard, like a trumpet speaking with me, saying: Come up here. . . .

11:11-12   And after the three and a half days . . . they heard a loud Voice from heaven saying to them: Come up here. . . .

The story of the Two Witnesses is therefore the story of the witnessing Church, which has received the divine command to **Come up here** and has ascended with Christ into the Cloud of heaven, to the Throne (Eph. 1:20-22; 2:6; Heb. 12:22-24): She now possesses an imperial grant to exercise rule over the ends of the earth, discipling the nations to the obedience of faith (Matt. 28:18-20; Rom. 1:5).

13-14   One of the results of Christ's ascension, as He foretold, would be the crack of doom for apostate Israel, the shak-

---

15. This bears some similarity to Elijah's experience, with the major difference that it was his *friend*, and not his enemies, who saw his ascension (2 Kings 2:9-14).

16. Herbert Schlossberg, *Idols for Destruction: Christian Faith and Its Confrontation with American Society* (Nashville: Thomas Nelson Publishers, 1983), p. 304.

ing of heaven and earth. Scripture connects as one theological Event — the Advent — Christ's birth, life, death, resurrection, ascension, the outpouring of His Spirit upon the Church in A.D. 30, and the outpouring of His wrath upon Israel in the Holocaust of A.D. 66-70: Thus **in that Day there was a great earthquake** (cf. Rev. 6:12; Ezek. 38:19-20; Hag. 2:6-7; Zech. 14:5; Matt. 27:51-53; Heb. 12:26-28). Because the triumph of Christ meant the defeat of His enemies, **a tenth of the City fell.** Actually, the whole City of Jerusalem fell in A.D. 70; but, as we have seen, the Trumpet-judgments do not yet reach the final end of Jerusalem, but (apparently) go only as far as the first siege of Jerusalem, under Cestius. In conformity to the nature of the Trumpet as an alarm, God's taking a "tithe" of Jerusalem in the first siege was a warning to the City.

For clearly symbolic, Biblical-theological reasons, St. John tells us that **seven thousand people were killed** in the earthquake. Ultimately, the Earth-and-Heavenquake brought by the New Covenant killed many more than seven thousand. But the number represents the exact reverse of the situation in Elijah's day. In 1 Kings 19:18, God told Elijah that 7,000 in Israel remained faithful to the covenant. Even then, it was most likely a symbolic number, indicating *completeness* (seven) multiplied by *many* (one thousand). In other words, Elijah should not be discouraged, for he was not alone. God's righteous elect were numerous, and the whole number was present and accounted for. On the other hand, however, they were in the minority. But now, in the New Covenant, the situation is reversed. The latter-day Elijahs, the faithful witnesses in the Church, are not to be dismayed when it seems as if God is destroying all Israel, and the faithful are few in number. For this time it is the apostates, the Baal-worshipers, who are the "seven thousand in Israel." The tables have been turned. In the Old Testament, only "7000" faithful existed; in the New Testament, only "7000" are wicked. They are destroyed, and the rest — the overwhelming majority — are converted and saved: **The rest were terrified and gave glory to the God of heaven** — Biblical language for conversion and belief (cf. Josh. 7:19; Isa. 26:9; 42:12; Jer. 13:16; Matt. 5:16; Luke 17:15-19; 18:43; 1 Pet. 2:12; Rev. 14:7; 15:4; 16:9; 19:7; 21:24). The tendency in the New Covenant age is *judgment unto salvation.*

St. John closes the section of the Sixth Trumpet with these words: **The Second Woe is past; behold, the Third Woe is coming quickly.** St. John does not tell us explicitly when the Third Woe arrives. Since the First and Second Woes refer to the warnings Israel received in the full-scale demonic attack on the Land (9:1-12) and in the first Roman invasion under Cestius (9:13-21), it is possible to take the Third Woe as the Fall of Jerusalem itself; six Woes (in three pairs) are listed in rapid succession in 18:10, 16, 19. It is more in keeping with St. John's literary structuring, however, to see the Third Woe as a consequence of the Seventh Trumpet (just as the First and Second Woes correspond to the Fifth and Sixth Trumpets: cf. 8:13; 9:12); the Woe is declared in 12:12, after Michael's defeat of the Dragon, and continues through the end of Chapter 14, showing the Dragon's "great wrath" during his "short time" of dominance.

The Seventh Trumpet (11:15-19)

15 And the seventh angel sounded; and there arose loud voices in heaven, saying,
> The kingdom of the world has become the Kingdom of our Lord, and of His Christ; and He will reign forever and ever.

16 And the twenty-four elders, who sit on their thrones before God, fell on their faces and worshiped God,
17 saying,
> We give Thee thanks, O Lord God, the Almighty, who art and who wast, because Thou hast taken Thy great power and hast begun to reign.

18   And the nations were enraged, and Thy rage came, and the time came for the dead to be vindicated, and the time to give their reward to Thy servants the prophets and to the saints and to those who fear Thy name, the small and the great, and to destroy those who destroy the Land.

19 And the Temple of God in heaven was opened; and the ark of His covenant appeared in His Temple, and there were flashes of lightning and sounds and peals of thunder and an earthquake and a great hailstorm.

15   In conformity with the Biblical pattern uniting the ideas of sabbath and consummation, the Trumpet of **the seventh angel** announces that "the Mystery of God" has been fulfilled and accomplished (cf. 10:6-7). At this point in history God's plan is made apparent: He has placed Jews and Gentiles on equal footing in the Covenant. The destruction of apostate Israel and the Temple revealed that God had created a new nation, a new Temple, as Jesus had prophesied to the Jewish leaders: "Therefore I say to you, the Kingdom of God will be taken away from you, and be given to a nation producing the fruit of it" (Matt. 21:43). Later, Jesus told his disciples what would be the effect of the destruction of Jerusalem: "At that time will appear the sign of the Son of Man in heaven" (Matt. 24:30). Marcellus Kik explains: "The judgment upon Jerusalem was the sign of the fact that the Son of man was reigning in heaven. There has been misunderstanding due to the reading of this verse, as some have thought it to be 'a sign in heaven.' But this is not what the verse says; it says the sign of the *Son of Man in heaven.* The phrase 'in heaven' defines the locality of the Son of Man and not of the sign. A sign was not to appear in the heavens, but the destruction of Jerusalem was to indicate the rule of the Son of Man in heaven."[17]

Kik continues: "The apostle Paul states in the eleventh chapter of Romans that the fall of the Jews was a blessing to the rest of the world. He speaks of it as the enriching of the Gentiles and the reconciling of the world. The catastrophe of Jerusalem really signalized the beginning of a new and world-wide kingdom, marking the full separation of the Christian Church from legalistic Judaism. The whole system of worship, so closely associated with Jerusalem and the Temple, received, as it were, a death blow from God himself. God was now through with the Old Covenant made at Sinai: holding full sway was the sign of the New Covenant."[18]

Thus the Kingdom of God, the "Fifth Kingdom" prophesied in Daniel 2, becomes universalized, as the heavenly choir sings: **The kingdom of the world has become the Kingdom of our Lord, and of His Christ; and He will reign forever and ever. The**

---

17. Marcellus Kik, *An Eschatology of Victory* (Nutley, NJ: The Presbyterian and Reformed Publishing Co., 1971), p. 137. The common rendering in modern versions of the Bible ("then the sign of the Son of Man will appear in the sky") simply reflects the unbiblical biases of a few translators and editors. The more literal translation in the King James Version is what the Greek text *says*. Cf. the discussion in *Paradise Restored: A Biblical Theology of Dominion* (Ft. Worth, TX: Dominion Press, 1985), pp. 97-105.
18. Ibid., p. 138.

final dissociation of Christianity from Judaism means that it is now a worldwide religion. The Kingdom of Christ now begins the process of encompassing and enveloping all kingdoms of the world. The earth will be regenerated. This became clear with the fall of Jerusalem, the sign that Christ had indeed ascended to His heavenly throne and was ruling the nations, pouring out wrath and tribulation upon His enemies at the request of His praying Church. The Roman armies who annihilated Jerusalem, massacring and enslaving its inhabitants, were His armies (Dan. 9:26), fulfilling His Word (Deut. 28:49-68).

In terms of the Biblical calendar, the "seventh trumpet" was sounded on Tishri 1, the first day of the seventh month in the liturgical year, and of the first month in the civil year: *Rosh Hashanah*, the Day of Trumpets. Ernest L. Martin has pointed out a number of interesting aspects of the Day of Trumpets that bear directly on the significance of the Seventh Trumpet in Revelation: "Before the period of the Exodus in the time of Moses, *this* was the day which apparently began the biblical year. It also looks like this was the day when many people were advanced one year of life — no matter at what month of the year they were actually born. Notice that the patriarch Noah became 601 years of age 'in the first month [Tishri], the first day of the month [later to be called the Day of Trumpets]' (Gen. 8:13). That was the very day when 'Noah removed the covering of the ark, and looked, and, behold, the face of the ground was dry' (v. 13). This was not only Noah's official birthday, it became a new birth for the earth as well. . . . Even the first day of creation mentioned in Genesis 1:1-5 could be reckoned to this very day. . . . Since the Autumn apparently commenced all biblical years before the Exodus, and since all the fruit was on the trees ready for Adam and Eve to eat (Gen. 1:29; 2:9, 16-17), it suggests that . . . the first day of creation mentioned in Genesis was also the first of Tishri (at least Moses no doubt intended to give that impression). This means that not only the birthday of the new earth in Noah's day was what later became the Day of Trumpets, but it was also the day which ushered in the original creation of the earth.

". . . . The majority opinion of Jewish elders (which still dominates the services of the synagogues) was that the Day of Trumpets was the memorial day that commemorated the beginning of the world. Authorized opinion prevailed that the first of Tishri was the first day of Genesis 1:1-5. It 'came to be regarded as the birthday of the world' (M'Clintock & Strong, *Cyclopaedia*, vol. X, p. 568). It was even more than an anniversary of the physical creation. 'Judaism regards New Year's Day not merely as an anniversary of creation, but — more importantly — as a renewal of it. This is when the world is reborn' (Theodor H. Gaster, *Festivals of the Jewish Year*, p. 109). . . .

"Each of the Jewish months was officially introduced by the blowing of trumpets (Num. 10:10). Since the festival year (in which all the Mosaic festivals were found) was seven months long, the last month (Tishri) was the last month for a trumpet introduction. This is one of the reasons that the day was called 'the Day of trumpets.' The 'last trump' in the series was always sounded on *this* day — so, it was the final trumpets' day (Lev. 23:24; Num. 29:1).

"This was the exact day that many of the ancient kings and rulers of Judah reckoned as their inauguration day of rule . . . Indeed, it was customary that the final ceremony in the coronation of kings was the blowing of trumpets. For Solomon: 'Blow ye the trumpet, and say, God save king Solomon' (1 Kings 1:34). For Jehu: 'They blew with the trumpets, saying, Jehu is king' (2 Kings 9:13). At the enthronement of Jehoash: 'The people of the land rejoiced, and blew with trumpets' (2 Kings 11:14)."[19]

M. D. Goulder summarizes the significance of Rosh Hashanah: "New Year is the Jewish equivalent of the Christian Advent: it combines joy at the thought of the ultimate coming of God's reign with penitence at the thought of the judgment which that reign will bring. It is marked by the blowing of the Shofar (Lev. 23:24), to proclaim the day (*kēryxate*, Joel 2:15); and by three proper benedictions, the Malkuyot, the Zikronot, and the Shofarot. Each of these comprises ten verses from Scripture: the first on the kingship of God, looking forward to his ultimate reign (e.g. Zech. 14:9); the second on God's remembering of men's deeds to judge or reward, and his remembering of his covenant; the third on the blowing of the Shofar, from Sinai to the last trumpet which shall gather the dispersion to Jerusalem."[20]

---

19. Ernest L. Martin, *The Birth of Christ Recalculated* (Pasadena: Foundation for Biblical Research, second ed., 1980), pp. 155ff.

20. M. D. Goulder, *The Evangelists' Calendar: A Lectionary Explanation of the Development of Scripture* (London: SPCK, 1978), pp. 245f.

All this would naturally be in the minds of St. John and his first-century audience at the mention of the great Seventh Trumpet. Now, he adds a new dimension of symbolism, by showing the Christian significance of Rosh Hashanah, that to which it had always pointed: The Day of Trumpets is the Beginning of the New World, the New Creation, the coronation-day of the King of kings, when He is enthroned as supreme Judge over the whole world. In fact, as we will see in Chapter 12, the significance of Tishri 1 is regarded by St. John—theologically, if not "actually"—as the birthday of Jesus Christ. For now, however, he presents it as the Birthday of the New Creation, the fruit of the Resurrection and Ascension of Christ and His saints.

16-18   The choral declaration of Christ's universal Lordship and the worldwide triumph of His kingdom is joined by **the twenty-four elders, who sit on their thrones before God.** (Note the architectural reference: The characteristic posture of the teacher/ruler in the New Testament is *enthronement*; Jesus *stood up* to read the Scriptures, and *sat down* to teach, Luke 4:16, 20.) These elders **fell on their faces and worshiped God, saying: We give Thee thanks, O Lord God, the Almighty.** The verb for **give thanks** is *eucharisteō*, used throughout Christian history for the Communion of the Lord's Body and Blood: The Eucharist. This term acquires its technical meaning very early (cf. *Didache* 9-10), based on its usage in the New Testament accounts of the Lord's Supper (Matt. 26:26-27; Mark 14:22-23; Luke 22:17, 19; 1 Cor. 11:24). We would be blind indeed not to see it here. For St. John has shown us that the pattern of God's redemptive action in history is the same as that acted out on every Lord's Day: The Church, having died and resurrected in Christ (v. 7-11), ascends amid cosmic judgments to heaven at the divine command (v. 12-14). Surrounded by the heavenly host singing praises (v. 15), the Elders fall down before God's majesty, proclaiming: *Eucharistoumen! We give Thanks!* (v. 16-17).

The Elders continue the service with a confession of faith, praising the Lord for the inauguration of His Kingdom: **Thou hast taken Thy great power and hast begun to reign.** It was Christ the Lord who was stirring up the nations of the Roman Empire to do battle against Israel, for Israel had persecuted and slaughtered His saints. Thus **the nations were enraged, and Thy**

290

rage came, and apostate, persecuting Jerusalem suffers the brunt of both; **and the time came for the dead to be vindicated, and the time to give their reward to Thy servants the prophets and to the saints and to those who fear Thy name, the small and the great.** This is just a rephrasing of Christ's statement to Jerusalem in His last public discourse: "That upon you may fall all the righteous blood shed on the earth, from the blood of righteous Abel to the blood of Zechariah, the son of Berechiah, whom you murdered between the Temple and the altar. Truly I say to you, all these things will come upon this generation" (Matt. 23:35-36). God's **servants the prophets** (equivalent terms in Revelation: see 1:1; 10:7; 16:6; 18:24; 19:2, 10; cf. Dan. 9:6, 10; Amos 3:7; Zech. 1:6) would be vindicated and rewarded in the coming judgment — not the final judgment at the Last Day, but rather *the historical vindication and avenging of the martyred saints,* those who had suffered at the hands of ungodly Israel, as Jesus had foretold.[21] Just prior to the fall of Israel, the Apostle Paul had written of the Jews, who were constantly persecuting the Christians, that "wrath has come upon them to the utmost" (1 Thess. 2:16). Now, St. John's glimpse into the near future shows that as God's pent-up rage fell in all its fury, the Church rejoiced. Echoing the familiar theme of expulsion from Eden, the song closes with the observation that the destruction of Israel served **to destroy those who destroy the Land** (cf. Lev. 18:24-30).

19 Here is summed up the theological significance of the fall of Israel: It meant that **the Temple of God in heaven was opened** (Matt. 27:51; Eph. 2:19-22; Heb. 8:1-6; 9:8). The earthly Temple is gone, and now only the true Temple remains. God's Temple is revealed to be the Church; and now **the ark of His covenant appeared in His Temple,** as God's indwelling presence is manifested there (Eph. 2:22). Technically, a "saint" is someone who has *access to the sanctuary,* someone with sanctuary privileges. In the New Covenant, we are all saints; we all have access to the Throne (Heb. 4:16; 10:19-25), having ascended in Christ (defin-

---

21. The word *judgment,* when used of God's people, generally signifies *vindication and vengeance on their behalf* (see 1 Sam. 24:15; 2 Sam. 18:19, 31; Ps. 10:18; 26:1; 43:1; Isa. 1:17; Heb. 10:30-39).

itively in His Ascension, progressively each Lord's Day in worship). In the Old Covenant, the Ten Commandments were "hidden" in the Sanctuary, and no one was allowed in (although God's revelation was published provisionally by Moses). But now, in the New Covenant, the Mystery has been openly published, and man in Christ has access. With the sounding of the Seventh Trumpet the revelation is complete and definitive; the Mystery is no longer mysterious. St. Paul commended the saints of Rome "to Him who is able to establish you according to my Gospel and the preaching of Jesus Christ, according to the revelation of the Mystery which has been kept secret for long ages past, but now is manifested, and by the Scriptures of the prophets, according to the commandment of the eternal God, has been made known to all the nations, leading to obedience of faith" (Rom. 16:25-26).

For this reason all the meteorological phenomena that had been associated with the Cloud in the Old Covenant revelation (cf. Ps. 18) are now spoken of by St. John in relation to the Church: **There were flashes of lightning and voices and peals of thunder and an earthquake and a great hailstorm.** In the Church of Jesus Christ the door of heaven has opened up to us. Our sanctification is by means of the Church, through its ministry and sacraments, as St. Irenaeus wrote: "We receive our faith from the Church and keep it safe; and it is as it were a precious deposit stored in a fine vessel, ever renewing its vitality through the Spirit of God, and causing the renewal of the vessel in which it is stored. For this gift of God has been entrusted to the Church, as the breath of life to created man, to the end that all members by receiving it should be made alive. And herein has been bestowed upon us our means of communion with Christ, namely the Holy Spirit, the pledge of immortality, the strengthening of our faith, the ladder by which we ascend to God. For the Apostle says, 'God has set up in the Church Apostles, prophets, teachers' [1 Cor. 12:28] and all the other means of the Spirit's working. But they have no share in this Spirit who do not join in the activity of the Church. . . . For where the Church is, there is the Spirit of God; and where the Spirit of God is, there is the Church and every kind of grace. The Spirit is truth. Therefore those who have no share in the Spirit are not nourished and given life at their mother's breast; nor do they enjoy the sparkling fountain that issues from the body of Christ."[22]

The early Christians who first read the Book of Revelation, especially those of a Jewish background, had to understand that the destruction of Jerusalem would not mean the end of covenant or Kingdom. The fall of old Israel was not "the beginning of the end." Instead, it was the sign that Christ's worldwide Kingdom had truly begun, that their Lord was ruling the nations from His heavenly throne, and that the eventual conquest of all nations by the armies of Christ was assured. For these humble, suffering believers, the promised age of the Messiah's rule had arrived. And what they were about to witness in the fall of Israel was the end of the Beginning.

---

22. St. Irenaeus, *Against Heresies*, iii.xxiv.1; translation by Henry Bettenson, ed., *The Early Christian Fathers* (Oxford: Oxford University Press, 1956, 1969), p. 83.

12

THE HOLY WAR

The Book of Revelation, we have noted, is organized in terms of the five-part treaty structure of the Biblical covenant. Chapter 12 falls into the fourth main series of visions (Trumpets), proclaiming God's judgment on the false king and the false prophet (chapters 8-14). But Chapter 12 also marks the intersection of this fivefold structure with another overarching pattern of the book: the theme of the Bridegroom and the Bride. Chapters 1-11 deal with the victory of Christ over His enemies, culminating in the glorious establishment of the Church as His holy Temple. Chapters 12-22 deal with the victory of the Church over her enemies, ending with her glorious establishment as God's holy Temple. Thus the second half of the Book of Revelation covers much the same ground as the first, but from a different perspective. Milton S. Terry comments: "Part First has revealed the Lamb of God under various symbols, glorious in power, opening the book of divine mysteries, avenging the martyred saints, and exhibiting the fearful judgments destined to come upon the enemies of God. Everything is viewed as from the throne of the King of heaven, who sends forth his armies and destroys the defiant murderers of his prophets and burns up their city (comp. Matt. 22:7).

"Part Second reveals the Church in conflict with infernal and worldly principalities and powers, surviving all persecution, and triumphing by the word of her testimony, and, after Babylon the harlot falls and passes from view, appearing as the wife of the Lamb, the tabernacle of God with men, glorious in her beauty and imperishable as the throne of God."[1]

---

1. Milton S. Terry, *Biblical Apocalyptics: A Study of the Most Notable Revelations of God and of Christ in the Canonical Scriptures* (New York: Eaton & Mains, 1896), p. 381.

Thus, although there is a progressive development toward a climax in the second half of Revelation, we will also see both a repetition of familiar concepts and a diversity in portraying them, a device often used by the Biblical prophets (see examples of this in Gen. 37:5-11; 41:18-25, 32; Dan. 2, 7). "The great red Dragon (12:3) is not to be regarded as different from the angel of the abyss (9:11). The hundred and forty-four thousand on Mount Zion (14:1) are the same as the sealed Israelites of 7:4-8. The seven last plagues (chaps. 15 and 16) correspond noticeably to the seven trumpets of doom. 'Babylon the Great' is the same as the great city where the Lord was crucified (11:8), and the new Jerusalem, filled with the glory of God and the Lamb, is but another symbol of the temple of God in the heaven (11:19)."[2]

This point in the prophecy, therefore, is something of a new beginning; and to show the conflict between Satan and the Church, St. John goes back to the beginning, to the birth of Christ and to Satan's unsuccessful attempts to destroy Him, ending with Christ's victorious ascent into heaven. This sets the stage for, and reveals the origin and meaning of, Satan's persecution of the Christian Church throughout the world. The struggle will be fierce and bloody; but Satan is already doomed, for Christ is reigning from His heavenly throne, and His people are destined for complete victory on the basis of His work and through their own faithful and fearless proclamation of the Gospel.

The Serpent and the Seed of the Woman (12:1-6)

1 And a great sign appeared in heaven: a Woman clothed with the sun, and the moon under her feet, and on her head a crown of twelve stars;

2 and being with child she cried out, being in labor and in pain to give birth.

3 And another sign appeared in heaven: and behold, a great red Dragon having seven heads and ten horns, and on his heads were seven diadems.

4 And his tail sweeps away a third of the stars of heaven, and threw them to the Land. And the Dragon stood before the Woman who was about to give birth, so that when she gave birth he might devour her Child.

---

2. Ibid.

5 And she gave birth to a Son, a male, who is to rule all nations with a rod of iron; and her Child was caught up to God and to His Throne.

6 And the Woman fled into the wilderness where she has a place prepared by God, so that there they may nourish her for one thousand two hundred and sixty days.

1-2 St. John alerts us from the outset that we must give careful attention to the subject of this vision, for the symbol of the Woman here is **a great sign**.[3] "Literalists" would have it that the use of this term implies that *"most* of Revelation is to be taken literally."[4] But this is to miss the point. St. John is not saying that this passage, in contrast to the rest of the book, is a "sign," for he has already told us that *the entire book is composed of "signs"* (1:1). The point here is that this is a *great* sign, an important symbol, central to the interpretation of the prophecy as a whole. St. John is telling his readers to think carefully about the Biblical meaning of the sign.

This central symbol is **a Woman**,[5] a familiar Biblical image for the Church, the people of God. (Specifically, as we shall see, the Woman here stands for *the Church in the form of Old Covenant Israel.*) St. John's first readers would immediately have thought of previous prophetic uses of the Woman as representing the Church (see, e.g., Isa. 26; 49-50; 54; 66; Jer. 3-4; Lam. 1; Ezek. 16; Hos. 1-4; Mic. 4). Some of the prophetic passages about the Woman-Church are not particularly complimentary, for Israel had often descended into adultery with heathen gods. But the symbol in Revelation 12 is a glorious vision of the Church in her purity, as the wife of God: She is, in the image of her Husband (Ps. 104:2; Rev. 1:16; 10:1), **clothed** (the same word as in 10:1) **with the sun** (cf. Isa. 60:1-2). **The moon under her feet** and her **crown of twelve stars** enhance the picture of glory and

---

3. The word *sign* is used seven times in chapters 12-19; three are in heaven (21:1, 3; 15:1), four are on earth (13:13, 14; 16:14; 19:20).

4. Henry M. Morris, *The Revelation Record: A Scientific and Devotional Commentary on the Book of Revelation* (Wheaton: Tyndale House Publishers, Inc., 1983), p. 213.

5. The word *woman* (or *women*) is used 19 times in Revelation, prompting Ford to suggest that "the woman symbol is almost as important as the Lamb" (*Revelation: Introduction, Translation, and Commentary* [Garden City: Doubleday and Company, 1975]), p. 188.

dominion—indeed, of her ascent from glory to glory (1 Cor. 15:41; 2 Cor. 3:18). Solomon proclaims that the Bride is "lovely as Jerusalem, terrible as an army with banners" (Cant. 6:4); she

> looks forth like the dawn,
> Beautiful as the full moon,
> Resplendent as the sun,
> Terrible as an army with banners. (Cant. 6:10)

This Woman, St. John says, is the Mother of Christ: She is seen to be **with child** (the same Greek expression used of the Virgin Mary in Matthew 1:18, 23), carrying in her womb the Messiah who is destined "to rule all the nations with a rod of iron" (v. 5). The image of the Woman/Mother has its origins all the way back to the Garden of Eden and the *protevangelium*—the first proclamation of the Gospel, in which God revealed that through the Woman would come the Redeemer to crush the Serpent's head (Gen. 3:15). The picture then becomes a regular *motif* in the historical outworking of God's purposes with Israel. One familiar example occurs in the story of Jael and Sisera, which tells how the enemy of God's people is destroyed, his head shattered, by a woman (Jud. 4:9, 17-22; 5:24-27; cf. the death of Abimelech in Jud. 9:53). This is also a major theme in the story of Esther and her deliverance of Israel. The definitive fulfillment of this prophecy took place in the Virgin Birth, as Mary clearly recognized:

> He has done mighty deeds with His arm;
> He has scattered those who were proud in the thoughts of their heart.
> He has brought down rulers from their thrones,
> And has exalted those who were humble.
> He has filled the hungry with good things;
> And sent away the rich empty-handed.
> He has given help to Israel His servant,
> In remembrance of His mercy,
> As He spoke to our fathers,
> To Abraham and his seed forever. (Luke 1:51-55)

Isaiah's prophecy of the Virgin Mother is the specific Biblical background for St. John's vision of the Woman, as Philip Carrington explains: "The actual words are drawn not from any heathen myth, but from the prophet Isaiah, *Moreover the LORD spake again unto Ahaz, saying, Ask thee a Sign of the LORD thy God; ask it either in the Depth, or in the Height above* (7:10-11); *or*, to translate it into Johannine language, either in the Abyss or in Heaven. In Isaiah the language appears to be purely a rhetorical flourish; but it is obviously the origin of St. John's Sign in Heaven.

"This is made perfectly clear by what follows in Isaiah. The king refuses to ask for the Sign, and Isaiah replies, *The LORD himself shall give you a Sign; Behold, a Virgin shall conceive, and bear a Son, and shall call his name Immanuel* [7:14]. The words of St. John are simply a quotation from the earlier prophet: *There appeared a great Sign in the Sky, a Woman . . . with child, and she cried in her pain and was in torment to be delivered.* More than this, St. John has given us a much closer translation of the Hebrew than our Authorized Version, which is influenced by the Septuagint; the Greek translation does, indeed, say, *A Virgin shall conceive*, but the original Hebrew only says, *A Woman is with Child*, and St. John has given it to us exactly. And, what is more, the words *Crying in her pain and was in torment* come from Isaiah also (26:17).

"St. John is therefore announcing the birth of the male child, the warrior king, foretold by . . . Isaiah."[6]

St. John thus brings together all the Woman-imagery of the Bible for this composite portrait of the covenant community, laboring to bring forth the Messiah: She is Eve, the Mother of all living, whose Seed will crush the Dragon's head; she is also Sarah, Rebekah, Rachel, Jochebed, Hannah, and the other women of the covenant who gave birth to deliverers, forerunners of the Seed; she is the Virgin Mary, through whom the promises to the fathers met their fulfillment. But this great cosmic figure cannot simply be identified with any one of these women; rather, each of them individually embodied and portrayed before the world a different facet of the Woman's meaning, imaging the labors of the Church to give birth to the Messiah:

---

6. Philip Carrington, *The Meaning of the Revelation* (London: SPCK, 1931), pp. 204f.

As the pregnant woman approaches the time to give birth,
She writhes and cries out in her labor pains,
Thus were we before Thee, O LORD. (Isa. 26:17)

As prophetic revelation progresses in Scripture, it becomes increasingly clear that the Old Covenant Church is laboring to bring forth the Christ (cf. Mic. 4:9-5:9): He was the basic promise of the Abrahamic covenant. This is what Israel was waiting for, **being in labor and pain** throughout her existence. This is the most essential meaning of Israel's history, apart from which it has no significance: the bearing of the Manchild (cf. John 16:20-22), the Savior of the world. From the *protevangelium* to the Flood, from the Abrahamic Covenant through the slavery in Egypt, the Exodus, the settling of Canaan, the Babylonian Captivity, the return from exile, and the suffering under the Greeks and the Romans, Israel was laboring to give birth to the Christ, to bring in the Messianic age.

In the midst of the Church's struggles, therefore, **she cried out**. This verb (*krazō*) has special significance in Scripture, generally being used for an oath or the solemn proclamation of God's revelation; it is often used of God's servants speaking in the face of opposition.[7] Here it has reference to the Church's official declaration of the Word of God, the prophecy that she uttered as she travailed in birth. This was the essence of all prophetic revelation, to bear witness to the Christ (John 5:39, 45-46; Luke 24:25-27; Acts 3:24; 13:27).

It is important to recognize the relationship of all this to the very obvious astronomical symbolism in the text. The word St. John uses for **sign** was the term used in the ancient world to describe the constellations of the Zodiac; St. John's model for this vision of the Church is the constellation of Virgo, which does have a "crown" of **twelve stars**.[8] It seems likely that the

---

7. See, e.g., Matt. 27:50; Mark 3:11; 5:7; 9:24; 10:48; 15:13; John 1:15; 7:28; 12:13, 44; Acts 19:28, 32, 34; Rom. 9:27; Gal. 4:6; James 5:4; and see its use especially in Revelation: 6:10; 7:2, 10; 10:3; 14:15; 18:2,18-19; 19:17.

8. The twelve stars are: "(1) Pi, (2) Nu, (3) Beta (near the ecliptic), (4) Sigma, (5) Chi, (6) Iota — these six stars form the southern hemisphere around the head of Virgo. Then there are (7) Theta, (8) Star 60, (9) Delta, (10) Star 93, (11) Beta (the second magnitude star), (12) Omicron — these last six form the northern hemisphere around the head of Virgo. All these stars are visible ones that could have been seen by observers." Ernest L. Martin, *The Birth of Christ Recalculated* (Pasadena, CA: Foundation for Biblical Research, 2nd ed., 1980), p. 159.

twelve stars also represent the twelve signs of the Zodiac, from ancient times regarded as symbols of the twelve tribes of Israel; in Joseph's famous dream his father, mother, and the twelve tribes were symbolized by the sun, the moon, and twelve stars or constellations (Gen. 37:9).[9] We have already seen how the divine arrangement of Israel's tribes around the Tabernacle (Num. 2) corresponded to the zodiacal order of the constellations.[10] The Seventh Trumpet of 11:15 brought us to Rosh Hashanah: the Day of Trumpets, the first day of the seventh month, the first day of the new year, the Day of the enthronement of the King of kings in the New Creation. The statement that Virgo is "crowned" with the twelve constellations, therefore, "means that she is the one among the twelve who reigns at the time," i.e. during the seventh month, just as "the Scorpion's claws seem about to catch the Virgin."[11] In terms of astral symbolism, therefore, the birth of the Messiah takes place on the Day of Trumpets.

It is interesting that by pursuing several lines of very convincing evidence, Prof. Ernest Martin carefully and painstakingly narrows down the probable date of Christ's birth to sometime in September, 3 B.C.[12] Martin then adds the icing to the cake: "In the period of Christ's birth, the Sun entered the head-position of the Woman about August 13, and exited from her feet about October 2. But the Apostle John saw the scene when the Sun 'clothes' or 'adorns' the Woman. This surely indicates that the position of the Sun in the vision was located somewhere mid-bodied of the Woman — between the neck and knees. (The Sun could hardly be said to 'clothe' the Woman if it were situated in her face or near her feet.)

"The only time in the year that the Sun could be in a position to 'clothe' this celestial Woman (to be mid-bodied) is when it was

---

9. See Josephus, *Antiquities of the Jews*, iii.vii.7, where he explains the twelve stones in the high priest's breastplate, representing the twelve tribes of Israel (Ex. 28:17-21), in terms of the Zodiac.

10. See comments on Revelation 4:7; cf. Ernest L. Martin, *The Birth of Christ Recalculated*, pp. 168f.

11. Farrer, *The Revelation of St. John the Divine* (Oxford: At the Clarendon Press, 1964), p. 141.

12. It is generally held that Herod the Great died in 4 B.C., and therefore that Christ was born in 6 or 7 B.C. Martin, however, presents a detailed and persuasive case for Herod's death occurring in 1 B.C. See his *Birth of Christ Recalculated*, pp. 26-131.

located between about 150 and 170 degrees along the ecliptic. This 'clothing' of the Woman by the Sun occurs for a 20-day period each year. This 20-degree spread could indicate the general time when Christ was born. In 3 B.C., the Sun would have entered this celestial region about August 27 and exited from it about September 15. If John in the Book of Revelation is associating the birth of Christ with the period when the Sun is mid-bodied to the Woman, then Christ would have had to be born within that 20-day period. From the point of view of the Magi (who were astrologers), this would have been the only logical sign under which the Jewish Messiah might be born—especially if he were to be born of a virgin. Even today, astrologers recognize that the sign of Virgo is the one which has reference to a messianic world ruler to be born of a virgin. . . .

"But there is a way to arrive at a much closer time for Christ's birth than a simple 20-day period. The position of the Moon in John's vision could pinpoint the nativity to within a day —perhaps to an hour period or less. This may seem absurd, but it is entirely possible.

"The key is the Moon. The apostle said it was located 'under her feet.' What does the word 'under' signify in this case? Does it mean the Woman of the vision was standing on the Moon when John observed it or does it mean her feet were positioned slightly above the Moon? John does not tell us. This, however, is not of major consequence in using the Moon to answer our question because it would only involve the difference of a degree or two. Since the feet of Virgo the Virgin represent the last 7 degrees of the constellation (in the time of Christ this would have been between about 180 and 187 degrees along the ecliptic), the Moon has to be positioned somewhere under that 7-degree arc. But the Moon also has to be in that exact location when the Sun is mid-bodied to Virgo. In the year 3 B.C., these two factors came to precise agreement for less than two hours, as observed from Palestine or Patmos, on September 11. The relationship began about 6:15 P.M. (sunset), and lasted until around 7:45 P.M. (moonset). This is the *only* day in the whole year that this could have taken place."[13]

---

13. Ibid., pp. 146f. What about December 25, the traditional date of the Nativity? As Martin demonstrates, there were numerous startling astronom-

An added bonus: Sundown on September 11, 3 B.C., was the beginning of Tishri 1 in the Jewish calendar—Rosh Hashanah, the Day of Trumpets![14] Martin summarizes: "The central theme of the Day of Trumpets is clearly that of enthronement of the great King of kings. This was the general understanding of the day in early Judaism—and it certainly is that of the New Testament. In Revelation 11:15 the seventh angel sounds his 'last trump' and the kingdoms of this world become those of Christ. This happens at a time when a woman is seen in heaven with twelve stars around her head and the Sun mid-bodied to her, with the Moon under her feet. This is clearly a New Moon scene for the Day of Trumpets."[15]

3 St. John sees **another sign . . . in heaven: a great red Dragon.** As he explains in v. 9, the Dragon is none other than "the Serpent of old who is called the devil and Satan," the enemy of God and His people. St. John reveals him as the power behind the imperial thrones of the ancient world that persecuted the Church; for, like the four Beast-empires of Daniel's prophecy, the Dragon has **seven heads and ten horns:** Daniel's beasts possessed seven heads among them (the third beast having four), and the fourth beast had ten horns (Dan. 7:3-7). Babylon, Medo-Persia, Greece, and Rome were all stages in the Dragon's attempt to establish his illicit empire over the world. (The significance of the seven heads is thus not simply that the Dragon is hard to kill, but rather that he is identified with the terrible beasts of Daniel's vision; cf. the "heads" of the Dragon in Ps. 74:13-15.) He was the great Beast, of which they had been only partial images. It was he who had been the agelong enemy of the people of God. In all Israel's struggles against Beasts,

---

ical phenomena taking place during the years 3-2 B.C. Chief among these celestial events was the fact that Jupiter, recognized by Jews and Gentiles alike as the "Planet of the Messiah," was located in Virgo's womb and standing still, directly over Bethlehem, on December 25, 2 B.C., when the Child was a little over a year old. (Matthew states that the holy family was settled in a house, not in a stable, by the time the Magi visited [Matt. 2:11]. Moreover, Herod ordered the slaughter of the innocents "from two years old and under, according to the time which he had ascertained from the Magi" [Matt. 2:16], indicating that the Child was no longer a newborn.) For a full account of the astronomical events of 3-2 B.C., see Martin, pp. 4-25, 144-77.

14. Ibid., pp. 152ff.
15. Ibid., p. 158.

through all the attempts by human empires to destroy the Seed of the Covenant, the Dragon had been their foe. He wore the **diadems** of the persecuting empires.

Why is the devil portrayed as a Dragon? In order to understand this, we must consider the Biblical theology of dinosaurs, which is surprisingly very detailed. While the Bible does speak of land dinosaurs (cf. *behemoth* in Job 40:15-24),[16] our focus here will be on *dragons and sea serpents* (cf. Job 7:12; 41:1-34).[17] Essentially, as part of God's good creation (see Gen. 1:21: *sea monsters*), there is nothing "evil" about these creatures (Gen. 1:31; Ps. 148:7); but, because of the Fall, they are used in Scripture to symbolize rebellious man at the height of his power and glory.

Three kinds of dragons are spoken of in Scripture: *Tannin* (*Dragon*; Ps. 91:13), *Leviathan* (Ps. 104:26), and *Rahab* (Job 26:12-13).[18] The Bible relates each of these monsters to *the Serpent*, who stands for the subtle, deceitful enemy of God's people (Gen. 3:1-5, 13-15). Thus, to demonstrate the divine victory and dominion over man's rebellion, God turned Moses' rod into a "serpent" (Ex. 4:1-4), and Aaron's rod into a "dragon" (*tannin*; Ex. 7:8-12). The Dragon/Serpent, therefore, becomes in Scripture a symbol of Satanically inspired, rebellious pagan culture (cf. Jer. 51:34), especially exemplified by Egypt in its war against the Covenant people. This is particularly true with regard to the monster Rahab (meaning *the proud one*), which is often a synonym for Egypt (Ps. 87:4; 89:10; Isa. 30:7). God's Covenant-making deliverance of His people in the Exodus is described in terms of both the original creation and God's triumph over the Dragon:

---

16. Some mistakenly suppose this to be a hippopotamus. Its description in the Biblical text indicates that it was much closer to a brontosaurus.

17. The creature mentioned in the latter reference, a huge, fire-breathing dragon called Leviathan, is actually thought by some to be a crocodile! It is clear from the statements in Job, however, that at least some great dinosaurs were contemporaries of this early patriarch. For a sober-minded examination of supposed sightings of sea monsters in more recent times, see Bernard Heuvelmans, *In the Wake of the Sea-Serpents* (New York: Hill and Wang, 1968). Duane T. Gish has proposed a possible explanation for the biology of "breathing fire" in his *Dinosaurs: Those Terrible Lizards* (San Diego: Creation-Life Publishers, 1977), pp. 50ff.

18. In Hebrew, this is a completely different word from the name of Rahab, the Canaanite harlot who saved the Hebrew spies in Joshua 2.

Awake, awake, put on strength, O arm of the LORD;
Awake as in the days of old, the generations of long ago.
Was it not Thou who cut Rahab in pieces,
Who pierced the Dragon?
Was it not Thou who dried up the sea,
The waters of the great deep;
Who made the depths of the sea a pathway
For the redeemed to cross over? (Isa. 51:9-10)

The Bible also speaks of the Exodus as a salvation from Leviathan:

Thou didst divide the sea by Thy strength;
Thou didst break the heads of the Dragons in the waters.
Thou didst crush the heads of Leviathan;
Thou didst give him as food for the creatures of the wilderness.
(Ps. 74:13-14)

Thus, in provisional fulfillment of the promise in Eden, the Dragon's head was crushed when God saved His people from Egypt. Of course, the head-wound became healed, and the Dragon (accompanied by the Dragon-State in his image) kept coming back to plague and persecute the Seed of the woman. This happens again and again throughout the Old Testament, which records numerous provisional head-crushings of the Dragon (Judg. 4:21; 5:26-27; 9:50-57; 1 Sam. 5:1-5; 17:49-51; 2 Sam. 18:9; 20:21-22; Ps. 68:21; Hab. 3:13). In terms of this, the prophets looked forward to the coming definitive defeat of the Dragon in the work of Christ. Isaiah saw Israel as a pregnant woman, writhing and crying out in her labor pains, waiting for the Deliverer to be born (Isa. 26:17-21); the next verse reads:

In that Day the LORD will punish Leviathan the fleeing Serpent
With His fierce and great and mighty sword,
Even Leviathan the twisted Serpent;
And He will kill the Dragon who lives in the sea.
(Isa. 27:1)

Daniel repeats the same idea in what might be called his "commentary" on Moses' account of creation in Genesis 1. Writing of the fifth and sixth days of creation, Moses had said that

God *created*[19] the "sea monsters" (*tannin*) in the sea, and "cattle" (*behemoth*) on the earth (Gen. 1:20-25); but these were succeeded by Man, who, as the image of God, was created for dominion over the creatures (Gen. 1:26-28). Daniel 7 symbolically expands on this idea by showing us a series of Beasts—the mighty and terrible world powers that exercised ungodly dominion over the earth (v. 1-8). But Daniel sees that their reign is only "for an appointed period of time" (v. 12); and, as he keeps looking, the night visions end with the Ancient of Days giving over world dominion to the Son of Man, the Second Adam—"an everlasting dominion which will not pass away" (v. 13-14), for He is the last Work of God.

4 The Dragon's **tail sweeps away a third of the stars of heaven**. St. John is capitalizing on the fact that the Scorpion, with which the Dragon/Serpent is associated,[20] "has a third of the (zodiacal) stars at his tail, for four out of the twelve signs come after him."[21] What of the statement that he **threw them to the Land**? That, as Farrer justly remarks, "is theology, not astronomy."[22] St. John has already associated stars with angels, a familiar Biblical connection (see comments on 1:20); now he symbolically describes the fall of Satan and the evil angels, an event related in more direct language in 2 Peter 2:4, Jude 6, and St. John's own commentary on his allegory in verse 9. The Dragon's "stars" are the fallen angels, who joined him in rebellion.

Why does the Dragon sweep away **a third** of the angels? First, this is the form in which the Trumpet-judgments are cast (cf. 8:7-12; 9:15, 18). Christ is the Firstborn; the two-thirds portion (cf. Deut. 21:17) is reserved for Him and His Kingdom. Second, the Biblical principle of the two witnesses may also be involved (St. John uses some courtroom language in this chapter): For every false witness Satan can muster against the covenant, God has two angels on His side; the evil report is more than nullified by the testimony God and his angels can give.

---

19. The Hebrew word here is *bara,* used otherwise only of the creation of the heavens and the earth, v. 1, and of man, v. 27.
20. Cf. Deut. 8:15; Luke 10:19; 11:11-12; Rev. 9:3-11.
21. Farrer, p. 143.
22. Ibid.

The Dragon's goal is to abort the work of Christ, to devour and kill Him. So **the Dragon stood** (cf. Gen. 3:14) **before the woman** in order to **devour her Child**, to kill Christ as soon as He was born. Again St. John is using astronomy for allegorical purposes; for, as we have seen, it is just as the sun is "clothing" Virgo that the Scorpion's claws seem about to catch her;[23] indeed, he seems poised to pounce upon her Child as soon as He is born. This conflict between Christ and Satan was announced in Genesis 3:15, the war between the two seeds, the Seed of the Woman and the seed of the Serpent. From the first book of the Bible to the last, this is the basic warfare of history. The Dragon is at war with the Woman and her Seed, primarily Jesus Christ. All throughout history Satan was trying either to keep Christ from being born, or to kill Him as soon as He was born. This is why Cain killed Abel, under the inspiration of the Dragon: The attack on Abel was an attempt to destroy the Seed. It was unsuccessful, for Eve then gave birth to Seth, the Appointed One, "in place of Abel" (Gen. 4:25), and the Seed was preserved in him. Satan's next tactic was to corrupt the line of Seth; thus, within ten generations from Adam, virtually all Seth's descendants apostatized through intermarriage with the heathen (Gen. 6:1-12), and the whole earth was corrupted except for one righteous man and his family. Satan's mad rage to attack the Seed was so great that the entire world was destroyed, yet still he failed. The Seed was preserved within a single family in the Ark.

The Dragon again tried to murder the Seed in his attacks on the family of Abraham. On two occasions Satan attempted to have Sarah raped by a heathen king (Gen. 12:10-20; 20:1-18); he tried again with Rebekah (Gen. 26:1-11). The Draconic enmity against the Seed is manifest also in the enmity of Esau against Jacob, a struggle between the two seeds that began in the womb (Gen. 25:22-23). We can also see Satan's attempts to obstruct the Seed in Isaac's sinful plan to cheat Jacob out of his divinely appointed inheritance (Gen. 27). Again, when the children of Israel were in Egypt, the Dragon tried to destroy the Seed by having all the male children killed (Ex. 1). Five hundred years

---

23. The constellation Libra (the Scales) was also regarded in the ancient world as the Claws of Scorpio; see Richard Hinckley Allen, *Star Names: Their Lore and Meaning* (New York: Dover Publications, 1963), pp. 269ff.

later, the Seed was being carried in a shepherd-boy, and again
the Dragon attacked, twice inspiring a demon-possessed king to
throw javelins at him (1 Sam. 18:10-11). In fact, the whole
machinery of Saul's kingdom went into effect just to try to kill
David (1 Sam. 18-27). Similarly, the wicked Queen Athaliah
"destroyed all the seed royal of the House of Judah" (2 Chron.
22:10), yet the Seed was preserved in the infant Joash. Haman,
the evil Prime Minister of Persia, would have succeeded in his
attempt to launch a full-scale pogrom to destroy all the Jews,
had it not been for the courage and wisdom of Queen Esther
(Est. 3-9). The most striking example of this pattern on a large
scale occurs throughout the history of Israel, from the Exodus
to the Exile: the covenant people's perennial, consistent temptation to murder their own children, to offer them up as sacrifices
to demons (Lev. 18:21; 2 Ki. 16:3; 2 Chron. 28:3; Ps. 106:37-38;
Ezek. 16:20). Why? It was the war of the two seeds. The Dragon
was trying to destroy the Christ.

This pattern comes to a dramatic climax at the birth of
Christ, when the Dragon possesses King Herod, the Edomite
ruler of Judea, and inspires him to slaughter the children of
Bethlehem (Matt. 2:13-18); indeed, St. John's vision of the
Woman, the Child, and the Dragon seems almost an allegory of
that event. The Dragon tried again, of course: tempting the
Lord (Luke 4:1-13), seeking to have Him murdered (Luke
4:28-29), subjecting Him to human and demonic oppression
throughout His ministry, possessing one of the most trusted disciples to betray Him (John 13:2, 27), and finally orchestrating
His crucifixion. Even then—rather, especially then—the Dragon
was defeated, for the Cross was God's way of tricking Satan
into fulfilling His purposes, according to His wisdom—"the hidden wisdom," St. Paul says, "which God predestined before the
ages to our glory, the wisdom which none of the rulers of this
age has understood; for if they had understood it, they would
not have crucified the Lord of glory" (1 Cor. 2:7-8). In wounding
the Seed's heel, the Serpent's head was crushed.

5　And she gave birth to a Son, a male (cf. Isa. 66:7-8) **who is
to rule all nations with a rod of iron.** St. John returns to Psalm
2, one of his favorite texts, to explain his symbolism. The Son
is, obviously, Jesus Christ, the Seed of the Woman, the Child of

the Virgin, born of Israel to rule the nations. In this verse St. John telescopes the entire history of Christ's earthly ministry, stating (as if it had happened all at once) that **her Child was caught up to God and to His Throne.** It is as if Christ's Incarnation had led directly to His Ascension to the Throne of glory. St. John's point is not to belittle the atonement and the resurrection, but to stress that the Lord's Anointed completely escapes the power of the Dragon; and we should note that St. John's order follows that of the Psalm. Telling of His exaltation to the heavenly Throne, the Christ says:

> I will surely tell of the decree of the LORD:
> He said to Me, "Thou art My Son,
> Today *I have begotten Thee.*[24]
> Ask of Me, and I will surely give the nations as Thine inheritance,
> And the very ends of the earth as Thy possession.
> Thou shalt rule them with a rod of iron,
> Thou shalt shatter them like earthenware." (Ps. 2:7-9)

"The Psalm makes Messiah's heavenly birth all one with his enthronement; if he is fathered by God, he reigns."[25] In spite of everything that the Dragon does, the Seed is caught up to the Throne and now rules the nations with a rod of iron, just as if He had gone straight from the Incarnation to the Throne; Satan had no power to stop Him. The Ascension was the goal of Christ's Advent.

6   And the Woman fled into the wilderness where she has a place prepared by God. As will become apparent below, the Woman's flight into the wilderness is a picture of the flight of the Judean Christians from the destruction of Jerusalem, so that the Dragon's wrath is expended upon apostate rather than faithful Israel. While she is in the wilderness, the Woman is nourished **for twelve hundred and sixty days,**[26] a period equivalent to the "time, times, and half a time" (3½ years) of verse 14, and sym-

---

24. Some will argue that this phrase refers not to the incarnation or physical birth of Christ, but to His eternal generation instead; for John's purposes of Biblical allusion, however, that question is beside the point. His emphasis is, with the Psalmist, that the Child goes from birth to reign.

25. Farrer, p. 141.

26. For the relationship of the 1,260 days to the number of the Beast (666), see comments on 13:18.

bolically related to the 42 months/1,260 days of 11:2-3 and 13:5. We saw on 11:2 that the Scriptures use this terminology to speak of a limited period of ascendant, triumphant wickedness, a period of wrath and judgment due to apostasy from the Covenant. During this time, therefore, when Satan seems to be dominant, the Church is protected. The Woman's flight into the wilderness calls up associations with Elijah's wilderness sojourn during the three and a half years of drought, when he was miraculously fed by ravens (1 Kings 17:3-6); similarly, St. John says, the Woman's flight does not signify God's abandonment of her but rather His loving provision. The faithful Bride **has a place prepared by God** (cf. 2 Sam. 7:10; 1 Chron. 17:9; John 14:2-3). He gives His messengers charge concerning her (Ps. 91:11-13) and sends her into the wilderness **so that there they may nourish her.** St. John also means for us to think, as we will see below, of Israel's flight into the wilderness from the face of the Egyptian Dragon; and of the flight of the Virgin Mary into Egypt from the murderous wrath of King Herod (Matt. 2:13-21).

War in Heaven (12:7-12)

7 And there was war in heaven, Michael and His angels waging war with the Dragon. And the Dragon and his angels waged war,

8 and they were not strong enough, and there was no longer a place found for them in heaven.

9 And the great Dragon was thrown down, the Serpent of old who is called the devil and Satan, who deceives the whole world; he was thrown down to the Land, and his angels were thrown down with him.

10 And I heard a loud Voice in heaven, saying: Now have come the salvation, and the power, and the Kingdom of our God, and the authority of His Christ, for he has been thrown down—the accuser of our brethren, who accused them before our God day and night.

11 And they conquered him by the blood of the Lamb and by the word of their testimony, and they did not love their life even to death.

12 For this reason, rejoice, O heavens and you who tabernacle in them. Woe to the Land and the Sea, because the devil has come down to you, having great wrath, knowing that he has only a short time.

7-9   The scene changes abruptly: St. John now sees **war in heaven, Michael and His angels waging war with the Dragon**. This is not, as some suppose, a sequel to the preceding vision, as if Satan, frustrated in his attempt to devour the Messiah, now directs his assault toward heaven. On the contrary, St. John unveils this scene in order to explain the preceding verse — to show why the Woman had to flee into the wilderness. Once that is explained, in verses 7-12, he returns to the theme of the flight of the Woman. In addition, St. John uses the imagery in this passage to display another aspect of the Child's conflict with the Dragon. Chronologically, this explanatory section fits in between verses 5 and 6.

We should note to begin with that the Holy War is initiated, not by the Dragon, but by **Michael and His angels**. There should be little question that this Captain of the angelic host is a symbol for the Seed of the Woman, the Son of God — represented now not as a Child, but as Michael, the great Warrior-Protector who leads the armies of heaven in battle against the demons. St. John's symbolism is not casual; it is intentional, and very precise. He carefully chose to reveal Christ in terms of the specific Biblical connotations associated with Michael.

The name **Michael** (meaning *Who is like God?*) occurs elsewhere in the Scriptures only in Daniel and Jude. Michael is portrayed in Daniel as "the great Prince" who stands as the special Protector of the people of God. War breaks out in heaven between the good and evil angels, and even Gabriel is unable to overcome the demons until Michael comes to do battle with the enemy (Dan. 10:12-13, 20-21). In view of what is revealed about Michael in the latter part of Daniel 10, it is likely that the otherwise unexplained vision in the first part of the chapter refers to Him as well: Daniel saw a man

> dressed in linen, whose waist was girded with a belt of pure gold of Uphaz. His body also was like beryl, His face like lightning, His eyes were like flaming torches, His arms and feet like the gleam of polished bronze, and the sound of His words like the sound of a tumult. (Dan. 10:5-6)

The closing passage of Daniel's prophecy refers to Michael as the Guardian over God's people, who will arise to fight on

311

their behalf during a time of great tribulation, saving all whose names are written in the Book of Life (Dan. 12:1).[27] Michael's name does not appear again in the Bible until an offhanded mention by Jude, who tells us that He "disputed with the devil and argued about the Body of Moses" (Jude 9).[28] Jude also calls Him *The Archangel*, a term which—contrary to some speculations that have developed about the various ranks of angels— does not necessarily mean "member of a superior class of angels," but rather simply "the Chief of the angels," an expression equivalent to "Captain of the LORD's hosts" (Josh. 5:13-15). This would also tend to identify Michael with the Angel of the LORD (cf. Ex. 23:20-23), a figure who is, in most cases, a preincarnate appearance of Christ.[29] The only other Biblical occurrence of the word *Archangel* is in 1 Thessalonians 4:16, where Christ descends in the Second Coming "with a shout, with the voice of the Archangel," or, better, "with a shout, with Archangelic Voice." The clear implication is that Christ Himself shouts with the Archangelic Voice.[30] (The fact that there are superior ranks of angels [cf. Rom. 8:38; Eph. 1:21; Col. 1:16] means that a more general use of the term *archangel* is theologically valid. But the Bible itself does not seem to use it in this way.) Carrington observes that the term *Archangel* "may even be compared with 'Lord of hosts,' and it may perhaps have meant that manifestation of God in which He appears as leader of the armies of Israel or of the heavens."[31] Accordingly, in the Book of Revelation we find Him leading the armies of heaven in victorious conflict with Satan, actions clearly predicated of Christ throughout the New Testament (cf. Matt. 12:22-29; Luke 11:14-22; Col. 2:15; Heb. 2:14-15; 1 John 3:8; Rev. 19:11-16).

Even at first glance, therefore, there is much to commend

---

27. Calvin recognized that this description of Michael must be a reference to Jesus Christ; see his *Commentaries on the Book of the Prophet Daniel* (Grand Rapids: Baker Book House, 1979), Vol. 2, pp. 369ff.

28. By "Body of Moses" Jude probably means the Old Testament Covenant community, the equivalent of the "Body of Christ": cf. the "houses" of Moses and Christ in Heb. 3:2-6.

29. See the discussion of this point in Herman Bavinck, *The Doctrine of God*, translated by William Hendriksen (Grand Rapids: William B. Eerdmans Publishing Co., 1951), pp. 256ff.

30. A most helpful discussion of this whole issue is in Carrington, pp. 218-24. See also E. W. Hengstenberg, *The Revelation of St. John* (Cherry Hill, NJ: Mack Publishing Co., [1851] 1972), Vol. 1, pp. 464-72.

31. Carrington, p. 222.

the view that **Michael** is a symbolic representation of Christ, a name that emphasizes His divine nature and power; and that the "angels" who accompany Him are His apostles, "together with all the angelic forces in sympathy and cooperation with them."[32] This view both explains, and is reinforced by, the passage as a whole. As Philip Carrington argues, "It makes sense of the chapter. Of course if you want the book to be a Chinese puzzle, this will not weigh with you; but if you think that the author (or even the final editor) of the book intended this chapter to have a meaning, then you will think it reasonable to consider an interpretation of it which removes confusion. A Woman who is pictured as the Bride of the Lord bears a Son; she is the new Eve, and therefore her son is to crush the Serpent; she is the Virgin of Isaiah, and therefore he is a warrior-king. There follows a war with the Serpent, in which an opponent casts him out of heaven; the Serpent then *went off to make war with the rest of the seed of the woman.* Clearly, then, the person he had first fought with was also the seed of the woman. Why drag in anyone else?

"The battle royal is followed by a choric song out of heaven, and, as we have seen, the function of these choric songs is to make clear the main action which is depicted in symbols. It says, *Now is come Salvation and Power and the Kingdom of our God and the Authority of His Messiah,* and then (going on to think of the followers of Christ rather than Christ himself), *They conquered him through the Blood of the Lamb and the Word of His Witness.* Now this admittedly means that it is the Christ whose power has come, and that it is through his blood that victory has been obtained. It tells us who conquered Satan and how; it was Jesus on the cross."[33]

We have already noted that the Holy War was initiated by the attack of Michael and the army of heaven. In response, **the Dragon and his angels waged war.** But this defensive action by the forces of evil proved an utter failure: **They were not strong enough, and there was no longer a place found for them in heaven. And the great Dragon was thrown down,** in abject defeat. For the forces of evil, the battle is lost. This is exactly what Jesus prophesied about the prospects for His Church Militant: "The gates of hell shall not prevail against it" (Matt. 16:18).

---

32. Terry, p. 386.
33. Carrington, p. 219.

Jesus pictures the Church, not as a city under siege by the forces of evil, but rather as a great army, besieging the capital city and headquarters of the enemy; and it is the forces of evil that succumb to the onslaught of the Church. The people of God are the aggressors: They take the initiative in the warfare, and are successful in their assault on the gates of hell. Satan and all his forces **are not strong enough**, while the Christian can say with St. Paul, *I am strong enough for everything, in Him who strengthens me* (Phil. 4:13).

St. John interjects detailed information about the Dragon's identity: He is **the Serpent of old**, the ancient Tempter who seduced Eve in the beginning (Gen. 3:1-15). The Dragon is known as **the devil**, a term meaning *The Slanderer*, for he is, as the Lord said, "a liar, and the father of the lie" (John 8:44). A related term for the Dragon is **Satan** (or, more properly, *the satan*), the Hebrew word for an adversary, especially in legal matters. The being whom we call *Satan* is the attorney for the prosecution, the Accuser who brings up legal charges against men in God's court, the evil one who tirelessly accuses the brethren "day and night" (v. 10). Satan was the accuser of Job (Job 1:6-11; 2:1-5) and of Joshua the high priest (Zech. 3:1-10) — and, as can be seen from both of those cases, his supposedly legal accusations are mere lies. The Accuser of God's people is a slanderer, the Father of the Lie.[34] Because he is the Liar *par excellence*, he **deceives the whole world**. It was Satan who was behind the slanderous accusations against the early Christians, the scurrilous rumors and criminal charges alleging that they were apostates, atheists, ritual murderers, cannibals, social revolutionaries, and haters of mankind.[35]

But, St. John says, the great Dragon **was thrown down to the Land, and his angels were thrown down with him**. Three times the expression **thrown down** is used in verse 9, emphasizing the significance and finality of this event. The principle of *lex talionis* (an eye for an eye) is put into force here: In 12:4 the

---

34. On the essential character of Satan as a slanderous "accuser of the brethren," see Greg Bahnsen, "The Person, Work, and Present Status of Satan," in *The Journal of Christian Reconstruction*, Vol. I, No. 2 (Winter, 1974).

35. Cf. Robert L. Wilken, *The Christians as the Romans Saw Them* (New Haven: Yale University Press, 1984), pp. 17ff., 117ff.

Dragon's tail swept a third of the stars of heaven and threw them to the Land; now the Dragon himself is thrown down to the Land with his evil angels. In the following verses, St. John explains the vision, telling us clearly when this great ejection of the demons took place.

10-11   The explanation comes, as it often does with St. John, in a call to worship from **a loud Voice in heaven,** exhorting the assembly to praise the Lord for His marvelous works. The result of Michael's victory over the Dragon is fourfold, covering the earth: **Now have come the salvation** — the victorious deliverance into a "wide, open space" — **and the power, and the Kingdom of our God, and the authority of His Christ.** The outcome of the Holy War is this: The Kingdom has arrived! The power of God and the authority of Christ **have come,** have been made manifest in history, because **the Accuser of our brethren has been thrown down, the one who accused them before our God day and night.**

This great apocalyptic battle, the greatest fight in all history, has already been fought and won by the Lord Christ, St. John says, and the Dragon has been overthrown. Moreover, the martyrs who spent their lives in Christ's service did not die in vain; they are partakers in the victory: They **conquered** the Dragon **by the blood of the Lamb** — by means of[36] His definitive, once-for-all victory — **and by the word of their testimony.** The martyrs' faithfulness to Christ is demonstrated in that **they did not love their life even to death,** knowing that "he who loves his life loses it; and he who hates his life in this world shall keep it to life eternal" (John 12:25).

The Holy War between Michael and the Dragon therefore cannot possibly be a portrayal of the final battle of history at the end of the world. It cannot be future at all. It is not a battle to take place at the Second Coming. The victory over the Dragon, according to St. John, does not take place by means of a cataclysmic event at the end of history, but by means of *the* cataclys-

---

36. *Blood* and *word* are both in the accusative case, but the preposition should be read in the sense of *means* as well as *grounds* here (cf. Matt. 15:6; John 6:57; 15:3; Eph. 5:18; Rev. 13:14); see Isbon T. Beckwith, *The Apocalypse of John: Studies in Introduction with a Critical and Exegetical Commentary* (Grand Rapids: Baker Book House, [1919] 1979), p. 627.

mic event that took place in the middle of history: the sacrifice of the Lamb. The language used to describe the basis of Michael's conquest has nothing to do with the Second Coming, but it has everything to do with the First Coming. The martyrs overcome by means of the shed blood of Christ, and by means of the fearless proclamation of the Gospel. The cosmic victory over the Dragon takes place through the Gospel, and the Gospel alone — the Gospel in its objective aspect (the work of Christ), and the Gospel in its subjective aspect (the proclamation of the work of Christ).

When, therefore, did Satan fall from heaven? He fell, definitively, during the ministry of Christ, culminating in the atonement, the resurrection, and the ascension of the Lord to His heavenly throne. We can see the stages of the Holy War throughout the message of the Gospels. Whereas the activity of demons seems relatively rare in the Old Testament, the New Testament records numerous outbreaks of demonism. Open the pages of the New Testament, and demons are almost inescapable. Why? What made the difference? It was the presence of Christ. He went on the offensive, entering history to do battle with the Dragon, and immediately the Dragon counterattacked, fighting back with all his might, wreaking as much havoc as possible. And when we see the Lord warring against the devil, we also see Him being given angelic assistance (cf. Matt. 4:11; 26:53; Luke 22:43). As Michael leading the angels, Christ led His apostles against the Dragon, driving him out of his position. The message of the Gospels is that in the earthly ministry of Christ and His disciples, Satan lost his place of power and fell down to the earth:

> And the seventy returned with joy, saying, "Lord, even the demons are subject to us in Your name." And He said to them, "I was watching Satan fall from heaven like lightning. Behold, I have given you authority to tread upon serpents and scorpions, and over all the power of the enemy, and nothing shall injure you. Nevertheless, do not rejoice in this, that the spirits are subject to you, but rejoice that your names are recorded in heaven." (Luke 10:17-20)

What Revelation 12 portrays is just that: not only the subjection of the demons to the saints, but the recording of the saints'

names in heaven—their sentence of justification, of right standing in heaven's hall of justice, for their accuser has been thrown
out of court, his false testimony invalidated. The word for **conquer** in this verse (*nikaō*) carries the connotation, not only of a
military victory, but of a legal victory as well; the winning of a
favorable verdict (cf. Rom. 3:4). The definitive accomplishment
of this, of course, was Christ's atonement for the sins of His people; thus, just before He offered up Himself as the sacrifice, our
Lord said: "Now judgment is upon this world; now the ruler of
this world shall be thrown out" (John 12:31). In Christ's victory,
salvation and the Kingdom came to earth. Satan was defeated.

The very language of the Gospels bears this out. The stand-
ard term for Christ's "casting out" of the demons throughout
His ministry (*ekballō*; cf. Matt. 8:16, 31; 9:33-34; 10:1, 8; 12:24,
26-28) is simply an intensive form of the word used repeatedly in
Revelation 12 for the "throwing down" of the Dragon (*ballō*).
And Jesus announced: "If I cast out demons by the Spirit of
God, then the Kingdom of God has come upon you" (Matt.
12:28). The message of Revelation is consistent with that of the
New Testament as a whole: Christ has arrived, Satan has been
thrown down, and the Kingdom has come. By His death and
resurrection, Christ "disarmed" the demons, triumphing over
them (Col. 2:15). Satan has been rendered powerless (Heb.
2:14-15), and so St. Paul was able to assure the believers in
Rome that "the God of peace will soon crush Satan under your
feet" (Rom. 16:20). The Cross was the mark, Jesus said, of the
judgment of the world (John 12:31)—or, as John Calvin rendered it, the reformation and restoration of the world.[37] The illegitimate ruler of the world was cast out by the coming of
Christ. As He announced at His Ascension, "All authority (*exousia*) in heaven and on earth has been given to Me" (Matt.
28:18). St. John's vision declares the same thing: **The Kingdom
of our God and the authority (*exousia*) of His Christ have come!**

12 The Voice from heaven exhorts the congregation to exultant worship: **For this reason, rejoice, O heavens, and you who
tabernacle in them.** Who are these who *tabernacle* (not just

---

37. John Calvin, *Commentary on the Gospel According to John* (Grand
Rapids: Baker Book House, 1979), Vol. 2, p. 36; cf. Ronald S. Wallace, *Calvin's Doctrine of the Christian Life* (Tyler, TX: Geneva Ministries, [1959]
1982), p. 110.

dwell) in heaven? St. John has made it plain by this time that the Church's worship takes place, really and truly, before the heavenly throne of God (4:4-11; 5:8-14; 7:9-17). The New Testament clearly reflects this understanding on the part of the apostles and the early Church, declaring that God has raised us up with Christ to the heavenly places (Eph. 2:6), where we have our citizenship (Phil. 3:20). Our worship is beheld by the angelic multitude (1 Cor. 11:10; Eph. 3:10), for we have come to the heavenly Jerusalem, where innumerable angels are gathered in festal assembly with the Church (Heb. 12:22-23). Those who are called to joyful praise for the coming of the Kingdom and the defeat of the Dragon, therefore, are the Church. We have followed the Child in His victorious Ascension (Eph. 1:20-22; 2:6), and have become His Tabernacle (cf. 7:15; 13:6).

But Christ's definitive conquest of the Dragon does not mean the end of his activity altogether. Indeed, like a cornered rat he becomes even more frantically vicious, his snarling rage increasing with his frustration and impotence. The Voice from heaven thus declares: **Woe to the Land and the Sea, because the Dragon has come down to you, having great wrath, knowing that he has only a short time.** The Seventh Trumpet has sounded (11:15), and the Third Woe has arrived (see 8:13; 11:14). The domain of the Dragon, following his defeat at the Ascension of Christ, has now become the Land and the Sea; he has lost forever the Edenic sanctuary, which had been surrendered to him by Adam. Thus, in Chapter 13, St. John sees two great Beasts in the Dragon's image, arising from the Sea and the Land. The Sea, in St. John's imagery, will turn out to be the heathen nations (see below, on 13:1-2), raging and foaming in their hatred against the Lord and His Christ (cf. Ps. 2:1). And, as we have seen repeatedly, Israel is represented by the Land. The Voice is warning that both Israel and the Empire will become demonized in Satan's mad frenzy to hold on to the decayed, withering remnants of his illicit rule. The Dragon has only a brief period left in which to bring about the ruin of the Church, while she is still connected to old Israel; he will seek to stir up Land and Sea, first in a demonic partnership against the Church, and then in a war against each other, in order to crush the Church between them. Like a deposed gangster on the run, the Dragon tries to consolidate his power for a last, desperate stand. But he knows he is doomed; time has almost run out.

318

The Dragon Attacks the Church (12:13-17)

13 And when the Dragon saw that he was thrown down to the Land, he persecuted the Woman who gave birth to the male Child.

14 And two wings of the great Eagle were given to the Woman, in order that she might fly into the wilderness to her place, so that she might be nourished for a time and times and half a time, from the face of the Serpent.

15 And the Serpent threw water like a river out of his mouth after the Woman, so that he might cause her to be swept away with the flood.

16 And the Land helped the Woman, and the Land opened its mouth and drank up the river which the Dragon threw out of his mouth.

17 And the Dragon was enraged with the Woman, and went off to make war with the rest of her seed, who keep the commandments of God and hold to the testimony of Jesus.

13 St. John returns to the theme mentioned in verse 6: the Woman's flight from the Dragon. This happens as a direct result of the Dragon's defeat at the hands of Michael, for **when the Dragon saw that he was thrown down to the Land, he persecuted the Woman who had given birth to the male Child**. It cannot be emphasized too greatly that for St. John and his audience this is one of the most crucial points of the entire chapter. *The Dragon persecutes the Church precisely because Christ defeated him.* We must remember this as we read of the Dragon's hatching of conspiracies, his crafty backstage machinations to bring about the Church's destruction; all of his attacks on the Church are rooted in the fact that he has already been conquered!

It is important for our interpretation to note also that the persecution of the Woman arises in connection with the Dragon's fall to **the Land** of Israel. It is there, first of all, that he seeks to destroy the Church.

14 But the Woman is delivered, flying **into the wilderness** on **two wings of the great Eagle**. St. John again uses imagery from the Exodus, in which the angel-filled pillars of the Glory-Cloud were described as "eagles' wings," by which God had brought Israel to Himself in the wilderness, to be a people for His own possession, a Kingdom of priests to God, a holy nation (Ex. 19:4-6; cf. 1 Pet. 2:9-10). The picture is developed further when Moses, surveying the history of the Covenant people at the end of his life, speaks of how God saved Israel in the wilderness:

> He found him in a desert land,
> And in the howling waste of a wilderness;
> He encircled him, He cared for him,
> He guarded him as the pupil of His eye.
> Like an eagle that stirs up its nest,
> That hovers over its young,
> He spread His wings and caught them,
> He carried them on His pinions. (Deut. 32:10-11)

Moses uses two key words in this passage: *waste* and *hover.* Both of these words occur only one other time in the entire Pentateuch, and again they occur together, in Genesis 1:2. *Waste* is used to describe the uninhabitable condition of the earth at its creation ("without form"); and *hover* is Moses' term for the Spirit's activity of "moving" in creative power over the face of the deep. God is not careless with language. His prophet Moses had a specific reason for repeating those key words in his farewell address. He was underscoring the message that the salvation of Israel was a creation event. The Covenant on Sinai was a re-creation, a reorganization of the world.[38] Similarly, St. John borrows terminology from the same passage in Moses to present that message to the Church: God has brought to fulfillment the provisional re-creations of the old order. The coming of Christ has brought about the definitive re-creation, the New Covenant. And, as in the days of old when God miraculously preserved Israel in all her afflictions, providing her a Paradise in the midst of a wilderness, so He will now nourish and cherish the Church, His Bride and the Mother of His only begotten Son. His Covenant people dwell in the shade of the Glory-Cloud, in the shadow of His wings (Ps. 17:8; 36:7; 57:1; 61:4; 91:4, 11). The wings of the Eagle, which signify death and destruction to the enemies of the covenant (Deut. 28:49; Job 39:27-30; Jer. 48:40;

---

38. David Chilton, *Paradise Restored: A Biblical Theology of Dominion* (Ft. Worth, TX: Dominion Press, 1985), p. 59; Meredith G. Kline, *Images of the Spirit* (Grand Rapids: Baker Book House, 1980), pp. 13ff.

Hos. 8:1; Hab. 1:8; Matt. 24:28), are an emblem of peace, security, and blessing to the heirs of Covenant grace.

Again (cf. v. 6), St. John makes the point that the Woman's flight into the wilderness is not evidence of her abandonment by God; it is not a sign that she has lost the battle, or that events are out of control. Rather, she flies on eagle's wings above the waters (v. 15) **to her place, so that she might be nourished** during the period of tribulation (cf. Luke 4:25-26), the standard three and a half years of judgment mentioned in the prophets — or, as St. John gives it here in the language of Daniel 7:25 and 12:7, **a time and times and half a time.**

Preterist commentators have traditionally seen this passage in terms of the escape of the Judean Church from the Edomite and Roman invasions during the Jewish War, when, in obedience to Christ's commands (Matt. 24:15-28), the Christians escaped to shelter in the caves of the desert.[39] There is nothing wrong with this view, as far as it goes, but it does not go far enough. For St. John's allegory of the Woman is the story of the Church, not only a particular branch of it. The deliverance of the Judean Church must be seen as the primary historical referent of this text, but with the realization that her experience is representative and illustrative of the deliverance of the Church as a whole in this difficult period, when the Lord prepared a table for her in **the face** of her enemies (Ps. 23:5).

15-16 St. John continues his Exodus imagery, reminding us of when the children of Israel had been trapped "between the devil and the deep Red Sea": **And the Serpent threw water like a river out of his mouth after the Woman, so that he might cause her to be swept away with the flood.** Farrer says: "The woman is treated as the congregation of Israel, saved from Egypt, lifted by the Lord on eagle's pinions and brought to Sinai. The dragon's pursuit of her by throwing a waterflood after her is a generalized image for the action of Pharaoh, who (1) commands Israelite children and especially Moses to be washed down the Nile, (2) comes out after escaping Israel with a host, and (3)

---

39. Eusebius, *Ecclesiastical History*, iii.v.

counts on the Red Sea to shut Israel in."[40] The Biblical imagery was familiar: a menacing river seeking to overwhelm God's people, flowing from the mouth of her enemies (Ps. 18:4, 16; 124:3-6; Isa. 8:5-8; 59:19; Jer. 46:7-8; 47:2; Hos. 5:10).

But again, as in the Exodus, the Dragon's plan is foiled: **The Land helped the Woman, and the Land opened its mouth and drank up the river which the Dragon threw out of his mouth.**[41] The picture is partially based on the incident recorded in Numbers 16:28-33, when the earth opened its mouth and swallowed the instigators of a rebellion against Moses. Milton Terry summarizes the point of St. John's Old Testament allusions in this passage: "The great thought in all these images is that divine power is put forth to deliver and sustain the New Testament Church of God in the day of her persecution — the same power that of old wrought the miracles of Egypt, and of the Red Sea, and of the wilderness."[42] That is indeed St. John's emphasis here. The Church is divinely protected and preserved through all her tribulations. No matter what the Dragon does in his attempts to destroy the Church — even bringing about the Jewish Revolt, causing the Edomites and the Romans to slaughter the inhabitants of Israel — the Church escapes his power. By the time Rome attacks, the Woman is long gone; the Land of Israel swallows up the river of wrath, absorbing the blow in her place. The destruction of Jerusalem left the true City and Temple unharmed, for they were safe with the Woman under the shadow of the Almighty.

---

40. Farrer, p. 148. Farrer also points out the astronomical imagery involved here: "There is the great Eagle of the starry heaven, with his two wings, and the Lady of the Zodiac may well receive their help in fleeing from the pursuing Scorpion; for we all hope to escape the baleful omen of his name by accepting the Eagle in his place, when we reckon the four faces of the sky. . . . It is after the woman has received the Eagle's wings that the Dragon shoots a river at her. This is astrological, too; the great river of the sky, the Milky Way, goes up from the Scorpion and sweeps over the Eagle" (ibid.).

41. Interestingly, both Christ and the Dragon are pictured in Revelation as spitting people out of their mouths: Christ vomits out the apostates (3:16), and the Dragon throws out floods of armies (12:16-17) (just as he had *thrown* the stars to earth in 12:4). In a related figure, the Land vomits out Canaanites and apostate Israelites in Leviticus 18:28, but here it swallows the river spat out by the Dragon.

42. Terry, p. 390.

17 The Dragon had only "a short time" (v. 12) to destroy the Church, and he failed again. Frustrated in his attempt to destroy the Mother Church, he **was enraged with the Woman, and went off to make war with the rest of her seed**, the Christians who were unharmed by the Dragon's war with the Woman. How is the Church symbolized by both the Woman and her children? "These distinctions are easily made and maintained. The Church, considered as an institution and an organic body, is distinguishable from her children, as Isaiah 66:7-8 and Galatians 4:22-26 clearly show. . . . We accordingly observe that the Church is in one point of view the totality of all her members of children; in other ways, familiar to the Scripture, her individual members are thought of as related to her as children to a mother."[43]

Having been thwarted in his designs to destroy both the Mother and her Seed, the Dragon turns in rage against **the rest of her seed**, the (predominantly Gentile) Christian Church throughout the Empire. Let us note well St. John's description of these brothers and sisters of the Lord Jesus Christ: They **keep the commandments of God and hold to the testimony of Jesus**. The definition of the Christian, from one perspective, is that he is a member of the organized assembly of the people of God; just as importantly, he is defined in terms of his ethical conformity to the law of God.

> And by this we know that we have come to know Him, if we keep His commandments. The one who says, "I have come to know Him," and does not keep His commandments, is a liar, and the truth is not in him. (1 John 2:3-4)

> For this is the love of God, that we keep His commandments; and His commandments are not burdensome. (1 John 5:3)

As St. John has already informed us, the saints overcome the Dragon through the word of their testimony and their faithful obedience, even unto death (v. 11). The following chapters will detail several crucial stages in the continuing war between the seed of the Serpent and the seed of the Woman. The passage

---

43. Ibid., p. 391. A related example is the Biblical use of the expressions *Zion* and *Daughter of Zion* (cf. Ps. 9:11, 14; Cant. 3:11) and *children of Zion* (cf. Ps. 149:2).

is not meant to be chronologically accurate, as if the Dragon turns against the rest of the Church only after the failure of the Jewish War. Rather, the flight of the Judean Church is only the culmination of a series of deliverances throughout the Last Days, symbolized by the flight of the Woman. St. John is describing in images the various stratagems devised by Satan for destroying the Church, and he shows them all to be complete failures. The Dragon is fighting a losing battle, for he has already been defeated at the Cross and at the Tomb. There is not a square inch of ground in heaven or on earth or under the earth where there is peace between the Serpent and the Seed of the Woman, and Christ has already won overwhelmingly, on every front. Ever since Christ's ascension, world history has been a mopping-up operation. The Church Militant, so long as she is the Church Obedient, will be the Church Triumphant as well.

13

LEVIATHAN AND BEHEMOTH

The Book of Revelation is a Covenant document. It is a prophecy, like the prophecies of the Old Testament. This means that it is not concerned with making "predictions" of astonishing events as such. As prophecy, its focus is redemptive and ethical. Its concern is with the Covenant. The Bible is God's revelation about His Covenant with His people. It was written to show what God has done to save His people and glorify Himself through them.

Therefore, when God speaks of the Roman Empire in the Book of Revelation, His purpose is not to tell us titillating bits of gossip about life at Nero's court. He speaks of Rome only in relation to the Covenant and the history of redemption. "We should keep in mind that in all this prophetic symbolism we have before us *the Roman empire as a persecuting power*. This Apocalypse is not concerned with the history of Rome. . . . The Beast is not a symbol of Rome, but of the great *Roman world-power*, conceived as the organ of the old serpent, the Devil, to persecute the scattered saints of God."[1] The most important fact about Rome, from the viewpoint of Revelation, is not that it is a powerful state, but that it is *Beast*, in opposition to the God of the Covenant; the issue is not essentially political but religious (cf. comments on 11:7). The Roman Empire is not seen in terms of itself, but solely in terms of 1) *the Land* (Israel), and 2) *the Church*.

---

1. Milton Terry, *Biblical Apocalyptics: A Study of the Most Notable Revelations of God and of Christ in the Canonical Scriptures* (New York: Eaton and Mains, 1898), pp. 393f.

The Beast from the Sea (13:1-10)

1 And I was stationed on the sand of the sea. And I saw a Beast coming up out of the sea, having ten horns and seven heads, and on his horns were ten diadems, and on his heads were blasphemous names.

2 And the Beast which I saw was like a leopard, and his feet were like those of a bear, and his mouth like the mouth of a lion. And the Dragon gave him his power and his throne and his great authority.

3 And I saw one of his heads as if it had been smitten to death, and his fatal wound was healed. And the whole Land wondered after the Beast;

4 and they worshiped the Dragon, because he gave his authority to the Beast; and they worshiped the Beast, saying: Who is like the Beast, and who is able to wage war with him?

5 And there was given to him a mouth speaking great things and blasphemies; and authority to make war for forty-two months was given to him.

6 And he opened his mouth in blasphemies against God, to blaspheme His Name and His Tabernacle, those who tabernacle in heaven.

7 And it was given to him to make war with the saints and to overcome them; and authority over every tribe and people and tongue and nation was given to him.

8 And all who dwell on the Land will worship him, everyone whose name has not been written from the foundation of the world in the Book of Life of the Lamb who has been slain.

9 If anyone has an ear, let him hear.

10 If anyone is destined for captivity, to captivity he goes; if anyone kills with the sword, with the sword he must be killed. Here is the perseverance and the faith of the saints.

1-2   St. John tells us that, just as he had ascended to God's Throneroom in order to behold the heavenly world (4:1; cf. Ezek. 3:14; 8:3), the Spirit now **stationed** him **on the sand of the sea,** the vantage point from which he is able to view the **Beast coming up out of the sea.** In a visual, dramatic sense, the mighty Roman Empire did seem to arise out of the sea, from the Italian peninsula across the ocean from the Land. More than this, however, the Biblical symbolism of the sea is in view here. The sea is, as we saw in 9:1-3, associated with the Abyss, the abode of the demons, who were imprisoned there after having been expelled

326

from the Garden. The Abyss is the "Deep" of Genesis 1:2, "without form and void," uninhabitable by man. It is away from the dry land of human environment, and is the place where the demons are kept imprisoned as long as men are faithful to God. When men apostatize, the demons are released; as man is progressively restored, the evil spirits are sent back into the Abyss (Luke 8:26-33). Here we see the ultimate source of the "beastliness" of the Beast: In essence, he comes from the sea, from the chaotic deep-and-darkness of the Abyss, which had to be conquered, formed, and filled by the light of the Spirit (Gen. 1:2; John 1:5). This is not to suggest that there was any real conflict between God and His creation; in the beginning, everything was "very good." The sea is most fundamentally an image of life. But after the Fall, the picture of the raging deep is used and developed in Scripture as a symbol of the world in chaos through the rebellion of men and nations against God: "The wicked are like the tossing sea; for it cannot be quiet, and its waters toss up refuse and mud" (Isa. 57:20; cf. Isa. 17:12). St. John is told later that "the waters which you saw . . . are peoples and multitudes and nations and tongues" (17:15). Out of this chaotic, rebellious mass of humanity emerged Rome, an entire empire founded on the premise of opposition to God.

The Beast has **ten horns and seven heads**, a mirror-image (cf. Gen. 1:26) of the Dragon (12:3), who gives the Beast **his power and his throne and great authority.** The ten crowned horns (powers)[2] of the Beast are explained in 17:12 in terms of the governors of the ten imperial provinces, while the seven heads are explained as the line of the Caesars (17:9-11): Nero is one of the "heads." We must keep in mind the logical distinction already drawn between *sense* (the meaning and associations of a symbol) and *referent* (the special significance of the symbol as it is used in a particular case). The connotations of heads and horns are the same in both the Dragon and the Beast, but they refer to different objects.

In a nightmarish parody of the Biblical High Priest, who wore the divine Name on his forehead (Ex. 28:36-38), the Beast displays **on his heads blasphemous names:** According to the Roman imperial theology, the Caesars were gods. Each emperor

---

2. Cf. 1 Kings 22:11; Zech. 1:18-21; Ps. 75:10.

was called *Augustus* or *Sebastos*, meaning *One to be worshiped*; they also took on the name *divus* (god) and even *Deus* and *Theos* (God). Many temples were erected to them throughout the Empire, especially, as we have noted, in Asia Minor. The Roman Caesars received honor belonging only to the one true God; Nero commanded *absolute* obedience, and even erected a 120-foot-high image of himself. For this reason St. Paul called Caesar "the man of sin"; he was, St. Paul said, "the son of destruction, who opposes and exalts himself above every so-called god or object of worship, so that he takes his seat in the temple of God, displaying himself as being God" (2 Thess. 2:3-4). St. John emphasizes this aspect of the Beast: **And there was given to him a mouth speaking arrogant words and blasphemies. . . . And he opened his mouth in blasphemies against God** (13:5-6). The Christians were persecuted because they refused to join in this idolatrous Emperor-cult.

The Roman Empire is further symbolized as a ravenous, ferocious animal, untamed and under the Curse. St. John says the appearance of the Beast was **like a leopard**, with **feet like those of a bear**, and a **mouth like the mouth of a lion**: "The three animals, thus combined by the writer, symbolize swiftness and ferocity in springing upon the prey, tenacity in holding it and dragging it away, and a ravenous appetite for devouring."[3] These are also the very animals (listed in reverse order) used to describe the first three of the four great world empires in Daniel 7:1-6 (Babylon, Medo-Persia, and Greece; cf. Daniel's description of the same empires under a different symbol, in Dan. 2:31-45). The fourth empire, Rome, partakes of the evil, beast-like characteristics of the other empires, but it is much worse: "Behold, a fourth Beast, dreadful and terrifying and extremely strong; and it had large iron teeth. It devoured and crushed, and trampled down the remainder with its feet; and it was different from all the beasts that were before it, and it had ten horns" (Dan. 7:7).[4] This, as we noted at 12:3, is the origin of the

---

3. Moses Stuart, *A Commentary on the Apocalypse* (Andover: Allen, Morrill and Wardwell, two vols., 1845), Vol. 2, p. 276.

4. According to Moses Stuart and Milton Terry, Daniel's beasts are Babylon, Media, Persia, and Greece. Even if this were the case (which I doubt), its "rebirth" in the imagery of Revelation would mean simply that Rome combines the worst characteristics of the four preceding world empires.

Dragon's (and thus the Beast's) **ten horns and seven heads** (the three heads of beasts 1, 2, and 4, plus the four heads of beast 3: Dan. 7:6). The Beast of Revelation is clearly the Roman Empire, which "combined in itself all the elements of the terrible and the oppressive, which had existed in the aggregate in the other great empires that preceded it; its extension too was equal to them all united."[5]

This Beast, however, is not just an institution, but a person; specifically, as we shall see, it is the Emperor Nero. This is because, particularly the way the Bible looks at things, the two could be considered as one. Rome was, to some extent, covenantally identified with its leader, as the human race was with Adam; the Empire was embodied and represented in the reigning Caesar (Nero). Thus St. John's prophecy can shift back and forth between them, or consider them both together, under the same designation. And both Nero and the Empire were sunk in degrading, degenerate, bestial activities. Nero, who murdered numerous members of his own family (including his pregnant wife, whom he kicked to death); who was a homosexual, the final stage in degeneracy (Rom. 1:24-32); whose favorite aphrodisiac consisted of watching people suffer the most horrifying and disgusting tortures; who dressed up as a wild beast in order to attack and rape male and female prisoners; who used the bodies of Christians burning at the stake as the original "Roman candles" to light up his filthy garden parties; who launched the first imperial persecution of Christians at the instigation of the Jews, in order to destroy the Church; *this* animalistic pervert was the ruler of the most powerful empire on earth. And he set the tone for his subjects. Rome was the moral sewer of the world.[6]

3-4   And I saw one of his heads as if it had been slain, and his fatal wound was healed. Some have pointed out that, after Nero was killed, the rumor began to spread that he would rise

---

5. Ibid.
6. See Suetonius, *The Twelve Caesars*, Robert Graves, trans. (New York: Penguin Books, revised ed., 1979), pp. 213-46; Tacitus, *The Annals of Imperial Rome*, Michael Grant, trans. (New York: Penguin Books, revised ed., 1977), pp. 252-397; Miriam T. Griffin, *Nero: The End of a Dynasty* (New Haven: Yale University Press, 1984).

again and recapture the throne; in some way, they suppose, St. John must be referring to this *Nero redivivus* myth. This, it seems to me, is a very unsatisfactory method of dealing with Scripture. St. John mentions the Beast's "death-wound" three times in this passage (see v. 12, 14); clearly, this is much more than a casual symbol, and we should attempt a Biblical explanation for it.[7]

The Beast, as we saw, resembles the Dragon. The fact that he receives a *head wound* should make us think of the scene in the Garden of Eden, when God promised that Christ would come and crush the Dragon's head (Gen. 3:15). Daniel had prophesied that in the days of the Roman rulers, Christ's Kingdom would crush the Satanic empires and replace them, filling the earth. Accordingly, apostolic testimony proclaimed that Christ's Kingdom had come, that the devil had been defeated, disarmed, and bound, and that all nations would begin to flow toward the mountain of the Lord's House. Within the first generation, the Gospel spread rapidly around the world, to all the nations; churches sprang up everywhere, and members of Caesar's own household came into the faith (Phil. 4:22). In fact, Tiberius Caesar even formally requested that the Roman Senate officially acknowledge Christ's divinity.[8] For a time, therefore, it looked

---

7. This point is brought up by virtually every commentary that espouses (or even takes notice of) the preterist interpretation. It is generally considered to be a crucial argument; the impression is given that the case as a whole stands or falls with the *Nero redivivus* myth. My objections to its use as the interpretive crux are, briefly, as follows: John was writing while Nero was still alive, and could not have been appealing to a myth which had not yet arisen; more importantly, such an approach is flawed since it uses pagan fables rather than Scripture as its *primary* source for interpretation. The Bible itself is the broad hermeneutical context for the canonical books. The value of extrabiblical literature is, at best, secondary. (Thus the *redivivus* myth may be of some minor importance as a historical complement to the theological perspective; indeed, it is possible that a mistaken interpretation of John's prophecy gave rise to the myth in the first place.)

8. This is reported by Tertullian in his *Apology*, chapter 5 (*The Ante-Nicene Fathers*, Alexander Roberts and James Donaldson, eds.; Eerdmans, 1973): "Unless gods give satisfaction to men, there will be no deification for them: the god will have to propitiate the man. Tiberius accordingly, in whose days the Christian name made its entry into the world, having himself received intelligence from Palestine of events which had clearly shown the truth of Christ's divinity, brought the matter before the Senate, with his own decision in favor of Christ. The Senate, because it had not given the approval itself, rejected his proposal. Caesar held to his opinion, threatening wrath against all accusers of

as if a *coup* were taking place: Christianity was in the ascendant, and soon would gain control. Satan's head had been crushed, and with it the Roman Empire had been wounded to death with the sword (see 13:14) of the Gospel.[9]

But then the tables were reversed. Although the Gospel had spread everywhere, so had heresy and apostasy; and under persecution by the Jews and the Roman State, great masses of Christians began falling away (1 Tim. 1:3-7, 19-20; 4:1-3; 6:20-21; 2 Tim. 2:16-18; 3:1-9, 13; 4:10, 14-16; Tit. 1:10-16; 1 John 2:18-19). The New Testament gives the definite impression that *most* of the churches fell apart and abandoned the faith; under Nero's persecution, the Church seemed to have been stamped out entirely. The Beast had received the head-wound, the wound unto death — yet it still lived. The reality, of course, was that Christ *had* defeated the Dragon and the Beast; but the implications of His victory still had to be worked out; the saints had yet to overcome, and take possession (cf. Dan. 7:21-22; Rev. 12:11).

And the whole Land wondered after the Beast; and they worshiped the Dragon, because he gave his authority to the Beast; and they worshiped the Beast, saying: Who is like the Beast, and who is able to make war against him? St. John is not speaking of the *world* (the "earth") following the Beast; the word he uses here should be translated *Land*, meaning *Israel*. We know this because the context identifies his worshipers as *those who dwell on the Land* (Rev. 13:8, 12, 14) — a technical phrase used twelve times in Revelation to denote apostate Israel (see above on 3:10). It is true, of course, that Nero was loved all over the Empire as the benevolent provider of welfare and entertainment. But it is *Israel* in particular which is condemned for Emperor-worship. Faced with a choice between Christ and Caesar, they had proclaimed: *We have no king but Caesar!*

---

the Christians. Consult your histories . . ." (pp. 21f.). A. Cleveland Coxe comments: "Great stress is to be placed on the fact that Tertullian was probably a juriconsult, familiar with the Roman archives, and influenced by them in his own acceptance of Divine Truth. It is not supposable that such a man would have hazarded his bold appeal to the records, in remonstrating with the Senate and in the very faces of the Emperor and his colleagues, had he not known that the evidence was irrefragable" (pp. 57f.).

9. The Biblical head-crushing theme is especially prominent in the Book of Judges; see James B. Jordan, *Judges: God's War Against Humanism* (Tyler, TX: Geneva Ministries, 1985).

(John 19:15). "With this cry Judaism was, in the person of its representatives, guilty of denial of God, of blasphemy, of apostasy. It committed suicide."[10] Their reaction to Caesar's apparently victorious war against the Church (Rev. 11:7) was awe and worship. *Israel sided with Caesar and the Empire against Christ and the Church.* Ultimately, therefore, they were worshiping the Dragon, and for this reason Jesus Himself called their worship assemblies *synagogues of Satan* (Rev. 2:9; 3:9).

5-7 Again St. John draws our attention to the Beast's **blasphemies against God** (cf. 13:1). Specifically, he says, the Beast seeks **to blaspheme His Name and His Tabernacle, those who tabernacle in heaven.** Our citizenship is in heaven (Phil. 3:20), we are enthroned there in Christ, our representative (Eph. 1:20; 2:6), and, as we have seen, the Church's official worship takes place in the heavenlies, with myriads of angels in festal assembly (Heb. 12:22-23; cf. comments on 8:1-2). In contrast to those who reject the faith, who "dwell on the earth," the New Covenant people tabernacle in heaven around the throne of God. In the same breath, therefore, St. John tells the Church of both the Beast's cruel opposition to them and their certainty of protection around the Throne in the heavenly court.

Alexander Schmemann has beautifully drawn attention to the nature of worship as the Church's weekly ascension to heaven (cf. Ex. 24:9-11; 34:1-8, 29-35; Mark 9:1-29): "The early Christians realized that in order to become the temple of the Holy Spirit they must *ascend to heaven* where Christ has ascended. They realized also that this ascension was the very condition of their mission in the world, of their ministry to the world. For there—in heaven—they were immersed in the new life of the Kingdom; and when, after this 'liturgy of ascension,' they returned into the world, their faces reflected the light, the 'joy and peace' of that Kingdom and they were truly its witnesses. They brought no programs and no theories; but wherever they went, the seeds of the Kingdom sprouted, faith was kindled, life was transfigured, things impossible were made possible. They were witnesses, and when they were asked, 'Whence shines this light, where is the source of its power?' they knew what to answer and where to lead men. In church today, we so often find we meet

---

10. Alfred Edersheim, *The Life and Times of Jesus the Messiah* (McLean, VA: MacDonald Publishing Company, two vols., n.d.), Vol. 2, p. 581.

only the same old world, not Christ and His Kingdom. We do not realize that we never get anywhere because we never leave any place behind us."[11]

The Beast was given **authority to act for forty-two months and to make war with the saints and to overcome them**. As I observed above (see comments on 11:2), the period of 42 months (or three and a half years, a broken seven) is a symbolic figure in prophetic language, signifying a time of trouble, when the enemies of God are in power, or when judgment is being poured out, while God's people wait for the coming of the Kingdom (as we have already noted, the Beast oppressed the Old Covenant saints for 42 generations, according to Matthew 1:1-17). Its prophetic usage is not primarily literal, although it is interesting that Nero's persecution of the Church did in fact last a full 42 months, from the middle of November 64 to the beginning of June 68. This period of 42 months thus corresponds (but is not necessarily identical) to the 42 months/1,260 days of 11:2-3 and the "time, times, and half a time" of 12:14. During the time of the Beast's triumph he wields **authority over** the fourfold earth: **every tribe and people and tongue and nation**. This was true of the Roman Empire, as it was true of *Beast* in general. Satan ruled "all the kingdoms of the world" (cf. Matt. 4:8-9) as their "prince" (John 12:31; cf. Dan. 10:13, 20). His authority was "legal," after a sort, since Adam had abdicated the throne; yet it was illegitimate as well. The Church Fathers make much of the fact that the Second Adam won back the world from Satan's dominion by just and lawful means, and not by force.[12]

---

11. Alexander Schmemann, *For the Life of the World: Sacraments and Orthodoxy* (New York: St. Vladimir's Seminary Press, revised ed., 1973), p. 28.

12. Cf. the words of St. Irenaeus: "The all-powerful Word of God, who never fails in justice, acted justly even in dealing with the Spirit of Rebellion. For it was by persuasion, not by force, that He redeemed His own property . . . for thus it behoved God to achieve His purpose: with the result that justice was not infringed, and God's original handiwork was saved from perishing" (*Against Heresies*, v.i.1). St. Augustine adds: "Christ demonstrated justice by his death, he promised power by his resurrection. What could be more just than to go as far as the death of the cross, for the sake of justice? What greater act of power than to rise from the dead, and ascend to heaven with the very flesh in which he was slain? First justice conquered the devil, then power; justice, because he had no sin and was most unjustly put to death by the devil; power, because he lived again after death, never to die thereafter" (*On the Trinity*, xiii.18).

8 St. John repeats what he has told us in v. 3-4: **All who dwell on the Land** (i.e., the apostate Israelites) **will worship him.** We must remember that the Bible speaks of worship in terms of both official, liturgical adoration (a "worship service") and everyday, practical allegiance and obedience. When faced with the practical choice between Caesar and their Lord, the Jews chose Caesar. Idolatry—worship of the creature rather than the Creator—is the mark of the one **whose name has not been written from the foundation of the world in the Book of Life of the Lamb who has been slain.** From the beginning, the wicked have been predestined to damnation. This is not only a necessary correlative to the Biblical doctrines of God's sovereignty and His unconditional election of His people (see, e.g., Acts 13:48), but it is explicitly taught as such in Scripture (see Prov. 16:4; Matt. 11:25; Mark 4:11-12; John 12:37-40; Rom. 9:13; 11:7-10; 1 Pet. 2:7-8; Jude 4; Rev. 17:8, 17). God's heavenly Church Membership Roll has existed from the foundation of the world, eternal and immutable. From the viewpoint of God's eternal decree, therefore, these circumcised covenant-breakers who worship the Beast have never been included in the Book of Life. Those who seek to excommunicate the followers of the Lamb are themselves locked out of the Covenant instead.

9-10 St. John interrupts his description of the Beast's worshipers to exhort his readers to pay close attention to what he is going to say next: **If anyone has an ear, let him hear** (the probable origin of this expression is a reference to the "circumcision," or boring open, of the "homeborn" slave's ear, representing covenantal death and resurrection, rebirth, and renewed obedience to the word of the master; see Ex. 21:5-6; Deut. 15:16-17; Ps. 40:6-8).[13] He then declares the doom of the followers of the Beast, of those who dwell on the Land: **If anyone is destined for captivity, to captivity he goes; if anyone kills with the sword, with the sword he must be killed.** St. John is quoting loosely from Jeremiah 15:2, a verse that occurs in an extended passage detailing God's rejection of Jerusalem. Jeremiah is instructed not to pray for the nation, because they have been destined for destruction (Jer. 14:10-12); in fact, even if those great interces-

---

13. For an extensive study of the circumcision of the ear, see James B. Jordan, *The Law of the Covenant: An Exposition of Exodus 21-23* (Tyler, TX: Institute for Christian Economics, 1985), pp. 77-84.

sors Moses (cf. Ex. 32:11-14; Num. 14:13-24) and Samuel (cf. 1 Sam. 7:5-9; 12:9-15) were to pray for them, God says He will not hear (Jer. 15:1). There will be no place to hide from the judgment, and when the terrified people asked, "Where shall we go?" Jeremiah was to answer:

> Those destined for death, to death;
> And those destined for the sword, to the sword;
> And those destined for famine, to famine;
> And those destined for captivity, to captivity.
> (Jer. 15:2; cf. 42:11, in context)

In language reminiscent of Jesus' foreboding words to the women of Jerusalem (Luke 23:28-31), Jeremiah goes on to describe the coming destruction of the Land (Jer. 15:5-9). Reminding his readers of this passage and its historical fulfillment in the destruction of Jerusalem and the first Temple by the Babylonians (587 b.c.), St. John hammers home the certainty of the coming judgment on the apostate Jews of the first century, those who are in league with the Beast in persecuting the saints. The wicked cannot escape: They have been destined for captivity and the sword.

Confidence in God's government is of the essence of the patient faith to which God's people are called. We are to place our trust not in man, not in the evil machinations of diabolical conspirators, but in God, who is ruling the world for His glory. His judgment will surely come. The patient expectation of this is **the perseverance and the faith of the saints.**

The Beast from the Land (13:11-18)

11 And I saw another Beast coming up from the Land; and he had two horns like a Lamb, and he spoke as a Dragon.

12 And he exercises all the authority of the First Beast in his presence. And he makes the Land and those who dwell in it to worship the First Beast, whose fatal wound was healed.

13 And he performs great signs, so that he even makes fire come down out of heaven to the Land in the presence of men.

14 And he deceives those who dwell in the Land because of the signs which it was given him to perform in the presence of the Beast, telling those who dwell in the Land to make an

335

Image to the Beast who has the wound of the sword and has
come to life.

15 And there was given to him to give breath to the Image of
the Beast, that the Image of the Beast might even speak and
cause as many as do not worship the Image of the Beast to
be killed.

16 And he causes all, the small and the great, and the rich and
the poor, and the free men and the slaves, to be given a mark
on their right hand, or on their forehead,

17 and that no one should be able to buy or to sell, except the
one who has the mark, either the name of the Beast or the
number of his name.

18 Here is wisdom. Let him who has understanding calculate
the number of the Beast, for the number is that of a man;
and his number is 666.

11 Just as the Beast from the sea was in the Image of the
Dragon, so we see another creature who is in the Image of the
Beast. St. John saw this one **coming up from the Land**, arising
from within Israel itself. In 16:13 and 19:20, we are told the identity of this Land Beast. He is the False Prophet, representing
what Jesus had foretold would take place in Israel's last days:
"Many will come in My name, saying, 'I am the Christ,' and will
mislead many. . . . Many false prophets will arise, and will mislead many" (Matt. 24:5, 11). The rise of the false prophets paralleled that of the antichrists; but whereas the antichrists had
apostatized into Judaism from within the Church, the false
prophets were Jewish religious leaders who sought to seduce
Christians from the outside. As Cornelis Vanderwaal has noted,
"In Scripture, false prophecy appears only within the covenant
context";[14] it is the imitation of true prophecy, and operates in
relation to the Covenant people. Moses had warned that false
prophets would arise *from among* the Covenant people, performing signs and wonders (Deut. 13:1-5).

It is important to remember that Judaism is not Old Testament religion at all; rather, it is a rejection of the Biblical faith
altogether in favor of the Pharisaical, Talmudic heresy. Like
Mormons, Jehovah's Witnesses, the Unification Church, and

---

14. Cornelis Vanderwaal, *Search the Scriptures,* Vol. 10: *Hebrews-Revelation*
(St. Catherines, Ontario: Paideia Press, 1979), p. 89; cf. p. 100.

other cults, it claims to be based on the Bible; but its actual authority comes from the traditions of men. Jesus was quite clear: Judaism denies *Christ* precisely because it denies *Moses* (John 5:45-47). Orthodox Christianity *alone* is the true continuation and fulfillment of Old Testament religion (see Matt. 5:17-20; 15:1-9; Mark 7:1-13; Luke 16:29-31; John 8:42-47).

The Jewish false prophets had the appearance of **a Lamb,** as Jesus had warned: "Beware of the false prophets, who come to you in sheep's clothing, but inwardly are ravening wolves" (Matt. 7:15). This is a reference not only to the false prophet's disguise as a member of God's flock, but to his specifically messianic pretensions. In reality, he was a wolf, a Beast, who **spoke as a Dragon.** How does the Dragon speak? He uses deceptive, subtle, seductive speech to draw God's people away from the faith and into a trap (Gen. 3:1-6, 13; 2 Cor. 11:3; Rev. 12:9); furthermore, he is a liar, a slanderer, and a blasphemer (John 8:44; Rev. 12:10). The Book of Acts records numerous examples of Draconian false witness by the Jews against Christians, a major problem for the early Church (Acts 6:9-15; 13:10; 14:2-5; 17:5-8; 18:6, 12-13; 19:9; 21:27-36; 24:1-9; 25:2-3, 7).

12 The Jewish leaders, symbolized by this Beast from the Land, joined forces with the Beast of Rome in an attempt to destroy the Church (Acts 4:24-28; 12:1-3; 13:8; 14:5; 17:5-8; 18:12-13; 21:11; 24:1-9; 25:2-3, 9, 24). Thus the Land Beast **exercises all the authority of the First Beast:** "As the first beast is the agent of the dragon, so the second beast is the agent of the first beast. 'All the authority' makes the second beast the complete agent of the first."[15] Apostate Judaism became completely subservient to the Roman State. This is emphasized by St. John's statement (repeated in v. 14) that the False Prophet exercised the Beast's authority **in his presence.** This is in direct contrast to the function of the true prophet, who stood "before [*the face of*] the Lord," in God's presence, under His authority and blessing (1 Sam. 1:22; 2:18; 1 Kings 17:1; cf. Num. 6:24-26; Hos. 6:2; Jonah 1:3, 10), just as the seven Trumpet-angels are said to "stand before God" (8:2). The prophet was privileged to enter God's

---

15. R. C. H. Lenski, *The Interpretation of St. John's Revelation* (Minneapolis: Augsburg Publishing House, 1943, 1963), p. 404.

throneroom in the Glory-Cloud as a member of the heavenly council, where the divine policy was formulated (cf. Ex. 33:8-11; 1 Kings 22:19-23; Jer. 23:18; Ezek. 1, 10; Amos 3:7; this is also indicated in the fact that prophets are called *angels*: 2 Chron. 36:15-16; Hag. 1:13; Mal. 3:1).[16] "The true prophet lives in the presence of God, taking his orders from Him and doing His pleasure; the False Prophet stands before the Beast, whose interpreter and servant he is."[17] That such a thing could ever be said of the religious leadership of Israel, the people of the Covenant, shows how far they had fallen from the faith of their fathers. They led Israel in worship of the Emperor, making **the Land and those who dwell in it to worship the First Beast, whose fatal wound was healed** (a counterfeit Resurrection of a counterfeit Son). Interestingly, it is the resurrection of the Beast that is given (here and in verse 14) as the reason for worship — just as Christian worship is ultimately founded on the Resurrection of Christ as the proof of His Messianic character and office (1 Cor. 15). The counterfeit resurrection of Rome served as Israel's false Testimony, their "proof" that Christ was *not* the Messiah.

13-14   The False Prophet also performed great miracles in the service of the Empire: Unlike the powerless false prophets of Baal, **he even makes fire come down out of heaven to the earth;** thus this false Elijah **deceives those who dwell on the Land.** Jesus had warned that "false Christs and false prophets will arise and will show great signs and wonders, so as to mislead, if possible, the very elect" (Matt. 24:24), and this was fulfilled numerous times as the period of Israel's "Last Days" progressed to its climax. The Book of Acts records several instances of miracle-working Jewish false prophets who came into conflict with the Church (cf. Acts 8:9-24) and worked under Roman officials (cf. Acts 13:6-11); as Jesus had foretold (Matt. 7:22-23), some of them even used His name in their incantations (Acts 19:13-16). In imitation of the Biblical prophets, who called down God's

---

16. The most detailed exposition of this is in Meredith G. Kline, *Images of the Spirit* (Grand Rapids: Baker Book House, 1980), pp. 57-96.

17. Henry Barclay Swete, *Commentary on Revelation* (Grand Rapids: Kregel Publications, third ed. [1911] 1977), p. 169.

fiery wrath against apostates and lawbreakers (Lev. 10:1-2; Num. 16:28-35; 1 Kings 18:36-40; 2 Kings 1:9-16; Amos 1:3-2:5; Rev. 11:5), the Jewish leaders appeared to exercise God's judgment against the Church, excommunicating Christians from the synagogues and persecuting them to the point of death. Again St. John underscores the apostate condition of these Jewish prophets, by observing that they perform their wonders **in the presence of men** and **in the presence of the Beast** rather than "before the Throne and before the Lamb" (7:9; cf. 3:5; 4:10; 5:8; 7:11, 15; 8:2; 11:4, 16; 14:3, 10; 15:4).

The perversity of Israel's leadership is such that they encourage **those who dwell on the Land** — the Jewish people — **to make an Image to the Beast**, as Nebuchadnezzar had erected an image to himself (Dan. 3). Before we can make a full identification of this Image it will be necessary to examine the religious background and context in which it is set. The depth of Israel's apostasy must first of all be seen in their rejection of the Lord Jesus Christ, the true God and Savior, in favor of Caesar. St. John reveals this in its true light as idolatry (cf. 9:20). It is not necessary to suppose that the Jews literally bowed down to a graven image; the point is that they were worshiping and serving an alien god.

Some would object that the Jews were never guilty of "idolatry" after the Exile. In answer, we repeat again Herbert Schlossberg's excellent summary of the essence of idolatry: "Idolatry in its larger meaning is properly understood as any substitution of what is created for the creator. People may worship nature, money, mankind, power, history, or social and political systems instead of the God who created them all. The New Testament writers, in particular, recognized that the relationship need not be *explicitly* one of cultic worship; a man can place anyone or anything at the top of his pyramid of values, and that is ultimately what he serves. The ultimacy of that service profoundly affects the way he lives."[18] Moreover, it is clear that the postexilic prophets did consider the Jews of their own day to be idolaters (cf. Zech. 13:1-3; Mal. 3:5-7).

The idolatrous character of apostate Israel is assumed

---

18. Herbert Schlossberg, *Idols for Destruction: Christian Faith and its Confrontation with American Society* (Nashville: Thomas Nelson, 1983), p. 6.

throughout the message of the New Testament. The Apostle Paul specifically accuses the Jews of lawlessness and apostasy in Romans 2. In verses 21-22, he says: "You, therefore, who teach another, do you not teach yourself? You that preach that one should not steal, do you steal? You who say that one should not commit adultery, do you commit adultery? *You who abhor idols, do you rob temples?*" Clearly, St. Paul is charging apostate Israel with committing idolatry (or its equivalent). It is crucial to note that all the accusations in Romans 2 refer to *Israel as a whole*; obviously, if they applied only to a select few his argument would have no force. (Since he also accuses them of committing adultery, it is at least possible that he has in mind "religious" adultery against their true Husband, Jesus Christ). In general, commentators have supposed the charge of idolatry to mean either that the Jews were guilty of robbing from heathen temples (e.g., St. Chrysostom, Henry Alford, John Murray; cf. Acts 19:37, which indicates that the Jews may have been considered liable to this offense), or that they were committing "sacrilege" in a more general sense, by their impiety, irreverence, and unbelief (e.g., John Calvin, Charles Hodge; cf. 1 Samuel 15:23; Neh. 13:4-12; Mal. 1:6-14; 3:8-9; Col. 3:5). What is not generally noticed is that the whole list of crimes in Romans 2:20-23 is taken from Malachi 2-3, indicating that the charge of "robbing temples" (and thus of idolatry) is related to the Israelites' failure to tithe, their refusal to honor Him as God (cf. Matt. 15:7-9). God says through Malachi:

> From the days of your fathers you have turned aside from My statutes, and have not kept them. Return to Me, and I will return to you, says the LORD of hosts. But you say, "How shall we return?" Will a man rob God? Yet you are robbing Me! But you say, "How are we robbing Thee?" In tithes and offerings! You are cursed with a curse, for you are robbing Me, the whole nation of you! (Mal. 3:7-9)

A good part of the Westminster Larger Catechism's definition of idolatry (virtually every word of which is abundantly referenced to Scripture) is applicable to the religious character of Israel during the Last Days: "The sins forbidden in the second commandment are, all devising, counselling, commanding, using, and any wise approving, any religious worship not instituted by God Himself; tolerating a false religion; . . . all superstitious devices, corrupting the worship of God, adding to it, or taking from it, whether invented and taken up of ourselves, or received by tradition from others, though under the title of antiquity, custom, devotion, good intent, or any other pretense whatsoever; simony; sacrilege; all neglect, contempt, hindering, and opposing the worship and ordinances which God hath appointed" (cf. Matt. 15:3-9; Acts 13:45; 1 Thess. 2:15-16).[19] The essential point for our purpose is simply that St. Paul is accusing the Jewish people of some sort of idolatry. It is certainly a broad enough term to cover their rejection of Jesus Christ.

15-17 The extent of the False Prophet's demonic power is such that he is able **to give breath** (or **spirit) to the Image of the Beast, that the Image of the Beast might even speak.** While some have argued that this refers to some trick of machinery or ventriloquism (and thus a seeming refutation of Psalm 135:15-16: "The idols of the nations . . . have mouths, but they do not speak"), it is more likely that the passage as a whole is intended to convey the idea of an apostate Jewish attempt to re-create the world. In the beginning, when God created the earth, He gave breath/Spirit to His Image and placed him in His garden-temple (Gen. 2:7-8); and the first thing we see the Image doing is *speaking,* naming and defining the creation in terms of God's mandate (Gen. 2:19-20).

The Beast's spirit-inspired Image itself is able to **cause as many as do not worship the Image of the Beast to be killed.** The Jewish synagogues enforced submission to the Emperor. Indeed, their leaders' charge against Christ Himself was that He was a rival to the all-embracing authority of Caesar (John 19:12-15). Similarly, they organized economic boycotts against those who refused to submit to Caesar as Lord, the leaders of the synagogues "forbidding all dealings with the excommunicate,"[20] and going so far as to put them to death.

And he causes all, (note the six categories) **the small and the**

---

19. *The Confession of Faith* (Free Presbyterian Church of Scotland, 1970), pp. 193ff.

20. Austin Farrer, *The Revelation of St. John the Divine* (London: Oxford University Press, 1964), p. 157.

great, and the rich and the poor, and the free men and the slaves, to be given a mark on their right hand, or on their forehead, and he provides that no one should be able to buy or to sell, except the one who has the mark, either the name of the Beast or the number of his name. The Book of Acts is studded with incidents of organized Jewish persecution of the Church (Acts 4:1-3, 15-18; 5:17-18, 27-33, 40; 6:8-15; 7:51-60; 9:23, 29; 13:45-50; 14:2-5; 17:5-8, 13; 18:17; 20:3; 22:22-23; 23:12, 20-21; 24:27; 26:21; 28:17-29; cf. 1 Thess. 2:14-16). All of this ultimately served the interests of Caesar against Christ and the Church; and the "mark of the Beast," of course, is the Satanic parody of the "seal of God" on the foreheads and hands of the righteous (3:12; 7:2-4; 14:1), the mark of wholehearted obedience to the Law in thought and deed (Deut. 6:6-8), the mark of blessing and protection (Ezek. 9:4-6), the sign that one is *HOLY TO THE LORD* (cf. Ex. 28:36). Israel has rejected Christ, and is "marked" with the seal of Rome's total lordship; she has given her allegiance to Caesar, and is obedient to his rule and law. Israel chose to be saved by the pagan state, and persecuted those who sought salvation in Christ.

The New Testament gives abundant testimony of this fact. The Jewish hierarchy was involved in a massive, organized attempt to destroy the Church by both deceit and persecution. In pursuit of this diabolical goal, they united in a conspiracy with the Roman government against Christianity. Some of them were able to perform miracles in the service of Satan. All this is exactly what is told us of the Beast from the Land. The False Prophet of Revelation represents none other than the leadership of apostate Israel, who rejected Christ and worshiped the Beast.

There is an interesting reversal of imagery in the text. The Book of Job has prepared us for St. John's prophecy, for it too tells us of a Land Beast (*Behemoth*, Job 40:15-24) and a Sea Beast (*Leviathan*, Job 41:1-34). In the Greek Old Testament which the early Church used, the Hebrew word *Behemoth* is translated *Thērion*, the same word St. John uses for *Beast*; and *Leviathan* is translated *Drakōn* (*Dragon*). But St. John's visions expand on Job's descriptions of these dinosaurs, and the order of their appearance is reversed. Job first saw the Behemoth (Job 40), then Leviathan (Job 41), and finally God (Job 42). In Revelation, St. John shows us the demonic reverse of this pattern:

First we see Satan as the Dragon, the Leviathan; then comes the Sea Beast, who is in the Dragon's image; finally, trailing behind and serving them, comes the Land Beast, in the image of the Sea Beast, bringing along yet another Image of the Beast. By listing the Beasts in reverse order, St. John underscores his point: Israel, which was to have been a kingdom of priests to the nations of the world, has surrendered her position of priority to Leviathan and the Beast. Instead of placing a godly imprint upon every culture and society, Israel has been remade into the image of the pagan, antichristian State, becoming its prophet. Abraham's children have become the seed of the Serpent.

During three years of ministry in Ephesus, the Apostle Paul continually suffered persecution because of "the plots of the Jews" (Act 20:19); in describing his conflicts with them, he called them "wild beasts" (1 Cor. 15:32). The Jewish Beast was the early Church's most deceptive and dangerous enemy. St. Paul strenuously warned the Church about Judaizers who propagated "Jewish myths": "They profess to know God, but by their deeds they deny Him, being detestable and disobedient, and worthless for any good deed" (Tit. 1:14, 16).

We are now in a position to attempt a more precise identification of **the Image of the Beast,** which is a continuation of the Satanic counterfeit, the demonic reversal of God's order. Just as the Son of God is the Image of the Father (John 1:18; Col. 1:15), so the Church has been redemptively re-created as the Image of the Son (Rom. 8:29; Eph. 4:24; Col. 3:10). The vision of the prophetic, priestly, and dominical Church seen by St. John parallels that of the Lord Jesus Christ: Like her Lord, she is robed in glorious light (cf. 1:13-16; 10:1; 12:1; 19:6-8; 21:9-22:5). Assisting the Son in His work throughout Revelation are the Seven Stars/Angels of the Presence (8:2), led by the Holy Spirit (the Seven Spirits, connected with the angels in 3:1). The divine order is thus:

Father
Son (Image of the Father)
Angels/Bishops
Church (Image of the Son)

The Satanic parody of this is:

343

Dragon
Beast (Image of the Dragon)
False Prophet
Synagogue of Satan (Image of the Beast)

Throughout the Book of Revelation the Church speaks liturgically, and the angels then act in history to bind and loose by
Trumpet and Chalice, bringing judgment on the disobedient;
similarly, the Synagogue "speaks," and the False Prophet brings
its false judgments upon those who defy its authority. The
Church has been resurrected, brought to life by the very Spirit/
Breath of God (11:11; cf. Gen. 2:7; John 20:22); the Synagogue
of Satan was animated by a spirit/breath as well (13:15). And,
just as the Angel of God marked the foreheads of the righteous
for protection (7:3), so the Beast's "angel" stamped the wicked
with its own branding mark of evil. The leaders of Israel worked
to enforce worship, not of the true God, as in the Christian
churches, but of *the Synagogue itself* — the **Image of the Beast.**

18 It was by now clear to St. John's readers that the Sea
Beast was the Roman Empire. St. John now provides his readers
with an identification of the Beast in a very different form: **Here
is wisdom. Let him who has understanding calculate the number
of the Beast, for the number is that of a man; and his number is
666.** As we shall see, 666 (literally, $\chi\xi\varsigma'$)[21] is the numerical value
of the name *Nero Caesar.*[22] While this is a convenient (and, so
far as it goes, perfectly correct) solution, it also poses several
problems. If the Beast is to be identified with the Roman Empire

---

21. In New Testament times the obsolete letter ς (*stigma*, which made the
sound *st*) was used for the numeral 6; see A. T. Robertson and W. Hersey
Davis, *A New Short Grammar of the Greek Testament* (New York: Harper &
Brothers, 1931, 1933) p. 109.

22. It is sometimes objected that, by using various systems of computation,
it is possible to give practically anyone's name the value of 666; thus, interpreters have identified the Beast with the Pope, Martin Luther, Napoleon, Adolf
Hitler, and Henry Kissinger (among a host of others). The point should be understood, however, that "*not any possible solution* of the name, but rather *a
relevant solution*, is required. Having already shown that the Roman Empire is
the Beast described in verses 1-8 of this chapter, we naturally look for some
name that gives specific designation of that power" (Milton Terry, *Biblical
Apocalyptics*, p. 401).

as a whole, rather than with Nero alone, does this not change the "number of the Beast" when another Caesar is on the throne? Moreover, is this not merely an example of "newspaper exegesis"—using first-century newspapers?[23] The answer is that Nero's name is *not* the primary reference of *666;* rather, the number of the Beast is based on several strands of Biblical data which point ultimately to the Roman Empire. The name *Nero Caesar* by no means exhausts the significance of the riddle. The Bible itself gives us enough information to allow us to identify Rome as the Beast, the fulfillment of 666.

We begin with the simple number 6, which is associated with both *Beast* and *Man* from the beginning, since they were both created on the sixth day of the week (Gen. 1:24-31). Six days out of seven are given to man and beast for labor (Ex. 20:8-11); the Hebrew slave was in bondage for six years before his release in the seventh year (Ex. 21:2); six cities of refuge were appointed for the accidental slaying of a man (Num. 35:9-15). *Six* is thus **the number of Man,** i.e. **a human number.** Lenski explains: "John writes the number not in words but in Greek letters: $\chi' =$ 600, $\xi' = 60$, $\varsigma' = 6$, thus 666. This is the number 6, plus its multiple by 10, namely 60, again plus its multiple by 10×10 (intensified completeness), namely 600—thus 666, three times falling short of the divine 7. In other words, *not* 777, but competing with 777, seeking to obliterate 777, but doing so abortively, its failure being as complete as was its expansion by puffing itself up from 6 to 666."[24] *Six* is thus the number Man was born with, the number of his creation; the repetition of the number reveals Man in opposition to God, trying to increase his number, attempting to transcend his creaturehood. But, try as he might, he can be nothing more than a six, or a series of sixes.

And this is exactly what we see in Scripture, as apostate man attempts to deify himself. Goliath, the ancient enemy of God's

23. There is, of course, some justification for a first-century "newspaper exegesis," for the Book of Revelation itself leads us to expect a first-century fulfillment of its prophecies. We *should* look — carefully — for historical events in the first century which correspond to the apocalyptic visions. This does not necessarily lend itself to undue speculation, for it is simply taking John's own statements about his book seriously. He said it would be fulfilled "shortly."

24. R. C. H. Lenski, *The Interpretation of St. John's Revelation* (Minneapolis: Augsburg Publishing House, 1943, 1963), pp. 411f.

people, is as tall as "six cubits and a span" (1 Sam. 17:4) — i.e., *six, plus a hand grasping for more*; the head of his spear weighs 600 shekels of iron. (Goliath is, on several counts, a Beast; as the seed of the Dragon, he wears *scale-armor*, 1 Sam. 17:5; but the Seed of the Woman destroys him by inflicting a head-wound, 1 Sam. 17:49-51.) Another striking example of this pattern takes place when King Nebuchadnezzar erects an image of himself measuring 60 cubits high and 6 cubits across (Dan. 3:1).[25] The impact of this is magnified when we consider that the numerical value of the Hebrew letters[26] in Daniel 3:1 (which describes Nebuchadnezzar's image) add up to 4,683 — which is 7 times 666 (4,662), plus 21, the *triangular* of 6 (triangulation will be explained presently).

A brief digression here will serve to place this point in its larger symbolic framework, for — in contrast to the multiplied sixes of Nebuchadnezzar's image — the names of Daniel and his three friends who refused to worship the idol add up to 888 in Hebrew.[27] This is also the number of *Jesus* in Greek.[28] The Fall of man occurred on the seventh day of creation (man's first full

---

25. St. Irenaeus sees 666 as a combination of Noah's age at the Flood (600) — symbolizing "all the commixture of wickedness which took place previous to the deluge" — with the 60 + 6 of Nebuchadnezzar's image, symbolizing "every error of devised idols since the flood, together with the slaying of the prophets and the cutting off of the just." *Against Heresies*, in Alexander Roberts and James Donaldson, eds., *The Ante-Nicene Fathers* (Grand Rapids: Wm. B. Eerdmans Publishing Co., 1973 reprint), Vol. 1, p. 558.

26. In Hebrew (as in most ancient languages), the alphabet served double duty: each letter was also a numeral. Thus any given word or group of words had a numerical value, which could be computed simply by adding up the numerals. The language-system of the West avoids this by using the Roman alphabet for its letters and the Arabic alphabet for its numerals. It is thus difficult and artificial for us to imagine going back and forth between the letter-use and numeral-use of the characters in our language, but for the ancients it was quite natural. In all probability, they did not need to engage in any great mental shifts back and forth, but simply saw and comprehended both aspects at once.

27. See Ernest L. Martin, *The Original Bible Restored* (Pasadena, CA: Foundation for Biblical Research, 1984), p. 110. In his vision of the great image which represented the heathen empires leading up to Christ's kingdom, Nebuchadnezzar was the "head of gold" (Dan. 2:37-38); Martin has pointed out that 666 years after Nebuchadnezzar inaugurated his reign (604 B.C.), Israel's last sabbatical cycle began (Autumn, A.D. 63), which ended in the destruction of Jerusalem and the Temple in the Autumn of 70.

28. ΙΗΣΟΥΣ (Ι = 10 + Η = 8 + Σ = 200 + Ο = 70 + Υ = 400 + Σ = 200) = 888.

day of life); Jesus Christ, the Second Adam, spent the seventh day in the grave, to pay for Adam's sin. His Resurrection took place on the eighth day, which becomes the replacement Sabbath for the New Creation.[29] Austin Farrer comments: "Jesus rose on the *third* day, being the *eighth* of that week: he is the Resurrection and the Life. For *eight* signifying resurrection, see 1 Peter 3:20-21, and 2 Peter 2:5. But the third day on which Jesus rose is third from that sixth day (Friday) on which Antichrist had his apparent triumph; so if Christ has a name valuing 888, Antichrist should have a name valuing 666."[30]

Farrer expands on this point: "Why should Antichrist be so emphatically *six*? The whole arrangement of the Apocalypse explains this. The divine work with which it deals is a work of judgment: it is judgment which has the sixfold pattern of the working-days, and always on the sixth day there is the culmination of judgment.[31] On the sixth day of the week, and at the sixth hour, says St. John [John 19:13-22; Rev. 13:16-14:1], the kingdoms of Christ and Antichrist looked one another in the face in Pilate's court, and the adherents of the false prophet (Caiphas) firmly wrote on their foreheads the mark of the Beast, when they said, 'We have no king but Caesar.' Presently they saw the Lamb uplifted with his true Name over his head, 'King of the Jews': and for all they could do, they could not get it erased: 'What I have written,' said Pilate, 'I have written.' Christ's Friday victory is the supreme manifestation also of Antichrist."[32]

There is an interesting mathematical property of the number 666, which would not have escaped St. John's readers: *666 is the triangular of the square of 6.* That is, the *square* of 6 (6×6) is 36. The *triangular* of 36 is 666. Triangulation is a method of computation that was popular in the ancient world, and very familiar to people in the first century, but it has been largely forgotten in our day. It works like this:

---

29. See James B. Jordan, *The Law of the Covenant: An Exposition of Exodus 21-23* (Tyler, TX: Institute for Christian Economics, 1984), p. 164.

30. Austin Farrer, *The Revelation of St. John the Divine* (London: Oxford University Press, 1964), p. 156; Farrer is, of course, referring to the Beast by the common (but technically inaccurate) term *Antichrist*, which is really the designation given by St. John to apostates from the Christian faith.

31. Cf. Gen. 1:31; Rev. 6:12-17; 9:13-21.

32. Farrer, *A Rebirth of Images*, p. 259.

These diagrams, both of which have six units on each side, show that 36 is the *square* of 6, while 21 is the *triangular* of 6. If we extend the triangle one more line, we would get the triangular of seven (28); another line would give us the triangular of eight (36). Extending it all the way up to 36 lines results in the number 666.[33] The number of the Beast, therefore, is a full "exposition" of the number of Man.

But there is more. If we were to strip off the outer edge of fifteen stars in the triangle above, we would be left with a "triangle within a triangle," made up of six stars; one could therefore say that the triangular 21 is the "filling in," or fulfillment, of 15 (the number of units in the outer triangle, or periphery).

Now, the triangular 666 contains 12 of these triangles, one inside the other, with the outermost triangle made up of 105 units; thus the triangular 666 is the "fulfillment" of 105. This brings us to the interesting part, for the factors of 105 are $30 \times 3\frac{1}{2}$. *Three and a half* years of *twelve* months in each year and *thirty* days in each month equals the *twelve hundred and sixty* days, the period of the Beast's triumph.

Austin Farrer explains: "666, therefore, is a 12-fold triangle with a periphery of $30 \times 3\frac{1}{2}$. . . . The coincidence between this reckoning and the factors of the 666 triangle is no mere accident. St. John's reckoning of the period is artificial, devised for the sake of conformity with the factors of the 666 triangle. There neither is nor was any calendar in which $3\frac{1}{2}$ years are $3\frac{1}{2}$

---

33. Incidentally, the easy way to figure out the triangular of any number is to multiply it by the next higher number, then divide by two; thus $\frac{36 \times 37}{2} = 666$.

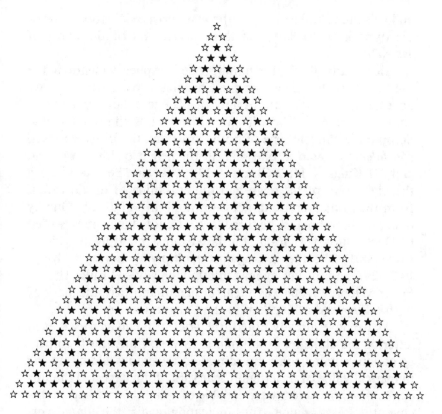

times twelve months of thirty days each.[34] The purpose of the artificial reckoning is to exhibit the Beast's fatally limited reign as a function of his number."[35]

F. W. Farrar described how the first readers of the Revelation would thus have regarded the mysterious 666 (χξϛ′): "The very look of it was awful. The first letter was the initial letter of the name of Christ. The last letter was the first double-letter (*st*) of the Cross (*st*auros). Between the two the Serpent stood confessed with its writhing sign and hissing sound. The whole formed a triple repetition of 6, the essential number of toil and imperfection;

---

34. Farrer's note at this point reads: "A solar calendar requires that about every other month shall be of 31 days, not 30. A lunar calendar must have every other month of 29 days and an intercalary month a little more frequently than every third year. So by lunar reckoning, 3½ years is either about 1,270, or about 1,300 days: or, if we neglect intercalation entirely, it is about 1,240 days. In no case is it 1,260 days."

35. Farrer, *A Rebirth of Images*, pp. 259f.

and this numerical symbol of the Antichrist, 666, stood in terrible opposition to 888 — the three perfect 8's of the name of Jesus."[36]

More than all this, the number 666 is explicitly mentioned in the books of the Kings and the Chronicles, from which, as we have seen, St. John takes many of his symbolic numbers (see comments on 4:4). These inspired historical writings tell us that Solomon (a Biblical type of both Christ and the Beast) received *666 talents of gold* in one year, at the height of his power and glory (1 Kings 10:14; 2 Chron. 9:13). That number marks both the high point of his reign and the beginning of his downfall; from then on, everything goes downhill into apostasy. One by one, Solomon breaks the three laws of godly kingship recorded in Deuteronomy 17:16-17: the law against multiplying gold (1 Kings 10:14-25); the law against multiplying horses (1 Kings 10:26-29); and the law against multiplying wives (1 Kings 11:1-8). For the Hebrews, 666 was a fearful sign of apostasy, the mark of both a king and a kingdom in the Dragon's image.

As we have already noted, the ancient languages used each letter of the alphabet as a numeral as well; thus, the "number" of anyone's name could be computed by simply adding up the numerical value of its letters. Clearly, St. John expected that his *contemporary* readers were capable of using this method to discover the Beast's name — thus indicating, again, the *contemporary message* of Revelation; he did not expect them to figure out the name of some 20th-century official in a foreign government. At the same time, however, he tells them that it will not be as easy as they might think: it will require someone "who has understanding." For St. John did not give a number that could be worked out in Greek, which is what a Roman official scanning Revelation for subversive content would expect. The unexpected element in the computation was that it had to be worked out in *Hebrew*, a language that at least some members of the churches would know. His readers would have guessed by now that he was speaking of Nero, and those who understood Hebrew probably grasped it instantly. The numerical values of the Hebrew letters in *Neron Kesar* (Nero Caesar) are:

---

36. F. W. Farrar, *The Early Days of Christianity* (Chicago and New York: Belford, Clarke & Co., 1882), p. 539.

נ = 50   ר = 200   ו = 6   נ = 50   ק = 100   ס = 60   ר = 200

thus:

נְרוֹן קֶסֶר = 666

As I mentioned earlier, the point is not that Nero's name is the primary identification of 666. The point is, instead, what the number meant to the churches. St. John's Biblically informed readers will have already recognized many clear indications of the Beast's identity as Rome (indeed, they already knew this from reading the Book of Daniel). Now Nero has arrived on the scene as the first great persecutor of the Church, the embodiment of the "666-ness" of the Empire, and — Lo and behold! — his very name spells out 666.[37]

It is significant that "all the earliest Christian writers on the Apocalypse, from Irenaeus down to Victorinus of Pettau and Commodian in the fourth, and Andreas in the fifth, and St. Beatus in the eighth century, connect Nero, or some Roman emperor, with the Apocalyptic Beast."[38] There should be no reasonable doubt about this identification. St. John was writing to first-century Christians, warning them of things that were "shortly" to take place. They were engaged in the most crucial battle of his-

---

37. It is charged by some that *Neron Kesar* is merely a convenient "misspelling" of Nero's name in Hebrew. This objection overlooks the fact that before the modern introduction of dictionaries the world was simply not as concerned as we are about uniformity in the spelling of names. *Alternate spellings* were common (e.g. "Joram" and "Jehoram" in the Old Testament), especially in the transliteration of words into a foreign tongue. But the allegation of misspelling is wholly wrong anyway. The form *Neron Kesar* (1) *is* the linguistically "correct" Hebrew form, (2) is the form found in the Talmud and other rabbinical writings, and (3) was used by Hebrews in the first century, as archaeological evidence has shown. As F. W. Farrar observed, "the Jewish Christian would have tried the name as he *thought* of the name — that is *in Hebrew letters*. And the moment he did this the secret stood revealed. No Jew ever thought of Nero except as 'Neron Kesar,' and this gives at once . . . 666" (*The Early Days of Christianity*, Chicago and New York: Belford, Clarke & Co., 1882, p. 540). Of some related interest is the fact that if Nero's name is written without the final *n* (i.e., the way it would occur to a Gentile to spell it in Hebrew), it yields the number *616* — which is exactly the variant reading in a few New Testament manuscripts. The most reasonable explanation for this variant is that it arose from the confusion over the final *n*.

38. F. W. Farrar, *The Early Days of Christianity* (Chicago and New York: Belford, Clarke & Co., 1882), p. 541. See, e.g., Sulpitius Severus (A.D. 363-420), who clearly cites Rev. 13 in his description of Nero: *Sacred History*, in *A Select Library of Nicene and Post-Nicene Fathers of the Christian Church* (Grand Rapids: Eerdmans, 1973 reprint), pp. 110f.

tory, against the Dragon and the evil Empire which he possessed. The purpose of the Revelation was to comfort the Church with the assurance that God was in control, so that even the awesome might of the Dragon and the Beast would not stand before the armies of Jesus Christ. Christ was wounded in His heel on Friday, the sixth day, the Day of the Beast — yet that is the day He crushed the Dragon's head. At his most powerful, St. John says, the Beast is just a *six*, or a series of sixes; never a *seven*. His plans of world dominion will never be fulfilled, and the Church will overcome through her Lord Jesus, the 888, who conquered on the Eighth Day.

TABLE OF NUMERALS IN USE
DURING THE BIBLICAL PERIOD

	Hebrew	*Greek*
1	א	α
2	ב	β
3	ג	γ
4	ד	δ
5	ה	ε
6	ו	ς
7	ז	ζ
8	ח	η
9	ט	θ
10	י	ι
20	כ	κ
30	ל	λ
40	מ	μ
50	נ	ν
60	ס	ξ
70	ע	ο
80	פ	π
90	צ	ϟ
100	ק	ρ
200	ר	σ
300	ש	τ
400	ת	υ
500	ך ם	φ
600		χ
700		ψ
800		ω

THE KING ON MOUNT ZION

St. John has just revealed the evil triad of enemies facing the early Church: the Dragon, the Sea Beast, and the Land Beast. He has made it clear that these enemies are implacable, that the conflict with them will require faithfulness unto death. The question again naturally arises: Will the Church survive such an all-out attack? In this closing section of the fourth major division of his prophecy, therefore, John again addresses these fears of his audience. The action of the book comes to a halt as the apostle gives comfort and provides reasons for confidence in the coming victory of the Church over all her opposition. "The revelation of the three great foes, the dragon, the beast from the sea, and the beast from the land, is followed immediately by a sevenfold disclosure of victory and judgment in the heavens. The purpose of these visions and voices from heaven is obviously to show that the powers of the heavens are mightier than those of the infernal serpent and his associates. The trinity of hostile forces, armed with many lying wonders, might seem from a human point of view invincible. But John, like the young servant of Elisha when confronted with the horses and chariots and immense host of the king of Syria, is here admonished that they which are with the persecuted Church are more and mightier than they which make war against her (comp. 2 Kings 6:15-17)."[1]

The Lamb with His Fair Army (14:1-5)

1 And I looked, and behold, the Lamb was standing on
Mount Zion, and with Him one hundred and forty-four

---

1. Milton Terry, *Biblical Apocalyptics: A Study of the Most Notable Revelations of God and of Christ in the Canonical Scriptures* (New York: Eaton and Mains, 1898), p. 402.

thousand, having His name and the name of His Father written on their foreheads.

2 And I heard a Voice from heaven, like the sound of many waters and like the sound of loud thunder, and the Voice which I heard was like harpists playing on their harps.

3 And they sing a New Song before the Throne and before the four living creatures and the elders; and no one could learn the Song except the one hundred and forty-four thousand who had been purchased from the Land.

4 These are the ones who have not been defiled with women, for they are chaste men. These are the ones who follow the Lamb wherever He goes. These have been purchased from among men as first fruits to God and to the Lamb.

5 And no lie was found in their mouth, for they are blameless.

1   We are back in Psalm 2 again: St. John has shown us the heathen raging against the Lord and against His Christ, rebelling against the authority of the Godhead; and now the Lord says: "But as for Me, I have installed My King upon Zion, My holy mountain," guaranteeing that the nations will submit to His all-embracing rule. In opposition to the Beasts rising from Sea and Land, **the Lamb** is **standing** (cf. 5:6) **on Mount Zion**, already enthroned as King of kings, the Ruler of all nations. The Mountain-imagery of the Bible is clearly a reference to the original Holy Mountain, the location of the Garden of Eden (Ezek. 28:13-14). The prophetic promises of the restoration of the Mountain to the earth (Isa. 2:2-4; Dan. 2:32-35, 44-45; Mic. 4:1-4), as well as the numerous redemptive activities on mountains (Gen. 22:2; Ex. 19:16-19; 2 Chron. 3:1; Matt. 28:16-20), signified the fulfillment and consummation of Paradise through the Messiah's atonement, when God's Kingdom would fill the earth (Isa. 11:9).[2] The Lamb standing on the Mountain is a symbol of Christ's victory over all His enemies, with His people restored to Eden and fellowship with God. The fact that the Mountain is **Zion** (mentioned seven times in the New Testament: Matt. 21:5; John 12:15; Rom. 9:33; 11:26; Heb. 12:22; 1 Pet. 2:6) serves to highlight this victory, for Zion is the special "holy mountain" of Jerusalem, the symbol of God's presence with His

---

2. See David Chilton, *Paradise Restored: A Biblical Theology of Dominion* (Ft. Worth, TX: Dominion Press, 1985), pp. 29-32.

354

people and His victorious reign over the earth, when all kingdoms are gathered together to serve Him in the New Covenant
(cf. Ps. 9:1-20; 14:7; 20:1-2; 48:1-14; 69:35; 87:1-3; 99:1-9;
102:13-22; Isa. 24:21-23; 51-52; 59:16-20; Jer. 31:10-37; Zech.
9:9-17).[3]

The Lamb is thus not alone on Zion, for his people share in
His victory. They are there with Him, the **one hundred and
forty-four thousand**, the Remnant of Israel ordered for battle
according to the thousands of her tribes (see on 7:4-8). We saw
that the Mark of the Beast (13:16-17) was the parody of the
divine sealing of the true Israel (7:2-8); now St. John reminds us
of the original sealing, the mark of God's ownership and protection of His obedient people. That the 144,000 are regarded as
members of the Church, and not ultimately as a separate cate-
gory of ethnic Israelites, is underscored by John's combination
of previous imagery. We were told before that the 144,000 are
sealed **on their foreheads** (7:3), while it is all Christ's overcomers
who have **His name and the name of His Father written on their
foreheads** (3:12). The 144,000, therefore, belong to the Church,
the army of overcomers. Yet they are also a special group: the
Remnant-Church of the first generation.

2-3   With his eyes on the Lamb and His army, St. John hears
a Voice from heaven, the familiar reminder of God's presence in
the Glory-Cloud: **like the sound of many waters and like the
sound of loud thunder, and . . . like the sound of harpists playing on their harps,** the heavenly orchestra playing accompaniment to the victory song of the army of saints, who **sing a New
Song before the Throne and before the four living creatures and**

---

3. Once we understand that the Garden of Eden was on a mountain, we can
more easily understand the basis for the amazing agreement among the myth-
ologies of the different cultures. All cultures originated from the dispersal at
Mount Ararat, and later at Babel; and they took with them the memories of
the original Paradise. Thus, in every ancient culture, there are myths of the
dwelling-place of God on the Cosmic Mountain (e.g., Mount Olympus), and
of man's expulsion from Paradise, and his attempts to return (e.g., the almost
universal preoccupation with building tower-gardens, pyramids, and mounds;
cf. the "groves" and "high places" of apostate Israel). See R. J. Rushdoony,
The One and the Many: Studies in the Philosophy of Order and Ultimacy
(Tyler, TX: Thoburn Press, [1971] 1978), pp. 36-53; cf. Mircea Eliade, *The
Myth of the Eternal Return: or, Cosmos and History* (Princeton: Princeton
University Press, 1954, 1971), pp. 12-17.

the elders. The **New Song** is, as we saw on 5:9, the new liturgy necessitated and brought about by the new epoch in the history of redemption. And this liturgy, the exultant response of the redeemed, belongs to the Church alone (cf. 2:17): **No one could learn the Song except the one hundred and forty-four thousand who have been purchased from the Land,** redeemed as slaves from the tyranny of the Land Beast.

4-5 St. John gives further descriptions of the redeemed: **These are the ones who have not been defiled with women, for they are chaste men.** Several strands of Biblical imagery are involved in this statement. We must dispense with the idea that John is speaking of literal celibacy by calling them "chaste men" (or "virgins"), as Carrington pointed out: " 'Virgins' here is obviously a violent symbol for purity, just as 'eunuchs' in Matthew [19:12] is a violent symbol for celibacy; neither is meant to be taken literally. They are not men who have had no intercourse with women, but men *who have not defiled themselves with women*, which is quite a different idea, and is certainly not meant to describe marriage."[4] *Virgin* is frequently used in the Old Testament for Zion, the people of God (2 Kings 19:21; Isa. 23:12; 37:22; Jer. 14:17; 18:13; 31:4, 21; Lam. 1:15; 2:13). More particularly, the chastity here is a symbolic reference to the requirement of sexual abstinence by soldier-priests during holy war (cf. Ex. 19:15; Lev. 15:16; Deut. 20:7; 23:10-11; 1 Sam. 21:4-5; 2 Sam. 11:8-11). In addition, the context condemns the "fornication" committed by the nations, in connection with the worship of the Beast (v. 8-10). Fornication and harlotry, throughout the Bible, are potent metaphors for apostasy and idolatry (cf. Isa. 1:21; Jer. 2:20-3:11; Ezek. 16:15-43; Rev. 2:14, 20-22), while religious fidelity is called chastity (2 Cor. 11:2). The Lamb's army, gathered about Him on Mount Zion, is chaste, faithful to Him, and singlemindedly consecrated to the Holy War.

St. John tells us further that these soldiers **are the ones who follow the Lamb wherever He goes,** the term **follow** being a typical metaphor for the obedience of a disciple (Matt. 9:9; 10:38;

---

4. Philip Carrington, *The Meaning of the Revelation* (London: SPCK, 1931), p. 237.

16:24; Mark 9:38; 10:21, 28; Luke 9:23; John 8:12; 10:4-5, 27; 21:22). A precise statement of those who comprise this group, however, is given in the next phrase: **These have been purchased from among men as first fruits to God and to the Lamb**. The expression **first fruits** refers essentially to a sacrifice, the offering up of the first harvest of the land to the Lord, claimed by Him as His exclusive property (Ex. 22:29; 23:16, 19; Lev. 23:9-21; Deut. 18:4-5; Neh. 10:35-37; Prov. 3:9-10); these Christians have offered themselves up to God's service for Christ's sake. More than this, though, the New Testament uses *first fruits* to describe the Church of the Last Days, the "first-generation" Church (Rom. 16:5; 1 Cor. 16:15), especially the faithful Remnant from the twelve tribes of Israel (James 1:1, 18): "The confessors and martyrs of the apostolic Church, who overcame by reason of their testimony and the blood of the Lamb, are thus declared to be a *first fruits,* a choice selection out of the innumerable company of saints. The purpose of this Apocalypse was to give special encouragement to these virgin spirits."[5]

The characteristics of this group are strikingly similar to those of Israel when she first became God's Bride:

> I remember concerning you the fidelity of your *youth*,
> The love of your *betrothals*,
> Your *following after* Me in the wilderness,
> Through a land not sown.
> Israel was holy to the LORD,
> The *first of His harvest*. . . . (Jer. 2:2-3; cf. v. 32)

Finally, St. John says, **no lie was found in their mouth, for they are blameless**. It is the Dragon who is the deceiver, the false accuser, the father of the Lie (John 8:44; Rev. 12:9); God's people are characterized by truthfulness (Eph. 4:24-27). As St. Paul declared regarding the heathen, the basic Lie is idolatry: "Professing themselves to be wise, they became fools, and exchanged the glory of the incorruptible God for an image in the form of corruptible man and of birds and four-footed animals and crawling creatures. . . . For they exchanged the Truth of God for the Lie, and worshiped and served the creature rather than the

---

5. Terry, p. 404.

Creator, who is blessed forever" (Rom. 1:22-25). At root, the Lie is false prophecy (cf. Jer. 23), the rendering of honor and glory to the creature in place of the Creator. We have seen that the conflict between true and false prophecy, between the witnessing servant-prophets and the False Prophet, is central to the concerns of the Book of Revelation. In opposition to her enemies, the Church carries and proclaims the Truth. As the prophets had foretold, God raised up a faithful Remnant during the time of wrath and tribulation on Jerusalem:

> But I will leave among you
> A humble and lowly people,
> And they will take refuge in the name of the LORD.
> The Remnant of Israel will do no wrong
> And tell no lies,
> Nor will a deceitful tongue
> Be found in their mouths. . . . (Zeph. 3:12-13)

Commentators have often been vexed over the question of whether this picture is meant to represent the Church as seen on earth, or the Church as seen at rest, in heaven. It should be obvious that both aspects of the Church are in view here—especially since, as we have seen, the Church on earth *is* "in heaven" (12:12; 13:6). The famous statement in Hebrews 12:22-23 provides compelling evidence: "*You have come* to Mount Zion and to the City of the living God, the heavenly Jerusalem, and to myriads of angels in festal assembly, and to the Church of the firstborn who are enrolled in heaven. . . ." Milton Terry rightly remarks: "The heaven of our apocalyptist is the visional sphere of the glory and triumph of the Church, and no marked distinction is recognized between the saints on earth and those in heaven. They are conceived as one great company, and death is of no account to them. . . . Thus the entire passage serves to illustrate how saints 'dwelling in heavenly places in Christ Jesus' are all one in spirit and triumph, no matter what physical locality they may occupy."[6] For St. John, Zion "is neither in Jerusalem nor above the clouds; it is the whole assembly of the saints, living and departed."[7]

---

6. Terry, p. 404.
7. Carrington, p. 236.

In fact, Stuart Russell held that Hebrews 12:22-23 was based on this passage in Revelation: "The points of resemblance are so marked and so numerous that it cannot possibly be accidental. The scene is the same — Mount Zion; the *dramatis personae* are the same — 'the general assembly and church of the first-born, which are written in heaven,' corresponding with the hundred and forty and four thousand who bear the seal of God. In the epistle they are called 'the church of the *first-born*'; the vision explains the title — they are 'the *first-fruits* unto God and to the Lamb'; the first converts to the faith of Christ in the Land of Judea. In the epistle they are designated 'the spirits of just men made perfect'; in the vision they are 'virgins undefiled, in whose mouth was found no guile; for they are without fault before the throne of God.' Both in the vision and the epistle we find 'the innumerable company of angels' and 'the Lamb,' by whom redemption was achieved. In short, it is placed beyond all reasonable doubt that since the author of the Apocalypse cannot be supposed to have drawn his description from the epistle, the writer of the epistle must have derived his ideas and imagery from the Apocalypse."[8]

Thus, while the specific *application* of the 144,000 is to the Church of the first generation, *in principle* they are seen as the Church in her entirety (which, at the time St. John was writing, they precisely were). This is confirmed by a comparison of the parallels between this passage and the description of the redeemed in 5:6-11:

14:1-5	*5:6-11*
1 And I looked, and behold, the Lamb was standing. . . .	6 And I saw . . . a Lamb standing. . . .
3 . . . before the throne and before the four living creatures and the elders.	6 . . . between the throne (with the four living creatures) and the elders.

---

8. J. Stuart Russell, *The Parousia: A Critical Inquiry into the New Testament Doctrine of Our Lord's Second Coming* (Grand Rapids: Baker Book House, [1887] 1983), pp. 469f. It may be admitted that Russell has not proved his case "beyond all reasonable doubt." But he has clearly established at least a conceptual relationship (if not a dependent one) between Hebrews 12 and Revelation 14.

14:1-5	*5:6-11*
2 the Voice . . . was like harpists playing on their harps.	8 the twenty-four elders . . . having each one a harp.
3 And they sing a New Song.	9 And they sing a New Song.
4 These have been purchased from among men as firstfruits to God and to the Lamb.	9 [The Lamb] purchased us for God . . . from every tribe and tongue and people and nation.

The Gospel and the Poisoned Cups (14:6-13)

6 And I saw another angel flying in midheaven, having an eternal Gospel to preach to those who sit over the Land, and to every nation and tribe and tongue and people;

7 and he said with a loud Voice: Fear God, and give Him glory, because the hour of His judgment has come; and worship Him who made the heaven and the earth and the sea and springs of waters.

8 And another angel, a second one, followed, saying: Fallen, fallen is Babylon the Great! She has made all the nations drink of the wine of the heat of her fornication.

9 And another angel, a third one, followed them saying with a loud Voice: If anyone worships the Beast and his image, and receives a mark on his forehead or upon his hand,

10 he also will drink of the wine of the heat of God, which is mixed in full strength in the cup of His anger; and he will be tormented with fire and brimstone in the presence of the holy angels and in the presence of the Lamb.

11 And the smoke of their torment goes up forever and ever; and they have no rest day and night, those who worship the Beast and his image, and whoever receives the mark of the Beast.

12 Here is the perseverance of the saints who keep the commandments of God and the faith of Jesus.

13 And I heard a Voice from heaven, saying, Write: Blessed are the dead who die in the Lord from now on! Yes, says the Spirit, that they may rest from their labors; and their deeds follow with them.

6-7 The rest of this chapter is divided into seven sections — a vision of the glorified Christ, flanked on each side by three angels. St. John is about to make the transition between the

Trumpet-visions (proclamations of judgment) and the Chalice-visions (applications of judgment). Foreshadowing this change, the first three angels make special *proclamations* regarding the Lamb's victory, and the last three angels perform special *actions* to assist Him in implementing His conquest. As we would expect, these angelic proclamations and actions parallel the duties of the Church, particularly of her rulers and governors.

First, St. John sees **another angel flying in midheaven,** the sphere of the Eagle's cries of woe to the Land (8:13). But this angel preaches peace: The coming judgment is not an end in itself, but part of the proclamation of the **eternal Gospel.** Contrary to the speculations of several expositors, there is no reason to suppose that this is something other than the Gospel of which the New Testament constantly speaks. It is the message of the coming of the Kingdom, as John and Jesus had announced from the beginning: "Now in those days John the Baptizer came, preaching in the wilderness of Judea, saying, Repent, for the Kingdom of heaven is at hand" (Matt. 3:1-2); "And after John had been taken into custody, Jesus came into Galilee, preaching the Gospel of the Kingdom of God, and saying, The time is fulfilled, and the Kingdom of God is at hand; repent and believe in the Gospel" (Mark 1:14-15). And this is the Gospel preached by the angel, every element in it an aspect of the New Testament message: **Fear God** (Luke 1:50; 12:5; Acts 10:35), **and give Him glory** (Matt. 5:16; 9:8; 15:31), **because the hour of His judgment has come** (John 12:23, 31-32; 16:8-11); **and worship Him who made the heaven and the earth and the sea** (the world, Gen. 1) **and springs of waters** (Paradise, Gen. 2). All this bears striking resemblance to what is recorded of the apostolic Gospel (cf. Acts 14:15; 17:24-31).

The angel preaches this Gospel **to those who sit over the Land.** The usual expression for the Israelite apostates is *those who dwell in the Land* (3:10; 13:8, 12, 14; 17:2, 8). This time, attention is focused on the message to the authorities of Israel, those who are seated or enthroned over the Land (the verb is the same as that used in v. 14, of the Son of Man enthroned on the Cloud). The Gospel message commanded the rulers of Palestine to submit to the lordship of Christ, to honor Him, rather than Caesar, as God. But the rulers and authorities rejected Him, saying "We will not have this Man to rule over us!" (Luke 19:14).

361

The Lord Himself proclaimed the glory and judgment of God to the authorities of Israel (Matt. 26:64), and warned His disciples that they would preach an unpopular Gospel to the rulers: "But beware of men; for they will deliver you up to the courts, and scourge you in their synagogues; and you shall even be brought before governors and kings for My sake, as a testimony to them and to the Gentiles" (Matt. 10:17-18). Moreover, "this Gospel of the Kingdom shall be preached in the whole world for a witness to all the nations, and then the end shall come" (Matt. 24:14). And this was the Gospel order – to the Jews first, and then to the Gentiles (Acts 3:26; 11:18; 13:46-48; 28:23-29; Rom. 1:16; 2:9): The angel preaches to the rulers of Palestine, and then **to every nation and tribe and tongue and people.** Before the end came in A.D. 70, St. Paul tells us, the Gospel was indeed preached to all the world (Rom. 1:8; 10:18; Col. 1:5-6, 23). In spite of the attempts of the Dragon and his two Beasts to thwart the progress of the Gospel, the mission of the apostles, evangelists, martyrs, and confessors of the early Church was successful. The world was evangelized.[9]

8   Another angel, a second one follows, presenting another aspect of the early Church's proclamation: **Fallen, fallen is Babylon the Great!** This is the first mention of "Babylon" in Revelation, a proleptic reference foreshadowing the full exposition to come in later chapters (similar to the early reference to the Beast in 11:7). It is certainly possible, however, that St. John's readers understood his meaning immediately. In his first epistle, presumably written before the Revelation, St. Peter described the local church from which he wrote as "she who is in Babylon" (1 Pet. 5:13). Many have supposed this to be Rome, where St. Peter was (according to tradition) later martyred; but it is much more likely that the apostle was in Jerusalem when he wrote these words. Based on data from the New Testament itself, our natural assumption should be that "Babylon" was Jerusalem, since that was where he lived and exercised his ministry (Acts 8:1; 12:3; Gal. 1:18; 2:1-9; cf. 1 Pet. 4:17). Moreover, St. Peter's first epistle also sends greetings from Mark and Silas [Silvanus]

---

9. See David Chilton, *Paradise Restored: A Biblical Theology of Dominion* (Ft. Worth, TX: Dominion Press, 1985), pp. 90f.

(1 Pet. 5:12-13), both of whom lived in Jerusalem (Acts 12:12; 15:22-40).[10]

In any case, the primary thrust of the prophecy has been directed against Jerusalem; it has dealt with Rome only insofar as Rome was related to Israel. John gives us no indication that the subject has been changed. As we shall see in Chapters 17 and 18, the evidence that the prophetic **Babylon** was Jerusalem is nothing short of overwhelming. The term is used of the apostate city just as "Sodom" and "Egypt" were used in 11:8 to describe "the Great City . . . where the Lord was crucified" (note also that the same expression *the Great City* is used in 16:19 to describe "Babylon"). St. John's reason for applying the word to Jerusalem is that Jerusalem has become a Babylon, a replica of the proud, idolatrous, persecuting oppressor of God's people. Terry rightly observes that "as Jesus in Matthew 24:14 said that the end of this city and the pre-Messianic age would follow the preaching of the Gospel among the nations, so in this Apocalypse the proclamation of the fall of **Babylon the Great** follows immediately after that of the eternal Gospel."[11]

This great Harlot-City (17:1) **has made all the nations drink of the wine of the heat of her fornication** (an ironic contrast to the legitimate and blessed "wine of love" celebrated by Solomon, Cant. 1:2-4; 4:10; 5:1; 7:2, 9). The word usually translated *wrath* (as in KJV) basically means **heat** (NASV renders it as *passion*). In verse 10 the idea is definitely one of wrath, but here John is simply using the familiar Biblical picture of apostate Israel as a harlot, inflaming men's passions with the heat of lust. Israel has abused her privileged position as the divinely ordained "guide to the blind" and "light to those in darkness" (Rom. 2:19). The nations looked to her for instruction, yet ended up blaspheming the name of God because of her wickedness (Rom. 2:24). God had intended her to be Lady Wisdom, summoning all men to eat of her food, to drink of her wine, and to live in the way of understanding (Prov. 9:1-6). Instead, she had become Madam Folly, using stolen goods to tempt men into the depths of hell (Prov. 9:13-18). Like the Beast from the Land (the False

---

10. For further material on the meaning of St. Peter's reference to "Babylon," see J. Stuart Russell, *The Parousia*, pp. 346ff.

11. Terry, p. 407.

Prophet who speaks like the Dragon), Babylon's primary occupation is seducing others into **fornication**, the worship of false gods.

9-11   And another angel, a third one, followed them, with an appropriate message of doom for **anyone** who **worships the Beast and his image, or receives a mark in his forehead or upon his hand** (see above, on 13:15-18). The great offense of the Land Beast — apostate Israel's religious leadership — was the promotion and enforcement of the worship of the Beast (13:11-17). St. John is thus giving a clue to the great city's identity by repeating his words about the Land Beast immediately after his first statement about "Babylon." He is also reminding the Christians, especially the "angels," the Church officers, of their duty in proclaiming the whole counsel of God. They must preach the uncompromising message of the exclusive, all-encompassing lordship of Jesus Christ against all pretenders to the Throne. They must speak prophetically to their generation, sternly condemning the worship of the Beast, warning that those who drink of Babylon's heretical cup of State-worship **also will drink of the wine of the wrath of God, which is mixed in full strength** — literally, **mixed unmixed** (or, as one commentator delightfully translates it, **mixed neat**[12]) — **in the cup of His anger.** The warning is clear: You cannot drink one cup without the other.

Moses Stuart explains the imagery: "God is often said to give the *cup of inflammation* or *indignation* to nations whom He is about to destroy (e.g. Isa. 51:17; Lam. 4:21; Jer. 25:15-16; 49:12; 51:7; Ezek. 23:31-34; Job 21:20; Ps. 75:8). Persons intoxicated are unable to destroy or even resist those that assail them; so that to represent them as intoxicated in the way of punishment is to represent them as devoted to irremedial destruction. Or we may present the matter in another light. Criminals about to suffer were often through compassion of executioners or bystanders presented with a stupefying potion which would diminish their sensibility to pain, but which of course was the index or precursor of certain death. Thus in Mark 15:23 it is recorded

---

12. Carrington, pp. 248f. With the British sense of propriety, Carrington admits to a certain degree of trepidation in this rendering.

that Jesus refused to drink 'the wine mingled with myrrh,' which was proffered Him when He was about to be nailed to the cross. The holy Savior would not abate any portion of His agonies by the use of an intoxicating drink. But in whichever of these two ways the expression in our text is accounted for, the meaning remains substantially the same — for the drinking of such an intoxicating cup is the prelude to certain death."[13]

As we saw in verse 8, the word rendered **wrath** is really **heat**; those who desire Babylon's cup of "heat" will get a hotter drink than they bargained for, the cup of God's undiluted wrath. Those who fornicate with the Beast **will be tormented with fire and brimstone in the presence of the holy angels and in the presence of the Lamb. And the smoke of their torment goes up forever and ever.** The imagery of their permanent doom is taken from the utter destruction of Sodom and Gomorrah by fire and brimstone, when "the smoke of the land ascended like the smoke of a furnace" (Gen. 19:28; cf. its symbolic use in Isa. 34:9-10, describing the fall of Edom). Incredibly, Ms. Ford claims that "the allusion to the Lamb is embarrassing for the Christian."[14] Not nearly so embarrassing as the inane remarks of certain commentators! The real reason for the embarrassment some scholars feel at finding these Beast-worshipers destroyed with fire and brimstone in the presence of the Lamb is their own modern form of Marcionism, a heretical dichotomy between the "gentle and loving" Christ of the New Testament and the "wrathful" Deity of the Old Testament. Such a distinction is completely alien to the Bible. St. John, with more sense (and no apparent embarrassment), has simply been faithful to his Old Testament source, recasting it in New Testament terms: "Then *the* LORD *rained* on Sodom and Gomorrah brimstone and fire *from the* LORD out of heaven, and *He overthrew* those cities, and all the valley, and all the inhabitants of those cities, and what grew on the ground" (Gen. 19:24-25). Certainly, the text itself emphasizes that the torment of the Sodomites took place in the presence of the LORD (just as the Altar is before the Throne in the Tabernacle). And St. John is fully aware, even if

---

13. Moses Stuart, *A Commentary on the Apocalypse* (Andover: Allen, Morrill and Wardwell, 1845), pp. 297f.

14. J. Massyngberde Ford, *Revelation: Introduction, Translation, and Commentary* (Garden City: Doubleday and Co., 1975), p. 237.

his commentators are not, that the Lamb is the LORD.

There is a grim contrast here: The worshipers of the Beast, and those who receive his mark, **have no rest day and night** from their torments. The words are repeated from the description of the cherubim in 4:8, who **have no rest day and night**, eternally engaged in a sacrifice of praise.

12-13   Here is the perseverance of the saints. The patient confidence, hope, expectation, and faith of God's people is in the justice of His continual government over the earth and the certainty of His coming judgment (cf. 13:10). The saints are not to fret because of evildoers, for they will wither like the grass; we are to trust in the Lord and do good, to rest in the Lord and wait patiently for Him, and we eventually will inherit the earth (Ps. 37). The wicked persecutors will be destroyed, St. John tells his readers, and that shortly; with St. James he can say:

> Be patient, therefore, brethren, until the coming of the Lord. Behold, the farmer waits for the precious produce of the soil, being patient about it, until it gets the early and the late rains. You too be patient; strengthen your hearts, for the coming of the Lord is at hand. Do not complain, brethren, against one another, that you yourselves may not be judged; behold, the Judge is standing right at the door! (James 5:7-9)

The perseverance of the saints is necessarily bound up in the fact that they **keep the commandments of God and the faith of Jesus.** In opposition to all forms of creature worship, Christians keep the commandments; they keep the faith. The New Testament knows nothing of a lawless Christianity, or of a devotion that denies the objective content of "the faith which was once for all delivered to the saints" (Jude 3). Christianity demands obedient and faithful perseverance in the face of opposition. Naturally that has consequences, not all of them pleasant. St. John's readers knew that keeping the faith could well mean their death. For their sakes he records the next words of the **Voice from heaven, saying, Write: Blessed are the dead who die in the Lord from now on!** By the work of Christ, heaven has been opened to God's people. The *limbus patrum*, the afterlife abode of the Old Testament faithful (the "bosom of Abraham" of Luke 16:22), has been unlocked and its inhabitants freed (cf.

1 Pet. 3:19; 4:6). Death is now the entrance to communion in glory with Christ and the departed saints. Jesus Christ has delivered us from the ultimate fear of death; we can say, in the famous lines of John Donne's "Death Be Not Proud":

> One short sleepe past, wee wake eternally,
> And death shall be no more; death, thou shalt die.

The early Christians understood that death had been conquered by the resurrection of Christ; this theme recurs repeatedly in their writings. Again and again one is struck with the note of victory in the attitude of the martyrs as they faced death. St. Athanasius wrote of this fact in his famous defense of the Christian faith: "All the disciples of Christ despise death; they take the offensive against it and, instead of fearing it, by the sign of the cross and by faith in Christ trample on it as on something dead. Before the divine sojourn of the Saviour even the holiest of men were afraid of death, and mourned the dead as those who perish. But now that the Saviour has raised His body, death is no longer terrible, but all those who believe in Christ tread it underfoot as nothing, and prefer to die rather than to deny their faith in Christ, knowing full well that when they die they do not perish, but live indeed, and become incorruptible through the resurrection. But that devil who of old wickedly exulted in death, now that the pains of death are loosed, he alone it is who remains truly dead. There is proof of this too; for men who, before they believe in Christ, think death horrible and are afraid of it, once they are converted despise it so completely that they go eagerly to meet it, and themselves become witnesses of the Saviour's resurrection from it. Even children hasten thus to die, and not men only, but women train themselves by bodily discipline to meet it. So weak has death become that even women, who used to be taken in by it, mock it now as a dead thing robbed of all its strength. Death has become like a tyrant who has been completely conquered by the legitimate monarch; bound hand and foot as he now is, the passers-by jeer at him, hitting him and abusing him, no longer afraid of his cruelty and rage, because of the king who has conquered him. So has death been conquered and branded for what it is by the Saviour on the cross. It is bound hand and foot, all who are in Christ trample it as they pass and as witnesses to Him deride it, scoffing and saying, 'O Death, where is thy victory? O Grave, where is thy sting?' "[15]

Bishop Eusebius, the great Church historian, was an eyewitness of many early martyrdoms, and recorded what often took place when Christians were placed on trial: "We were witnesses to the most admirable ardor of mind, and the truly divine energy and alacrity of those that believed in the Christ of God. For as soon as the sentence was pronounced against the first, others rushed forward from other parts to the tribunal before the judge, confessing they were Christians, most indifferent to the dreadful and multiform tortures that awaited them, but declaring themselves fully and in the most undaunted manner on the religion which acknowledges only the one Supreme God. They received, indeed, the final sentence of death with gladness and exultation, so far as even to sing and send up hymns of praise and thanksgiving, until they breathed their last."[16]

The same cheerful hope is evident in St. Ignatius, Bishop of Antioch, the early martyr who was torn apart by wild beasts in Rome (around A.D. 107). In one of his famous letters, he pleaded with his Christian brethren in Rome not to seek his release, but to allow him to be "poured out a libation to God, while there is still an altar ready": "I write to all the churches, and I bid all men know, that of my own free will I die for God, unless ye should hinder me. I exhort you, be ye not an unseasonable kindness to me. Let me be given to the wild beasts, for through them I can attain unto God. I am God's wheat, and I am ground by the teeth of wild beasts that I may be found pure bread of Christ. Rather entice the wild beasts, that they may become my sepulchre and may leave no part of my body behind, so that I may not, when I am fallen asleep, be burdensome to anyone. Then shall I be truly a disciple of Jesus Christ, when the world shall not so much as see my body. Supplicate the Lord for me, that through these instruments I may be found a sacrifice to God. I do not enjoin you, as Peter and Paul did. They were

---

15. St. Athanasius, *On the Incarnation*, translated and edited by Sister Penelope Lawson, C.S.M.V. (New York: Macmillan Publishing Co., 1946, 1981), pp. 42f.

16. Eusebius, *Ecclesiastical History*, viii.ix.5, trans. Christian Frederick Cruse (Grand Rapids: Baker Book House, [n.d.] 1955), p. 328.

Apostles, I am a convict; they were free, but I am a slave to this very hour. Yet if I shall suffer, then am I a freed-man of Jesus Christ, and I shall rise free in Him. Now I am learning to put away every desire.

"From Syria even unto Rome I fight with wild beasts, by land and sea, by night and day, being bound amidst ten leopards, even a company of soldiers, who only wax worse when they are kindly treated. Howbeit through their wrongdoings I become more completely a disciple; yet am I not hereby justified. May I have joy of the beasts that have been prepared for me; and I pray that I may find them prompt; nay, I will entice them that they may devour me promptly, not as they have done to some, refusing to touch them through fear. Yea, though of themselves they should not be willing while I am ready, I myself will force them to it. Bear with me. I know what is expedient for me. Now I am beginning to be a disciple. May naught of things visible and things invisible envy me; that I may attain unto Jesus Christ. Come fire and cross and grapplings with wild beasts, cuttings and manglings, wrenching of bones, hacking of limbs, crushings of my whole body, come cruel tortures of the devil to assail me. Only be it mine to attain unto Jesus Christ.

"The farthest bounds of the universe shall profit me nothing, neither the kingdoms of this world. It is good for me to die for Jesus Christ rather than to reign over the farthest bounds of the earth. Him I seek, who died on our behalf; Him I desire, who rose again for our sake. The pangs of a new birth are upon me. Bear with me, brethren. Do not hinder me from living; do not desire my death. Bestow not on the world one who desireth to be God's, neither allure him with material things. Suffer me to receive the pure light. When I am come thither, then shall I be a man. Permit me to be an imitator of the passion of my God. If any man hath Him within himself, let him understand what I desire, and let him have fellow-feeling with me, for he knows the things which straiten me."[17]

Alexander Schmemann reminds us, however, that "Christianity is not reconciliation of death. It is the revelation of death,

---

17. St. Ignatius, *Epistle to the Romans*, iv-vi, ed. and trans. J. B. Lightfoot, *The Apostolic Fathers* (Grand Rapids: Baker Book House, [1891] 1956), pp. 76f. On the early Christian attitude toward martyrdom, see Louis Bouyer, *The Spirituality of the New Testament and the Fathers* (Minneapolis: The Seabury Press, 1963), pp. 190-210.

and it reveals death because it is the revelation of Life. Christ is this Life. And only if Christ is Life is death what Christianity proclaims it to be, namely the enemy to be destroyed, and not a 'mystery' to be explained."[18]

Yes, says the Spirit, that they may rest from their labors; and their deeds follow with them. Again there is a contrast with the fate of the Beast-worshipers, who will have *no rest day and night* from their torments. The persevering saints are encouraged to continue in faithfulness, for their eternal rest is coming and their works will be rewarded. Biblical perseverance is determined by the rewards of eternity, not by the tribulations of the moment. Biblical hope transcends the battle. This does not mean that the Bible commands an other-worldly neglect of the present life; but neither does it countenance a perspective that is only, or primarily, this-worldly. Our sinful tendency is to go in one direction rather than the other, but God calls us to be both this-worldly and other-worldly. Biblical faith calls us to work in this world for dominion with all our might (Gen. 1:28; Eccl. 9:10), and at the same time reminds us constantly of our eternal hope, our ultimate rest.

The Son of Man, the Harvest, and the Vintage (14:14-20)

14 And I looked, and behold, a white Cloud, and sitting on the Cloud One like the Son of Man, having a golden crown on His head, and a sharp sickle in His hand.

15 And another angel came out of the Temple, crying out with a loud Voice to Him who sat on the Cloud: Put in your sickle and reap, because the hour to reap has come, because the harvest of the Land is ripe.

16 And He who sat on the Cloud threw His sickle over the Land; and the Land was reaped.

17 And another angel came out of the Temple which is in heaven, and he also had a sharp sickle.

18 And another angel, the one who has power over the fire, came out from the altar; and he called with a loud shout to him who had the sharp sickle, saying: Send forth your sharp sickle, and gather the clusters from the vine of the Land, because her grapes are ripe.

19 And the angel threw out his sickle to the Land, and gathered

---

18. Alexander Schmemann, *For the Life of the World: Sacraments and Orthodoxy* (Crestwood, NY: St. Vladimir's Seminary Press, 1973), pp. 99f.

the vine of the Land, and threw it into the great winepress of the wrath of God.

20 And the winepress was trodden outside the City, and blood came out from the winepress, up to the horses' bridles, for sixteen hundred stadia.

14-16 These verses form the centerpiece of the whole section, verses 6-20. We have seen three angels making proclamations to the Land of Israel (v. 6-13); three more will appear, to perform symbolic actions over the Land (v. 15, 17-20); and in the center is **a white Cloud, and sitting on the Cloud One like a Son of Man, having a golden crown on His head.** This is the familiar Glory-Cloud, with which Christ was clothed in 10:1; now it is **white,** and not dark as on Sinai (Ex. 19:16-18; cf. Zeph. 1:14-15). St. John's reason for referring to the Cloud in this context can be discerned from his connecting it with the **Son of Man.** The reference is to Daniel's prophecy of the Coming of the Messiah to His inauguration as universal King—a vision which follows his prophecy of the Beasts with seven heads and ten horns:

> I kept looking in the night visions,
> And behold, with the Clouds of heaven
> One like a Son of Man was coming,
> And He came up to the Ancient of Days
> And was presented before Him.
> And to Him was given dominion,
> Glory, and a kingdom,
> That all the peoples, nations, and men of every language
> Might serve Him.
> His dominion is an everlasting dominion
> Which will not pass away;
> And His kingdom is one
> Which will not be destroyed. (Dan. 7:13-14)

St. John's point is clear: Let the Beasts do their worst—the Son of Man has ascended in the Clouds and received everlasting dominion over all peoples and nations! His Kingdom will never be overthrown; He will never have a successor. It is clear also that this is a vision, not of some future coming to earth, but of

371

the result of Christ's original Ascension in the Clouds to the Father — the definitive *Parousia*.[19] The Son of Man reigns now as the Second Adam, the King of kings. St. John does not show Christ *coming* in the Cloud, but in fact already *seated* on the Cloud, installed on His heavenly throne. Earlier (v. 6), he showed us the Israelite officials *sitting* over the Land; over against them sits the Lord Christ, enthroned on the Glory-Cloud (cf. Ps. 2:2-6).

The King has not only a crown on His head, but also **a sharp sickle in His hand. And another angel came out of the Temple, crying out with a loud voice to Him who sat on the Cloud: Put in your sickle and reap, because the hour to reap has come, because the harvest of the Land is ripe.** The first angel in this triad repeats what the first angel of the other triad had said (v. 7): **The hour has come!** This time, however, the emphasis falls not on judgment but on blessing, the gathering in of the elect. This, too, is connected with the work of the Son of Man in His Parousia, when He sends out His "angels," His apostolic messengers, to gather in the elect (Matt. 24:30-31). The word for *gather* is, literally, *to synagogue*; His meaning is that Israel, which refused to be synagogued under Christ (Matt. 23:37-38), will be replaced by the Church as the new Synagogue. The first churches were simply Christian "synagogues" (James 2:2), and looked forward to the soon-approaching Day when apostate Israel would be thoroughly disinherited, and the Church revealed as the true Synagogue, "gathered together" in the final, New Covenant form (2 Thess. 2:1). Jesus described the Kingdom of God as a great harvest (Mark 4:26-29), and told His disciples: "Behold, I say to you, lift up your eyes, and look on the fields, that they are white for harvest. Already he who reaps is receiving wages [cf. Rev. 14:13], and is gathering fruit [cf. Rev. 14:4] for life eternal; that he who sows and he who reaps may rejoice together" (John 4:35-36).

Accordingly, the first angel (representing his earthly counterparts) calls on the Son of Man to put in His **sickle** (mentioned seven times in this passage) and **reap,** praying in obedience to Christ's command: "The harvest is plentiful, but the workers are

---

19. See David Chilton, *Paradise Restored: A Biblical Theology of Dominion* (Ft. Worth, TX: Dominion Press, 1985), pp. 68ff., 102f.

few; therefore beseech the Lord of the harvest to send out workers into His harvest" (Matt. 9:37-38). From His Cloud-Throne the King answers the Church's prayer: Throwing His sickle over the earth, He sends out harvesters; the Land is reaped, and the fruit is brought into His Kingdom. The image of the sickle is connected in Scripture with Pentecost, celebrated after the grain had been harvested (Deut. 16:9), when the Spirit is poured out in salvation and blessing (Acts 2).

17-18 St. John returns to the theme of judgment, for the concomitant of the gathering of the Church is the excommunication of Israel. Genesis 21 records how the recognition of Isaac as the child of promise required the casting out of the bondwoman Hagar and her son, Ishmael; and St. Paul saw in this story an allegory of the rejection of old Israel and the recognition of the Church as the "heir of the promise." He spelled it out to the churches of Galatia, which had been infiltrated by Judaistic teachings: "It is written that Abraham had two sons, one by the bondwoman and one by the free woman. But the son by the bondwoman was born according to the flesh, and the son by the free woman through the promise. This is allegorically speaking: for these women are two covenants, one proceeding from Mount Sinai bearing children who are to be slaves; she is Hagar. Now this Hagar is Mount Sinai in Arabia, and corresponds to the present Jerusalem, for she is in slavery with her children. But the Jerusalem above is free; she is our Mother. . . . And you, brethren, like Isaac, are children of promise. But as at that time he who was born according to the flesh persecuted him who was born according to the Spirit, so it is now also. But what does the Scripture say? 'Cast out the bondwoman and her son, for the son of the bondwoman shall not be an heir with the son of the free woman.' So then, brethren, we are not children of a bondwoman, but of the free woman" (Gal. 4:22-31). Old Jerusalem, the capital city of apostate, persecuting Judaism, was cast out, excommunicated from the Covenant, even as the Church was being recognized as the legitimate heir of the promise. Christians, born of the Spirit, are the true children of the heavenly Jerusalem.

A second angel, therefore, comes **out of the Temple which is**

373

in heaven to assist in the harvest with his **sharp sickle**. At first this appears to be simply a continuation of the first harvest, but St. John makes a subtle shift, going all the way back to the beginning of this section of Revelation in order to draw on its imagery of wrath. Christ instructed his disciples to pray, not just for the conversion of Israel, but for its destruction as well; and thus in 6:9-11 we saw the saints gathered around the golden altar of incense, offering up their imprecatory prayers for vengeance. Shortly after that scene, at the beginning of the Trumpet visions, an angel took the censer of the saint's prayers, filled it with the fire of the altar, and threw it onto the Land; "and there followed peals of thunder and voices and flashes of lightning and an earthquake" (8:3-5). Now, at the close of the Trumpet section, St. John sees the same angel, **the one who has power**, not just "over fire," as most translations render it, but **over *the* fire**, the fire burning on the altar; and he comes specifically **from the altar** of the saints' prayers in order to render judgment, to bring about the historical response to the worship and the prayers of the Church. He too prays for a harvest—but this time it will be a harvest of the wicked, the "grapes of wrath" (Joel 3:13 similarly combines the images of harvest and vintage). So this third angel calls to the second angel, the one holding the sickle, and says: **Put in your sharp sickle, and gather the clusters from the vine of the Land, because her grapes are ripe**. God's Vineyard, Israel, is ripe for judgment.

> My well-beloved had a vineyard on a fertile hill.
> And He dug it all around, removed its stones,
> And planted it with a bright red grape.
> And He built a tower in the middle of it,
> And hewed out a wine press in it;
> Then He expected it to produce good grapes,
> But it produced only worthless ones.
> And now, O inhabitants of Jerusalem and men of Judah,
> Judge between Me and My vineyard.
> What more was there to do for My vineyard that I have not done
>   in it?
> Why, when I expected it to produce good grapes did it produce
>   worthless ones?
> So now let Me tell you what I am going to do to My vineyard:
> I will remove its hedge and it will be consumed;

I will break down its wall and it will become trampled ground.
And I will lay it waste;
It will not be pruned or hoed;
But briars and thorns will come up.
I will also charge the clouds to rain no rain on it.
For the Vineyard of the LORD of hosts is the House of Israel,
And the men of Judah His delightful plant.
Thus He looked for justice, but behold, bloodshed;
For righteousness, but behold, a cry of distress. (Isa. 5:1-7)

19-20   The Vineyard is judged: **The angel threw his sickle to the Land, and gathered the vine of the Land, and threw it into the great wine press of the wrath of God** to produce the substance that will be poured from the chalices in Chapter 16. The repeated references to **the Land** (six times in verses 15-19), combined with the imagery of **the vine of the Land**, emphasize that this is a judgment on the Land of Israel. Reviewing the extensive Biblical background of the vineyard idea, Carrington concludes: "It does not seem possible to suppose that St. John could have intended to apply these words to any other country than Israel, or to any other city than Jerusalem. They echo the words of St. John the Baptist, with which the whole Christian prophetic movement began, *Even now is the axe laid to the root of the tree*. What is contingent in the Baptist is absolute in Revelation. Israel is rejected."[20]

The imagery of this passage is based on Isaiah's prophecy of the destruction of Edom, where God is described as a man crushing grapes in a wine press. He explains why His robe is stained with "juice":

I have trodden the wine trough alone,
And from the peoples there was no man with Me.
I also trod them in My anger,
And trampled them in My wrath;
And their juice is sprinkled on My garments,
And I stained all My raiment.
For the Day of Vengeance was in My heart,
And My year of redemption has come.
And I looked, and there was no one to help,

---

20. Carrington, p. 256. On Christ's use of vineyard imagery in His parables, see Chilton, *Paradise Restored*, pp. 76-82.

And I was astonished and there was no one to uphold;
So My own arm brought salvation to Me,
And My wrath upheld Me.
And I trod down the peoples in My anger,
And made them drunk in My wrath,
And I brought down their juice to the earth. (Isa. 63:1-6)

And the wine press was trodden outside the City, and blood came out from the wine press, up to the horses' bridles, for a distance of sixteen hundred stadia. It is unfortunate that translations such as the New American Standard Version, due to literalist presuppositions, render this measurement into a modern American measurement: *two hundred miles.* While that translation does provide a good idea of the magnitude of the bloodshed, it entirely misses the important symbolic figure of **sixteen hundred**, a number which again emphasizes the Land: *four* squared (the Land), times *ten* squared (largeness). Sixteen hundred stadia is slightly more than the length of Palestine: The whole Land of Israel is thus represented as overflowing with blood in the coming nationwide judgment. The streams of running blood become a great Red Sea, reaching **up to the horses' bridles** in a recapitulation of the overthrow of Pharaoh's horses and chariots (Ex. 14:23, 28; 15:19; cf. the extensive use of Exodus imagery in the following chapter). Zechariah had foretold of a day when all things throughout the Land would be holy, when the Land would be filled with pure worshipers, when *HOLY TO THE LORD* would be inscribed even "on the bells of the horses" of Israel (Zech. 14:20-21). But God had raised up on Mount Zion a new, pure Israel, in whom the promises would be fulfilled. Old Israel had become apostate and unclean, her horses swimming in blood.

The bloodshed covers the Land, yet it is **outside the City.** The historical fulfillment of this was, from one perspective, when "Galilee was all over filled with fire and blood," as the troops of Vespasian and Titus overran the country. The whole Land, except for Jerusalem, was covered with death and devastation.[21] Theologically, however, the fulfillment of this text must also be related to the sacrifice of Christ, for that was the defini-

---

21. See Josephus, *The Jewish War*, Book iii.

tive bloodshedding "outside the City." In the Old Testament sacrificial system, "the bodies of those animals whose blood is brought into the holy place by the high priest as an offering for sin, are burned outside the camp. Therefore Jesus also, that He might sanctify the people through His own blood, suffered outside the gate. Hence, let us go to Him outside the camp, bearing His reproach. For here we do not have a lasting City, but we are seeking the City which is to come" (Heb. 13:11-14). Outside the City, therefore, was the place of judgment, where the bodies of sacrificed animals were disposed of; and it was *the* Place of Judgment, where Christ's blood was shed by rebellious Israel. In this layered imagery, then, the blood flowing outside the City belongs to Christ, sacrificed outside the camp; and it is to be the blood of apostate Israel as well, cast out and excommunicated from "the Jerusalem above" and disinherited by the Father. Here is the doctrine of Limited Atonement, and with a vengeance: Blood will flow — if the blood is not Christ's, shed on our behalf, it will be ours! "In A.D. 70 the Vine of Israel is cut down and trampled in the Winepress; but this destruction is the culmination of a process which has lasted over forty years; it began Outside the City, when one whom they despised and rejected trod the Winepress alone, and of the people there was none with Him. It was in that moment that Jerusalem fell."[22]

---

22. Carrington, p. 261.

Part Five

COVENANT SUCCESSION AND
CONTINUITY: THE SEVEN CHALICES
(Revelation 15-22)

Introduction

As we have seen, the final section of Revelation corresponds
to Christ's letter to the angel of the church at Thyatira, which
speaks of His judgment on "Jezebel," the False Bride; and, like
the letter to the angel of the church at Laodicea, it speaks
against the economically wealthy yet spiritually wretched church
(Judaism), which Christ is about to spit out of His mouth. This
section also corresponds to the last of the four living creatures,
the man-cherub, and (in St. John's order) the last quarter of the
Zodiac, ruled by the constellation of Aquarius the Water-
Pourer; accordingly, the symbol of judgment in this section is
that of the angels pouring out God's wrath from their Chalices.

We have also noted that the last division in Revelation corresponds to the fifth and final part of the covenantal treaty structure: the succession arrangements. This deals with the continuity
of the Covenant, the disinheritance of illegitimate members,
and the inheritance of those who are faithful to their sworn obligations (cf. Deut. 31-34).[1] Moses begins this section of Deuteronomy with orders for extending the Covenant into the future.
He charges the people (31:1-6), Joshua (31:7-8), and the priests
(31:9-13) with the duty of following the Covenant program and

---

1. See Meredith G. Kline, *Treaty of the Great King: The Covenant Structure
of Deuteronomy* (Grand Rapids: William B. Eerdmans Publishing Co., 1963),
pp. 135-49; cf. Ray R. Sutton, *That You May Prosper: Dominion By Covenant* (Tyler, TX: Institute for Christian Economics, 1987).

379

ensuring its transmission to the coming generations. Then (31:14-15) God appears in the Glory-Cloud at the doorway of the Tabernacle to meet with Moses and Joshua, and instructs them to teach a Song of Witness to the children of Israel. He says to Moses: "Behold, you are about to lie down with your fathers; and this people will arise and play the harlot with the strange gods of the Land, into the midst of which they are going, and will forsake Me and break My Covenant which I have made with them. Then My anger will be kindled against them in that day, and I will forsake them and hide My face from them, and they shall be consumed, and many evils and troubles shall come upon them. . . . Now therefore, write this Song for yourselves, and teach it to the sons of Israel; put it in their mouths, in order that this Song may be a witness for Me against the sons of Israel. . . . Then it shall come about, when many evils and troubles have come upon them, that this Song will testify before them as a witness" (31:16-21).

As Kline shows, the Song of Witness (Deut. 32) is "Yahweh's covenant lawsuit against his ungrateful and unfaithful people, prophetically delivered through Moses, 'the man of God' (see Deut. 33:1, 'the man of X' being a title for the messengers of great kings)."[2] A model Covenant Lawsuit, the Song itself is structured according to the standard form of the treaty document. Thus we have the familiar outline:

    I. *Preamble* (32:1-4)
    II. *Historical Prologue* (32:5-14)
    III. *Record of Rebellion Against Covenant Stipulations* (32:15-18)
    IV. *Sanctions:*
        A. *Curses Against Covenant-Breakers* (32:19-25)
        B. *Blessings on the Remnant Through Redemptive Judgment* (32:26-43)
    V. *Succession Arrangements* (32:44-34:12)[3]

Both Moses and Joshua taught the Song of Witness to the people (32:44); it might well be called "the Song of Moses and Joshua." Accordingly, in the corresponding fifth section of Rev-

---

2. Kline, *Treaty of the Great King*, p. 139.
3. See ibid., pp. 140-49; I have slightly amended Kline's outline.

elation, St. John begins with a manifestation of God's glory at "the Sanctuary of the Tabernacle of the Testimony," where God gives a covenantal commission to seven angel-priests; as choral accompaniment to all this the Remnant sings "the Song of Moses the bond-servant of God and the Song of the Lamb." The Lamb, as all St. John's readers know, is *Jesus*, the Greek form of the Hebrew name *Joshua*; the Song is therefore "the Song of Moses and (the Greater) Joshua."

In Revelation 15 and 16 the Tabernacle is opened and the priests are sent forth to pour out their Chalice-judgments upon Israel as punishment for her harlotry—the chief crime that called forth the original Song of Witness (Deut. 31:16). Here we should note one important element that ties Chapters 15-22 together as a literary unit. After the seven angels have poured out their Chalices of wrath, one of the same seven angels comes to show St. John "the judgment of the Great Harlot" (17:1). Later, in the final vision of the book, another of these Chalice-angels shows St. John the Harlot's opposite number: "the Bride, the Wife of the Lamb" (21:9). Clearly, the visions relating to both the Harlot and the Bride are extensions of the Seven Chalices section of the prophecy.

As God had declared in Moses' Song of Witness, He is the Jealous Husband, betrayed by the infidelity of this "perverse generation" (Deut. 32:5, 16, 20-21; cf. Matt. 17:17; Acts 2:40). The punishment He sends will be that already threatened in Deuteronomy 28:49-57: A fearful enemy nation will arise to destroy Israel, bringing vengeance upon God's apostate "wife" (Deut. 32:21-25).[4] This theme is taken up and enlarged in Revelation 17-18, where the Harlot Bride is destroyed for her unfaithfulness. Yet the Remnant is saved; and, as we have seen, this "remnant" is ultimately larger than its original, being transformed into a great multitude that no one can count, vastly outnumbering the old Israel (Rev. 7). God guarantees the covenantal succession by establishing the transcendent New Covenant. Distinguishing His true heirs, He incorporates them into the Bride of the Lamb, the New Jerusalem; and Bride and

---

4. Nevertheless, the nation used as the rod of God's anger will itself be smashed for its own disobedience, and the Remnant of Israel will be saved (Deut. 32:26-43; cf. Isa. 10:5-34; Rev. 17:16-17; 19:17-21).

Bridegroom meet in the sacramental meal, the Marriage Supper of the Lamb (Rev. 19:1-10).

After singing the Song of Witness, Moses outlines the future of the twelve tribes in a final Testament (Deut. 33; cf. Rev. 21:12), which proclaims the Coming of the Lord in salvation (Deut. 33:2), and exults in the priestly and regal dominion God will provide for His people:

> There is none like the God of Jeshurun,
> Who rides the heavens to your help,
> And through the skies in His majesty.
> The eternal God is a dwelling place,
> And underneath are the everlasting arms;
> And He drove out the enemy from before you,
> And said, "Destroy!"
> So Israel dwells in security,
> The fountain of Jacob secluded,
> In a land of grain and new wine;
> His heavens also drop down dew.
> Blessed are you, O Israel;
> Who is like you, a people saved by the Lord,
> Who is the shield of your help,
> And the sword of your majesty!
> So your enemies shall cringe before you,
> And you shall tread upon their high places.
> (Deut. 33:26-29; cf. Rev. 19:11-22:5)

Finally, the Lord takes Moses to the top of Mount Nebo, showing him the Promised Land, but informing him again that he will not be able to lead the people into it; his place must be taken by Joshua the Conqueror (Deut. 34:1-9). Nevertheless, Moses' status remains unique, for "since then no prophet has risen in Israel like Moses, *whom the Lord knew face to face*" (Deut. 34:10). St. John's message in Revelation, however, is that (as Moses wished), all the Lord's people are prophets (Num. 11:29). Christians, as "bond-servants" like Moses (Rev. 15:3; 19:2, 5), are not inferior even to angels in their sanctuary privileges (19:10), but have complete access to God, exercising the same outspoken freedom of speech (cf. Heb. 10:19) that he enjoyed. Before God's heavenly Throne "His bond-servants shall serve Him, *and they shall see His face*, and His name shall be on their foreheads" (Rev. 22:4).

SEVEN LAST PLAGUES

The Song of Victory (15:1-4)

1 And I saw another sign in heaven, great and marvelous, seven angels who had seven plagues, which are the last, because in them the wrath of God is finished.

2 And I saw, as it were, a Sea of glass mixed with fire, and those who had come off victorious from the Beast and from his image and from the number of his name, standing on the Sea of glass, holding harps of God.

3 And they sing the song of Moses the bond-servant of God and the song of the Lamb, saying:
Great and marvelous are Thy works,
O Lord God, the Almighty;
Righteous and true are Thy ways,
Thou King of the nations.

4 Who will not fear Thee, O Lord, and glorify Thy name?
For Thou alone art holy;
For all the nations will come and worship before Thee,
For Thy righteous acts have been revealed.

1 St. John now tells us of **another sign in heaven, great and marvelous**. Twice before he has shown us a *great sign in heaven*: the Woman clothed with the sun (12:1), and the great red Dragon (12:3). As Farrer says, it is "as though everything in 12-14 had been the working out of that mighty conflict, and the next act were now to begin."[1] This new sign initiates the climax of the book: **seven plagues, which are the last, because in them the wrath of God is finished.** There is no reason to assume that these must be the "last" plagues in an ultimate, absolute, and

---

1. Austin Farrer, *The Revelation of St. John the Divine* (Oxford: At the Clarendon Press, 1964), p. 169.

universal sense; rather, in terms of the specifically limited purpose and scope of the Book of Revelation, they comprise the final outpouring of God's wrath, His great cosmic Judgment against Jerusalem, abolishing the Old Covenant world-order once and for all. Like that of the Trumpets, this series of judgments is to be performed by **seven angels** (as we shall see in the following chapter, there are several parallels between the proclamations sounded by the Trumpets and the libations poured from the Chalices). This opening statement is more or less the superscription to the rest of the book, and is explained in the following verses.

2 The vision begins: St. John sees, **as it were, a Sea of glass,** the crystal Sea before God's Throne (4:6), corresponding to the sapphire "pavement" seen by Moses on the Holy Mountain (Ex. 24:10), the blue crystal "firmament" through which Ezekiel passed in his ascension in the Glory-Cloud (Ezek. 1:26), and the brazen Sea (the Laver) in the Temple (1 Kings 7:23-26). In this vision, however, the Sea is no longer blue, but *red*: The glass is **mixed with fire.** The imagery ties this vision to the last scene in Chapter 14, that of the great river of blood running the whole length of the Land, a truly *Red* Sea, through which the righteous have been delivered, but in which their enemies were destroyed. Now St. John pictures the saints rejoicing at the water's edge like Moses and the Israelites after the original Red Sea crossing (Ex. 14:30-31; 15:1-21), **victorious** over the monster from the deep; literally, they are **those overcoming** or **the conquerors**, "for it is the abiding character of 'conqueror' on which emphasis is laid, and not the fact of conquest."[2] The description of their conquest is threefold: They have come off victorious **from the Beast and from his image and from the number of his name.**

At the seashore, on the lip of the font, the conquerors offer praise: **Standing on the Sea of glass, holding harps of God,** they comprise the new priestly Temple choir that stands at the cleansing Laver, by which they were sanctified. St. Paul described the Red Sea deliverance as a "baptism" of God's people (1 Cor. 10:1-2), and the Tribulation was indeed the Church's baptism of

---

2. Henry Barclay Swete, *Commentary on Revelation* (Grand Rapids: Kregel Publications, [1911] 1977), p. 194.

fire: "So the great glass bowl of the sea is seen 'filled with a fiery mixture.' What the Israelites are brought through to salvation, their persecutors undergo to their destruction; Pharaoh and his hosts perish in the returning waters. And so we know that the baptism of fire must fall on the people of Antichrist; the vision of the bowls [Chalices] will show us how."[3]

A further interesting aspect of the Laver image comes from the Chronicler's story of the dedication of the Temple by King Solomon: "Then he stood before the altar of the LORD in the presence of all the assembly of Israel and spread out his hands. Now Solomon had made a bronze *laver*,[4] five cubits long, five cubits wide, and three cubits high, and had set it in the midst of the court; and he stood on it, knelt on his knees in the presence of all the assembly of Israel, and spread out his hands toward heaven" to perform the prayer of dedication (2 Chron. 6:12-13). This was not *the* great Laver in the southeast corner of the Temple (the dimensions of which are recorded in 2 Chron. 4:2-5), but one of several bronze lavers constructed by Solomon (cf. 2 Chron. 4:6, 14). Solomon stood on this "sea" before the Altar and offered his supplication, thanking God for His mighty works, invoking His righteous judgments, and entreating Him for the conversion of all nations (2 Chron. 6:14-42; cf. Rev. 15:3-4). Immediately afterward, we read: "When Solomon had finished praying, fire came down from heaven and consumed the burnt offering and the sacrifices; and the Glory of the LORD filled the House. And the priests could not enter into the House of the LORD, because the Glory of the LORD filled the LORD's House" (2 Chron. 7:1-2). Similarly, at the end of the prayer of the saints standing on the Sea, the seven angels are given chalices filled with fiery wrath, which will fall upon the Land to consume apostate Israel as a whole burnt sacrifice; the Glory fills the Temple, and no one is able to enter until the sacrifice is consumed (Rev. 15:5-8).

Another passage parallel to this is Zechariah 12, which pictures Jerusalem as a cup of drunkenness to the nations (Zech. 12:2; cf. Rev. 14:8-10), a *laver of fire* that will consume the heathen (Zech. 12:6; Rev. 15:2). The irony of Revelation, as we

---

3. Farrer, pp. 170f.
4. Heb. *kiyyor*, the standard word for laver: e.g. Ex. 30:18, 28; 40:7, 11, 30.

have seen repeatedly, is that first-century Israel herself has taken the place of the heathen nations in the prophecies: She is consumed in the fiery laver—the Lake of Fire—while the Church, having passed through the holocaust, inherits salvation.

3 We saw in the Introduction to Part Five that **the Song of Moses . . . and the Song of the Lamb** refers to the Song of Witness which Moses and Joshua (= Jesus, the Lamb) taught to the children of Israel at the border of the Promised Land (Deut. 31-32). The imagery, however, is taken from Exodus 15, which records Moses' Song of triumph at the defeat of Pharaoh and his army in the Red Sea (two other Biblical paraphrases of Moses' Song in Exodus are Isaiah 12 and Habakkuk 3). It is important to note that both Songs of Moses are firmly rooted in history: Both proclaim that the salvation God provides is His victory in this world, over the heathen of this world. These saints through Christ are *overcomers*, in time and on earth. As R. J. Rushdoony says, "The earth is the Lord's, and the area of His victory. The issue of the kingdom's battle will be no more a flight from history than was the incarnation and the atonement. God the Son did not enter history in order to surrender it. He came to redeem His elect, assert His crown rights, make manifest the implications of His victory, and then to re-create all things in terms of His sovereign will."[5]

St. John's text of the Song of Moses does not actually quote from either Exodus 15 or Deuteronomy 32, although some of its phrasing contains faint echoes of the latter; however, as Farrer observes, "it is characteristic of St. John that he is content with having made the references; the beautiful psalm he puts into the mouths of the saints is a cento of phrases from all over the psalter and elsewhere."[6] Edersheim comments on the relationship of this scene to the Sabbath services in the Temple: "It is the Sabbath of the Church; and as on the Sabbath, besides the psalm for the day [Ps. 92] at the ordinary sacrifice, they sang at the additional Sabbatic sacrifice [Num. 28:9-10], in the morning, the Song of Moses, in Deuteronomy 32, and in the evening that in

---

5. Rousas John Rushdoony, *Thy Kingdom Come: Studies in Daniel and Revelation* (Tyler, TX: Thoburn Press, [1970] 1978), p. 93.
6. Farrer, p. 171.

Exodus 15, so the victorious Church celebrates her true Sabbath of rest by singing this same 'Song of Moses and of the Lamb,' only in language that expresses the fullest meaning of the Sabbath songs in the Temple."[7]

It is probably impossible to track down the Song's Old Testament allusions completely, but I have at least noted some of them: **Great and marvelous are Thy works, O Lord God, the Almighty** (Ex. 34:10; Deut. 32:3-4; 1 Chron. 16:8-12; Ps. 92:5; 111:2; 139:14; Isa. 47:4; Jer. 10:16; Amos 4:13; cf. Rev. 1:8); St. John makes it clear that the saints are not merely making a general statement of fact, but instead are specifically referring to the "great and marvelous" *final judgments* in which "the wrath of God is finished" (15:1). **Righteous and true are Thy ways** (Deut. 32:4; Ps. 145:17; Hos. 14:9); again, God is said to be "righteous and true" with special reference to His saving judgments, delivering the Church and destroying His enemies (cf. 16:7). "In seasons of tribulation on earth, when the worldly power appears to triumph over the church, she has often been led to doubt the greatness of God's works, the justice and truth of His ways; to doubt whether He were really the king of the heathen. Now this doubt is put to shame; it is dispelled by deeds; the clouds, which veiled the glory of God from her eyes, are made entirely to vanish."[8] **Thou King of the nations** (Ps. 22:28; 47:2, 7-8; 82:8; cf. 1 Tim. 1:17; 6:15; Rev. 1:5; 19:16); as Ruler of all nations He moves the armies of earth to fulfill His purposes in judgment; He smashes them for their rebellion; and He brings them to repentance.

4 Who will not fear Thee, O Lord, and glorify Thy name? (Ex. 15:14-16; Jer. 10:6-7; cf. Rev. 14:7); this means, in language we are more familiar with: Who will not be converted? Who will not serve God, worship Him, and obey Him? The clear implication (to be made explicit in the next sentence) is that the overwhelming majority of all men will come into the salvation that God has provided in Jesus Christ. This is the great hope of the

---

7. Alfred Edersheim, *The Temple: Its Ministry and Services As They Were at the Time of Jesus Christ* (Grand Rapids: William B. Eerdmans Publishing Co., 1980), p. 76.

8. E. W. Hengstenberg, *The Revelation of St. John*, two vols. (Cherry Hill, NJ: Mack Publishing Co., [1851] 1972), Vol. 2, pp. 146f.

Old Covenant fathers, as numerous passages abundantly attest. **For Thou alone art holy** (Ex. 15:11; 1 Sam. 2:2; Ps. 99:3, 5, 9; Isa. 6:3; 57:5, 15; Hos. 11:9; cf. Matt. 19:17; 1 Tim. 6:16). God's "holiness" in Scripture often refers not so much to His ethical qualities as to His unique majesty, His absolute transcendence and "otherness." Yet this very "unapproachableness" is here stated to be the precise reason for His immanence, His nearness, His accessibility to all peoples. The doctrine is declared positively: **For all the nations will come and worship before Thee, for Thy righteous acts have been revealed** (1 Chron. 16:28-31; Ps. 2:8; 22:27; 65:2; 66:4; 67:1-7; 86:8-9; 117:1; Isa. 26:9; 66:23; Jer. 16:19); the conversion of all nations is both the ultimate goal and inevitable result of God's judgments. The fall of Israel, St. John is telling the Church, will bring about the salvation of the world (and St. Paul extended the logic: Israel's fall must therefore eventually produce her own restoration to the covenant; Rom. 11:11-12, 15, 23-32).

The Sanctuary Is Opened (15:5-8)

5 After these things I looked, and the Temple of the Tabernacle of the Testimony in heaven was opened,

6 and the seven angels who had the seven plagues came out of the Temple. They were clothed in linen, clean and bright, and girded around their breasts with golden girdles.

7 And one of the four living creatures gave to the seven angels seven golden bowls full of the wrath of God, who lives forever and ever.

8 And the Temple was filled with smoke from the Glory of God and from His power; and no one was able to enter the Temple until the seven plagues of the seven angels were finished.

5 Now the scene changes, and we are shown **the Temple of the Tabernacle of the Testimony in heaven**, the "*true* Tabernacle" (Heb. 8:2), the divine Pattern, of which the Tabernacle on earth was a "copy and shadow" (Heb. 8:5; 9:11-12, 23-24; 10:1; Ex. 25:9, 40; 26:30; Num. 8:4; Acts 7:44). St. John is very careful to use correct technical expressions for his imagery here, based on the Old Covenant order. The basic treaty document of the Covenant was the Decalogue; this was often called **the Testimony,** emphasizing its legal character as the record of the Covenant oath (Ex. 16:34; 25:16, 21-22; 31:18; 32:15; cf. Ps. 19:7; Isa. 8:16, 20). The Tabernacle, in which the Testimony was kept, was therefore called the **Tabernacle of the Testimony** (Ex. 38:21; Num. 1:50, 53; 9:15; 10:11; Acts 7:44). As we have seen, in Revelation the **Temple** (Greek *naos*) is the **Sanctuary**, or Holy Place (cf. 3:12; 7:15; 11:1-2, 19; 14:15, 17).

A major aspect of St. John's message in Revelation is the coming of the New Covenant. In his theology (as in the rest of the New Testament), the Church is the *naos*, the Temple. The writer to the Hebrews shows that the Mosaic Tabernacle was both a copy of the heavenly Original and a foreshadowing of the Church in the New Covenant (Heb. 8:5; 10:1); St. John draws the conclusion, showing that these two, the heavenly Pattern and the final form, coalesce in the New Covenant age: The Church tabernacles in heaven. And, if the **Temple** is the Church, the **Testimony** is the New Covenant, the *Testimony of Jesus* (1:2, 9; 6:9; 12:11, 17; 19:10; 20:4).

6-7 The seven angels who had the seven plagues came out of the Temple, in order to apply the Curses proclaimed by the Trumpets. As priests of the New Covenant, these angel-ministers are **clothed in linen, clean and bright, and girded around their breasts with golden girdles,** in the image and likeness of their Lord (1:13; cf. Ex. 28:26-29, 39-43; Lev. 16:4).

And one of the four living creatures gave to the seven angels seven golden Chalices; presumably, this cherub is the one with the man's face (4:7), since the other three have already appeared on the stage of the drama, and since St. John is proceeding systematically through the quarters of the Zodiac. We saw that he began in the Spring (Easter), with the sign of Taurus governing the Preamble and the Seven Letters; moved through Summer with Leo ruling the Seven Seals; continued through Autumn under Scorpio (the Eagle/Scorpion) and the Seven Trumpets; and now he arrives in Winter, with Aquarius, the Waterer, supervising the outpouring of **the wrath of God** from the Seven Chalices.

I have called these seven containers **Chalices** (rather than *vials* [KJV] or *bowls* [NASV]) to emphasize their character as a "negative sacrament." From one perspective, the substance in the Chalices (God's wrath, which is "hot," cf. 14:10) seems to be *fire*, and several commentators have therefore seen the containers as incense-bowls (5:8; cf. 8:3-5). Yet the wicked are condemned in 14:10 to "drink of the *wine* of the wrath of God, which is mixed in full strength in the cup of His anger"; and, when the plagues are poured out, the "Angel of the waters" exults in the appropriateness of God's justice: "For they poured out the blood of saints and prophets, and Thou hast given them *blood* to drink" (16:6). A few verses later, St. John returns to the image of "the cup of the *wine* of His fierce wrath" (16:19). What is being modeled in heaven for the Church's instruction on earth is the final excommunication of apostate Israel, when the Communion of the Body and Blood of the Lord is at long last denied to her. The angel-bishops, entrusted with the Sacramental sanctions of the covenant, are sent from the heavenly Temple itself, and from the Throne of God, to pour out upon her the Blood of the Covenant. Jesus warned the rebels of Israel that he would send His martyrs to them to be killed, "so that *upon you may fall all the righteous blood* shed on earth, from the *blood* of righteous Abel to the *blood* of Zechariah, the son of Berechiah, whom you murdered between the Temple and the Altar. Truly I say to you, all these things shall come upon this generation" (Matt. 23:35-36). Drinking Blood is inescapable: Either the ministers of the New Covenant will serve it to us in the Eucharist, or they will pour it out of their Chalices upon our heads.

Austin Farrer explains some of the Old Covenant imagery behind the symbol of the Chalices. "The 'bowls,' *phialae*, are libation-bowls. Now the libation, or drink-offering, was poured at the daily sacrifice just after the trumpets had begun to sound, so that by placing bowls in sequence to trumpets St. John maintains the sequence of ritual action that began with the slaughtered Lamb, continued in the incense-offering and passed into the trumpet-blasts. Because the drink-offering had such a position, it was the last ritual act, completing the service of the altar, and was proverbial in that connexion (Phil. 2:17). The drink-offering, as St. Paul implies, was poured upon the slaughtered victim, burning in the fire. Because there is no bloody sacrifice in heaven, the angels pour their libations upon the terrible holocaust of vengeance which divine justice makes on earth."[9]

---

9. Farrer, p. 174.

We should be reminded in this context of the purification offering, designed to atone for the defilement of a *place*, so that God could continue to dwell with His people (cf. comments on 9:13). If the whole nation sinned, so that the entire Land was defiled, the priests were required to perform special rites of purification: The blood of the sacrifice was sprinkled seven times toward the veil before the Holy of Holies, then smeared on the four horns of the altar, and the remainder poured out at the foot of the altar (Lev. 4:13-21).[10] But in the outpoured plagues of the Chalice-judgments, this is reversed, as Philip Carrington points out: "This Blood, instead of bringing reconciliation, brings rejection and vengeance. Instead of being sprinkled seven times towards the veil, it is poured seven times on the Land. Instead of the appearance of the High Priest with the blood of reconciliation, we have Seven Angels with the Blood of Vengeance."[11]

Why is the blood in Revelation no longer sprinkled toward the veil? Because Jesus' blood has already been offered, and Israel has rejected it. As the writer to the Hebrews warned just before the Holocaust: "If we go on sinning wilfully after receiving the knowledge of the truth, *there no longer remains a sacrifice for sins*, but a certain terrifying expectation of judgment, and the fury of a fire that will consume the adversaries. Anyone who has set aside the Law of Moses dies without mercy on the testimony of two or three witnesses. How much severer punishment do you think he will deserve who has trampled under foot the Son of God, and has regarded as unclean the blood of the covenant by which he was sanctified, and has insulted the Spirit of grace? For we know Him who said: Vengeance is Mine, I will repay! And again: The Lord will judge His people! It is a terrifying thing to fall into the hands of *the living God*" (Heb. 10:26-31).

That is precisely St. John's point here: Blood and fire are about to be poured out upon the Land of Israel from the Seven Chalices, which are **full of the wrath of God, who lives forever and ever.** Indeed, God's eternal nature ("As I live forever!") was

---

10. See Gordon J. Wenham, *The Book of Leviticus* (Grand Rapids: William B. Eerdmans Publishing Co., 1979), pp. 86-103.

11. Philip Carrington, *The Meaning of the Revelation* (London: SPCK, 1931), p. 262.

given in the Song of Moses as a pledge of His vengeance against His enemies, and those who shed the blood of His servants (Deut. 32:40-43). Thus we are shown that the seven angels with the plagues come from *the Tabernacle of the Testimony*, bearing in their hands the curses of the Covenant; they come from the *Temple*, the Church, as ministers binding on earth the decrees of heaven against those who have rejected the Testimony of Jesus; and they come from *the Throne of God* Himself, having received their Chalices of wrath from one of the cherubs who carry God's Throne (cf. 4:6).

8   At the dedication of both the Tabernacle of Moses and the Temple of Solomon, the Sanctuary **was filled with smoke from the Glory of God and from His power; and no one was able to enter** (see Ex. 40:34-35; 1 Kings 8:10-11; 2 Chron. 5:11-14; 7:1-3). As we have seen, this phenomenon happened in connection with heavenly fire descending and consuming the sacrifices (Lev. 9:23-24; 2 Chron. 7:1-3). The filling of the Temple was thus both a sign of God's gracious presence with His people and an awesome revelation of His terrible wrath against sinners, a warning that His fiery judgment would be sent forth from the Temple against those who rebelled against Him (for examples of this, see Lev. 10:1-3; Num. 11:1-3; 16:35).

With the coming of the New Covenant, the Church of Jesus Christ became the Temple of God. This new redemptive event was signaled by the Spirit's filling the Church on the Day of Pentecost, as He had filled the Tabernacle and the Temple. As St. Peter declared, however, the Pentecostal outpouring would be accompanied at the end of the age by a Holocaustal outpouring as well: "Blood, and fire, and vapor of smoke" (Acts 2:16-21; cf. Joel 2:28-32). For the Church to take full possession of her inheritance, for her to assume her proper place as the New Covenant Temple, the corrupt scaffold of the Old Covenant had to be thrown down and demolished. The first-generation Christians were continually exhorted to look forward to the fast-approaching Day when their adversaries would be consumed, and the Church "synagogued" as the definitive Temple (cf. 2 Thess. 2:1; Heb. 10:25). In the complete sense of New Covenant fullness and "perfection" (cf. 1 Cor. 13:12), **no one was able to enter the Temple until the seven plagues of the seven angels were finished** in the destruction of Old Covenant Israel.

E. W. Hengstenberg mentions a related aspect of this symbol: "So long as Israel was the people of the Lord the pillar of cloud exclaimed to all his enemies, 'Touch not Mine anointed, and do My prophets no harm.' So here; that the temple is full of smoke, and no one is able to go into it, this is 'a sign for believers, that the Lord in love to them was now going to complete the destruction of their enemies.'[12] Besides, we see quite plainly in Isaiah 6 the reason why none could enter in. If God manifests Himself in the whole glory of His nature, in the whole energy of His punitive righteousness, the creature must feel itself penetrated by a deep feeling of its nothingness — not merely the *sinful* creature, as there in the case of Isaiah, but also the *finite*, according to Job 4:18; 15:15. . . . Bengel[13] remarks, 'When God pours out His fury, it is fit that even those who stand well with Him should withdraw for a little, and should restrain their inquiring looks. All should stand back in profound reverence, till by and by the sky become clear again.' "[14]

---

12. C. F. J. Züllig, *Die Offenbarung Johannis erklärt* (Stuttgart, 1834-40).
13. J. A. Bengel, *Erklärte Offenbarung Johannis* (Stuttgart, 1740).
14. Hengstenberg, Vol. 2, p. 153.

16

JUDGMENT FROM THE SANCTUARY

The Seventh Trumpet was the sign that "there shall be no more delay" (cf. 10:6-7). Time has run out; wrath to the utmost has now come upon Israel. From this point on, St. John abandons the language and imagery of warning, concentrating wholly on the message of Jerusalem's impending destruction. As he describes the City's doom, he extends and intensifies the Exodus imagery that has already been so pervasive throughout the prophecy. Again he mentions "the Great City" (16:19), reminding his readers of a previous reference: "the Great City, which Spiritually is called Sodom and Egypt, where also their Lord was crucified" (11:8). Jerusalem is called Sodom because of its sensual, luxurious apostasy (cf. Ezek. 16:49-50), and because it is devoted to total destruction as a whole burnt sacrifice (Gen. 19:24-28; Deut. 13:12-18). But St. John's more usual metaphors for the Great City are taken from the Exodus pattern: Jerusalem is not only Egypt, but also the other enemies of Israel. He has shown us the Egyptian Dragon chasing the Woman into the wilderness (Chapter 12); a revived Balak and Balaam seeking to destroy God's people by war and by seduction to idolatry (Chapter 13); the sealed armies of the New Israel gathered on Mount Zion to celebrate the feasts (Chapter 14); and the saints standing in triumph at the "Red Sea," singing the Song of Moses (Chapter 15). Now, in Chapter 16, seven judgments corresponding to the ten Egyptian Plagues are to be poured out on the Great City.

There is also a marked correspondence between these Chalice-judgments and the Trumpet-judgments of Chapters 8-11.[1] Be-

---

1. The correspondence is not exact, however; and Russell characteristically goes too far when, after a superficial comparison, he categorically declares:

cause the Trumpets were essentially warnings, they took only a third of the Land; with the Chalices, the destruction is total.

Chalices	Trumpets	Plagues on Egypt
1. On the Land, becoming sores (16:2)	1. On the Land; ⅓ earth, trees, grass burned (8:7)	1. Boils (sixth plague: Ex. 9:8-12)
2. On the sea, becoming blood (16:3)	2. On the sea; ⅓ sea becomes blood, ⅓ sea creatures die, ⅓ ships destroyed (8:8-9)	2. Waters become blood (first plague: Ex. 7:17-21)
3. On rivers and springs, becoming blood (16:4-7)	3. On the rivers and springs; ⅓ waters become wormwood (8:10-11)	3. Waters become blood (first plague: Ex. 7:17-21)
4. On the sun, causing it to scorch (16:8-9)	4. ⅓ of sun, moon, and stars darkened (8:12)	4. Darkness (ninth plague: Ex. 10:21-23)
5. On the throne of the Beast, causing darkness (16:10-11)	5. Demonic locusts tormenting men (9:1-12)	5. Locusts (eighth plague: Ex. 10:4-20)
6. On the Euphrates, drying it up to make way for kings of the east; invasion of frog-demons; Armageddon (16:12-16)	6. Army from Euphrates kills ⅓ mankind (9:13-21)	6. Invasion of frogs from river (second plague: Ex. 8:2-4)
7. On the air, causing storm, earthquake, and hail (16:17-21)	7. Voices, storm, earthquake, hail (11:15-19)	7. Hail (seventh plague: Ex. 9:18-26)

The First Four Chalices: God's Creation Takes Vengeance (16:1-9)

1 And I heard a loud Voice from the Temple, saying to the seven angels: Go and pour out the seven Chalices of the wrath

---

"This cannot be mere casual coincidence: it is *identity*, and it suggests the inquiry, For what reason is the vision thus repeated?" (J. Stuart Russell, *The Parousia: A Critical Inquiry into the New Testament Doctrine of Our Lord's Second Coming* [Grand Rapids: Baker Book House, 1983], p. 476).

of God into the Land.

2 And the first angel went and poured out his Chalice into the Land; and it became a loathsome and malignant sore upon the men who had the mark of the Beast and who worshiped his image.

3 And the second angel poured out his Chalice into the sea, and it became blood like that of a dead man; and every living soul in the sea died.

4 And the third angel poured out his Chalice into the rivers and the springs of waters; and it became blood.

5 And I heard the Angel of the Waters saying: Righteous art Thou, who art and who wast, O Holy One, because Thou didst judge these things;

6 for they poured out the blood of saints and prophets, and Thou hast given them blood to drink: They are worthy!

7 And I heard the altar saying: Yes, O Lord God, the Almighty, true and righteous are Thy judgments.

8 And the fourth angel poured out his Chalice upon the sun; and it was given to it to scorch the men with fire.

9 And the men were scorched with great heat; and the men blasphemed the name of God who has the power over these plagues; and they did not repent, so as to give Him glory.

1   The command authorizing the judgments is given by **a loud Voice from the Temple**, again underscoring both the divine and ecclesiastical origin of these terrible plagues (cf. 15:5-8).[2] "The judgments of the vials are the overflow of the wrath of God blazing forth and filling his temple, a visitation or presence vouchsafed in response to the prayers of his saints."[3] The **seven angels** (cf. 15:1) are told to **pour out** the Chalices of God's wrath: The Septuagint uses this verb (*ekcheō*) in the directions to the priest to pour out the blood of the sacrifice around the base of the altar (cf. Lev. 4:7, 12, 18, 25, 30, 34; 8:15; 9:9). The term is used in Ezekiel with reference to apostate Israel's fornication with the heathen (Ezek. 16:36; 23:8), of her shedding of innocent blood through oppression and idolatry (Ezek. 22:3-4, 6, 9, 12, 27), and of God's threat to pour out His wrath upon her

---

2. Cf. Isa. 66:6 — "A Voice of uproar from the City, a Voice from the Temple: The Voice of the LORD who is rendering recompense to His enemies!"

3. Austin Farrer, *The Revelation of St. John the Divine* (Oxford: At the Clarendon Press, 1964), p. 175.

(Ezek. 14:19; 20:8, 13, 21; 21:31). In the New Testament, it is similarly used in contexts that parallel major themes in Revelation: the spilling of wine (Matt. 9:17; Mark 2:22; Luke 5:37), the shedding of Christ's blood (Matt. 26:28; Mark 14:24; Luke 22:20), the shedding of the martyrs' blood (Matt. 23:35; Luke 11:50; Acts 22:20; Rom. 3:15), and the outpouring of the Spirit (Acts 2:17-18, 33; 10:45; Rom. 5:5; Tit. 3:6; cf. Joel 2:28-29; Zech. 12:10). All these different associations are in the background of this outpouring of plagues **into the Land** that has spilled the blood of Christ and His witnesses, the people who have resisted and rejected the Spirit: The old wineskins of Israel are about to split open.

2   As the first angel pours out his Chalice into the Land, it becomes **a loathsome and malignant sore upon the men who had the mark of the Beast and who worshiped his image.** The sores are a fitting retribution for apostasy, "a hideous stamp avenging the mark of the Beast"[4] — as if the mark had "broken out in a deadly infection."[5] Just as God had poured out boils on the ungodly, state-worshiping Egyptians who persecuted His people (Ex. 9:8-11), so He is plaguing these worshipers of the Beast in the Land of Israel — the Covenant people who have now become Egyptian persecutors of the Church. This plague is specifically mentioned by Moses in his list of the curses of the Covenant for idolatry and apostasy: "The LORD will smite you with the boils of Egypt and with tumors and with the scab and with the itch, from which you cannot be healed. . . . The LORD will strike you on the knees and legs with sore boils, from which you cannot be healed, from the sole of your foot to the crown of your head" (Deut. 28:27, 35).

3   The second angel pours out his Chalice **into the sea**, and it becomes **blood**, as in the first Egyptian plague (Ex. 7:17-21) and the Second Trumpet (Rev. 8:8-9). This time, however, the blood is not running in streams, but instead is **like that of a dead man:**

---

4. Ibid., p. 175.

5. J. P. M. Sweet, *Revelation* (Philadelphia: The Westminster Press, 1979), p. 244.

clotted, coagulated, and putrefying.[6] Blood is mentioned four times in this chapter; it covers the face of Israel, spilling over the four corners of the Land.

While the primary significance of this plague is symbolic, referring to the uncleanness of contact with blood and death (cf. Lev. 7:26-27; 15:19-33; 17:10-16; 21:1; Num. 5:2; 19:11-19), there are close parallels in the actual events of the Great Tribulation. On one occasion, thousands of Jewish rebels fled to the Sea of Galilee from the Roman massacre of Tarichaeae. Setting out on the lake in small, flimsy boats, they were soon pursued and overtaken by the sturdy rafts of Vespasian's superior forces. Then, as Josephus recounts, they were mercilessly slaughtered: "The Jews could neither escape to land, where all were in arms against them, nor sustain a naval battle on equal terms. . . . Disaster overtook them and they were sent to the bottom, boats and all. Some tried to break through, but the Romans could reach them with their lances, killing others by leaping upon the barks and passing their swords through their bodies; sometimes as the rafts closed in, the Jews were caught in the middle and captured along with their vessels. If any of those who had been plunged into the water came to the surface, they were quickly dispatched with an arrow or a raft overtook them; if, in their extremity, they attempted to climb on board the enemy's rafts, the Romans cut off their heads or their hands. So these wretches died on every side in countless numbers and in every possible way, until the survivors were routed and driven onto the shore, their vessels surrounded by the enemy. As they threw themselves on them, many were speared while still in the water; many jumped ashore, where they were killed by the Romans.

---

6. In passing, we may note here an example of the constant tendency of the so-called "literalist" interpretation to indulge in fanciful speculations regarding the fulfillment of these prophecies. Dr. Henry Morris, who has written what his publishers have called "the most literal exposition of Revelation you will ever read!" offers his interpretation of this phenomenon: "It is merely a chemical solution, water containing iron and other chemicals which give it a blood-red appearance" (*The Revelation Record: A Scientific and Devotional Commentary on the Book of Revelation* [Wheaton: Tyndale House Publishers, 1983], p. 298). This is especially interesting in light of his stated principle of interpretation: "Actually, a 'literal interpretation' is a contradiction in terms, since one does not *interpret* (that is, 'translate' saying 'this means that') if he simply accepts a statement as meaning precisely what it says. Furthermore, the terms 'more literal' or 'most literal' are redundancies. Literal is *literal*" (p. 24).

"One could see the whole lake stained with blood and crammed with corpses, for not a man escaped. During the days that followed a horrible stench hung over the region, and it presented an equally horrifying spectacle. The beaches were strewn with wrecks and swollen bodies, which, hot and clammy with decay, made the air so foul that the catastrophe that plunged the Jews in mourning revolted even those who had brought it about."[7]

4-7   The plague of the Third Chalice more directly resembles the first Egyptian plague (and the Third Trumpet: cf. 8:10-11), since it affects **the rivers and the springs of waters**, turning all the drinking water to **blood**. Water is a symbol of life and blessing throughout Scripture, beginning from the story of creation and the Garden of Eden.[8] In this plague, the blessings of Paradise are reversed and turned into a nightmare; what was once pure and clean becomes polluted and unclean through apostasy.

The Angel of the Waters responds to this curse by praising God for His just judgment: **Righteous art Thou, who art and who wast, O Holy One, because Thou didst judge these things.** We should not be embarrassed by a passage such as this. The whole Bible is written from the perspective of cosmic personalism — the doctrine that God, who is absolute personality, is constantly active throughout His creation, everywhere present with the whole of His being, bringing all things to pass immediately by His power and mediately through His angelic servants. There is no such thing as natural "law"; rather, as Auguste Lecerf has said, "the constant relations which we call natural laws are simply 'divine habits': or, better, the habitual order which God imposes on nature. It is these habits, or this habitual process, which constitute the object of the natural and physical sciences."[9]

This is what guarantees the validity and reliability of both scientific investigation and prayer: On the one hand, God's angels have *habits* — a cosmic dance, a liturgy involving every

---

7. Flavius Josephus, *The Jewish War*, iii.x.9.
8. David Chilton, *Paradise Restored: A Biblical Theology of Dominion* (Ft. Worth, TX: Dominion Press, 1985), pp. 18ff, 30f.
9. Auguste Lecerf, *An Introduction to Reformed Dogmatics*, trans. André Schlemmer (Grand Rapids: Baker Book House, [1949] 1981), p. 147.

aspect of the whole universe, that can be depended upon in all of man's technological labors as he exercises dominion under God over the world. On the other hand, God's angels are personal beings, constantly carrying out His commands; in response to our petitions, He can and does order the angels to change the dance.[10]

There is, therefore, an "Angel of the Waters" (in terms of St. John's zodiacal progression, this is presumably the cherub of the fourth quarter, Aquarius);[11] he, along with all of God's personal creation, rejoices in God's righteous government of the world. God's strict justice, summarized in the principle of *lex talionis*, is evidenced in this judgment; the punishment fits the crime. **They poured out the blood of saints and prophets, and Thou hast given them blood to drink.** As we have seen, the characteristic crime of Israel was always the murder of the prophets (cf. 2 Chron. 36:15-16; Luke 13:33-34; Acts 7:52): Jesus named this fact as the specific reason why *the blood of the righteous* would be poured out in judgment upon that generation (Matt. 23:31-36).

The Angel of the Waters concludes with an interesting statement: By the apostates' shedding of blood, **they are worthy!** This is a deliberate parallel to the message of the New Song: *"Worthy art Thou to take the Book, and to break its seals; for Thou wast slain*, and didst purchase us for God *with Thy blood"* (5:9). Just as the Lamb received His reward on the basis of the blood He shed, so these persecutors have now received the just recompense for their bloodshed.

God had once promised the oppressed of Israel that He would render to their enemies according to their evil works:

> I will feed your oppressors with their own flesh,
> And they will become drunk with their own blood as with
>   sweet wine;
> And all flesh will know that I, the LORD, am your Savior,
> And your Redeemer, the Mighty One of Jacob. (Isa. 49:26)

This has, as usual, become reversed: Now it is Israel, the

---

10. Cf. ibid., pp. 147-49.

11. The mention of the Angel of the Waters also serves as another of the many subtle connections between the Book of Revelation and St. John's Gospel; see John 5:3-4.

Persecutor *par excellence,* that will be forced to drink its own blood and devour its own flesh. This was true in much more than a figurative sense: As God had foretold through Moses (Deut. 28:53-57), during the siege of Jerusalem the Israelites actually became cannibals; mothers literally ate their own children.[12] Because they shed the blood of the saints, God gives them their own blood to drink (cf. 17:6; 18:24).

Joining the angel in praise comes the voice of **the Altar** itself, where the blood of the saints and prophets had been poured out. The Altar rejoices: **Yes, O Lord God, the Almighty, true and righteous are Thy judgments!** The saints gathered round the base of the Altar had cried out for justice, for vengeance on their oppressors (6:9-11). In the destruction of Israel that prayer is answered; the witnesses are vindicated. It is more than coincidental that these prayers in verses 5-7 (along with the text of the Song of Moses in 15:3-4) are actually "based on the song sung by the priests and levites during the interval between the preparation and the offering of the sacrifice."[13] Ironically — just as God Himself is preparing for the Whole Burnt Sacrifice of A.D. 70 — the very angels of heaven were singing apostate Israel's own liturgy against her.

8-9   The fourth angel now pours out his Chalice **upon the sun; and it was given to it to scorch the men with fire.** Whereas the Fourth Trumpet resulted in a plague of darkness (8:12), now the heat of the sun is increased, so that **the men were scorched with great heat.** This too is a reversal of a basic covenantal blessing that was present in the Exodus, when Israel was shielded from the heat of the sun by the Glory-Cloud, the Shadow of the Almighty (Ex. 13:21-22; cf. Ps. 91:1-6). This promise is repeated again and again throughout the prophets:

> The LORD is your keeper;
> The LORD is your shade on your right hand.
> The sun will not smite you by day,
> Nor the moon by night.
> The LORD will protect you from all evil;
> He will keep your soul. (Ps. 121:5-7)

---

12. See Josephus, *The Jewish War,* vi.iii.3-4.
13. J. Massyngberde Ford, *Revelation: A New Translation with Introduction and Commentary* (Garden City, NY: Doubleday and Co., 1975), p. 266.

They will not hunger or thirst,
Neither will the scorching heat or sun strike them down;
For He who has compassion on them will lead them,
And will guide them to springs of water. (Isa. 49:10)

Blessed is the man who trusts in the LORD,
And whose trust is the LORD.
For he will be like a tree planted by the water,
That extends its roots by a stream
And will not fear when the heat comes;
But its leaves will be green,
And it will not be anxious in a year of drought
Nor cease to yield fruit. (Jer. 17:7-8)

And He who sits on the Throne shall spread His Tabernacle over them. They shall hunger no more, neither thirst anymore; neither shall the sun beat down on them, nor any heat; for the Lamb in the center of the Throne shall be their Shepherd, and shall guide them to springs of the waters of life; and God shall wipe away every tear from their eyes. (Rev. 7:15-17)

We have noticed several times already that St. John uses the passive voice to indicate divine control. He again stresses God's sovereignty by telling us that **it was given** to the sun to scorch the men; and, in the very next line, he is even more explicit: **God . . . has the power over these plagues.** St. John knows nothing of a "God" who sits helplessly on the sidelines, watching the world go by; nor does he acknowledge a "God" who is too nice to send judgments on the wicked. He knows that the plagues falling upon Israel are "the works of the LORD, who has wrought desolations in the earth" (Ps. 46:8).

In his book on the Trinity, St. Augustine emphasizes the same point: "The whole creation is governed by its Creator, from whom and by whom and in whom it was founded and established. And thus the will of God is the first and supreme cause of all corporal appearances and motions. For nothing happens in the visible and sensible sphere which is not ordered, or permitted, from the inner, invisible, and intelligible court of the most high Emperor, in this vast and illimitable commonwealth of the whole creation, according to the inexpressible justice of His rewards and punishments, graces and retributions."[14]

But the apostates refuse to submit to God's lordship over them. Like the Beast, whose head is crowned with "names of blasphemy" (13:1) and whose image they worship, **the men blasphemed the name of God who has the power over these plagues.** And, like the impenitent Pharaoh (cf. Ex. 7:13, 23; 8:15, 19, 32; 9:7, 12, 34-35; 10:20, 27; 11:10; 14:8), **they did not repent so as to give Him glory.** Israel has become an Egypt, hardening its heart; and, like Egypt, it will be destroyed.

The Last Three Chalices: It Is Finished! (16:10-21)

10 And the fifth angel poured out his Chalice upon the throne of the Beast; and his kingdom became darkened; and they gnawed their tongues because of pain,

11 and they blasphemed the God of heaven because of their pains and their sores; and they did not repent of their deeds.

12 And the sixth angel poured out his Chalice upon the great river, the Euphrates; and its water was dried up, that the way might be prepared for the kings from the rising of the sun.

13 And I saw coming out of the mouth of the Dragon and out of the mouth of the Beast and out of the mouth of the False Prophet, three unclean spirits like frogs;

14 for they are spirits of demons, performing signs, which go out to the kings of the whole world, to gather them together for the War of that great Day of God, the Almighty.

15 Behold, I am coming like a thief. Blessed is the one who stays awake and keeps his garments, lest he walk about naked and they see his shame.

16 And they gathered them together to the place which in Hebrew is called Armageddon.

17 And the seventh angel poured out his Chalice upon the air; and a loud Voice came from the Temple of heaven, from the throne, saying: It is done.

18 And there were flashes of lightning and peals of thunder and voices; and there was a great earthquake, such as there had not been since the men came to be upon the Land, so mighty an earthquake, and so great.

19 And the Great City was split into three parts, and the cities

---

14. St. Augustine, *On the Trinity*, iii.9; Henry Bettenson, ed. and trans., *The Later Christian Fathers* (Oxford: Oxford University Press, [1972] 1977), p. 191.

of the Gentiles fell. And Babylon the Great was remembered before God, to give her the cup of the wine of His fierce wrath.

20 And every island fled away, and the mountains were not found.

21 And great hail, about the weight of a talent, comes down from heaven upon the men; and the men blasphemed God because of the plague of the hail, because its plague is exceedingly great.

The symbolic targets of the first four Chalices were the elements of the physical creation: Land, sea, waters, and the sun. With the last three plagues, the consequences of the angelic attack are more "political" in nature: the disruption of the Beast's kingdom; the War of the great Day of God; and the Fall of "Babylon."

10-11 Although most of the judgments throughout Revelation are aimed specifically at apostate Israel, the heathen who join Israel against the Church come under condemnation as well. Indeed, the Great Tribulation itself would prove to be "the hour of testing, that hour which is to come upon *the whole world*, to test those who dwell upon *the Land*" (3:10). The fifth angel therefore pours out his Chalice **upon the throne of the Beast**; and, even as the sun's heat is scorching those who worship the Beast, the lights are turned out on **his kingdom**, and it becomes **darkened** — a familiar Biblical symbol for political turmoil and the fall of rulers (cf. Isa. 13:9-10; Amos 8:9; Ezek. 32:7-8). The primary significance of this plague is still the judgment on Israel, for (in terms of the message of Revelation) that was the **throne** and **kingdom** of the Beast. Moreover, as we shall see, the people who suffer from the Fifth Chalice are identified as suffering as well from the First Chalice, which was poured out upon the Land, upon the Israelite worshipers of the Beast (v. 2).

It is also likely, however, that this judgment partially corresponds to the wars, revolutions, riots, and "world-wide convulsions"[15] that racked the Empire after Nero committed suicide in June 68. F. W. Farrar writes in this connection of "the horrors inflicted upon Rome and Romans in the civil wars by provincial

---

15. Cornelius Tacitus, *The Histories*, iii.49.

governors — already symbolized as the horns of the Wild Beast, and here characterized as kings yet kingdomless. Such were Galba, Otho, Vitellius, and Vespasian.[16] Vespasian and Mucianus deliberately planned to starve the Roman populace;[17] and in the fierce struggle of the Vitellians against Sabinus and Domitian, and the massacre which followed, there occurred the event which sounded so portentously in the ears of every Roman — the burning to the ground of the Temple of the Capitoline Jupiter, on December 19th, A.D. 69.[18] It was not the least of the signs of the times that the space of one year saw wrapped in flames the two most hallowed shrines of the ancient world — the Temple of Jerusalem and the Temple of the great Latin god."[19]

One brief passage from Tacitus provides some idea of the chaotic conditions in the capital city: "Close by the fighting stood the people of Rome like the audience at a show, cheering and clapping this side or that in turns as if this were a mock battle in the arena. Whenever one side gave way, men would hide in shops or take refuge in some great house. They were then dragged out and killed at the instance of the mob, who gained most of the loot, for the soldiers were bent on bloodshed and massacre, and the booty fell to the crowd.

"The whole city presented a frightful caricature of its normal self: fighting and casualties at one point, baths and restaurants at another, here the spilling of blood and the litter of dead bodies, close by prostitutes and their like — all the vice associated with a life of idleness and pleasure, all the dreadful deeds typical of a pitiless sack. These were so intimately linked that an observer would have thought Rome in the grip of a simultaneous orgy of violence and dissipation. There had indeed been times in the past when armies had fought inside the city, twice when Lucius Sulla gained control, and once under Cinna. No less cruelty had been displayed then, but now there was a brutish indifference, and not even a momentary interruption in the pursuit of pleasure. As if this were one more entertainment in the festive season, they gloated over horrors and profited by them,

---

16. The rulers during 69, "the year of the four emperors."
17. Tacitus, *The Histories*, iii.48; Josephus, *The Jewish War*, iv.x.5.
18. Tacitus, *The Histories*, iii.71-73; Josephus, *The Jewish War*, iv.xi.4.
19. F. W. Farrar, *The Early Days of Christianity* (Chicago and New York: Belfors, Clarke & Co., 1882), pp. 555f.

careless which side won and glorying in the calamities of the state."[20]

Again St. John draws attention to the impenitence of the apostates. Their response to God's judgment is only greater rebellion—yet their rebellion is becoming increasingly impotent: **And they gnawed their tongues because of pain, and they blasphemed the God of heaven because of their pains and their sores; and they did not repent, so as to give Him glory.** A distinguishing mark of the Chalice-plagues is that they come all at once, with no "breathing space" between them. The plagues are bad enough one at a time, as in the judgments on Egypt. But these people are still gnawing their tongues and blaspheming God on account of their sores—the sores that came upon them when the First Chalice was poured out. The judgments are being poured out so quickly that each successive plague finds the people still suffering from all those that preceded it. And, because their character has not been transformed, they do not repent. The notion that great suffering produces godliness is a myth. Only the grace of God can turn the wicked from rebellion; but Israel has resisted the Spirit, to its own destruction.

12 Corresponding to the Sixth Trumpet (9:13-21), the Sixth Chalice is poured out **upon the great river, the Euphrates; and its water was dried up, that the way might be prepared for the kings from the rising of the sun.** As we saw on 9:14, the Euphrates was Israel's northern frontier, from which invading armies would come to ravage and oppress the Covenant people. The image of the drying of the Euphrates for a conquering army is taken, in part, from a stratagem of Cyrus the Persian, who conquered Babylon by temporarily turning the Euphrates out of its course, enabling his army to march up the riverbed into the city, taking it by surprise.[21] The more basic idea, of course, is the drying up of the Red Sea (Ex. 14:21-22) and the Jordan River (Josh. 3:9-17; 4:22-24) for the victorious people of God. Again there is the underlying note of tragic irony: Israel has become

---

20. Tacitus, *The Histories*, iii.83; trans. Kenneth Wellesley (New York: Penguin Books, 1964, 1975), pp. 197f.

21. Herodotus, *History*, i.191; see the prophecies of this in Jer. 50:38; 51:32, 36.

the new Babylon, an enemy of God that must now be conquered by a new Cyrus, as the true Covenant people are miraculously delivered and brought into their inheritance. As Carrington observes, the coming of the armies from the Euphrates "surely represents nothing but the return of Titus to besiege Jerusalem with further reinforcements";[22] and it is certainly more than coincidental that thousands of these very troops actually did come from the Euphrates.[23]

13-14 St. John now sees **three unclean spirits** proceeding **out of the mouth of the Dragon and out of the mouth of the Beast and out of the mouth of the False Prophet** (the Land Beast of 13:11; cf. 19:20). A connection with the second Egyptian plague is established here, for the multitude of frogs that infested Egypt came from the river (Ex. 8:1-7). St. John has combined these images in these verses: First, an invasion from a river (v. 12); second, a plague of **frogs** (in the Old Covenant dietary laws, frogs are **unclean**: Lev. 11:9-12, 41-47). But these "frogs" are really **spirits of demons, performing signs** in order to deceive mankind. Again there is a multiple emphasis on the Dragon (imitated by his cohorts) throwing things from his **mouth** (cf. 12:15-16; 13:5-6; contrast 1:16; 11:5; 19:15, 21); and the triple repetition of **mouth** here serves also as another point of contact with the Sixth Trumpet (9:17-19). These unclean spirits from the devil, the Roman government, and the leaders of Israel **go out to the kings of the whole world** (cf. Ps. 2) **to gather them together for the War of that great Day of God.** By their false prophecy and miraculous works they incite the armies of the world to join together in war against God. What they do not realize is that the battle is the Lord's, and that the armies are being brought to fulfill God's purposes, not their own. It is He who prepares the way for them, even drying up the Euphrates for their passage.

Micaiah the prophet gave a much similar message to the evil king Ahab of Israel, explaining why he would be killed in battle against the Aramaeans:

22. Philip Carrington, *The Meaning of the Revelation* (London: SPCK, 1931), p. 265.
23. See Josephus, *The Jewish War*, iii.i.3; iii.iv.2; v.i.6; vii.i.3.

I saw the LORD sitting on His Throne, and all the host of heaven standing by Him on His right and on His left. And the LORD said, "Who will entice Ahab to go up and fall at Ramoth-gilead?" And one said this while another said that. Then a spirit came forward and stood before the LORD and said, "I will entice him." And the LORD said to him, "How?" And he said, "I will go out and be a deceiving spirit in the mouth of all his prophets." Then He said, "You are to entice him and also prevail. Go and do so." (1 Kings 22:19-22)

This is echoed in St. Paul's prophecy to the Thessalonians:

For the mystery of lawlessness is already at work; only he who now restrains will do so until he is taken out of the way. And then that lawless one will be revealed whom the Lord will slay with the Breath of His mouth and bring to an end by the appearance of His Coming; that is, the one whose coming is in accordance with the activity of Satan, with all power and signs and false wonders, and with all the deception of wickedness among those who perish, because they did not receive the love of the truth so as to be saved.

And for this reason God will send upon them a work of error so that they might believe the lie, in order that they all may be condemned who did not believe the truth, but took pleasure in wickedness. (2 Thess. 2:7-12)

Ultimately, the "work of error" performed by these lying spirits is sent by God in order to bring about the destruction of His enemies in **the War of that great Day of God,** a Biblical term for a Day of Judgment, of calamity for the wicked (cf. Isa. 13:6, 9; Joel 2:1-2, 11, 31; Amos 5:18-20; Zeph. 1:14-18). Specifically, this is to be the Day of Israel's condemnation and execution; the Day, as Jesus foretold in His parable, when the King would send His armies to destroy the murderers and set their City on fire (Matt. 22:7). St. John underscores this point again by referring to the Lord as **God the Almighty,** the Greek translation of the Hebrew expression *God of Hosts*, the Lord of the *armies* of heaven and earth (cf. 1:8). The armies coming to bring about Israel's destruction — regardless of their motivation — are God's armies, sent by Him (even through lying spirits, if necessary) to bring about His purposes, for His glory. The evil frog-demons perform their false wonders and works of error because God's angel poured out his Chalice of wrath.

15   The narrative is suddenly interrupted: **Behold, I am coming like a thief!** This is the central theme of the Book of Revelation, summarizing Christ's warnings to the churches in the Seven Letters (cf. 2:5, 16, 25; 3:3, 11). The coming of the Roman armies will be, in reality, Christ's Coming in terrible wrath against His enemies, those who have betrayed Him and slain His witnesses. The specific wording and imagery seem to be based on the Letter to the church in Sardis: *"I will come like a thief, and you will not know at what hour I will come upon you"* (3:3; cf. Matt. 24:42-44; Luke 12:35-40; 1 Thess. 5:1-11). That Letter also says: *"Wake up,* and strengthen the things that remain, which were about to die; for I have not found your deeds completed in the sight of My God. . . . But you have a few people in Sardis *who have not soiled their garments*; and they will walk with Me in white; for they are worthy. He who overcomes shall thus be *clothed in white garments. . . ."* (3:2, 4-5). Similarly, the text of the Sixth Chalice continues, in Revelation's third beatitude: **Blessed is the one who stays awake and keeps his garments, lest he walk about naked and men see his shame** (cf. 3:18, in the Letter to Laodicea: "I advise you to buy from Me . . . *white garments, that you may clothe yourself, and that the shame of your nakedness may not be revealed"*). John Sweet comments: "Here the tense of **go naked** and **be seen** is present subjunctive = 'go about naked habitually.' The danger is of being caught not momentarily but habitually off guard — not, to put it crudely, with trousers down, but without trousers at all."[24]

Philip Carrington explains the origin of St. John's allusion: "There was an officer on duty at the Temple whose business it was to walk round and see that those who were on watch kept awake; if he found them asleep he beat them; if he found them a second time, he burnt their clothes. This is the only possible explanation of this passage. It means, Now is the time for those who are guarding the Temple to keep awake. The whole symbolism of the Sixth Bowl, therefore, of which this is a part, has to do with an attack on the Temple."[25] Judgment and destruction

---

24. Sweet, p. 249.
25. Carrington, pp. 265f.; cf. Alfred Edersheim, *The Temple: Its Ministry and Services As They Were at the Time of Jesus Christ* (Grand Rapids: William B. Eerdmans Publishing Co., 1980), pp. 142, 148.

are approaching rapidly; there is no time left to waste. The churches must be awake and on the alert.

16 The narrative is resumed: The demons gather the kings of earth together **to the place which in Hebrew is called Armageddon.**[26] Literally, this is spelled **Har-Magedon**, meaning **Mount Megiddo.** A problem for "literalists" arises here, for Megiddo is a city on a plain, not a mountain. There never was or will be a literal "Battle of Armageddon," for there is no such place. The mountain nearest to the plain of Megiddo is Mount Carmel, and this is presumably what St. John had in mind. Why didn't he simply say "Mount Carmel"? Farrer answers: "One can only suppose that St. John wants to refer to Megiddo and to Carmel in one breath"[27] — Carmel because of its association with the defeat of Jezebel's false prophets, and Megiddo because it was the scene of several important military engagements in Biblical history. Megiddo is listed among the conquests of Joshua (Josh. 12:21), and it is especially important as the place where Deborah defeated the kings of Canaan (Jud. 5:19). King Ahaziah of Judah, the evil grandson of King Ahab of Israel, died at Megiddo (2 Kings 9:27). Perhaps the most significant event that took place there, in terms of St. John's imagery, was the confrontation between Judah's King Josiah and the Egyptian Pharaoh Neco. In deliberate disobedience to the Word of God, Josiah faced Neco in battle at Megiddo and was mortally wounded (2 Chron. 35:20-25). Following Josiah's death, Judah's downward spiral into apostasy, destruction, and bondage was swift and irrevocable (2 Chron. 36). The Jews mourned for Josiah's death, even down through the time of Ezra (see 2 Chron. 35:25), and the prophet Zechariah uses this as an image of Israel's mourning

---

26. Cf. the similar phrasing in John 19:13: "Pilate . . . sat down at the judgment seat at a place called The Pavement, but in Hebrew, Gabbatha." Carrington (p. 267) comments: "Whatever may be our views about the authorship of the Johannine literature, it is certain that the resemblances in thought, plan, and diction between the Revelation and the Gospel are at times extraordinarily close, and those scholars who hold that they are from different authors and are inspired by different motives have some difficult points to explain. In the present case there is a contrast intended between Jesus, judged and going to his death at the hands of the Emperor's procurator, and Jerusalem, judged and going to her destruction at the hands of the Emperor."

27. Farrer, p. 178.

for the Messiah: After promising to "destroy all the nations that come against Jerusalem" (Zech. 12:9), God says:

> And I will pour out on the house of David and on the inhabitants of Jerusalem the Spirit of grace and of supplication, so that they will look on Me whom they have pierced; and they will mourn for Him, as one mourns for an only son, and they will weep bitterly over Him, like the bitter weeping over a first-born. In that day there will be great mourning in Jerusalem, like the mourning of Hadadrimmon in the plain of Megiddo. And the Land will mourn, every family by itself. . . . (Zech. 12:10-11)

This is then followed by God's declaration that He will remove from Israel the idols, the false prophets, and the evil spirits (Zech. 13), and that He will bring hostile armies to besiege Jerusalem (Zech. 14).[28]

"Megiddo" thus was for St. John a symbol of defeat and desolation, a "Waterloo" signifying the defeat of those who set themselves against God, as Farrer explains: "In sum, Mt. Megiddo stands in his mind for a place where lying prophecy and its dupes go to meet their doom; where kings and their armies are misled to their destruction; and where all the tribes of the earth mourn, to see Him in power, whom in weakness they had pierced."[29]

17   Finally, the seventh angel pours out his Chalice **upon the air**. The reason for this does not seem to be that the air is the domain of Satan, "the prince of the power of the air" (Eph. 2:2), but rather that it is the element in which the lightning and thunder (v. 18) and hail (v. 21) are to be produced. Again a **Voice** comes **from the Temple of heaven, from the Throne**, signifying God's control and approval. St. John told us in 15:1 that these seven plagues were to be "the last, because in them the wrath of God is finished"; with the Seventh Chalice, therefore, the Voice

---

28. Carrington (pp. 268-71) provides an extensive list of St. John's allusions to Zechariah, observing that "next to Ezekiel it has influenced St. John most. It is important to realize, therefore, that it speaks of the destruction of this Jerusalem and a vengeance upon its inhabitants; it looks forward to the glory of a New Jerusalem under the house of David, and the gentiles coming to worship there" (p. 271).

29. Farrer, p. 178.

proclaims: **It is done!** (cf. 21:6). "The utterance is a single word, *ghegonen*, which is as thunderlike as the word *uai* is like the scream of an eagle (8:13). 'It is come to pass' is the seal of an accomplishment, like that other one-word speech, 'It is achieved,' *tetelestai* [John 19:30], uttered by the Johannine Christ, as He dies upon the cross."[30]

18 Again appear the phenomena associated with the Day of the Lord and the covenant-making activity of the Glory-Cloud: **flashes of lightning and peals of thunder and voices; and there was a great earthquake.** Seven times in Revelation St. John mentions an earthquake (6:12; 8:5; 11:13 [twice]; 11:19; 16:18 [twice]), emphasizing its covenantal dimensions. Christ came to bring the definitive earthquake, the great cosmic earthquake of the New Covenant, one **such as there had not been since the men came to be upon the Land, so mighty an earthquake, and so great** (cf. Matt. 24:21; Ex. 9:18, 24; Dan. 12:1; Joel 2:1-2).

This was also the message of the writer to the Hebrews. Comparing the covenant made at Sinai with the coming of the New Covenant (which would be established at the destruction of the Temple and the complete passing of the Old Covenant), he said:

> See to it that you do not refuse Him who is speaking. For if those did not escape when they refused Him who warned them on earth, much less shall we escape who turn away from Him who warns from heaven. And His Voice shook the earth then, but now He has promised, saying: Yet once more I will shake not only the earth, but also the heaven [Hag. 2:6]. And this expression, "Yet once more," denotes the removing of those things that can be shaken, as of created things, in order that those things that cannot be shaken may remain. Therefore, since we receive a Kingdom that cannot be shaken, let us show gratitude, by which we may offer to God an acceptable service with reverence and awe; for our God is a consuming fire. (Heb. 12:25-29)

The eminent Puritan theologian John Owen commented on this text about this definitive "earthquake": "It is the dealing of God with *the church,* and the alterations which he would make

---

30. Farrer, p. 179.

in the state thereof, concerning which the apostle treats. It is therefore *the heavens and earth of Mosaical worship*, and the Judaical church-state, with the *earth of their political state* belonging thereunto, that are here intended. These were they that were shaken at the coming of Christ, and so shaken, as shortly after to be removed and taken away, for the introduction of the more heavenly worship of the gospel, and the immovable evangelical church-state. This was the greatest commotion and alteration that God ever made in the heavens and earth of the church, and which was to be made once only. . . .

"This is the conclusion of the whole argumentative part of this epistle, that which was aimed at from the beginning. Having fully proved the excellency of the gospel, and state of the church therein, above that under the law, and confirmed it by an examination of all the concernments of the one and of the other, as we have seen; he now declares from the Scripture, according to his usual way of dealing with those Hebrews, that all the *ancient institutions* of worship, and the whole church-state of the old covenant, were now to be *removed and taken away*; and that to make way for a better state, more glorious, and that which should never be obnoxious [i.e., subject] to change or alteration."[31]

19 As we have seen, **the Great City** is the Old Jerusalem, where the Lord was crucified (11:8; cf. 14:8); originally intended to be "the light of the world, a City set on a hill," she is now an apostate murderess, condemned to perish. Under the judgment

---

31. John Owen, *An Exposition of the Epistle to the Hebrews*, W. H. Goold ed., seven vols. (Grand Rapids: Baker Book House, [1855] 1980), Vol. 7, pp. 366f. Owen further observes: "Although the removal of Mosaical worship and the old church-state be principally intended, which was effected at the coming of Christ, and the promulgation of the gospel from heaven by him, yet all other oppositions unto him and his kingdom are included therein; not only those that then were, but all that should ensue unto the end of the world. The 'things that cannot be moved' are to remain and be established against all opposition whatever. Wherefore, as the heavens and the earth of the idolatrous world were of old shaken and removed, so shall those also of the antichristian world, which at present in many places seem to prevail. All things must give way, whatever may be comprised in the names of heaven and earth here below, unto the gospel, and the kingdom of Christ therein. For if God made way for it by the removal of his own institutions, which he appointed for a season, what else shall hinder its establishment and progress unto the end?" (p. 368).

of the Seventh Chalice, she is to be **split into three parts.** The imagery is drawn from the fifth chapter of Ezekiel, in which God instructs the prophet to stage a drama portraying the coming destruction of Jerusalem. Ezekiel was to shave his head with a sharp sword and then carefully divide the hair into three parts:

> One third you shall burn in the fire at the center of the city. . . . Then you shall take one third and strike it with the sword all around the city, and one third you shall scatter to the wind; and I will unsheathe a sword behind them. Take also a few in number from them and bind them in the edges of your robes. And take again some of them and throw them into the fire, and burn them in the fire; from it a fire will spread to all the house of Israel.
>
> Thus says the Lord GOD: This is Jerusalem; I have set her at the center of the nations, with lands around her. But she has rebelled against My ordinances more wickedly than the nations and against My statutes more than the lands that surround her; for they have rejected My ordinances and have not walked in My statutes.
>
> Therefore, thus says the Lord GOD: Because you have more turmoil than the nations that surround you, and have not walked in My statutes, nor observed My ordinances, nor observed the ordinances of the nations that surround you; therefore, thus says the Lord GOD: Behold, I, even I, am against you, and I will execute judgments against you in the sight of the nations. And because of all your abominations, I will do among you what I have not done, and the like of which I will never do again. Therefore, fathers will eat their sons among you, and sons will eat their fathers; for I will execute judgments on you, and scatter all your remnant to every wind.
>
> So as I live, declares the Lord GOD, surely, because you have defiled My sanctuary with all your detestable idols and with all your abominations, therefore I will also withdraw, and My eye shall have no pity and I will not spare. One third of you will die by plague or be consumed by famine among you, one third will fall by the sword around you, and one third I will scatter to every wind, and I will unsheathe a sword behind them. (Ezek. 5:1-12)

While St. John's image of the City's division into three parts is clearly taken from Ezekiel, the specific referent may be that conjectured by Carrington: "This refers to the division into three factions, which became acute after the return of Titus. While Titus was besieging it from without, the three leaders of rival factions were fighting fiercely within: but for this the city might have staved off defeat for a long time, even perhaps indefinitely, for no great army could support itself for long in those days in the neighborhood of Jerusalem; there was no water and no supplies. This fighting within the city delivered it quickly into the hands of Titus; 'the days were shortened.' "[32]

Another indication that the Great City is Jerusalem is the fact that St. John distinguishes her from **the cities of the Gentiles**, which **fell** with her. Jerusalem, we must remember, was the capital city of the kingdom of priests, the place of the Temple; within her walls sacrifices and prayers were offered up for all nations. The Old Covenant system was a *world-order*, the foundation on which the whole world was organized and maintained in stability. She covenantally represented all the nations of the world, and in her fall they collapsed. The new organization of the world was to be based on the New Jerusalem, built on the Rock.

And Babylon the Great (cf. on 14:8) **was remembered before God, to give her the cup of the wine of His fierce wrath.** As Ford observes, "the phrase suits the liturgical setting of the text. The libations have been poured, but instead of the memorial being a turning of God towards his people with grace and mercy, it is for judgment. God's 'remembering' is always an efficacious and creative act, not a mere intellectual activity; he remembers in the act of blessing (transmitting vitality or life) and cursing (destroying). The irony of vs. 19 lies in the exhortation to Israel to 'remember' God's covenant and kindness in general. She was especially admonished, as in Deuteronomy 6, to keep a perpetual remembrance of the Exodus and Sinai events, to recall them day and night, and never to forget God who brought them to pass. . . .

"In this chapter the author intimates that because Israel forgot and became arrogant, the Egyptian plagues were turned back on her. Even then she did not repent but blasphemed (cf. Job 1:22; 2:10), and God remembered her for judgment."[33]

---

32. Carrington, p. 266; cf. Josephus, *The Jewish War*, v.v.1-5.
33. Ford, p. 275.

20 In this final judgment, every false refuge disappears; the mountains and rocks no longer can hide the wicked "from the face of Him who sits on the Throne, and from the wrath of the Lamb" (6:16): **Every island fled away, and the mountains were not found.**

21 We have noted several times the close relationship between Revelation and the prophecy of Ezekiel. Here again there is a parallel: Ezekiel declared that Jerusalem's false prophets would bring her destruction by a violent hailstorm (Ezek. 13:1-16). St. John foretells the same fate: **And great hail, about the weight of a talent [100 lbs.], comes down from heaven upon the men; and the men blasphemed God because of the plague of the hail, because its plague is exceedingly great.** As with the other plagues, the imagery is borrowed from the plagues that Moses brought upon Egypt (in this case, the seventh plague: Ex. 9:18-26). The plague of hailstones also calls up associations with "the large stones from heaven" that God threw down upon the Canaanites when the Land was being conquered under Joshua (Josh. 10:11); as Deborah sang, the very stars of heaven make war against the enemies of God (Jud. 5:20).

A specific historical referent of this "hailstorm" may have been recorded by Josephus, in his strange account of the huge stone missiles thrown by the Roman catapults into the city: "The stone missiles weighed a talent and traveled two furlongs or more, and their impact not only on those who were hit first, but also on those behind them, was enormous. At first the Jews kept watch for the stone — for it was white — and its approach was intimated to the eye by its shining surface as well as to the ear by its whizzing sound. Watchmen posted on the towers gave the warnings whenever the engine was fired and the stone came hurtling toward them, shouting in their native tongue: *'The Son is coming!'* Those in the line of fire made way and fell prone, a precaution that resulted in the stone's passing harmlessly through and falling in their rear. To frustrate this, it occurred to the Romans to blacken the stones so that they could not be seen so easily beforehand; then they hit their target and destroyed many with a single shot."[34]

After considering various theories about the meaning of this

---

34. Josephus, *The Jewish War*, v.vi.3.

phrase, Stuart Russell writes: "It could not but be well known to the Jews that the great hope and faith of the Christians was the speedy coming of the Son. It was about this very time, according to Hegesippus, that St. James, the brother of our Lord, publicly testified in the temple that 'the Son of Man was about to come in the clouds of heaven,' and then sealed his testimony with his blood. It seems highly probable that the Jews, in their defiant and desperate blasphemy, when they saw the white mass hurtling through the air, raised the ribald cry, 'The Son is coming,' in mockery of the Christian hope of the Parousia, to which they might trace a ludicrous resemblance in the strange appearance of the missile."[35]

And the men blasphemed God — their consistent reaction throughout the pouring out of the Chalices, revealing not only their wickedness but their downright stupidity: When hundred-pound stones are falling from heaven, it is surely the wrong time to commit blasphemy! But God has abandoned these men to their own self-destruction; their vicious, hateful rebellion consumes them to such a degree that they can depart into eternity with curses on their lips.

The Chalices containing the last of the plagues have been poured out; but the end is not yet. The chapters that follow will close in on the destruction of the great Harlot-City and her allies, and conclude with the revelation of the glorious Bride of Christ: the true Holy City, New Jerusalem. (Chapters 17-22 may therefore be considered a continuation of the Seventh Chalice, or an exposition of its meaning; in any case, the events are clearly governed by the angels of the Chalices; see 17:1; 21:9.) "Thus the whole book from beginning to end teaches the great truths — Christ shall triumph! Christ's enemies shall be overcome! They who hate him shall be destroyed; they who love him shall be blessed unspeakably. The doom alike of Jew and of Gentile is already imminent. On Judea and Jerusalem, on Rome and her Empire, on Nero and his adorers, the judgment shall fall. Sword and fire, and famine and pestilence, and storm and earthquake, and social agony and political terror are nothing but the woes which are ushering in the Messianic reign. Old things are rapidly passing away. The light upon the visage of the old dispensation

---

35. Russell, p. 482.

is vanishing and fading into dimness, but the face of him who is as the sun is already dawning through the East. The new and final covenant is instantly to be established amid terrible judgments; and it is to be so established as to render impossible the continuance of the Old. Maranatha! The Lord is at hand! Even so come, Lord Jesus!"[36]

36. F. W. Farrar, *The Early Days of Christianity* (Chicago and New York: Belford, Clarke & Co., 1882), p. 557.

17

THE FALSE BRIDE

While some in recent years have attempted to see the Great Harlot of Revelation as the City of Rome, the Church throughout Christian history has generally understood that she is in some sense a False Bride, a demonic parody of the True Bride, the Church. The Biblical *motif* of the Bride falling into adultery (apostasy) is so well-known that such an identification is all but inescapable. The metaphor of harlotry is exclusively used in the Old Testament for a city or nation that has abandoned the Covenant and turned toward false gods; and, with only two exceptions (see on v. 1-2, below), the term is always used for faithless Israel. The Harlot is, clearly, the False Church. At this point, however, agreement shatters into factionalism. To the Donatist heretics of the fourth century, the Catholic Church was the Whore. Some Greek Orthodox and Protestant theologians have seen her in the Roman papacy, while many fundamentalists have spotted her tinsel charms in the World Council of Churches. Although it is true that there may be (and certainly have been) false churches in the image of the Harlot, we must remember the historical context of the Revelation and the preterist demands it makes upon its interpreters. Merely to find some example of a false church and identify her as the Whore is not faithful exegesis. St. John has set our hermeneutical boundaries firmly within his own contemporary situation, in the first century. He has, in fact, stated definitely that the Harlot was a current phenomenon (17:18), from which he expects his current readers to separate themselves. Whatever modern applications are made of this passage, we must see them as just that: *applications*. The primary significance of the vision must refer to the False Church of St. John's day.

421

We have seen that the Book of Revelation presents us with two great cities, set in antithesis to each other: *Babylon* and *New Jerusalem*. As we shall see in a later chapter, the New Jerusalem is Paradise Consummated, the community of the saints, the City of God. The other city, which is continually contrasted to the New Jerusalem, is the *old* Jerusalem, which has become unfaithful to God. Another way to view this is to understand that Jerusalem was intended from the beginning to be the true fulfillment of *Babylon*, a word meaning "Gate of God." The place of God's gracious revelation of Himself and of His covenant should be a true Babylon, a true "Gate of Heaven" and "House of God," as Jacob understood when he saw God's staircase to heaven, the true Tower of Babel, the true pyramid which foretold of Jesus Christ (Gen. 28:10-22; cf. John 1:51). But Jerusalem did not walk worthy of the calling with which it had been called. Like the original Babylon, Jerusalem turned its back on the true God and sought autonomous glory and dominion; like the original Babylon, it was apostate; and thus the "Gate of God" became "Confusion" instead (Gen. 11:9).

How did the faithful City become a Harlot? It began with the apostasy of the priesthood in Israel. The primary responsibility of the priest (God's *representative*), is to *re-present* the Bridegroom to the Bride, and to guard her from danger. Instead, the priesthood led the people in apostasy from their Lord (Matt. 26:14-15, 47, 57-68; 27:1-2, 20-25, 41-43, 62-66). Because of the priesthood's failure to bring the Bridegroom to Israel, the Bride became a Harlot, in search of other husbands. The apostasy of the priesthood is described in 13:11-17, under the figure of the Beast from the Land. But the False Bride is not absolved of responsibility. She is guilty as well, and St. John's prophecy rightly turns now to consider her judgment and destruction.[1]

The symbolic "Babylon" was destroyed when the seventh angel poured out his Chalice, the drink-offering of annihilation (16:17-21). As we have seen, this vision is part of the fourth Seven of Revelation — the Seven Chalices containing the seven plagues. The connection is provided in 17:1 (cf. 21:9), which tells

---

1. The failure of the priesthood, and the consequences of this for the Bride, are recurring themes in Scripture. See James B. Jordan, *Judges: God's War Against Humanism* (Tyler, TX: Geneva Ministries, 1985).

us that it is one of the seven Chalice-angels who gives St. John the vision of the judgment of the Great Harlot. This vision, therefore, opens up the meaning of the Seventh Chalice, the destruction of Jerusalem.

The Identity of the Harlot (17:1-7)

1 And one of the seven angels who had the Seven Chalices came and spoke with me, saying: Come here, I will show you the judgment of the great Harlot who sits on many waters,

2 with whom the kings of the earth committed fornication, and those who dwell on the Land were made drunk with the wine of her fornication.

3 And he carried me away in the Spirit into a wilderness; and I saw a Woman sitting on a scarlet Beast, full of blasphemous names, having seven heads and ten horns.

4 And the Woman was clothed in purple and scarlet, and adorned with gold and precious stones and pearls, having in her hand a gold cup full of abominations and of the unclean things of her fornication,

5 and upon her forehead a name written: MYSTERY, BABYLON THE GREAT, THE MOTHER OF THE HARLOTS AND OF THE ABOMINATIONS OF THE LAND.

6 And I saw the woman drunk with the blood of the saints, and with the blood of the witnesses of Jesus. And when I saw her, I wondered with great wonder.

7 And the angel said to me, Why do you wonder? I will tell you the mystery of the Woman and of the Beast that carries her, which has the seven heads and the ten horns.

1-2   The vision of the Seven Chalices continues: **One of the seven angels who had the Seven Chalices** shows St. John the fall of **the Great Harlot who sits on many waters.** St. John's readers have already been told of a Harlot-City named "Babylon the Great" (14:8; 16:19), and the Harlot's resemblance to the original Babylon is underscored by the information that she **sits on many waters,** an image taken from Jeremiah's description of Babylon in his famous oracle of judgment against her (Jer. 50-51). The expression *many waters* of Jeremiah 51:13 refers both to the Euphrates, which ran through the middle of the city, and to the canals surrounding it. Ultimately, it refers to the blessings which

423

God had bestowed on Babylon, and which she prostituted for her own glory. Thus St. John describes the Great Harlot of his day in terms of her prototype and model. Later, in 17:15, we are informed of one aspect of the symbolic meaning of the "many waters," but for now the point is merely the identification of the Harlot with Babylon.

At the same time, however, we must recognize that at every other point in Revelation where the expression **many waters** is used, it is set within a description of God's covenantal relationship and liturgical interaction with His people. We have noted that the Voice from the Glory-Cloud sounds like many waters, and that this Voice is produced by the innumerable angels in the heavenly council (Ezek. 1:24). Similarly, in Revelation 1:15 Christ's Voice is "like the sound of many waters" (cf. Ezek. 43:2); in 14:2 St. John again hears the Voice from heaven as "the sound of many waters"; and in 19:6 the great multitude of the redeemed, having entered the angelic council in heaven, joins in a song of praise, which St. John hears as "the sound of many waters." The expression is thus reminiscent of both God's gracious revelation and His people's liturgical response of praise and obedience. Given the Biblical background and context of the phrase, it would come as no surprise to St. John's readers that the Woman should be seen seated on "many waters." The surprise is that she is a whore. She has taken God's good gifts and prostituted them (Ezek. 16:6-16; Rom. 2:17-24).

The Harlot-City has **committed fornication** with **the kings of the earth**. This expression is taken from Isaiah's prophecy against Tyre, where it primarily refers to her international commerce (Isa. 23:15-17); Nineveh as well is accused of "many harlotries" with other nations (Nahum 3:4).[2] Most often, however, the image of a city or nation playing the harlot with the kingdoms of the world is used in reference to the rebellious Covenant people. Speaking against apostate Jerusalem, Isaiah mourned:

---

2. It is noteworthy that Tyre and Nineveh — the only two cities outside of Israel that are accused of harlotry — had both been in covenant with God. The kingdom of Tyre in David and Solomon's time was converted to the worship of the true God, and her king contracted a covenant with Solomon and assisted in the building of the Temple (1 Kings 5:1-12; 9:13; Amos 1:9); Nineveh was converted under the ministry of Jonah (Jon. 3:5-10). The later apostasy of these two cities could rightly be considered harlotry.

How the faithful City has become a Harlot,
She who was once full of justice!
Righteousness once lodged in her,
But now murderers. (Isa. 1:21)

The imagery of Israel's adultery is fairly common in the
prophets, as they bring God's Covenant Lawsuit against the Bride
who has abandoned her Husband.[3] Jeremiah spoke against
Israel as the Harlot, seeking after the false gods of the heathen
in place of her true Husband:

For long ago I broke your yoke
And tore off your bonds;
But you said, "I will not serve!"
For on every high hill
And under every green tree
You have lain down as a harlot. . . .
You are a swift young camel entangling her ways,
A wild donkey accustomed to the wilderness,
That sniffs the wind in her passion.
In the time of her heat who can turn her away?
All who seek her will not become weary;
In her month they will find her. . . .
Your sword has devoured your prophets
Like a destroying lion.
O generation, hear the Word of the LORD.
Have I been a wilderness to Israel,
Or a land of thick darkness?
Why do My people say, "We are free to roam;
We will come no more to Thee"?
Can a virgin forget her ornaments,
Or a Bride her attire?
Yet My people have forgotten Me
Days without number.
How well you prepare your way
To seek love!
Therefore even the wicked women
You have taught your ways. . . .

---

3. For a brief survey of the harlot motif in Scripture, see Francis Schaeffer's
excellent little book *The Church Before the Watching World* (Downers Grove,
IL: InterVarsity Press, 1971), Chapter 2: "Adultery and Apostasy—The Bride
and the Bridegroom Theme."

God says, If a husband divorces his wife,
And she goes from him
And belongs to another man,
Will he still return to her?
Will not that land be completely polluted?
But you are a harlot with many lovers;
Yet you turn to Me, declares the LORD.
Lift up your eyes to the bare heights and see;
Where have you not been violated?
By the roads you have sat for them
Like an Arab in the desert,
And you have polluted a land
With your harlotry and with your wickedness.
Therefore the showers have been withheld,
And there has been no spring rain.
Yet you had a harlot's forehead;
You refused to be ashamed. (Jer. 2:20-24, 30-33; 3:1-3)

Israel's adulteries, Hosea said, took place "on every thresh-ing floor" (Hos. 9:1): The picture is that of a woman prostituting herself for money in the grain house in harvest-time. This car-ries a double meaning. First, Israel was apostatizing into Baal-worship, seeking harvest blessing and fertility from false gods (forgetting that fertility, and blessing in every area, can come only from the one true God). Second, the Temple was built on a threshing floor (2 Chron. 3:1), symbolizing God's action throughout history in separating the chaff from His holy wheat (Job 21:18; Ps. 1:4; 35:5; Isa. 17:13; Luke 3:17). The threshing floor is also symbolic of the marriage relationship: The union of Boaz and Ruth took place on his threshing floor (Ruth 3), and the action of grinding at a mill is a Biblical image of sexual rela-tions (Job 31:10; Isa. 47:2; Jer. 25:10).[4] Thus, instead of consum-mating her marriage to God through worship at His threshing floor, the Bride went whoring after every other threshing floor, prostrating herself before strange gods and alien altars.

Apostate Jerusalem is the Harlot-city; this theme becomes even more prominent in the prophecy of Ezekiel, particularly in Ezekiel 16 and 23, where it is clear that her "adulteries" consist

---

4. For a full discussion of this point, see Calum M. Carmichael, "Treading in the Book of Ruth," ZAW 92 (1980), pp. 248-66.

of religious-political alliances with powerful heathen kingdoms (see, e.g., Ezek. 16:26-29). The people of Jerusalem in Ezekiel's day had abandoned the true faith and had turned to heathen gods and ungodly nations for help, rather than trusting in God to be their protector and deliverer. It is important to note that while Israel herself seems to have regarded these relationships in primarily political terms, the prophets emphasized that the religious issue was central. The reliance of the Covenant nation on heathen powers could not be viewed as mere political expediency; it was nothing less than harlotry. Using language so graphic and explicit that most modern pastors won't preach from these chapters,[5] Ezekiel condemns Jerusalem as a degraded, wanton whore: "You spread your legs to every passerby to multiply your harlotry" (Ezek. 16:25). Ezekiel's sarcastic portrayal of Israel's adultery is sharp and vivid: She lusts after the (supposedly) well-endowed Egyptians, whose sex organs are the size of donkeys' genitals, and who produce semen in such prodigious amounts that it rivals that of a horse (16:26; 23:20). Her adulterous desire (inflamed by pornographic pictures, 23:14-16) is so great that she is willing to pay strangers to come to her, rather than the other way around (16:33-34); she even masturbates with the "male images" she has made (16:17). Ezekiel's prophecy was crude, and he most certainly offended many of his listeners; but he was simply giving them a faithful description of how offensive they were to God. In the view of the all-holy God who spoke through Ezekiel, nothing could be more obscene than the

---

5. The attitude of the Rev. H. Foster, Rector of Clerkenwell in the early nineteenth century, is probably representative. Discussing the propriety of preaching from Canticles (the Song of Solomon), he says: "I have preached from various independent texts in the Canticles. I once went through Ezekiel 16, but dared not do it again." Quoted in John H. Pratt, ed., *The Thought of the Evangelical Leaders: Notes of the Discussions of the Eclectic Society, London, During the Years 1798-1814* (Edinburgh: The Banner of Truth Trust, [1856] 1978), p. 441. In a more down-to-earth age, John Calvin was able to be much more explicit in his lectures — so much so that his nineteenth-century translator simply deleted several passages, with this note: "The Reformer dwells so minutely on the language of the Prophet, that the refined taste of modern days will not bear a literal translation of some clauses." Thomas Myers, in Calvin's *Commentaries on the First Twenty Chapters of the Book of the Prophet Ezekiel* (Grand Rapids: Baker Book House, 1979 reprint), Vol. 2, p. 127. Cf. another translator's omission of Calvin's comments on Gen. 38:8-10 (*Commentaries on the First Book of Moses*, Baker Book House, 1979, Vol. 2, p. 281).

Bride's apostasy from her divine Husband.

The same was true of Israel in the first century. At the very moment when the promised Bridegroom arrived, Israel was fornicating with Caesar. The sight of her true Husband only drove her further into adulterous union with "the kings of the earth." Rejecting Christ's kingship (cf. 1 Sam. 8:7-8), the chief priests cried: "We have no King but Caesar!" (John 19:15).

The apostasy of Jerusalem led the whole nation into religious and political fornication. **Those who dwell on the Land** — the Jewish people (see comments on 3:10) — **were made drunk with the wine of her fornication**, seduced into such a spiritual stupor that they did not recognize their own Christ. Intoxicated by their apparently successful relationship with the imperial power-state, the Jews did not realize that it was a trap: They were being drugged in preparation for their own execution.

3   We have already seen the Woman in the **wilderness**, where she fled from the oppression of the seven-headed Dragon (12:6, 14). But that wilderness sojourn was out of necessity, and for a specified time. The True Bride does not dwell in the wilderness — the sign of the Curse, the habitation of demons (Matt. 12:43)[6] — by preference. To the False Bride, however, the wilderness is her element; she chooses to remain there rather than follow the Spirit to the promised land. The wilderness is thus her heritage, and her destiny (cf. Num. 13-14; Zech. 5:5-11). This is, again, a familiar prophetic picture: Apostate Jerusalem is a Harlot, plying her obscene trade alongside wilderness roads like a wild ass in heat (cf. Jer. 2-3; Hos. 2).

It is as if the Woman of Revelation 12, having fled to the wilderness for protection, has become accustomed to desert life and established an intimate relationship with the Dragon. St. John sees her **sitting on a scarlet Beast**. It is not immediately clear whether the Scarlet Beast is the Dragon or the Sea Beast. Like the Sea Beast, it is **full of blasphemous names** (cf. 13:1); and like the Dragon, it has **seven heads and ten horns** (cf. 12:3; the order is reversed for the Sea Beast, which has *ten horns and*

---

6. See on 12:6; cf. remarks on the wilderness theme in David Chilton, *Paradise Restored: A Biblical Theology of Dominion* (Ft. Worth, TX: Dominion Press, 1985), pp. 24, 46, 50-53.

seven heads, 13:1). Since she is seated "on many waters" (v. 1) *and* on the Scarlet Beast as well, the imagery seems to suggest that the Beast has risen up out of the sea (cf. 11:7; 13:1). The most likely solution is simply to see the passage as a reference to Jerusalem's apostate intimacy with both Satan and the Empire. Rome was the devil's reigning political incarnation, and the two could certainly be considered together under one image. Israel was dependent upon the Roman Empire for her national existence and power; from the testimony of the New Testament there is no doubt that Jerusalem was politically and religiously "in bed" with institutionalized paganism, cooperating with Rome in the crucifixion of Christ and the murderous persecution of Christians.

Incidentally, this is one of many indications that the Harlot is not Rome, for she is clearly distinct from it. She is *seated* on the Beast, supported and maintained by him whose seven heads represent—among other things— the famed "seven hills" of Rome (17:9). It is worth noting too that there is a contrast between the Throne of God, supported by the Living Creatures who are "full of eyes" and who are day and night engaged in God's praise (4:6-8; cf. Ezek. 10:12), and the Harlot Queen, whose throne is supported by a Beast who is **full of blasphemous names**.

4 The Woman is **clothed in purple and scarlet**, garments of splendor and royalty for one who sits as a queen (18:7; see Jud. 8:26; 2 Sam. 1:24; Dan. 5:7, 16, 29; Luke 16:19). She is **gilded with gold and precious stones and pearls**, in keeping with the Biblical descriptions of the glorious City of God (Isa. 54:11-12; 60:5-11; Rev. 21:18-21), based further on the pattern of the jewel-littered Garden of Eden (Gen. 2:11-12; Ezek. 28:13). Jewelry is also a feature both of the high priest's garments (Ex. 28:9-29) and of the throne of God (4:3-4). There is thus no need to see the Woman's garments and jewels as merely the loud, bold, and extravagant decking-out of a harlot's costume. Instead, these are *originally* the clothes of the righteous Woman—the Bride— who is supposed to be arrayed in glorious dress (cf. Ex. 3:22; Ezek. 16:11-14; Prov. 31:21-22). St. John wants his readers to see the Harlot adorned in the beautiful garments of the Church. He wants them to understand that this degenerate whore who forni-

cates with beasts is still carrying the trappings of the pure and chaste Bride. We should note, however, that the enormous veil covering the Temple gate (over 80 feet high and 24 feet wide) was "a *Babylonian* tapestry, embroidered with blue, and *fine linen* [cf. 18:16], and *scarlet*, and *purple*."[7]

The False Bride celebrates a communion of sorts: She holds **in her hand a gold cup full of abominations and of the unclean things of her fornication**, combining the images of unclean *food* (cf. Lev. 11) and unclean *marriage* (cf. Lev. 20; see esp. Lev. 20:22-26).[8] The picture is slightly changed from that of Jeremiah 51:7, where the original Babylon is described as "a golden cup in the hand of the LORD, intoxicating all the earth," but the basic idea is similar. Jerusalem still has the beautiful chalice of the Covenant, but the communion she offers leads men to death and destruction. Her cup is full of "abominations," a word which the Bible often uses in connection with the worship of false gods (Deut. 29:17; Ezek. 5:11). Pharisaic Jerusalem prides itself on its observance of the ceremonial cleanliness regulations, but in reality it is radically unclean, defiled from within by its apostasy and fornication (Matt. 23:25-28; Mark 7:1-23). The overall picture may well be, as Ford has observed, "a parody of the high priest on the Day of Atonement wearing the vestments specially reserved for that occasion and holding the libation offering. However, instead of the sacred name upon his brow the 'priest-harlot' bears the name Babylon, mother of harlots and the abominations of the earth, a title illustrating Ezek. 16:43-45 [RSV], where Yahweh speaks of the lewdness of Jerusalem."[9]

5 The Harlot has **on her forehead a name written.** By now the writing on the forehead is a familiar image in Revelation. We have seen it on the saints (3:12; 7:3; 14:1) and on the followers of

---

7. Josephus, *The Jewish War*, v.v.4.

8. For an extended, though preliminary, discussion of the relationships between culinary and sexual purity in the Law, see Mary Douglas, *Purity and Danger: An Analysis of the Concepts of Pollution and Taboo* (London: Routledge & Kegan Paul, [1966] 1969), Ch. 3: "The Abominations of Leviticus" (pp. 41-57); idem, *Implicit Meanings: Essays in Anthropology* (London: Routledge & Kegan Paul, 1975), Ch. 16: "Deciphering a Meal" (pp. 249-75).

9. J. Massyngberde Ford, *Revelation: A New Translation with Introduction and Commentary* (Garden City, NY: Doubleday and Co., 1975), p. 288.

the Beast (13:16-17). The forehead is especially singled out as a symbol of rebellion (Isa. 48:4; Ezek. 3:9); rebellious Israel is said to have "a harlot's forehead" (Jer. 3:3). But the name written there begins with the word **Mystery.** Corsini has properly noted the significance of this much-overlooked fact: "If the prostitute is called 'mystery,' that means that she, even in the moment in which she is judged and condemned, still forms an integral and important part in the divine plan of salvation. This cannot be the case for Rome or any other pagan city, but only for Jerusalem. Only she, and no other city, will be renewed and will descend from heaven upon Mt. Sion to celebrate a marriage with the Lamb (21:2, 10ff.), because 'in the days of the trumpet call to be sounded by the seventh angel, the mystery of God . . . should be fulfilled' (10:7)."[10]

The Harlot's symbolic name continues: **Babylon the Great,** for she is heiress and namesake of the ancient city which was the epitome of rebellion against God (Gen. 11:1-9; Jer. 50-51). The name also serves to remind us of her high calling, that she was created to be the True Babylon, the Gate of God. Instead, however, she has followed the path of the old Babylon in her apostate rejection of God's lordship over her. Now identified with bestiality and confusion, she has become "the Mystery of Lawlessness" (2 Thess. 2:7), **the Mother of Harlots** (corresponding to "Jezebel" and her "children," spoken of in 2:20-23; cf. the description of Jerusalem as a mother of harlots in Ezek. 16:44-48).

6-7 Now we see what the Harlot has in her cup, the demonic communion with which she and her paramours (v. 2; cf. 14:8) are becoming **drunk:** It is **the blood of the saints, and . . . of the witnesses of Jesus.** This is "the wine of her fornication," the sacrament of her apostasy from the true faith; the ultimate unclean food (cf. Lev. 17:10-14). While it is true that Rome became a great persecutor of the Church, we must remember that Jerusalem was the preeminent transgressor in this regard. The Roman persecution came about through the Jews' instigation and connivance, as the Book of Acts constantly informs us. Jerusalem's whole history, in fact, was one of relentless persecu-

---

10. Eugenio Corsini, *The Apocalypse: The Perennial Revelation of Jesus Christ* (Wilmington, DE: Michael Glazier, 1983), p. 335.

tion of the godly, and especially of the prophets (Matt. 21:33-44; 23:29-35; Acts 7:51-53). As St. John tells us in 18:24, "in her was found the blood of prophets and of saints and of all who have been slain on the earth." Jerusalem was the persecutor of the prophets *par excellence*.

But it is not always easy to look at things with "theological" eyes. At the moment of her glory, a successful harlot is beautiful, alluring, seductive. God's Word is realistic, and does not pretend that evil always appears repulsive. The temptation to sin, as we all know, can be very attractive (Gen. 3:6; 2 Cor. 11:14). As St. John beheld the Great Harlot, therefore, he was quite taken in, fascinated with her beauty: He **wondered with great wonder** (cf. Rev. 13:3-4: "And the whole Land *wondered* after the Beast; and they worshiped the Dragon . . ."). The angel therefore rebukes him: **Why do you wonder?** St. John records this to warn his readers against being seduced by the Harlot, for she *is* beautiful and impressive. The antidote to being deceived by the wiles of the False Bride is to understand **the Mystery of the Woman and of the Beast that carries her.** The angel will now reveal the nature of the Harlot's alliance with the Beast, her opposition to Christ, and her approaching destruction. St. John's readers must understand that there is no longer any hope of "reform from within." Jerusalem is implacably at war with Jesus Christ and His people. The once-Holy City is now a Whore.

The Angel Explains the Mystery (17:8-18)

8 The Beast that you saw was and is not, and is about to ascend out of the Abyss and to go to destruction. And those who dwell on the Land will wonder, whose name has not been written in the Book of Life from the foundation of the world, when they see the Beast, that he was and is not and will come.

9 Here is the mind which has wisdom. The seven heads are seven mountains on which the Woman sits,

10 and they are seven kings; five have fallen, one is, the other has not yet come; and when he comes, he must remain a little while.

11 And the Beast which was and is not, is himself also an eighth, and is of the seven, and he goes to destruction.

12 And the ten horns which you saw are ten kings, who have not yet received a kingdom, but they receive authority as kings with the Beast for one hour.

13 These have one purpose and they give their power and authority to the Beast.

14 These will wage war against the Lamb, and the Lamb will overcome them, because He is Lord of lords and King of kings, and those who are with Him are the called and chosen and faithful.

15 And he said to me: The waters which you saw, where the Harlot sits, are peoples and multitudes and nations and tongues.

16 And the ten horns which you saw, and the Beast, these will hate the harlot and will make her desolate and will make her naked, and will eat her flesh and will burn her up with fire.

17 For God has put it into their hearts to execute His purpose, to execute one purpose, and to give their kingdom to the Beast, until the words of God should be fulfilled.

18 And the Woman whom you saw is the Great City, which has a Kingdom over the kings of the earth.

8 The angel begins his explanation by speaking about the Beast, since the Harlot's intimacy with the Beast is so integral to her character and destiny. Again, we must note that this is a composite Beast (cf. v.3 above), comprising the attributes of both the Roman Empire and its original, the Dragon. Milton Terry says: "In his explanation the angel seems to point our attention particularly to the spirit which actuated the dragon, the beast from the sea, and the false prophet alike; and so what is here affirmed of the beast has a special reference to the different and successive manifestations of Satan himself. . . . Hence we understand by the beast that *was and is not* an enigmatical portraiture of the great red dragon of 12:3. He is the king of the Abyss in 9:11, and the beast that killed the witnesses in 11:7. He appears for a time in the person of some great persecutor, or in the form of some huge iniquity, but is after a while cast out. Then he again finds some other organ for his operations and enters it with all the malice of the unclean spirit who wandered through dry places, seeking rest and finding none until he discovered his old house, empty, swept, and garnished as if to invite his return."[11]

The angel represents the Beast as a parody of "Him who is and who was and who is to come" (1:4): **The Beast . . . was and is not and is about to ascend up out of the Abyss.** At this point, it is likely that the specific human referent of **the Beast** is Vespasian, who became Caesar after the chaos which followed upon the death of Nero. Ford comments: "The beast 'was' (Vespasian was in favor with Nero) and 'is not' (he fell from favor) and will come from the abyss (he was restored with the help of the 'men of the pit,' an epithet for perverse men from Qumran). Vespasian stands parallel to 'he who is to come.' In a sense the empire passed through the same stages; 'it was,' from Caesar to Nero, 'was not' in the critical year of the four emperors, and came again with Vespasian."[12]

Ultimately, as we have seen, this is a description of the original Beast, the Dragon, the ancient enemy of God and His people. If at the moment there is a temporary respite from his cruel opposition, the Christians must be aware that he is about to ascend again out of the Abyss to attack and persecute them again; nevertheless, St. John reminds them that the Beast's defeat is assured, for his ascension is not to power and glory at the right hand of God, but only in order **to go to destruction.** The word **destruction** is *apoleian*, the root of *Apollyon*, the "king of the Abyss" in 9:11. St. John is pointing out that although the Beast is allowed, for a time, to ascend out of the abyss, he is just as certain to return there. His destiny is utter destruction, and he cannot succeed in destroying the Church.

But the Dragon/Beast will be successful in carrying off apostate Israel into his idolatrous cult. **Those who dwell on the Land will wonder . . . when they see the Beast, that he was and is not and will come.** The word used earlier for the Beast's rise from the Abyss is *anabainō,* in mimicry of Christ's *Resurrection/ Ascension*; the word *come* here is *paristēmi* (the verb form of *parousia*), in imitation of Christ's *Coming* in power and glory, bringing judgment and salvation (the definitive Parousia

---

11. Milton S. Terry, *Biblical Apocalyptics: A Study of the Most Notable Revelations of God and of Christ in the Canonical Scriptures* (New York: Eaton & Mains, 1898), pp. 429f.
12. Ford, p. 289.

occurred at the Ascension, resulting in Christ's Parousia against Jerusalem in A.D. 70). Thus, just as the first-century Christians lived in expectation of their Lord's near Parousia, so the apostate Jews looked to the Beast for deliverance and salvation. The "second coming" of the Dragon, after his apparent (and real) defeat by Christ, was an occasion of wonder, astonishment, and worship by the Christ-rejecting Jews. The rise of the total state, in opposition to the Kingdom of Christ, was for rebellious Israel an ascension to glory, a parousia, a day of the lord. The Beast was their Messiah, and his Anti-Parousia delivered them — into the hands of Apollyon, the perdition and destruction of the Abyss. The only ultimate issue of the Beast's ascension from the Abyss is the greater damnation of himself and his worshipers.

Why, ultimately, did the Jews reject Christ and worship the Dragon? Because, in contrast to Christ's elect, who were "chosen in Him before the foundation of the world" (Eph. 1:4) apostate Israel's **name has not been written in the Book of Life from the foundation of the world** (cf. 13:8). St. Peter wrote that Jesus Christ, the great Cornerstone, was for the Jews "a Stone of stumbling and a rock of offense; for they stumble because they are disobedient to the Word, and to this doom they were also appointed" (1 Peter 2:8).[13] Instead, the Church has inherited the former status (Ex. 19:6) held by Israel: "But you are a chosen race, a royal priesthood, a holy nation, a people for God's own possession . . ." (1 Pet. 2:9).

9-10   The angel turns to speak of the Dragon's incarnation in the Beast from the Sea. **Here is the mind which has wisdom. The seven heads are seven mountains on which the woman sits.** The "seven mountains" again identify the Beast as Rome, famous

---

13. In context (v. 6-8), St. Peter is quoting from Isaiah's prophecies of the Jews' rejection of Christ (Isa. 8:14; 28:16; see Matt. 28:12-15). John Brown of Edinburgh commented on 1 Peter 2:8: "The direct reference in the term disobedient is, no doubt, to the unbelieving Jews. When God proclaimed to them, 'Behold, I lay in Zion for a foundation a stone, a tried stone, a precious corner-stone, a sure foundation; he that believeth shall not make haste,'—they disbelieved the declaration. They disobeyed the command. They rejected the stone. They would not build on it. They would not receive Jesus as the Messiah; on the contrary, they 'took him, and with wicked hands they crucified and slew him.'" (*Expository Discourses on 1 Peter*, two vols.; Edinburgh: The Banner of Truth Trust, [1848] 1975, Vol. 1, p. 314).

for its "seven hills"; [14] but these also correspond to the line of the Caesars, for **they are seven kings; five have fallen**: The first five Caesars were Julius, Augustus, Tiberius, Caligula, and Claudius.[15] **One is**: Nero, the sixth Caesar, was on the throne as St. John was writing the Revelation. **The other has not yet come; and when he comes, he must remain a little while**: Galba, the seventh Caesar, reigned for less than seven months.

11 But the fall of the Julio-Claudian dynasty and the severe political chaos attending it must not be interpreted by Christians to mean the end of troubles. For their real enemy is **the Beast**, who will become incarnated in other Caesars as well. He is **also an eighth** king, yet is **of the seven**: the antichristian brutality of succeeding tyrants will mark them as being of the same stripe as their predecessors. *Eight* is the number of resurrection in the Bible; St. John is warning that even though the Empire will seem to disintegrate after the rule of the seven kings, it will be "resurrected" again, to live on in other persecutors of the Church. Yet the Empire's comeback will not result in victory for the Beast, for even the eighth, the resurrected Beast, **goes to de-**

---

14. It is not at all necessary, with Russell (*The Parousia*, p. 492), to seek seven mountains in Jerusalem as the fulfillment of this statement. The Harlot is seated on the Beast, and thus on the seven hills of Rome; in other words, apostate Judaism, centered in the City of Jerusalem, is supported by the Roman Empire.

15. This has been called into question by some, since, in a technical sense, the Empire began with Augustus, not Julius (cf. Tacitus, *The Annals*, i.1). Yet that was a technicality which, as far as the normal conversation and writing of the first century were concerned, was irrelevant. For all practical purposes, Julius Caesar was Emperor: He claimed the title *imperator*, and most early Roman, Christian, and Jewish writers count him as the first Emperor. Suetonius begins his *Lives of the Twelve Caesars* with Julius as the first Emperor, as does Dio Cassius in his *Roman History*. Book 5 of the *Sibylline Oracles* calls Julius "the first king," and 4 Ezra 12:15 speaks of Augustus as "the second" of the emperors. For our purposes, Josephus seems to provide the most convincing testimony, since he wrote for both a Roman and a Jewish audience, in the common parlance of the day. In his *Antiquities of the Jews* he clearly speaks of Augustus and Tiberius as the second and third emperors (xviii.ii.2), of Caligula as the fourth (xviii.vi.10), and of Julius as the first (xix.i.11). The most extensive discussion of all the evidence is in Moses Stuart, *Commentary on the Apocalypse*, two vols. (Andover: Allen, Morrill, and Wardwell, 1845), Vol. 2, pp. 445-52; cf. Isbon T. Beckwith, *The Apocalypse of John: Studies in Introduction with an Exegetical and Critical Commentary* (Grand Rapids: Baker Book House, [1919] 1979), pp. 704f.

struction. The Church will have to exercise patience during the period of the Beast's ascendancy, but she has the assurance that her enemies will not succeed. Their King will be victorious; His servants have been predestined to share in His triumph.

12 The ten horns which St. John saw on the Beast **are ten kings.** The number *10* in the Bible, as we have noted on other occasions, is related to the concept of "manyness," of quantitative or numerical fullness. That these "kings" are associated with the Beast, adorning his heads as "crowns," and that **they receive authority with the Beast** (i.e., by virtue of their relationship with him) indicates that they are rulers subject to, or allied with, the Empire. Rome actually had ten imperial provinces, and some have read this as a reference to them.[16] It is not necessary, however, to attempt a precise definition of these ten subject kings; the symbol simply represents "the *totality* of those allied or subject kings who aided Rome in her wars both on Judaism and Christianity."[17] The burden of the text is to point to these kings, with whom the Harlot has plied her trade (v. 2), as the instruments of her eventual destruction (v. 16-17).

13-14 St. John records that the "ten kings" join with the Beast against Christ, persecuting the Church throughout the provinces and subordinate kingdoms of the Empire: **These have one purpose, and they give their power and authority to the Beast** in order to **wage war against the Lamb,** as Michael and His angels had waged war with the Dragon (12:7). This has always been the ultimate goal of reprobate man's exercise of government: the attempt to dethrone God. As the Psalmist foretold, "The kings of the earth take their stand, and the rulers take counsel together, against the LORD and against His *Christ*" (Ps. 2:2; cf. Acts 2:26). The apostolic commentary on this text is revealed in an early prayer of the persecuted Church. After quoting Psalm 2, they said: "For truly in this city there were gathered together against Thy holy servant Jesus, whom Thou didst

---

16. These were: Italy, Achaia, Asia, Syria, Egypt, Africa, Spain, Gaul, Britain, and Germany. See F. W. Farrar, *The Early Days of Christianity* (Chicago and New York: Belford, Clarke & Co., 1882), p. 532.

17. Terry, p. 433.

437

anoint, both Herod and Pontius Pilate, along with the Gentiles and the peoples of Israel, to do whatever Thy hand and Thy purpose predestined to occur" (Acts 4:27-28). The ungodly are united in the bond of hatred against the Son of God, the Anointed One. That is why we are told the outcome of the conspiracy of Herod and Pilate against Christ: "Now Herod and Pilate became friends with one another that very day; for before they had been at enmity with one another" (Luke 23:12). Enemies will unite in fighting a common foe, and in the Advent of Christ we see the world of pagans and apostates joining together in rebellion against Him. But the Psalmist long before had warned kings and rulers to "worship the LORD with reverence, and rejoice with trembling. Kiss the Son, lest He become angry, and you perish in the way, for His wrath may soon be kindled. How blessed are all who take refuge in Him!" (Ps. 2:11-12). The outcome of this cosmic struggle is thus assured, and inevitable: **And the Lamb will overcome them, because He is Lord of lords and King of kings, and those who are with Him are the called and chosen and faithful.** St. John assures the Church that in their terrible and terrifying conflict with the awesome might of imperial Rome, *the victory of Christianity is guaranteed.*

15 The angel now explains the significance of **the waters . . . where the Harlot sits.** These are described in terms of a fourfold designation: **peoples and multitudes and nations and tongues,** i.e. the world. The identification of the ungodly, rebellious nations of the world with the raging sea is a familiar one in Scripture (cf. 13:1). Isaiah wrote of "the uproar of many peoples who roar like the roaring of the seas, and the rumbling of nations who rush on like the rumbling of mighty waters! The nations rumble on like the rumbling of many waters, but He will rebuke them and they will flee far away, and be chased like chaff in the mountains before the wind, or like whirling dust before a gale" (Isa. 17:12-13). "The wicked are like the tossing sea; for it cannot be quiet, and its waters toss up refuse and mud. There is no peace for the wicked, says my God" (Isa. 57:20-21).

Jerusalem could truly be portrayed as seated on "many waters" (i.e., the nations) because of the great and pervasive influence the Jews had in all parts of the Roman Empire before the destruction of Jerusalem. Their synagogues were in every

THE FALSE BRIDE 17:16

city, and the extent of their colonization can be seen in the record of the Day of Pentecost, which tells us that "there were Jews staying in Jerusalem, devout men, from every nation under heaven" (Acts 2:5).[18]

16 In their war against Christ, the raging nations turn against the Harlot, *because of her connection with Him.*[19] The angel portrays this new enmity toward the Harlot by a fourfold description: The peoples of the Empire **will hate the Harlot and will make her desolate and will make her naked, and will eat her flesh and burn her up with fire** (cf. Jer. 13:26; Lam. 1:8-9; Nah. 3:5). Jerusalem had committed fornication with the heathen nations, but in A.D. 70 they turned against her and destroyed her, making her **desolate** (the same word is used in Matthew 24:15, Mark 13:14, and Luke 21:20, reflecting the Greek version of Daniel 9:26-27: the abomination of desolation). One of the punishments for a convicted adulteress in the ancient world was the public humiliation of being stripped **naked** (cf. Isa. 47:2-3; Jer. 13:26; Lam. 1:8; Ezek. 16:37, 39; 23:29; Hos. 2:10; Nah. 3:5).

Another connection with "Jezebel" (2:20; cf. on 17:5) is made here: The nations **eat her flesh**, as the dogs (cf. 22:15) had eaten the flesh of the original Jezebel (1 Kings 21:23-24; 2 Kings 9:30-37). The prophets who spoke of Jerusalem as the Whore had said that just as a priest's daughter who became a harlot was to be "burned with fire" (Lev. 21:9), so God would use Jerusalem's former "lovers," the heathen nations, to destroy her and **burn her** to the ground (Jer. 4:11-13, 30-31; Ezek. 16:37-41; 23:22, 25-30). Russell observed that "Tacitus speaks of the bitter animosity with which the Arab auxiliaries of Titus were filled against the Jews,[20] and we have a fearful proof of the intense

---

18. Luke goes on to list some of these nationalities: "Parthians and Medes and Elamites, and residents of Mesopotamia, Judea and Cappadocia, Pontus and Asia, Phrygia and Pamphylia, Egypt and the districts of Libya around Cyrene, and visitors from Rome, both Jews and proselytes, Cretans and Arabs" (Acts 2:9-11).

19. The destruction of the Harlot by her former "lovers" is inexplicable apart from the hypothesis that she is Jerusalem. There is clearly a contextual connection between the nations' war against Christ and their war against the Harlot. Their opposition is, first and foremost, against Him; their destruction of her is represented as an aspect of their attempt to destroy Him.

20. Cornelius Tacitus, *The Histories*, v.1.

hatred felt towards the Jews by the neighbouring nations in the wholesale massacres of that unhappy people perpetrated in many great cities just before the outbreak of the war. The whole Jewish population of Caesarea were massacred in one day. In Syria every city was divided into two camps, Jews and Syrians. In Scythopolis upwards of thirteen thousand Jews were butchered; in Ascalon, Ptolemais, and Tyre, similar atrocities took place. But in Alexandria the carnage of the Jewish inhabitants exceeded all the other massacres. The whole Jewish quarter was deluged with blood, and fifty thousand corpses lay in ghastly heaps in the streets.[21] This is a terrible commentary on the words of the angel-interpreter: 'The ten horns which thou sawest upon the beast, these shall hate the whore,' etc."[22]

It is important to realize, as we noted above, that the Beast destroyed Jerusalem as part of his war against Christ; the Roman leaders' motive in destroying the Temple was not only to put down the Jewish rebellion, but to obliterate Christianity, as Sulpitius Severus recorded:

> Titus is said, after calling a council, to have first deliberated whether he should destroy the temple, a structure of such extraordinary work. For it seemed good to some that a sacred edifice, distinguished above all human achievements, ought not to be destroyed, inasmuch as, if preserved, it would furnish an evidence of Roman moderation, but, if destroyed, would serve for a perpetual proof of Roman cruelty. But on the opposite side, others and Titus himself thought that the temple ought specially to be overthrown, in order that the religion of the Jews and of the Christians might more thoroughly be subverted; for that these religions, although contrary to each other, had nevertheless proceeded from the same authors; that the Christians had sprung up from among the Jews; and that, if the root were extirpated, the offshoot would speedily perish.[23]

---

21. Josephus, *The Jewish War*, ii.xviii.

22. J. Stuart Russell, *The Parousia: A Critical Inquiry into the New Testament Doctrine of Our Lord's Second Coming* (Grand Rapids: Baker Book House, [1887] 1983), p. 503.

23. *The Sacred History of Sulpitius Severus*, in *A Select Library of Nicene and Post-Nicene Fathers of the Christian Church* (Grand Rapids:Eerdmans, [n.d.] 1973), Second Series, Vol. 11, p. 111. This information from Sulpitius seems to have been derived from Tacitus's record of eyewitness accounts. See Michael Grant, *The Twelve Caesars* (New York: Charles Scribner's Sons, 1975), pp. 228f.

The Beast thought that he could kill the Whore and the Bride in one stroke! But when the dust settled, the scaffolding of old, apostate Jerusalem lay in ruins, and the Church was revealed as the new and most glorious Temple, God's eternal dwelling place.

17 The sovereign Lord is thus not at the mercy of the Beast and his minions; rather, all these events have been predestined for God's glory, through the execution of His decrees. **For God has put it into their hearts to execute His purpose by having a common purpose, and by giving their kingdom to the Beast.** Obviously, it is a *sin* for these kings to give their kingdoms to the Beast, for the purpose of making war against the Lamb. And yet it is God who put it into their hearts! Some will complain, of course, that this makes God "the Author of sin." The obvious answer to such an objection is that the text *says* that God placed the evil purpose into their hearts; at the same time, we are assured that "the LORD is righteous in all His ways." If we believe the Bible, we must believe both Revelation 17:17 and Psalm 145:17. We must hold firmly to two (seemingly contradictory) points: First, God is not responsible for sin; Second, *nothing* happens in spite of Him, or in opposition to His purpose.[24] Thus, to those who fight against the Word of God, the Biblical response is blunt: "On the contrary, who are you, O man, who answers back to God? The thing molded will not say to the molder, 'Why did you make me like this,' will it? Or does not the

---

24. These seem contradictory to us because we are *creatures*. Problems such as the relationship of God's sovereignty and human responsibility, or of God's sovereignty and God's righteousness, or of unity and diversity within the Trinity, cannot be "solved" by us because we are not capable of comprehending God. Cornelius Van Til writes: "Human knowledge can never be completely comprehensive knowledge. Every knowledge transaction has in it somewhere a reference point to God. Now since God is not fully comprehensible to us we are bound to come into what seems to be contradiction in all our knowledge. Our knowledge is analogical and therefore must be paradoxical" (*The Defense of the Faith,* Philadelphia: Presbyterian and Reformed, third revised ed., 1967, p. 44). For this reason, "all teaching of Scripture is apparently contradictory" (*Common Grace and the Gospel,* Nutley, NJ: Presbyterian and Reformed, 1972, p. 142; cf. pp. 9ff.; cf. Van Til's *Introduction to Systematic Theology,* Presbyterian and Reformed, pp. 247ff.). For a full consideration of this matter, see John Frame, "The Problem of Theological Paradox," in Gary North, ed., *Foundations of Christian Scholarship* (Vallecito, CA: Ross House Books, 1976), pp. 295-330.

potter have a right over the clay, to make from the same lump one vessel for honor, and another vessel for dishonor?" (Rom. 9:20-21). St. Augustine observed: "It is, therefore, in the power of the wicked to sin; but that in sinning they do this or that is not in their power, but in God's, who divides the darkness and regulates it; so that hence *even what they do contrary to God's will is not fulfilled except it be God's will.*"[25]

The whole purpose for the heathen kings' wrath, for their joining in conspiracy against both the Bride and the Harlot, for their surrendering their kingdoms to the Beast and receiving power for one hour with him, is now revealed. God has put it into their hearts to fulfill His purpose, **until the words of God should be fulfilled.** The war between Christ and the Beast, culminating in the desolation of the Harlot, took place in fulfillment of God's announcements through His prophets. The curses of the Covenant (Deut. 28) were executed on Israel through the Beast and the ten horns. They were the instruments of God's wrath, as Christ had foretold in His discourse on the Mount of Olives. During these horrifying "days of vengeance," He said, *all things that were written* would be fulfilled (Luke 21:22). Vision and prophecy would be sealed and completed in the destruction of the old world order (Dan. 9:24).

18   The angel now identifies the Harlot as **the Great City,** which, as we have seen, St. John uses as a term for Jerusalem, where the Lord was crucified (11:8; 16:19). Moreover, says the angel, this City **has a Kingdom over all the kings of the earth.** It is perhaps this verse, more than any other, which has confused expositors into supposing, against all other evidence, that the Harlot is Rome. If the City is Jerusalem, how can she be said to wield this kind of worldwide political power? The answer is that *Revelation is not a book about politics; it is a book about the Covenant.* Jerusalem *did* reign over the nations. She *did* possess a Kingdom which was above all the kingdoms of the world. She had a covenantal priority over the kingdoms of the earth. Israel was a Kingdom of priests (Ex. 19:6), exercising a priestly minis-

---

25. St. Augustine, *Anti-Pelagian Works*, Peter Holmes and Robert Ernest Wallis, trans. (Grand Rapids: William B. Eerdmans, reprinted 1971), p. 514, italics added; cf. John Calvin, *Institutes of the Christian Religion*, ii.iv.4.

try of guardianship, instruction, and intercession on behalf of the nations of the world. When Israel was faithful to God, offering up sacrifices for the nations, the world was at peace; when Israel broke the Covenant, the world was in turmoil. The Gentile nations recognized this (1 Kings 10:24; Ezra 1; 4-7; cf. Rom. 2:17-24).[26] Yet, perversely, they would seek to seduce Israel to commit whoredom against the Covenant – and when she did, they would turn on her and destroy her. That pattern was repeated several times over until Israel's final excommunication in A.D. 70, when Jerusalem was destroyed. The desolation of the Harlot was God's final sign that the Kingdom had been transferred to His new people, the Church (Matt. 21:43; 1 Pet. 2:9; Rev. 11:19; 15:5; 21:3). The Kingdom over the kingdoms will never again be possessed by national Israel.

---

26. Josephus points out repeatedly that the nations had historically recognized the sanctity and centrality of the Temple: "This celebrated place . . . was esteemed holy by all mankind" (*The Jewish War*, v.i.3; cf. v.ix.4; v.xiii.6). In fact, the action of Jewish rebels, in the summer of A.D. 66, of halting the daily sacrifices for the Emperor (in violation, Josephus points out, of long-standing practice) was the single event which finally precipitated the Roman war against the Jews (ii.xvii.2-4). Even at the very end, as Titus prepared to raze the city to the ground, he was still pleading with the Jewish priests to offer up the sacrifices, which by now had been entirely discontinued (vi.ii.1).

18

BABYLON IS FALLEN!

Come Out of Her! (18:1-8)

1 After these things I saw another Angel coming down from heaven, having great authority, and the earth was illumined with His glory.

2 And He cried out with a mighty voice, saying: Fallen, Fallen is Babylon the great! And she has become a dwelling place of demons and a prison of every unclean spirit, and a prison of every unclean and hateful bird.

3 For all the nations have drunk of the wine of the wrath of her fornication, and the kings of the earth have committed fornication with her, and the merchants of the earth have become rich by the wealth of her sensuality.

4 And I heard another voice from heaven, saying: Come out of her, My people, that you may not participate in her sins and that you may not receive of her plagues;

5 for her sins have piled up as high as heaven, and God has remembered her iniquities.

6 Pay her back even as she has paid, and give back double according to her deeds; in the cup which she has mixed, mix twice as much for her.

7 To the degree that she glorified herself and lived sensuously, to the same degree give her torment and mourning; for she says in her heart: I sit as a queen and am not a widow, and will never see mourning.

8 For this reason in one Day her plagues will come, pestilence and mourning and famine, and she will be burned up with fire; for strong is the Lord God who judges her.

1 St. John is now introduced to **another Angel** — probably the Lord Jesus Christ, considering the description of Him, compared with statements about Christ in St. John's Gospel: He comes down from heaven (John 3:13, 31; 6:38, 58), He has great authority (John 5:27; 10:18; 17:2), and the earth was illumined with His glory (John 1:4-5, 9, 14; 8:12; 9:5; 11:9; 12:46; cf. 1 Tim. 6:16). The expressions parallel those in 10:1, which, as we have seen, are clearly speaking of the Son of God. The last phrase is virtually a repetition of Ezekiel 43:2, where it says of God that "the earth shone with His glory." Christ Himself, who brings the wrath of god upon the Harlot-City, comes to proclaim her judgment. The destruction of the covenant apostates manifests His authority and glory in the Land.

2 The proclamation of God's Messenger is consistent (cf. 14:8): **Fallen, fallen is Babylon the great!** Her doom is certain, and thus is spoken of as already completed. This is similar to the funeral dirge Amos sang against Israel:

> She has fallen, she will not rise again —
> The virgin Israel.
> She lies neglected on her land;
> There is none to raise her up. (Amos 5:2)

Jerusalem's apostasy has become so great that her judgment is permanent and irrevocable. She is **Babylon,** the implacable enemy of God, having **become a dwelling place of demons and a prison of every unclean spirit, and a prison of every unclean and hateful bird,** in contrast to the New Jerusalem in 21:27 ("nothing unclean . . . shall ever come into it"). The Harlot is in a *wilderness* (17:3), having been made *desolate* for her sins (17:16; cf. Matt. 24:15; our words *wilderness, desert, desolation,* and *desolate* are basically the same word in Greek). The desert is, as we have already noted, the place of sin and demons (Matt. 12:43; cf. Luke 8:27). An important source for this is the original desolation of the world through the demon-inspired rebellion against God (Gen. 3:17-18). Following from this, on the Day of Atonement a goat was driven into the wilderness, bearing the sins of the people. This "scapegoat" was, literally, said to be sent *to* or *for* "Azazel" (Lev. 16:8, 10, 26),[1] a name for the "goat-demon"

---

1. See the discussion of this point in Gordon J. Wenham, *The Book of Leviticus* (Grand Rapids: William B. Eerdmans Publishing Co., 1979), pp. 231, 234f., 243.

who lived in the wilderness.[2] Isaiah had prophesied about the desolation of Babylon:

> Desert creatures will lie down there,
> And their houses will be full of owls,
> Ostriches also will live there,
> And goat-demons will frolic there. (Isa. 13:21)

God's wrath against Edom was phrased in much the same language:

> It shall not be quenched night or day;
> Its smoke shall go up forever;
> From generation to generation it shall be desolate;
> None shall pass through it forever and ever.
> But pelican and hedgehog shall possess it,
> And owl and raven shall dwell in it;
> And He shall stretch over it the measuring line of desolation
> And the plumb line of void. . . .
> And thorns shall come up on its fortified towers,
> Nettles and thistles in its fortified cities;
> It shall also be a haunt of jackals
> And an abode of ostriches.
> And the desert creatures shall meet with the wolves,
> The goat-demon also shall cry to its kind;
> Yes, the night demon [*Lilith*] shall settle there
> And shall find herself a resting place. (Isa. 34:10-14)

Now the Angel's decree applies the ancient curses to the rebellious Jews of the first century. Because Israel rejected Christ, the entire nation becomes demon-possessed, utterly beyond hope of reformation (cf. Matt. 12:38-45; Rev. 9:1-11). Underscoring the tragedy of this is John's use of the term **dwelling place** (*katoikētērion*), a word elsewhere used for the place of God's special Presence, in heaven, in the holy city, in the Temple, and in the Church; "the *Place* (*katoikētērion*) O Lord, which Thou hast made for Thy dwelling, the sanctuary, O Lord, which Thy hands have established" (Ex. 15:17; cf. 1 Kings

---

2. This was not to be interpreted as a sacrifice to the demon himself (Lev. 17:7). Centuries later, the apostate Northern Israelites under Jeroboam did in fact offer worship to this goat-demon (2 Chron. 11:15).

8:39, 43, 49; 2 Chron. 30:27; Ps. 33:14; 76:2; 107:7; Eph. 2:22). Jerusalem, which had been God's dwelling place, has now become the unclean dwelling place of demons.

3 Israel's abandonment and perversion of her calling as teacher-priest to the nations is again stated to be the reason for her destruction (cf. 14:8; 17:2, 4). She has committed **fornication** with the **nations**, with the **kings**, and with the **merchants**, prostituting her gifts instead of leading the nations to the Kingdom, joining with them in the attempted overthrow of the King. The stress on the merchants is most likely related to the commercial activities around the Temple (see below, on 18:11-17a). The corruption of Temple commerce affected the liturgy of the nation. All of life flows from the religious center of culture;[3] if the core is rotten, the fruit is worthless. This is why Jesus came into conflict with the Temple moneychangers (Matt. 21:12-13; John 2:13-22). Observing that many of the shops belonged to the family of the high priest, Ford cites Josephus' characterization of the high priest Ananias as "the great procurer of money." In particular, "the court of the Gentiles appears to have been the scene of a flourishing trade in animal sacrifice, perhaps supported by the high priestly family."[4] This would agree with the observation already made, that Babylon is no ordinary prostitute: Her punishment by fire indicates that she is of the priestly class (see on 17:16).

4-5 Since Israel was to be destroyed, the apostles spent much of their time during the Last Days summoning God's people to a religious separation from her, urging them to align themselves instead with the Church (cf. Acts 2:37-40; 3:19-26; 4:8-12; 5:27-32). This is St. John's message in Revelation. God's people must not seek to reform Israel, with its new religion of Judaism, but must abandon her to her fate. The Jews had "tasted the good Word of God and the powers of the Age to come" — the

---

3. See Henry R. Van Til, *The Calvinistic Concept of Culture* (Philadelphia: The Presbyterian and Reformed Publishing Co., 1959); Abraham Kuyper, *Lectures on Calvinism* (Grand Rapids: William B. Eerdmans Publishing Co., 1931).

4. J. Massyngberde Ford, *Revelation: Introduction, Translation, and Commentary* (Garden City: Doubleday and Co., 1975), pp. 301f.

Age brought in by Christ's redemptive act—and had fallen away. It would be "impossible to renew them again to repentance." Judaism—the vain attempt to continue the Old Covenant while rejecting Christ "is worthless and close to being cursed, and it ends up being burned" (Heb. 6:4-8). Old Covenant religion cannot be revivified; it is impossible to have the Covenant without Christ. There can be no turning "back" to something which never existed, for even the fathers under the Old Covenant worshiped Christ under the signs and seals of the provisional age (1 Cor. 10:1-4). Now that "the Age to come" has arrived, salvation is with Christ and the Church. Only destruction awaits those who are identified with the Harlot: **Come out of her, My people, that you may not participate in her sins and that you may not receive of her plagues** (cf. Heb. 10:19-39; 12:15-29; 13:10-14). Time for Israel's repentance has run out, and by now **her sins have piled up** [literally, *have adhered*] **to heaven** (cf. Gen. 19:13; 2 Chron. 28:9; Ezra 9:6; Jer. 51:9; Jon. 1:2). Jesus had foretold that this crucifying generation would "fill up the measure of the guilt" of their rebellious fathers, and thus that upon them would fall "all the righteous blood shed on earth" (Matt. 23:32-35). This prophecy was fulfilled within the first century, as St. Paul observed: "They are not pleasing to God, but hostile to all men, hindering us from speaking to the Gentiles that they might be saved; with the result that *they always fill up the measure of their sins. But wrath has come upon them to the uttermost*" (1 Thess. 2:15-16).

Therefore, not only religious separation was demanded—**that you may not participate in her sins**—but physical, geographical separation was necessary as well (cf. Matt. 24:16-21), **that you may not receive of her plagues.** The language is reminiscent of God's call to His people to come out of Babylon at the end of the captivity. The Old Testament texts speak in terms of three ideas: the coming destruction of Babylon, the coming redemption of the faithful Covenant people, and the rebuilding of the Temple (Ezra 1:2-3; Isa. 48:20; 52:11-12; Jer. 50:8; 51:6, 9, 45). Similarly, the New Covenant people were to separate themselves from Israel. The persecutors were about to suffer destruction at God's hands, the Church's redemption was drawing near (Luke 21:28, 31), and the new Temple was about to be fully established.

6-8 The righteous Judge demands full restitution: **Pay her back even as she has paid, and give back double according to her deeds; in the cup which she has mixed, mix twice as much for her** (cf. Jer. 50:15, 29; Ps. 137:8; Isa. 40:2). This command, presumably, is spoken either to the angels of heaven, or to the Roman armies who are the agents of God's wrath. The expression translated **give back double** actually has a Hebraic duplication of the term, providing a "double witness," for purposes of emphasis: **Double to her double things.** This is the ordinary restitution required by Biblical law (Ex. 22:4, 7).[5] Thus, **to the degree that she glorified herself and lived sensuously, to the same degree give her torment and mourning.** Double (or multiple) restitution in the Bible is not more than the criminal deserves. It is exactly what he deserves—a strict, proportional accounting of wrath according to God's *lex talionis* principle of equivalence: "life for life, eye for eye, tooth for tooth, hand for hand, foot for foot, burn for burn, wound for wound, bruise for bruise" (Ex. 21:23-25).

This punishment comes on the Harlot because **she says in her heart: I sit as a queen and am not a widow, and will never see mourning**—paralleling the boast of the Laodicean church: "I have become rich, and have become wealthy, and have need of nothing" (3:17). The text is based on God's condemnation of Babylon in Isaiah 47:6-11, a pronouncement of judgment which would come upon her for mistreating the Covenant people:

> You did not show mercy to them,
> On the aged you made your yoke very heavy.
> Yet you said, "I shall be a queen forever."
> These things you did not consider,
> Nor remember the outcome of them.
> Now, then, hear this, you sensual one,

---

5. Cf. God's declaration of judgment against Judah: "And I will first *doubly repay* their iniquity and their sin, because they have polluted My land" (Jer. 16:18); "Bring on them a day of disaster, and crush them with *twofold* destruction!" (Jer. 17:18). Contrast with this Isa. 40:2: "Speak to the heart of Jerusalem, and call out to her that her warfare has ended, that her iniquity has been removed, that she has received of the LORD's hand double for all her sins." On the pleonasm as a double witness, see James B. Jordan, *The Law of the Covenant: An Exposition of Exodus 21-23* (Tyler, TX: Institute for Christian Economics, 1984), pp. 96, 106; on the laws of restitution, see pp. 134ff.

Who dwells securely,
Who says in your heart,
"I am, and there is no one besides me.
I shall not sit as a widow,
Nor shall I know the loss of children."
But these two things shall come on you suddenly in one day:
Loss of children and widowhood.
They shall come on you in full measure
In spite of your many sorceries,
In spite of the great power of your spells.
And you felt secure in your wickedness and said,
"No one sees me."
Your wisdom and your knowledge, they have deluded you;
For you have said in your heart,
"I am, and there is no one besides me."
But evil will come on you
Which you will not know how to charm away;
And disaster will fall on you
For which you cannot atone,
And destruction about which you do not know
Will come on you suddenly.

Jerusalem has committed the sin of Eve, who committed fornication with the Dragon, in seeking to make herself God (Gen. 3:5); for when she says, "I am," she contradicts the declaration of the Most High God: "I, even I, am the LORD; and there is no Savior besides Me" (Isa. 43:11). **For this reason in one Day her plagues will come, pestilence and mourning and famine, and she will be burned up with fire; for strong is the Lord God who judges her.** The Day of the Lord would come upon Israel in fiery judgment, bringing swift destruction (1 Thess. 5:2-3). The term **Day** here does not signify some specific duration of time; but it is used here to indicate relative suddenness, as well as emphasizing that the destruction of Jerusalem would be no random occurrence: it was coming as the Day of Judgment. As the priest's daughter who turned Harlot, she would be burned with fire (Lev. 21:9). After that awful Day came, "there was left nothing to make those who came there believe it had ever been inhabited."[6]

---

6. Josephus, *The Jewish War*, vii.i.1.

Reactions to Babylon's Fall (18:9-20)

9 And the kings of the earth, who committed fornication and lived sensuously with her, will weep and lament over her when they see the smoke of her burning,

10 standing at a distance because of the fear of her torment, saying: Woe, woe, the great City, Babylon, the strong City! For in one hour your judgment has come.

11 And the merchants of the earth weep and mourn over her, because no one buys their cargoes any more;

12 cargoes of gold, silver, precious stones, and pearls; of fine linen, purple, silk, and scarlet; and every kind of citron wood, every article of ivory, and every article made from very costly wood, bronze, iron, and marble;

13 and cinnamon, incense, perfume, and frankincense; and wine, olive oil, fine flour, and wheat; and sheep and cattle, of horses, of chariots, and of bodies; and souls of men.

14 And the fruit of your soul's desire has gone from you, and all things that were luxurious and splendid have passed away from you and men will no longer find them.

15 The merchants of these things, who became rich from her, will stand at a distance because of the fear of her torment, weeping and mourning,

16 saying: Woe, woe, the Great City, she who was clothed in fine linen and purple and scarlet, and adorned with gold and precious stones and pearls;

17 for in one hour such great wealth has been laid waste! And every shipmaster and everyone who sails anywhere, and every sailor, and as many as make their living by the sea, stood at a distance,

18 and were crying out as they saw the smoke of her burning, saying: Who is like the Great City?

19 And they threw dust on their heads and were crying out, weeping and mourning, saying: Woe, woe, the Great City, in which all who had ships at sea became rich by her costliness, for in one hour she has been laid waste!

20 Rejoice over her, O heaven, and you saints and apostles and prophets, because God has judged your judgment against her!

9-10   Three classes of people lament for the destruction of Jerusalem. The first group comprises **the kings of the earth**, the nations of the empire who aided and abetted the faithless Cove-

452

nant people in their apostasy from God. The destruction of the Harlot is a fearful sign to them of God's rigorous and inexorable judgment. They see **the smoke of her burning** — a symbol borrowed from the destruction of Sodom (Gen. 19:28) and the later, metaphorical description of the fall of Edom (Isa. 34:10) — and are reminded that a similar judgment on themselves cannot be long in coming. God declared to the prophet Jeremiah that the nations of the earth would be forced to drink the cup of His fierce wrath: "And it will be, if they refuse to take the cup from your hand to drink, then you will say to them, Thus says the LORD of hosts: You shall surely drink! For behold, I am beginning to work calamity in this City which is called by My name, and shall you be completely free from punishment? You will not be free from punishment; for I am summoning a sword against all the inhabitants of the earth, declares the LORD of hosts" (Jer. 25:28-29).

The lament of each group ends with the words, **Woe, woe, the Great City!** This expression would turn out to have great significance for those living in Jerusalem in the years before and during the Tribulation. Josephus tells of a Jewish prophet (interestingly, his name was Jesus) in the Last Days, whose cry of "Woe, woe!" became a familiar aspect of life in the City.

> A portent still more alarming had appeared four years before the war at a time when profound peace and prosperity still prevailed in the city [i.e., A.D. 62]. One Jesus, the son of Ananias, an uncouth peasant, came to the feast at which every Jew is expected to put up a tabernacle for God [i.e., the Feast of Tabernacles, or *Sukkoth*]; as he stood in the Temple courts he suddenly began to cry out: "A voice from the east, a voice from the west, a voice from the Four Winds, a voice against Jerusalem and the Sanctuary, a voice against the Bridegroom and the Bride, a voice against the whole people!" Day and night he uttered this cry as he went about all the alleys.
>
> Some of the leading citizens, seriously annoyed at these ominous pronouncements, laid hold of the man and beat him savagely. But he, without uttering a word in his own defense, or for the private information of those who were beating him, persisted in uttering the same warnings as before. Thereupon, the magistrates, rightly concluding that some supernatural impulse was responsible for his behavior, took him before the Roman

governor. There, although flayed to the bone with scourges, he neither begged for mercy nor shed a tear, but, raising his voice to a most mournful cry, answered every stroke with "Woe, woe, to Jerusalem!" When Albinus, the governor, asked him who he was and whence he came and why he uttered these cries, he made no reply whatever, but endlessly repeated his dirge over the city, until Albinus released him because he judged him insane.

Throughout this time, until the war broke out, he never approached another citizen nor was he seen talking to any, but daily, like a prayer that he had memorized, he recited his lament: "Woe, woe, to Jerusalem!" He never cursed any of those who beat him from day to day, nor did he thank those who gave him food; his only response to anyone was that melancholy prediction.

His voice was heard most of all at the festivals. So, for seven years and five months he continued his wail, his voice as strong as ever and his vigor unabated, till, during the siege, after seeing the fulfillment of his foreboding, he was silenced. He was going his rounds, shouting in penetrating tones from the wall, "Woe, woe, once more to the city, and the people and the Temple!" Then, when he added a last word—"And woe to me also!"—a stone hurled from the ballista struck him, killing him on the spot. Thus, with those same forebodings still upon his lips, he met his end.[7]

11-17a   The second and largest group of mourners is comprised of **the merchants of the Land**, weeping **because no one buys their cargoes any more.** The wealth of Jerusalem was a direct result of the blessings promised in Leviticus 26 and Deuteronomy 28. God had made her a great commercial center, but she had abused the gift. While there are similarities between the list of goods here and that in Ezekiel 27:12-24 (a prophecy against Tyre), it is likely that the items primarily reflect the Temple and the commerce surrounding it. Ford observes that "foreign trade had a great influence on the holy city, and the temple drew the largest share. The chief items were food supplies, precious metals, luxury goods, and clothing materials."[8] Josephus described the luxurious wealth of the Temple's facade (cf. Luke 21:5): "The first gate was 70 cubits high and 25 broad; it had no doors, displaying unhampered the vast expanse of heaven; the entire

---

7. Josephus, *The Jewish War*, vi.v.3.
8. Ford, p. 305.

face was covered with gold, and through it the arch of the first hall was fully visible to an onlooker without in all its grandeur, and the surroundings of the inner gate, all gleaming with gold, struck the beholder's eye. . . . The gate opening into the building was, as I said, completely overlaid with gold, as was the whole wall surrounding it. Above it, moreover, were the golden grapevines from which hung grape clusters as tall as a man. In front of these hung a veil of equal length of Babylonian tapestry embroidered with blue, scarlet and purple, and fine linen, wrought with marvelous craftsmanship. . . . The exterior of the sanctuary did not lack anything that could amaze either mind or eye. Overlaid on all sides with massive plates of gold, it reflected in the first rays of the sun so fierce a flash that those looking at it were forced to look away as from the very rays of the sun. To strangers as they approached it, it seemed in the distance like a mountain clad with snow; for any part not covered with gold was of the purest white."[9]

Josephus also records that one of the priests, named Jesus, turned over the treasures of the Temple to Titus: "He came out and handed from over the wall of the sanctuary two lampstands resembling those deposited in the sanctuary, as well as tables, bowls, and platters, all of solid gold and very heavy. He also handed over the curtains, the vestments of the high priests, set with precious stones, and a multitude of other objects required for the Temple services. In addition, the Temple treasurer, Phineas by name, when taken prisoner, disclosed the tunics and girdles of the priests, a large supply of purple and scarlet kept in store for repairing the curtain of the Temple, together with a large supply of cinnamon and cassia and a multitude of other spices, which were blended and burned daily as incense to God. He delivered many other treasures, with an abundance of sacred ornaments. . . ."[10]

In the midst of a lengthy passage describing Jerusalem's extensive commerce, Edersheim reports: "In these streets and lanes everything might be purchased: the production of Palestine, or imported from foreign lands—nay, the rarest articles from the remotest parts. Exquisitely shaped, curiously designed

9. Josephus, *The Jewish War*, v.v.4, 6.
10. Ibid., vi.viii.3.

and jewelled cups, rings, and other workmanship of precious metals; glass, silks, fine linen, woolen stuffs, purple, and costly hangings; essences, ointments, and perfumes, as precious as gold; articles of food and drink from foreign lands—in short, what India, Persia, Arabia, Media, Egypt, Italy, Greece, and even the far-off lands of the Gentiles yielded, might be had in these bazaars. Ancient Jewish writings enable us to identify no fewer than 118 different articles of import from foreign lands, covering more than even modern luxury has devised."[11]

St. John's list of trade goods divides into several sections, generally of four items each; the prosaic, businesslike enumeration concludes with a shock:

1) **cargoes of gold, silver, precious stones, and pearls;**
2) **of fine linen, purple, silk, and scarlet;**[12]
3) **and every kind of citron wood, every article of ivory, and every article made from very costly wood, bronze, iron, and marble;**
4) **and cinnamon, incense, perfume, and frankincense;**
5) **and wine, olive oil, fine flour, and wheat;**
6) **and sheep and cattle, even of horses, of chariots, and of bodies;**
7) **and souls of men.**

The final phrase, adapted from the description of Tyre's slave traffic in Ezekiel 27:13, is applied to Jerusalem's spiritual bondage of men's souls. As St. Paul noted in his contrast of the earthly, apostate Jerusalem with the Church, the heavenly City of God: "The present Jerusalem . . . is in slavery with her children," while "the Jerusalem above is free; She is our Mother" (Gal. 4:25-26). Jerusalem trafficked in many goods, from all over the world. In keeping with the promises of Leviticus 26 and Deuteronomy 28, God had made her into a great commercial center. But she abused God's gifts: Her most basic trade was in human souls. Instead of fulfilling her proper function as the

---

11. Alfred Edersheim, *The Life and Times of Jesus the Messiah*, two vols. (McLean, VA: MacDonald Publishing Co., n.d.), Vol. 1, p. 116.

12. As mentioned earlier (on 17:4), this may well be a reference to the Temple curtain, a "Babylonian tapestry embroidered with blue, scarlet and purple, and fine linen, wrought with marvelous craftsmanship." Josephus, *The Jewish War*, v.v.4.

mother of all mankind, she prostituted herself, and led her children into demonic bondage, statist oppression, and finally annihilation.

Briefly, the narrative turns to address Jerusalem herself: **And the fruit of your soul's desire has gone from you, and all things that were luxurious and splendid have passed away from you and men will no longer find them.** By heeding the Serpent and seeking to become as God, the Bride committed apostasy and thus lost access to the fruit she desired [cf. Matt. 21:19, 43]; barred from the Tree of Life, she lost also the other blessings of the Garden, "all things that were luxurious and splendid."

The merchants of Israel had been enriched, Spiritually and (therefore) materially, from their relationship with Jerusalem; now, at the sight of her destruction, they are helpless to do anything but weep and mourn for **the Great City, she who was clothed in fine linen and purple and scarlet, and adorned with gold and precious stones and pearls.** Again, the description of the Harlot City indicates her identity as apostate Jerusalem, arrayed in the glory of the Temple and dressed in the fine linen of the righteous Bride (19:8). Those who have profited from Jerusalem's riches are shocked at the suddenness of her destruction: **for in one hour such great wealth has been laid waste!** The expression translated **laid waste** is, as we should by now expect, **desolated:** It is the promised *desolation* of Jerusalem (Matt. 23:38; 24:15, etc.) that is being described. The term **hour** is not to be taken in a strictly literal sense here, any more than in many other metaphorical uses of the word; rather, it is often used, especially in St. John, to refer to a particularly critical time (cf. Matt. 25:13; Mark 14:41; John 2:4; 5:25, 28; 7:30; 8:20; 12:23; 17:1; 1 John 2:18). There is, however, the sense of swiftness. Jerusalem's destruction was sudden, and even unexpected: right up to the end the people were looking for a miraculous deliverance. The world of apostate Judaism was stunned at the desolation of its City and Temple. The fall of Jerusalem was a shock to the system from which it has never recovered.

17b-19 The third group that mourns for the fallen City is made up of **every shipmaster and everyone who sails anywhere and every sailor, and as many as make their living by the sea.** They too weep over the loss of Jerusalem, because **all who had**

457

ships at sea became rich by her wealth. Obviously, investment in Israel's economy ceased to be profitable after A.D. 70, but it seems likely that the mourning of the "seafarers" points to the nations of the world (of which seafaring men would in any case be representatives).

St. John has already spoken of the sea in relation to the Great City: the waters, over which the Harlot is straddled on the Beast, "are peoples and multitudes and nations and tongues" (17:15). He has also listed three classes of people affected by the Harlot's destruction: "the kings of the earth," "the merchants of the Land," and "all who had ships at sea." These seem to correspond to the threefold designation of those who had been corrupted by the Harlot, given in verse 3: *all the nations . . . the kings of the earth . . . the merchants of the Land.* "Those who go down to the sea in ships, who do business on great waters" should have been instructed in the ways of the Lord, that they might call upon Him in their distress, that He might show them His Covenant mercy (Ps. 107:23-32). And, indeed, when Israel walked worthy of her calling, the whole world was enriched by her wealth: she had been "a guide to the blind, a light to those in darkness, a corrector of the foolish, a teacher of children, having in the Law the embodiment of knowledge and truth" (Rom. 2:19-20). When Israel was in fellowship with God and under His Spiritual and material blessing, the nations had come to her both for wisdom and for trade and commerce (Deut. 28:12; 1 Kings 10:23-25). In apostasy, however, trade became a snare, a means of committing fornication with idolaters, and Israel corrupted not only her own children, but the nations of the world as well. She had arrogated to herself the honors of deity, so that the seafarers cried out: **Who is like the Great City?** (cf. the cry of the worshipers in 13:4: "Who is like the Beast?"). But because she had said in her heart, "I will ascend to heaven. . . . I will make myself like the Most High," Jerusalem was cast down to hell (Isa. 14:13-15). In **one hour** she was **laid waste,** desolate, never again to be the Great City.

20 There is a fourth response to Jerusalem's downfall: that of the Church. God's people are instructed by the angel to **rejoice over her.** The Church tabernacling in **heaven — saints and apostles and prophets —** had prayed for the destruction of the apostate, demonized City that led the world in rebellion against God and persecution of His children. As the smoke of the whole burnt offering ascends to heaven, the saints are to rejoice that their prayers have been answered: **God has judged your judgment against her!** the angel announces, employing a Hebraic pleonasm to express the divine Court's "double witness" against her. Again we find that the Biblical image of the Church, tabernacled in heaven, is firm in its opposition to evil, praying for God to vindicate His people in the earth. Note well: the judgment on the Harlot is called *"your* judgment," the Church's judgment. It was the just retribution to Israel for her oppression of saints, apostles, and prophets throughout her history, and culminating in the Last Days in her war against Christ and His Church. It was she who had inspired the Roman persecution of Christians; but the heathen wrath which she had stoked up had been poured out on her head instead. If the Church in our age is to proceed from victory to victory as did the Church in the apostolic age, she must recover the triumphalistic perspective of the early saints. The Church must pray for her enemies' defeat—a defeat that must come either by conversion or by destruction. We are at war, a war in which the definitive victory has been won by our King. All of history is now a mopping-up operation in terms of that victory, looking forward to the conversion of the world and the final overcoming of Death itself. Our opposition is doomed to perish, and the Church is called to rejoice in the certain knowledge of her earthly vindication and ultimate triumph.

Babylon is Thrown Down (18:21-24)

21 And a strong angel took up a stone like a great millstone and threw it into the sea, saying: Thus will Babylon, the great City, be thrown down with violence, and will not be found any longer.

22 And the sound of harpists and musicians and flute-players and trumpeters will not be heard in you any longer; and no craftsman of any craft will be found in you any longer; and the sound of a mill will not be heard in you any longer;

23 and the light of a lamp will not shine in you any longer; and the Voice of Bridegroom and Bride will not be heard in you any longer; for your merchants were the great men of the earth, because all nations were deceived by your sorcery.

459

24 And in her was found the blood of prophets and of saints
and of all who have been slain on the earth.

21   Jesus had instructed His disciples to pray for the mountain of Jerusalem to be cast into the sea (Matt. 21:21); He had warned the Pharisees that the man who opposed the Gospel and hindered the "little ones" from receiving it would be better off "if he had a millstone hung around his neck and he were thrown into the sea" (Luke 17:2; cf. Matt. 18:6; Mark 9:42). Here, in similar language, Jerusalem's destruction is symbolically portrayed by the dramatic action of **a strong angel**, the third and final occurrence of this expression in Revelation. In the first (5:2), he is heard calling for someone to open the scroll declaring God's covenantal judgments on Jerusalem; in the second (10:1ff.), he is seen as the Witness to the New Creation, holding the "little scroll" which spoke of the New Covenant and of the Church's role in the history of redemption, in the "finishing" of "the Mystery of God" in the Last Days. A related expression is used in 18:1-2, in which an angel with a "strong voice" announces the final doom of Babylon. Now, in fulfillment of all of these, the strong angel casts **a great millstone . . . into the sea.** All productivity (the millstone) is gone (cf. v. 23); in contrast to the Church (1 Cor. 15:58), Jerusalem's labor *has* been in vain. She and her works are hurled into the Abyss. The Old Testament background of this image comes from the destruction of the Egyptians in the Red Sea, according to Moses' song on the shore, echoed by the song of the Levites at the return from the Babylonian captivity:

> The LORD is a warrior;
> The LORD is His name.
> Pharaoh's chariots and his army He has cast into the sea;
> And the choicest of his officers are drowned in the Red Sea.
> The deeps cover them;
> They went down into the depths like a stone. . . .
> Thou didst blow with Thy wind, the sea covered them;
> They sank like lead in the mighty waters. (Ex. 15:3-5, 10)

> Thou didst see the affliction of our fathers in Egypt,
> And didst hear their cry by the Red Sea. . . .
> And Thou didst divide the sea before them,

So they passed through the midst of the sea on dry ground;
And their pursuers Thou didst hurl into the depths,
Like a stone into raging waters. (Neh. 9:9-11)

The symbol is also based on the prophetic drama performed
by Seraiah, Jeremiah's messenger of judgment (Jer. 51:61-64).
After reading the prophecy of Babylon's "perpetual desolation,"
he tied the scroll to a stone and threw it into the Euphrates, declaring: "Just so shall Babylon sink down and not rise again. . . ."
Applying Seraiah's words to the Harlot, the angel says: **Thus
will Babylon, the great city, be thrown down with violence, and
will not be found any longer.** How was this fulfilled in A.D. 70, if
"Jerusalem" is still standing in the twentieth century? In a physical sense, of course, Jerusalem was not destroyed *forever* in A.D.
70, any more than Babylon or Edom or Egypt was destroyed
"forever." But prophecy is covenantally and ethically oriented; it
is not primarily concerned with geography as such. For example, consider Isaiah's prophecy against Edom:

Its streams shall be turned into pitch,
And its loose earth into brimstone,
And its land shall become burning pitch.
It shall not be quenched night or day;
Its smoke shall go up forever;
From generation to generation it shall be desolate;
None shall pass through it forever and ever. (Isa. 34:9-10)

This is evocative language, associating the desolation of
Edom with the destruction of Sodom and Gomorrah. In a
"literal," physical sense, the prophecy was not fulfilled; but it
has been fulfilled, in terms of its actual meaning and intent. The
ancient territory of Edom still contains trees and flowers, portions of it are used as cropland, and travelers continue to pass
through it. As Patrick Fairbairn observed, "Edom was to be
stricken with poverty and ruin: Edom, however, not simply, nor
chiefly as a land, but as a people. This was what the prophecy
foretold, and it has been amply verified. . . . The Edom of
prophecy — Edom considered as the enemy of God, and the rival
of Israel — has perished forever; all, in that respect, is an untrod-
den wilderness, a hopeless ruin; and *there*, the veracity of God's

461

word finds its justification."[13]

Fairbairn explained how Edom is used in prophetic symbolism: "In the latter stages of the history of Israel, the Edomites surpassed all their enemies in keenness and intensity of malice; and hence they naturally came to be viewed by the Spirit of prophecy as the personification of that godless malignity and pride which would be satisfied with nothing less than the utter extermination of the cause of God — the heads and representatives of the whole army of the aliens, whose doom was to carry along with it the downfall and destruction of everything that opposed and exalted itself against the knowledge of God. This is manifestly the aspect presented of the matter in verse 15 of the prophecy of Obadiah; the fate of all the heathen is bound up with that of Edom:

> For the Day of the LORD draws near on all the nations;
> As you [Edom] have done, it will be done to you;
> Your dealings will return on your head;

— that is, in Edom, the quintessence of heathenism, all heathenism was to receive, as it were, its death-blow."[14]

Moreover, the prophet Amos foretold the subjugation of "Edom" under the rule of the House of David (Amos 9:11-12), and the New Testament interpretation of this text explains it as a prophecy of the conversion of the nations under the government of Christ (Acts 15:14-19). "This clearly implies that the Edom of prophecy, which was doomed to utter prostration and eternal ruin, is only the Edom of bitter and unrelenting hostility to the cause and people of God; that insofar as the children of Edom ceased from this, and entered into a friendly relation to the covenant of God, and submitted to the yoke of universal sovereignty committed to the house of David, instead of breaking it, as of old, from their necks, they should participate in the blessing, and have their interests merged in those of the people on whom God puts His name to do them good. A promise and prospect like this can never be made to harmonize with the result that is obtained from the predicted judgments upon

---

13. Patrick Fairbairn, *The Interpretation of Prophecy* (London: The Banner of Truth Trust, [1865] 1964), p. 221.

14. Ibid., pp. 221f.

Edom, as read by the strictly literal style of interpretation; for, according to it, there should be no remnant to be possessed, no seed or place of blessing, as connected with Edom, but one appalling scene of sterility, desolation, and cursing."[15]

Similarly, the "forever" desolation of Jerusalem means that Israel, as *the* covenant people, will cease to exist. Jerusalem—as *the Great City,* the *Holy* City—**will not be found any longer.**[16] True, as Romans 11 clearly shows, the descendants of Abraham will be grafted into the covenant again.[17] But they will *not* be a distinct, holy nation of special priests. They will join the peoples of the world in the saved multitude, with no distinction (Isa. 19:19-25). By His finished work Christ "made both groups [Hebrew and Gentile believers] into one" (Eph. 2:14). They have been united "in one Body," the Church (Eph. 2:16). There is one salvation and one Church, in which all believers, regardless of ethnic heritage, become children of God and heirs of the promises to Abraham (Gal. 3:26-29; cf. Eph. 2:11-22). Old Jerusalem, the apostate harlot, has been replaced by New Jerusalem, the pure Bride of Christ. There is no salvation outside of the Church.

22-23 As a further indication of the removal of the Harlot's covenantal status, the angel announces that the blessings of the Garden of Eden will be forever taken away. Alluding both to Jeremiah's prophecies against the rebellious Jerusalem of his day (Jer. 7:34; 16:9; 25:10; cf. Isa. 24:7-12), and to Ezekiel's prophecy against the king of Tyre (Ezek. 28:11-19), he pronounces the City's doom in five parts:

First, there is a fourfold description of the loss of music throughout the entire Land: **And the sound of harpists and musicians and flute-players and trumpeters will not be heard in you any longer** (cf. the mention of "tambourines" and "flutes" in Ezek. 28:13 [margin]).

---

15. Ibid., pp. 224f.

16. This expression is used six times in verses 21-23, connoting the fact that Jerusalem has fallen short—that, like Babylon of old, it has been weighed in the scales and found deficient, and is about to be overthrown, with its kingdom given to others (Dan. 5:25-28).

17. See David Chilton, *Paradise Restored: A Biblical Theology of Dominion* (Ft. Worth, TX: Dominion Press, 1985), pp. 125-31.

Second, the productivity of the Land disappears, as the workman is taken from Israel and cast into the Abyss: **No craftsman of any craft will be found in you any longer.** According to Zechariah, the tyranny of heathen nations over Israel would be restrained by her craftsmen (Zech. 1: 18-21). But, for apostate Israel, this bulwark against oppression will no longer exist.

The third and middle item in the list is significant: **The sound of a mill will not be heard in you any longer.** The image of the Mill was, throughout the ancient world, a symbol of the foundation of the cosmos, grinding out peace and prosperity; the Mill's destruction signifies the End of the Age.[18] The centrality of the **mill** in this passage may indicate that the Temple, as the Mill that supports the world, is to be destroyed; Christ has brought in the Final Age.

Fourth, Israel will suffer the loss of God's Word, of discernment and wisdom, and of eschatological hope: **The light of a lamp will not shine in you any longer.**

Fifth, the summing-up of Jerusalem's desolation is that, as the unfaithful wife, the Harlot, she has been cast out and replaced by another: **The Voice of Bridegroom and Bride will not be heard in you any longer.**

These five points mark several important characteristics of the Jerusalem Temple:

1. *Music* — the Levitical orchestra and choir (1 Chron. 25)
2. *Craftsmen* — cf. Bezalel, Oholiab, Hiram, etc. (Ex. 31:1-11; 1 Kings 5)
3. *Mill* — the Temple itself (the "threshingfloor"; 2 Chron. 3:1)
4. *Lamp* — the Lampstand(s) (Ex. 25:31-40; 2 Chron. 4:19-22)
5. *Marriage* — the marriage of the Lord and Israel (Ezek. 16:1-14)

The desolation of Jerusalem is said to fall on her for two reasons. First, her **merchants were the great men of the Land.** This should not seem strange at first glance; much the same could be said of any city in history. In any prosperous economy,

---

18. See Giorgio de Santillana and Hertha von Dechend, *Hamlet's Mill: An Essay on Myth and the Frame of Time* (Ipswich: Gambit, 1969). On the symbolism of Samson's grinding at the mill (Jud. 16:21), see James B. Jordan, *Judges: God's War Against Humanism* (Tyler, TX: Geneva Ministries, 1985), p. 273.

merchants will be prominent. But what, in the final analysis, were Israel's "merchants" trading in? The souls of men (v.13). As Jesus had thundered to the "great men of the Land": "Woe to you, scribes and Pharisees, hypocrites, because you travel about on sea and land to make one convert; and when he becomes one, you make him twice as much a son of hell as yourselves!" (Matt. 23:15).

The second reason for Jerusalem's punishment flows from the first: **all the nations were deceived by your sorcery.** Israel had been the priest to the nations of the world, ordained both to bring them the light of salvation and to offer up sacrifices on their behalf. This should have culminated in the presentation of Christ to the nations as the Light of the world and the true sacrifice for their sins. Instead, Israel rejected Christ, the sum and substance of Biblical religion. By attempting to retain the formal structure of the Old Covenant in its rejection of the New, Israel essentially created a hybrid religion of occult Satan-worship and statism.[19] And she was torn in pieces by her own gods.

24 St. John provides a final clue to the Harlot's identity in this verse, confirming our interpretation that she represents Jerusalem: **In her was found the blood of prophets and of saints and of all who have been slain on the earth.** This is a clear allusion to Christ's condemnation of Jerusalem, at the close of His final discourse in the Temple:

> Therefore, behold, I am sending you prophets and wise men and scribes; some of them you will kill and crucify, and some of them you will scourge in your synagogues, and persecute from city to city, that upon you may fall *all the righteous blood shed on the earth,* from the blood of righteous Abel to the blood of Zechariah, the son of Berechiah, whom you murdered between the sanctuary and the altar. Truly I say to you, all these things shall come upon this generation. *O Jerusalem, Jerusalem, who kills the prophets* and stones those who are sent to her! (Matt. 23:34-37)

---

19. On the intimate historical relationship between occultism and statism, see Gary North, *Unholy Spirits: Occultism and New Age Humanism* (Ft. Worth, TX; Dominion Press, 1986).

This language cannot be used of Rome or any other city. Only Jerusalem was guilty of "all the righteous blood shed on the earth," from Abel onward. Historically, it was Jerusalem that had always been the great Harlot, continually falling into apostasy and persecuting the prophets (Acts 7:51-52); Jerusalem was the place where the prophets were killed: as Jesus Himself said, "It cannot be that a prophet should perish outside of Jerusalem. O Jerusalem, Jerusalem, the city that kills the prophets and stones those sent to her!" (Luke 13:33-34). St. John's "Covenant Lawsuit" was true, and effective. Jerusalem was found guilty as charged, and from A.D. 66-70 she suffered the "days of vengeance," the outpouring of God's wrath for her agelong shedding of innocent blood.

19

THE FEASTS OF THE KINGDOM

The Marriage Supper of the Lamb (19:1-10)

1 After these things I heard, as it were, a loud voice of a great multitude in heaven, saying: Hallelujah! Salvation and power and glory belong to our God;

2 because His judgments are true and righteous; for He has judged the great Harlot who was corrupting the earth with her fornication, and He has avenged the blood of His servants at her hand!

3 And a second time they said: Hallelujah! Her smoke rises up forever and ever!

4 And the twenty-four elders and the four living creatures fell down and worshiped God who sits on the Throne saying: Amen! Hallelujah!

5 And a Voice came from the Throne, saying: Praise our God, all you His servants and those who serve Him, both the small and the great.

6 And I heard, as it were, the voice of a great multitude and as the sound of many waters and as the sound of mighty peals of thunder, saying: Hallelujah! For the Lord our God, the Almighty, reigns.

7 Let us rejoice and be glad and give the glory to Him, for the marriage of the Lamb has come, and His Bride has made herself ready.

8 And it was given to her to clothe herself in fine linen, bright and clean; for the fine linen is the righteous acts of the saints.

9 And he said to me, Write: Blessed are those who are invited to the marriage supper of the Lamb. And he said to me, These are the true words of God.

10 And I fell at his feet to worship him. And he said to me, Don't do that! I am a fellow servant of yours and of your

brethren who hold the Testimony of Jesus; worship God! For the Testimony of Jesus is the Spirit of prophecy.

There are several similarities in language between this passage and that in 11:15-19, the announcement of the seventh angel's theme of the completion of "the Mystery of God": the opening of the Kingdom and the heavenly Temple to the whole world in the New Covenant. We can easily see the message of these verses as an expansion of that idea when we take note of the parallels:

11:15 — loud voices in heaven.	19:1 — a loud voice of a great multitude in heaven.
11:15, 17 — He will reign forever and ever. . . . Thou hast taken Thy great power and didst reign.	19:1, 6 — Hallelujah! Salvation and power and glory belong to our God. . . . Hallelujah! For the Lord our God, the Almighty, reigns.
11:16 — The twenty-four elders . . . fell on their faces and worshiped God.	19:4 — The twenty-four elders . . . fell down and worshiped God.
11:18 — The time came for the dead to be vindicated, and the time to give their reward to Thy servants the prophets and to the saints.	18:24-19:2 — In her was found the blood of prophets and of saints. . . . His judgments are true and righteous; for . . . He has avenged the blood of His servants.
11:18 — Thy servants . . . those who fear Thy name, the small and the great.	19:5 — All you His servants, you who fear Him, the small and the great.
11:19 — There were lightnings, noises, thunderings. . . .	19:6 — The voice of a great multitude and as the sound of many waters and as the sound of mighty peals of thunder. . . .

The appearance of the Bride, prepared for marriage, is thus equivalent to the opening of the Temple and the full establishment of the New Covenant. These same images are brought together again at the close of this series of visions, when the City of God descends from heaven, "made ready as a Bride adorned for her Husband; and I heard a loud voice from the Throne, saying: Behold, the Tabernacle of God is among men, and He shall dwell among them. . . ." (21:2-3). The Church, the Bride of Christ and City of God, is the New Covenant Temple—or, rather, "the Lord God, the Almighty, and the Lamb, are its Temple" (21:22).

1-2 God's people had prayed for Jerusalem's destruction (6:9-11). Now that their prayers have been answered, the great multitude of the redeemed breaks out into antiphonal praise, in obedience to the angelic command in 18:20: "Rejoice over her, O Heaven, and you saints and apostles and prophets, because God has judged your judgment against her!" We should note carefully what St. John is doing here. The Revelation is a prophecy, and therefore intended "for edification and exhortation and consolation" (1 Cor. 14:3): Its readers were commanded to "*heed* the things that are written in it*" (Rev. 1:3). In revealing the heavenly Church's imprecatory prayers against her enemies, St. John was instructing his brethren on earth to do the same; now, having revealed the certain destruction of the Harlot, he shows the Church of the first century what their duty must be when Jerusalem falls. They are not to mourn her passing, but to praise God for the execution of His vengeance upon her. God's will is to be performed on earth as it is performed in heaven. In showing the pattern of heavenly worship, St. John reveals God's will for earthly worship as well.

The antiphonal liturgy is divided into five distinct parts. The number five is, as we have seen (cf. 9:5), connected with strength, especially in terms of military action. Appropriately, this five-part song is a "battle-hymn," based on Old Testament songs of triumph over the enemies of God and the Covenant. The heavenly multitude sings: **Hallelujah!** The only New Testament uses of this Hebrew expression (meaning *Praise ye the Lord!*) are in this passage, where it occurs four times, in praise for the divine reconquest of the earth. As Hengstenberg notes, "the preservation of the Hebrew word, as in the case also of *Amen* and *Hosanna,* serves like a visible finger-post to mark the internal connection between the Church of the New Testament and that of the Old."[1] The word itself recalls the Old Testament *Hallel*-psalms (Ps. 113-118), songs of victory that were sung at the festivals of Passover and Tabernacles. These psalms celebrated the greatness of God, especially as revealed in the deliverance of His people from Egypt and their restoration to true worship; and they look forward to the day when all nations will praise the Lord. Except for minor allusions to a couple of *Hallel*-psalms in verses 5 and 7, St. John does not construct this liturgy on their pattern; rather, the use of *Hallelujah!* alone is enough to make the connection. The first Biblical occurence of the expression, however, is in Psalm 104:35, which strikingly parallels the juxtaposition of judgment and praise in Revelation:

> Let sinners be consumed from the earth,
> And let the wicked be no more.
> Bless the LORD, O my soul.
> Hallelujah!

The destruction of apostate Jerusalem on behalf of Christ and His Church will be the demonstration that **salvation and power and glory belong to our God** — a phrase that recalls David's exultation when the preparations for building the Temple had been completed: "Thine, O LORD, is the greatness and the power and the glory and the victory and the majesty, indeed everything that is in the heavens and the earth; Thine is the dominion, O LORD, and Thou dost exalt thyself as head over all" (1 Chron. 29:11; Christ also alluded to David's text in the Lord's Prayer, Matt. 6:13: "Thine is the Kingdom and the power and the glory forever and ever, Amen"). The song also quotes David's celebration of the Law's all-embracing authority in Psalm 19:9: "The judgments of the Lord are true and righteous altogether." In the fulfillment of the Law's curses on the apostate city, God's new Israel takes up the chant, affirming that **His judgments are true and righteous**.

Israel's destruction is the showcase of God's righteousness. God's honor could not endure the blasphemy of His name occa-

---

1. E. W. Hengstenberg, *The Revelation of St. John*, two vols. (Cherry Hill, NJ: Mack Publishing Co., n.d.), vol. 2, p. 238.

sioned by the rebellion of His people (Rom. 2:24). The proof that "His judgments are true and righteous" is precisely the fact that He has avenged Himself upon His own people, rejecting those who had been called by His name: **for He has judged the Great Harlot who was corrupting the earth with her fornication, and He has avenged the blood of His servants at her hand!** This establishes the connection between the Harlot and the "Jezebel" who was seeking to destroy the churches (see 2:20-24). Jezebel, the harlot queen (2 Kings 9:22), had drawn Israel from the worship of the true God into a cult of statism and idolatry (1 Kings 16:29-34). She had persecuted and murdered the prophets (1 Kings 18:4, 13), and raised up false witnesses to slander the righteous in court (1 Kings 21:1-16). Thus Jehu was ordained by God's messenger to destroy the house of Ahab, *"that I may avenge the blood of My servants the prophets*, and the blood of all the servants of the LORD, *at the hand of Jezebel"* (2 Kings 9:7). Israel's adulterous flirtations and dalliances with paganism are likened by the prophets to Jezebel's "harlotries and witchcrafts" (2 Kings 9:22): just as she "painted her eyes and adorned her head" in a futile attempt to ward off her destruction (2 Kings 9:30-37), Israel vainly did the same:

> And you, O desolate one, what will you do?
> Although you dress in scarlet,
> Although you decorate yourself with ornaments of gold,
> Although you enlarge your eyes with paint,
> In vain you make yourself beautiful;
> Your lovers despise you;
> They seek your life. (Jer. 4:30; cf. Ezek. 23:40)

Nothing short of repentance could have saved Jerusalem. This she adamantly refused to do, and so God took vengeance on her for her persecution of the righteous. Again it must be emphasized that Jesus specifically marked out Jerusalem as the object of God's vengeful wrath. Speaking of the outpouring of covenantal curses which would culminate in the A.D. 70 destruction of Jerusalem, He said: *"These are the days of vengeance*, in order that all things that are written may be fulfilled"* (Luke 21:22). Through Moses God had warned of Israel's future apostasy, when they would make Him jealous by serving other gods (Deut. 32: 15-22), bringing certain destruction upon themselves

471

and their land (Deut. 32:23-43). Four times in this passage God threatens that His vengeance will overtake the apostates: *"Vengeance* is mine, and retribution" (v. 35); "I will render *vengeance* on My adversaries, and I will repay those who hate Me" (v. 41); "Rejoice, O nations, with His people; for *He will avenge the blood of His servants*, and will render *vengeance* on His adversaries, and will atone for His land and His people" (v. 43).

3   In the second division of the song, the great multitude repeats the refrain: **Hallelujah!** The reason for praise is, again, a godly rejoicing at the destruction of the Church's enemy, for **her smoke rises up forever and ever.** As we have noted (see on 14:11; 18:2, 9), this expression is based on the destruction of Sodom and Gomorrah (Gen. 19:28), while the specific phraseology is borrowed from Isaiah's description of the punishment of Edom (Isa. 34:10). It is used here to indicate the permanent nature of Babylon's fall.[2]

4   The third section of the liturgy finds **the twenty-four elders and the four living creatures** — representing the Church and all the earthly creation (see on 4:4-11) — taking up their distinctive part in the song. First, we are told, they **fell down and worshiped;** again we notice the importance of posture, of physical attitude, in our religious activity. The modern Church's affliction of "spiritualistic" neoplatonism — not to mention simple laziness — has resulted in her all-too-casual approach to the Most High. At the very least, our physical position in public, official worship should be one that corresponds to the godly fear and reverence which is appropriate in those who are admitted to an audience with **God who sits on the throne.**

5   We are not told whose **Voice** pronounces the fourth section of the liturgy **from the Throne.** It could be that of one of the elders, leading the congregation from a position close to the throne; but it is more likely to be that of Jesus Christ (cf. 16:17), calling upon His brethren (Rom. 8:29; Heb. 2:11-12) to **praise**

---

2. The phrase thus cannot be pressed into service as a literal description of the eternal state of the wicked in general. The actual flames that consumed "Babylon" burned out long ago; but her punishment was eternal. She will never be resurrected.

472

our God (cf.John 20:17, where Jesus says, "I ascend to My Father and your Father, and My God and your God"). That this is addressed to the Church as a whole is clear from the description of the worshipers: **His servants, those who fear Him, the small and the great.**

6-8 As the entire Church responds to the officiant's invitation, she speaks with the familiar Voice of the Glory-Cloud (cf. Ex. 19:16; Ezek. 1:24), indicating her full identification with the glorious Image of God: St. John hears, **as it were, the voice of a great multitude and as the sound of many waters and as the sound of mighty peals of thunder.** The Cloud has assumed the Church into itself.

The first *Hallelujah!* of the "great multitude" had praised God for His sovereignty, as shown in the judgment of the great Harlot. The fourth **Hallelujah!**, in this fifth and final portion of the liturgy, praises God again for His sovereignty, this time as shown in the **marriage of the Lamb** to **His Bride.** *The destruction of the Harlot and the marriage of the Lamb and the Bride* — the divorce and the wedding — *are correlative events.* The existence of the Church as the congregation of the New Covenant marks an entirely new epoch in the history of redemption. God was not now merely taking Gentile believers into the Old Covenant (as He had often done under the Old Testament economy). Rather, He was bringing in "the age to come" (Heb. 2:5; 6:5), the age of fulfillment, during these Last Days. Pentecost was the inception of a *New* Covenant. With the final divorce and destruction of the unfaithful wife in A.D. 70, the marriage of the Church to her Lord was firmly established; the Eucharistic celebration of the Church was fully revealed in its true nature as "the Marriage Supper of the Lamb" (v. 9).

The multitude of the redeemed exults: **His Bride has made herself ready!** The duty of the apostles during the Last Days was to prepare the Church for her nuptials. Paul wrote of Christ's sacrifice as the redemption of the Bride: He "loved the Church and gave Himself up for her; that He might sanctify her, having cleansed her by the washing of water with the Word; that He might present to Himself the glorious Church, having no spot or wrinkle or any such thing; but that she should be holy and blameless" (Eph. 5:25-27). Paul extended this imagery in speaking to the Corinthians about the goal of his ministry: "I am jealous for you with a godly jealousy; for I betrothed you to one Husband, that to Christ I might present you as a pure virgin." Yet there was the danger that the Church would be seduced into fornication with the Dragon; the Apostle was "afraid, lest as the Serpent deceived Eve by his craftiness, your minds should be led astray from the simplicity and purity of devotion to Christ" (2 Cor. 11:2-3). As the crisis of those days was drawing to its conclusion, when many were departing the faith and following after various heresies, Jude penned a hurried emergency message to the Church (see Jude 3), in which he enjoined the Bride to remain faithful to her Lord, committing her "to Him who is able to keep you from stumbling, and to make you stand in the presence of His glory blameless with great joy" (Jude 24).

But now St. John sees a vision of the Church in her glory and purity, having successfully met her trials and temptations, having passed through great tribulations into her possession of the Kingdom as the Bride of Christ. Contrary to the expectations of Rome, the destruction of Jerusalem was not the end for the Church. Instead, it was the Church's full establishment as the new Temple, the final declaration that God had taken to Himself a new Bride, a faithful, chaste virgin who had successfully resisted the seductive temptations of the Dragon. She had made herself ready, and this was her wedding day. The early Christians learned well the lesson that was later stated by the third-century bishop St. Cyprian: "The spouse of Christ cannot be adulterous; she is uncorrupted and pure. She knows one home; she guards with chaste modesty the sanctity of one couch. She keeps us for God. She appoints the sons whom she has born for the kingdom. Whoever is separated from the Church and is joined to an adulteress, is separated from the promises of the Church; nor can he who forsakes the Church of Christ attain to the rewards of Christ. He is a stranger; he is profane; he is an enemy. He can no longer have God for his Father, who has not the Church for his mother. If anyone could escape who was outside the ark of Noah, then he also may escape who shall be outside of the Church. The Lord warns, saying, 'He who is not with me is against me, and he who gathereth not with me scattereth' [Matt. 12:30]. He who breaks the peace and the concord of Christ, does so in opposition to Christ; he who gathereth elsewhere than in the Church, scatters the Church of Christ. . . . He who does not hold this unity does not hold God's law, does not hold the faith of the Father and the Son, does not hold life and salvation."[3]

The song of praise continues: **And it was given to her to clothe herself in fine linen, bright and clean; for the fine linen is the righteous acts of the saints**. We have already seen linen used as a symbol (15:6; cf. 3:4; 4:4; 7:9, 14); now, its symbolic meaning is explicitly stated to be the saints' **righteous acts**.[4] Two important points are made here about the saints' obedience: first, **it was given to her** — our sanctification is due wholly to the gracious work of God's Holy Spirit in our hearts; second, she was graciously enabled **to clothe herself** in the linen of righteous acts — our sanctification is performed by ourselves. This dual emphasis is found throughout the Scriptures: "You shall sanctify yourselves. . . . I am the LORD who sanctifies you" (Lev. 20:7-8); "Work out your salvation with fear and trembling; for it is God who is at work in you, both to will and to work for His good pleasure" (Phil. 2:12-13).

9 St. John is instructed to write the fourth and central beatitude of the Book of Revelation: **Blessed are those who are invited to the Marriage Supper of the Lamb**. God's people have been saved from the whoredoms of the world to become the Bride of His only begotten Son; and the constant token of this fact is the Church's weekly celebration of her sacred feast, the Holy Eucharist. The absolute fidelity of this promise is underscored by the angel's assurance to St. John that **these are the true words of God**.

It should go without saying (but, unfortunately, it cannot),

---

3. Cyprian, *On the Unity of the Church*, 6; in Alexander Roberts and James Donaldson, eds., *The Ante-Nicene Fathers* (Grand Rapids: William B. Eerdmans, reprinted 1971), Vol. 5, p. 423.

4. The Greek word is generally used in the New Testament to mean God's "statute" or "ordinance" (Luke 1:6; Rom. 1:32; 8:4; Heb. 9:1, 10; Rev. 15:4); the related meaning, used here, is "fulfillment of God's statute" (cf. Rom. 5:18). A further meaning is the "judicial sentence that one has met God's requirement" and hence "justification" (cf. Rom. 5:16). While some have argued for "justification" as the proper meaning here, both the context and the fact that the plural form of the word is employed indicate its most natural meaning to be "righteous acts."

that the Eucharist is the center of Christian worship; the Eucharist is what we are commanded to do when we come together on the Lord's Day. Everything else is secondary. This is not to suggest that the secondary things are unimportant. The teaching of the Word, for example, is very important, and in fact necessary for the growth and well-being of the Church. Doctrine has long been recognized as one of the essential marks of the Church. Instruction in the faith is therefore an indispensable part of Christian worship. But it is not the heart of Christian worship. The heart of Christian worship is the Sacrament of the Body and Blood of our Lord Jesus Christ. This is assumed by St. Paul in 1 Corinthians 10:16-17 and 11:20-34. We can see it reflected in Luke's simple statement in Acts 20:7: "And on the first day of the week, when we were gathered together to break bread. . . ." It is also described in the *Didache*: "But every Lord's Day do ye gather yourselves together, and break bread, and give thanksgiving after having confessed your transgressions, that your sacrifice may be pure."[5] Justin Martyr reports the same pattern as the standard for all Christian assemblies: "On the day called Sunday, all who live in cities or in the country gather together to one place, and the memoirs of the apostles or the writings of the prophets are read, as long as time permits; then, when the reader has ceased, the president verbally instructs, and exhorts to the imitation of these good things. Then we all rise and pray, and, as we before said, when our prayer is ended, bread and wine and water are brought, and the president in like manner offers prayers and thanksgivings, according to his ability, and the people assent, saying, Amen; and there is a distribution to each, and a participation of that over which thanks have been given, and to those who are absent a portion is sent by the deacons."[6]

The greatest privilege of the Church is her weekly participation in the Eucharistic meal, the Marriage Supper of the Lamb. It is a tragedy that so many churches in our day neglect the

---

5. *The Teaching of the Twelve Apostles*, xiv.1, in Alexander Roberts and James Donaldson, eds., *The Ante-Nicene Fathers* (Grand Rapids: Wm. B. Eerdmans, reprinted 1971), Vol. 7, p. 381.

6. Justin Martyr, *The First Apology*, chap. lxvii, in Alexander Roberts and James Donaldson, eds., *The Ante-Nicene Fathers* (Grand Rapids: Wm. B. Eerdmans, reprinted 1971), Vol. 1, p. 186.

Lord's Supper, observing it only on rare occasions (some so-called churches have even abandoned Communion altogether). What we must realize is that the official worship service of the Church on the Lord's Day is not merely a Bible study or some informal get-together of like-minded souls; to the contrary, it is the formal wedding feast of the Bride with her Bridegroom. *That* is why we meet together on the first day of the week. In fact, one of the primary issues in the controversy of the Protestant Reformation was the fact that the Roman Church admitted its members to the Eucharist only once a year.[7] Ironically, the practice of the Roman Church now excels that of most "Protestant" churches; on the issue of frequent communion at least, it is Rome which has "reformed."

Commenting on the dictum of the German materialistic philosopher Ludwig Feuerbach that "man is what he eats," the great Orthodox theologian Alexander Schmemann wrote: "With this statement . . . Feuerbach thought he had put an end to all 'idealistic' speculations about human nature. In fact, however, he was expressing, without knowing it, the most religious idea of man. For long before Feuerbach the same definition of man was given by the Bible. In the biblical story of creation man is presented, first of all, as a hungry being, and the whole world as his food. Second only to the direction to propagate and have dominion over the earth, according to the author of the first chapter of Genesis, is God's instruction to men to eat of the earth: 'Behold I have given you every herb bearing seed . . . and every tree, which is the fruit of a tree yielding seed; to you it shall be for meat. . . .' Man must eat in order to live; he must take the world into his body and transform it into himself, into flesh and blood. He is indeed that which he eats, and the whole world is presented as one all-embracing banquet table for man. And this image of the banquet remains, throughout the whole Bible, the central image of life. It is the image of life at its creation and also the image of life at its end and fulfillment: '. . . that you eat and drink at my table in my Kingdom.' "[8]

---

7. See John Calvin, *Institutes of the Christian Religion*, iv.xvii.43-46; cf. idem., *Selected Works: Tracts and Letters*, ed. by Henry Beveridge and Jules Bonnet, seven vols. (Grand Rapids: Baker Book House, reprinted 1983), Vol. 2, p. 188.

8. Alexander Schmemann, *For the Life of the World: Sacraments and Orthodoxy* (New York: St. Vladimir's Seminary Press, 1973), p. 11.

The Eucharist is at the center of our life, and all of life flows out of this central liturgy. The "shape" of the eucharistic liturgy, therefore, gives shape to the rest of life, the daily liturgy we follow as we pursue our calling to exercise dominion over the earth. The "rite of life" is patterned after the central ritual of communion, which is itself patterned after the liturgy of creation set forth in Genesis 1: God took hold of the creation, separated it, distributed it, evaluated the work, and enjoyed it in sabbath rest. And this is the pattern of Holy Communion, as James B. Jordan observes: "When we perform this rite on the Lord's Day, we are becoming readjusted, rehabituated, retrained in the right way to use the world. For Jesus Christ, on the night of His betrayal, (1) took bread and wine, (2) *gave thanks,* (3) broke the bread, (4) distributed the bread and wine, naming it His body and blood; then the disciples (5) tasted and evaluated it, eleven approving of it, and one rejecting it; and finally (6) the faithful rested and enjoyed it.

"It is because the act of thanksgiving is the central difference between the Christian and the non-Christian that the liturgy of the Christian churches is called 'Holy Eucharist.' Eucharist means Thanksgiving. It is the restoration of true worship (thanksgiving) that restores the work of man (the six-fold action in all of life). This explains why the restoration of true worship takes primacy over cultural endeavors."[9]

10 St. John falls at the angel's feet **to worship him,** and the angel tersely replies: **Don't do that!** Why is this incident (repeated in 22:8-9) recorded in the Book of Revelation? While it might seem to be unrelated to the great, cosmic issues of the prophecy, it actually comes close to the heart of St. John's message. At first glance, it appears to be a polemic against idolatry, certainly a central concern of the Book of Revelation. On closer inspection, however, such an interpretation presents serious difficulties. In the first place, we must remember that it is an in-

---

9. James B. Jordan, "Studies in Genesis One: God's Rite for Life," in *The Geneva Review,* No. 21 (August 1985), p. 3; cf. idem, "Christian Piety: Deformed and Reformed," *Geneva Papers* (New Series), No. 1 (September 1985); on the centrality of worship, see idem, *The Law of the Covenant: An Exposition of Exodus 21-23* (Tyler, TX: Institute for Christian Economics, 1984), pp. 10f., 41f., 217f.

spired Apostle who performs this act of worship, in the course of receiving divine revelation; while it is not absolutely impossible that St. John would commit the crime of idolatry in such a situation, it seems highly unlikely. In the second place, the angel's reason for refusing worship seems strange. Why does he not simply quote the commandment against having false gods, as Jesus did (Matt. 4:10) when the devil demanded that He worship him? Instead of this, he launches into a brief explanation of the nature of prophecy: **I am a fellow servant of yours and your brethren who hold the Testimony of Jesus; worship God! For the Testimony of Jesus is the Spirit of prophecy.**

The solution is to be found, first, in the fact that the term *worship* (in Greek, *proskuneō*) simply means "the custom of prostrating oneself before a person and kissing his feet, the hem of his garment, the ground, etc.,"[10] and can be used not only for the homage paid to God (or, sinfully, to a false god), but also for the proper reverence due superiors (see, e.g., the LXX usage in Gen. 18:2; 19:1; 23:7, 12; 27:29; 33:3, 6-7; 37:7, 9-10; 42:6; 43:26, 28; 49:8). It was completely appropriate for Lot to "worship" the angels who visited him, and for the sons of Israel to "worship" Joseph. Matthew uses the word to describe a slave's obeisance before his master (Matt. 18:26), and St. John employs it to record Christ's promise to the faithful Philadelphians, that the Jews would be forced "to come and *bow down* [*proskuneō*]" at their feet (Rev. 3:9).

Assuming, therefore, that St. John was not offering divine worship to the angel, but rather reverence to a superior, the angel's reply can be more clearly understood. A common theme throughout the Book of Revelation is that "all the LORD's people are prophets" (cf. Num. 11:29). All have ascended into the Lord's presence, taking their places at the heavenly Council around the throne in the Glory-Cloud. Before Pentecost it was appropriate for mere men to bow down before angels, but no longer. "Don't do that!" the angel cries: **I am a fellow servant of yours and your brethren who hold the Testimony of Jesus.** The angel is on an equal level with St. John and the rest of the Chris-

---

10. William F. Arndt and F. Wilbur Gingrich, *A Greek-English Lexicon of the New Testament and Other Early Christian Literature* (Chicago: University of Chicago Press, 1957), p. 723.

tian community; thus he urges St. John to worship God, to "draw near with confidence to the Throne of grace" (Heb. 4:16). The fact that St. John's brethren **hold the Testimony of Jesus** demonstrates that they are members of the Council, indwelt by the Spirit; for **Jesus' Testimony is the Spirit of prophecy**; the Spirit is wherever Jesus' Testimony is held and proclaimed.

"With perfect justice, therefore, does Bossuet remark, 'that the angel rejects the worship in order to place the apostolical and prophetical ministry on a footing with that of the angels.' . . . The dissuasion is not based on the consideration that the worship trenches on God's glory, but on the consideration that it trenches on John's honour. It is as if it were said, go directly to God with thy worship, so that thou mayest not throw into the shade the glorious dignity bestowed on thee, and represented by thee."[11]

But what is it about the angel's proclamation that induced St. John to bow at his feet in the first place? "It is the eucharistic reference which it contains. The primitive Church consecrated the eucharist by the great thanksgiving-prayer which names the rite. Lifting their hearts to heaven, they blessed God for his mighty acts of salvation, thereby both assuring their ultimate possession of Christ, and making real the foretaste they were about to receive in his sacramental body and blood. The exultation of victory has passed into eucharistic prayer in 19:1-8, but it is the angel's beatitude which first makes explicit the allusion to that blessed feast eaten in the kingdom of God and anticipated in the Church. St. John falls to adore, and every intermediary vanishes between himself and Christ."[12]

The Son of God Goes Forth to War (19:11-21)

11 And I saw heaven opened; and behold, a white horse, and the One sitting upon it called Faithful and True; and in righteousness He judges and wages war.

12 And His eyes are a flame of fire, and upon His head are many diadems; and He has a name written which no one knows except Himself.

---

11. E. W. Hengstenberg, *The Revelation of St. John*, two vols. (Cherry Hill, NJ: Mack Publishing Co., [1851] 1972), Vol. 2, p. 256.

12. Austin Farrer, *The Revelation of St. John the Divine* (Oxford: At the Clarendon Press, 1964), pp. 195f.

13 And He is clothed with a robe dipped in blood; and His name is called the Word of God.

14 And the armies that are in heaven, clothed in fine linen, white and clean, were following Him on white horses.

15 And from His mouth comes a sharp two-edged sword, so that with it He may smite the nations; and He Himself will rule them with a rod of iron; and He Himself treads the wine press of the wine of the fierce wrath of God, the Almighty.

16 And on His robe and on His thigh He has a name written: *KING OF KINGS, AND LORD OF LORDS.*

17 And I saw one angel standing in the sun; and he cried out with a loud voice, saying to all the birds that fly in mid-heaven: Come, assemble for the great supper of God;

18 in order that you may eat the flesh of kings and the flesh of commanders and the flesh of mighty men and the flesh of horses and of those who sit on them and the flesh of all men, both free men and slaves, and small and great.

19 And I saw the Beast and the kings of the earth and their armies, assembled to make war against the One sitting upon the horse, and against His army.

20 And the Beast was seized, and with him the False Prophet who performed the signs in his presence, by which he deceived those who had received the mark of the Beast and those who worshiped his image; these two were thrown alive into the lake of fire which burns with brimstone.

21 And the rest were killed with the sword that came from the mouth of the One sitting upon the horse, and all the birds were filled with their flesh.

11 This begins the final section of seven visions, each one opening with the phrase *kai eidon*, **And I saw** (19:11, 17, 19; 20:1, 4, 11; 21:1). With the revelation of the Holy Eucharist St. John sees, as he has not seen before, **heaven opened**, and, as Farrer observes, "every intermediary vanishes between himself and Christ." It is the invitation to Communion with Christ that opens heaven to the Church and reveals her Lord.

St. John sees **a white horse**, the symbol of Christ's victory and dominion (6:2; cf. 14:14). It is important for the proper understanding of this passage to note that **the One sitting upon it** is **called Faithful and True**: Christ rides forth to victory in His character as "the faithful and true *Witness*" (3:14), as "the Word of God" (19:13). St. John is not describing the Second Coming

481

at the end of the world. He is describing the progress of the Gospel throughout the world, the universal proclamation of the message of salvation, which follows the First Advent of Christ. The connection with the message to Laodicea (3:14-22) is further established when we understand that this part of the prophecy contains several parallels with the Laodicean message. Farrer says: "The ill-founded boast of present possession made by the Laodicean angel in 3:17 is echoed by the boast of the Jezebel-city in 18:7ff. And St. John has no sooner done with Jezebel in 19:3 than he provides the saints with pure raiment (19:8, 3:18), invites them to the supper of the Lamb (19:9, 3:20), and, opening the doors of heaven, reveals Christ as the Amen, the Faithful and True (19:9-13, 3:14)."[13]

In righteousness He judges and makes war: Christ rides forth to do battle in the earth, subduing us to Himself, ruling and defending us, "restraining and conquering all His and our enemies," as the Westminster Shorter Catechism says (Q. 26), rendering justice throughout the world according to the law of God, in fulfillment of the Messianic prophecies:

> He will judge Thy people with righteousness,
> And Thine afflicted with justice. (Ps. 72:2)

> Let the heavens be glad, and let the earth rejoice;
> Let the sea roar, and all its fulness;
> Let the field exult, and all that is in it.
> Then all the trees of the forest will sing for joy
> Before the LORD, for He is coming;
> For He is coming to judge the earth.
> He will judge the world in righteousness,
> And the peoples in His faithfulness. (Ps. 96:11-13)

> He will not judge by what His eyes see,
> Nor make a decision by what His ears hear;
> But with righteousness He will judge the poor,
> And decide with fairness for the afflicted of the earth;
> And He will strike the earth with the rod of His mouth,
> And with the breath of His lips He will slay the wicked.
> (Isa. 11:3-4)

---

13. Ibid., p. 85.

Behold, days are coming, declares the LORD,
When I shall raise up for David a righteous Branch;
And He will reign as King and act wisely
And do justice and righteousness in the land.
In His days Judah will be saved,
And Israel will dwell securely;
And this is His name by which He will be called:
The LORD Our Righteousness. (Jer. 23:5-6)

12   The figure on the white horse is the same as the Son of Man, the First and the Last, the Living One, of St. John's first vision, for **His eyes are a flame of fire** (cf. 1:14): He is the omniscient Lord whose discerning scrutiny is "able to judge the thoughts and intentions of the heart" (Heb. 4:12). This majestic figure is already victorious, many times over, as symbolized by the **many diadems** He wears.

The gold plate on the forehead of the high priest bore the sacred Name of the LORD; appropriately, after taking note of the many diadems on Christ's brow, St. John sees that **He has a name written.** But this is a name **which no one knows except Himself.** How are we to understand this? As we saw at 2:17, the New Testament use of the words for *know* (*ginōskō* and *oida*) is influenced by a Hebrew idiom, in which the verb *to know* acquires related meanings: *to acknowledge, to acknowledge as one's own,* and *to own* (see, e.g., Gen. 4:1; Ex. 1:8; Ps. 1:6; Jer. 28:9; Ezek. 20:5; Zech. 14:7; Matt. 7:23; John 10:4-5; Rom. 8:29; 1 Cor. 8:3; 2 Tim. 2:19).[14] Thus, the point in this verse is not that no one can know what the name is (for in fact, as we shall see, we *do* "know" the name, in the cognitive sense), but that He alone properly owns the name; it belongs only to Him. This is reinforced by the chiastic structure of the passage:

A.   He has a name written which no one owns except Himself (v. 12b)
   B.   He is clothed with a robe dipped in blood (v. 13a)
      C.   His name is called the Word of God (v. 13b)
      C.   From His mouth comes a sharp two-edged sword (v. 15a)
   B.   He treads the wine press of the fierce wrath of God (v.15b)
A.   On His robe and on His thigh He has a name written: *KING OF KINGS AND LORD OF LORDS* (v.16)

---

14. See the brief discussion in Meredith G. Kline, *Images of the Spirit* (Grand Rapids: Baker Book House, 1980), p. 130.

The sharp, two-edged sword of 15a answers to 13b's characterization of Christ as the Word of God; 15b's information that Christ treads the wine press of wrath explains how His robe became stained with blood in 13a; and 16 tells us the name that 12b says Christ uniquely owns.[15]

13   As we have noted above, Christ's **robe dipped in blood** is explained by v. 15b. The blood is, clearly, that of Christ's enemies, the "grapes of wrath"; yet (as we saw on 14:20), there is a sense in which the bloody robe is stained by Christ's own sacrifice of Himself as well. For the vision is truly an allegory of the Incarnation: Here alone in Revelation, as in the Prologue to His Gospel (John 1:1, 14), St. John calls Christ **the Word,** speaking of His pre-existence and divine nature, and of His becoming flesh, tabernacling among us. In the passage before us, moreover, we have not only an allegory of His Incarnation, but of His Atonement, Resurrection, Ascension, and Enthronement as well. This is not "only" the story of the outpouring of wrath on Israel. It is the story of Jesus Christ, the King of kings. We see here the Advent of the Son of Man: The heavens are opened, and He descends to earth to do battle with His enemies; stained with blood, He wins the victory.

14   But Christ is not alone in this victory. He is followed by **the armies that are in heaven,** "the called and chosen and faithful" who are with Him in battle (17:14). Again we must remember that from the perspective of the New Testament, the Church is "in heaven": We are God's tabernacle in heaven (7:15; 12:12; 13:6), we are seated with Christ in the heavenly places (Eph. 2:6), we have come to the heavenly Jerusalem, and to myriads of angels in festal assembly, and to the Church of the first-born who are enrolled in heaven (Heb. 12:22-23). The armies are composed of Christians (it is possible that angels are in view here as well), riding **on white horses** with their Lord in His aggressive and triumphant campaign through the earth, bringing the Word of God to the world. Because the armies of heaven are the Bride, they are **clothed in fine linen, white and clean.**

---

15. Ibid.

15 From the **mouth** of the incarnate Word of God proceeds **a sharp two-edged sword**. St. John has used this imagery before (1:16; 2:16); the sword (especially as it comes from the *mouth*) is a clear Biblical symbol for the powerful "prophetic word which is creative and dynamic and brings to pass what it pronounces. The word of a true prophet, such as the rider, transforms word into action; that of the false prophet, such as the second beast, is ineffectual."[16] The Word of God is used not only in battle, to slay God's enemies (Eph. 6:17), but also in the Church, to cut apart the sacrifice (Rom. 12:1-2): "For the Word of God is living and active and sharper than any two-edged sword, and piercing as far as the division of soul and spirit, of both joints and marrow, and able to judge the thoughts and intentions of the heart. And there is no creature hidden from His sight, but all things are open and laid bare to the eyes of Him with whom we have to do" (Heb. 4:12-13). The pre-incarnate Christ says:

> Listen to Me, O islands,
> And pay attention, you peoples from afar.
> The LORD called Me from the womb;
> From the inward parts of My mother He named Me.
> And He has made My mouth like a sharp sword. (Isa. 49:1-2)

In the same way, God wields His prophets like a sword:

> I have hewn them in pieces by the prophets;
> I have slain them by the words of My mouth. (Hos. 6:5)

Christ uses the Sword of the Spirit to **smite the nations**: He conquers by His mouth. Again, it is not the Second Coming that is portrayed here, but rather Christ's defeat of the nations by His bare Word. In Matthew 24:29-31, it is "immediately after" the destruction of Jerusalem that the conversion of the nations begins, as Christ sends his angels/ministers throughout the world to gather in the elect.[17]

The Wisdom of Solomon (18:15-16) speaks of God's deliverance of Israel from Egypt with imagery similar to St. John's pic-

---

16. J. Massyngberde Ford, *Revelation: Introduction, Translation, and Commentary* (Garden City, NY: Doubleday & Co., 1975), p. 323.

17. See David Chilton, *Paradise Restored: A Biblical Theology of Dominion* (Ft. Worth, TX: Dominion Press, 1985), pp. 103ff.

ture in this passage: "Thine Almighty Word leaped down from heaven out of Thy royal throne, as a fierce man of war into the midst of a land of destruction, and brought Thine unfeigned commandment as a sharp sword, and standing up filled all things with death; and it touched the heaven, but it stood upon the earth." As Isaiah wrote, "He will strike the earth with the rod of His mouth, and with the breath of His lips He will slay the wicked" (Isa. 11:4). "The 'mouth like a sharp sword' is the symbol of the prophet, whose utterance has a cutting edge to it, because he speaks the word of God. . . . Thus the only weapon the Rider needs, if he is to break the opposition of his enemies, and establish God's reign of justice and peace, is the proclamation of the gospel."[18] Thus "the whole course of 'the expansion of Christianity' is here in a figure: the conversion of the Empire; the conversion of the Western nations which rose on the ruins of the Empire; the conversion of the South and the far East, still working itself out in the history of our own time. In all St. John would have seen Christ using the Sword of His mouth; the white horse and his Rider, the diadem-crowned head, the invisible armies of heaven."[19]

Christ conquers the nations in order to **rule [or, shepherd] them with a rod of iron**. "The work of the Pastor, the Guide and Ruler of souls (1 Pet. 2:25), follows that of the Evangelist; the heathen are first to be reduced to obedience, and then brought under the discipline of Christ."[20] His Father had commanded Him:

> Ask of Me, and I will surely give the nations as Thine inheritance,
> And the very ends of the earth as Thy possession.
> Thou shalt rule[21] them with a rod of iron,
> Thou shalt shatter them like earthenware. (Ps. 2:8-9)

Psalm 2 goes on to declare that the kings of the earth must

---

18. G. B. Caird, *A Commentary on the Revelation of St. John the Divine* (New York: Harper and Row, 1966), p. 245.

19. H. B. Swete, *Commentary on Revelation* (Grand Rapids: Kregel Publications, [1911] 1977), p. 254.

20. Ibid.

21. The Hebrew verb can be read either as *break* or *rule* (*shepherd*), depending on the vowel-points used. The LXX translated it as *rule*, and this reading was adopted by the New Testament writers.

submit to the Son or else perish under His wrath. Christ has come into His inheritance; He has received His Kingdom from the Father (Dan. 7:13-14), having been installed on His heavenly throne "far above all rule and authority and power and dominion" (Eph. 1:21). As universal Sovereign **He Himself treads the wine press of the wine of the fierce wrath of God, the Almighty** (cf. 14:19-20):

> Who is this who comes from Edom,
> With garments of glowing colors from Bozrah,
> This One who is majestic in His apparel,
> Marching in the greatness of His strength?
> It is I who speak in righteousness, mighty to save.
> Why is Your apparel red,
> And Your garments like the one who treads in the wine press?
> I have trodden the wine trough alone,
> And from the peoples there was no man with Me.
> I also trod them in My anger,
> And trampled them in My wrath;
> And their juice is sprinkled on My garments,
> And I stained all My raiment.
> For the Day of Vengeance was in My heart,
> And My year of redemption has come.
> And I looked, and there was no one to help,
> And I was astonished and there was no one to uphold;
> So My own arm brought salvation to Me;
> And My wrath upheld Me.
> And I trod down the peoples in My anger,
> And I made them drunk in My wrath,
> And I brought down their juice to the earth. (Isa. 63:1-6)

The text in Isaiah emphasizes that Christ singlehandedly accomplishes this work: "I have trodden . . . alone"; "there was no one to help"; "My own arm brought salvation to Me," etc.; St. John similarly uses the expression **He Himself** twice in this verse, stressing that while Christ is accompanied by His heavenly armies, the victory is based on His work alone. The work of salvation is performed solely by the Lord Jesus Christ; the blessings and judgments that attend the salvation of the elect are set in place by Him.

Come, behold the works of the LORD,
Who has wrought desolations in the earth.
He makes wars to cease to the end of the earth;
He breaks the bow and cuts the spear in two;
He burns the chariots with fire. (Ps. 46:8-9)

"We are thus bound to believe that those occurrences by which guilty nations are scourged and chastised for their sins, are not merely brought about in providence, but ordered and directed by the Mediator. And whether, therefore, we behold the desolating sword cutting off the inhabitants, or the blasting mildew destroying the crops, or commercial stagnation obstructing the sources of wealth, or wasting disease stalking with ghastly power over a land, or the upheavings of popular commotion overturning the foundations of social order, we recognize the wisdom, and might, and righteous retribution of Prince Messiah, carrying into execution the divine decree, *The nation and kingdom that will not serve thee shall perish: yea, those nations shall be utterly wasted"* (Isa. 60:12).[22]

16 St. John sees Christ's title "which no one knows except Himself" (v. 12) written **on His robe and on His thigh,** the place where the sword is worn (cf. Ps. 45:3). "The title is the ground, not the result, of the coming victory; he will conquer the monster and the kings because he is already **King of kings and Lord of lords.**"[23] Riding out on His war-horse, followed by His army of saints, He conquers the nations with the Word of God, the Gospel. This is a symbolic declaration of hope, the assurance that the Word of God will be victorious throughout the world, so that Christ's rule will be established universally. Jesus Christ will be acknowledged everywhere as King of all kings, Lord over all lords. From the beginning of Revelation, Christ's message to His Church has been a command to overcome, to *conquer* (2:7, 11, 17, 26-28; 3:5, 12, 21); now He assures the suffering Church that, regardless of the fierce persecution by Israel and Rome, He and His people will in fact be victorious over all enemies.

---

22. William Symington, *Messiah the Prince: or, The Mediatorial Dominion of Jesus Christ* (Philadelphia: The Christian Statesman Publishing Co., [1839] 1884), p. 224.
23. Caird, p. 246.

All nations are absolutely required to be Christian, in their official capacity as well as in the personal character of their individual citizens. Any nation that does not submit to the all-embracing rule of King Jesus will perish; all nations *shall* be Christianized some day. It is only a matter of time. Jesus Christ is the universal Sovereign, and He will be recognized as such throughout the earth, in this world as well as in the next, in time as well as in eternity. He has promised: "I will be exalted among the nations, I will be exalted in the earth" (Ps. 46:10). The LORD of hosts is with us.

17-18 This is the second of the final seven visions, each of which begins with the phrase **And I saw**; thus, while it is certainly related to the subject of the previous vision, it is not simply a continuation of it. As we have seen, the chapter begins with a feast, the Marriage Supper of the Lamb, the sacred Eucharistic meal of the Church before her Lord. But another great feast is proclaimed here. The Sun of Righteousness has arisen, with healing in His wings (Mal. 4:2); but He also brings **an angel standing in the sun** (the ruler of the Day, Gen. 1:16) who issues an invitation to **all the birds that fly in midheaven**, the birds of prey. We have seen "midheaven" as the place in which the Eagle warned of woe (8:13), and in which an angel invited the rulers of the earth to embrace the eternal Gospel (14:6). Now the angel invites the eagles to **the Great Supper of God**, where they may glut themselves on the flesh of Christ's enemies: **the flesh of kings and the flesh of commanders and the flesh of mighty men and the flesh of horses and of those who sit on them and the flesh of all men, both free men and slaves, and small and great.** We noted at 8:13 that a basic curse of the covenant is that of being eaten by birds of prey (cf. Deut. 28:26, 49). Israel is now a sacrificial corpse (Matt. 24:28), and there is no longer anyone who can drive away the scavengers (cf. Gen. 15:11; Deut. 28:26).[24]

---

24. Genesis 15 describes the ratification ceremony of God's covenant with Abram. After Abram cuts the sacrificial animals apart and arranges the halves opposite each other, the unclean birds of prey descend to attack the carcasses, and Abram drives them away (v. 11). Gordon Wenham interprets this as a promise that Israel, through Abramic faith and obedience (cf. Gen. 26:5), will be protected from the attacks of unclean nations; Gordon Wenham, "The Symbolism of the Animal Rite in Genesis 15: A Response to G. F. Hasel, *JSOT* 19 (1981) 61-78," in *Journal for the Study of the Old Testament* 22 (1981), 134-37.

St. John's language is borrowed from God's invitation through Ezekiel "to every bird and beast of the field" to devour the corpses of His enemies, the armies of the heathen who had made war upon Israel:

> Assemble and come, gather from every side to My sacrifice which I am going to sacrifice for you, as a great sacrifice on the mountains of Israel, that you may eat flesh and drink blood. You shall eat the flesh of mighty men, and drink the blood of the princes of the earth, as though they were rams, lambs, goats, and bulls, all of them fatlings of Bashan. So you will eat fat until you are glutted, and drink blood until you are drunk, from My sacrifice which I have sacrificed for you. And you will be glutted at My table with horses and charioteers, with mighty men and all the men of war, declares the LORD. (Ezek. 39:17-20)

The meaning is clear: Those nations that refuse to submit to the lordship of Christ, as Psalm 2 commands, will be utterly destroyed. God requires of all men and institutions nothing less than complete subservience to His ordained Christocracy.

Peter J. Leithart observes that the feasting of the scavengers in Ezekiel 39 has a cleansing effect on the Land. "The expanded invitation to the birds of prey in verses 17-20 comes immediately after a discussion of cleansing the land through the burial of the dead (cf. Deut. 21:22f.). Perhaps the birds help to cleanse the land by feeding on the dead bodies which defile it. Moreover, the Lord invites the birds to eat a sacrificial meal. Sacrifice implies cleansing and restoration. Thus, in Ezekiel 39, the image of the birds of prey not only emphasizes the totality of the judgment, but also points to the obverse of judgment, cleansing and redemption."[25]

Leithart continues: "Is the idea of cleansing found also in Revelation 19:17-18? There is no direct mention of cleansing, nor of sacrifice. Still, for several reasons, the Revelation passage can be understood as a cleansing. First, the events of 20:4-6 suggest that by His victory, the Warrior cleanses the earth of the influence of the beast and the false prophet, and this, combined with the fall of Babylon and the binding of the dragon, inaugur-

---

25. Peter J. Leithart, "Biblical-Theological Paper: Revelation 19:17-18," Westminster Theological Seminary, 1985, p. 11.

ates a period of unprecedented power for the Church. Second, the totality of the Warrior's victory is so great that not even the slain bodies of His opponents remain. All traces of the beast's armies are obliterated. Finally, considered systematically, judgment never occurs apart from accompanying grace. The judgment of Pharaoh is the liberation of Israel. So also here, the judgment of the beasts and their armies cleanses the earth of their idolatry and liberates the saints."[26]

19-21   The third vision in this section, marked again by the words **And I saw,** reveals the defeat of Leviathan and Behemoth in their war against the Kingdom of Christ: The two Beasts are **seized** and **thrown alive into the lake of fire,** the fiery Laver (cf. 15:2) **which burns with brimstone.** The imagery is borrowed from the story of the destruction of Sodom and Gomorrah ("fire and brimstone") combined with that of the rebels Korah, Dathan, and Abiram, who with their households were swallowed up by the earth's mouth: "So they and all that belonged to them went down alive into Sheol; and the earth closed over them, and they perished from the midst of the assembly" (Num. 16:31-33). St. John's point, therefore, is not to provide a detailed personal eschatology of the Beast and the False Prophet; still less is he attempting to describe the Fall of Rome in 410 or 476. Rather, the Lake of Fire is his symbolic description of the utter defeat and complete destruction of these enemies in their attempt to seize the Kingdom: The evil personifications of pagan Rome and apostate Israel are ruined and overthrown. Rome, like Sodom, is destroyed by fire and brimstone; Israel's false prophets, like Korah, Dathan, and Abiram, are swallowed up alive.

There is one notable contrast, however: Whereas the rest of Korah's followers were consumed by a blast of fire "from the LORD," **the rest** of the Beasts' followers—the kings of the earth —are **killed with the sword that came from the mouth of Him who sat upon the horse.** The message of the Gospel, the Word-sword of the Spirit, goes out from Christ's mouth and destroys His enemies by converting them, piercing them to the dividing asunder of soul and spirit, of joints and marrow, judging the thoughts and intentions of their hearts. The Beasts are doubly

---

26. Ibid., p. 12.

losers: Not only are they defeated, but the very nations that they led in battle against Christ are conquered by His victorious Word.

At their very worst, Leviathan, Behemoth, and their co-conspirators could do no more than fulfill the decrees of the sovereign God (17:17). He ordained their every move, and He ordained their destruction. The nations rage, but God laughs: He has already set up His King on His holy mountain, and all nations will be ruled by Him (Psalm 2). *All power in heaven and earth* has been given to Christ (Matt. 28:18); as Martin Luther sang, "He *must* win the battle." As the Gospel progresses throughout the world it will win increasing victories, until all kingdoms become the kingdoms of our Lord, and of His Christ; and He will reign forever and ever. We must not concede to the enemy even one square inch of ground in heaven or on earth. Christ and His army are riding forth, conquering and to conquer, and we through Him will inherit all things.

20

THE MILLENNIUM AND THE JUDGMENT

What is the position of the historic, orthodox Church on the question of the Millennium? Can the doctrine of the Church be accurately described as either postmillennialist or amillennialist? In general, the difference between those traditionally called "amillennialists" and those traditionally called "postmillennialists" has been set in terms of their interpretations of the "thousand years" (in Latin, the *millennium*) of Revelation 20. "Amillennialists" have usually seen this text as a reference to the condition of the saints reigning in heaven, while "postmillennialists" have understood it as a description of the saints' dominion on earth. As we shall see, however, this way of framing the question can actually obscure some very important facts about the *Christian* view of "the Millennium." If we wish to gain an understanding of the orthodox position, we must understand that the answer to this precise question cannot be determined *primarily* by the exegesis of particular texts. For example, "amillennialists" often disagree with each other about the precise nature of the resurrection(s) in Revelation 20 (to cite only one of several major points in dispute). And Benjamin Warfield, perhaps the leading "postmillennialist" scholar of the early part of this century, proposed an exegesis of Revelation 20 which most theologians would consider to be classically "amillennialist"![1]

Our framing of the question, therefore, should be broad enough to account for the diversity of approach among the various amillennialist and postmillennialist camps. In essence, the question of the Millennium centers on the mediatorial Kingdom of Christ: When did (or will) Christ's Kingdom begin? And once we pose the question this way, something amazing happens—

---

1. Benjamin B. Warfield, "The Millennium and the Apocalypse," *Biblical Doctrines* (New York: Oxford University Press, 1929), pp. 643-64.

something almost unheard of in Christian circles: Unity! From the Day of Pentecost onward, orthodox Christians have recognized that Christ's reign began at His Resurrection/Ascension and continues until all things have been thoroughly subdued under His feet, as St. Peter clearly declared (Acts 2:30-36). "The Millennium," in these terms, is simply the Kingdom of Christ. It was inaugurated at Christ's First Advent, has been in existence for almost two thousand years, and will go on until Christ's Second Advent at the Last Day. In "millennial" terminology, this means that the return of Christ and the resurrection of all men will take place *after* "the Millennium." In this objective sense, therefore, *orthodox Christianity has always been postmillennialist.* That is to say, regardless of how "the Millennium" has been conceived (whether in a heavenly or an earthly sense)—i.e., regardless of the technical exegesis of certain points in Revelation 20—orthodox Christians have always confessed that Jesus Christ will return after (*"post"*) the period designated as "the thousand years" has ended. In this sense, all "amillennialists" are also "postmillennialists." At the same time, *orthodox Christianity has always been amillennialist* (i.e., non-millenarian). The historic Church has always rejected the heresy of Millenarianism (in past centuries, this was called *chiliasm*, meaning *thousand-year-ism*). The notion that the reign of Christ is something wholly future, to be brought in by some great social cataclysm, is not a Christian doctrine. It is an unorthodox teaching, generally espoused by heretical sects on the fringes of the Christian Church.[2] Now,

---

2. Premillennialism seems to have been originated by the Ebionite archheretic Cerinthus, a "false apostle" who was an opponent of both St. Paul and St. John. Cerinthus claimed that his doctrine of the Millennium had been revealed to him by angels; and it is interesting that St. Paul's epistle to the Galatians—which is greatly concerned to refute the legalistic heresies of Cerinthus—begins with these words: "But even though we, *or an angel from heaven,* should preach to you a gospel contrary to that which we have preached to you, let him be accursed" (Gal. 1:8)! St. Irenaeus records that St. John ran out of a public bathhouse upon encountering Cerinthus, and cried: "Let us flee, lest even the bath-house fall, because Cerinthus, the enemy of the truth, is within!" For àn account of Cerinthus and his heresies, see St. Irenaeus, *Against Heresies,* i.xxvi.1-2; iii.iii.4; cf. Eusebius, *Ecclesiastical History,* iii.xxviii.1-6; iv.xiv.6; vii.xxv.2-3. As Louis Bouyer points out in *The Spirituality of the New Testament and the Fathers* (Minneapolis: The Seabury Press, 1963, p. 173), some early Church Fathers (e.g. Justin Martyr) adopted premillennial literalism because of their heathen background, to which the Biblical literary genres and imagery were unfamiliar. The orthodox, "Augustinian" view represents a more mature understanding of Scriptural symbolism and a more consistent Christian worldview.

Millenarianism can take two general forms. It can be either *Pre*-millenarianism (with the Second Coming as the cataclysm that ushers in the Millennium), or *Post*millennarianism (with the Social Revolution as the cataclysm). Examples of the first branch of Chiliasm would be, of course, the Ebionite movement of the Early Church period, and the modern Dispensationalism of the Scofield-Ryrie school.[3] Examples of the Postmillennarian heresy would be easy to name as well: the Münster Revolt of 1534, Nazism, and Marxism (whether "Christian" or otherwise).[4] Orthodox Christianity rejects both forms of the Millenarian heresy. Christianity opposes the notion of any new redemptive cataclysm occurring before the Last Judgment. Christianity is anti-revolutionary. Thus, while Christians have always looked forward to the salvation of the world, believing that Christ died

---

3. Perhaps the most basic argument against premillennialism is simply that the Bible never speaks of a thousand-year reign of the saints — outside of Revelation 20, a highly symbolic and complex passage in the most highly symbolic and complex book of the Bible! Graeme Goldsworthy observes in *The Lamb and the Lion: The Gospel in Revelation* (Nashville: Thomas Nelson Publishers, 1984): "It is highly unlikely, to say the least, that something so dramatically significant as a thousand year reign of a reappeared Christ on earth before this age ends should nowhere else be mentioned in the New Testament" (p. 127). Some works that refute premillennialism, from various perspectives, are: Jay Adams, *The Time Is at Hand* (Nutley, NJ: Presbyterian and Reformed Publishing Co., [1966] 1970); Oswald T. Allis, *Prophecy and the Church* (Nutley, NJ: Presbyterian and Reformed Publishing Co., 1945, 1947); Loraine Boettner, *The Millennium* (Phillipsburg, NJ: Presbyterian and Reformed Publishing Co., revised ed., 1984); David Brown, *Christ's Second Coming: Will It Be Premillennial?* (Grand Rapids: Baker Book House, [1876] 1983); W. J. Grier, *The Momentous Event: A Discussion of Scripture Teaching on the Second Advent* (Edinburgh: The Banner of Truth Trust, [1945] 1970); Arthur H. Lewis, *The Dark Side of the Millennium: The Problem of Evil in Rev. 20:1-10* (Grand Rapids: Baker Book House, 1980); Rousas John Rushdoony, *God's Plan for Victory: The Meaning of Postmillennialism* (Tyler, TX: Thoburn Press, 1977); Ralph Woodrow, *His Truth Is Marching On: Advanced Studies on Prophecy in the Light of History* (Riverside, CA: Ralph Woodrow Evangelistic Association, 1977).

4. For accounts of heretical (post)millenarian movements, see Igor Shafarevich, *The Socialist Phenomenon*, William Tjalsma, trans. (New York: Harper and Row, Publishers, 1980); Norman Cohn, *The Pursuit of the Millennium: Revolutionary Millenarians and Mystical Anarchists of the Middle Ages* (New York: Oxford University Press, 1957; revised, 1970); Otto Friedrich, *The End of the World: A History* (New York: Coward, McCann & Geoghegan, 1982), pp. 143-77; David Chilton, *Productive Christians in an Age of Guilt-Manipulators: A Biblical Response to Ronald J. Sider* (Tyler, TX: Institute for Christian Economics, third ed., 1985), pp. 321-42.

and rose again for that purpose, they have also seen the Kingdom's work as a leavening influence, gradually transforming the world into the image of God. *The definitive cataclysm has already taken place, in the finished work of Christ.* Depending on the specific question being asked, therefore, orthodox Christianity can be considered either amillennial or postmillennial—because, in reality, it is both.

One further point should be understood: In addition to being both "amillennialist" and "postmillennialist," the orthodox Christian Church has been generally *optimistic* in her view of the power of the Gospel to convert the nations. In my book *Paradise Restored: A Biblical Theology of Dominion* (Ft. Worth, TX: Dominion Press, 1985), I opened each chapter with a quotation from the great St. Athanasius on the subject of the victory of the Gospel throughout the world and the inevitable conversion of all nations to Christianity. The point was not to single out St. Athanasius as such; numerous statements expressing the Hope of the Church for the worldwide triumph of the Gospel can be found throughout the writings of the great Fathers and teachers, in every age of Christianity.[5] Even more significantly, the universal belief in the coming victory can be seen in the *action* of the Church in history. Christians never supposed that their high calling was to work for some sort of détente with the Enemy. "Pluralism" was never regarded by the orthodox as a worthy goal. The Church has always recognized that God sent His only begotten Son in order to redeem the world, and that

---

5. See St. Augustine, *The City of God*, Book XX. On St. Augustine and the influence of his postmillennial philosophy of history, see Peter Brown, *Augustine of Hippo* (Berkeley and Los Angeles: University of California Press, 1967); Charles Norris Cochrane, *Christianity and Classical Culture: A Study of Thought and Action from Augustus to Augustine* (London: Oxford University Press, [1940, 1944], 1957); Robert Nisbet, *History of the Idea of Progress* (New York: Basic Books, 1980), pp. 47-76. On the extensive Reformed heritage of postmillennialism, from John Calvin to the late nineteenth century, see Greg L. Bahnsen, "The *Prima Facie* Acceptability of Postmillennialism," *The Journal of Christian Reconstruction*, Vol. III, No. 2 (Winter, 1976-77), pp. 48-105, esp. pp. 68-105; James B. Jordan, "A Survey of Southern Presbyterian Millennial Views Before 1930," *The Journal of Christian Reconstruction*, Vol. III, No. 2 (Winter, 1976-77), pp. 106-21; J. A. de Jong, *As the Waters Cover the Sea: Millennial Revival and the Interpretation of Prophecy* (Kampen: J. H. Kok, 1970); J. Marcellus Kik, *An Eschatology of Victory* (Nutley, NJ: Presbyterian and Reformed Publishing Co., 1971), pp. 3-29; Iain Murray, *The Puritan Hope: A Study in Revival and the Interpretation of Prophecy* (London: The Banner of Truth Trust, 1971).

He will be satisfied with nothing less than what He paid for.

When the early missionaries from the East first ventured into the demonized lands of our pagan forefathers, they had not the slightest intention of developing peaceful coexistence with warlocks and their terrorizing deities. When St. Boniface came up against Thor's sacred oak tree in his mission to the heathen Germans, he simply chopped it down and built a chapel out of the wood. Thousands of Thor-worshipers, seeing that their god had failed to strike St. Boniface with lightning, converted to Christianity on the spot. As for St. Boniface, he was unruffled by the incident. He knew that there was only one true God of thunder – the Triune Jehovah.

There is nothing strange about this. The attitude of Hope, the expectation of victory, is an absolutely fundamental characteristic of Christianity.[6] The advance of the Church through the ages is inexplicable apart from it – just as it is also inexplicable apart from the fact that the Hope is *true*, the fact that Jesus Christ *has* defeated the powers and *shall* reign "from the River to the ends of the earth." W. G. T. Shedd wrote: "Apart from the power and promise of God, the preaching of such a religion as Christianity, to such a population as that of paganism, is the sheerest Quixotism. It crosses all the inclinations, and condemns all the pleasures of guilty man. The preaching of the Gospel finds its justification, its wisdom, and its triumph, only in the attitude and relation which the infinite and almighty God sustains to it. It is *His* religion, and therefore it must ultimately become a universal religion."[7]

With the rise of divergent eschatologies over the last two centuries, the traditional evangelical optimism of the Church was tagged with the term "postmillennialism," whether the so-called "postmillennialists" liked it or not. This has had positive and negative results. On the plus side, it is (as we have seen) a *technically* accurate description of orthodoxy; and it carries the connotation of optimism. On the minus side, it can too often be confused with heretical millenarianism. And, while "amillen-

---

6. Consider the fact that the compilers of *The Book of Common Prayer* provided "Tables for Finding Holy Days" all the way to A.D. 8400! Clearly, they were digging in for the "long haul," and did not expect an imminent "rapture" of the Church.

7. W. G. T. Shedd, *Sermons to the Spiritual Man* (London: The Banner of Truth Trust, [1884] 1972), p. 421.

nialism" rightly expresses the orthodox abhorrence of apocalyptic revolution, it carries (both by name and by historic association) a strong connotation of defeatism.[8] The present writer therefore calls himself a "postmillennialist," but also seeks to be sensitive to the inadequacies of current theological terminology.[9]

This "generic" postmillennialism holds that Jesus Christ established His mediatorial Kingdom by His death, resurrection, and ascension to the heavenly Throne, and as the Second Adam rules over all creation until the end of the world, when He shall come again to judge the living and the dead; that He is conquering all nations by the Gospel, extending the fruits of His victory throughout the world, thereby fulfilling the dominion mandate originally given by God to Adam; that eventually, through the outpouring of the Holy Spirit, "the earth will be full of the knowledge of the LORD, as the waters cover the sea" (Isa. 11:9); and that the Biblical promises of abundant blessing, in every area of life, will be poured out by God upon the whole world, in covenantal response to the faithfulness of His people.[10]

---

8. Some have sought to remedy this by styling themselves "optimistic amillennialists," a term that has nothing wrong with it except a mouthful of syllables (the term "non-chiliastic postmillennialist" suffers from the same problem).

9. The foregoing is not intended to minimize certain other areas of dispute among the various eschatological schools of thought. The vexed issue of "common grace"—which James Jordan has more accurately termed "crumbs from the children's table" (Mark 7:27-28)—is particularly crucial to the debate, and so I have included Gary North's essay on "Common Grace, Eschatology, and Biblical Law" as an appendix to this volume.

10. This is perhaps as good a place as any to comment on what is currently the most intellectually disrespectable "objection" to postmillennialism: the notion that the earth cannot experience a future period of great physical blessing because the world is "running out" of natural resources, becoming overpopulated, and/or dying of pollution (etc.)—popularized by heavily slanted and even deliberately deceptive "studies" such as *Global 2000* and *Limits to Growth*. In the first place, this objection completely disregards the fact that, according to the Bible, both abundance and famine, productivity and pollution, come from the hand of Almighty God; that He can and does reward obedience with blessing, and disobedience with the curse (Deut. 8:1-20; 28:1-68; Isa. 24:1-6). Secondly, the "running-out-of-resources" and "overpopulation" (etc., etc.) arguments are completely baseless in both hard data and sound economic theory. See Warren T. Brookes, *The Economy in Mind* (New York: Universe Books, 1982); Edith Efron, *The Apocalyptics: Cancer and the Big Lie* (New York: Simon and Schuster, 1984); Herbert I. London, *Why Are They Lying to Our Children?* (New York: Stein and Day, 1984); Charles Maurice and Charles W. Smithson, *The Doomsday Myth: 10,000 Years of Economic*

The Binding of Satan (20:1-3)

1 And I saw an Angel coming down from heaven, having the key of the Abyss and a great chain in His hand.

2 And He laid hold of the Dragon, the Serpent of old, who is the devil and Satan, who deceives the whole world, and bound him for a thousand years,

3 and threw him into the abyss, and shut it and sealed it over him, so that he should not deceive the nations any longer, until the thousand years were completed; after these things he must be released for a short time.

1   The importance of the imagery in this passage is heightened by its centrality as the fourth of seven visions introduced by the expression **And I saw** (*kai eidon*; cf. 19:11, 17, 19; 20:4, 11; 21:1). St. John sees **an Angel coming down from heaven, having the key of the Abyss and a great chain in His hand.** Again, as in 10:1 and 18:1 (cf. 12:7), this is the Lord Jesus Christ, who as Mediator is the Angel (Messenger) of the Covenant (Mal. 2:7; 3:1). His absolute control and authority over the Abyss are symbolized by **the key** and the **great chain.** The author sets up a striking contrast: Satan, the evil star that *fell* from heaven, was briefly *given* the key to the Abyss (9:1); but Christ **descended** from heaven, **having** as His lawful possession "the keys of death and of Hades" (1:18).

2-3   St. John brings together the various descriptions of the evil one that he has used throughout the prophecy: **the Dragon** (12:3-4, 7, 9, 13, 16-17; 13:2, 4, 11; 16:13), **the Serpent of old** (9:19; 12:9, 14-15), **the devil** (2:10; 12:9, 12), **Satan** (2:9, 13, 24; 3:9; 12:9), **the deceiver of the whole world** (2:20; 12:9; 13:14; 18:23; 19:20). But the terrifying power of this enemy only serves to display the surpassing greatness of his Conqueror, who has so easily rendered him impotent: Jesus Christ, in His mission as the "Angel from heaven," **laid hold of the Dragon . . . and bound**

Crises (Stanford: Hoover Institution Press, 1984); Julian L. Simon, *The Ultimate Resource* (Princeton: Princeton University Press, 1981); Julian L. Simon and Herman Kahn, eds., *The Resourceful Earth: A Response to "Global 2000"* (Oxford: Basil Blackwell, 1984); William Tucker, *Progress and Privilege: America in the Age of Environmentalism* (Garden City, NY: Anchor Press/Doubleday, 1982). The fact is that Christianity, by producing the science and technology of the West, has vastly increased the earth's resources.

him for a thousand years, and threw him into the Abyss, and shut it and sealed it over him. As St. John declared in his first epistle, Christ "appeared for this purpose, that He might destroy the works of the devil" (1 John 3:8). In terms of this purpose, the Lord began "binding the strong man" during His earthly ministry; having successfully completed His mission, *He is now plundering Satan's house and carrying off his property:*

> If I cast out demons by the Spirit of God, then the Kingdom of God has come upon you. Or how can anyone enter the strong man's house and carry off his property, unless he first binds the strong man? And then he will plunder his house. (Matt. 12:28-29; cf. Luke 11:20-22)

Herman Ridderbos comments on the significance of this statement, and goes on to provide an excellent summary of the Gospel accounts of Christ's victory over the devil: "This passage [Matt. 12:28; Luke 11:20] is not an isolated one. The whole struggle of Jesus against the devils is determined by the antithesis between the kingdom of heaven and the rule of Satan, and time and again Jesus' superior power over Satan and Satan's dominion proves the break-through on the part of the kingdom of God. This is already proved at the start by the temptation in the wilderness. There can be no doubt that in it the issue is Jesus' messianic kingship. Three times in succession it is Satan's point of departure, referring back to the divine words about Jesus at his baptism (Matt. 3:17; Mark 1:11; Luke 3:22; Matt. 4:3, 6; Luke 4:3, 9). Especially the temptation with respect to 'all the kingdoms of the world' (Matt. 4:8ff.; Luke 4:5ff.) shows what is at issue in the struggle between Jesus and Satan. Here Satan appears as 'the prince of the world' (cf. John 12:31; 14:30; 16:11), who opposes God's kingdom, and who knows that Jesus will dispute that power with him in the name of God. Here, then, together with the Messiahship, the kingdom of God is at issue. At the same time it appears that the victory over Satan to be gained by the kingdom of God is not only a matter of *power*, but first and foremost one of *obedience* on the part of the Messiah. The Messiah must not make an arbitrary use of the authority entrusted to him. He will have to acquire the power that Satan offers him only in the way ordained by God. That is why

Jesus' rejection of the temptation is already the beginning of his victory and of the coming of the kingdom, although this victory will have to be renewed again and again during his life on earth (cf. Luke 4:13; Matt. 16:23, and parallels; 26:38, and parallels; 27:40-43, and parallels). From the beginning of his public activity Jesus' power over Satan had already asserted itself. This is not only proved by the casting out of devils in itself, but also by *the manner in which those possessed by the devil behave in his presence* (cf. Mark 1:24; Luke 4:34; Mark 5:7; Matt. 8:29; Luke 8:28, 31). When Jesus approaches they raise a cry, obviously in fear. They show that they have a supernatural knowledge of his person and of the significance of his coming (cf. Mark 1:34; 3:11). They call him 'the Holy One of God,' 'the Son of God,' 'Son of the most high God.' By this they recognize his messianic dignity (cf. Luke 4:41). They consider his coming as their own destruction (Mark 1:24; Luke 4:34); their torment (Matt. 8:29; Mark 5:7; Luke 8:28). They feel powerless and try only to lengthen their existence on earth (Matt. 8:29; Mark 5:10), and implore him not to send them into 'the deep,' that is to say, the place of their eternal woe (Luke 8:31, cf. Rev. 20:3ff.). All this shows that in Jesus' person and coming the kingdom has become a present reality. For the exercise of God's power over the devil and his rule has the coming of the kingdom for its foundation.

"And finally we must refer in this context to Luke 10:18-19. Jesus has sent out the seventy (or seventy-two) who come back to him and joyfully tell him of the success of their mission. And then Jesus says: 'I beheld Satan as lightning fall from heaven.' Thus he accepts the joy of those he had sent out and shows them the background of their power over the devils. The general meaning of this is clear: Satan himself has fallen with great force from his position of power. This is what Jesus had seen with his own eyes. Satan's supporters cannot maintain themselves. . . . The thing that counts in this connection is that what is said here is essentially the same thing as in Matthew 12:28 and Luke 11:20, i.e., the great moment of the breaking down of Satan's rule has come and at the same time that of the coming of the kingdom of heaven. The redemption is no longer future but has become *present*. In this struggle it is Jesus himself who has broken Satan's power and who continues to do so. Such appears from what follows when he discusses the power of the disciples which they have received from him to tread on serpents and scorpions and over all the power of the enemy, so that, in the future also, nothing will be impossible to them. By this *enemy* Satan is again meant. *Serpents* and *scorpions* are mentioned here as his instruments (Ps. 91:13) by which he treacherously tries to ruin man. But any power Satan has at his disposal to bring death and destruction (cf., e.g., Heb. 2:14) has been subjected to the disciples. All this implies and confirms that the great moment of salvation, the fulfillment of the promise, the kingdom of heaven, has come."[11]

The whole message of the New Testament (cf. Eph. 4:8; Col. 2:15; Heb. 2:14) stresses that Satan was definitively defeated in the life, death, resurrection, and ascension of Jesus Christ. It is absolutely crucial to remember that in speaking of Christ's "Ascension"—His Coming to the Throne of the Ancient of Days (Dan. 7:13-14)—we are speaking not only of His single act of ascending into the Cloud, but also of the direct and immediate consequences of that act: the outpouring of the Spirit on the Church in A.D. 30 (Luke 24:49-51; John 16:7; Acts 2:17-18, 33), and the outpouring of wrath upon Jerusalem and the Temple in A.D. 70 (Dan. 9:24-27; Acts 2:19-20). Pentecost and Holocaust were the Ascension applied. The final act in the drama of the *definitive* (as distinguished from the *progressive* and *consummative*)[12] binding of Satan was played out in the destruction of the Old Covenant system. This is why St. Paul, writing a few years before the event, could assure the Church that "the God of peace will soon crush Satan under your feet" (Rom. 16:20).

For all these reasons, it is generally suggested by both post-millennial and amillennial authors that the binding of Satan, **so that he should not deceive the nations any longer,** refers to his

---

11. Herman Ridderbos, *The Coming of the Kingdom* (St. Catherines, Ontario: Paideia Press, [1962] 1978), pp. 62ff.

12. Satan is bound *progressively* as Christ's Kingdom grows throughout history, extending its influence to transform every aspect of life (Matt. 5:13-16; 13:31-33), and in the daily experience of Christians as we successfully resist the devil (James 4:7) and proclaim the Word of God (Rev. 12:11). Satan will be bound *consummatively* at the Last Day, when death itself is destroyed in the Resurrection (John 6:39-40; 1 Cor. 15:22-26, 51-54). On the definitive-progressive-final pattern in general, see David Chilton, *Paradise Restored: A Biblical Theology of Dominion* (Ft. Worth, TX: Dominion Press, 1985), pp. 24f., 42, 73, 136, 146ff., 206, 209, 223.

inability to prevent the message of the Gospel from achieving success. And, as far as it goes, this interpretation certainly has Biblical warrant: Before the coming of Christ, Satan controlled the nations;[13] but now his death-grip has been shattered by the Gospel, as the good news of the Kingdom has spread throughout the world. The Lord Jesus sent the Apostle Paul to the Gentile nations "to open their eyes so that they may turn from darkness to light and from the dominion of Satan to God, in order that they may receive forgiveness of sins and an inheritance among those who have been sanctified by faith in Me" (Acts 26:18). Christ came "to rule over the Gentiles" (Rom. 15:12). That Satan has been bound does not mean that all his activity has ceased. The New Testament tells us specifically that the demons have been disarmed and bound (Col. 2:15; 2 Pet. 2:4; Jude 6) — yet they are still active. It is just that their activity is restricted. And, as the Gospel progresses throughout the world, their activity will become even more limited. Satan is unable to prevent the victory of Christ's Kingdom. We will overcome (1 John 4:4). "Let it be known to you therefore, that this salvation of God has been sent to the Gentiles, and they will listen" (Acts 28:28).

The great fathers and teachers of the Church have always recognized that Christ definitively defeated Satan in His First Coming. As St. Irenaeus said, "The Word of God, the Maker of all things, conquering him by means of human nature, and showing him to be an apostate, has put him under the power of man. For He says, 'Behold, I confer upon you the power of treading upon serpents and scorpions, and upon all the power of the enemy' [Luke 10:19], in order that, as he obtained power

---

13. A good account of the pervasiveness of demonic activity and control throughout the ancient heathen world is contained in the first ten books of St. Augustine's *City of God*, but the fact is obvious even in the writings of the pagans themselves. Virtually every page of Herodotus' *History* or Virgil's *Aeneid* bears eloquent and explicit testimony of the tyranny the "gods" exercised over every aspect of pagan life and thought. Yet it all came to a halt with the Resurrection of Christ: The gods suddenly stopped talking, as the pagan writer Plutarch observed in his work *On Why Oracles Came to Fail*, and as St. Athanasius constantly remarks in his classic treatise *On the Incarnation of the Word of God*. Cf. the wide-ranging discussion of the demise of the archaic worldview in Giorgio de Santillana and Hertha von Dechend, *Hamlet's Mill: An Essay on Myth and the Frame of Time* (Ipswich: Gambit, 1969), pp. 56-75, 275-87, 340-43.

over man by apostasy, so again his apostasy might be deprived of power by means of man turning back again to God."[14] St. Augustine agreed: "The devil was conquered by his own trophy of victory. The devil jumped for joy, when he seduced the first man and cast him down to death. By seducing the first man, he slew him; by slaying the last man, he lost the first from his snare. The victory of our Lord Jesus Christ came when he rose, and ascended into heaven; then was fulfilled what you have heard when the Apocalypse was being read, 'The Lion of the tribe of Judah has won the day' [Rev. 5:5]. . . . The devil jumped for joy when Christ died; and by the very death of Christ the devil was overcome: he took, as it were, the bait in the mousetrap. He rejoiced at the death, thinking himself death's commander. But that which caused his joy dangled the bait before him. The Lord's cross was the devil's mousetrap: the bait which caught him was the death of the Lord."[15]

But the precise thrust of Revelation 20 seems to be dealing with something much more specific than a general binding and defeat of Satan. St. John tells us that the Dragon is **bound** with reference to his ability to **deceive the nations** — in particular, as we learn from verse 8, the Dragon's power "to deceive the nations . . . *to gather them together for the war.*" The stated goal of the Dragon's deception is to entice the nations to join forces against Christ for the final, all-out war at the end of history. Satan's desire from the beginning has often been to provoke a premature eschatological cataclysm, to bring on the end of the world and the Final Judgment *now*. He wants to rush God into judgment in order to destroy Him, or at least to short-circuit His program and destroy the wheat with the chaff (cf. Matt. 13:24-30). In a sense, he can be considered as his own *agent provocateur*, leading his troops headlong into an end-time rebellion that will call down God's judgment and prevent the full maturation of God's Kingdom.

Writing of Jesus' parable of the leaven — "The Kingdom of heaven is like leaven, which a woman took, and hid in three

---

14. St. Irenaeus, *Against Heresies*, v.xxiv.4.
15. St. Augustine, *Sermons*, 261; trans. by Henry Bettenson, ed., *The Later Christian Fathers: A Selection From the Writings of the Fathers from St. Cyril of Jerusalem to St. Leo the Great* (Oxford: Oxford University Press, 1970, 1977), p. 222.

pecks of meal, until it was all leavened" (Matt. 13:33)—Gary North observes: "The kingdom of God is like leaven. Christianity is the yeast, and it has a leavening effect on pagan, satanic cultures around it. It permeates the whole of culture, causing it to rise. The bread which is produced by this leaven is the *preferred bread*. In ancient times—indeed, right up until the advent of late-nineteenth century industrialism and modern agricultural methods—leavened bread was considered the staff of life, the symbol of God's sustaining hand. 'Give us this day our daily bread,' Christians have prayed for centuries, and they have eaten leavened bread at their tables. So did the ancient Hebrews. The kingdom of God is the force that produces the fine quality bread which all men seek. The symbolism should be obvious: *Christianity makes life a joy for godly men. It provides men with the very best.*

"Leaven takes time to produce its product. It takes time for the leaven-laden dough to rise. *Leaven is a symbol of historical continuity, just as unleavened bread was Israel's symbol of historical discontinuity.* Men can wait for the yeast to do its work. God gives man time for the working of His spiritual leaven. Men may not understand exactly how the leaven works—how the spiritual power of God's kingdom spreads throughout their culture and makes it rise—but they can see and taste its effects. If we really push the analogy (pound it, even), we can point to the fact that dough is pounded down several times by the baker before the final baking, almost as God, through the agents of Satan in the world, pounds His kingdom in history. Nevertheless, the yeast does its marvelous work, *just so long as the fires of the oven are not lit prematurely.* If the full heat of the oven is applied to the dough before the yeast has done its work, both the yeast and the dough perish in the flames. God waits to apply the final heat (2 Pet. 3:9-10). First, His yeast—His church—must do its work, in time and on earth. The kingdom of God (which includes the institutional church, but is broader than the institutional church) must rise, having 'incorrupted' the satanic dough of the kingdom of Satan with the gospel of life, including the life-giving reconstruction of all the institutions of culture.

"What a marvelous description of God's kingdom! Christians work inside the cultural material available in any given culture, seeking to refine it, permeate it, and make it into some-

505

thing fine. They know they will be successful, just as yeast is eventually successful in the dough, if it is given sufficient time to do its work. This is what God implicitly promises us in the analogy of the leaven: *enough time to accomplish our individual and collective assignments.* He tells us that His kingdom will produce the desirable bread of life. It will take time. It may take several poundings, as God, through the hostility of the world, kneads the yeast-filled dough of men's cultures. But the end result is guaranteed. God does not intend to burn His bread to a useless crisp by prematurely placing it in the oven. He is a better baker than that."[16]

As Tertullian stated in his masterful defense of the Christian faith: "We are a body united by a common religious profession, by a godly discipline, by a bond of hope. We meet together as an assembly and congregation that as an organized force we may assail God with our prayers. Such violence is acceptable to God. We pray also for emperors, for their ministers and those in authority, for man's temporal welfare, *for the peace of the world, for the delay of the end of all things.*"[17]

The specific point of the binding of the Dragon, therefore, is to prevent him from inciting the eschatological "war to end all wars," the final battle — until God is ready. When God's Kingdom-City is fully matured, then He will once more release Satan and allow him to deceive the nations for the final conflagration. But the fire will fall according to God's schedule, not the Dragon's. At every point, God is controlling events for His own glory.

Satan is to remain bound, St. John tells us, for **a thousand years** — a large, rounded-off number. We have seen that, as the number *seven* connotes a fullness of *quality* in Biblical imagery, the number *ten* contains the idea of a fullness of *quantity*; in other words, it stands for *manyness.* A thousand multiplies and intensifies this $(10 \times 10 \times 10)$, in order to express great vastness

16. Gary North, *Moses and Pharaoh: Dominion Religion Versus Power Religion* (Tyler, TX: Institute for Christian Economics, 1985), pp. 169f.

17. Tertullian, *Apology,* 39; trans. by Henry Bettenson, *The Early Christian Fathers: A Selection from the Writings of the Fathers from St. Clement of Rome to St. Athanasius* (Oxford: Oxford University Press, 1956, 1969), p. 141. Italics added.

(cf. 5:11; 7:4-8; 9:16; 11:3, 13; 12:6; 14:1, 3, 20).[18] Thus, God claims to own "the cattle on a thousand hills" (Ps. 50:10). This of course does not mean that the cattle on the 1,001st hill belongs to someone else. God owns all the cattle on all the hills. But He says "a thousand" to indicate that there are many hills, and much cattle (cf. Deut. 1:11; 7:9; Ps. 68:17; 84:10; 90:4). Similarly, the **thousand years** of Revelation 20 represent a vast, undefined period of time (although its limited, provisional nature as a pre-consummation era is underlined by the fact that the phrase is mentioned only *six* times in this chapter). It has already lasted almost 2,000 years, and will probably go on for many more. Milton Terry observes: "The *thousand years* is to be understood as a symbolical number, denoting a long period. It is a round number, but stands for an indefinite period, an eon whose duration it would be a folly to attempt to compute. Its beginning dates from the great catastrophe of this book, the fall of the mystic Babylon. It is the eon which opens with the going forth of the great Conqueror of 19:11-16, and continues until he shall have put all his enemies under his feet (1 Cor. 15:25). It is the same period as that required for the stone of Daniel's prophecy (Dan. 2:35) to fill the earth, and the mustard seed of Jesus' prophecy to consummate its world-wide growth (Matt. 13:31-32). How long the King of kings will continue His battle against evil and defer the last decisive blow, when Satan shall be 'loosed for a little time,' no man can even approximately judge. It may require a million years."[19]

The binding of the Dragon prevents him from deceiving the nations any longer, until the thousand years are **completed; after these things he must be released for a short time**, in which he again goes forth to deceive the nations. The story of the Dragon will be picked up again in verse 7, and so here we need notice only St. John's use of the word **must** (literally, **it is necessary**; cf. 1:1; 4:1; 10:11; 11:5; 13:10; 17:10; 22:6). At every point, Satan's activity takes place under the strict government of the Providence of God. As Swete observes, "it is in vain to speculate on the grounds of this necessity" (upon which he immediately

---

18. An analogy of this Scriptural usage is the way we, with a more inflationary mentality, use the term *million*: "I've told you a million times!" (I suspect that even "literalists" talk that way on occasion.)

19. Milton Terry, *Biblical Apocalyptics: A Study of the Most Notable Revelations of God and of Christ in the Canonical Scriptures* (New York: Eaton and Mains, 1898), p. 451.

goes on to speculate!);[20] it is enough that God has decreed its necessity. The Dragon is not his own master. He has been seized and bound and shut up in the Abyss, and someday he will be released for a brief time—but all this takes place according to God's good and holy purposes. All the Dragon's hatred and rage against Christ's Kingdom are utterly impotent and ineffectual; he is powerless to do anything until he is deliberately **released** by the One who holds the key to the Abyss.

The First Resurrection (20:4-6)

4 And I saw thrones, and they sat upon them, and judgment was given to them. And I saw the souls of those who had been beheaded because of the testimony of Jesus and because of the Word of God, and those who had not worshiped the Beast or his Image, and had not received his mark upon their forehead and upon their hand; and they lived and reigned with Christ for a thousand years.

5 (The rest of the dead did not live until the thousand years were completed.) This is the First Resurrection.

6 Blessed and holy is the one who has a part in the First Resurrection; over these the Second Death has no power, but they will be priests of God and of Christ and will reign with Christ for a thousand years.

4 The new vision is of the thousand-year Kingdom: **And I saw thrones, and they sat on them.** We are not explicitly told who **"they"** are, but there should be no doubt about their identity, for they are enthroned. St. John uses the word **thrones** (plural) only with reference to the twenty-four elders:

And around the Throne were twenty-four thrones; and upon the thrones twenty-four elders sitting, clothed in white garments, and golden crowns on their heads. (4:4)

And the twenty-four elders, who sit on their thrones before God, fell on their faces and worshiped God. (11:16)

As we have seen, St. John's twenty-four elders are the representative assembly of the Church, the Royal Priesthood. Throughout the prophecy God's people are seen reigning as

---

20. Henry Barclay Swete, *Commentary on Revelation* (Grand Rapids: Kregel Publications, [1911] 1977), p. 261.

priests with Christ (1:6; 5:10), wearing crowns (2:10; 3:11), possessing kingly authority over the nations (2:26-27), seated with Christ on His Throne (3:21). These things are all symbolized in the picture of the heavenly presbytery (4:4): As *kings*, the elders sit on thrones; as *priests*, they are twenty-four in number (cf. 1 Chron. 24), and they wear crowns (cf. Ex. 28:36-41).

The relationship between the priesthood of the elders and that of the Church at large has been well summarized by T. F. Torrance in his excellent study of the *Royal Priesthood*: "In the Old Testament Church there was a twofold priesthood, the priesthood of the whole body through initiation by circumcision into the royal priesthood, although that priesthood actually functioned through the first-born. Within that royal priesthood there was given to Israel an institutional priesthood in the tribe of Levi, and within that tribe, the house of Aaron. The purpose of the institutional priesthood was to serve the royal priesthood, and the purpose of the royal priesthood, that is of Israel as a kingdom of priests, was to serve God's saving purpose for all nations. So with the Christian Church. The real priesthood is that of the whole Body, but within that Body there takes place a membering of the corporate priesthood, for the edification of the whole Body, to serve the whole Body, in order that the whole Body as Christ's own Body may fulfill His ministry of reconciliation by proclaiming the Gospel among the nations. Within the corporate priesthood of the whole Body, then, there is a particular priesthood set apart to minister to the edification of the Body until the Body reaches the fulness of Christ (Eph. 4:13). . . . This ministry is as essential to the Church as Bible and sacramental ordinances, but like them, this order of the ministry will pass away at the *parousia*, when the real priesthood of the one Body, as distinct from the institutional priesthood, will be fully revealed."[21]

We therefore are not forced to choose whether those who are enthroned in the Millennium are elders *or* the Church, because both are true. In St. John's vision, he sees the elders on thrones — but they represent the whole Church.[22] Related to this is the

---

21. T. F. Torrance, *Royal Priesthood* (Edinburgh: Oliver and Boyd Ltd., 1955), p. 81.

22. It might be asked: Why didn't St. John simply *say* that those whom he saw on thrones were the twenty-four elders? There are at least two reasons — first, the various clues in the text (the mention of thrones, judgment, and a

promise Jesus made to His disciples: "Truly I say to you, that you who have followed Me, in the Regeneration when the Son of Man will sit on His glorious Throne, you also shall sit upon twelve thrones, judging the twelve tribes of Israel" (Matt. 19:28; cf. Luke 22:30, where the term *kingdom* is used instead of *regeneration*). By His death, resurrection, and ascension to His glorious Throne (Eph. 1:20-22), Jesus inaugurated the Kingdom Age (Col. 1:13) — the Regeneration — in which all nations are being brought to feast at His Table with the patriarchs and apostles (Isa. 52:15; Luke 13:28-29; 22:29-30). In this age, the apostles reign over the New Israel; they are the very foundation of the Church (Eph. 2:20), which itself is a nation of kingly priests (1 Pet. 2:9).

Jesus gave His disciples two promises regarding the Messianic era: that they would sit on *thrones*, and that they would *judge*. This is precisely what St. John shows us in this text. He tells of those who sit on the thrones of the Kingdom, and adds that **judgment was given to them**, paralleling his statement in 11:18 that the saints are "judged" or "vindicated"; further, however, there is the sense here that the privilege of judging (ruling) is **given** into the hands of the saints. Before Christ's victory over Satan, the Church was judged and ruled over by the heathen nations, because Adam had abdicated his position of judgment and surrendered it to the Dragon. But now the Son of Man, the Second Adam, has ascended to the Throne as ruler of the kings of the earth, and His people have ascended to rule with Him (Eph. 2:6). Definitively — and increasingly as the age progresses — judgment is given to God's people.[23] The Dominion Mandate of Genesis 1:26-28 (cf. Ps. 8; Heb. 2) will be fulfilled through the triumph of the Gospel; as the Gospel progresses, so does the dominion of the saints. The two go together. In His Great Commission (Matt. 28:18-20), Jesus commanded us to *teach* and *dis-*

---

priesthood reigning with Christ) make an explicit identification unnecessary; second, in keeping with the symbolism of the Church as the New Israel, St. John uses the term *elder* twelve times (4:4, 10; 5:5, 6, 7, 11, 14; 7:11, 13; 11:16; 14:3; 19:4). At this point in the Book of Revelation, he has already used up his "quota"!

23. See two essays by Gary North: "Witnesses and Judges," *Biblical Economics Today*, Vol. VI, No. 5 (Aug./Sept. 1983); "Christ's Mind and Economic Reconstruction," *Biblical Economics Today*, Vol. VII, No. 1 (Dec./Jan. 1984). These are available for a donation to the Institute for Christian Economics, P.O. Box 8000, Tyler, TX 75711.

ciple the nations, and as the earth is gradually discipled to the commands of God's Word, the boundaries of the Kingdom will expand. Eventually, through evangelism, the reign of Christians will become so extensive that "the earth will be full of the knowledge of God, as the waters cover the sea" (Isa. 11:9). Edenic blessings will abound across the world as God's law is increasingly obeyed by the converted nations (Lev. 26:3-13; Deut. 28:1-14).[24]

It must be stressed, however, that the road to Christian dominion does not lie primarily through political action. While the political sphere, like every other aspect of life, is a valid and necessary area for Christian activity and eventual dominance, we must shun the perennial temptation to grasp for political power. Dominion in civil government cannot be obtained before we have attained maturity in wisdom—the result of generations of Christian *self*-government. As we learn to apply God's Word to practical situations in our personal lives, our homes, our schools, and our businesses; as Christian churches exercise Biblical judgment over their own officers and members, respecting and enforcing the discipline of other churches; *then* Christians will be able to be trusted with greater responsibilities. Those who are faithful in a few things will be put in charge of many things (Matt. 25:21, 23), but "from everyone who has been given much shall much be required" (Luke 12:48; cf. Luke 16:10-12; 19:17). One of the distinguishing marks of heretical movements throughout Church history has been the attempt to grab the robe of political power before it has been bestowed.

This whole issue has been thoughtfully explored in an excellent essay by James Jordan, and the best service I can provide the interested reader at this point is simply to refer him to it.[25] Jordan concludes his study with these words: "When we are ready, God will give the robe to us. That He has not done so proves that we are not ready. Asserting our readiness will not

---

24. Iain Murray has shown in *The Puritan Hope: Studies in Revival and the Interpretation of Prophecy* (London: The Banner of Truth Trust, 1971) how this view of worldwide conversion has provided a basic inspiration for missionary activity throughout the history of the Church, particularly since the Protestant Reformation.

25. James B. Jordan, "Rebellion, Tyranny, and Dominion in the Book of Genesis," in Gary North, ed., *Tactics of Christian Resistance*, Christianity and Civilization No. 3 (Tyler, TX: Geneva Ministries, 1983), pp. 38-80.

fool Him. Let us pray that He does not crush us by giving us such authority before we are ready for it. Let us plan for our great-grandchildren to be ready for it. Let us go about our business, acquiring wisdom in family, church, state, and business, and avoiding confrontations with the powers that be. . . . For as sure as Christ is risen from the grave and is ascended to regal glory on high, so sure it is that His saints will inherit the kingdom and rule in His name, when the time is right."²⁶ *When the time is right.*

St. John tells us that, in addition to the enthroned elders, he saw those whom the elders represent: First, **the souls of those who had been beheaded because of the Testimony of Jesus and because of the Word of God.** This expression is almost identical to his description of the martyrs underneath the altar:

> I saw . . . the souls of those who had been slain because of the Word of God, and because of the Testimony they had maintained. (6:9)

There is a significant difference, however: the use of the word **beheaded.** While most commentators are surely correct in seeing this as a general reference to all the martyrs for the Faith (by whatever means they were slain), we should attempt to do justice to St. John's choice of this particular term. The Greek verb (*pelekizō*) is not used anywhere else in the Bible, but the act of beheading is mentioned, under a synonym (*apokephalizō*), in Matthew 14:10, Mark 6:16, 27, and Luke 9:9. The subject of the beheading, of course, was John the Baptizer, the last of the Old Covenant prophets and the Forerunner of Jesus Christ. As the latter-day Elijah (Mal. 4:5; Matt. 11:14; 17:10-13; Luke 1:17), he

---

26. Ibid., p. 74. In this connection, Jordan's remarks on the so-called "patriotic" tax-resistance movement are also worth repeating: "We must keep in mind that the pagan is primarily interested in *power.* This means that the maintenance of force (the draft) and the seizure of *money* (excessive taxation) are of absolute primary interest to him. If we think these are the most important things, then we will make them the point of resistance (becoming 'tax patriots' or some such thing). To think this way is to think like pagans. For the Christian, the primary things are righteousness (priestly guarding) and diligent work (kingly dominion). Generally speaking, the pagans don't care how righteous we are, or how hard we work, so long as they get their tax money. This is why the Bible everywhere teaches to go along with oppressive taxation, and nowhere hints at the propriety of tax resistance" (p. 79).

summed up the message of all the preceding witnesses: "For all the prophets and the Law prophesied until John" (Matt. 11:13). It seems likely, therefore, that St. John is here drawing our attention to the fact that the Old Covenant witnesses, symbolized by John the Forerunner, are to be counted among the faithful martyrs who "live and reign with Christ."

A question immediately arises: Did the Old Covenant faithful really bear the Testimony of *Jesus*? It is striking that St. John uncharacteristically emphasizes the name of Jesus, as if to highlight the specifically *Christian* standing of these "beheaded" witnesses. And the New Testament rings clear that, like John, all the Old Covenant witnesses were Forerunners of Jesus Christ, testifying of Him:

> And He said to them, "O foolish men and slow of heart to believe in all that the prophets have spoken! Was it not necessary for the Christ to suffer these things and to enter into His glory?" And beginning with Moses and from all the prophets, He explained to them the things concerning Himself in all the Scriptures. (Luke 24:25-27)

> Do not think that I will accuse you before the Father; the one who accuses you is Moses, in whom you have set your hope. For if you believed Moses, you would believe Me; for he wrote of Me. (John 5:45-46)

> Of Him all the prophets bear witness that through His name everyone who believes in Him receives forgiveness of sins. (Acts 10:43)

> Paul, a bondservant of Jesus Christ, called as an apostle, set apart for the Gospel of God, which He promised beforehand through His prophets in the holy Scriptures concerning His Son. . . . (Rom. 1:1-3)

> But now apart from the Law the righteousness of God has been manifested, being witnessed by the Law and the Prophets, even the righteousness of God through faith in Jesus Christ to all and on all those who believe. (Rom. 3:21-22)

The ranks of those who reign with Christ are also filled by the New Covenant faithful, the overcomers of St. John's day who also bore the Testimony of Jesus: **those who had not worshiped the Beast or his image, and had not received the mark**

upon their forehead and upon their hand (cf. 1:2, 9; 2:13; 12:9-11, 17; 15:2; 19:10). All these **lived and reigned with Christ for a thousand years**. Man's life has always fallen short of a thousand years: Adam lived 930 years (Gen. 5:5), and Methuselah, whose life was the longest recorded in the Bible, lived only 969 years before he died in the Great Flood (Gen. 5:27).[27] If his heirs had been faithful, David's kingdom should have endured "forever" — meaning that it should have lasted a thousand years, until the Coming of Christ (2 Sam. 7:8-29; 1 Chron. 17:7-27; 2 Chron. 13:5; 21:7; Ps. 89:19-37; Isa. 9:7; 16:5; Jer. 30:9; Ezek. 34:23-24; Hos. 3:5; Luke 1:32-33); but, again, man fell short. No one was able to bring in "the Millennium" — the Thousand-Year Kingdom — until the Son of God appeared as the Son of Man (the Second Adam) and Son of David. He obtained the Kingdom for all His people.

Does this reign of the saints take place in heaven or on earth? The answer should be obvious: *both!* The saints' thrones are in heaven, with Christ (Eph. 2:6); yet, with their Lord, they exercise rule and dominion on earth (cf. 2:26-27; 5:10; 11:15). Those who reign with Christ in His Kingdom are all those whom He has redeemed, the whole Communion of Saints, whether they are now living or dead (including Old Covenant believers). In His Ascension, Jesus Christ brought us all to the Throne. As the *Te Deum* exults:

> When Thou hadst overcome the sharpness of death
> Thou didst open the Kingdom of Heaven to all believers.

The reign of the saints is thus analogous to their worship: The whole Church, in heaven and on earth, worships together before the Throne of God, "tabernacling" in heaven (7:15; 12:12; 13:6). To ask whether or not the saints' worship is heavenly or earthly is to propose a false dilemma, for the Church is both heavenly and earthly. Similarly, the Church's sphere of rule in-

---

27. Based on a strict chronology, this seems to be a reasonable conclusion, since Methuselah died in the Flood year (Methuselah was 187 when his son Lamech was born, 369 when his grandson Noah was born, and hence 969 when the Flood came; see Gen. 5:25, 28; 7:6). More than a century before the Flood, God declared the entire human race (except for Noah) to be worthy of destruction (Gen. 6:1-8; 7:1); there is no apparent reason to exclude Methuselah from this sweeping condemnation.

cludes the earth, but it is exercised *from the Throne in heaven*. Jesus said to Pilate, "My Kingdom is not from this world. If My Kingdom were from this world, then My servants would be fighting, that I might not be delivered up to the Jews; but as it is, My Kingdom is not from here" (John 18:36). The text does *not* say, as some foolishly teach, that Christ's Kingdom is irrelevant to the world; rather, it affirms that the Kingdom is not *derived* from earth: "He was speaking of the *source* of His authority, not the place of His legitimate reign. His kingdom is not *of* this world but it *is* in this world and over it."[28]

5-6 The first part of verse 5 is a parenthetical statement about those who are excluded from the privilege of living and reigning with Christ. Now, if "those who had been beheaded" (v. 4) are the Old Covenant faithful, **the rest of the dead** are the (primarily) Old Covenant *un*faithful, the non-saints who were dead at the time St. John was writing. The figure can be logically extended to include all the unredeemed, of every age, but that is not the specific point St. John is making. Rather, he is stressing the fact that the dead believers of the Old Covenant have been included in Christ's Ascension and glorious reign from the heavenly Throne; they **live**, while the wicked are **dead**.

Ultimately, St. John tells us, there are two classes of people: 1) The elders and those whom they represent (the faithful of the Old and New Covenants), who live and reign with Christ "for a thousand years" in His Kingdom; and 2) the rest of the dead, the unbelievers. These **did not live until the thousand years were completed**. While some interpreters have leaped to the conclusion that "the rest of the dead" will live *after* the Millennium has ended, there is no such implication here. St. John is concerned simply to tell us about the Millennium itself, and his phrase means nothing more than that the rest of the dead are excluded from life and dominion for the whole period. We all know, from such passages as John 5:28-29 and Acts 24:15, that there will be a general resurrection of both the just and the unjust; but we must remember that St. John is not writing a comprehensive Systematic Theology of the end of the world. He is writing a

---

28. Gary North, *Backward, Christian Soldiers? An Action Manual for Christian Reconstruction* (Tyler, TX: Institute for Christian Economics, 1984), p. 4.

Prophecy to the Church, dealing with certain aspects of the blessings of the righteous and the curses of the wicked.

The narrative thus continues with St. John's definition of the saints' millennial living and reigning with Christ: **This is the First Resurrection** — first in both temporal order and importance. The imagery of two resurrections is solidly rooted in Scripture. In the Levitical system it was typologically set forth in the law prescribing purification after the defilement of death:

> The one who touches the corpse of any person shall be unclean for seven days. That one shall purify himself from uncleanness with the water on the third day and on the seventh day, and then he shall be clean; but if he does not purify himself on the third day and on the seventh day, he shall not be clean. (Num. 19:11-12)

As James Jordan has shown, this cleansing ritual was a symbolic *resurrection*: The man who was defiled by contact with the dead was ceremonially dead, and had to be resurrected from death.[29] The resurrection was accomplished by the sprinkling of water (see Num. 19:13)[30] on both the Third and Seventh days — in other words, *a first and second resurrection*. This "double resurrection" pattern is repeated in different ways throughout the Bible. St. John's Gospel records Jesus' words on the subject:

> Truly, truly, I say to you, he who hears My Word, and believes Him who sent Me, has eternal life, and does not come into judgment, but has passed out of death into life. Truly, truly, I say to you, *an hour is coming and now is, when the dead shall hear the voice of the Son of God; and those who hear shall live....*
>
> Do not marvel at this; for *an hour is coming in which all who are in the tombs shall hear His voice and shall come forth*; those who did the good deeds to a resurrection of life, those who committed evil deeds to a resurrection of judgment. (John 5:24-25, 28-29)

---

29. James B. Jordan, *The Law of the Covenant: An Exposition of Exodus 21-23* (Tyler, TX: Institute for Christian Economics, 1984), pp. 56ff.

30. On the significance of this passage for the mode of baptism, see Duane Edward Spencer, *Holy Baptism: Word Keys Which Unlock the Covenant* (Tyler, TX: Geneva Ministries, 1984), pp. 14ff.

Jesus here claims to be inaugurating the Age of the Resurrection, in which those who believe in Him are *now* to be participants; later, another "hour" will come in which all men, the just and the unjust, will rise out of the graves (cf. John 11:24-25). St. Paul drew the same distinction between two resurrections:

> But now Christ has been raised from the dead, the first fruits of those who are asleep. For since by a man came death, by a man also came the resurrection of the dead. For as in Adam all die, so also in Christ all shall be made alive. But each in his own order: Christ the first fruits, after that those who are Christ's at His coming. (1 Cor. 15:20-23)

There is thus to be a resurrection at the end of history, at the Second Coming of Christ on the Last Day (John 6:38-40, 44, 54; Acts 24:15; 1 Thess. 4:14-17). But before that final resurrection there is another, a First Resurrection: the resurrection of "Christ the first fruits." He rose from the dead, and resurrected all believers with Him. Note: St. John does not say that the believer himself as such is resurrected, but that he **has a part in the First Resurrection.** He is *sharing in* the Resurrection of Another — the Resurrection of the Lord Jesus Christ.[31] St. Paul told the Colossian Christians how they had been made partakers in Christ's resurrection:

> Having been buried with Him in baptism, in which you were also raised up with Him through faith in the working of God, who also raised Him from the dead. (Col. 2:12)

Christ's resurrection is the definitive resurrection, the First Resurrection, which took place on the Third Day. We participate in His resurrection through covenantal baptism, so that now we "walk in newness of life" (Rom. 6:4). When we were dead in our transgressions, God "made us alive together with Christ . . . and raised us up with Him, and seated us with Him in the heavenly places, in Christ Jesus" (Eph. 2:5-6; cf. Col. 3:1). It is this definitive resurrection on the Third Day, in the middle

---

31. See Philip Edgcumbe Hughes, "The First Resurrection: Another Interpretation," *The Westminster Theological Journal*, XXXIX (Spring 1977) 2, pp. 315-18.

of history, that both guarantees and is consummated by the "Seventh Day" resurrection at the end of history. Those who are baptized in Christ and thus united with Him in the likeness of His resurrection (Rom. 6:4-14) will be joined with Him in that final resurrection as well (Rom. 8:11).

Yet, as Norman Shepherd has observed, St. John in Revelation 20 "does not even describe the bodily resurrection of the just expressly as the second resurrection. This may well be indicative of the fact that contrary to much popular thought on the subject, baptism is even more properly resurrection than is the resurrection of the body. The just who are alive at the return of the Lord will not be resurrected in the body but will be transformed. The righteous dead who do rise bodily at the last day do not again assume mortality but immortality. Not resuscitation but transformation is the leading feature of resurrection, and the foundational transformation and transition takes place at baptism, the first resurrection."[32]

The First Resurrection is thus Spiritual and ethical, our regeneration in Christ and union with God, our re-creation in His image, our participation in His Resurrection. This interpretation is confirmed by St. John's description of those in the First Resurrection — it completely corresponds with everything he tells us elsewhere about the elect: They are **blessed** (1:3; 14:13; 16:15; 19:9; 22:7, 14) **and holy**, i.e. *saints* (5:8; 8:3-4; 11:18; 13:7, 10; 14:12; 16:6; 17:6; 18:20, 24; 19:8; 20:9; 21:2, 10); as Christ promised all the faithful, **the Second Death** (v. 14) **has no power** over them (2:11); and they are **priests** (1:6; 5:10) who **reign with Christ** (2:26-27; 3:21; 4:4; 11:15-16; 12:10). Indeed, St. John began his prophecy by telling his readers that all Christians are royal priests (1:6); and the consistent message of the New Testament, as we have seen repeatedly, is that God's people are now seated with Christ, reigning in His Kingdom (Eph. 1:20-22; 2:6; Col. 1:13; 1 Pet. 2:9). The greatest error in dealing with the Millennium of Revelation 20 is the failure to recognize that it speaks of present realities of the Christian life. The Bible is clear: Through baptism, we have been resurrected to eternal life

---

32. Norman Shepherd, "The Resurrections of Revelation 20," *The Westminster Theological Journal*, XXXVII (Fall, 1974) 1, pp. 37f. St. Gregory of Nyssa said: "It is necessary for us to undergo, by means of water, this preparatory rehearsal of the grace of the resurrection, so that we may realize that it is as easy for us to rise again from death as to be baptized with water." *The Great Catechism*, xxv.

and rule with Christ now, in this age. The First Resurrection is taking place now. Jesus Christ is reigning now (Acts 2:29-36; Rev. 1:5). And this means, of necessity, that *the Millennium is taking place now as well.*

The Last Battle (20:7-10)

7 And when the thousand years are completed, Satan will be released from his prison,

8 and will come out to deceive the nations which are in the four corners of the earth, Gog and Magog, to gather them together for the War; the number of them is like the sand of the sea.

9 And they came up on the breadth of the earth and surrounded the camp of the saints and the beloved City, and fire came down from heaven and devoured them.

10 And the devil who deceived them was thrown into the Lake of fire and brimstone, where the Beast and the False Prophet are; there they will be tormented day and night forever and ever.

7-8 At last **the thousand years are completed,** and God's timetable is ready for the final defeat of the Dragon. According to God's sovereign purpose, the devil is **released from his prison** in order to **deceive the nations.** Biblical postmillennialism is not an absolute universalism; nor does it teach that at some future point in history absolutely everyone living will be converted. Ezekiel's prophecy of the River of Life suggests that some outlying areas of the world—the "swamps" and "marshes"—will not be healed, but will be "given over to salt," remaining unrenewed by the living waters (Ezek. 47:11). To change the image: Although the Christian "wheat" will be dominant in world culture, both the wheat and the tares will grow together until the harvest at the end of the world (Matt. 13:37-43). At that point, as the potential of both groups comes to maturity, as each side becomes fully self-conscious in its determination to obey or rebel, there will be a final conflict. The Dragon will be released for a short time, to deceive the nations in his last-ditch attempt to overthrow the Kingdom.

We noted at verse 3 that the specific purpose of Satan's deception of the nations is **to gather them together for the War.** This had been at least one of Satan's goals from the beginning: to provoke the final war between God and His rebellious creatures, in order to "spike" God's work and prevent it from attaining fruition and maturity. That is why there was a sudden outbreak of demonic activity when Christ began His earthly ministry; that was Satan's motivation for tempting Him, for entering into Judas to betray Him, and for inspiring the Jewish and Roman authorities to slay Him. His plan backfired, of course (1 Cor. 2:6-8), and the Cross became his own destruction. Throughout the Book of Revelation St. John has shown the devil frantically working to bring about the final battle, and invariably being frustrated in his designs. Only after God's Kingdom has realized its earthly potential, when the full thousand years have been completed, will Satan be released to foment the last rebellion — thus engendering his own final defeat and eternal destruction.

In describing the eschatalogical war, St. John uses the vivid "apocalyptic" imagery of Ezekiel 38-39, which prophetically depicts the Maccabees' defeat of the Syrians in the second century B.C.: The ungodly forces are called **Gog and Magog**. According to some popular premillennial writers, this expression refers to Russia, and foretells a war between the Soviets and Israel during a future "Tribulation." Even apart from the fact that this interpretation is based on a radically inaccurate reading of Matthew 24 and the other "Great Tribulation" passages,[33] it is beset with numerous internal inconsistencies. First, premillennialists tend to speak of this coming war with the Soviet Union as synonymous with the "Battle of Armageddon" (16:16). Yet, on premillennialist assumptions, the Battle of Armageddon takes place before the Millennium begins — more than 1,000 years before St. John's "Gog and Magog" finally appear! Thus, premillennial prophecy buffs are treated to prolonged discussions of present Soviet military might and their supposed preparations for assuming the role of "Gog and Magog."[34] At the

---

33. This should be obvious by now; cf. Chilton, *Paradise Restored*, pp. 77-102.

34. It is certainly true that the Soviet Union's aggressive imperialism and its worldwide sponsorship of terrorism pose a grave danger to the Western nations; see Jean-François Revel, *How Democracies Perish* (Garden City: Doubleday and Co., 1984). This, however, has nothing to do with fulfilled prophecy, and everything to do with the fact that the West has simultaneously engaged in an increasing renunciation of Christian ethics and a progressive military and technological outfitting of her enemies; on the latter, see Antony Sutton, *Western*

same time, there is virtually a complete neglect of what the Book of Revelation actually says about the war with Gog and Magog; apparently, the specific facts of Biblical revelation occasionally get in the way of "prophetic truth."[35]

Second, those who interpret the war of "Gog and Magog" as an end-time war involving the Soviet Union usually pride themselves on being "literalists." Yet we should take note of what a strictly literal interpretation of Ezekiel 38-39 requires:

1. Gog's reason for invading Israel is to plunder her silver and gold, and *to take away her cattle* (38:11-13); contrary to much premillennialist exposition, nothing is said about expropriating Israel's oil or extracting minerals from the Dead Sea.

2. *All* of Gog's soldiers are on horseback (38:15); there are no soldiers in trucks, jeeps, tanks, helicopters, or jets.

3. *All* of Gog's soldiers are carrying swords, wooden shields, and helmets (38:4-5); their other weapons are *wooden* bows and

---

Technology and Soviet Economic Development, 1917-67, three vols. (Stanford: Hoover Institution Press, 1968-73); idem, *National Suicide* (New Rochelle, NY: Arlington House, 1973); cf. Richard Pipes, *Survival Is Not Enough: Soviet Realities and America's Future* (New York: Simon and Schuster, 1984). Those who are shocked that the possible future conquest of the United States by the Soviets might not be included in Bible prophecy would do well to consider the large number of important conflicts throughout the last thousand years of Western history that have also been omitted — such as the Norman Conquest, the Wars of the Roses, the Thirty Years' War, the English Civil War, the American Revolution, the French Revolution, the Napoleonic War, the Seminole War, the Revolutions of 1848, the Crimean War, the War between the States, the Sioux Indian War, the Boer War, the Spanish-American War, the Mexican Revolution, the First World War, the Spanish Civil War, the Italo-Ethiopian War, the Second World War, the Korean War, and the Vietnam War, to name a few; many of which were viewed by contemporary apocalyptists as notable fulfillments of Biblical prophecy.

35. The obvious example, of course, is Hal Lindsey, whose *Late Great Planet Earth* (Grand Rapids: Zondervan Publishing House, 1970) spends about thirty pages (pp. 59-71, 154-68) detailing how the Soviet Union will soon fulfill the prophecy of "Gog and Magog" in the Battle of Armageddon, and takes only two or three sentences to deal with Rev. 20:8 — not once even mentioning that the *only* reference to Gog and Magog in the entire Book of Revelation is in that verse. Cf. idem, *There's a New World Coming: A Prophetic Odyssey* (Eugene, OR: Harvest House, 1973), pp. 222-25, 278. Another example is the usually more circumspect Henry M. Morris, whose *Revelation Record: A Scientific and Devotional Commentary on the Book of Revelation* (Wheaton: Tyndale House Publishers, 1983) discusses Gog and Magog under Rev. 6:1 (pp. 108-110) and 16:12 (p. 310), but strives mightily to dismiss the significance of the reference in 20:8 (pp. 422f.).

arrows, clubs, and spears (39:3, 9).

4. Instead of using firewood (apparently no one even considers using gas, electricity, or solar power), the victorious Israelites will burn Gog's wooden weapons for fuel for seven years (39:9-10).

Third, the expression **Gog and Magog** does not, and never did, refer to Russia. That has been entirely made up from whole cloth, and simply repeated so many times that many have assumed it to be true. Ostensible reasons for this interpretation are based on a peculiar reading of Ezekiel 38:3, which speaks of "Gog, the chief prince of Meshech and Tubal." The word *chief* is, in the Hebrew, *rosh*; some have therefore translated the text as "Gog, the prince of Rosh." *Rosh* sounds something like *Russia*; therefore Gog is the prince (or premier) of Russia. Unfortunately for this ingenious interpretation, *rosh* simply means *head*, and is used over 600 times in the Old Testament — never meaning "Russia."[36]

Those who hold that "Gog" (a name supposedly derived from Soviet Georgia, since they both start with a "G"!) is the Soviet Premier generally make the further claim that "Meshech" is really Moscow, "Tubal" is Tobolsk, and "Gomer" (of Ezek. 38:6) is Germany. In his very helpful examination of this issue,[37] Ralph Woodrow comments: "This is doubtful. 'Moscow' comes from the Moscovites and is a Finnish name. Moscow was first mentioned in ancient documents in 1147 A.D., when it was a small village. Some think Tubal means Tobolsk, but this is only a similarity in sound. Tobolsk was founded in 1587 A.D. Some think Gomer [Ezek. 38:6] means Germany. It is true the words 'Gomer' and 'Germany' both begin with a 'G.' So does guesswork."[38]

Woodrow goes on to give reasons why the war of "Gog and Magog" spoken of in Revelation cannot be identical to that prophesied in Ezekiel:

---

36. Here is a complete list of its uses in Ezekiel alone: 1:22, 25, 26; 5:1; 6:13; 7:18; 8:3; 9:10; 10:1, 11; 11:21; 13:18; 16:12, 25, 31, 43; 17:4, 19, 22; 21:19, 21; 22:31; 23:15, 42; 24:23; 27:22, 30; 29:18; 32:27; 33:4; 38:2-3; 39:1; 40:1; 42:12; 43:12; 44:18, 20.

37. Ralph Woodrow, *His Truth Is Marching On: Advanced Studies on Prophecy in the Light of History* (Riverside, CA: Ralph Woodrow Evangelistic Association, 1977), pp. 32-46.

38. Ibid., p. 41.

1. In Ezekiel, Gog is a prince. In Revelation, Gog is a nation. [But see Farrer's alternative explanation, below.]

2. In Ezekiel, Gog is spoken of as coming against Israel with people from various countries around Israel; in Revelation, Gog and Magog are pictured as nations in the four quarters of the earth, in number as the sands of the sea.

3. In Ezekiel, Gog and his troops come against Israel, a people who have returned from captivity and are dwelling without walls; in Revelation, Gog and Magog go up on the breadth of the earth and compass the city of the saints.

4. In Ezekiel the enemy is Gog *of* the land of Magog; in Revelation Gog *and* Magog.

5. In Ezekiel, Gog's troops are defeated in Israel and the people burn the remaining weapons for *seven years*; in Revelation, Gog and Magog are destroyed by fire from God out of heaven. . . . Wooden weapons would be destroyed *then and there*.

It is not uncommon for the imagery of Revelation to be based on Old Testament subjects or places. The "Jezebel" of Revelation is not the same woman as in Kings. The "Sodom" in Revelation is not the same Sodom as in Genesis. The "Babylon" in Revelation is not the Babylon of Daniel. The "New Jerusalem" in Revelation cannot mean the old Jerusalem. But, in each instance, the former serves as a *type*. The woman Jezebel had already died, the cities of Sodom and Babylon had already been overthrown, and (in our opinion) the battle of Ezekiel 38 and 39 (if a literal battle) had already met its fulfillment within an Old Testament setting.[39]

As Caird points out, in Jewish writings "Gog and Magog" was a frequent, standard expression for the rebellious nations of Psalm 2, which gather together "against the LORD and against His Anointed."[40] Austin Farrer comments: "St. John takes the story from Ezekiel and leaves the symbol undecoded. St. John

---

39. Ibid., p. 42; cf. T. Boersma, *Is the Bible a Jigsaw Puzzle? An Evaluation of Hal Lindsey's Writings* (St. Catherines, Ont.: Paideia Press, 1978), pp. 106-25; see also Cornelis Vanderwaal's discussion of "Goggology" in *Hal Lindsey and Biblical Prophecy* (St. Catherines, Ont.: Paideia Press, 1978), pp. 78-80.

40. G. B. Caird, *A Commentary on the Revelation of St. John the Divine* (New York: Harper & Row, Publishers, 1966), p. 256. Caird cites the following references in the Talmud: *Ber.* 7^b, 10^a, 13^a; *Shab.* 118^a; *Pes.* 118^a; *Meg.* 11^a; *San.* 17^a, 94^a, 97^b; '*Abodah Z.* 3^b; '*Ed.* II 10.

says that the nations, or 'gentiles' beguiled by Satan are 'in the four *corners* of the earth' and perhaps he means this, i.e. that the unreconciled are tucked away in lands remote from the centre. The simple pairing of 'Gog and Magog' must not be taken as fixing on St. John the error of understanding both names either as tribes or as princes. In Ezekiel it is perfectly clear that Gog is the prince, Magog the people. St. John is innocent of the mistake; he says simply 'the nations in the four corners of the earth, Gog and Magog,' i.e. the power so described by Ezekiel—as an English orator might have said 'the forces of frustrated nationalism, Hitler and Germany.' It is certainly curious that St. John equates without explanation the tribes in the four corners with a tribe in one corner; only he does exactly the same thing in the Armageddon vision. Euphrates is dried to let the kings of the East pass; the three demons beguile *all the kings of the earth* to come to Armageddon. The old biblical picture of invasion from the North East is in both cases given an ecumenical interpretation."[41]

This is reinforced by St. John's observation that **the number of them is like the sand of the sea**—the same hyperbolic image used for the Canaanite nations conquered by Joshua (Josh. 11:4) and the Midianites overthrown by Gideon (Jud. 7:12)—two of the greatest triumphs in the history of the Covenant people. Rather than being a reason for panic and flight, the surrounding of the saints by a rebellious horde "like the sand of the sea" is a signal that God's people are about to be victorious, completely and magnificently. God's reason for bringing a vast multitude to fight against the Church is not in order to destroy the Church, but in order to bring the Church a speedier victory. Instead of God's people having to seek out her enemies and engage them in combat one by one, God allows Satan to incite them into concerted opposition, so that they may be finished off quickly, in one fell swoop.

9-10   And they came up on the breadth of the earth: This is reminiscent of Isaiah's prophecy of a coming Assyrian invasion, which "will fill *the breadth of your land*" (Isa. 8:8); yet, as Isaiah goes on to say, the land belongs to *Immanuel*. If the people trust

---

41. Austin Farrer, *The Revelation of St. John the Divine* (Oxford: At the Clarendon Press, 1964), pp. 207f.

in Him, all the power of the enemy will be shattered. Faithful Israel can taunt her attackers:

> Be broken, O peoples, and be shattered;
> And give ear, all remote places of the earth.
> Gird yourselves, yet be shattered;
> Gird yourselves, yet be shattered.
> Devise a plan, but it will be thwarted;
> State a proposal, but it will not stand,
> For God is with us! (Isa. 8:9-10)

Yet St. John's allusion to Isaiah's prophecy is also a reminder that old Israel is now apostate. For her there is no longer an Immanuel. She has definitively rejected her Maker and Husband, and He has abandoned her. Instead, God is now with the Church, and it is the Church's opponents who will be shattered, though they be as many in number as the sands of the sea (Gen. 32:12)! Jesus Christ is the Seed of Abraham, and He will possess the gate of His enemies, for the sake of His Church (Gal. 3:16, 29; Gen. 22:17).

St. John's image for the gathered people of God combines Moses' **camp of the saints** with David and Solomon's **beloved City**. This City is the New Jerusalem, described in detail in 21:9-22:5. The significance of this should not be missed: The City exists during the Millennium (i.e. the period between the First and Second Advents of Christ), which means that the "new heaven and new earth" (21:1) are a present as well as future reality. The New Creation will exist in consummate form after the Final Judgment, but it exists, definitively and progressively, in the present age (2 Cor. 5:17).

The apostates rebel, and Satan's forces briefly **surround** the Church; but there is not a moment of doubt about the outcome of the conflict. In fact, there is no real conflict at all, for the rebellion is immediately crushed: **Fire came down from heaven and devoured them,** as it had the wicked citizens of Sodom and Gomorrah (Gen. 19:24-25), and the soldiers of Ahaziah who came against Elijah (2 Kings 1:10, 12). Is this to be a literal **fire** at the end of the world? That seems probable, although we must remember that St. John is now showing us "a world of symbols too shadowy and distant even to be disputed."[42] Acknowledging that this firefall may refer to "that blow wherewith Christ in His coming is to strike those persecutors of the Church whom He shall then find alive upon earth," St. Augustine proposed another explanation: "In this place 'fire out of heaven' is well understood of the firmness of the saints [cf. 11:5], wherewith they refuse to yield obedience to those who rage against them. For the firmament is 'heaven,' by whose firmness these assailants shall be pained with blazing zeal, for they shall be impotent to draw away the saints to the party of Antichrist. This is the fire which shall devour them, and this is 'from God'; for it is by God's grace the saints become unconquerable, and so torment their enemies."[43]

In any case, the basic point of the text is that, in contrast to the armies of the Beast who were "killed" (i.e., converted) by the sword from the mouth of the Word of God (19:15, 21), these self-conscious rebels of the end are utterly destroyed. All opposition to the Kingdom of God is completely eliminated. The Dragon never really had a chance—his release from the Abyss had been a trap from the very beginning, intended merely to draw his forces out into the open, to make them visible in order to destroy them. Terry comments: "It is a great symbolic picture, and its one great teaching is clear beyond the possibility of doubt or misunderstanding, namely, that Satan and his forces must all ultimately perish. This is written for the comfort and confidence of the saints. But that final victory is in the far future, at the close of the Messianic age, and it is here simply outlined in apocalyptic symbols. Any presumption, therefore, of determining specific events of the future from this grand symbolism must be regarded as in the nature of the case a species of worthless and misleading speculation."[44]

Without descending into "misleading speculation," it is valid to ask: *Why* will the nations rebel after living in a Christianized world-order? In his thought-provoking study of "Common Grace, Eschatology, and Biblical Law," Gary North explains that both the regenerate culture and the unregenerate culture, as "wheat" and

---

42. Farrer, p. 208.
43. St. Augustine, *The City of God*, xx.12.
44. Terry, *Biblical Apocalyptics*, p. 455.

"tares," develop historically toward greater consistency to their presuppositions—in Cornelius Van Til's phrase, "epistemological self-consciousness." Over time, as Christians conform themselves more fully to God's commands and thereby receive His blessings, they become more powerful and attain increasing dominion. But what will happen to the unbelievers, as they become more self-conscious? North writes: "In the last days of this final era in human history [i.e., at the end of the Millennium], the satanists will still have the trappings of Christian order about them. Satan has to sit on God's lap, so to speak, in order to slap His face—or try to. Satan cannot be consistent to his own philosophy of autonomous order and still be a threat to God. An autonomous order leads to chaos and impotence. He knows that there is no neutral ground in philosophy. He knew Adam and Eve would die spiritually on the day that they ate the fruit. He is a good enough theologian to know that there is one God, and he and his host tremble at the thought (James 2:19). When demonic men take seriously his lies about the nature of reality, they become impotent, sliding off (or nearly off) God's lap. It is when satanists realize that Satan's official philosophy of chaos and antinomian lawlessness is a *lie* that they become dangerous. . . . They learn more of the truth, but they pervert it and try to use it against God's people.

"Thus, the biblical meaning of epistemological self-consciousness is not that the satanist becomes consistent with Satan's official philosophy (chaos), but rather that Satan's host becomes consistent with what Satan *really* believes: that order, law, power are the product of God's hated order. They learn to use law and order to build an army of conquest. In short, *they use common grace*—knowledge of the truth—*to pervert the truth and to attack God's people.* They turn from a false knowledge offered to them by Satan, and they adopt a perverted form of truth to use in their rebellious plans. They *mature,* in other words. Or, as C. S. Lewis has put into the mouth of his fictitious character, the senior devil Screwtape, when materialists finally believe in Satan but not in God, then the war is over. Not quite; when they believe in God, know He is going to win, and nevertheless strike out in fury—not blind fury, but *fully self-con-*

527

scious fury—at the works of God, *then* the war is over."[45]

North concludes: "Does the postmillennialist believe that there will be faith in general on the earth when Christ appears? Not if he understands the implications of the doctrine of common grace. Does he expect the whole earth to be destroyed by the unbelieving rebels before Christ strikes them dead—doubly dead? No. The judgment comes before they can do their work. Common grace is extended to allow unbelievers to fill up their cup of wrath. They are vessels of wrath. Therefore, the fulfilling of the terms of the dominion covenant through common grace is the final step in the process of filling up these vessels of wrath. The vessels of grace, believers, will also be filled. Everything is full. Will God destroy His preliminary down payment on the New Heavens and the New Earth? Will God erase the sign that His word has been obeyed, that the dominion covenant has been fulfilled? Will Satan, that great destroyer, have the joy of seeing God's word thwarted, His handiwork torn down by Satan's very hordes? The amillennialist answers yes. The postmillennialist must deny it with all his strength.

"There is continuity in life, despite discontinuities. The wealth of the sinner is laid up for the just. Satan would like to burn up God's field, but he knows he cannot. The tares and wheat grow to maturity, and then the reapers go out to harvest the wheat, cutting away the chaff and tossing chaff into the fire. . . . When [Satan] uses his gifts to become finally, totally destructive, he is cut down from above. *This final culmination of common grace is Satan's crack of doom.*

"And the meek—meek before God, active toward His creation—shall at last inherit the earth. A renewed earth and renewed heaven is the final payment by God the Father to His Son and to those He has given to His Son. This is the postmillennial hope."[46]

So **the devil who deceived them was thrown into the Lake of fire and brimstone, where the Beast and the False Prophet are; there they will be tormented day and night forever and ever.**

---

45. Gary North, "Common Grace, Eschatology, and Biblical Law," Appendix C, below, pp. 657f.
46. Ibid., pp. 663f.

Satan's cause will be finally and thoroughly overthrown. To picture this St. John again uses imagery based on the holocaust of Sodom and Gomorrah (Gen. 19:24-25, 28) and the destruction of the rebels in the wilderness of Kadesh (Num. 16:31-33), based on Isaiah's similar usage to describe the utter ruin of Edom (Isa. 34:9-10). He has already represented the eternal destruction of the Beast and the False Prophet and their followers by such imagery (see 14:10-11; 19:20); now he shows that the prime instigator of the cosmic conspiracy is inevitably doomed to suffer the same fate.

The Judgment of the Dead (20:11-15)

11 And I saw a great white Throne and Him who sat upon it, from whose face earth and heaven fled away, and no place was found for them.

12 And I saw the dead, the great and the small, standing before the Throne. And books were opened; and another book was opened, which is the Book of Life; and the dead were judged from the things which were written in the books, according to their works.

13 And the Sea gave up the dead which were in it, and Death and Hades gave up the dead which were in them; and they were judged, each one according to his works.

14 And Death and Hades were thrown into the lake of fire. This is the Second Death, the lake of fire.

15 And if anyone was not found written in the Book of Life, he was thrown into the lake of fire.

11 The sixth vision begins with the familiar formula: **And I saw** (*kai eidon*). History has ended; the crack of doom has fallen; and now the apostle's vision is filled with **a great white Throne, and Him who sat upon it**. Usually, it is implied in Revelation that the One seated on the Throne in heaven is the Father (cf. 4:2-3; 5:1, 7); but in this case St. John may have in mind the Son, since He is seated on a **white** Throne, and He has been seen previously seated on a white cloud (14:14) and a white horse (6:2; 19:11). The Lord Jesus Christ is the great "Shepherd and Bishop" (I Pet. 2:25); Farrer points out that "the idea of a 'white throne' may perhaps have been familiar to St. John's hearers as the distinguishing character of the local bishop's chair in the church. The practice of spreading a white cover over it was certainly early;

529

whether so early as St. John's date, we cannot prove."[47]

Prof. Berkhof summarizes the New Testament evidence regarding the Judge at the Last Day: "Naturally, the final judgment, like all God's *opera ad extra*, is a work of the triune God, but Scripture ascribes it particularly to Christ. Christ in His mediatorial capacity will be the future Judge, Matt. 25:31-32; John 5:27; Acts 10:42; 17:31; Phil. 2:10; 2 Tim. 4:1. Such passages as Matt. 28:18; John 5:27; Phil. 2:9-10 make it abundantly evident that the honor of judging the living and the dead was conferred on Christ as Mediator in reward for His atoning work and as part of His exaltation. This may be regarded as one of the crowning honors of His kingship. In His capacity as Judge, too, Christ is saving His people to the uttermost: He completes their redemption, justifies them publicly, and removes the last consequences of sin."[48]

With this agree the great ecumenical creeds:

The Apostles' Creed:

[Jesus Christ] ascended into heaven,
And sitteth on the right hand of God the Father Almighty;
From thence He shall come to judge the quick and the dead.

The Nicene Creed:

He ascended into heaven,
And sitteth on the right hand of the Father;
And He shall come again with glory to judge both the quick
and the dead;
Whose Kingdom shall have no end.

The *Te Deum Laudamus*:

Thou sittest at the right hand of God in the glory of the Father.
We believe that Thou shalt come to be our Judge.
We therefore pray Thee, help Thy servants, whom Thou hast
redeemed with Thy precious blood.
Make them to be numbered with Thy Saints in glory everlasting.
O Lord, save Thy people, and bless Thine heritage.
Govern them, and lift them up forever.

---

47. Farrer, p. 208.
48. L. Berkhof, *Systematic Theology* (Grand Rapids: William B. Eerdmans Publishing Co., 1939, 1941), pp. 731f.

The Athanasian Creed:

> He ascended into heaven; He sitteth on the right hand of the Father, God Almighty; from whence He shall come to judge the quick and the dead.
>
> At whose coming all men shall rise again with their bodies and shall give an account of their own works.
>
> And they that have done good shall go into life everlasting; and they that have done evil, into everlasting fire.
>
> This is the catholic faith; which except a man believe faithfully and firmly, he cannot be saved.

I have emphasized this point because it has become popular in some otherwise apparently orthodox circles to adopt a heretical form of "preterism" that denies any future bodily Resurrection or Judgment, asserting that all these are fulfilled in the Resurrection of Christ, the regeneration of the Church, the coming of the New Covenant, and the destruction of Jerusalem in A.D. 70.[49] Whatever else may be said about those who hold such notions, it is clear that they are not in conformity with any recognizable form of orthodox Christianity. The one, holy, catholic, and apostolic Church has always and everywhere insisted on the doctrine of the Last Judgment at the end of time. Its inclusion into all the historic definitions of the Faith is a universal testimony to its importance as an article of belief.

St. John heightens our sense of awe at the terrible majesty of the Judge: **From whose face earth and heaven fled away, and no place was found for them.** The allusion is to Psalm 114, which shows us that it is in light of the Final Judgment that we can see the significance of its precursors in preliminary historic judgments:

---

49. The most influential figure in this movement is Max R. King, a Church of Christ minister who has authored *The Spirit of Prophecy* (Warren, OH: Max R. King, 1971), a work that is both insightful and frustrating. King's hermeneutic is hampered by neoplatonic presuppositions (God wouldn't bother to resurrect a physical body because He is interested only in "spiritual," i.e. incorporeal, things) and by a "code" approach to Biblical symbolism. Cf. Jim McGuiggan and Max R. King, *The McGuiggan-King Debate* (Warren, OH: Parkman Road Church of Christ, n.d.). See also the similar views espoused by J. Stuart Russell, *The Parousia: A Study of the New Testament Doctrine of Our Lord's Second Coming* (Grand Rapids: Baker Book House, [1887] 1983). James B. Jordan has responded to King and Russell in two taped lectures, available from Geneva Ministries, P.O. Box 131300, Tyler, TX 75713.

When Israel went forth from Egypt,
The house of Jacob from a people of strange language,
Judah became His sanctuary,
Israel, His dominion.
The sea looked and fled;
The Jordan turned back.
The mountains skipped like rams,
The hills, like lambs.
What ails you, O sea, that you flee?
O Jordan, that you turn back?
O mountains, that you skip like rams?
O hills, like lambs?
Tremble, O earth, before the LORD,
Before the God of Jacob,
Who turned the rock into a pool of water,
The flint into a fountain of water. (Ps. 114)

Earth and heaven flee from before His face, terrified at His approach; yet the people of the covenant need have no fear. For them, God's judgment is redemptive, not destructive. If the earth trembles, it is for our sake, so that God may give us the water of salvation. In fact, as we shall see, the judgment portrayed in these verses is concerned with the wicked dead, those who come under the judgment of the Second Death. The elect, who reign with Christ, are not in view here. Rejoicing in the fruit of Christ's final victory, they do not come into judgment, but have passed out of death into life (John 5:24).

12 Although we are still in the sixth vision, verse 12 contains the seventh *kai eidon*, **And I saw** — allowing the seventh vision to begin with the eighth *kai eidon* (see on 21:1). We must remember that St. John is not writing of the general judgment of all men, but of the fate of the wicked, called here **the dead** (cf. v. 5). Hengstenberg comments: "The *dead* can only be the ungodly dead. It must alone appear singular, that here the dead are still spoken of, although they must have been raised up, before they could stand before the throne. If only the ungodly dead are meant, then there is nothing strange in the matter. For *their* life after the resurrection is but a life in semblance, as it was also before in Hades."[50]

---

50. E. W. Hengstenberg, *The Revelation of St. John*, two vols. (Cherry Hill, NJ: Mack Publishing Co., n.d.), Vol. 2, p. 310.

St. John tells us he saw men of all classes and conditions, both **the great and the small, standing before the Throne. And books were opened; and another book was opened, which is the Book of Life**, the membership roll of the covenant, in which the names of the elect are inscribed (cf. 3:5; 13:8; 17:8). The function of the Book of Life in this context is simply to reveal that the names of "the dead" do not appear therein.

And the dead were judged from the things which were written in the books, according to their works. This can seem strange to modern evangelical ears; we are not used to reading such statements in Scripture, yet they actually exist in abundance (cf. Ps. 62:12; Prov. 24:12; Matt. 16:27; John 5:28-29; Rom. 2:6-13; 14:12; 1 Cor. 3:13; 2 Cor. 5:10; Eph. 6:8; Col. 3:25; Rev. 2:23; 22:12). The point of the text is not, of course, "salvation by works." The point is, instead, *damnation by works.*

It is true that we are not saved by works (Eph. 2:8-9), but it is also true that we are not saved *without* works (Eph. 2:10; Phil. 2:12-13). The Christian is "justified by faith alone"—but genuine justifying faith is never alone, as the *Westminster Confession of Faith* declares: "Faith, thus receiving and resting on Christ and His righteousness, is the alone instrument of justification; yet is it not alone in the person justified, but is ever accompanied with all other saving graces, and is no dead faith, but worketh by love" (xi.2). In a similar vein, John Murray wrote: "Faith alone justifies but a justified person with faith alone would be a monstrosity which never exists in the kingdom of grace. Faith works itself out through love (cf. Gal. 5:6). And faith without works is dead (cf. James 2:17-20). It is living faith that justifies and living faith unites to Christ both in the virtue of his death and in the power of his resurrection."[51]

13   For this judgment **the Sea gave up the dead which were in it**—those who perished in the judgments of the Flood and the Red Sea symbolizing all the wicked, drowned in the "torrents of Belial" (Ps. 18:4); **and Death and Hades**, the "cords of Sheol" (Ps. 18:5) **gave up the dead which were in them,** God suddenly emptying "all supposable places where the dead could be

---

51. John Murray, *Redemption: Accomplished and Applied* (Grand Rapids: William B. Eerdmans Publishing Co., 1955), p. 161.

found."[52] **And they were judged, each one according to his works:** Again St. John emphasizes that men's actions will come into judgment at the Last Day.

14-15   St. Paul proclaimed that when Christ returns at the end of His mediatorial Kingdom, "the last enemy that will be abolished is Death" (1 Cor. 15:26). Thus, St. John saw **Death and Hades,** which were paired in 1:18 and 6:8, **thrown into the lake of fire.** As Terry says, "the entire picture of judgment and perdition is wrapped in mystic symbolism, and the one certain revelation is the final overthrow in remediless ruin of all who live and die as subjects of sin and death."[53] Further, as Morris observes, "death and Hades are ultimately as powerless as the other forces of evil. Finally there is no power but that of God. All else is completely impotent."[54]

This is the Second Death, the lake of fire. And if anyone was not found written in the Book of Life, he was thrown into the lake of fire. Universalists have tried for centuries to evade the plain fact that Scripture slams the furnace lid shut over those who are finally impenitent, whose names are not inscribed (from the foundation of the world, 13:8; 17:8) in the Lamb's Book of Life. Using a metaphor similar to St. John's, Jesus said: "If anyone does not abide in Me, he is thrown away as a branch, and dries up; and they gather them, and cast them into the fire, and they are burned" (John 15:6). "The rest of the dead" will never live, for there is no life outside of Jesus Christ.

---

52. Milton Terry, *Biblical Apocalyptics,* p. 457.
53. Terry, *Biblical Apocalyptics,* p. 458.
54. Leon Morris, *The Revelation of St. John* (Grand Rapids: William B. Eerdmans Publishing Co., 1969), pp. 241f.

21

THE NEW JERUSALEM

The Bible is a Storybook, with one Story to tell. That Story, which is of Jesus Christ and His salvation of the world, is presented again and again throughout the Bible, with innumerable variations on the same basic theme. One important aspect of that Story is of God as the Warrior-King, who raises His people from death, defeats His enemies, takes for Himself the spoils of war, and builds His House. For example, there is the story of the Exodus: "Moses said to the people, 'Do not fear! Stand by and see the salvation of the LORD which He will accomplish for you today; for the Egyptians whom you have seen today, you will never see them again forever. The LORD will fight for you while you keep silent' " (Ex. 14:13-14). Accordingly, after the successful Red Sea crossing (the baptismal resurrection of Israel and the baptismal destruction of Egypt), Moses exulted: "The LORD is a Warrior!" (Ex. 15:3). Egypt and all its wealth and glory were completely wiped out; all that was left was what the Israelites had "plundered," of silver and gold, and articles of clothing (Ex. 3:21-22; 11:1-2; 12:35-36). Much of this was later turned over to the Lord for the construction of the Tabernacle, God's House (Ex. 35:21-29; 36:3-8), which He entered in flaming Glory (Ex. 40:34).

The pattern is repeated many times, another well-known example being the story of David and Solomon: David acts as God's Warrior, fighting the Lord's battles with Him (cf. 2 Sam. 5:22-25), and his son Solomon builds the Lord's House (2 Sam. 7:12-13); and again, the sign that God has moved in is the descent of fire (2 Chron. 7:1-3). All these were provisional victories and House-buildings, anticipations of the definitive Victory in the work of Jesus Christ.

535

One of the most striking announcements of the coming Warrior-King occurs in the prophecy of Ezekiel. As we have seen, the Book of Revelation is self-consciously tied to Ezekiel at many points; and the last twelve chapters of Ezekiel are especially in the background of St. John's concluding chapters. In Ezekiel 37, the prophet sees a vision of Israel in exile, represented as a valley full of dry bones; humanly speaking, all hope is gone. But as Ezekiel preaches to the bones and intercedes for the people with the Spirit of God, the Lord performs the miracle of re-creation, raising up the people of Israel to life, bringing them out of their graves, and turning them into "an exceedingly great army." A united Israel is restored to her Kingdom, with David again ruling as King, forever.

After this Resurrection, however, there is the War: "Gog of the land of Magog" comes with the armies of the heathen nations to make war against the restored Israel (Ezek. 38). He is destroyed by fire and brimstone from heaven, his spoils are taken by the victorious Israelites, and his armies are devoured by the birds of the air and the beasts of the field (Ezek. 39). Following this scene, Ezekiel writes some of the most elaborately detailed chapters in the Bible (Ezek. 40-48), in which he describes an ideal Temple-City, a New Jerusalem in which God Himself dwells among His people and sends blessings out from His Throne to the ends of the earth.

St. John has already used the resurrection-battle-Temple theme several times in Revelation (one of the most notable examples is Chapter 11, in which the two witnesses are resurrected, the Kingdom comes, God's wrath falls upon the nations, the destroyers are destroyed, and the Temple is opened). But Ezekiel's specific outline is clearly in mind in Revelation 20: The saints share in the First Resurrection and reign in the Kingdom with their greater "David"; then they are attacked by Gog and Magog. The enemy is destroyed by fire from heaven—the sign that God is entering His holy Temple. All this brings us up to 21-22, St. John's vision of the final Temple, the consummate Paradise that has become the City of God, where God dwells with His people in perfect communion. Adam's original task has been accomplished, and its cultural implications are fully realized as the nations willingly bring their treasures into God's House and the River of Life flows out to heal the world.

536

All Things New (21:1-8)

1 And I saw a new heaven and a new earth; for the first heaven and the first earth passed away, and there is no longer any Sea.

2 And I saw the Holy City, New Jerusalem, coming down out of heaven from God, made ready as a Bride adorned for her Husband.

3 And I heard a loud Voice from heaven, saying: Behold, the Tabernacle of God is among men, and He shall dwell among them, and they shall be His people, and God Himself shall be among them,

4 and He shall wipe away every tear from their eyes; and there shall no longer be any death; there shall no longer be any mourning, or crying, or pain; the first things have passed away.

5 And He who sits on the throne said: Behold, I am making all things new. And He said: Write, for these words are faithful and true.

6 And He said to me: It is done! I am the Alpha and the Omega, the Beginning and the End. I will give to the one who thirsts from the spring of the Water of Life without cost.

7 He who overcomes shall inherit these things, and I will be his God and he shall be My son.

8 But for the cowardly and unbelieving and sinners and abominable and murderers and fornicators and sorcerers and idolaters and all liars, their part will be in the lake that burns with fire and brimstone, which is the Second Death.

1 St. John begins this, the last and lengthiest in the final series of visions, with the words **And I saw.** Although this is the seventh vision in the series, it is the eighth occurrence of the phrase *kai eidon* — the number 8, as we have already noted, being associated with resurrection and regeneration (e.g., Hebrew males were circumcised on the eighth day; Jesus [888], was resurrected on the eighth day, etc.). St. John uses it here in order to underscore the picture of cosmic resurrection and regeneration: He sees **a new heaven and a new earth, for the first heaven and the first earth passed away,** having fled from the face of the Judge (20:11). The old world is completely replaced by the **new**; the word used is not *neos* (chronological newness) but *kainos* (newness in kind, of superior quality). Adam's task of heavenizing the earth has been completed, established on an entirely new basis in the work of Christ. Earth's original uninhabitable condition of deep-and-darkness has been utterly done away with: **There is no longer any Sea** or Abyss. There is heaven and earth, but no "under-the-earth," the abode of Leviathan. What St. John reveals to us is the eschatological outcome of the comprehensive, cosmic reconciliation celebrated by St. Paul: "For it was the Father's good pleasure for all the fulness to dwell in Him, and through Him to reconcile all things to Himself, having made peace through the blood of His cross; through Him, whether things on earth or things in heaven" (Col. 1:19-20).[1]

Yet this vision of the new heaven and earth is not to be interpreted as wholly future. As we shall see repeatedly throughout our study of this chapter, that which is to be absolutely and completely true in eternity is definitively and progressively true *now*. Our enjoyment of our eternal inheritance will be a continuation and perfection of what is true of the Church in this life. We are not simply to look forward to the blessings of Revelation 21 in an eternity to come, but to enjoy them and rejoice in them and extend them here and now. St. John was telling the early Church of present realities, of blessings that existed already and would be on the increase as the Gospel went forth and renewed the earth.

Salvation is consistently presented in the Bible as *re-creation*.[2] This is why creation language and symbolism are used in Scripture whenever God speaks of saving His people. We have seen how God's deliverances of His people in the Flood and the Exodus are regarded by the Biblical writers as provisional New Creations, pointing to the definitive New Creation in the First Advent of Christ. Thus, God spoke through Isaiah of the blessings of Christ's coming Kingdom:

> For, behold, I create *new heavens and a new earth*;
> And the former things shall not be remembered or come to mind.
> But be glad and rejoice forever in what I create;
> For behold, I create Jerusalem for rejoicing,

---

1. See John Murray, "The Reconciliation," *The Westminster Theological Journal*, XXIX (1966) 1, pp. 1-23; *Collected Writings*, 4 vols. (Edinburgh: The Banner of Truth Trust, 1976-82), Vol. 4, pp. 92-112.

2. See David Chilton, *Paradise Restored: A Biblical Theology of Dominion* (Ft. Worth, TX: Dominion Press, 1985), pp. 23-26.

And her people for gladness.
I will also rejoice in Jerusalem, and be glad in My people;
And there will no longer be heard in her
The voice of weeping and the sound of crying.
No longer will there be in it an infant who lives but a few days,
Or an old man who does not live out his days;
For the youth will die at the age of one hundred,
And the one who does not reach the age of one hundred
Shall be thought accursed.
And they shall build houses and inhabit them;
They shall also plant vineyards and eat their fruit.
They shall not build, and another inhabit;
They shall not plant, and another eat;
For as the lifetime of a tree, so shall be the days of My people,
And My chosen ones shall wear out the work of their hands.
They shall not labor in vain,
Or bear children for calamity;
For they are the offspring of those blessed by the LORD,
And their descendants with them.
It will also come to pass
That before they call, I will answer;
And while they are still speaking, I will hear.
The wolf and the lamb shall graze together,
And the lion shall eat straw like the ox;
And dust shall be the serpent's food.
They shall do no evil or harm in all My Holy Mountain.
(Isa. 65:17-25)

This cannot be speaking of heaven, or of a time after the end of the world; for in this "new heaven and earth" there is still death (though at a very advanced age — "the lifetime of a tree"); people are building, planting, working, and having children. Isaiah is clearly making a statement about *this* age, *before* the end of the world, showing what future generations can expect as the Gospel permeates the world, restores the earth to Paradise, and brings to fruition the goals of the Kingdom. Isaiah is describing the blessings of Deuteronomy 28 in their greatest earthly fulfillment. Thus, when St. John tells us that he saw "a new heaven and earth," we should recognize that the *primary* significance of that phrase is symbolic, and has to do with the blessings of salvation.

Perhaps the definitive New Testament text on the "new

heaven and earth" is 2 Peter 3:1-14. There, St. Peter reminds his readers that Christ and all the apostles had warned of accelerating apostasy toward the end of the "last days" (2 Pet. 3:2-4; cf. Jude 17-19)—which, as we have seen, was the forty-year transitional period (cf. Heb. 8:13) between Christ's Ascension and the destruction of the Old Covenant Temple, when the nations were beginning to flow toward the Mountain of the LORD (Isa. 2:2-4; Acts 2:16-17; Heb. 1:2; James 5:3; 1 Pet. 1:20; 1 John 2:18). As St. Peter made clear, these latter-day "mockers" would be *Covenant apostates*: Jews who were familiar with Old Testament history and prophecy, but who had abandoned the Covenant by rejecting Christ. Upon this evil and perverse generation would come the great "Day of Judgment" foretold in the prophets, a "destruction of ungodly men" like that suffered by the wicked of Noah's day (2 Pet. 3:5-7; cf. the same analogy drawn in Matt. 24:37-39; Luke 17:26-27). Just as God had destroyed the "world" of that day by the Flood, so would He destroy the "world" of first-century Israel by fire in the fall of Jerusalem.

St. Peter describes this as the destruction of "the present heavens and earth" (2 Pet. 3:7), making way for "new heavens and a new earth" (v. 13). Because of the "collapsing-universe" terminology used in this passage, many have mistakenly assumed that St. Peter is speaking of the final end of the physical heaven and earth, rather than the dissolution of the Old Covenant world order. The great seventeenth-century Puritan theologian John Owen answered this view by referring to the Bible's metaphorical usage of *heavens and earth*, as in Isaiah's description of the Mosaic Covenant:

> But I am the LORD thy God, that divided the sea, whose waves roared: The LORD of hosts is His name.
> And I have put my words in thy mouth, and I have covered thee in the shadow of mine hand, that I may plant the *heavens*, and lay the foundations of the *earth*, and say unto Zion, Thou art my people. (Isa. 51:15-16)

Owen writes: "The time when the work here mentioned, of planting the heavens, and laying the foundation of the earth, was performed by God, was when he 'divided the sea' (v. 15), and gave the law (v. 16), and said to Zion, 'Thou art my people'—that is, when he took the children of Israel out of

Egypt, and formed them in the wilderness into a church and state. Then he planted the heavens, and laid the foundation of the earth—made the new world; that is, brought forth order, and government, and beauty, from the confusion wherein before they were. This is the planting of the heavens, and laying the foundation of the earth in the world."[3]

Another such text, among many that could be mentioned, is Jeremiah 4:23-31, which speaks of the imminent fall of Jerusalem (587 B.C.) in similar language of *decreation*: "I looked on the *earth*, and behold, it was formless and void; and to the *heavens*, and they had no light. . . . For thus says the LORD, the whole land shall be a desolation [cf. Matt. 24:15], yet I will not execute a complete destruction. For this the *earth* shall mourn, and the *heavens* above be dark. . . ." God's Covenant with Israel had been expressed from the very beginning in terms of a *new creation*; thus the Old Covenant order, in which the entire world was organized around the central sanctuary of the Jerusalem Temple, could quite appropriately be described, before its final dissolution, as "the present heavens and earth."

Owen continues: "And hence it is, that when mention is made of the destruction of a state and government, it is in that language that seems to set forth the end of the world. So Isaiah 34:4; which is yet but the destruction of the state of Edom. The like is also affirmed of the Roman empire, Revelation 6:14; which the Jews constantly affirm to be intended by Edom in the prophets. And in our Saviour Christ's prediction of the destruction of Jerusalem, Matthew 24, he sets it out by expressions of the same importance. It is evident then, that, in the prophetical idiom and manner of speech, by 'heavens' and 'earth,' the civil and religious state and combination of men in the world, and the men of them, are often understood. So were the heavens and earth that world which was then destroyed by the flood.

"On this foundation I affirm that the heavens and earth here intended in this prophecy of Peter, the coming of the Lord, the day of judgment and perdition of ungodly men, mentioned in the destruction of that heaven and earth, do all of them relate, not to the last and final judgment of the world, but to that utter

---

3. John Owen, *Works*, 16 vols. (London: The Banner of Truth Trust, 1965-68), Vol. 9, p. 134.

desolation and destruction that was to be made of the Judaical church and state."[4]

This interpretation is confirmed by St. Peter's further information: In this imminent "Day of the Lord" which is about to come upon the first-century world "like a thief" (cf. Matt. 24:42-43; 1 Thess. 5:2; Rev. 3:3), "the elements will be destroyed with intense heat" (v. 10; cf. v. 12). What are these *elements*? So-called "literalists" will have it that the apostle is speaking about physics, referring the term to atoms (or perhaps subatomic particles), the actual physical components of the universe. What these "literalists" fail to recognize is that although the word *elements* is used several times in the New Testament, it is *never* used in connection with the physical universe! The term is *always* used in connection with the Old Covenant order (see Gal. 4:3, 9; Col. 2:8, 20). The writer to the Hebrews chided them: "For though by this time you ought to be teachers, you have need again for someone to teach you the *elements* of the oracles of God, and you have come to need milk and not solid food" (Heb. 5:12). In context, the writer is clearly speaking of Old Covenant truths—particularly since he connects it with the term *oracles of God*, an expression generally used for the provisional, Old Covenant revelation (see Acts 7:38; Rom. 3:2). St. Peter's message, Owen argues, is that "the heavens and earth that God himself planted—the sun, moon, and stars of the Judaical polity and church—the whole old world of worship and worshippers, that stand out in their obstinacy against the Lord Christ—shall be sensibly dissolved and destroyed."[5] Thus "the Land and its works will be burned up" (v. 10).

Owen offers two further reasons ("of many that might be insisted on from the text") for adopting the A.D. 70 interpretation of 2 Peter 3. First, he observes, "whatever is here mentioned was to have its particular influence on the men of that generation." St. Peter is especially concerned that the first-century believers remember the apostolic warnings about "the last days" (v. 2-3); Jewish scoffers, clearly familiar with the Biblical prophecies of judgment, refuse to heed the warnings (v. 3-5); St. Peter's readers are exhorted to live holy lives in the light of this imminent

---

4. Ibid.
5. Ibid., p. 135.

judgment (v. 11, 14); and it is *these* early Christians who are repeatedly mentioned as actively "looking for and hastening" the judgment (v. 12, 13, 14). It is precisely the *nearness* of the approaching conflagration that St. Peter cites as a motive to diligence in godly living.

Second, Owen cites 2 Peter 3:13: "But *according to His promise* we are looking for new heavens and a new earth, in which righteousness dwells." Owen asks: "What is that promise? Where may we find it? Why, we have it in the very words and letter, Isaiah 65:17. Now, when shall this be that God will create these 'new heavens and new earth, wherein dwelleth righteousness'? Saith Peter, 'It shall be after the coming of the Lord, after that judgment and destruction of ungodly men, who obey not the Gospel, that I foretell.' But now it is evident, from this place of Isaiah, with chapter 66:21-22, that this is a prophecy of Gospel times only; and that the planting of these new heavens is nothing but the creation of Gospel ordinances, to endure forever. The same thing is so expressed in Hebrews 12:26-28."[6]

Owen is right on target, asking the question that so many expositors fail to ask: *Where* had God promised to bring "new heavens and a new earth"? The answer, as Owen correctly states, is in Isaiah 65 and 66 — passages which clearly prophesy the period of the Gospel, brought in by the work of Christ. According to Isaiah, this New Creation cannot be the eternal state, since it contains birth and death, building and planting (65:20-23). The "new heavens and earth" promised to the Church comprise the age of the Gospel's triumph, when all mankind will come to bow down before the Lord (66:22-23). St. Peter's encouragement to the Church of his day was to be patient, to wait for God's judgment to destroy those who are persecuting the faith and impeding its progress. Once the Lord comes to destroy the scaffolding of the Old Covenant structure, the New Covenant Temple will be left in its place, and the victorious march of the Church will be unstoppable. The world will be converted; the earth's treasures will be brought into the City of God, as the Paradise Mandate (Gen. 1:27-28; Matt. 28:18-20) is consummated (Rev. 21:24-27).

This is why the apostles constantly affirmed that the age of

---

6. Ibid., pp. 134f.

consummation had already been implemented by the resurrection and ascension of Christ, who poured out the Holy Spirit. Once the old order had been swept away, St. Peter declared, the Age of Christ would be fully established, an era "in which righteousness dwells" (2 Pet. 3:13). The distinguishing characteristic of the new age, in stark contrast to what preceded it, would be righteousness — *increasing* righteousness, as the Gospel would be set free in its mission to the nations. Norman Shepherd shows how this is foreshadowed in the provisional new creation after the Flood: "Just as Noah sets foot with his family after the first household baptism (1 Peter 3:20f.) on a new earth in which once again righteousness dwells, so also Christ by his baptism — his death and resurrection — introduces his children by their baptism into him, to a new existence in which they can begin to see and participate in a new earth characterized by righteousness and holiness. In the power of the Spirit they cultivate the earth for the glory of God."[7]

It is certainly true that righteousness does not dwell in the earth in an absolute sense; nor will this world ever be absolutely righteous, until the final enemy is defeated at the Second Coming of Christ. The war between Christ and Satan for dominion over the earth is not over yet. There have been many battles throughout the history of the Church, and many battles lie ahead. But these must not blind us to the very real progress that the Gospel has made and continues to make in the world. The war has been won definitively; the New World Order of the Lord Jesus Christ has arrived; and, according to God's promise, the saving knowledge of Him will yet fill the earth, as the waters cover the sea.

Moreover, the phrase *heaven and earth* in these contexts does not, as Owen pointed out, refer to the physical heaven and the physical world, but to the *world-order*, the religious organization of the world, the "House" or Temple God builds in which He is worshiped. The consistent message of the New Testament is that the House of the New Covenant, over which Jesus presides as Apostle and High Priest, is infinitely superior to the House of the Old Covenant, presided over by Moses (cf. 1 Cor.

---

7. Norman Shepherd, "The Resurrections of Revelation 20," *The Westminster Theological Journal*, XXXVII (Fall 1974) 1, p. 40.

3:16; Eph. 2:11-22; 1 Tim. 3:15; Heb. 3:1-6). In fact, as the writer to the Hebrews insists, "the world to come" *has come*; it is the present salvation, brought in by the Son of God in the Last Days (Heb. 1:1-2:5). In this specific sense, righteousness does dwell in "heaven and earth."

2 St. John next sees, as the central aspect of this New Creation, **the Holy City, New Jerusalem.** Again we must remember that Jesus Christ has accomplished one salvation, one New Creation, with definitive, progressive, and consummative aspects. The final reality of the eschatological New Creation is also the present reality of the definitive-progressive New Creation. No aspect of this salvation should be emphasized to the exclusion or undue minimization of the others. The New Testament teaches that, with Old Jerusalem about to be excommunicated and executed for her violation of the covenant, Christians have become citizens and heirs of the New Jerusalem, the City whose origin is in heaven, which comes **down out of heaven from God** (3:12; cf. Gal. 4:22-31; Eph. 2:19; Phil. 3:20; Heb. 11:10, 16; 12:22-23). The New Testament then goes on to say: All this, and heaven too! (cf. Phil. 3:21); the New Creation is not only a state established definitively by Christ, and progressively unfolding now; someday it will be established finally, in consummate, absolute perfection![8]

The City is **made ready as a Bride adorned for her Husband.** The Bride is not just *in* the City; the Bride *is* the City (cf. v. 9-10). St. John's clear identification of the City as the Bride of Christ serves as another demonstration that the City of God is a present as well as future reality. The "Bride" of the weekly eucharistic Wedding Feast (19:7-9) is the "beloved City" of the Kingdom of Christ (cf. 20:9). We are in the New Jerusalem *now*, as the Bible categorically tells us: "*You have come* to Mount Zion

---

8. Unfortunately, the almost exclusively futuristic interpretation of such passages in the recent past — and the accompanying neoplatonic outlook, as if to say that it is useless and even sinful to work for the "heavenization" of this world — has meant that a proper emphasis on the present reality of the Kingdom appears to reverse the movement of the New Testament. Where the Bible says: "Not in this age only, but also in the age to come," our zeal to recover the Biblical perspective sometimes leads us to say: "Not in the age to come only, but also in this age." The danger in this, obviously, is that it can produce contempt for a truly Biblical eschatology.

and to the City of the living God, the heavenly Jerusalem, and to myriads of angels in festal assembly, and to the Church of the firstborn who are enrolled in heaven. . . ." (Heb. 12:22-23).

3   If we are citizens of heaven, as St. Paul declared (Eph. 2:19), it is also true that heaven dwells within us (Eph. 2:20-22). Indeed, the Word Himself has tabernacled among us (John 1:14); He and His Father have made Their abode with us (John 14:23); and thus we are the Temple of the Living God (2 Cor. 6:16). Accordingly, St. John's vision of the Holy City is followed by **a loud Voice from heaven, saying: Behold, the Tabernacle of God is among men, and He shall dwell among them, and they shall be His people, and God Himself shall be among them.** Again, this is a repetition of what we have already learned in this prophecy (3:12; 7:15-17). In the New Testament Church the promise of the Law and the prophets is realized: "I will make My Tabernacle among you, and My soul will not reject you; I will also walk among you and be your God, and you shall be My people" (Lev. 26:11-12); "And I will make a Covenant of peace with them; it will be an everlasting Covenant with them. And I will establish them and multiply them, and will set My sanctuary in their midst forever. My dwelling place also will be with them; and I will be their God, and they will be My people. And the nations will know that I am the LORD who sanctifies Israel, when My sanctuary is in their midst forever" (Ezek. 37:26-28).

As verse 9 makes explicit, this passage is the conclusion of the Chalices-section of the prophecy. At its beginning, St. John saw the Sanctuary of the Tabernacle filling with smoke, so that no one was able to enter it (15:5-8), and then he heard "a loud Voice" from the Sanctuary order the seven angels to pour out their Chalices of wrath into the Land (16:1). At the outpouring of the seventh Chalice "a loud Voice" again issued from the Sanctuary, saying: "It is done!" — producing a great earthquake, in which the cities fell and every mountain and island "fled away" as the vision turned to focus on the destruction of Babylon, the False Bride (16:17-21). Now, toward the close of the Chalices-section, earth and heaven have "fled away" (20:11; 21:1), and again St. John hears **a loud Voice from heaven,** announcing that access to the Sanctuary has been provided to the greatest possible degree, for **the Tabernacle of God is among**

men. Soon, that same Voice will again announce: "It is done" (v. 6), as the vision turns our attention to the establishment of the True Bride, New Jerusalem.

4-5 The Voice St. John heard continues: **And He shall wipe away every tear from their eyes; and there shall no longer be any death; there shall no longer be any mourning, or crying, or pain.** We can look forward to the absolute and perfect fulfillment of this promise at the Last Day, when the last enemy is destroyed. But, in principle, it is true already. Jesus said: "I am the Resurrection and the Life; he who believes in Me shall live even if he dies, and everyone who lives and believes in Me shall never die" (John 11:25-26). God *has* wiped away our tears, for we are partakers of His First Resurrection. One striking evidence of this is the obvious difference between Christian and pagan funerals: We grieve, but not as those who have no hope (1 Thess. 4:13). God has taken away the sting of death (1 Cor. 15:55-58).

All these blessings have come because **the first things have passed away. And He who sits on the Throne said: Behold, I am making all things new.** Here is another connection to the teaching of St. Paul: "Therefore, if anyone is in Christ, there is *a New Creation; the old things have passed away; behold, all things have become new*" (2 Cor. 5:17). Again, of course, we are confronted with the fact that this is true now, as well as on the Last Day. The only essential difference between the subjects of 2 Corinthians 5 and Revelation 21 is that St. Paul is speaking of *the redeemed individual*, while St. John is speaking of *the redeemed community*. Both the individual and the community are re-created, renewed, and restored to Paradise in salvation, and this cosmic restoration has already begun. St. John sees that what has begun in seemingly (to the eyes of the first century) isolated instances is really the wave of the future. The New Creation will fill the earth; the whole creation will be renewed. This is true definitively, it will be absolutely true eschatologically — and it gives us the pattern for our work in between, for it is also to be worked out progressively. The New Creation must be unfolded, its every implication understood and applied, by the royal priesthood in this age.

The great Church Historian Philip Schaff understood this: "To the Lord and his kingdom belongs the whole world, with all that lives and moves in it. *All* is yours, says the apostle [1 Cor. 3:22]. Religion is not a single, separate sphere of human life, but the divine principle by which the entire man is to be pervaded, refined, and made complete. It takes hold of him in his undivided totality, in the center of his personal being; to carry light into his understanding, holiness into his will, and heaven into his heart; and to shed thus the sacred consecration of the new birth, and the glorious liberty of the children of God, over his whole inward and outward life. No form of existence can withstand the renovating power of God's Spirit. There is no rational element that may not be sanctified; no sphere of natural life that may not be glorified. The creature, in the widest extent of the word, is earnestly waiting for the manifestation of the sons of God, and sighing after the same glorious deliverance. The whole creation aims toward redemption; and Christ is the second Adam, the new universal man, not simply in a religious but also in an absolute sense. The view entertained by Romish monasticism and Protestant pietism, by which Christianity is made to consist in an abstract opposition to the natural life, or in *flight from the world*, is quite contrary to the spirit and power of the Gospel, as well as false to its design. Christianity is the redemption and renovation of the *world*. It must make *all things* new."⁹

6   And He said to me: It is done! This is the flip side of the declaration of Babylon's destruction (16:17), both texts serving as echoes of His cry on the Cross: "It is finished!" (John 19:30). By His redemption, Christ has won the everlasting defeat of His enemies and the eternal blessing of His people.

The One who sits on the Throne names Himself (as in 1:8) **the Alpha and the Omega** (in English, "the A and the Z"), meaning **the Beginning and the End,** the Source, Goal, and Meaning of all things, the One who guarantees that the promises will be fulfilled. This is said here in order to confirm what is to follow, in Christ's promise of the Eucharist.

We noted above that our Lord's final announcement from the Cross from St. John's Gospel ("It is finished!") is echoed here; but there is more. For after Jesus made that proclamation

---

9. Philip Schaff, *The Principle of Protestantism,* trans. John Nevin (Philadelphia: United Church Press, [1845] 1964), p. 173.

He gave up the ghost; and when the Roman soldiers came and saw that he had died, "one of the soldiers pierced His side with a spear, and immediately there came out blood and water" (John 19:34). St. John Chrysostom commented: "Not without a purpose, or by chance, did these founts come forth, but because the Church was formed out of them both: The initiated are reborn by water, and are nourished by the Blood and the Flesh. Here is the origin of the Sacraments; that when you approach that awful cup, you may so approach as if drinking from the very side."[10] For this reason the Lord says: **I will give to the one who thirsts from the spring of the Water of Life without cost.** "Without cost," that is, to us; because the fountain of Life springs forth from His own flesh. Our redemption was purchased, "not with perishable things like silver or gold . . . but with precious blood, as of a Lamb unblemished and spotless, the blood of Christ" (1 Pet. 1:18-19). The water feeds us freely, springing up within us and then flowing out from us to give Life to the whole world (John 4:14; 7:37-39).

7   The theme of the Seven Letters is repeated in the promise to the overcomer, the victorious Christian conqueror: **He who overcomes shall inherit these things.** This prophecy has never lost sight of its character as a practical, ethical message to the churches (rather than a bare "prediction" of coming events). We must also note that the inheritance of all these blessings is exclusively the right of the overcomer. As we have already seen, St. John does not allow for the existence of a defeatist Christianity. There is only one kind of Christian: the conqueror. The child of God is characterized by victory against all opposition, against the world itself (1 John 5:4).

Further, God assures the overcomer of His faithfulness to His covenantal promise of salvation: **I will be his God and he shall be My son** (cf. Gen. 17:7-8; 2 Cor. 6:16-18). The highest and fullest enjoyment of communion with God will take place in heaven for eternity. But, definitively and progressively, it is true now. We are already living in the new heaven and the new earth; we are citizens of the New Jerusalem. The old things have passed away, and all things have become new.

---

10. St. John Chrysostom, *Homilies on St. John*, lxxxv.

8 Any possibility of a universalistic interpretation is denied by this grim verse. God Himself gives nine[11] descriptions of the finally impenitent and unredeemed—a summary accounting of His enemies, the Dragon's followers—who "shall not inherit the Kingdom of God" (1 Cor. 6:9; cf. Gal. 5:21), but whose **part will be in the lake that burns with fire and brimstone, which is the Second Death.** Those condemned to final perdition are the **cowardly,** in contrast to the godly conquerors; **unbelieving,** in contrast to those who have not denied the faith (cf. 2:13, 19; 13:10; 14:12); **sinners,** in contrast to the saints (cf. 5:8; 8:3-4; 11:18; 13:7, 10; 14:12; 18:20; 19:8); **abominable** (cf. 17:4-5; 21:27; Matt. 24:15); **murderers** (cf. 13:15; 16:6; 17:6; 18:24); **fornicators** (cf. 2:14, 20-22; 9:21; 14:8; 17:2, 4-5; 18:3; 19:2); **sorcerers** (*pharmakoi*), a word meaning "poisonous magicians or abortionists" (cf. 9:21; 18:23; 22:15);[12] **idolaters** (cf. 2:14, 20; 9:20; 13:4, 12-15); **and all liars** (cf. 2:2; 3:9; 16:13; 19:20; 20:10; 21:27; 22:15). As Sweet points out, "the list belongs, like similar lists in the epistles, to the context of baptism, the putting off of the 'old man' and putting on of the new" (cf. Gal. 5:19-26; Eph. 4:17-5:7; Col. 3:5-10; Tit. 3:3-8).[13]

The New Jerusalem (21:9-27)

9 And one of the seven angels who had the Seven Chalices full of the seven last plagues came and spoke with me, saying: Come here, I will show you the Bride, the Wife of the Lamb.

10 And he carried me away in the Spirit to a great and high Mountain, and showed me the holy City, Jerusalem, coming down out of heaven from God,

---

11. Nine, that is, if the "Majority Text" reading of *and sinners* be accepted; both the Textus Receptus and the so-called "critical text" (Nestle, etc.) omit these words, leaving eight descriptions. According to some students of symbolism, the number 9 is associated with judgment in the Bible, but the evidence for this seems slim and arbitrary; see E. W. Bullinger, *Number in Scripture* (Grand Rapids: Kregel Publications, [1894] 1967), pp. 235-42.

12. J. Massyngberde Ford, *Revelation: Introduction, Translation, and Commentary* (Garden City, NY: Doubleday and Co., 1975), p. 345. On the use of *pharmakeia* and its cognates with reference to abortion in both pagan and Christian writings, see Michael J. Gorman, *Abortion and the Early Church: Christian, Jewish, and Pagan Attitudes in the Greco-Roman World* (Downers Grove, IL: InterVarsity Press, 1982), p. 48.

13. J. P. M. Sweet, *Revelation* (Philadelphia: The Westminster Press, 1979), p. 300.

11 having the glory of God. Her luminary was like a very costly stone, as a stone of crystal-clear jasper.

12 She had a great and high wall, with twelve gates, and at the gates twelve angels; and names were written on them, which are those of the twelve tribes of the sons of Israel.

13 There were three gates on the east and three gates on the north and three gates on the south and three gates on the west.

14 And the wall of the City had twelve foundation stones, and on them were the twelve names of the twelve apostles of the Lamb.

15 And the one who spoke with me had a measure, a gold reed to measure the City, and its gates and wall.

16 And the City is laid out as a square, and its length is as great as the width; and he measured the City with the reed, twelve thousand stadia; its length and width and height are equal.

17 And he measured its wall, one hundred forty-four cubits, according to human measurements, which are also angelic measurements.

18 And the material of the wall was jasper; and the City was pure gold, like clear glass.

19 The foundation stones of the City were adorned with every kind of precious stone. The first foundation stone was jasper; the second, sapphire; the third, chalcedony; the fourth, emerald;

20 the fifth, sardonyx; the sixth, sardius; the seventh, chrysolite; the eighth, beryl; the ninth, topaz; the tenth, chrysoprase; the eleventh, jacinth; the twelfth, amethyst.

21 And the twelve gates were twelve pearls; each one of the gates was a single pearl. And the street of the City was pure gold, like transparent glass.

22 And I saw no Sanctuary in it, for the Lord God, the Almighty, and the Lamb, are its Sanctuary.

23 And the City has no need of the sun or of the moon to shine upon it, for the glory of God has illumined it, and its lamp is the Lamb.

24 And the nations shall walk by its light, and the kings of the earth shall bring their glory and honor into it.

25 And in the daytime (for there shall be no night there) its gates shall never be closed;

26 and they shall bring the glory and honor of the nations into it;

27 and nothing unclean and no one who practices abomination and lying, shall ever come into it, but only those whose names are written in the Lamb's Book of Life.

9 This verse ties the final section of Revelation together, establishing the literary relationship of chapters 15-22. It is **one of the seven angels who had the Seven Chalices** who reveals to St. John the New Jerusalem, just as one of the same seven angels had shown him the vision of Babylon (17:1); and here **the Bride, the Wife of the Lamb,** is contrasted to the Harlot, the unfaithful wife.

10-11 St. John is **carried away in the Spirit** (cf. 1:10; 4:2; 17:3) **to a great and high Mountain,** a deliberate contrast to the wilderness where he saw the Harlot (17:3). We have seen (on 14:1) that the image of the Mountain speaks of Paradise, which was located on a high plateau from whence the water of life flowed out to the whole world (cf. 22:1-2). The apostle sees **the Holy City, Jerusalem, coming down out of heaven from God.** The picture is not, of course, intended to evoke images of space stations, or of cities literally floating in the air; rather, it indicates the divine origin of "the City which has *foundations*, whose Architect and Builder is God" (Heb. 11:10).

During Judah's apostasy, the prophet Ezekiel saw the Glory-Cloud depart from the Temple and travel east, to the Mount of Olives (Ezek. 10:18-19; 11:22-23); later, in his vision of the New Jerusalem, he sees the Glory-Cloud returning to dwell in the new Temple, the Church (Ezek. 43:1-5). This was fulfilled when Christ, the incarnate Glory of God, ascended to His Father in the Cloud from the Mount of Olives (Luke 24:50-51), thereupon sending His Spirit to fill the Church at Pentecost. There was probably a later image of this transfer of God's Glory to the Church when on Pentecost of A.D. 66, as the priests in the Temple were going about their duties, there was heard "a violent commotion and din" followed by "a voice as of a host crying, 'We are departing hence!' "[14] Ernest Martin comments: "This departure of the Deity from the Temple at Pentecost of A.D. 66 was exactly 36 years (to the very day) after the Holy Spirit was first given in power to the apostles and the others at the first Christian Pentecost recorded in Acts 2. And now, on the same Pentecost day, the witness was given that God himself was aban-

---

14. Josephus, *The Jewish War*, vi.v.3. On this and other events of A.D. 66, see above, pp. 252-55.

doning the Temple at Jerusalem. This meant that the Temple was no longer a holy sanctuary and that the building was no more sacred than any other secular building. Remarkably, even Jewish records show that the Jews had come to recognize that the Shekinah glory of God left the Temple at this time and remained over the Mount of Olives for 3½ years. During this period a voice was heard to come from the region of the Mount of Olives asking the Jews to repent of their doings (*Midrash* Lam. 2:11). This has an interesting bearing on the history of Christianity because we now know that Jesus Christ was crucified and resurrected from the dead on the Mount of Olives[15] — the exact region the Jewish records say the Shekinah glory of God remained for the 3½ years after its departure from the Temple on Pentecost, A.D. 66. . . . The Jewish reference states that the Jews failed to heed this warning from the Shekinah glory (which they called a *Bet Kol*— the voice of God), and that it left the earth and retreated back to heaven just before the final seige of Jerusalem by the Romans in A.D. 70.

". . . From Pentecost A.D. 66, no thinking person among the Christians, who respected these obvious miraculous signs associated with the Temple, could believe that the structure was any longer a holy sanctuary of God. Josephus himself summed up the conviction of many people who came to believe that God 'had turned away even from his sanctuary' (*War*, II.539), that the Temple was 'no more the dwelling place of God' (*War*, V.19), because 'the Deity has fled from the holy places' (*War*, V.412)."[16]

Writing while these events are still uppermost in the minds of the Jews, St. John declares that the *Shekinah*, **the Glory of God**, now rests on the true Holy Temple/City, the consummate Paradise — the Bride of Christ.

The New Jerusalem is further described as possessing a **luminary** (*phōstēr*) — literally, a *star* or light-bearer (cf. Gen. 1:14, 16 [LXX], where it is used with reference to the sun, moon, and stars); St. Paul uses the same term when he says that Christians "shine as *luminaries* in the world" (Phil. 2:15; cf. Dan. 12:3). This parallels the sun with which the Woman is clothed in 12:1 —

15. See Ernest L. Martin, *The Place of Christ's Crucifixion: Its Discovery and Significance* (Pasadena, CA: Foundation for Biblical Research, 1984).

16. Ernest L. Martin, *The Original Bible Restored* (Pasadena, CA: Foundation for Biblical Research, 1984), pp. 157f.

except that now the Bride's luminary, brighter than even the sun, shines with the Glory of God Himself: **like a very costly stone, as a stone of crystal-clear jasper,** in the image of Him who was "like a jasper stone and a sardius in appearance" (4:2-3). C. S. Lewis wrote: "It is a serious thing to live in a society of possible gods and goddesses, to remember that the dullest and most uninteresting person you can talk to may one day be a creature which, if you saw it now, you would be strongly tempted to worship, or else a horror and a corruption such as you now meet, if at all, only in a nightmare. All day long we are, in some degree, helping each other to one or the other of these destinations. It is in the light of these overwhelming possibilities, it is with the awe and circumspection proper to them, that we should conduct all our dealings with one another, all friendships, all loves, all play, all politics. There are no *ordinary* people. You have never talked to a mere mortal. . . . Next to the Blessed Sacrament itself, your neighbour is the holiest object presented to your senses. If he is your Christian neighbour, he is holy in almost the same way, for in him also Christ *vere latitat* — the glorifier and the glorified, Glory Himself, is truly hidden."[17]

12-14   The Woman of 12:1, in addition to her glorious clothing, wore a crown of twelve stars; this is now to be replaced with another twelve-starred crown — this time a "crown" of jewelled walls. But inasmuch as the Bride's clothing also corresponds to that of the enthroned Glory of 4:3, St. John is careful to make her "crown" correspond to the circle of twelve in that passage as well. There, the Throne was ringed about with two twelves, the twenty-four enthroned elders. So here, the Bride-City is crowned with a double twelve: the patriarchs and the apostles. "The transition from a crown on the lady's brows to a ring of city walls was mere routine for St. John's contemporaries; the standing emblem for a city was the figure of a lady with a battlemented crown."[18]

It is implied in Ezekiel's vision that the City has **a great and high wall,** for "the gates about which the prophet speaks [Ezek. 48: 31-34] are the gatehouses, porches or gate towers which con-

---

17. C. S. Lewis, *The Weight of Glory: And Other Addresses* (New York: Macmillan Publishing Co., 1949; revised ed., 1980), pp. 18f.

18. Austin Farrer, *The Revelation of St. John the Divine* (Oxford: At the Clarendon Press, 1964), p. 215.

stitute a city wall"; [19] this is made explicit in St. John's account. The **twelve gates** of the City are guarded by **twelve angels** (cf. the cherubim who guarded Eden's gate in Gen. 3:24), and are inscribed with the **names . . . of the twelve tribes of the sons of Israel,** another feature in common with Ezekiel's vision (Ezek. 48:31-34). Sweet comments: "The twelve portals of the Zodiac in the city of the heavens are brought under the control of the Bible: Israel is the nucleus of the divine society." [20]

The City has **three gates on the east and three gates on the north and three gates on the south and three gates on the west.** We saw in the discussion of 7:5-8 that the twelve tribes of Israel are listed by St. John (and before him, by Ezekiel) in such a way as to "balance" the sons of Leah and Rachel. The order in which the gates are listed (east, north, south, west) corresponds to this tribal list—which we would naturally expect, since St. John mentions the gates, with their unusual order, immediately after mentioning the twelve tribes. In other words, he intends for us to use the information in this verse in order to go back and solve the riddle of 7:5-8 (see the charts on pp. 210-11).

There is another intriguing point about this verse: St. John tells us that the gates are, literally, *from* the east, *from* the north, *from* the south, and *from* the west — giving, as Sweet suggests, "the picture of many coming from the four points of the compass (Isa. 49:12; Luke 13:29)." [21] As St. John later shows, the nations will walk by the City's light, the kings of the earth will bring their wealth into her, and her gates will always be open to them (v. 24-26).

St. John extends his imagery: **The wall of the City had twelve foundation stones, and on them were the names of the twelve apostles of the Lamb.** This, of course, is straight Pauline theology: "So then, you are no longer strangers and aliens, but you are fellow citizens with the saints, and are of God's household, having been built upon the foundation of the apostles and prophets, Jesus Christ Himself being the Cornerstone, in whom the whole building, being fitted together is growing into a holy Temple in the Lord; in whom you also are being built together

---

19. Ford, p. 341.
20. Sweet, p. 304.
21. Ibid.

into a dwelling of God in the Spirit" (Eph. 2:19-22). It should be needless to say also that both St. Paul's and St. John's concept of the City of God, the Church, is that it comprehends both Old and New Covenant believers within its walls. As the historic Church has always recognized, there is only one way of salvation, one Covenant of Grace; the fact that it has operated under various administrations does not affect the essential unity of the one people of God through the ages.

15-17 And the one who spoke with me — one of the seven Chalice-angels (v. 9) — **had a measure, a gold reed to measure the City, and its gates and wall.** The Sanctuary had been measured earlier, as an indication of its sanctity and protection (11:1-2); now the City itself is to be measured, for the entire City itself is the Temple. To demonstrate this, St. John tells us that **the City is laid out as a square, and its length is as great as the width:** It is perfectly foursquare. **And he measured the City with the reed . . . ; its length and width and height are equal.** Like the Holy of Holies — the divine model for all culture — the City is a perfect cube (cf. 1 Kings 6:20): New Jerusalem is itself a cosmic Holy of Holies. At the same time, however, we should note another dimension of this imagery. The combination of a *square* with a *mountain* (v. 10) indicates the idea of a pyramid, the "cosmic mountain" which appears in ancient cultures throughout the world. The original Paradise was the first "pyramid," a Garden-Temple-City on top of a mountain; and when the prophets speak of the salvation and renovation of the earth it is almost always in terms of this imagery (Isa. 2:2-4; 25:6-9; 51:3; Ezek. 36:33-36; Dan. 2:34-35, 44-45; Mic. 4:1-4).

Each side of the City — length, breadth, and height — measures **twelve thousand stadia;** the City wall is **one hundred forty-four cubits.** The absurdity of "literalism" is embarrassingly evident when it attempts to deal with these measurements. The numbers are obviously symbolic, the multiples of twelve being a reference to the majesty, vastness, and perfection of the Church. But the "literalist" feels compelled to *translate* those numbers into modern measurements, resulting in a wall *1,500* miles long and *216* feet (or *72* yards) high.[22] St. John's clear sym-

---

22. See, e.g., the New American Standard Bible.

bols are erased, and the unfortunate Bible reader is left with just a jumble of meaningless numbers (what in the world does "216 feet" signify?). Ironically, the "literalist" finds himself in the ridiculous position of deleting the *literal* numbers of God's Word and replacing them with meaningless *symbols!*

St. John makes the seemingly casual, offhand, and intriguing remark that these **human measurements** (stadia and cubits) **are also angelic measurements**. But this is not as mysterious as it appears at first. St. John is simply making explicit what has been assumed throughout his prophecy: that there are divinely ordained *correspondences* between angels and men. The angelic activity seen in the Revelation is a pattern for our own activity; as we see God's will being done in heaven, we are to image that activity on earth. Heaven is the pattern for earth, the Temple is the pattern for the City, the angel is the model for man. Just as the Spirit hovered over the original creation, fashioning it into the image of the heavens, so our task is to "heavenize" the world, bringing God's blueprint to its most complete realization.

18-21 The City is now described in terms of jewelry, as the perfect consummation of the original Edenic pattern (cf. Gen. 2:10-12; Ezek. 28:13):[23] **The material of the wall was jasper**, an image of God Himself (4:3; 21:11); **and the City was pure gold, like clear glass** (gold is an image of the Glory of God, and was therefore used in the Tabernacle and the Temple, and on the garments of the priests; and the gold associated with Paradise is said to be "good," i.e. pure, unmixed: Gen. 2:12). **The twelve foundation stones of the City were adorned with every kind of precious stone**, like the High Priest's breastplate, which has four rows of three gems each, representing the twelve tribes of Israel (Ex. 28:15-21): The Bride has become adorned for her Husband (v. 2). The expression **precious** (or **costly**) **stones** is used in 1 Kings 5:17 for the **foundation stones** of Solomon's Temple; now, in the eschatological City-Temple, they are truly "precious stones," in every sense.

The first foundation stone was jasper; the second, sapphire; the third, chalcedony; the fourth, emerald; the fifth, sardonyx; the sixth, sardius; the seventh, chrysolite; the eighth, beryl; the

---

23. See Chilton, *Paradise Restored*, pp. 32-36.

ninth, topaz; the tenth, chrysoprase; the eleventh, jacinth; the twelfth, amethyst. There have been several attempts to discover St. John's rationale for listing the stones in this order, the most well-known being R. H. Charles' suggestion that the jewels are connected to the signs of the Zodiac, and that *"the signs or constellations are given in a certain order, and that exactly the reverse order of the actual path of the sun through the signs."* This demonstrates, he says, that St. John *"regards the Holy City which he describes as having nothing to do with the ethnic speculations of his own and past ages regarding the city of the gods."*[24] Charles has been followed on this point by several commentators,[25] but later research has disproved this theory.[26] Sweet points out that "Philo (*Special Laws* I.87) and Josephus (*Ant.* III.186) link the jewels with the Zodiac, but only as part of the cosmic symbolism which they claim for the high priest's vestments; cf. Wisd. 18:24. John's aim is similar. Any direct astrological reference is destroyed by his linking them not with the twelve *gates* of the heavenly city but with the foundations."[27]

The most sensible explanation for the order of the stones comes, as we would expect, from Austin Farrer. He shows that the stones are laid out in four rows of three gems in each row, as on the high priest's breastplate: "St. John does not adhere either to the order or to the names of the stones in the LXX Greek of Exodus, and any query we may raise about translations of the Hebrew names which he might have preferred to those offered by the LXX can only land us in an abyss of uncertainty. It is reasonable to suppose that he did not trouble to do more than give a euphonious list in some general correspondence with the Exodus catalogue. He has so arranged the Greek names, as to emphasize the division by threes. All but three of them end with *s* sounds, and the three exceptions with *n* sounds. He has placed the *n* endings at the points of division, thus:

---

24. R. H. Charles, *A Critical and Exegetical Commentary on the Revelation of St. John*, 2 vols. (Edinburgh: T. & T. Clark, 1920), pp. 167f. Italics his.
25. See, e.g., G. B. Caird, *The Revelation of St. John the Divine* (New York: Harper and Row, 1966), pp. 274-78; Rousas John Rushdoony, *Thy Kingdom Come: Studies in Daniel and Revelation* (Tyler, TX: Thoburn Press, [1970] 1978), pp. 221f.
26. See T. F. Glasson, "The Order of Jewels in Rev. xxi. 19-20: A Theory Eliminated," *Journal of Theological Studies* 26 (1975), pp. 95-100.
27. Sweet, p. 306.

Jaspis, sapphiros, chalcedon;
smaragdos, sardonyx, sardion;
chrysolithos, beryllos, topazion;
chrysoprasos, hyacinthos, amethystos.

"Why should he trouble to do more? If he had made a list
perfectly worked out, what could it have done but answer exactly to the list of tribes which he has already arranged for us in
[Chapter] 7? And how would our wisdom be increased by that?
St. John wishes to give body to his vision by listing the tribes;
but he has already listed the tribes. So he lists stones which (as
we know from Exodus) are to be deemed equivalent to the
tribes. He makes two points: first, that the names of the apostles
can be substituted for those of the tribes – and, after all, the
new mystical twelvefold Israel is more truly to be described as
companies gathered round the Apostles, than as the actual
descendants of Reuben, Simeon, Levi, and the rest. Second, he
puts the jasper up to be head of the list and so, no doubt, to
stand for Judah and its apostle (cf. 7:5). And jasper is both the
general stuff of the walls above, and the colour of the divine
glory. The meaning of the allegory is plain. Messiah is the chief
corner-stone; it is by being founded on him that the whole city,
or Church, acquires the substance and colour of the divine
glory."[28]

Instead of being aligned with the signs of the Zodiac and
their twelve portals, **the twelve gates were twelve pearls; each
one of the gates was a single pearl.** Obviously, these gates are
decorative and ornamental only, not designed to withstand attack; but since the City is to comprehend the whole world, there
is no danger of attack anyway. Emphasizing the tremendous
wealth and glory of the New Jerusalem, St. John tells us that **the
street of the City was pure gold, like transparent glass.** We may
note here that the value which men have always placed on gold
and precious stones derives from the prior value which God has
imputed to it. God has built into us a desire for gems, but His
Word makes it clear that wealth is to be gained as a by-product

---

28. Farrer, *The Revelation of St. John the Divine,* p. 219. Fifteen years earlier, Farrer's views on the subject were much more elaborate, as evidenced by
his chapter on the order of the jewels in *A Rebirth of Images: The Making of
St. John's Apocalypse* (London: Dacre Press, 1949), pp. 216-44.

of the Kingdom of God, and His righteousness (Matt. 6:33). The Harlot was adorned with jewels, and she perished with them; the Bride is adorned with jewels because of her union with the Bridegroom. It is God who gives the power to get wealth, for His glory (Deut. 8:18); when we turn our God-given wealth into an idol, he takes it away from us and stores it up for the righteous, who use it for God's Kingdom and are generous to the poor (Job 27:16-17; Prov. 13:22; 28:8; Eccl. 2:26).

Eight centuries before St. John wrote, the prophet Isaiah described the coming salvation in terms of a City adorned with jewels:

> O afflicted one, storm-tossed, and not comforted,
> Behold, I will set your stones in fair colors,
> And your foundations I will lay in sapphires.
> Moreover, I will make your battlements of rubies,
> And your gates of sparkling jewels,
> And your entire wall of precious stones. (Isa. 54:11-12)

It is interesting that the word translated *fair colors* is, in Hebrew, *eye shadow* (cf. 2 Kings 9:30; Jer. 4:30); again, the wall of the City of God is merely decorative: built with jewels, with cosmetics for "mortar." The point is that the Builder is fabulously wealthy, and supremely confident against attack. This, Isaiah says, is the future of the Church, the City of God. She will be rich and secure from enemies, as the rest of the passage explains:

> And all your sons will be taught of the LORD;
> And the well-being of your sons will be great.
> In righteousness you will be established;
> You will be far from oppression, for you will not fear;
> And from terror, for it will not come near you. . . .
> No weapon that is formed against you shall prosper;
> And every tongue that accuses you in judgment you will condemn.
> This is the heritage of the servants of the LORD,
> And their vindication is from Me, declares the LORD.
> (Isa. 54:13-17)

22-23   The whole City is the Temple, as we have seen — but there is **no Sanctuary in it, for the Lord God, the Almighty, and the Lamb, are its Sanctuary.** This is really another way of stating the blessings described earlier: "He who overcomes, I will make him a pillar in the Sanctuary of My god, and he will not go out from it anymore" (3:12); "For this reason, they are before the Throne of God; and they serve Him day and night in His Sanctuary; and He who sits on the Throne shall spread His Tabernacle over them" (7:15). "Their city of residence is their temple; it contains within it no temple whose walls or doors intervene between them and the God they adore. God is temple to the city, and the city is temple to God."[29]

Indwelt by God in the Glory-Cloud, the City shines with the original, uncreated Light of the Spirit. Thus **the City has no need of the sun or of the moon to shine upon it, for the Glory of God has illumined it, and its lamp is the Lamb**, as Isaiah had foretold:

> Arise, shine; for your Light has come,
> And the Glory of the LORD has risen upon you.
> For behold, darkness will cover the earth,
> And deep darkness the peoples;
> But the LORD will rise upon you,
> And His Glory will appear upon you.
> And nations will come to your Light,
> And kings to the brightness of your rising. . . .
> No longer will you have the sun for light by day,
> Nor for brightness will the moon give you light;
> But you will have the LORD for an everlasting Light,
> And the days of your mourning will be finished.
> Then all your peoples will be righteous;
> They will possess the land forever,
> The branch of His planting,
> The work of My hands,
> That I may be glorified. (Isa. 60:1-3, 19-21)

24-27 In the same passage, Isaiah prophesies that the nations of the earth will flow into the City of God, bringing all the wealth of their cultures:

> The wealth on the seas will be brought to you,
> To you the riches of the nations will come.
> Herds of camels will cover your land,

---

29. Farrer, *The Revelation of St. John the Divine*, p. 221.

Young camels of Midian and Ephah.
And all from Sheba will come,
Bearing gold and incense
And proclaiming the praise of the LORD. . . .
Surely the islands look to me;
In the lead are the ships of Tarshish,
Bringing your sons from afar,
With their silver and gold,
To the honor of the LORD your God,
The Holy One of Israel,
For He has endowed you with splendor. . . .
Your gates will always stand open,
They will never be shut, day or night,
So that men may bring you the wealth of the nations.
(Isa. 60:5-6, 9, 11)

St. John applies this prophecy to the New Jerusalem: **The nations shall walk by its Light, and the kings of the earth shall bring their glory and honor into it. And in the daytime (for there shall be no night there) its gates shall never be closed; and they shall bring the glory and honor of the nations into it; and nothing unclean and no one who practices abomination and lying, shall ever come into it, but only those whose names are written in the Lamb's Book of Life.** This is what Jesus commanded His Church to be: the City on the Hill (Matt. 5:14-16), the light of the world, shining before men so that they will glorify God the Father. Obviously, the New Jerusalem cannot be seen simply in terms of the eternal future, after the final judgment. In St. John's vision the nations still exist as nations; yet the nations are all converted, flowing into the City and bringing their treasures into it. Of course, "the other side to the fact that the Gentiles bring in their honour and glory, is that they do not bring in their abominations. . . . The access of the Gentiles here is in strong contrast with their access in 11:2. The mere presence of unregenerate heathen in the outer court spelled the ruin of Old Jerusalem; the New admits them sanctified, to her undivided precinct."[30]

In another striking prophecy of the Gospel's effect on the world, Isaiah wrote:

---

30. Ibid.

Thus says the Lord GOD:
Behold, I will lift up My hand to the nations,
And set up My standard to the peoples;
And they will bring your sons in their bosom,
And your daughters will be carried on their shoulders.
And kings will be your guardians,
And their princesses your nurses.
They will bow down to you with their faces to the earth,
And lick the dust of your feet;
And you will know that I am the LORD;
Those who hopefully wait for Me will not be put to shame.
(Isa. 49:22-23).

William Symington commented: "The prophecy refers to New Testament times, when the Gentiles are to be gathered unto the Redeemer. A prominent feature of these times shall be the subserviency of civil rulers to the Church, which surely supposes their subjection to Christ her Head. *Kings shall be thy nursing-fathers* is a similitude which imports the most tender care, the most enduring solicitude; not mere protection, but active and unwearied nourishment and support. If, according to the opinions of some, the best thing the state can do for the Church is to let her alone, to leave her to herself, to take no interest in her concerns, it is difficult to see how this view can be reconciled with the figure of a nurse, the duties of whose office would certainly be ill discharged by such a treatment of her feeble charge."[31]

As the Light of the Gospel shines through the Church to the world, the world is converted, the nations are discipled, and the wealth of the sinners becomes inherited by the just. This is a basic promise of Scripture from beginning to end; it is the pattern of history, the direction in which the world is moving. This is our future, the heritage of generations to come. The gift of His Holy Spirit guarantees the fulfillment of His promise: not that He will make new things, but that He will make all things new.[32]

---

31. William Symington, *Messiah the Prince: or, The Mediatorial Dominion of Jesus Christ* (Philadelphia: The Christian Statesman Publishing Co., [1839] 1884), pp. 199f.
32. See Alexander Schmemann, *For the Life of the World: Sacraments and Orthodoxy* (Crestwood, NY: St. Vladimir's Seminary Press), p. 123.

22

COME, LORD JESUS!

As we saw in the Introduction, St. John wrote the Book of Revelation as an annual cycle of prophecies, meant to be read to the congregation (coinciding with serial Old Testament readings, especially Ezekiel) from one Easter to the next.[1] Chapter 22 thus brings us full circle, verses 6-21 being read exactly one year after Chapter 1 was read. For that reason, as well as recapitulating many of the themes of the prophecy, Chapter 22 also has much in common with Chapter 1. We read again, for example, that the prophecy is of "things that must shortly take place" (22:6; cf. 1:1); that it is communicated by an angel (22:6; cf. 1:1) to St. John (22:8; cf. 1:1, 4, 9); that it is a message intended for God's "bond-servants" (22:6; cf. 1:1); that there is a special blessing for those who "keep" its words (22:7; cf. 1:3); and that it specifically involves the Testimony of Christ (22:16, 18, 20; cf. 1:2, 5, 9), the Alpha and the Omega, the First and the Last (22:13; cf. 1:8, 17), who is "coming quickly" (22:7, 12, 20; cf. 1:7).

Paradise Restored (22:1-5)

1 And he showed me a River of the Water of Life, clear as crystal, coming from the Throne of God and of the Lamb,

2 in the middle of its street. And on each side of the River was Tree of Life, bearing twelve crops of fruit, yielding its fruit every month; and the leaves of the Tree were for the healing of the nations.

3 And there shall no longer be any Curse; and the Throne of God and of the Lamb shall be in it, and His servants shall serve Him;

---

1. See M. D. Goulder, "The Apocalypse as an Annual Cycle of Prophecies," *New Testament Studies* 27, No. 3 (April 1981), pp. 342-67.

4 and they shall see His face, and His name shall be in their
foreheads.

5 And there shall no longer be any Night; and they shall not
have need of the light of a lamp nor the light of the sun, because the Lord God shall illumine them; and they shall reign
forever and ever.

1-2 The vision of the New Jerusalem continues: the Chalice-
angel (21:9) shows St. John **a River of the Water of Life, clear as
crystal, coming from the Throne of God and of the Lamb, in
the middle of its street.** The scene is based, first, on the Garden
of Eden, in which springs bubbled up out of the ground (Gen.
2:6) to form a river, which then parted into four heads and went
out to water the earth (Gen. 2:10-14). This image is later adopted
by Ezekiel in his vision of the New Covenant Temple. In the Old
Covenant, people had to journey to the Temple to be cleansed,
but that will no longer be true; for in New Covenant times the
great bronze Laver in the southeast corner of the House (2 Chron.
4:10) tips over and spills its contents out under the door, becoming a mighty river of grace and life for the world, even transforming the waters of the Dead Sea:[2]

> Then he brought me back to the door of the House; and
> behold, water was flowing from under the threshold of the
> House toward the east, for the House faced east. And the water
> was flowing down from under, from the right side of the House,
> from south of the altar. And he brought me out by way of the
> north gate and led me around on the outside to the outer gate by
> way of the gate that faces east. And behold, water was trickling
> from the south side.
> When the man went out toward the east with a line in his
> hand, he measured a thousand cubits, and led me through the
> water, water reaching the ankles.
> Again he measured a thousand and led me through the water,
> water reaching the knees.
> Again he measured a thousand and led me through the water,
> water reaching the loins.

---

2. On the symbolism associated with the Dead Sea (the site of Sodom and
Gomorrah) see David Chilton, *Paradise Restored: A Biblical Theology of Dominion* (Ft. Worth, TX: Dominion Press, 1985), pp. 52f. For another illustration of
the difference between the 'static' grace of the Old Covenant and the 'dynamic'
grace of the New Covenant, compare Hag. 2:10-14 with Mark 5:25-34.

Again he measured a thousand; and it was a river that I could not ford, for the water had risen, enough water to swim in, a river that could not be forded.

And he said to me, "Son of man, have you seen this?" Then he brought me back to the bank of the river. Now when I had returned, behold, on the bank of the river there were very many trees on the one side and on the other. Then he said to me, "These waters go out toward the eastern region and go down into the Arabah; then they go toward the sea, being made to flow into the sea, and the waters of the sea become fresh. And it will come about that every living creature that swarms in every place where the river goes will live. And there will be very many fish, for these waters go there, and the others become fresh; so everything will live where the river goes." (Ezek. 47:1-9)

Ezekiel said that "on the bank of the river there were very many trees on the one side and on the other"; St. John expands on this and tells us that **on each side of the River was Tree of Life**—not a single tree only, but forests of Tree-of-Life lining the riverbanks. The blessing which Adam forfeited has been restored in overwhelming superabundance, for what we have gained in Christ is, as St. Paul said, "much more" than what we lost in Adam:

For if by the transgression of the one the many died, *much more* did the grace of God and the gift by the grace of the one man, Jesus Christ, abound to the many. . . . For if by the transgression of the one, death reigned through the one, *much more* those who receive the abundance of grace and of the gift of righteousness will reign in life through the One, Jesus Christ. . . . Where sin increased, grace abounded *all the more*, that, as sin reigned in death, even so grace might reign through righteousness to eternal life through Jesus Christ our Lord. (Rom. 5:15-21; cf. v. 9-10)

Paradise is not, therefore, only "restored"; it is consummated, its every implication brought to complete fruition and fulfillment.

The word **Tree** is *xulon*, often used with reference to the Cross (cf. Acts 5:30; 10:39; 13:29; 1 Pet. 2:24); in fact, it is likely that Christ was crucified on a living tree, as His words in Luke 23:31 imply: "For if they do these things in the green tree, what will happen in the dry?" St. Paul saw Christ's crucifixion as the fulfillment of the Old Testament curse on one who is hanged on a tree (Gal. 3:13; cf. Deut. 21:23; Josh. 10:26-27).[3] St. Irenaeus saw the Cross as the Tree of Life, contrasting it with the Tree of the Knowledge of Good and Evil, through which man fell: Jesus Christ "has destroyed the handwriting of our debt, and fastened it to the Cross [Col. 2:14]; so that, just as by means of a tree we were made debtors to God, so also by means of a tree we may obtain the remission of our debt."[4] The image was quickly adopted in the symbolism of the early Church: "Early Christian art indicates a close relationship between the tree of life and the cross. The cross of Christ, the wood of suffering and death, is for Christians a tree of life. In the tomb paintings of the 2nd century it is thus depicted for the first time as the symbol of victory over death. It then recurs again and again. The idea that the living trunk of the cross bears twigs and leaves is a common motif in Christian antiquity."[5]

As in Ezekiel's vision (Ezek. 47:12), the Tree of Life is continuously productive, **bearing twelve crops of fruit, yielding its fruit every month** in a never-ending supply of life for the overcomers (2:7), those who do His commandments (22:14). St. John goes on to make it clear that the power of Christ's Tree will transform the whole world: **The leaves of the Tree were for the healing of the nations.** Again, St. John does not conceive of this as a blessing reserved only for eternity, although its effects continue into eternity. The Tree of Life is sustaining believers now, as they partake of Christ:

> Truly, truly, I say to you, he who hears My Word, and believes in Him who sent Me, has eternal life, and does not come

---

3. The word *cross* (*stauros*) can refer either to the tree itself (considered as the instrument of execution) or to the *patibulum,* (the upper crosspiece to which Christ's hands were nailed, and which was then nailed to the tree). For a discussion of this whole issue, see Ernest L. Martin, *The Place of Christ's Crucifixion: Its Discovery and Significance* (Pasadena, CA: Foundation for Biblical Research, 1984), pp. 75-82.

4. St. Irenaeus, *Against Heresies,* v.xvii.3.

5. Johannes Schneider, in Gerhard Kittel and Gerhard Friedrich, eds., *Theological Dictionary of the New Testament,* 10 vols., trans. Geoffrey W. Bromily (Grand Rapids: William B. Eerdmans Publishing Co., 1964-76), Vol. 5, pp. 40-41.

into judgment, but has passed out of death into life. Truly, truly, I say to you, an hour is coming, and now is, when the dead shall hear the Voice of the Son of God; and those who hear shall live. (John 5:24-25)

In the same way, St. John expects the healing virtues of the Cross to give Life to the nations as nations, in this world; the nations, he has told us, are made up of "those whose names are written in the Lamb's Book of Life," since the nations as such are admitted into the Holy City (21:24-27). The River of Life is flowing now (John 4:14; 7:37-39), and will continue to flow in an ever-increasing stream of blessing to the earth, healing the nations, bringing an end to lawlessness and warfare (Zech. 14:8-11; cf. Mic. 4:1-4). This vision of the Church's glorious future, earthly and heavenly, mends the fabric that was torn in Genesis. In Revelation we see Man redeemed, brought back to the Mountain, sustained by the River and the Tree of Life, regaining his lost dominion and ruling as a priest-king over the earth. This is our privilege and heritage now, definitively and progressively, in this age; and it will be ours fully in the age to come.

3-4   Thus **there shall no longer be any Curse**, in fulfillment of the ancient promises:

> Thus says the Lord GoD: On the Day that I cleanse you from all your iniquities, I will cause the cities to be inhabited, and the waste places will be rebuilt. And the desolate land will be cultivated instead of being a desolation in the sight of everyone who passed by. And they will say, "This desolate land has become like the Garden of Eden; and the waste, desolate, and ruined cities are fortified and inhabited." Then the nations that are left round about you will know that I, the LORD, have rebuilt the ruined places; I, the LORD, have spoken and will do it. (Ezek. 36:33-36)

The Throne of God and of the Lamb shall be in the Holy City, as St. John implied in 21:3, 11, 22-23. It is striking that the citizens are called **His servants** — an expression that is primarily used to describe *prophets* (cf. 1:1; 10:7; 11:18; 15:3; 19:2, 5 [cf. 18:24]; 22:6, 9). As we have seen, this has been a significant theme in Revelation, the fulfillment of the Old Covenant hope of communion with God: All the LORD's people are prophets, for the LORD has put His Spirit upon them (Num. 11:29). Therefore **they shall see His face, and His name shall be in their fore-heads.** Kline comments: "Behind the imagery of Revelation 22:4 are the figures of Moses and Aaron. Aaron bore on his forehead the name of the Lord inscribed on the crown on the front of the priestly mitre. The very countenance of Moses was transformed into a reflective likeness of the Glory-Face, the Presence-Name of God, when God talked to him 'mouth to mouth' (Num. 12:8) out of the Glory-cloud. As the Name and the Glory are alike designations of the Presence of God in the theophanic cloud, so both name and glory describe the reflected likeness of God. To say that the overcomers in the New Jerusalem bear the name of Christ in their forehead is to say that they reflect the glory of Christ, which is to say that they bear the image of the glorified Christ."[6] Thus, says St. Paul, all the saints now see His face: "We all, with unveiled face beholding as in a mirror the Glory of the Lord, are being transformed into the same image from glory to glory, just as from the Lord, the Spirit" (2 Cor. 3:18). And, because all the saints are priests (Rev. 1:6; 20:6), we wear His name in our forehead (3:12; 7:3; 14:1), serving Him in His Temple (7:15).

5 As St. John told us in 21:22-25, within the walls of the Holy City **there shall no longer be any Night; and they shall not have need of the light of a lamp nor the light of the sun, because the Lord God shall illumine them.** In our study of "the new heaven and earth" in Chapter 21, we took note of how St. Peter urged the churches to holy living in light of the approaching age of righteousness, which was to be ushered in at the fall of the Old Covenant with the destruction of the Temple (2 Pet. 3:1-14). Similarly, St. Paul exhorted the Christians of Rome to godly living in view of the imminent dawning of the Day:

> And this do, knowing the time, that it is already the hour for you to awaken from sleep; for now salvation is nearer to us than when we first believed. The Night is almost gone, and the Day is at hand. Let us therefore lay aside the deeds of darkness and put on the armor of light. (Rom. 13:11-12)

---

6. Meredith G. Kline, *Images of the Spirit* (Grand Rapids: Baker Book House, 1980), pp. 54f.

In much the same way he wrote to the Thessalonians, arguing that their lives must be characterized by the approaching Dawn rather than by the fading Night:

> For you yourselves know full well that the Day of the Lord will come just like a thief in the night. While they are saying, "Peace and safety!" then destruction will come upon them suddenly like birth pangs upon a woman with child; and they shall not escape. But you, brethren, are not in darkness, that the Day should overtake you like a thief; for you are all sons of Light and sons of Day. We are not of Night nor of Darkness; so then let us not sleep as others do, but let us be alert and sober. For those who sleep do their sleeping at night, and those who get drunk get drunk at night. But since we are of Day, let us be sober, having put on the breastplate of faith and love, and as a helmet, the hope of salvation. For God has not destined us for wrath, but for obtaining salvation through our Lord Jesus Christ. (1 Thess. 5:2-9)

The era of the Old Covenant was the time of the world's dark Night; with the Advent of Jesus Christ has come the age of Light, the great Day of the Lord, established at His Ascension and His full inauguration of the New Covenant:

> Arise, shine; for your Light has come,
> And the Glory of the LORD has risen upon you.
> For behold, Darkness will cover the earth,
> And deep Darkness the peoples;
> But the LORD will rise upon you,
> And His Glory will appear upon you.
> And nations will come to your Light,
> And kings to the brightness of your rising. (Isa. 60:1-3)

> For behold, the Day is coming, burning like a furnace; and all the arrogant and every evildoer will be chaff; and the Day that is coming will set them ablaze, says the LORD of hosts, so that it will leave them neither root nor branch. But for you who fear My name the Sun of righteousness will rise with healing in His wings; and you will go forth and skip about like calves from the stall. (Mal. 4:1-2)

> Blessed be the Lord God of Israel,
> For He has visited us and accomplished redemption for His people. . . .

Because of the tender mercy of our God,
With which the Sunrise from on high shall visit us,
To shine upon those who sit in Darkness and the shadow of Death,
To guide our feet into the way of peace. (Luke 1:68, 78-79)

In Him was Life, and the Life was the Light of men. And the Light shines in the darkness, and the Darkness did not overpower it. (John 1:4-5)

Again therefore Jesus spoke to them, saying, "I am the Light of the world; he who follows Me shall not walk in the Darkness, but shall have the Light of Life." (John 8:12)

The god of this age has blinded the minds of the unbelieving, that they might not see the Light of the Gospel of the glory of Christ, who is the Image of God. . . . For God, who said, "Light shall shine out of darkness," is the One who has shone in our hearts to give the Light of the knowledge of the glory of God in the face of Christ. (2 Cor. 4:4, 6)

Giving thanks to the Father, who has qualified us to share in the inheritance of the saints in Light. For He delivered us from the domain of Darkness, and transferred us to the Kingdom of His beloved Son. (Col. 1:12-13)

Let us hold fast the confession of our hope without wavering, for He who promised is faithful; and let us consider how to stimulate one another to love and good deeds, not forsaking our own assembling together, as is the habit of some, but encouraging one another; and all the more, as you see the Day drawing near. (Heb. 10:23-25)

And so we have the prophetic word made more sure, to which you do well to pay attention as to a lamp shining in a dark place, until the Day dawns and the Morning Star arises in your hearts. (2 Pet. 1:19)

Again we must remember that the New Covenant age is regarded in Scripture as definitively and progressively an era of Light, in contrast to the relative Darkness of pre-Messianic times. In the absolute and ultimate sense, the Light will come only at the end of the world, at the Second Coming of Christ. But, as the apostles contemplated the end of the Old Covenant era, during which the nations were enslaved to demons, they spoke of the imminent Dawn as *the* age of righteousness, when the power of the Gospel would sweep across the earth, smashing idolatry and flooding the nations with the Light of God's grace. Relatively speaking, the whole history of the world from Adam's Fall to Christ's Ascension was Night; relatively speaking, the whole future of the world is bright Day. This follows the pattern laid down at the creation, in which the heavens and earth move eschatologically from evening to morning, the lesser light being succeeded by the greater light, going from glory to Glory (Gen. 1:5, 8, 13, 19, 23, 31): Now, St. John tells us, Jesus Christ has appeared, and is "coming quickly," as the bright Morning Star (v. 16).

In his concluding comment on the restoration of Paradise, St. John tells us that the royal priesthood **shall reign**, not just for a "millennium," but **forever and ever**: "The reign of the thousand years (20:4-6) is but the beginning of a regal life and felicity which are to continue through all aeons to come. And so the kingdom of the saints of the Most High will be most truly, as Daniel wrote, 'an everlasting kingdom' (Dan. 7:27). This is the 'eternal life' of Matthew 25:46, just as the second death, the lake of fire, is the 'eternal punishment' into which the 'cursed' go away."[7]

Final Warnings and Blessings (22:6-21)

6 And he said to me: These words are faithful and true. And the Lord, the God of the spirits of the prophets, sent His angel to show to His servants the things which must shortly take place.

7 And behold, I am coming quickly. Blessed is he who keeps the words of the prophecy of this book.

8 And I, John, am the one who heard and saw these things. And when I heard and saw, I fell down to worship at the feet of the angel who showed me these things.

9 And he said to me: Don't do that! I am a fellow servant of yours and of your brethren the prophets and of those who keep the words of this book; worship God.

10 And he said to me: Do not seal up the words of the prophecy of this book, for the time is near.

11 Let the one who does wrong, still do wrong; and let the one who is filthy, still be filthy; and let the one who is righteous,

---

7. Milton Terry, *Biblical Apocalyptics: A Study of the Most Notable Revelations of God and of Christ in the Canonical Scriptures* (New York: Eaton and Mains, 1898), p. 471.

still practice righteousness; and let the one who is holy, still keep himself holy.

12 Behold, I am coming quickly, and My reward is with Me, to render to every man according to what he has done.

13 I am the Alpha and the Omega, the First and the Last, the Beginning and the End.

14 Blessed are those who do His commandments, that they may have the right to the Tree of Life, and may enter by the gates into the City.

15 Outside are the dogs and the sorcerers and the fornicators and the murderers and the idolaters, and everyone who loves and practices lying.

16 I, Jesus, have sent My angel to testify to you these things for the churches. I am the Root and the Offspring of David, the bright Morning Star.

17 And the Spirit and the Bride say: Come. And let the one who hears say: Come. And let the one who is thirsty come; let the one who wishes take the water of life without cost.

18 I testify to everyone who hears the words of the prophecy of this book: If anyone adds to them, God shall add to him the plagues which are written in this book;

19 and if anyone takes away from the words of the book of this prophecy, God shall take away his part from the Tree of Life and from the Holy City, which are written in this book.

20 He who testifies to these things says: Yes, I am coming quickly! Amen. Come, Lord Jesus!

21 The grace of the Lord Jesus Christ be with all the saints. Amen.

6-7 The apostle's final section reviews and summarizes the central messages of the book. Appropriately, St. John's angelic guide begins by testifying that **these words are faithful and true**, in keeping with the character of their Author (1:5; 3:14; 19:11; cf. 19:9; 21:5); they cannot fail to be fulfilled. **And the Lord, the God of the spirits of the prophets, sent His angel to show to His servants the things which must shortly take place.** The word **spirits** here may refer to the "Seven Spirits" (cf. 1:4; 4:5), i.e. the Holy Spirit in His manifold operation through the prophets (cf. 19:10: "the Spirit of prophecy"), but it is possible also to understand the expression in the sense of 1 Corinthians 14:32 — the spirit of each prophet in particular. In any case, St. John has repeatedly emphasized throughout his prophecy that "all the

LORD's people are **prophets"** in this age, having ascended with Christ to the heavenly Council-chamber. The function of the Book of Revelation is that of an official "memo" to all members of the Council, telling them what they need to know regarding imminent events. The consistent message of the whole book is that the things of which it speaks—the final end of the Old Covenant and the firm establishment of the New—are on the verge of fulfillment, irrevocably destined to take place **shortly.**

Speaking on behalf of Christ, the angel repeats the theme of the prophecy, underscoring its immediacy: **Behold, I am coming quickly** (cf. 1:7; 2:5, 16; 3:11; 16:15); in fact, the word *come* or *coming* (*erchomai*) is used seven times in Chapter 22 alone: "The *frequency* of the assurance now before us, shows with what earnestness it was made."[8] Our study of the New Testament is drastically off-course if we fail to take into account the apostolic expectation of an imminent Coming of Christ (not the Second Coming) which would destroy "this generation" of Israel and fully establish the New Covenant Church. This message was not to be taken lightly, and there is an implicit warning in Revelation's Sixth Beatitude, a promise that echoes the First (1:3): **Blessed is he who keeps the words of the prophecy of this book.** Again, St. John stresses the ethical response of his audience to the truths they have heard. He has given them commandments to obey (cf. v. 14), not only explicitly but implicitly: He has revealed the activity of heaven as a pattern for life on earth (cf. Matt. 6:10).

8-9 St. John emphasizes that he, the Apostle, is **the one who heard and saw these things** (cf. his similar language in 1 John 1:1-3; 4:14). **And when I heard and saw, I fell down to worship at the feet of the angel who showed me these things. And he said to me: Don't do that! I am a fellow servant of yours and of your brethren the prophets and of those who keep the words of this book; worship God.** As at 19:10, it is the angelic declaration of a Beatitude which causes St. John to fall down in reverence before the messenger. As we saw on that passage, St. John was not offering divine worship to the angel, but rather honor to a

---

8. Moses Stuart, *Commentary on the Apocalypse*, 2 vols. (Andover: Allen, Morrill, and Wardwell, 1845), Vol. 2, p. 390.

superior. Even so, in the New Covenant age that is no longer appropriate. Angelic superiority over man was intended only to be temporary, an expedient after Adam forfeited his responsibility as guardian of the sanctuary (Gen. 2:15; 3:24). Now that Christ has ascended to the Throne, His people are saints, with access to the sanctuary as God's counselors and confidants; indeed, says St. Paul, the saints are destined to rule not only the world but angels as well (1 Cor. 6:1-3). The angel, though exalted and powerful, is no more than a **fellow servant** of the apostle and his **brethren the prophets** — the other members of the Christian Church, all **those who keep the words of this book.** The believer is a member of the heavenly council, and is able to **worship God** face to face (cf. v. 4). Again, this shows that the blessings enumerated in these closing chapters are not reserved for the consummation alone, but have already been granted to God's people; otherwise, the angel would have accepted St. John's act of reverence. We have direct access to God's Throne.

That this incident had to be repeated almost word-for-word demonstrates both the centrality of this concern to the apostle, and how hard it is for us to learn it. It may well be said that the most important teaching of the Book of Revelation is that Jesus Christ has ascended to the Throne; and the second most important lesson is that we have ascended to heaven with Him.

10 And he said to me: Do not seal up the words of the prophecy of this book, for the time is near. Again the angel emphasizes the imminence of the prophecy's fulfillment. For this reason St. John is forbidden to seal up the words of the book. We have already had occasion (on 10:4) to contrast this with the command to Daniel to "conceal the words and seal up the book until the time of the end" (Dan. 12:4). Because his prophecy spoke of the distant future, Daniel was ordered to seal it up; because St. John's prophecy refers to the imminent future, he is ordered to set it loose. "Indeed, these are the very days for which Daniel wrote, and St. John has been inspired to 'unseal' him."[9]

---

9. Austin Farrer, *The Revelation of St. John the Divine* (Oxford: At the Clarendon Press, 1964), p. 225.

11 Let the one who does wrong, still do wrong; and let the one who is filthy, still be filthy; and let the one who is righteous, still practice righteousness; and let the one who is holy, still keep himself holy. The great battle of the first century was reaching its climax, and the angel calls for the differentiation of the righteous and the wicked, the attainment of "epistemological self-consciousness" through differing responses to God's grace;[10] it constitutes a prayer "that the world may come out black and white, so as to be ripe for judgment."[11] Self-consciousness on both sides of the contest is always a prelude to judgment (cf. Ezek. 3:27: "He who hears, let him hear; and he who refuses, let him refuse").

12-13 The Lord again promises the imminence of His coming judgment on Israel and deliverance of His Church: **Behold, I am coming quickly, and My reward is with Me, to render to every man according to what he has done** (cf. 2:23; 20:12-13). Christ had promised that this would be the result of His first-century Coming in His Kingdom (Matt. 16:27-28). Confirming the promise with an oath, He swears by Himself as the Lord of history, the sovereign Controller of all things: **I am the Alpha and the Omega, the First and the Last, the Beginning and the End.**

14 Continuing to speak through the angel, Christ pronounces the Seventh Beatitude of Revelation: **Blessed are those who do His commandments,** the present participle emphasizing the ongoing duty of obedience. God requires not just a one-time profession of faith, but a continuing life of repentance and confessing Christ. Obedience characterizes the redeemed, as St. John declares elsewhere:

> And by this we know that we have come to know Him, if we keep His commandments. The one who says, "I have come to know Him," and does not keep His commandments, is a liar, and the truth is not in him; but whoever keeps His Word, in him the love of God has truly been perfected. By this we know that

---

10. See Gary North, "Common Grace, Eschatology, and Biblical Law," Appendix C (below).
11. Farrer, p. 225.

577

we are in Him: The one who says he abides in Him ought himself to walk in the same manner as He walked. (1 John 2:3-6)

These alone **have the right to the Tree of Life** (promised to the overcomers in 2:7) **and may enter by the gates into the City** (promised to the overcomers in 3:12). Again, we should note that the nations of the earth will enter into the City (21:24-26), which means that the nations and their rulers will be characterized by righteousness, by the world-conquering faith of the overcomer.

15 Christ provides another catalogue (cf. 21:8), a sevenfold one this time, of those who are excluded from blessing, banished **outside** the City, into the fiery Gehenna (Isa. 66:24; Mark 9:43-48). First are mentioned **the dogs**, scavengers that are regarded with disgust and revulsion throughout the Bible (cf. Prov. 26:11). In Deuteronomy 23:18, sodomites are called "dogs,"[12] and Christ equated dogs with the unclean nations (Mark 7:26-28). St. Paul applies the term, in what must have been a shocking reference, to *the false circumcision*, the Jews who had betrayed the Covenant by rejecting Christ (Phil. 3:2) and have thus joined the heathen and the perverts. That is probably the reference here (cf. 2:9; 3:9). God does not give what is holy unto dogs (Matt. 7:6). The other categories mentioned in this verse, **the sorcerers and the fornicators and the murderers and the idolaters, and everyone who loves and practices lying**, are also listed at 21:8, 27. Christians have renounced all these ungodly actions by their baptism to newness of life.

16 **I, Jesus, have sent My angel to testify to you these things for the churches**; the word **you** is plural, meaning that St. John's audience is directly addressed by the Lord; and the message is for **the churches** generally ("all the saints," v. 21). Christ repeats the lesson of 5:5, that He is the bringer of the New Covenant, the "Charter for Humanity" through which all nations will be blessed: **I am the Root and the Offspring of David**, both the Source and Culmination of the Davidic line. Hengstenberg comments: "Because Jesus is the root, he is also the *race* of

---

12. See Rousas John Rushdoony, *The Institutes of Biblical Law* (Nutley, NJ: The Craig Press, 1973), pp. 89f.

COME, LORD JESUS!   22:17

David. *In him alone is the race preserved*; while otherwise it
would have vanished without a trace. The race of David is more
than his offspring; it indicates that the race of David should,
save for Christ, have ceased to exist. The race of David is here
brought into view in respect to the unconquerable strength and
everlasting dominion promised it by God (comp. Luke 1:32-33).
What he testifies, in whom the glorious race of David culmin-
ates, will assuredly go into fulfillment."[13]

In Numbers 24:17, Balaam prophesied of Christ under the
symbols of a star and a scepter; Christ's scepter is promised to
the overcomer in Thyatira (2:26-27), in an allusion to Psalm
2:8-9; then, as the promise to the overcomer continues, Christ
offers Himself as **the Morning Star** (2:28), and that promise is
repeated here, partly in order to complement the promise of
Light in verse 5, and partly in keeping with other connections
which this passage shares with the Letters to both Pergamum
(the mention of idolatry and the allusion to Balaam) and Thyatira (the mention of sorcery and fornication).

17   And the Spirit and the Bride say: Come! This is a prayer
to Jesus, the Spirit inspiring the Bride to call for Him (cf. Cant.
8:14: "Hurry, my beloved!") to come in salvation and judgment,
even as the four living creatures called forth the Four Horsemen
(6:1, 3, 5, 7). The liturgical response is then set forth: **And let
the one who hears say: Come!** Finally, the expression is inverted
(cf. 3:20-21, where Christ first asks to dine with us, then invites
us to sit with Him), for the certainty of Christ's coming to us in
salvation enables us to come to Him for the Water of Life: **And
let the one who is thirsty come; let the one who wishes take the
Water of Life without cost.** The expression **without cost** is
dōrean, meaning *as a gift,* used by Christ in a particularly telling
reference: "They hated me *without a cause*" (John 15:25). Our
salvation is free, "without a cause" as far as our own merit is
concerned; its source and reason are wholly in Him, and not at
all in us. We are "justified *as a gift* by His grace through the redemption which is in Christ Jesus" (Rom. 3:24).

---

13. E. W. Hengstenberg, *The Revelation of St. John*, 2 vols., trans. Patrick
Fairbairn (Cherry Hill, NJ: Mack Publishing Co., n. d.), Vol. 2, p. 373.

18-19   Now Jesus states what many regard as the most solemn and terrifying words in the entire prophecy: **I testify to everyone who hears the words of the prophecy of this book: If anyone adds to them, God shall add to him the plagues which are written in this book; and if anyone takes away from the words of the book of this prophecy, God shall take away his part from the Tree of Life and from the Holy City, which are written in this book** (cf. Deut. 4:2; 12:32; 29:20).[14] Rushdoony comments: "In a very real sense, Revelation concludes Scripture. It speaks deliberately as a final word. Moses, in Deuteronomy 4:2, declared, 'Ye shall not add unto the word which I command you, neither shall ye diminish ought from it. . . .' *Words* were to be added by others, but the revelation would be one unchanging *word*. Now, with the conclusion of Scripture, adding or removing the 'words' of the book is forbidden; words can no longer be added. The self-conscious parallel and alteration are too obvious to be accidental. The last words have been given of the unchanging word."[15]

20-21   **He who testifies to these things**, the True and Faithful Witness, **says: Yes, I am coming quickly!** In this closing liturgy, the Church answers: **Amen! Come, Lord Jesus!** The Church asks for judgment; she specifically requests her Lord to come (*Maranatha!*), bringing *Anathema* for all His enemies (1 Cor. 16:22), but with **grace** for **all the saints.** As we saw on 3:14, the familiar word **Amen** is an oath, a calling down upon oneself the curses of the covenant, and a solemn recognition that we would have no grace at all but for the fact that Jesus Christ is our "Amen," who underwent the Curse for us. Therefore, as St. Ambrose exhorted, "What the mouth speaks, let the mind within confess; what the tongue utters, let the heart feel."[16]

---

14. It seems most strange that, of all places, these two verses should have any variant readings at all; yet, in fact, there are, not one, but at least *thirteen* separate points in dispute! See Zane C. Hodges and Arthur L. Farstad, eds., *The Greek New Testament According to the Majority Text* (Nashville: Thomas Nelson Publishers, 1982).

15. Rousas John Rushdoony, *Thy Kingdom Come: Studies in Daniel and Revelation* (Tyler, TX: Thoburn Press, [1970] 1978), p. 225. Italics added.

16. St. Ambrose, *On the Mysteries*, 54.

CONCLUSION: THE
LESSONS OF REVELATION

If the Book of Revelation is primarily a prophecy to the first-century Church, is it of any value to Christians today? As a matter of fact, that question faces us with regard to every book in the Bible, not just Revelation; for all Scripture was written "to" someone else, and not "to" us. But St. Paul stated a fundamental principle of Biblical interpretation: "All Scripture is inspired by God and profitable for teaching, for reproof, for correction, for training in righteousness; that the man of God may be adequate, equipped for every good work" (2 Tim. 3:16-17). God's judgment on Israel for her disobedience can happen to us as well, if we do not persevere in faith and works. If even *Israel* could be broken off from the covenantal Tree of Life, so can we: "They were broken off for their unbelief, but you stand by your faith. Do not be conceited, but fear; for if God did not spare the natural branches, neither will He spare you. Behold then the kindness and severity of God: to those who fell, severity; but to you, God's kindness, if you continue in His kindness; otherwise you also will be cut off. And they also, if they do not continue in their unbelief, will be grafted in; for God is able to graft them in again" (Rom. 11:20-23).

The Book of Revelation therefore has continuing lessons for the Church of all ages. I have summarized some of these lessons below, providing references to the pages in the commentary where they are discussed. The following is not to be taken as an exhaustive list, but as a rough sketch for topical study and review.

The Interpretation of Prophecy

The purpose of prophecy is not simply "prediction"; rather, it is a summons to ethical living in terms of God's standards (p. 11). It is therefore not "history written in advance" (pp. 27-29). Our standard for interpreting prophecy must be the Bible itself

581

(pp. 29-31). The Book of Revelation is written in "signs," i.e. *symbols* (p. 53). Symbolism is inescapable; in fact, everything is symbolic (pp. 32-33). Symbolism is analogical, not realistic; it is fluid, not a "code" (pp. 33-34). The primary controls on undue speculation must be faithfulness to the Bible's *system of doctrine*, and faithfulness to the Bible's *system of symbolism* (pp. 38-39).

The Book of Revelation

The Book of Revelation has a contemporary focus; it is not about the Second Coming (pp. 39-44), but about the inauguration of the New Covenant era during the Last Days—the period A.D. 30-70, from the Ascension of Christ to the fall of Jerusalem (p. 51). Written sometime within the final decade of Israel's history (pp. 3-6) in the distinctive form of the Biblical Covenant Lawsuit (pp. 10-20, 46-47, 49-50, 85-86, 141-44, 225-27, 379-82), its main prophecies were to be fulfilled *shortly* (p. 51-55). The prophecy was intended to be read in the liturgical setting of the first-century churches (p. 54), and so begins with Seven Letters to the churches of Asia Minor. Each Letter recapitulates the five-part structure of the historic Biblical covenants (pp. 85-86). Taken together, the Letters recapitulate all of Covenant history, from Adam to Christ (pp. 86-89); and they also foreshadow the entire structure of Revelation (pp. 89-91). The Seven Seals set forth the period of the Last Days in general (p. 181); the Seven Trumpets warn of the Tribulation, up to the first siege of Jerusalem under Cestius (pp. 252-53, 286); and the Seven Chalices reveal the final outpouring of God's wrath upon Jerusalem and the Temple in A.D. 67-70 (pp. 383-84).

Revelation is written to comfort and instruct the churches that are plagued and oppressed by an occult, gnostic, statist form of apostate Judaism which had captured the religious hierarchy of Israel (pp. 94, 106-07, 115-16). St. John calls this movement various symbolic names—"Nicolaitans," "Balaamites," "Jezebelites," and "the Synagogue of Satan"—but all these expressions refer to the same cult (pp. 98, 101-03, 107-08, 113-14, 127-28).

The meaning of the main symbols in Revelation may be summarized as follows:

The Seven-Sealed Book is the New Covenant, which Christ obtained at His glorious Ascension and "opened" during the period of the Last Days, climaxing in the destruction of Jeru-

THE LESSONS OF REVELATION

salem (pp. 166-77). (The "Little Book," which explains the Seven-Sealed Book, is the Revelation to St. John: p. 268.) The sealed multitude of 144,000 are the Remnant, the believing Jews of the first century (pp. 206-8, 355-59), the core of the innumerable multitude of the redeemed from every nation (pp. 213-16). The "Two Witnesses" represent the faithful Church of the Old Covenant, "the law and the prophets" exemplified in Moses and Elijah, culminating in the witness-bearing of John the Forerunner (pp. 276-85). The Woman clothed with the Sun is faithful Israel, the Mother of Christ (pp. 297-300). In spite of the Dragon's wrath, the Messiah ascends to rule heaven and earth from the Throne (pp. 308-9). Christ's defeat of Satan in His life, death, and resurrection is portrayed by Michael's offensive "war in heaven" against the Dragon (pp. 311-18).

The Beast from the Sea is the Roman Empire, embodied in Nero Caesar (pp. 325-35); the Beast from the Land (also called the False Prophet) is Israel's religious leadership (pp. 336-44); and the Image of the Beast is the apostate Jewish Synagogue (pp. 339-44). Babylon, the Great Harlot-City, is old, apostate Jerusalem (pp. 362-63, 414-16, 421-43). The New Jerusalem, the pure Bride-City, is the Church (pp. 473-75, 545-46, 552-63), which celebrates her Marriage Supper with the Lamb in the Eucharist, the Communion Feast (pp. 475-78); then she follows her Lord, who, as the Word of God, conquers all nations by the Gospel (pp. 481-92).

Satan was bound in Christ's First Advent and thus prevented from prematurely instigating the eschatological War (pp. 499-508). The "Millennium" is Christ's Kingdom, which began at the Resurrection/Ascension and continues until the end of the world (pp. 494-98, 508-19). The "new heaven and earth" is a picture of salvation: brought in definitively by the finished work of Christ, developing progressively throughout the present age, and coming finally, in absolute fullness, at the consummation of all things (pp. 535-45).

Old Covenant Israel

All Biblical covenants were provisional re-creations, looking forward to the definitive New Creation: the New Covenant (pp. 266-67). The meaning of Israel's history is the bearing of the Manchild, Jesus Christ (pp. 297-300). Old Covenant believers

583

carried the Testimony of Christ (pp. 512-13). The war between the Seed of the Woman and the seed of the Serpent climaxed at the Cross and the Resurrection (pp. 307-8). Unbelieving Israel was excommunicated; and now the Gentiles are streaming in to the New Covenant (pp. 273-74). Israel will never have a covenantal identity apart from the Church (p. 269), for Old Covenant religion cannot be revivified; salvation is now only with Christ and the Church (pp. 448-49).

Christ's Resurrection, Ascension, and New Covenant Kingdom

The goal of Christ's Advent was His glorious Ascension to the heavenly Throne (p. 309) — His *definitive* "Coming in the Clouds" (pp. 64-67). By His Resurrection and Enthronement, He defeated the devil and destroyed his works (pp. 315-17, 502-4), opening heaven to all believers (pp. 366-67). Having been inaugurated at His First Advent (p. 117), Christ is the Ruler of all the kings of the earth (pp. 62-64); His Kingdom has begun and is going on now (pp. 63-64, 68-69).

Jesus Christ's definitive victory gives us progressive dominion (pp. 117-18, 178-79). His resurrection is the First Resurrection, in which all believers share (pp. 104, 516-19). The Kingdom is the Age of Regeneration (pp. 509-10), the era to be characterized by righteousness (pp. 543-45). All Christians are royal priests (pp. 64, 139, 508-9), ministering and reigning both in heaven and on earth (pp. 514-15).

Christ's Ascension opened the New Covenant (pp. 169-74), the New Creation of heaven and earth — a description of both our present and future inheritance (pp. 538-45). The New Jerusalem is the Kingdom City, the Church: Christ's Bride now and forever (pp. 525, 545-46). As the Old Covenant was the era of (relative) Night, the New Covenant is the era of the Day, for the world moves eschatologically from Darkness to Light (pp. 570-73). The New Covenant is thus the promised "age to come" (p. 473).

Orthodox Christians agree that Christ's Kingdom goes from His Ascension to the end of the world (pp. 493-94). Orthodox Christianity is both amillennialist and postmillennialist (pp. 494-96): For, while Christianity has always been staunchly anti-revolutionary (p. 495), it has also been strongly optimistic regarding the power of the Gospel to convert the nations of the world (pp. 496-97). Orthodox Christianity is therefore not "pluralistic" with respect to the Kingdom, holding that all men, nations, and institutions must bow down before the Lord Jesus Christ, obeying His commands in every area of life and thought (p. 496).

Judaism and the Fall of Jerusalem

The foremost enemy of the Church in New Testament times was apostate Judaism (pp. 106-7). First-century Judaism was not simply a continuation of Old Covenant religion; rather, it was an apostate religion, denying both the Old Testament and the New Testament (pp. 101-2, 336-37), promoting the heresy of salvation through chaos (pp. 115-16), committing idolatry by substituting the creation for the Creator (pp. 255-56). Israel's rejection of Christ corrupted the rest of the world (p. 458), turned God's blessings into curses (pp. 245-46), and led her into the slavery of occultism and statism (p. 465). Common Biblical metaphors for covenant-breaking are fornication and adultery; apostate Jerusalem is thus represented as the Great Harlot, the corrupter of the world (pp. 108-9, 114, 363-64, 421-31). Unbelieving Jews are therefore not God's chosen people (pp. 127-28).

Israel's greater privilege meant greater responsibility, and thus greater judgment (p. 128). After the Gospel was preached to the whole world (pp. 361-62), God poured out the Great Tribulation of A.D. 67-70 upon apostate Jerusalem and her Temple (p. 68), in direct response to the prayers of His Church (pp. 238-39). The destruction of Jerusalem was the sign to Israel and the world that the Son of Man is now reigning in heaven (pp. 286-87); and it was the necessary final act of ushering in the New Covenant (pp. 267-68). Christ brought in the Age of Righteousness after the fall of Jerusalem (p. 570); the salvation of the world came through Israel's fall (pp. 241-42); indeed, Israel's fall will eventually result in her own conversion (p. 388). The only way of salvation, for Jews and Gentiles, is in Jesus Christ (p. 128).

The Church

There is only one Covenant of Grace, operating through different administrations (pp. 555-56). With the coming of the New Covenant, God's Glory was transferred from the Temple to

585

the Church (pp. 552-53), and believing Jews and Gentiles united in one Body in Jesus Christ (p. 265). The Church is the True Israel (pp. 102-3, 152), the eschatological Synagogue (pp. 372, 392); as such, she is no longer tied to the earthly Jerusalem but multicentralized throughout the world (p. 83). In the Old Covenant, the world had been organized around the Old Jerusalem; the Church is the New Jerusalem, the City of God (p. 131), and so now the world is organized around the Church (p. 416). We cannot have God for our Father if we do not have His Church for our Mother (p. 474). The sanctification of God's people is carried on by means of the Church, through her ministry and sacraments (pp. 292-93).

The Church ascended to heaven with Christ (p. 284), and now "tabernacles" in heaven (pp. 318, 332), with the saints and angels (pp. 358-59). A *saint* is one who has sanctuary privileges; all Christians through the Ascension have access to the sanctuary (pp. 291-92). Christians and angels are now on an equal level as members of the heavenly Council (pp. 479-80): All Christians are prophets, seeing God face-to-face (p. 382).

The Church is the definitive re-creation of the world, the New Covenant (p. 320); she is the City on the Hill, the Light of the world (pp. 562-63). Salvation will flow out from her gates to convert the world (pp. 566-67). All nations will stream into her with the fruits of their culture (pp. 561-62); indeed, rulers have the duty to support the Church (p. 563). When states forsake their responsibility and seek to destroy the Church instead, such persecution is never merely "political"; it is always religious (pp. 279-80). Satan's persecution of the Church is not a sign of his power; rather, he attacks the Church precisely because Jesus Christ has already defeated him (p. 319). Therefore, the Church will be preserved through all her tribulations, and will gloriously overcome all her opposition (p. 322). There is therefore no excuse for failure: Christ condemns churches that are ineffective (pp. 134-35).

The heavenly Temple, the archetype for Israel's Tabernacle and Temple (pp. 150-51), has been inherited by the Church (pp. 272-74). Since God's will is to be performed on earth as it is in heaven, angelic activity is the pattern for our own (pp. 153-54, 557); in particular, the angels correspond to the pastors/bishops of the Church, and their judging/ruling activities are to be imitated by their earthly counterparts (pp. 81, 230-31, 361-62, 364).

586

Worship

The New Covenant inevitably resulted in a New Song: the New Covenant Liturgy (pp. 176-77). (The anti-liturgical bias is essentially pagan and Moslem in character, not Biblical: pp. 24-25). The Christian day of worship, "the Lord's Day," is the liturgical acting-out of the Day of the Lord (pp. 70-71); this is why the Book of Revelation has historically set the pattern for the Church's worship (p. 24). Biblical worship is corporate, responsorial, and orderly: This requires a formal liturgy (pp. 162-64). Every week, on the Lord's Day, the worshiping Church follows Christ in His Ascension to heaven (pp. 147-48); angels are present in our worship because the Church is standing in the Court of heaven (p. 231). Everything we do in worship has cosmic significance: According to the Scriptural pattern, our public prayer should be performed in a reverent physical posture (p. 219); and even our simple *Amen* is regarded as a legal oath (pp. 132-33). Because of the Ascension, all Christians are prophets, members of God's Advisory Council (pp. 148-49). The faithful Church prays imprecatory prayers against her oppressors (pp. 194-95), and God brings judgments on the earth in response to the Church's cries for justice (pp. 232-33).

Worship must be centered on Jesus Christ. This means the weekly celebration of the Eucharist, the heart of Christian worship (pp. 137-39, 476-77). The Eucharist is the center of life, and should give "shape" to everything else we do (p. 478).

Dominion

The Dominion Mandate, the task God assigned Adam, will be fulfilled by the triumph of the Gospel throughout the world (pp. 510-11). Christians rule with Christ in His Kingdom now, in this age (pp. 64, 68-69, 139, 508-11, 514-15), and Christianity is destined to take over all the kingdoms of the earth (pp. 287-88). God has given His people a "covenant grant" to take possession and exercise dominion over His creation (p. 85). All Christians are therefore commanded to overcome opposition; and, in fact, all Christians *are* overcomers (pp. 98-99). Political power, however, does not come first; the temptation to grasp it prematurely must be resisted (pp. 511-12). The Church is to take the initiative in fighting against the forces of evil — she must *attack*, and not

587

merely defend — and she will be successful (pp. 313-14). She must pray for, expect, and rejoice in her enemies' defeat (p. 459). God will give His Church enough time to accomplish her assignment (p. 506).

The Conversion of the World

For the most part, the world is still pre-Christian, not post-Christian (p. 57). Jesus Christ came to save the world (pp. 213-15), and His Resurrection and Ascension guarantee the triumph of the Gospel (p. 216). Christ is destined to smite and conquer all nations by His Word (pp. 481-92). His Cross, the Tree of Life, will heal all nations (pp. 567-69), as the Feast of Tabernacles symbolically sets forth (pp. 221-24). The overwhelming majority of people will be saved (pp. 387-88), and even Israel's fall will eventually result in her conversion (p. 388). The tendency in the New Covenant age is judgment unto salvation (p. 285).

Salvation and the Christian Life

The "age of accountability" doctrine is a myth; all men are accountable to God at every moment of their existence (pp. 124-25). From one perspective, the Book of Life is a baptismal-roll, a Covenant record-book from which apostates are erased (p. 125); from another perspective, however, it is the membership roll of those whom God has chosen from before the foundation of the world (p. 334). The Bible teaches perseverance, not "eternal security" (pp. 69-70). Perseverance requires faith in God's righteous government of the world (p. 335).

The Bible does not teach salvation by works, but it does teach damnation by works. We are justified by faith alone; but true faith is never alone (p. 533). Wealth is a by-product of God's Kingdom; the pursuit of it apart from Christ is idolatry (pp. 559-60). Christianity does not exempt us from suffering, but enables us to overcome it (pp. 220-21). Suffering does not produce godliness; only God's grace does (p. 407). Our sufferings serve one of two purposes: they either *prove* us or they *improve* us (pp. 236-37). God is more than willing to answer our prayers; our problem is that we don't pray (pp. 249-50). God has His secrets, but He has revealed what we need to know to obey Him (pp. 262-64).

Salvation is God's victory over His enemies, in this world and the next (p. 386). Salvation redeems both the individual and the community in the City of God (p. 547). All life and culture flow from a religious center (p. 448). Christianity applies to every area of life; it renovates the world (p. 548).

God and His World

In the most absolute sense, God is independent of His creation (pp. 160-62). The unity and diversity of the created order are reflections of the Trinity, in which unity and diversity are equally ultimate (pp. 58-59). God knows the future because He planned it (pp. 52-53). The meaning of predestination is that all facts are *created facts*, their meaning predetermined and wholly interpreted by God (p. 100). The opposite of predestination is not freedom but meaninglessness (p. 100). Although God is not responsible for sin, nothing happens outside His control (pp. 441-42).

Belief in autonomous "Natural Law" is the modern form of Baalism (pp. 156-58). Nothing in creation is autonomous; all things are personal and God-centered (p. 204). God rules His creation directly and personally (pp. 156-58). The very order of the constellations manifests the glory of God (pp. 158-60). God is King of the nations, and uses them to fulfill His purposes (p. 387); He rules even the heathen armies of the earth (p. 409). The world's judgments proceed, directly and personally, from His Throne (p. 192). God imposes restraints on man's wickedness; without these there would be no limit to hatred and warfare (pp. 188-89). God applies His standards of justice to the world, requiring multiple restitution (p. 450).

Last Things

The devil is not his own master; in the final analysis, he is governed by Christ (pp. 507-8). When God chooses to release him, Satan will bring the final War at the end of history (pp. 519-25), but this last rebellion will be crushed immediately (pp. 525-26). Both sides, the righteous and the wicked, will mature up to the very end; this is called *epistemological self-consciousness* (pp. 527-28).

Orthodox Christianity has always held to a future Second Coming of Christ and God's final Judgment of the world (pp.

589

263-64, 530-31). The Bible does not teach an absolute universalism; some people will never be converted and will perish everlastingly (p. 519). All those outside of Christ will be cast into eternal punishment (p. 534).

God is the great Warrior-King: He defeats His enemies, and uses the spoils of victory to build His Temple (pp. 535-36). The Dominion Mandate will be fulfilled, and earth will be completely "heavenized" (pp. 537-38). Salvation abolishes the Curse (pp. 569-70), and promises not only that Paradise will be restored, but that it will be utterly consummated (pp. 354-55): Our gain in Christ is much more than what we lost in Adam (p. 567). Christians will reign with Christ, not just for a "millennium," but forever (p. 573).

CHRISTUS VINCIT
CHRISTUS REGNAT
CHRISTUS IMPERAT

APPENDIXES

Appendix A

THE LEVITICAL SYMBOLISM IN REVELATION

PHILIP CARRINGTON

The liturgical character of sections in *Revelation* has often been pointed out; but I have seen no attempt to study and elucidate the liturgical scaffolding into which the visions are built. Archbishop Benson came very near to it when he treated the book as a drama, and printed it so as to display the choric structure. But *Revelation* is not a drama; it is a liturgy. A drama deals with the unfolding of personality, and the actors in it must use their own personalities to interpret it. In liturgy the hierophants must submerge their personalities and identities in the movement of the whole composition. It is a real literary triumph that a sustained poem like *Revelation* should grip the attention as it does without the assistance of human interest in character; and that triumph is liturgical in character.

The author of the *Revelation* frequented the temple and loved its liturgy; when he shut his eyes in Ephesus, he could see the priests going about their appointed tasks at the great altar of burnt-offering. That vision forms the background of the whole poem.

I am astonished to find so few discussions on the temple ritual, not only in connection with the *Revelation,* but also in connection with the Palestinian background of the New Testament generally. The recent advance in this study has concerned itself with the eschatological literature, and the oral teaching of the Rabbis; it has neglected the temple, its priesthood, and worship. But in the New Testament period the temple system was central; after its destruction the Rabbis organized a new Judaism on enlightened Pharisee lines. But it was a new religion, not the old. The old religion died in the year A.D. 70, and gave birth to

Reprinted from Philip Carrington, *The Meaning of the Revelation* (London: SPCK, 1931). I cannot recommend all of Carrington's opinions—for instance his ridiculous JEDP-style "documentary hypothesis" of Revelation's authorship, and his views on the supposed evolution and late date of the text—but I believe that his overall contribution to our understanding of St. John's meaning is very valuable and more than compensates for his shortcomings. Instead of registering my disagreement every time Carrington makes an objectionable statement, I shall take the risk of expecting the reader to think for himself.

two children; the elder was modern Judaism without temple or priest or sacrifice; the younger was Christianity, which was proud of possessing all three.

What links *Hebrews* with *Revelation* is its insistence on this fact. Christianity is the true heir of the old faith. To it have been transferred the priesthood and the sacrifice.

The New Universal Worship

When St. John came to the work of publishing his visions twenty years after Jerusalem had fallen, one of his main tasks was to provide a scheme or pattern for Christian worship. There can be no doubt that he set himself to do this consciously and deliberately; what is more, he was successful. The "Anaphora," as the consecration prayer of the Eucharist is called in the East, follows the pattern he laid down. The "Canon" of the Roman Mass and the Consecration Prayer of the English Prayer Book do so, though less faithfully.

It seems reasonable to suppose that his liturgical work was not done at random or in a spirit of theory. It must have borne some sort of relation to the way Christian worship was actually conducted at the time; analogy suggests that if the older part of the book reflected the worship of the old religion that had passed away, the newer part would reflect that of the new religion which had taken its place. Now the opening chapters 4 and 5, though they belong to the later period of St. John's inspiration, do seem to be built upon a foundation of older work, in which the following changes appear to have been made: (1) a Throne takes the place of an Altar, and (2) Twenty-four Elders on Thrones are added. (See Charles, *ad. loc.*) But these changes correspond to the picture of the Christian congregation of the period suggested in the writings of St. Ignatius (see Rawlinson in *Foundations,* on "The Origins of the Christian Ministry"). The Throne of God represents the chair of the bishop, and around him are grouped the Elders. The number is chosen because of the Twenty-four courses into which the Hebrew Priesthood (and even the Levites and people) had been divided; we may compare the picture of the High Priest Simon in *Ecclesiasticus* 1 with his "garland" of priests.

We may therefore feel some confidence that we have before us the actual arrangements of the Christian liturgy, which was in its turn dependent on Hebrew origins.

I have dealt in the text with the parallelisms between the Four Zoa [living creatures], the Seven Lamps, the Glassy Sea, etc., and the Cherubim, Candlestick, and Laver of the Temple. In *St. John* they are variously applied to the universal worship of all creation. This universal worship finds expression in the Sanctus (Holy, Holy, Holy), which is

594

also used in the morning prayers of the synagogue, where it is associated with the thought of creation; in the *Revelation* the praise of God for his creation is uttered by the Elders, who prostrate themselves at the sound of the Sanctus.

This is the "first movement" of the Anaphora, of the Christian Eucharist, in which men "join with angels and archangels and all the company of heaven." Most of the Greek liturgies show traces of the "Axios" or "Axion" (worthy) of *Revelation*; at rather a long remove it is reflected in "It is meet and right (*justum et dignum*) so to do."

The *Revelation of St. John* then proceeds to show us the Lamb as it had been slain for Sacrifice; and the Christian liturgies follow him by narrating the life and death of Christ, and so leading up to the consecration and offering. The word Standing, which is applied to the Lamb, is a translation of Tamid, the technical name for the lamb which was offered every morning in the temple as a whole burnt-offering. It was the "standing offering."

This is followed by the offering of Incense, which stands for intercessory prayer; and then comes a New Song. The New Song was also mentioned in a hymn used in the temple after the killing of the lamb, and before the Incense. I shall refer to it later.

The liturgy ends with praise to God and the Lamb, and the singing of the Amen, which was characteristic of the Eucharist at this point. All the liturgies follow this outline, and it is from this point onwards that they vary. The first two parts of the Te Deum follow the same lines of construction.

We now turn to chapter 7, verses 9 to 17, a short passage which is also the work of the latest period, anticipating the end of the book. It represents the worship of the Martyrs in heaven.

The thought of martyrdom as sacrifice is as early as the Maccabean period, and has behind it *Isaiah* 53. The man who gives his life for God or country is both priest and victim; he offers, but what he offers is himself. In *Revelation* his priesthood is dependent upon that of Christ.

In chapter 1 Christ has been shown as priest and King. He is wearing the long white robe and the girdle at the breast; he stands "in the midst of" the seven lamps; that is to say, he is in the sanctuary where the seven-branched candlestick is, and robed like a priest. This plain linen was worn by the high priest on the Day of Atonement. At the end of *Revelation* the same figure comes out of the sanctuary with the same robe splashed with blood.

The martyrs also wear white robes, which are connected with that of Christ by the statement that they are washed in the blood of the lamb; the same mixed character of priest and victim belongs both to

595

the martyrs and their lord; but their deaths are lifted to the level of sacrifice by association with his.

The martyrs offered their bodies, and more than their bodies: their lives, their courage, their *patient endurance*; this is the *living sacrifice* of *Romans* 12, *holy, acceptable, your logical worship.* Giving the word body this wide sense, we may well agree that the white robes mean all that the martyrs offered to God, purified now in the blood of the perfect sacrifice.

Later on the white robes are called *fine linen,* which is priestly material.

In the text of the book I have compared the palms and the hosanna (Salvation) to the triumphal entry of Christ into Jerusalem, his going up to be sacrificed. This is only part of a wider comparison. Both are connected with the ritual of the Feast of Tabernacles, which occurred at the time of Ingathering, when the vintage and all the other harvests were in. In this festival priests encircled the altar waving palms and singing Hosanna; here the martyr-priests are in the sanctuary waving palms and singing hosanna round the throne which has taken the place of the altar.

The thought of Tabernacles is carried further in the statement that God *will Tabernacle upon them*; they are themselves to be his Tabernacle or dwelling-place.

We turn to the end of the book for the fourth and last section dealing with Christian worship. In 21:3 the last statement is taken up again. It is, strange to say, a quotation from *Leviticus,* where it implies that the holy God will dwell among a holy people. Here it is widened to mean that men generally make up the sanctuary of God; his Tabernacling is with them. The noun and verb "Tabernacle" are connected with the Hebrew Shekinah, the visible glory of God which is said to have filled the tabernacle in the desert and the temple when Solomon consecrated it. St. John is announcing, therefore, that the old local sanctuary is gone, and henceforth the Presence is with men in general, and God is making himself visible in and through them.

The thought is developed in the Epilogue which begins with verse 9. It is first repeated in the language of symbolism. The holy city has the Glory of God; its lustre is like the Jasper Stone; in chapter 4 God was said to be like the Jasper Stone, so that all this only repeats the previous statement about the Tabernacling. God's "visible" Presence is in this city. It replaces the old temple. The whole city is filled with the Presence, not merely a sacred part of it. Even its foundation is Jasper — that is to say, divine.

The precious stones built into its walls mean the elect souls in which God dwells; the twelve foundations being the apostles of the lamb. The clear bright gold of its streets means that God's tabernacle is built out of the pure in heart; this symbolism corresponds to that of the white robes.

There was no sanctuary in it; that is to say, the Presence is not localised. There is no alternation of light and dark upon it; no need to calculate suns and moons; it lives in the perpetual light of the Presence. No seven-branched lamp needs to be kindled to burn through the night; the Lamb is the lamp.

Through the lives of the elect souls in which God dwells the light shall shine into the world. The community of the elect is wide open; its gates are never shut. It has no national distinctions. The kings of the earth bring their glory into it; a reference to the sacrifices offered by Roman emperors and others at Jerusalem. The honour they gave to that sanctuary shall come to this. Free to all shall be the waters and fruits of the spiritual paradise.

No hereditary and monopolist priesthood shall have sole possession of this sanctuary and mediate between God and his people. All his servants shall stand in his presence, and every one of them shall be like the high priest, and have his name on their foreheads. Open universal vision: open universal priesthood.

This epilogue builds up a picture of the Catholic church in which it is contrasted at every point with the old Jewish temple, and shown to be more glorious because every part of it is filled with the illumination of the Presence which had been confined to the Holy of Holies. St. John deliberately avoids all the ornaments of temple worship—white robes, golden girdles, harps, incense, altar; they are all gone. Note also its square shape, its gates, and its living waters, which are all taken from Ezekiel's temple.

The Temple Sacrifice

We have gone through the later additions to St. John's poem and seen how illuminating it is to test them from the liturgical point of view; we now turn to the older visions which are preserved within this scaffolding.

Chapters 1 to 5 are new material which forms an introduction to this older system; and no doubt older elements are to be found in them. I have pointed out already how the High Priest is to be seen in the vision of Christ in chapter 1, the sanctuary and its ornaments in chapter 4, and the slain lamb in chapter 5.

Let me now outline the course of the daily burnt-offering at the temple; it may be divided as follows:

1. The killing of the lamb.
2. The preparation of the offerings.
3. *Interval* for prayer.
4. Offering of Incense.
5. The burning of the offering.
6. Psalms, etc. The "shout."
7. Feasting on the sacrifice: if a sin-offering.

1. *The Killing of the Lamb.* —Four events took place simultaneously: the trumpet was blown three times, and the gates of the temple and the gates of the sanctuary were opened; at the same moment the lamb was killed and its blood dashed against the altar.

Of necessity St. John must begin with the lamb killed, as he wishes to work it into the Christian scheme of worship which he has prefixed to his older series of visions; v. 6 is therefore the culmination of one and the opening of the other. *I saw a lamb standing as sacrificed.* I have already pointed out that the word "standing" is a literal translation of Tamid, the technical name for the morning burnt-offering. The verse should therefore be translated, "I saw the lamb of the Tamid as slain." The expression recurs in 14:1.

(A "New Song" is sung by the Twenty-four Elders, who now have harps and incense as priests; but this has to do with the Christian scheme, which overlaps at this point. The "New Song" in the temple came a little later; and St. John has deferred it till 14:3.)

Passing over the non-liturgical episode of the Four Horsemen, we come to the souls under the altar (6:9). Immediately after the lamb was killed its blood was splashed on to the altar; there is a strong connection in Hebrew thought between blood and soul, and the souls here are described as the souls of the sacrificed. They pray also for vengeance on their blood. The blood is thought of as poured on the ground; the blood-soul is thought of as going up to Jehovah. The same thought ultimately underlies the blood sacrifice and blood vengeance. We see that already the deaths of the innocent dead are associated with the death of the Lamb; perhaps they are thought of as cleansed by his blood, for they are given a white robe (see above).

Passing over the sixth seal and the later Christian liturgical passage which has been linked to it, we come to the trumpets and the incense offering (8:1). The incense offering appears to be out of its place, and we will neglect it for the moment, noting, however, the feeling of St. John for correct and beautiful ceremonial. One of the beauties of ceremonial is simultaneous action designed to prevent delay while preparations are being made.

1. Seven angels are given seven trumpets.
2. The Incense is offered.
3. The trumpets are sounded.

The same particularity is shown in the case of the seven bowls (see 15:1).

Let us return to the killing of the lamb. The signal for the killing of the lamb was three blasts on the trumpet; these three blasts were also a signal for the gates of the temple and sanctuary to be opened. This is what we find in *St. John*:

Seven Trumpets (8:1 to 11:18).
Opening of the Sanctuary of God in Heaven (11:19).

We are justified in concluding, therefore, that he is following, though in a rough manner, the temple ceremonial. The likeness becomes more exact when we recollect that Dr. Charles has given very good reason to suppose that in *Revelation* also the number of trumpets was originally three. The argument from ceremonial converts Dr. Charles' hypothesis into a certainty. The series of seven seals and seven trumpets as I have observed in the text of my book, is *not* a key to the construction of *Revelation;* it obscures it; it was introduced to bind together visions that did not cohere.

In dealing with the Naos or Sanctuary in Heaven, we are on very delicate ground. Two things seem clear. One is that the "visible" Presence or Glory is departed from Jerusalem so that the Naos there is a Naos no longer; the other is that the Naos in heaven is the number of elect believers in which the Presence is henceforth to Tabernacle. It is universal, in the "heavens," open to all. I believe that the older series of visions was to have ended, or perhaps did end, with the descent of this *Temple not made with hands.* Two traces of it, I think, are to be found: the promise in 3:12, *I will make him a pillar in the Naos of my God,* and the statement about the triumphant martyrs, 7:15, *They serve him day and night in his Naos.*

This thought of the new Naos from heaven was superseded by something better, the vision of the New City which has no Naos, and no day or night either.

Now we see why the death of the lamb had to come first. It was the death of Christ that opened the way. *When thou hadst overcome the sharpness of death, thou didst open the Kingdom of heaven to all believers.* Comparing *St. John* with the temple ritual, we now get:

Temple. Simultaneous.	*St. John.*
Three trumpets.	Lamb killed.
Lamb killed.	Blood on altar.
Blood splashed on altar.	Three trumpets.
Gates opened.	Gates opened.

The Incense Offering (Rev. 8:3-5)

Why, then, is the incense offering put in its wrong place?

There are one or two suggestions which can be made on this point. The first is a literary point of some importance. St. John is following out several complicated systems in this book, and the logical order of one sometimes has to give way to another. I have shown how faithfully the order of *Revelation* follows the book of *Ezekiel*; now this passage is based on a vision of Ezekiel's which comes at this point. If he remains true to *Ezekiel* it must immediately succeed the vision of the sealing.

Further, there was one day of the year when the offering of incense did come earlier; and this day was the Day of Atonement, the only day when the high priest was bound to officiate in person. We shall find other reasons for supposing that St. John has the Day of Atonement in mind. We have had one already. The high priest (Christ) has been shown to us in chapter 1 wearing a white vestment, and the only day the high priest wore white was the Day of Atonement.

If this suggestion is true, St. John has not confined himself to the ceremonial of one type of sacrifice only. His ceremonial is conflate. We may note that he could not have used the Day of Atonement ceremonial only, as he would then have had to have symbolised Christ by a goat.

The ceremony described by St. John seems to be based on the daily ritual, as it is done by an angel, not by Christ the high priest; but possibly this need not be pressed, as the angel symbolises the whole process of intercession. The half-hour's silence which preceded the incense offering corresponds to the silence and prostration which followed it in the temple system. We may note that in the daily ritual the Naos was entered at this point, and the incense altar cleansed; the heavenly Naos would not need this. On the other hand, when we come to the point where the incense offering took place in the daily ritual, we find that St. John has a very significant passage corresponding to it.

To sum up. St. John desired at this spot to symbolise the prayers of the innocent dead coming before God and being answered. He therefore moves the incense offering to this point, as on the Day of Atonement. He thus preserves his parallelism with *Ezekiel*.

600

A long non-liturgical passage follows. The three trumpets are made to symbolise the voice of prophecy in its denunciation of sin. Lengthened to seven, they recall the fall of the city of Jericho (8:6 to 9:21).

Then comes the completion and fulfilment of the prophetic ministry in the Christian evangel, in connection with which he relates his own call, and his peculiar and distinctive work which is to prophesy against Jerusalem. Jerusalem is to be destroyed; the Naos only is to be preserved; and by the Naos we have seen that he means the community of elect souls in which the Presence of God is Tabernacling. The real Israel is now the Christian church (10:1 to 11:13).

All this is concluded by the last trumpet and the opening of the heavenly Naos (11:14-19).

The Great Interlude is also non-liturgical. It narrates the appearance of the Deliverer, his victory over Satan, the persecution of his followers in Jerusalem, and the appearance of the beast (the Roman god-emperor system) which persecutes his followers abroad (12 and 13).

2. *The Preparation of the Sacrifice.* – After the lamb had been killed and its blood splashed on the altar there was still much to be done. It had to be skinned and cut into pieces; its entrails and legs were washed in the laver; and it was laid out on the slope that led up to the altar. The priests then went to the Hall of Polished Stones for Prayers.

Chapter 14 opens with the *lamb standing on the Mount Sion,* or rather *the lamb of the Tamid on Mount Sion.* As Mount Sion is the site of the temple, I need not labour the sacrificial aspect of this verse.

With him are the hundred and forty and four thousand who were "sealed"; they have *the name of his father written on their foreheads.* These are the martyrs, who, together with the lamb, form the sacrifice. They are also priests. The high priest carried on his forehead a golden plate, the petalon, bearing the sacred name of Jehovah, *Holiness unto the Lord.* In verse 4 they are described as "firstfruits," a definitely sacrificial term; and in verse 5 they are said to be "without blemish"; a perfect material for sacrifice.

I have dealt in the text with the statement in verse 4 that they were not defiled with women. The priests at the sacrifice had to observe certain ceremonial taboos which kept them technically "holy"; among these was abstinence from intercourse with women.

Then follows the New Song, sung not in the Hall of Polished Stone, but before the Throne; but I shall deal with this later.

After the three woes which are non-liturgical, we find the coming of one like a son of man upon a white cloud, followed by the harvest and vintage of the land. These are stongly liturgical in tone. Let us set it out liturgically.

601

And I looked and lo a White Cloud, and upon the Cloud one Seated like a Son of Man, having upon his head a Golden crown and in his hand a sharp Sickle.

And another Angel came out of the Naos, crying in a loud voice to the one Seated on the Cloud,

Send thy Sickle and reap: for the hour is come to reap; for the Harvest of the Land is dried up.

And the one Seated on the Cloud put his Sickle to the Land and the Land was reaped.

And another Angel came out of the Naos in Heaven also having a sharp Sickle.

And another Angel came out of the Altar who had charge of the Fire and said with a loud voice to the one that had the Sickle, saying

Send thy sharp Sickle and cut the clusters of the Vine of the Land; for its Grapes are full-ripe.

And the Angel put his Sickle into the Land, and cut the Vine of the Land, and put it into the Great Winepress of the wrath of God.

And the Winepress was trodden outside the City, and there came out Blood from the Winepress.

The liturgical form and tone of this section are obvious, and invite closer study than we were able to give it in the text of the book. It is a very complicated passage.

1. Its primary reference is to *Mark* 13:26, which speaks: (*a*) of the Son of Man coming on the Clouds, (*b*) of his sending his Angels to gather the elect into his kingdom, and (*c*) of the sun darkened, etc., by which is meant the fall of Jerusalem.

2. The meaning of a resurrection of the just is impossible as the passage stands, though it may have meant that in an early recension of the poem. As it stands it means the separation of the elect, and their escape from the doom of Jerusalem.

3. There is a reference to the Jewish Calendar and the system of feasts observed at the Temple: (*a*) Passover at the beginning of the year, marking the beginning of harvest, and (*b*) Tabernacles or Ingathering at the end of the year, marked by the vintage. This allusion relates the vision to our previous supposition that the early recension J ended with symbolism based on Tabernacles. 14:1 ff. would have followed this vision.

4. The liturgical form suggests that it may be based on the ritual of gathering in the harvest. Now the cutting of the first sheaf was itself a ritual, known as the Omer of Firstfruit. It occurred on Nisan 15, the "high day" of *John* 19:31, and as it was done at night it was contemporaneous with the resurrection.

Nisan 14. Lamb killed.   Crucifixion.
          Passover eaten. Burial.
   15. High day.
          Firstfruit cut.   Resurrection.

In the year of the cruxifixion it chanced that Nisan 15 was also a sabbath; but this was, of course, a coincidence. I have dated the cruxifixion, etc., as in the fourth gospel, which I take to be correct; but in any case the references in *Revelation* are to the cruxifixion story as related in that gospel.

5. Lightfoot in his account of the Temple and its services gives an outline of the ritual for the Omer.

"Those that the Sanhedrin sent about it went out at the evening of the Holy Day (the first day of the Passover Week); they took baskets and sickles, etc.

"They went out on the Holy Day when it began to be dark, and a great company went out with them; when it was now dark, one said to them,

"On this Sabbath, On this Sabbath, On this Sabbath.

"In this Basket, In this Basket, In this Basket.

"Rabbi Eliezer the son of Zadok saith, With this Sickle, With this Sickle, With this Sickle, every particular three times over,

"And they answer him, Well, Well, Well; and he bids them reap."

This is not perhaps on first sight as close a parallel as one might have desired to the passage we are discussing; but there are points of likeness: (*a*) There was a dialogue which took place at the beginning of harvest. (*b*) It explicitly mentions the time: This Sabbath = The Hour is come. (*c*) It explicitly mentions the Sickle. (*d*) The reaper is then commanded to do his work; but the words of this command are not given. The two dialogues are of the same character, have the same purpose, involve similar speakers, and have points of resemblance; we could not expect much more.

(The word Sabbath demands a note. I think I am right in saying that Nisan 15, though not necessarily a Sabbath, might be called a Sabbath, because it was in every respect equal to a Sabbath and observed in the same way. The breach of the Sabbath involved in cutting the first sheaf was excused.)

6. A further very interesting parallel is afforded by the stage we have now reached in the Tamid, or daily offering. To the pieces of the lamb were added (*a*) the meal offering of fine flour, and (*b*) the daily offering of the high priest, which consisted of bread and wine. The Son of Man is, of course, the Christian high priest; the wheat harvest and the vintage afford some parallel to the bread and wine. The con-

nection, which seems rather fanciful, will amount to a certainty if we accept the relation proposed in the text of the book between the cutting of the Vine of the land and the murder of the high priest Ananus; for this provides a second point of contact with the thought of the high priest.

To a poet of St. John's type, the thought of the high priest's offering of bread and wine would prove a basis for rich and complex symbolism. (a) Considering the crucifixion, there is the thought of the high priest Jesus offering himself on Calvary, and antithetically the thought that his offering was the work of the official high priest Caiaphas; and linked with this the institution of the sacrament of bread and wine the night before the crucifixion. (b) Taking the murder of Ananus as the starting point of the ruin of Jerusalem, there is the thought of the official high priest lying dead, sacrificed, as Josephus describes it, in the courts of the temple itself; a vengeance of blood.

7. The Winepress imagery makes clear the blood-vengeance symbolism, and suggests at once the Edomites who murdered Ananus.

The words "outside the City" are the link with the crucifixion, and provide a connection with the sin-offering when it was offered for the high priest or for the whole nation, as in the special case of the Day of Atonement; for it was then that the body of the victim was taken outside the city to be burned. (*Note:* the Day of Atonement follows the festival of Ingathering.)

The parallelisms in the second section may therefore be summarised as follows:

Temple.	St. John.
Preparation of Lamb.	
Pieces laid on slope of altar.	Lamb of the Tamid on Mount Sion.
Meal offering.	
Offering of high priest.	Appearance of Son of Man.
Bread.	Harvest.
Wine.	Vintage.

Those with the Lamb in *St. John* may perhaps be compared to the numerous free-will offerings which accompanied the Tamid.

3. *Interval for Prayers, etc.* — At this point in the temple ritual, when all was ready for the sacrifice, the priests retired to the Hall of Polished Stone for prayers, which included the Ten Commandments and Shema. Amongst them was a "G'ullah," which includes the following verses in the form still used among the Jews:

604

True and firm it is that thou art Jehovah: our God and the God of our fathers.

Thy Name is from everlasting: and there is no God beside thee.

A new song did they that were delivered: sing to thy Name by the sea shore.

Together did all praise and own thee as king: and say Jehovah shall reign who hath redeemed Israel.

We are not surprised, therefore, to find St. John introducing at this point *the song of Moses the servant of God and of the Lamb.* It is sung by the martyrs standing by the glassy sea in heaven, which now appears as if mingled with fire, a clear reference to the Red Sea of the Mosaic deliverance. St. John's song is very like the temple ceremonial:

Great and wonderful are thy works; Jehovah God of hosts.

Just and true are thy ways; O king of the world.

Who shall not fear thee O Jehovah; and glorify thy Name? for thou only art holy.

For all the nations shall come and worship before thee: for thy righteous acts have been shown forth.

The "New Song" mentioned in the temple ritual is alluded to earlier in 14:3 by those who stand with the Lamb on Mount Sion; but this song is only known to those who sing it. The song at this point, however, serves to identify them as priests as well as victims.

A "New Song" has also been given to the twenty-four priestly elders who lead the Christian worship in chapter 5. This also follows the revelation of *the Lamb of the Tamid as slain for sacrifice* (5:9). *"Worthy art thou to take the book . . . for thou wast slain for sacrifice and redeemed to God in thy blood, out of every tribe and tongue and people and nation, and hast made them a royal priesthood to God and they reign upon the earth."*

It is impossible to say how much of this psalmody is based on the temple ritual, or how much it has influenced Christian liturgiology. May not the "True and firm" have suggested the "Meet and right?"

A form of the True and Firm is still used in the Synagogue morning prayers.

4. *The Incense Offering.* — The next section of the daily ritual of the temple was the offering of the incense at the golden altar inside the Naos. We have noted that St. John has placed this piece of ceremonial earlier; but that has enabled him to place something far more significant here.

Let us note first that he has arranged the ritual of the seven bowls exactly as he arranged the ritual of the seven trumpets. A comparison will suffice to show this:

605

The Trumpets	The Bowls
The Trumpets given	The Bowls ready
Incense offered	The Song of Moses and the Lamb
The Trumpets sounded	The Angels with Bowls appear
	The Smoke of the Glory
	The Bowls poured out

It will be noted that in the case of the bowls, to which we are now coming, the ritual is more elaborate, as the greater importance of the event warrants. They are, of course, the real answer to the prayers offered with the incense; the trumpets were warnings.

The point we have now reached was the most solemn in the daily ritual. The priest with the incense went in with four assistants, who placed everything in readiness and then withdrew; the priest in charge of the incense, who was now alone in the Naos, threw the incense on the coals, and the Naos was filled with smoke. Then came the solemn silence for intercession, the people and priests outside prostrating themselves. This was the moment for prayer and answer to prayer. St. Luke gives an account of it in the first chapter of his gospel.

In *St. John* we read that the Naos was filled with smoke from the Glory of God and his Power. As in the story of Solomon's dedication, the "visible" Presence of God appears in the temple, the outward signs which corresponded to the pillar of smoke by day and the pillar of fire by night in the temple. The Glory and the Power are both words which mean nothing else in Rabbinic Hebrew but God himself in his glory and power. After the incense and the trumpets in chapter 8 we read that the Naos appeared in heaven with the ark which was the outward sign of God's covenant; now the Naos is filled with the Shekinah.

Just as in the former case we saw some parallelism with the ceremonial of the Day of Atonement, so the same is to be found here: *No one could enter into the Naos till the seven plagues of the seven angels were completed.* On the Day of Atonement, once the high priest had entered the Naos, no one could enter it till he had finished his work.

But in St. John's ceremonies there is still no sign of the high priest. All is entrusted to angels; and the splendour of his coming is delayed.

The Pouring of the Blood

We now come to another point in which St. John deserts the order of the Tamid, which has no pouring of blood at this point; it has been done at the beginning.

There are several reasons for this.

St. John is bound to have two pourings of blood, because he is using the symbolism of blood avenging; blood has been shed, and more blood must avenge it.

It was at this point on the Day of Atonement that the High Priest came out, after cleansing the Naos and Holy of Holies, in order to smear blood upon the horns of the altar and cleanse that, following the custom in all sin-offerings.

The offering on the Day of Atonement was a special version of the sin-offering, a sin-offering for the High Priest and for the whole nation; in such cases it was directed that the carcase should be taken and burnt "outside the Camp"—that is to say, in historic times, "outside the City." I have pointed out how our author and the author of the *Epistle to the Hebrews* have brought out the likeness between this custom and the crucifixion of our Lord "outside the city."

In the sin-offering the whole of the remainder of the Blood was poured out at the foot of the altar; and this ceremony has provided the basis for what follows in *Revelation*. On the Day of Atonement the High Priest entered the Holy Place and sprinkled Blood Seven times towards the veil; he then came out with reconciliation and atonement for the people. Nothing of the sort occurs in *Revelation*, because there is no reconciliation. No High Priest appears. Only a "great voice" from within the Naos directs the seven angels to pour out their bowls, and the seven angels in "white stone" and golden girdles come out with a sevenfold libation to pour upon the land. It is to be presumed that in St. John's thought the land that has been soaked in the blood of Jesus and his martyrs is one great altar of burnt-and blood-offerings.

It is a reversal of all values and expectations. There is no atonement, no reconciliation; what is to follow is rejection, retribution, and destruction.

The blood-avenging symbolism recurs throughout the seven bowls. Under the second the sea becomes like the blood of a corpse. Under the third the rivers become blood, and a versicle and response follow:

And I heard the voice of the Angel of the Waters saying,

Righteous art thou, who art and who wast, the Holy; for thou hast judged these things.

For the blood of saints and prophets they poured out; and blood thou hast given them to drink.

They are worthy.

And I heard the Altar saying,

Yea, Jehovah God of hosts: true and just are thy judgments.

I pointed out in the text of the book that the altar here signifies the martyrs, or their blood spilt on the land.

When the seventh is poured out on the air, a Great Voice came out of the Naos from the Throne, saying, IT IS DONE . . . and Babylon the great was remembered before God to give her the cup of the wine of the anger of his wrath. Here too the liturgical tone cannot be missed. "Remembered before God" is a devotional phrase; and we shall recur to the cup.

5. *The Offerings Burnt.* — The next stage in the daily ritual was the burning of all the offerings except the drink-offering, which was poured out at the foot of the altar.

Babylon is priest as well as victim. Her fine linen is priestly. Her purple and gold and scarlet and blue are priestly. The fine linen recalls the stones of the temple gleaming white like snow. She is "gilded with gold," like the temple. There was in front of the door of the Naos a "Babylonian tapestry in which blue, purple, scarlet and linen were mingled with such skill that one could not look on it without admiration," as Josephus tells us.

The merchandise of 18:11, which critics say could never have come to a small town like Jerusalem, would all have been used in building and furnishing the temple; the merchandise of these things must have employed many ships. And note the irony at the end, *horses and chariots and slaves, yes and the souls of men.*

The conjunction of the desert and the scarlet in 17:3 suggests the scapegoat.

Her former lovers are *to make her desolate and naked and eat her flesh, and burn her with fire,* and the only excuse for this horrible symbolism is that it is drawn from the sin-offering.

A verse of masterly irony is found in 18:5: *Her sin-offerings have mounted up to heaven, and God has remembered her unrighteousness.* Hattah in Hebrew means both sin and sin-offering; not till the last word of the line, when we read unrighteousness, is the meaning of the first apparent: it means sins.

Babylon, falsely priestly, is herself the burnt-offering. It is another reversal of expectations. *In fire shall she be burnt, When they see the Smoke of her burning;* and finally when the shout of triumph goes up, *Alleluia: for her Smoke goeth up forever and ever.* She is turned into a continual burnt-offering. (Compare *Lev.* 6:13.)

Nor is that the end. One ceremony remains. The high priest's cup of wine, the drink-offering, must be poured out. This too is not forgotten, but it is turned into a communion. *To give her the cup of the wine of the anger of his wrath* for she is *drunk with the blood of the saints and with the blood of the martyrs of Jesus. Repay to her as she repaid; and double and redouble according to her works.* So ends the blood avenging. *In her was found the blood of prophets and saints and all who were slain for sacrifice upon the land* (18 and 19).

6. *The Psalms.* — After the drink-offering was poured out, came the psalms; there was a "shout"; there were trumpets; there were pros-

tration and silence; there was for the first time instrumental music. All this is reflected in the Alleluia chorus which goes up after the fall of Babylon. The detail of it need not detain us here, except that the Alleluias recall the last psalms of the book; and that each chorus begins with Alleluia, though in one case it has been translated into "Praise our God" (19:1-10).

7. *The Feast on the Sacrifice.* — Sin-offerings were followed by the eating of part of the sacrifice by the priest. Two feasts follow the psalmody here, one for God's friends, and one for his enemies. The first is the marriage feast of the lamb, with its obvious reference to the eucharist (19:9). The other is the invitation to the birds of heaven to feed on the flesh of those who fall in the wars of the messiah (19:17).

The Hebrew part of the book has two further liturgical points in it before it closes: (1) *The Coming Out of the Great High Priest* (19:11) in which the liturgical symbolism is already gone; he comes out of heaven, not out of the Naos. The Naos in heaven seems to vanish with the earthly temple. I have dealt with the symbolism of this passage; but it is worth noting again the fine linen, and the priestly garment splashed with blood. One fine point is the name written on the thigh; I have given an explanation in the text, which I think is the central one. But it is worth noting that priestly sacredness attached to the thigh; it was a part of the sin-offering that went to the priest. I have seen medieval Jewish drawings with a letter engraved on the thigh. But I do not know the explanation. (2) *The New Naos* (21:3). Here too the liturgical symbolism is gone, though the description of the new order which replaces the old Jerusalem is taken from Leviticus: "Behold the Tabernacle of God is with men, and he shall Tabernacle with them, and they shall be his peoples, and he (God with them) shall be their God."

The word Tabernacle is used, but there is only a ghost of the old priestly symbolism. The new sanctuary is universal, human, catholic, not national or local. He goes on to describe it more fully in chapter 22; but that belongs to the later part of the book, that deals with Christian worship.

I have dealt fairly fully in this appendix with the liturgical background of the book, because it seems to have been neglected and yet to be all important. It sheds a great deal of light on the tone and motives of the book. It reinforces the view that Babylon is priestly Jerusalem. It may shed some light on the development of Christian worship, and even on the worship in the temple.

I cannot pretend to have done more than blaze a trail through a dense forest of obscurities; and what I have revealed, I do not profess to understand. Until we know what a Jew felt when he saw the blood being splashed on the altar, or the fire consuming the lamb of the Tamid, we can hardly expect to enter into the complexities of the liturgical poetry of St. John.

THE LITURGICAL STRUCTURE OF REVELATION

A. Hebrew Sacrifice

Revelation.	The Jerusalem Sacrifices.
1-3 Introductory.	The High Priest.
4 Christian Worship A. The Creator.	The Temple Ornaments.
5 Christian Worship B. The Lamb.	1. *The lamb killed at dawn.*
6 (The Four Horsemen).	
Souls under Altar.	Blood splashed on altar.
(Sixth seal.)	
7 Christian Worship C. The Martyrs.	(Feast of Tabernacles.)
8 *The Trumpets.*	Three Trumpets.

Offering of Incense. This does not occur at this point in the daily ritual; but it does on the Day of Atonement. See below. In the Temple ritual the Silence *follows* the burning of the Incense.

9 (The Trumpets, orginally *three,* symbolise the prophetic message.)

11 (The Call of St. John, and his witness against Jerusalem.)

Opening of Sanctuary in Heaven.	Gates of Temple and Sanctuary opened.

12 and 13 (The Great Interlude.)

14 *The Lamb and his Followers on*	2. *Preparation of Sacrifice.*
Mount Sion.	Lamb skinned, cut up, washed,
First fruits. Without blemish.	laid by altar.
The Harvest (Passover).	The meal offering. Bread.
The Vintage (Ingathering).	The drink offering. Wine.
15 *Song of Moses and the Lamb.*	Pause for prayer and praise.
The Sanctuary Opens.	3. *Offering of Incense.*
The Smoke of the Glory.	Silence.
No one may enter the Sanctuary.	Intercession.

St. John has placed the Incense symbolism earlier, though the smoke recalls it here. On the Day of Atonement no one might enter the sanctuary till the High Priest had finished his work there.

16 *Pouring of the Blood.*

The Seven Bowls. In the daily ritual this is done at the beginning; but on the Day of Atonement the High Priest smeared the mercy seat and altar with blood at this point.

17, 18 *Babylon Burned.*	4. *The Burning of the Victim.*
Her Cup.	The Cup poured out.

17:16 refers to the ritual of the sin-offering;
17:2, 3 is reminiscent of the scapegoat.

19 *Alleluia Chorus.*	5. *The Psalms.*
	Song and Instruments.

The Marriage Supper of the Lamb.
The High Priest out of Heaven (cf. Ecclus. 50).

The Great Supper of God.	6. *The Feast on the Sacrifice.*

20 (Wars of the Messiah and Judgments.)

21, 22 *The Tabernacle of God with Men* (cf. Lev. 26:11-12).
Christian Worship D. The Universal Worship of Mankind.

Note — This chart shows how the structure of the older part of *Revelation* follows the events of the daily sacrifice, with variations suggested by the ritual of the Day of Atonement.

THE LITURGICAL STRUCTURE OF REVELATION

B. Christian Worship

1. SCHEME FOR CHRISTIAN SACRIFICIAL WORSHIP

A. *The Worship of the Creator.*

4:1	"Come up."	Lift up your hearts.
	In spirit, in heaven.	
4-6	Throne, Elders, Lamps, and Living Creatures.	The "Preface": With angels and archangels.
8	HOLY, HOLY, HOLY.	The Sanctus.
10	Elders join in: Worthy art thou, etc.	Conception of communion with heaven.
		It is meet and right.

B. *The Worship of the Lamb.*

5:6	The Lamb Sacrificed.	Recital of redeeming life and death.
8	Adoration of Lamb.	
14	Amen.	Amen.

2. THE WORSHIP OF THE TRIUMPHANT SAINTS

This is a literary anticipation of the vision with which St. John closes his poem; it symbolises his faith that the martyrs are triumphant and do anticipate the bliss prepared for all.

C. *The Martyrs in their Worship.*

Note that they are not included under A and B.

7:9	Robes and Palms.	
10	Hosanna.	Hosanna.
15	Worship him day and night in his Sanctuary.	Borrowed from ritual of the Feast of Tabernacles.
	God shall "Tabernacle upon them."	

3. THE IDEAL UNIVERSAL WORSHIP

St. John here sketches a worship free from the limitations of time and space or of a national religion and a hereditary priesthood. The symbolism of Jewish liturgical worship is deliberately excluded.

D. *The Universal Worship of Mankind.*

21:3	The Tabernacling with Men.	Not a temple made with hands.
10	The Glory of God.	His "visible" presence.
22	No Sanctuary in it.	Not local.
23	Its Candlestick the Lamb.	Seven-branch candlestick.
24	The kings of the earth.	Royal sacrifices by gentile kings at Jerusalem.
25	No night.	Free of times and seasons.
22:4	Worship him: see his face.	Open universal presence.
	Name on their forehead.	High priest's petalon: all are priests.

Note – In A and B St. John is consciously constructing a pattern for Christian worship, a pattern which was followed in every Eucharistic liturgy of the Catholic Church. It is based on Hebrew ritual, and no doubt reflects the custom of St. John's own day.

Appendix B

CHRISTIAN ZIONISM
AND MESSIANIC JUDAISM

James B. Jordan

One of the most grotesque aspects of the sociology of modern American protestantism is the phenomenon of Christian Zionism. While related to the theology of dispensationalism, Christian Zionism is actually something altogether different theologically. The purpose of this essay is to explore this movement, and in particular to point out its grievously heretical theoretical basis. To facilitate discussion, we shall interact with the expressed beliefs of a Christian Zionist, Jerry Falwell. We close with a brief note on Messianic Judaism.

Zionism

Zionism is a political movement built on the belief that the Jewish people deserve by right to possess the land of Palestine as their own. During the last part of the 19th and first part of the 20th centuries, Zionism gained support throughout the Christian West. This was due to two factors: the influence that Jewish wealth could purchase among politicians, and the emotional support that the history of Jewish tribulation could elicit from a Christianized public conscience.[1]

With this support, Zionist guerrillas succeeded in throwing Palestine into havoc during the late 1940s, and eventually took over that land. The result was the disenfranchisement of the people who had historically dwelt there. The Moslem Palestinians were formally disenfranchised, and the Palestinian Jews were effectively disenfranchised as a result of being swamped by larger numbers of European Jews who immigrated to the new State of Israel.

Reprinted from James B. Jordan, *The Sociology of the Church* (Tyler, TX: Geneva Ministries, 1986).

1. On the former aspect, see Ronald Sanders, *The High Walls of Jerusalem: A History of the Balfour Declaration and the Birth of the British Mandate for Palestine* (New York: Holt, Rinehart, & Winston, 1984).

It is important to realize that the most conservative Jews were anti-Zionists, believing that Palestine was not to become a Jewish land until made so by the coming of the Messiah. (This viewpoint was dramatized in the recent and rewarding film, *The Chosen*.) Much of the most severe criticism of the political Zionist movement has come from anti-Zionist Jews, the most noted being Alfred M. Lilienthal.[2]

Spurious criticisms of Zionism abound on the right. I have no wish to be associated with these, and so at the outset I want to critique them before dealing with the heresy of Christian Zionism. First of all, we hear from some rightist sources that it is a myth that 6,000,000 Jews were slaughtered by the National Socialists. It is argued that there were not that many Jews in Europe, that it would be impossible logistically to do away with that many people given the time and facilities that the Nazis had, and so forth. This may be true; I have absolutely no way of knowing. The argument, however, seems to be that virtually no Jews were slaughtered by Nazis, and this is nonsense. Even if the number is 600,000 rather than six million, the event is still a moral horror of astonishing magnitude. Even if only one man were killed simply because he was a Jew, this would be a moral horror. And there can be no doubt but that many, many Jews were slaughtered.

Of course, a blasphemous theology has been erected upon this in some Jewish circles, which is the notion that the Nazi persecutions fulfill the prophecy of Isaiah 53, and that the Jews suffered for the sins of the world. As Christians we can only abominate such a construction, and we must call it what it is: a Satanic lie. Still, it is not necessary to deny the event itself in order to argue against an evil theological construction put upon the event.

Perhaps more common is the assertion that most modern Jews are not Jews at all: They are Khazars.[3] The Khazari race seems to lie behind the Ashkenazik Jews of Eastern Europe. This kind of assertion can, of course, be debated. The real problem in the discussion is the notion that Jewishness is a blood or racial phenomenon. It is not.

Biblically speaking, a Jew is someone who is covenanted into the people of the Jews by circumcision, for better or for worse. When Abraham was commanded to circumcise, he was told to circumcise his entire household, including his 318 fighting men and his other domestic servants (Gen. 14:14; 17:10-14). Competent scholars imagine that Sheik Abraham's household probably included at the very least 3000 persons. These servants multiplied as the years went by, and Jacob in-

---

2. Lilienthal has authored several books on this subject. His magnum opus is *The Zionist Connection* (New York: Dodd, Mead, & Co., 1978).

3. On the Khazars, see Arthur Koestler, *The Thirteenth Tribe* (New York: Random House, 1976).

herited them all (Gen. 27:37). Although only 70 from the loins of Jacob went down into Egypt, so many servants went along that they had to be given the whole land of Goshen in which to live.

All these people were Jews, but only a small fraction actually had any of Abraham's blood in them. Later on we see many other people joining the Jews; indeed, the lists of David's men include many foreigners, of whom Uriah the *Hittite* is but the best known. What this demonstrates is that covenant, not race, has always been the defining mark of a Jew (as it also is of a Christian). Genealogical records were kept for the immediate family, of course, since the Messiah had to be of the actual blood of Abraham, and later of David; but this could not have applied to more than a fraction of the total number of people.

Thus, the Jews are those who claim to be Jews, who are covenanted with the Jews. The Khazari converted to Judaism in the Middle Ages, and they are Jews, British-Israelite rightist nonsense to the contrary.[4] (Of course, modern Zionists do not understand this religious principle any more than do their British-Israelite critics. Both conceive of everything in terms of blood and race.)

So then, it is spurious to criticize Zionism on the grounds that "Jews really didn't suffer during World War II," or "Who knows who the real Jews are?" It is pretty obvious who the Jews are, and they are, as always, a force to be reckoned with.

The third line of criticism against Zionism concerns the rightness or wrongness of its invasion and conquest of Palestine. We can listen to arguments to the effect that the Jews stole the land from its inhabitants, that they have persecuted the Palestinians, that they committed horrors during their guerrilla campaign, and the like. Then we can listen to arguments that say that the Jews in Palestine were mistreated under Moslem rule, that the Palestinians are better off today under enlightened Jewish government than they formerly were, that the Jews have exercised dominion over the land and the Moslems did not, thereby forfeiting their right to it, and the like.

Actually, none of this is any of our direct concern as Christians. As Christians we see both Jews and Moslems as groups that have rejected Christ as Messiah, and who have opposed the true faith. If they want to convert, we rejoice. If they want to kill each other off, then that is too bad, but let them have at it — there's nothing we can do about it.

---

4. British-Israelitism claims that the Anglo-Saxon people are the true Jews, and thus inherit the covenant promises by means of race alone. This weird, stupid idea is promoted by the Armstrong cult, but also crops up in right wing Christian circles. For a fine analysis and refutation of this viewpoint, see Louis F. DeBoer, *The New Phariseeism* (Columbus, NJ: The American Presbyterian Press, 1978).

But then, that brings us to the issue: Are Bible-believing Christians supposed to support a Jewish State, for theological reasons? Such is the assertion of Jerry Falwell, and of the heresy of Christian Zionism. Let us turn to this doctrine.

Orthodox Dispensationalism versus Christian Zionism

During the nineteenth century, a peculiar doctrinal notion known as "dispensationalism" arose. Its leading lights were Darby and Scofield; its Bible was the Scofield Reference Bible; and in recent years its primary headquarters has been Dallas Theological Seminary. Technically, dispensationalism teaches that God has two peoples in the history of the world: Israel and the "Church." We presently live in the "Church Age," and God's people today are Christians, the Church. At the present time, the Jews are apostate enemies of God and of Christ, and are under God's judgment until they repent.

Someday soon (It's always soon!), Christ will return to earth invisibly and snatch away all the Church-Christians (this is called the "Rapture" of the saints). At that point, God will go back to dealing with Israel. There will be a seven-year period called "The Tribulation," and during that period, apostate Jewry will form an anti-God alliance with the Beast, but God will begin to convert the Jews, and in time the Beast will turn and begin to persecute these converted Jews. Just when things look hopeless, Christ will return and inaugurate the Millennium.

One other point to note: There are absolutely no signs that the Rapture of the Church is near. It will come "as a thief in the night."

Now, this entire scheme, though popular in recent years, has no roots in historic Christian interpretation of the Scriptures, and at present it is collapsing under the weight of criticism from Bible-believing scholars of a more historically orthodox persuasion. All the same, there are several things to note.

First, by teaching that there are no signs that precede the Rapture, dispensationalism clearly implies that the modern State of Israel has nothing to do with Bible prophecy. If Israel collapsed tomorrow, it would make no difference. The existence of the State of Israel, while it may encourage dispensationalists to believe that the Rapture is near, is of no theologically prophetic importance.

Second, dispensationalism teaches that Jews of today, and even into the Tribulation period, are apostate, and this certainly implies that they are under the wrath and judgment of God. Christians should minister to them, and try to convert them, and show them all kindness as fellow human beings; but Christians should understand that *during the Church Age, the Jews are not the people of God*. Rather, the Church is the people of God today.

615

Third, by teaching that Israel is "set aside" during the Church Age, dispensationalism clearly implies that the promises made to Israel are also "set aside" during that period. The land promise, and the promise "those who bless you, I will bless," have been set aside, until we reenter "prophetic time." Thus, the Jews have no right to the land during the Church Age, and also there is no particular blessing for Gentiles who treat the Jews with especial favor.

Fourth, dispensational theologians are most strict on the point that the Church is a "new people," composed as one body in Christ of both Jew and Gentile. During the Church Age, the distinction between these two is not to be felt in the Church. Thus, dispensational theology is, by implication, opposed to the kind of standpoint articulated in many "Messianic Jewish" groups.

What I am setting forth is standard, consistent dispensationalism. As far as I am concerned, dispensationalism is sorely wrong in its prophetic view, but it is at least orthodox in its view of salvation and blessing. Blessing comes to the Jews when they repent and accept Christ; until then, they are under God's curse. How can it be otherwise? All blessings are in Christ. This is the teaching of orthodox Christianity, and Darby and the early dispensationalists were orthodox Christians on this point, as far as I can tell.

Jerry Falwell and Christian Zionism

My description of dispensationalism may seem rather strange, because this is not the teaching of Hal Lindsey, of the modern Dallas Theological Seminary, or of other modern dispensationalists. I call these people "pop-dispies," for short. In contrast to the dispensational system, these people hold that God *presently* has two peoples on the earth: the Church and Israel. The consistent dispensational system teaches that there are no prophecies whose fulfillment takes place during the Church Age, because the Church exists outside of prophetic time, but modern pop-dispies teach that the reestablishment of the nation of Israel in 1948 was a fulfillment of prophecy.

Consistent dispensationalism teaches that God is dealing with His "heavenly" people today (the Church), and that during the Church Age, God has "set aside" His apostate "earthly" people (Israel). Pop-dispies, on the contrary, hold that *even though apostate, Israel still must be regarded as being under God's present blessing*. They hold the heretical notion that the Jews do not need to repent in order to obtain the blessings of God's covenant. They hold the unBiblical notion that apostate Jewry is not today under the wrath of God.

A well-known advocate of this unfortunate position is the Rev. Jerry Falwell. A modern Zionist, Merrill Simon, has recognized this fact, and has written a book, *Jerry Falwell and the Jews.*[5] This book is a series of interviews with Rev. Falwell, designed to present him as a friend of Zionism, and to alleviate suspicions that liberal Zionist Jews naturally have when it comes to a supposedly orthodox, fundamental Christian preacher.

I should like to cite some quotations from this book, and make some appropriate comments. The books says, however, "No part of this book may be reproduced in any manner without prior written consent from the publishers," which rather cramps my style. You'll just have to believe me, as I summarize Falwell's comments. You can always go to your local library and look it up for yourself.

On page 13, Falwell is asked if he considers the destruction of Jerusalem in A.D. 70 as a sign of God's rejection of Israel. Falwell answers by saying that he surely does not believe a "vengeful" God brought the Roman army to Jerusalem to destroy the Jews. Falwell ascribes the event rather to anti-Semitism.

Now let's hear what the Bible says about it. We needn't quote Leviticus 26 and Deuteronomy 28 in their entirety. Read them at your leisure, and ask this question: Do we see an angry, "vengeful" God here threatening to bring horrors upon Israel if they apostatize? Also read Psalm 69:21 and ask Whom this refers to, and then continue reading until the end of the Psalm, remembering that the Romans surrounded Jerusalem at Passover time. Notice Psalm 69:25 speaks of the "desolation" of Jerusalem, and consider that in connection with Jesus' pronouncement of the desolation of Jerusalem in Matthew 23:38. Falwell is completely out of line with Scripture on this point.

On page 25, Falwell says that he believes anti-Semitism is inspired exclusively by Satan, as part of his opposition to God. Against this, read Job chapters 1 and 2. Here we find that Satan is never allowed to do anything without God's permission. Moreover, we find from the rest of the Bible that God frequently raises up enemies against His people, as scourges to punish them. Read the Book of Judges. Read Kings and Chronicles about Assyria and Babylon. Read Habakkuk. This is not some minor point tucked away in some obscure passage. Rather, this truth pervades the entire Scriptures.

It is true that anti-Jewish feelings are not part of the Christian message, and that Christians should be as considerate toward Jews as they are toward all other men. It is also true, however, that it is God Who stirs up the Babylonians and Assyrians. Until the Jews repent and convert (as Romans 11 promises that someday they shall), they remain God's enemies, and He does stir up pagans against them. Anti-Jewishness

---

5. Middle Village, NY: Jonathan David Publishers, Inc., 1984.

has been part and parcel of secular humanism from the time of Frederick II, through the Renaissance, down to today. The Christian church protected the Jews throughout the Middle Ages, and has continued to do so.[6]

On page 55, Falwell says that Jews and Christian may differ at some points, but they have a common heritage in the Old Testament. Would Falwell be willing to say the same to a Moslem? At any rate, the statement is incorrect. Judaism looks to the Talmud, not to the Bible, as its law. It shows extreme ignorance of Judaism, medieval or modern, to think that Christians can appeal to the Old Testament as common ground. Judaism never approaches the Bible except through the Talmud.

On page 62, Falwell says that the future of the State of Israel is more important than any other political question. He says that the Jews have a theological, historical, and legal right to Palestine. He affirms his personal commitment to Zionism, and says that he learned Zionism from the Old Testament.

The Bible teaches us that when Adam and Eve rebelled, they lost their right to the Garden, and God cast them out. God used the very same principle with Israel, giving them the land, but warning them over and over again that if they rebelled, they would be cast out. It is beyond me how Falwell can read the Old Testament Scriptures and fail to see this. Modern apostate Jews have absolutely no theological, and therefore no historical and legal right to the land of Palestine.

The church of all ages has always taught that the New Testament equivalent of the "land" is the whole world, in Christ, and ultimately the New Earth. God's people, Christ-confessors, are given the whole earth, in principle, and progressively will take dominion over it in time. Even if dispensationalism were correct in its assertion that someday the land of Palestine will be given back to the Jews, we should still have to say that they must convert to Christ first!

On page 68, Falwell says that one thing in modern Israel disturbs him. It is that Christians do not have the liberty to evangelize for the gospel. In other words, *Falwell is aware that Christians are being persecuted in Israel today, but he still supports Israel!* If this is not a betrayal of the faith, what is?

Finally, on p. 145, Falwell is asked about abortion, since modern Jews advocate abortion. Simon asks him whether or not the death penalty should be used against a woman who has an abortion, and her

---

6. On the church's protection of the Jews, see Harold J. Berman (himself a Jew), *Law and Revolution: The Formation of the Western Legal Tradition* (Cambridge: Harvard U. Press, 1983), pp. 90, 222.

physician. Falwell replies that he has never thought about this before, and that he thinks any action against the woman would be wrong.

Well, there we see it. Mr. Simon knows what the issues really are, but Rev. Falwell is so confused, befuddled, and blind that he cannot see them. Obviously, if abortion is murder, then we have to advocate the death penalty for it! Of course, Falwell here sounds just like most of the rest of the modern anti-abortion movement: They've never even thought about some of the most basic, elementary issues involved. "Abortion is murder," they cry. "Reinstitute the death penalty for murder," says the Moral Majority (Falwell's political group). Anybody with an IQ over 25 can figure out the implications of these two statements, but apparently Falwell has never thought of this before. We live in sorry times, when such a novice is the spokesman for the New Christian Right!

Christian Zionism is blasphemy. It is a heresy. Christians have no theological stake whatsoever in the modern State of Israel. It is an anti-God, anti-Christ nation. Until it repents and says "blessed is He Who comes in the Name of the Lord," it will continue to be under the wrath of God. The modern State of Israel permits the persecution of Christians and Christian missionaries. We must pray that God will change the hearts of Jews, as of all other pagans, to receive Christ. But to support the enemies of the Gospel is not the mark of a Gospel minister, but of an anti-Christ.

I've been pretty hard on Jerry. Somebody needs to be. This kind of thing is inexcusable, and needs to be repented of. A couple of years ago I wrote an essay defending Falwell against a somewhat liberal critic.[7] What I have said here does not change what I wrote then, because Falwell's critic was wrong; but I have certainly come to take a dimmer view of Mr. Falwell since. His trumpet is giving forth an uncertain sound. He needs to clean it out.

Messianic Judaism

In recent years, a large number of Jewish young people have turned to Jesus Christ as their Lord and Savior. Many of these young people have formed "Messianic Synagogues," and have articulated here and there various theologies of "Messianic Judaism." For many, Messianic Judaism is simply a way of keeping some Jewish cultural traditions while becoming Christian, and there is nothing wrong with this. It is proper for Christians of various tribes and tongues to give expression

---

7. See my essay, "The Moral Majority: An Anabaptist Critique," in James B. Jordan, ed. *The Failure of the American Baptist Culture*, Christianity and Civilization No. 1 (Tyler, TX: Geneva Ministries, 1982).

to the faith in a variety of cultural forms.

Unfortunately, for some, Messianic Judaism is seen as an alternative to historic Christianity. This is due to the influence of pop-dispyism. After all, if the Millennium is right around the corner, and Jewish culture will be imperialistically triumphant during the Millennium, then even today Jewish practices anticipate that superiority. In fact, some Messianic Jews apparently believe that they can claim unlimited financial support from Gentile Christians, because of this preeminence.[8]

Most of what I have written regarding Christian Zionism above applies to this group of Messianic Jews. I should like, however, to call attention to another facet of the matter. These Messianic Jews believe wrongly that Gentile Christianity (the historic church) departed from Biblical forms in the early days of the church. They see as their mission a restoration of these customs, which they believe they have preserved.

In fact, this is completely false. Anyone who has seen a presentation of "Christ in the Passover" is amazed at the number of non-Biblical rites that are discussed and exhibited (the use of eggs, bread broken in three pieces and hidden in cloth, etc.). These customs arose after the birth of the church, and do not preserve Old Testament ritual at all. Moreover, to try to place a Christian interpretation on the various features of these rituals is most misguided and artificial. Clever as such presentations are, they are grossly misleading.

As a matter of fact, the leading features of Temple and Synagogue worship were brought straight into the church, as she spoiled the new enemies of God: apostate Jewry. The period of this spoiling was A.D. 30 to A.D. 70. Once the church had completed her integration of the spoils of the Old Covenant into her new, transfigured body, God destroyed the remnants of the Old Covenant completely. Modern Jewish rituals and music owe far more to racial/cultural inheritance from the peoples of Eastern Europe than they do to the Old Covenant.[9]

Thus, while there is nothing wrong with converted Jews maintaining a cultural continuity with their past, there are no grounds for the assumption that post-Christian Jewry has preserved the musical and

8. See Gary North, "Some Problems with 'Messianic Judaism,'" in *Biblical Economics Today* 7:3 (Apr./May, 1984).

9. Louis Bouyer has shown at considerable length that the eucharistic prayer of the early church was a modification of the prayers of the Synagogue and Temple. See Bouyer, *Eucharist* (Notre Dame: U. of Notre Dame Press, 1968). Similarly, Eric Werner has shown that the plainchant of the Christian church preserves the style of music known among the Jews of the Old Testament period. See Werner, *The Sacred Bridge* (Columbia U. Press, 1959; the paperback by Schocken only reproduces the first half of this important study).

liturgical forms of the Bible. Those forms were preserved in the church, and in her alone. Jews who wish to recover their heritage would do well to study the early Church, not the traditions of Eastern European cultures.

Therefore thou shalt keep the commandments of the Lord thy God, to walk in his ways, and to fear him. For the Lord thy God bringeth thee into a good land, a land of brooks of water, of fountains and depths that spring out of valleys and hills; A land of wheat, and barley, and vines, and fig trees, and pomegranates; a land of oil olive, and honey; A land wherein thou shalt eat bread without scarceness, thou shalt not lack any thing in it; a land whose stones are iron, and out of whose hills thou mayest dig brass. When thou hast eaten and art full, then thou shalt bless the Lord thy God for the good land which he hath given thee. Beware that thou forget not the Lord thy God, in not keeping his commandments, and his judgments, and his statutes, which I command thee this day: Lest when thou hast eaten and art full, and hast built goodly houses, and dwelt therein; And when thy herds and thy flocks multiply, and thy silver and thy gold is multiplied, and all that thou hast is multiplied; Then thine heart be lifted up, and thou forget the Lord thy God, which brought thee forth out of the land of Egypt, from the house of bondage; Who led thee through that great and terrible wilderness, wherein were fiery serpents, and scorpions, and drought, where there was no water; who brought thee forth water out of the rock of flint; Who fed thee in the wilderness with manna, which thy fathers knew not, that he might humble thee, and that he might prove thee, to do thee good at thy latter end; And thou say in thine heart, My power and the might of mine hand hath gotten me this wealth. But thou shalt remember the Lord thy God: for it is he that giveth thee power to get wealth, that he may establish his covenant which he sware unto thy fathers, as it is this day. And it shall be, if thou do at all forget the Lord thy God, and walk after other gods, and serve them, and worship them, I testify against you this day that ye shall surely perish. As the nations which the Lord destroyeth before your face, so shall ye perish; because ye would not be obedient unto the voice of the Lord your God.

— **Deuteronomy 8:6-20**

For there is no respect of persons with God. For as many as have sinned without law shall also perish without law: and as many as have sinned in the law shall be judged by the law; (For not the hearers of the law are just before God, but the doers of the law shall be justified. For when the Gentiles, which have not the law, do by nature the things contained in the law, these, having not the law, are a law unto themselves: Which shew the work of the law written in their hearts, their conscience also bearing witness, and their thoughts the mean while accusing or else excusing one another;) In the day when God shall judge the secrets of men by Jesus Christ according to my gospel.

— **Romans 2:11-16**

Appendix C

COMMON GRACE, ESCHATOLOGY, AND BIBLICAL LAW

GARY NORTH

The concept of common grace is seldom discussed outside of Calvinistic circles, although all Christian theologies must come to grips eventually with the issues underlying the debate over common grace. The phrase itself goes back at least to the days of colonial American Puritanism. I came across it on several occasions when I was doing research on the colonial Puritans' economic doctrines and experiments. The concept goes back at least to John Calvin's writings.[1]

Before venturing into the forest of theological debate, let me state what I believe is the meaning of the word "grace." The Bible uses the idea in several ways, but the central meaning of grace is this: A gift given to God's creatures on the basis, first, of His favor to His Son, Jesus Christ, the incarnation of the second person of the Trinity, and second, on the basis of Christ's atoning work on the cross. Grace is not strictly unmerited, for Christ merits every gift, but in terms of the merit of the creation — merit deserved by a creature because of its mere creaturehood — there is none. In short, when we speak of any aspect of the creation, other than the incarnate Jesus Christ, grace is defined as an *unmerited gift*. The essence of grace is conveyed in James 1:17: "Every good gift and every perfect gift is from above, and cometh down from the Father of lights, with whom is no variableness, neither shadow of turning."

Special grace is the phrase used by theologians to describe the gift of eternal salvation. Paul writes: "For by grace are ye saved through faith; and that not of yourselves: it is the gift of God: Not of works, lest any man should boast" (Eph. 2:8-9). He also writes: "But God

---

The original version of this essay appeared in the Winter, 1976-77 issue of *The Journal of Christian Reconstruction*, published by the Chalcedon Foundation, P.O. Box 158, Vallecito, California 95251.
1. John Calvin, *Institutes of the Christian Religion* (1559), Book II, Section II, chapter 16; II:III:3; III:XIV:2.

commendeth his love toward us, in that, while we were yet sinners, Christ died for us" (Rom. 5:8). God selects those on whom He will have mercy (Rom. 9:18). He has chosen these people to be recipients of His gift of eternal salvation, and He chose them before the foundation of the world (Eph. 1:4-6).

But there is another kind of grace, and it is misunderstood. *Common grace* is equally a gift of God to His creatures, but it is distinguished from special grace in a number of crucial ways. A debate has gone on for close to a century within Calvinistic circles concerning the nature and reality of common grace. I hope that this essay will contribute some acceptable answers to the people of God, though I have little hope of convincing those who have been involved in this debate for 60 years.

Because of the confusion associated with the term "common grace," let me offer James Jordan's description of it. Common grace is the equivalent of the crumbs that fall from the master's table that the dogs eat. This is how the Canaanite woman described her request of healing by Jesus, and Jesus healed her because of her understanding and faith (Matt. 15:27-28).[2]

Background of the Debate

In 1924, the Christian Reformed Church debated the subject, and the decision of the Synod led to a major and seemingly permanent division within the ranks of the denomination. The debate was of considerable interest to Dutch Calvinists on both sides of the Atlantic, although traditional American Calvinists were hardly aware of the issue, and Arminian churches were (and are still) completely unaware of it. Herman Hoeksema, who was perhaps the most brilliant systematic theologian in America in this century, left the Christian Reformed Church to form the Protestant Reformed Church. He and his followers were convinced that, contrary to the decision of the CRC, there is no such thing as common grace.

The doctrine of common grace, as formulated in the disputed "three points" of the Christian Reformed Church in 1924, asserts the following:

1. There is a "favorable attitude of God toward mankind in general, and not alone toward the elect, . . ." Furthermore,

---

2. Dogs in Israel were not highly loved animals, so the analogy with common grace is biblically legitimate. "And ye shall be holy men unto me: neither shall ye eat any flesh that is torn of beasts in the field; ye shall cast it to the dogs" (Ex. 22:31). If we assume that God loves pagans the way that modern people love their dogs, then the analogy will not fit.

there is "also a certain favor or grace of God which he shows to his creatures in general."

2. God provides "restraint of sin in the life of the individual and in society, . . ."

3. With regard to *the performance of so-called civic right-eousness* . . . the unregenerate, though incapable of any saving good . . . can perform such civic good."[3]

These principles can serve as a starting point for a discussion of common grace. The serious Christian eventually will be faced with the problem of explaining the good once he faces the biblical doctrine of evil. James 1:17 informs us that all good gifts are from God. The same point is made in Deuteronomy, chapter 8, which is quoted as the intro-duction to this essay. It is clear that the unregenerate are the benefici-aries of God's gifts. None of the participants to the debate denies the existence of the gifts. What is denied by the Protestant Reformed crit-ics is that these gifts imply the *favor of God* as far as the unregenerate are concerned. They categorically deny the first point of the original three points.

For the moment, let us refrain from using the word grace. Instead, let us limit ourselves to the word *gift*. The existence of gifts from God raises a whole series of questions:

Does a gift from God imply His favor?

Does an unregenerate man possess the power to do good?

Does the existence of good behavior on the part of the unbe-liever deny the doctrine of total depravity?

Does history reveal a progressive separation between saved and lost?

Would such a separation necessarily lead to the triumph of the unregenerate?

Is there a common ground intellectually between Christians and non-Christians?

Can Christians and non-Christians cooperate successfully in certain areas?

Do God's gifts increase or decrease over time?

Will the cultural mandate (dominion covenant) of Genesis 1:28 be fulfilled?

---

3. Cornelius Van Til, *Common Grace* (Philadelphia: Presbyterian and Re-formed Publishing Co., 1954), pp. 20-22. This essay was reprinted in Van Til, *Common Grace and the Gospel* (Nutley, New Jersey: Presbyterian & Re-formed, 1974), same pagination.

The Favor of God

This is a key point of dispute between those who affirm and those who deny the existence of common grace. I wish to save time, if not trouble, so let me say from the outset that the Christian Reformed Church's 1924 formulation of the first point is defective. The Bible does not indicate that God in any way favors the unregenerate. The opposite is asserted: "He that believeth on the Son hath everlasting life: and he that believeth not the Son shall not see life; but the wrath of God abideth on him" (John 3:36). The prayer of Christ recorded in John 17 reveals His favor toward the redeemed and them alone. There is a fundamental ethical separation between the saved and the lost. God hated Esau and loved Jacob, before either was born (Rom. 9:10-13).

What are we to make of the Bible's passages that have been used to support the idea of limited favor toward creatures in general? Without exception, they refer to *gifts* of God to the unregenerate. They do not imply God's favor. For example, there is this affirmation: "The Lord is good to all: and his tender mercies are over all his works" (Ps. 145:9). The verse preceding this one tells us that God is compassionate, slow to anger, gracious. Romans 2:4 tells us He is longsuffering. Luke 6:35-36 says:

> But love ye your enemies, and do good, and lend, hoping for nothing again; and your reward shall be great, and ye shall be the children of the Highest: for he is kind unto the unthankful and to the evil. Be ye therefore merciful, as your Father also is merciful.

I Timothy 4:10 uses explicit language: "For therefore we both labour and suffer reproach, because we trust in the living God, who is the Saviour of all men, specially of those that believe." The Greek word here translated as "Saviour" is transliterated *sōtēr*: one who saves, heals, protects, or makes whole. God saves (heals) everyone, *especially* those who believe. Unquestionably, the salvation spoken of is universal—not in the sense of special grace, and therefore in the sense of common grace. This is probably the most difficult verse in the Bible for those who deny universal salvation from hell and who also deny common grace.[4]

The most frequently cited passage used by those who defend the

---

4. Gary North, "Aren't There Two Kinds of Salvation?", Question 75 in North, *75 Bible Questions Your Instructors Pray You Won't Ask* (Tyler, Texas: Spurgeon Press, 1984).

idea of God's favor to the unregenerate is Matthew 5:44-45:

> But I say unto you, Love your enemies, bless them that curse you, do good to them that hate you, and pray for them which despitefully use you, and persecute you; That ye may be the children of your Father which is in heaven: for he maketh his sun to rise on the evil and on the good, and sendeth rain on the just and on the unjust.

It is understandable how such verses, in the absence of other verses that more fully explain the nature and intent of God's gifts, could lead men to equate God's favor and gifts. Certainly it is true that God protects, heals, rewards, and cares for the unregenerate. But none of these verses indicates an attitude of favor toward the unregenerate beneficiaries of His gifts. Only in the use of the word "favor" in its slang form of "do me a favor" can we argue that a gift from God is the same as His favor. Favor, in the slang usage, simply means *gift* — an unmerited gift from the donor. But if favor is understood as an attitude favorable to the unregenerate, or an emotional commitment by God to the unregenerate for their sakes, then it must be said, God shows no favor to the unrighteous.

Coals of Fire

One verse in the Bible, above all others, informs us of the underlying attitude of God toward those who rebel against Him despite His gifts. This passage is the concomitant to the oft-quoted Luke 6:35-36 and Matthew 5:44-45. It is Proverbs 25:21-22, which Paul cites in Romans 12:20:

> **If thine enemy be hungry, give him bread to eat; and if he be thirsty, give him water to drink: For thou shalt heap coals of fire upon his head, and the Lord shall reward thee.**

Why are we to be kind to our enemies? First, because God instructs us to be kind. He is kind to them, and we are to imitate Him. Second, by showing mercy, we heap coals of fire on their rebellious heads. From him to whom much is given, much shall be required (Luke 12:47-48). Our enemy will receive greater punishment for all eternity because we have been merciful to him. Third, we are promised a reward from God, which is always a solid reason for being obedient to His commands. The language could not be any plainer. Any discussion of common grace which omits Proverbs 25:21-22 from consideration is not a serious discussion of the topic.

The Bible is very clear. The problem with the vast majority of interpreters is that they still are influenced by the standards of self-proclaimed autonomous humanism. Biblically, *love is the fulfilling of the law* (Rom. 13:8). Love thy neighbor, we are instructed. Treat him with respect. Do not oppress or cheat him. Do not covet his goods or his wife. Do not steal from him. In treating him lawfully, you have fulfilled the commandment to love him. In so doing, you have rendered him without excuse on the day of judgment. God's people are to become conduits of God's gifts to the unregenerate.

This is not to say that every gift that we give to the lost must be given in an attempt to heap coals of fire on their heads. We do not know God's plan for the ages, except in its broad outlines. We do not know who God intends to redeem. So we give freely, hoping that some might be redeemed and the others damned. We play our part in the salvation of some and the damnation of others. For example, regenerate marriage partners are explicitly instructed to treat their unregenerate partners lawfully and faithfully. "For what knowest thou, O wife, whether thou shalt save thy husband? or how knowest thou, O man, whether thou shalt save thy wife" (I Cor. 7:16)? We treat our friends and enemies lawfully, for they are made in the image of God. But we are to understand that our honest treatment does make it far worse on the day of judgment for those with whom we have dealt righteously than if we had disobeyed God and been poor testimonies to them, treating them unlawfully.

God gives rebels enough rope to hang themselves for all eternity. This is a fundamental implication of the doctrine of common grace. The law of God condemns some men, yet it simultaneously serves as a means of repentance and salvation for others (Rom. 5:19-20). The same law produces different results in different people. What separates men is the saving grace of God in election. The law of God serves as a tool of final *destruction* against the lost, yet it also serves as a tool of active *reconstruction* for the Christian. The law rips up the kingdom of Satan as it serves as the foundation for the kingdom of God on earth.

Christ is indeed the savior of all people prior to the day of judgment (I Tim. 4:10). Christ sustains the whole universe (Col. 1:17). Without Him, no living thing could survive. He grants to His creatures such gifts as *time, law, order, power,* and *knowledge.* He grants all of these gifts to Satan and his rebellious host. In answer to the question, "Does God show His grace and mercy to all creation?" the answer is emphatically yes. To the next question, "Does this mean that God in some way demonstrates an attitude of favor toward Satan?" the answer is emphatically no. God is no more favorable toward Satan and his demons than He is to Satan's human followers. But this does not mean that He does not bestow gifts upon them—gifts that they in no way deserve.

Total Depravity and God's Restraining Hand

Law is a means of grace: common grace to those who are perishing, special grace to those who are elect. *Law is also a form of curse*: special curse to those who are perishing, common curse to those who are elect. We are all under law as creatures, and because of the curse of Adam and the creation, we suffer the *temporal* burdens of Adam's transgression. The whole world labors under this curse (Rom. 8:18-23). Nevertheless, "all things work together for good to them that love God, to them who are the called according to his purpose" (Rom. 8:28). As men, we are all under law and the restraint of law, both physical and moral law, and we can use this knowledge of law either to bring us external blessings or to rebel and bring destruction. But we know also that all things work together for evil for them that hate God, to them who are the rejected according to His purpose (Rom. 9:17-22). Common grace—common curse, special grace—special curse: we must affirm all four.

The transgression of the law brings a *special curse* to the unregenerate. It is a curse of eternal duration. But this same transgression brings only a *common curse* to the elect. A Christian gets sick, he suffers losses, he is blown about by the storm, he suffers sorrow, but he does not suffer the second death (Rev. 2:11; 20:6, 14). For the believer, the common curses of life are God's chastening, signs of God's favor (Heb. 12:6). The difference between common curse and special curse is not found in the intensity of human pain or the extent of the loss; the difference lies in God's *attitude* toward those who are laboring under the external and psychological burdens. There is an attitude of favor toward the elect, but none toward the unregenerate. The common curse of the unregenerate is, in fact, a part of the special curse under which he will labor forever. The common curse of the elect man is a part of the special grace in terms of which he finally prospers. The common curse is nonetheless common, despite its differing effects on the eternal state of men. The law of God is sure. God does not respect persons (Rom. 2:11), with one exception: the person of Jesus Christ. (Christ was perfect, yet He was punished.)

But if the effects of the law are common in cursing, then the effects of the law are also common in grace. This is why we need a doctrine of common grace. This doctrine gives meaning to the doctrine of common curse, and vice versa. The law of God restrains men in their evil ways, whether regenerate or unregenerate. The law of God restrains "the old man" or old sin nature in Christians. Law's restraint is a true blessing for all men. In fact, it is even a temporary blessing for Satan and his demons. All those who hate God love death (Prov. 8:36b). This hatred of God is restrained during history. Evil men are given power, life, and time that they do not deserve. So is Satan. They cannot fully work out the implications of their rebellious, suicidal faith, for God's restraint will not permit it.

The common grace which restrains the totally depraved character of Satan and all his followers is, in fact, part of God's *special curse* on them. Every gift returns to condemn them on the day of judgment, heaping coals of fire on their heads. On the other hand, the common grace of God in law also must be seen as a part of the program of special grace to His elect. God's special gifts to His elect, person by person, are the source of varying rewards on the day of judgment (I Cor. 3:11-15). Common grace serves to condemn the rebels proportionately to the benefits they have received on earth, and it serves as the operating backdrop for the special grace given to the elect. The laws of God offer a source of order, power, and dominion. Some men use this common grace to their ultimate destruction, while other use it to their eternal benefit. It is nonetheless common, despite its differing effects on the eternal state of men.

The Good That Men Do

The Bible teaches that there is no good thing inherent in fallen man; his heart is wicked and deceitful (Jer. 17:9). All our self-proclaimed righteousness is as filthy rags in the sight of God (Isa. 64:6). Nevertheless, we also know that history has meaning, that there are permanent standards that enable us to distinguish the life of Joseph Stalin from the life of Albert Schweitzer. There are different punishments for different unregenerate men (Luke 12:45-48). This does not mean that God in some way favors one lost soul more than another. It only means that in the eternal plan of God there must be an eternal affirmation of the validity and permanence of His law. It is worse to be a murderer than a liar or a thief. Not every sin is a sin unto death (I John 5:16-17). History is not some amorphous, undifferentiated mass. It is not an illusion. It has implications for eternity. Therefore, the law of God stands as a reminder to unregenerate men that it is better to conform in part than not to conform at all, even though the end result of rebellion is destruction. There are degrees of punishment (Luke 12:47-48).

But what is the source of the good that evil men do? It can be no other than God (James 1:17). He is the source of all good. He restrains men in different ways, and the effects of this restraint, person to person, demon to demon, can be seen throughout all eternity. Not favor toward the unregenerate, but rather perfect justice of law and total respect toward the law of God on the part of God Himself are the sources of the good deeds that men who are lost may accomplish in time and on earth. There are, to use the vernacular, "different strokes for different folks," not because God is a respecter of persons, but because the deeds of different men are different.

The Knowledge of the Law

The work of the law is written on every man's heart. There is no escape. No man can plead ignorance (Rom. 2:11-14). But each man's history does have meaning, and some men have been given clearer knowledge than others (Luke 12:47-48). There is a *common knowledge* of the law, yet there is also *special knowledge* of the law — historically unique in the life of each man. Each man will be judged by the deeds that he has done, by every word that he has uttered (Rom. 2:6; Matt. 12:36). God testifies to His faithfulness to His word by distinguishing every shade of evil and good in every man's life, saved or lost.

Perhaps a biblical example can clarify these issues. God gave the people who dwelt in the land of Canaan an extra generation of sovereignty over their land. The slave mentality of the Hebrews, with the exceptions of Joshua and Caleb, did not permit them to go in and conquer the land. Furthermore, God specifically revealed to them that He would drive the people out, city by city, year by year, so that the wild animals could not take over the land, leaving it desolate (Ex. 23:27-30). Did this reveal God's favor toward the Canaanites? Hardly. He instructed the Hebrews to destroy them, root and branch. They were to be driven out of their land forever (Ex. 23:32-33). Nevertheless, they did receive a temporal blessing: an extra generation or more of peace. This kept the beasts in their place. It allowed the Hebrews to mature under the law of God. It also allowed the Hebrews to heap coals of fire on the heads of their enemies, for as God told Abraham, the Hebrews would not take control of the promised land in his day, "for the iniquity of the Amorites is not yet full" (Gen. 15:16). During that final generation, the iniquity of the Amorites was filled to the brim. Then came destruction.

The Canaanites did receive more than they deserved. They stayed in the land of their fathers for an extra generation. Were they beneficiaries? In the days of wandering for the Hebrews, the Canaanites were beneficiaries. Then the final payment, culturally speaking, came due, and it was exacted by God through His people, just as the Egyptians had learned to their woe. They cared for the land until the Hebrews were fit to take possession of it. As the Bible affirms, "the wealth of the

631

sinner is laid up for the just" (Prov. 13:22b). But this in no way denies the value of the sinner's wealth during the period in which he controls it. It is a gift from God that he has anything at all. God has restrained the sinners from dispersing their wealth in a flurry of suicidal destruction. He lets them serve as caretakers until that day that it is transferred to the regenerate.

The Hivites of Gibeon did escape destruction. They were wise enough to see that God's people could not be beaten. They tricked Joshua into making a treaty with them. The result was their perpetual bondage as menial laborers, but they received life, and the right to pursue happiness, although they forfeited liberty. They were allowed to live under the restraints of God's law, a far better arrangement culturally than they had lived under before the arrival of the Hebrews. They became the recipients of the cultural blessings given to the Hebrews, and perhaps some of them became faithful to God. In that case, what has been a curse on all of them—servitude—became a means of special grace. Their deception paid off (Josh. 9). Only the Hivites escaped destruction (Josh. 11:20).

In the day that Adam and Eve ate of the tree of knowledge, they died spiritually. God had told them they would die on that very day. But they did not die physically. They may or may not have been individually regenerated by God's Spirit. But they were the beneficiaries of a promise (Gen. 3:15). They were to be allowed to have children. Before time began, God had ordained the crucifixion. Christ was in this sense slain from the very beginning (Rev. 13:8). God granted them time on earth. He extended their lease on life; had they not sinned, they would have been able to own eternal life. God greatly blessed them and their murderous son Cain with a stay of execution. God respected Christ's work on the cross. Christ became a savior to Cain—not a personal savior or regenerating savior, but a savior of his life. God granted Cain protection (Gen. 4:15), one of the tasks of a savior.

Meaning in History

Once again, we see that history has meaning. God has a purpose. He grants favors to rebels, but not because He is favorable to them. He respects His Son, and His Son died for the whole world (John 3:16). He died to save the world, meaning to give it time, life, and external blessings. He did not die to offer a hypothetical promise of regeneration to "vessels of wrath" (Rom. 9:22), but He died to become a savior in the same sense as that described in the first part of I Timothy 4:10—not a special savior, but a sustaining, restraining savior. God dealt mercifully with Adam and Adam's family because He had favor for His chosen people, those who receive the blessings of salvation.

But this salvation is expressly *historical* in nature. Christ died in time and on earth for His people. They are regenerated in time and on earth. He therefore preserves the earth and gives all men, including rebels, time.

With respect to God's restraint of the total depravity of men, consider His curse of the ground (Gen. 3:17-19). Man must labor in the sweat of his brow in order to eat. The earth gives up her fruits, but only through labor. Still, this common curse also involves common grace. Men are compelled to cooperate with each other in a world of scarcity if they wish to increase their income. They may be murderers in their hearts, but they must restrain their emotions and cooperate. The division of labor makes possible the specialization of production. This, in turn, promotes increased wealth for all those who labor. Men are restrained by scarcity, which appears to be a one-sided curse. Not so; it is equally a blessing. This is the meaning of common grace; common curse and common grace go together.

The cross is the best example of the fusion of grace and curse. Christ was totally cursed on the cross. At the same time, this was God's act of incomparable grace. Justice and mercy are linked at the cross. Christ died, thereby experiencing the curse common to all men. Yet through that death, Christ propitiated God. That is the source of common grace on earth — life, law, order, power — as well as the source of special grace. The common curse of the cross — death — led to *special grace* for God's elect, yet it also is the source of that *common grace* which makes history possible. Christ suffered the "first death," not to save His people from the first death, and not to save the unregenerate from the second death of the lake of fire. He suffered the first death to satisfy the penalty of sin — the first death (which Adam did not immediately pay, since he did not die physically on the day that he sinned) and the second death (God's elect will never perish).

At some time in the future, God will cease to restrain men's evil (II Thess. 2:6-12). As He gave up Israel to their lusts (Ps. 81:12; 106:15), so shall He give up on the unregenerate who are presently held back from part of the evil that they would do. This does not necessarily mean that the unregenerate will then crush the people of God. In fact, it means precisely the opposite. When God ceased to restrain Israel, Israel was scattered. (True, for a time things went badly for God's prophets.) But the very act of releasing them from His restraint allowed God to let them fill up their own cup of iniquity. The end result of God's releasing Israel was their fall into iniquity, rebellion, and impotence (Acts 7:42-43). They were scattered by the Assyrians, the Babylonians, and finally the Romans. The Christian church became the heir to God's kingdom (Matt. 21:43). The Romans, too, were given up to their own lusts (Rom. 1:24, 26, 28). Though it took three centuries, they were finally replaced by the Christians. The empire collapsed. The Christians picked up the pieces.

When God ceases to restrain men from the evil that they are capable of committing, it seals their doom. Separated from restraint, they violate the work of the law written in their hearts. Separated from God's law, men lose God's tool of cultural dominion. Men who see themselves as being under law can then use the law to achieve their ends. Antinomians rush headlong into impotence, for, denying that they are under law and law's restraints, they throw away the crucial tool of external conquest and external blessings. They rebel and are destroyed.

Wheat and Tares

The parable of the tares is instructive in dealing with the question: Does history reveal a *progressive separation* between the saved and the lost? The parable begins with the field which is planted with wheat, but which is sown with tares by an enemy during the night (Matt. 13:24-30, 36-43). The parable refers to the kingdom of God, not to the institutional church. "The field is the world," Christ explained (Matt. 13:38). The good wheat, the children of God, now must operate in a world in which the tares, the unregenerate, are operating. The servants (angels) instantly recognize the difference, but they are told not to yank up the tares yet. Such a violent act would destroy the wheat by plowing up the field. To preserve the growing wheat, the owner allows the tares to develop. What is preserved is *historical development*. Only at the end of the world is a final separation made. Until then, *for the sake of the wheat*, the tares are not ripped out.

The rain falls on both the wheat and the tares. The sun shines on both. The blight hits both, and so do the locusts. Common grace and common curse: the law of God brings both in history. An important part of historical development is man's fulfillment of the dominion covenant. New productive techniques can be implemented through the common grace of God, once the care of the field is entrusted to men. The regularities of nature still play a role, but increasingly fertilizers, irrigation systems, regular care, scientific management, and even satellite surveys are part of the life of the field. Men exercise increasing dominion over the world. A question then arises: If the devil's followers rule, will they care tenderly for the needs of the godly? Will they exercise dominion for the benefit of the wheat, so to speak? On the other hand, will the tares be cared for by the Christians? If Christians rule, what happens to the unrighteous?

This is the problem of *differentiation in history*. Men are not passive. They are commanded to be active, to seek dominion over nature (Gen. 1:28; 9:1-7). They are to manage the field. As both the good and the bad work out their God-ordained destinies, what kind of development can be expected? Who prospers most, the saved or the lost? Who becomes dominant?

The final separation comes at the end of time. Until then, the two groups must share the same world. If wheat and tares imply slow growth to maturity, then we have to conclude that the radically discontinuous event of separation will not mark the time of historical development. It is an event of the last day: the final judgment. It is a discontinuous event that is the capstone of historical continuity. The death and resurrection of Christ was the last historically significant event that properly can be said to be discontinuous (possibly the day of Pentecost could serve as the last earth-shaking, kingdom-shaking event). The next major eschatological discontinuity is the day of judgment. So we should expect growth in our era, the kind of growth indicated by the agricultural parables.[5]

What must be stressed is the element of continuous development. "The kingdom of heaven is like to a grain of mustard seed, which a man took and sowed in his field: Which indeed is the least of all seeds: but when it is grown, it is the greatest among herbs, and becometh a tree, so that the birds of the air come and lodge in the branches thereof" (Matt. 13:31-32). As this kingdom comes into maturity, there is no physical separation between saved and lost. That total separation will come only at the end of time. There can be major changes, even as the seasons speed up or retard growth, but we should not expect a radical separation.

While I do not have the space to demonstrate the point, this means that the separation spoken of by premillennialists — the Rapture — is not in accord with the parables of the kingdom. The Rapture comes at the end of time. The "wheat" cannot be removed from the field until that final day, when we are caught up to meet Christ in the clouds (I Thess. 4:17). There is indeed a Rapture, but it comes at the end of time — when the reapers (angels) harvest the wheat and the tares. There is a Rapture, but it is a postmillennial Rapture.

Why a postmillennial Rapture, the amillennialist may say? Why not simply point out that the Rapture comes at the end of time and let matters drop? The answer is important: We must deal with the question of the development of the wheat and tares. We must see that this process of time leads to Christian victory on earth and in time.

---

5. Gary North, *Moses and Pharaoh: Dominion Religion vs. Power Religion* (Tyler, Texas: Institute for Christian Economics, 1985), ch. 12: "Continuity and Revolution."

Knowledge and Dominion

Isaiah 32 is a neglected portion of Scripture in our day. It informs us of a remarkable day that is coming. It is a day of "epistemological self-consciousness," to use Cornelius Van Til's phrase. It is a day when men will know God's standards and apply them accurately to the historical situation. It is not a day beyond the final judgment, for it speaks of churls as well as liberal people. Yet it cannot be a day inaugurated by a radical separation between saved and lost (the Rapture), for such a separation comes only at the end of time. This day will come before Christ returns physically to earth in judgment. We read in the first eight verses:

> Behold, a king shall reign in righteousness, and princes shall rule in judgment. And a man shall be as an hiding place from the wind, and a covert from the tempest; as rivers of water in a dry place, as the shadow of a great rock in a weary land. And the eyes of them that see shall not be dim, and the ears of them that hear shall hearken. The heart also of the rash shall understand knowledge, and the tongue of the stammerers shall be ready to speak plainly. The vile person shall be no more called liberal, nor the churl said to be bountiful. For the vile person will speak villany, and his heart will work iniquity, to practise hypocrisy, and to utter error against the LORD, to make empty the soul of the hungry, and he will cause the drink of the thirsty to fail. The instruments also of the churl are evil; he deviseth wicked devices to destroy the poor with lying words, even when the needy speaketh right. But the liberal deviseth liberal things: and by liberal things shall he stand.

To repeat, "The vile person shall be no more called liberal, nor the churl said to be bountiful" (v. 5). Churls persist in their churlishness; liberal men continue to be gracious. It does not say that all churls will be converted, but it also does not say that the liberals shall be destroyed. The two exist together. But the language of promise indicates that Isaiah knew full well that in his day (and in our day), churls are called liberal and vice versa. Men refuse to apply their knowledge of God's standards to the world in which they live. But it shall not always be thus.

At this point, we face two crucial questions. The answers separate many Christian commentators. First, should we expect this knowledge to come instantaneously? Second, when this prophesied world of epistemological self-consciousness finally dawns, which group will be the earthly victors, churls or liberals?

The amillennialist must answer that this parallel development of knowledge is gradual. The postmillenialist agrees. The premillennialist must dissent. The premil position is that the day of self-awareness comes only after the Rapture and the establishment subsequently of the earthly kingdom, with Christ ruling on earth in person. The amil position sees no era of pre-consummation, pre-final judgment righteousness. Therefore, he must conclude that the growth in self-awareness does separate the saved from the lost culturally, but since there is no coming era of godly victory culturally, the amillennialist has to say that this ethical and epistemological separation leads to the defeat of Christians on the battlefields of culture. Evil will triumph before the final judgment, and since this process is continuous, the decline into darkness must be part of the process of differentiation over time. This increase in self-knowledge therefore leads to the victory of Satan's forces over the church.

The postmillennialist categorically rejects such a view of knowledge. As the ability of Christians to make accurate, God-honoring judgments in history increases over time, more authority is transferred to them. As pagans lose their ability to make such judgments, as a direct result of their denial of and war against biblical law, authority will be removed from them, just as it was removed from Israel in 70 A.D. True knowledge in the postmillennial framework leads to blessing in history, not a curse. It leads to the victory of God's people, not their defeat. But the amillennialist has to deny this. The increase of true self-knowledge is a curse for Christians in the amillennial system. Van Til makes this fundamental in his book on common grace—his only systematically erroneous and debilitating book.

Van Til's Amillennial Version of Common Grace

We now return to the question of common grace. The slow, downward drift of culture parallels the growth in self-awareness, says the amillennialist. This has to mean that common grace is to be withdrawn as time progresses. The restraining hand of God will be progressively removed. Since the amillennialist believes that things get worse before the final judgment, he has to see common grace as *earlier* grace (assuming he admits the existence of common grace at all). This has been stated most forcefully by Van Til, who holds a doctrine of common grace and who is an amillennialist:

All common grace is earlier grace. Its commonness lies in its earliness. It pertains not merely to the lower dimensions of life. It pertains to all dimensions of life, but to all these dimensions ever decreasingly as the time of history goes on. At the very first

637

stage of history there is much common grace. There is a common good nature under the common favor of God. But this creation-grace requires response. It cannot remain what it is. It is conditional. Differentiation must set in and does set in. It comes first in the form of a common rejection of God. Yet common grace continues; it is on a "lower" level now; it is long-suffering that men may be led to repentance. . . . Common grace will diminish still more in the further course of history. With every conditional act the remaining significance of the conditional is reduced. God allows men to follow the path of their self-chosen rejection of Him more rapidly than ever toward the final consummation. God increases His attitude of wrath upon the reprobate as time goes on, until at the end of time, at the great consummation of history, their condition has caught up with their state.[6]

Van Til affirms the reality of history, yet it is the history of continuous decline. The unregenerate become increasingly powerful as common grace declines. But why? Why should the epistemological self-awareness described in Isaiah 32 necessarily lead to defeat for the Christians? By holding to a doctrine of common grace which involves the idea of the common favor of God toward all creatures (except Satan, says Van Til), he then argues that this favor is withdrawn, leaving the unregenerate a free hand to attack God's elect. If common grace is linked with God's favor, and God's favor steadily declines, then that other aspect of common grace, namely, God's restraint, must also be withdrawn. Furthermore, the third feature of common grace, civic righteousness, must also disappear. Van Til's words are quite powerful:

> But when all the reprobate are epistemologically self-conscious, the crack of doom has come. The fully self-conscious reprobate will do all he can in every dimension to destroy the people of God. So while we seek with all our power to hasten the process of differentiation in every dimension we are yet thankful, on the other hand, for "the day of grace," the day of undeveloped differentiation. Such tolerance as we receive on the part of the world is due to this fact that we live in the earlier, rather than in the later, stage of history. And such influence on the public situation as we can effect, whether in society or in state, presupposes this undifferentiated stage of development.[7]

---

6. Van Til, *Common Grace*, pp. 82-83.
7. *Ibid.*, p. 85.

Consider the implications of what Van Til is saying. *History is an earthly threat to Christian man.* Why? His amil argument is that common grace is earlier grace. It declines over time. Why? Because God's attitude of favor declines over time with respect to the unregenerate. With the decline of God's favor, the other benefits of common grace are lost. Evil men become more thoroughly evil.

Van Til's argument is the generally accepted one in Reformed circles. His is the standard statement of the common grace position. Yet as the reader should grasp by now, it is deeply flawed. It begins with *false assumptions*: 1) that common grace implies common favor; 2) that this common grace-favor is reduced over time; 3) that this loss of favor necessarily tears down the foundations of civic righteousness within the general culture; 4) that the amillennial vision of the future is accurate. Thus, he concludes that the process of differentiation is leading to the impotence of Christians in every sphere of life, and that we can be thankful for having lived in the period of "earlier" grace, meaning greater common grace.

It is ironic that Van Til's view of common grace is implicitly opposed to the postmillennialism of R. J. Rushdoony, yet his view is equally opposed to the amillennialism of the anti-Chalcedon amillennial theologian (and former colleague of Van Til's), Meredith G. Kline, who openly rejects Rushdoony's postmillennial eschatology.[8] It is doubly ironic that Rushdoony has adopted Van Til's anti-

---

8. Kline rejects Van Til's assertion that common grace declines over time. Kline says that this is what the Chalcedon postmillennialists teach — which simply is not true, nor even implied by their eschatology — and in doing so Kline breaks radically with Van Til. It is unlikely that Kline even recognizes the anti-Van Til implications of what he has written. "Along with the hermeneutical deficiencies of Chalcedon's millennialism there is a fundamental theological problem that besets it. And here we come around again to Chalcedon's confounding the biblical concepts of the holy and the common. As we have seen, Chalcedon's brand of postmillennialism envisages as the climax of the millennium something more than a high degree of success in the church's evangelistic mission to the world. An additional millennial prospect (one which they particularly relish) is that of a material prosperity and a world-wide eminence and dominance of Christ's established kingdom on earth, with a divinely enforced submission of the nations to the world government of the Christocracy. . . . The insuperable theological objection to any and every such chiliastic construction is that it entails the assumption of a premature eclipse of the order of common grace. . . . In thus postulating the termination of the common grace order before the consummation, Chalcedon's postmillennialism in effect attributes unfaithfulness to God, for God committed himself in his ancient covenant to maintain that order for as long as the earth endures." Meredith G. Kline, "Comments on an Old-New Error," *Westminster Theological Journal*, XLI (Fall 1978), pp. 183, 184.

postmillennial version of common grace, meaning "earlier grace."[9]

Van Til's amillennism colors his whole doctrine of common grace. Perhaps unconsciously, he selectively structured the biblical evidence on this question in order to make it conform with his Netherlands amillennial heritage. This is why his entire concept of common grace is incorrect. It is imperative that we scrap the concept of "earlier grace" and adopt a doctrine of common (crumbs for the dogs) grace.

A Postmillennial Response

In response to Van Til, I offer three criticisms. First, God does not favor the unregenerate at any time after the rebellion of man. Man is totally depraved, and there is nothing in him deserving praise or favor, nor does God look favorably on him. God grants the unregenerate man favors (not favor) in order to heap coals of fire on his head (if he is not part of the elect) or else to call him to repentance (which God's special grace accomplishes). Thus, God is uniformly hostile to the rebel throughout history. God hates unregenerate men with a holy hatred from beginning to end. "Earlier" has nothing to do with it.

Second, once the excess theological baggage of God's supposed favor toward the unregenerate is removed, the other two issues can be discussed: God's restraint and man's civic righteousness. The activity of God's Spirit is important in understanding the nature of God's restraint, but we are told virtually nothing of the operation of the Spirit. What we *are* told is that *the law of God restrains men*. They do the work of the law written on their hearts. This law is the primary means of God's external blessings (Deut. 28:1-14); rebellion against His law brings destruction (Deut. 28:15-68). Therefore, as the reign of biblical law is extended by means of the preaching of the whole counsel of God, as the law is written in the hearts of men (Jer. 31:33-34; Heb.

---

9. It is one of the oddities in the Christian reconstruction movement that R. J. Rushdoony categorically rejects amillennialism, calling it "impotent religion" and "blasphemy," and yet he affirms the validity of Van Til's common grace position, calling for the substitution of Van Til's "earlier grace" concept for "common grace." Rushdoony's anti-amillennial (and therefore by implication anti-Van Til) essay appeared in *The Journal of Christian Reconstruction*, III (Winter 1976-77: "Postmillennialism versus Impotent Religion." His pro-"earlier grace" statement appeared in his review of E. L. Hebden Taylor's book, *The Christian Philosophy of Law, Politics and the State*, in *The Westminster Theological Journal*, XXX (Nov. 1967): "A concept of 'earlier grace' makes remnants of justice, right, and community tenable; a concept of 'common grace' does not" (p. 100). "The term 'common grace' has become a shibboleth of Dutch theology and a passageway across the Jordan and into Reformed territory of those who can feign the required accent. Has not the time come to drop the whole concept and start afresh?" (p. 101).

8:10-11; 10:16), and as the unregenerate come under the sway and influence of the law, common grace must *increase*, not decrease. The central issue is the restraint by God inherent in the work of the law. This work is in every man's heart.

Remember, this has nothing to do with the supposed favor of God toward mankind in general. It is simply that as Christians become more faithful to biblical law, they receive more bread from the hand of God. As they increase the amount of bread on their tables, more crumbs fall to the dogs beneath.

Third, the amillennial view of the process of separation or differentiation is seriously flawed by a lack of understanding of the power which biblical law confers on those who seek to abide by its standards. Again, we must look at Deuteronomy, chapter eight. Conformity to the precepts of the law brings external blessings. The blessings can (though need not) serve as a snare and a temptation, for men may forget the source of their blessings. They can forget God, claim autonomy, and turn away from the law. This leads to destruction. The formerly faithful people are scattered. Thus, the paradox of Deuteronomy 8: covenantal faithfulness to the law — external blessings by God in response to faithfulness — temptation to rely on the blessings as if they were the product of man's hands — judgment. The blessings can lead to disaster and impotence. Therefore, *adherence to the terms of biblical law is basic for external success.*

Ethics and Dominion

As men become epistemologically self-conscious, they must face up to reality — God's reality. Ours is a moral universe. It is governed by a law-order which reflects the very being of God. When men finally realize who the churls are and who the liberals are, they have made a significant discovery. They recognize the relationship between God's standards and the ethical decisions of men. In short, they come to grips with the law of God. The *law* is written in the hearts of Christians. The *work of the law* is written in the hearts of all men. The Christians are therefore increasingly in touch with the source of earthly power: biblical law. To match the power of the Christians, the unregenerate must conform their actions externally to the law of God as preached by Christians, the work of which they already have in their hearts. The unregenerate are therefore made far more responsible before God, simply because they have more knowledge. They desire power. Christians will some day possess cultural power through their adherence to biblical law. Therefore, unregenerate men will have to imitate special covenantal faithfulness by adhering to the demands of God's external covenants. The unregenerate will thereby bring down

641

the final wrath of God upon their heads, even as they gain external blessings due to their increased conformity to the *external requirements* of biblical law. At the end of time, they revolt.

The unregenerate have two choices: Conform themselves to biblical law, or at least to the work of the law written on their hearts, or, second, abandon law and thereby abandon power. They can gain power only on God's terms: acknowledgement of and conformity to God's law. There is no other way. Any turning from the law brings impotence, fragmentation, and despair. Furthermore, it leaves those with a commitment to law in the driver's seat. Increasing differentiation over time, therefore, does not lead to the impotence of the Christians. It leads to their victory culturally. They see the implications of the law more clearly. So do their enemies. The unrighteous can gain access to the blessings only by accepting God's moral universe as it is.

The Hebrews were told to separate themselves from the people and the gods of the land. Those gods were the gods of Satan, the gods of chaos, dissolution, and cyclical history. The pagan world was faithful to the doctrine of cycles: there can be no straight-line progress. But the Hebrews were told differently. If they were faithful, God said, they would not suffer the burdens of sickness, and no one and no animal would suffer miscarriages (Ex. 23:24-26). Special grace leads to a commitment to the law; the commitment to God's law permits God to reduce the common curse element of natural law, leaving proportionately more common grace—the reign of *beneficent common law*. The curse of nature can be steadily reduced, but only if men conform themselves to revealed law or to the works of the law in their hearts. The blessing comes in the form of a more productive, less scarcity-dominated nature. There can be *positive feedback* in the relation between law and blessing: the blessings will confirm God's faithfulness to His law, which in turn will lead to greater convenantal faithfulness (Deut. 8:18). This is the answer to the paradox of Deuteronomy 8: it need not become a cyclical spiral. Of course, special grace is required to keep a people faithful in the long run. Without special grace, the temptation to forget the source of wealth takes over, and the end result is destruction. This is why, at the end of the millennial age, the unregenerate try once again to assert their autonomy from God. They attack the church of the faithful. They exercise power. And the crack of doom sounds—for the unregenerate.

Differentiation and Progress

The process of differentiation is not constant over time. It ebbs and flows. Its general direction is toward epistemological self-consciousness. But Christians are not always faithful, any more than the Hebrews were in the days of the judges. The early church defeated Rome, and then the secular remnants of Rome compromised the church. The Reformation launched a new era of cultural growth, the Counter-Reformation struck back, and the secularism of the Renaissance swallowed up both — for a time. This is not cyclical history, for history is linear. There was a creation, a fall, a people called out of bondage, an incarnation, a resurrection, Pentecost. There will be a day of epistemological self-consciousness, as promised in Isaiah 32. There will be a final rebellion and judgment. There has been a Christian nation called the United States. There has been a secular nation called the United States. (The dividing line was the Civil War, or War of Southern Secession, or War between the States, or War of Northern Aggression — take your pick.) Back and forth, ebb and flow, but with a long-range goal.

There has been progress. Look at the Apostles' Creed. Then look at the Westminster Confession of Faith. Only a fool could deny progress. There has been a growth in wealth, in knowledge, and culture. What are we to say, that technology as such is the devil's, that since common grace has been steadily withdrawn, the modern world's development is the creative work of Satan (since God's common grace cannot account for this progress)? Is Satan creative — autonomously creative? If not, from whence comes our wealth, our knowledge, and our power? Is it not from God? Is not Satan the great imitator? But whose progress has he imitated? Whose cultural development has he attempted to borrow, twist, and destroy? There has been progress since the days of Noah — not straight-line progress, not pure compound growth, but progress nonetheless. Christianity produced it, secularism borrowed it, and today we seem to be at another crossroad: Can the Christians sustain what they began, given their compromises with secularism? And can the secularists sustain what they and the Christians have constructed, now that their spiritual capital is running low, and the Christians' cultural bank account is close to empty?

Christians and secularists today are, in the field of education and other "secular" realms, like a pair of drunks who lean on each other in order not to fall down. We seem to be in the "blessings unto temptation" stage, with "rebellion unto destruction" looming ahead. It has happened before. It can happen again. In this sense, it is the *lack* of epistemological self-consciousness that seems to be responsible for the *reduction* of common grace. Yet it is Van Til's view that the increase of epistemological self-consciousness is responsible for, or at least parallels, the reduction of common grace. Amillennialism has crippled his analysis of common grace. So has his equation of God's gifts and God's supposed favor to mankind in general.

The separation between the wheat and the tares is progressive. It is not a straight-line progression. Blight hits one and then the other. Sometimes it hits both at once. Sometimes the sun and rain help both to grow at the same time. But there is maturity. The tares grow unto final destruction, and the wheat grows unto final blessing. In the meantime, both have roles to play in God's plan for the ages. At least the tares help keep the soil from eroding. Better tares than the destruction of the field, at least for the present. They serve God, despite themselves. There has been progress for both wheat and tares. Greek and Roman science became static; Christian concepts of optimism and an orderly universe created modern science. Now the tares run the scientific world, but for how long? Until a war? Until the concepts of meaningless Darwinian evolution and modern indeterminate physics destroy the concept of regular law—the foundation of all science?

How long can we go on like this? Answer: until epistemological self-consciousness brings Christians back to the law of God. Then the pagans must imitate them or quit. Obedience to God alone brings long-term dominion.

Law and Grace

The dual relationship between common law and common curse is a necessary backdrop for God's plan of the ages. Take, for example, the curse of Adam. Adam and his heirs are burdened with frail bodies that grow sick and die. Initially, there was a longer life expectancy for mankind. The longest life recorded in the Bible, that given to Methuselah, Noah's grandfather, was 969 years. Methuselah died in the year that the great flood began.[10] Thus, as far as human life is concerned, the greatest sign of God's common grace was given to men just before the greatest removal of common grace recorded in history.

This is extremely significant for the thesis of this essay. The *extension of common grace to man*—the external blessings of God that are given to mankind in general—is a *prelude to a great curse for the unregenerate*. As we read in the eighth chapter of Deuteronomy, as well as in the twenty-eighth chapter, men can be and are lured into a snare by

---

10. Methuselah was 969 years old when he died (Gen. 5:27). He was 187 years old when his son Lamech was born (5:25) and 369 years old when Lamech's son Noah was born (5:28-29). Noah was 600 years old at the time of the great flood (7:6). Therefore, from the birth of Noah, when Methuselah was 369, until the flood, 600 years later, Methuselah lived out his years (369 + 600 = 969). The Bible does not say that Methuselah perished in the flood, but only that he died in the year of the flood. This is such a remarkable chronology that the burden of proof is on those who deny the father-to-son relationship in these three generations, arguing instead for an unstated gap in the chronology.

looking upon the external gifts from God while forgetting the heavenly source of the gifts and the *covenantal terms* under which the gifts were given. The gift of long life was given to mankind in general, not as a sign of God's favor, but as a prelude to His almost total destruction of the seed of Adam. Only His special grace to Noah and his family preserved mankind.

Thus, the mere existence of external blessing is no proof of a favorable attitude toward man on the part of God. In the first stage, that of *covenantal faithfulness*, God's special grace is extended widely within a culture. The second state, that of *external blessings* in response to covenantal faithfulness, is intended to reinforce men's faith in the reality and validity of God's covenants (Deut. 8:18). But that second stage can lead to a third stage, covenantal or ethical *forgetfulness*. The key fact which must be borne in mind is that this third stage cannot be distinguished from the second stage in terms of measurements of the blessings (economic growth indicators, for example). An increase of external blessings should lead to the positive feedback of a faithful culture: victory unto victory. But it can lead to stage three, namely, forgetfulness. This leads to stage four, *destruction*. It therefore requires *special* grace to maintain the "faithfulness-blessing-faithfulness-blessing . . ." relationship of positive feedback and compound growth. But common grace plays a definite role in reinforcing men's commitment to the law-order of God.

Everyone in the Hebrew commonwealth, including the stranger who was within the gates, could benefit from the increase in external blessings. Therefore, the curse aspect of the "common grace-common curse" relationship can be progressively removed, and common grace either increases, or else the mere removal of common cursing makes it appear that common grace is increasing. (Better theologians than I can debate this point.)

The Reinforcement of Special Grace

Nevertheless, without special grace being extended by God — without continual conversions of men — the positive feedback of Deuteronomy 8 cannot be maintained. A disastrous reduction of blessings can be counted on by those who are not regenerate if their numbers are becoming dominant in the community. When regenerate Lot was removed from Sodom, and the unregenerate men who had been set up for destruction by God no longer were protected by Lot's presence among them, *their* crack of doom sounded (Gen. 18, 19). And the effects were felt in Lot's family, for his wife looked back and suffered the consequences of her disobedience (19:26), and his daughters committed sin (19:30-38). But it had been Lot's presence among them that

645

had held off destruction (19:21-22).

The same was true of Noah. Until the ark was completed, the world was safe from the great flood. The people seemed to be prospering. Methuselah lived a long life, but after him, the lifespan of mankind steadily declined. Aaron died at age 123 (Num. 33:39). Moses died at age 120 (Deut. 31:2). But this longevity was not normal, even in their day. In a psalm of Moses, he said that "The days of our years are threescore years and ten; and if by reason of strength they be fourscore years, yet is their strength labour and sorrow; for it is soon cut off, and we fly away" (Ps. 90:10). The common curse of God could be seen even in the blessing of extra years, but long life, which is a blessing (Ex. 20:12), was being removed by God from mankind in general.

The Book of Isaiah tells us of a future restoration of long life. This blessing shall be given to all men, saints and sinners. It is therefore a sign of extended common grace. It is a gift to mankind in general. Isaiah 65:20 tells us: "There shall be no more thence an infant of days, nor an old man that hath not filled his days: for the child shall die an hundred years old; but the sinner being an hundred years old shall be accursed." The gift of long life shall come, though the common curse of long life shall extend to the sinner, whose long life is simply extra time for him to fill up his days of iniquity. Nevertheless, the infants will not die, which is a fulfillment of God's promise to Israel, namely, the absence of miscarriages (Ex. 23:26). If there is any passage in Scripture that absolutely refutes the amillennial position, it is this one. This is not a prophecy of the New Heavens and New Earth in their post-judgment form, but it is a prophecy of the pre-judgment manifestation of the preliminary stages of the New Heavens and New Earth — an earnest (down payment) of our expectations. There are still sinners in the world, and they receive long life. But to them it is an ultimate curse, meaning a *special curse*. It is a special curse because this exceptionally long life is a common blessing — the reduction of the *common curse*. Again, we need the concept of common grace to give significance to both special grace and common curse. Common grace (reduced common curse) brings special curses to the rebels.

There will be peace on earth extended to men of good will (Luke 2:14). But this means that there will also be peace on earth extended to evil men. Peace is given to the just as a reward for their covenantal faithfulness. It is given to the unregenerate in order to heap coals of fire on their heads, and also in order to lure rebels living in the very last days into a final rebellion against God.

Final Judgment and Common Grace

An understanding of common grace is essential for an understanding of the final act of human history before the judgment of God. To

646

the extent that this essay contributes anything new to Christian theology, it is its contribution to an understanding of the final rebellion of the unregenerate. The final rebellion has been used by those opposing postmillennialism as final proof that there will be no faith on earth among the masses of men when Christ returns. The devil shall be loosed for a little season at the end of time, meaning his power over the nations returns to him in full strength (Rev. 20:3). However, this rebellion is short-lived. He surrounds the holy city (meaning the church of the faithful), only to be cut down in final judgment (Rev. 20:7-15). Therefore, conclude the critics of postmillennialism, there is a resounding negative answer to Christ's question: "Nevertheless when the Son of man cometh, shall he find faith on earth" (Luke 18:8)? Where, then, is the supposed victory?

The doctrine of common grace provides us with the biblical answer. *God's law is the main form of common grace.* It is written in the hearts of believers, we read in Hebrews, chapters eight and ten, but the work of the law is written in the heart of every man. Thus, the work of the law is universal — common. This access to God's law is the foundation of the fulfilling of the dominion covenant to subdue the earth (Gen. 1:28). The command was given to all men through Adam; it was reaffirmed by God with the family of Noah (Gen. 9:1-7). God's promises of external blessings are conditional to man's fulfillment of external laws. The reason why men can gain the blessings is because the knowledge of the work of the law is common. This is why there can be outward cooperation between Christians and non-Christians for certain earthly ends.

From time to time, unbelievers are enabled by God to adhere more closely to the work of the law that is written in their hearts. These periods of cultural adherence can last for centuries, at least with respect to some aspects of human culture (the arts, science, philosophy). The Greeks maintained a high level of culture inside the limited confines of the Greek city-states for a few centuries. The Chinese maintained their culture until it grew stagnant, in response to Confucian philosophy, in what we call the Middle Ages. But in the West, the ability of the unregenerate to act in closer conformity to the work of the law written in their hearts has been the result of the historical leadership provided by the cultural triumph of Christianity. In short, special grace increased, leading to an extension of common grace throughout Western culture. Economic growth has increased; indeed, the concept of linear, compound growth is unique to the West, and the foundations of this belief were laid by the Reformers who held to the eschatology known as postmillennialism. Longer lifespans have also appeared in the West, primarily due to the application of technology to living conditions.

Applied technology is, in turn, a product of Christianity[11] and especially Protestant Christianity.[12]

In the era prophesied by Isaiah, unbelievers will once again come to know the benefits of God's law. No longer shall they twist God's revelation to them. *The churl shall no longer be called liberal.* Law will be respected by unbelievers. This means that they will turn away from an open, consistent worship of the gods of chaos and the philosophy of ultimate randomness, including evolutionary randomness. They will participate in the blessings brought to them by the preaching of the whole counsel of God, including His law. The earth will be subdued to the glory of God, including the cultural world. Unbelievers will fulfil their roles in the achievement of the terms of the dominion covenant.

This is why a theology that is orthodox must include a doctrine of common grace that is intimately related to biblical law. Law does not save men's souls, but *it does save their bodies and their culture.* Christ is the savior of all, especially those who are the elect (I Tim. 4:10).

Antinomian Revivalism vs. Reconstruction

The blessings and cultural victory taught by the Bible (and adequately commented upon by postmillennialists) will not be the products of some form of pietistic, semi-monastic revivalism. The "merely soteriological" preaching of pietism — the salvation of souls by special grace — is not sufficient to bring the victories foretold in the Bible. The whole counsel of God must and will be preached. This means that the law of God will be preached. The external blessings will come in response to covenantal faithfulness of God's people. The majority of men will be converted. The unconverted will not follow their philosophy of chaos to logical conclusions, for such a philosophy leads to ultimate impotence. It throws away the tool of reconstruction, biblical law.

The great defect with the postmillennial revival inaugurated by Jonathan Edwards and his followers in the eighteenth century was their neglect of biblical law. They expected to see the blessings of God

---

11. Stanley Jaki, *The Road of Science and the Ways to God* (Chicago: University of Chicago Press, 1978); *Science and Creation: From eternal cycles to an oscillating universe* (Edinburgh and London: Scottish Academic Press, [1974] 1980).

12. Robert K. Merton, *Social Theory and Social Structure* (rev. ed.; New York: Free Press of Glencoe, 1957), ch. 18: "Puritanism, Pietism, and Science"; E. L. Hebden Taylor, "The Role of Puritanism-Calvinism in the Rise of Modern Science," *The Journal of Christian Reconstruction*, VI (Summer 1979); Charles Dykes, "Medieval Speculation, Puritanism, and Modern Science," *ibid*.

come as a result of merely soteriological preaching. Look at Edwards' *Treatise on the Religious Affections*. There is nothing on the law of God in culture. Page after page is filled with the words "sweet" and "sweetness." A diabetic reader is almost risking a relapse by reading this book in one sitting. The words sometimes appear four or five times on a page. And while Edwards was preaching the sweetness of God, Arminian semi-literates were "hot-gospeling" the Holy Commonwealth of Connecticut into political antinomianism.[13] Where sweetness and emotional hot flashes are concerned, Calvinistic preaching is no match for antinomian sermons. The hoped-for revival of the 1700s became the Arminian revivals of the early 1800s, leaving emotionally burned-over districts, cults, and the abolitionist movement as their devastating legacy. Because the postmillennial preaching of the Edwardians was culturally antinomian and pietistic, it crippled the remnants of Calvinistic political order in the New England colonies, helping to produce a vacuum that Arminianism and then Unitarianism filled.

Progress culturally, economically, and politically is intimately linked to the extension and application of biblical law. The blessings promised in Romans, chapter eleven, concerning the effects of the promised conversion of Israel (not necessarily the state of Israel) to the gospel, will be in part the product of biblical law.[14] But these bless-

---

13. On the opposition to Edwards' toleration of revivalism, not from theological liberals but from orthodox Calvinistic pastors, see Richard L. Bushman, *From Puritan to Yankee* (Cambridge, Massachusetts: Harvard University Press, 1967). Bushman also explains how the Great Awakening was a disaster for the legal remnants of biblical law in the colony of Connecticut. The political order was forced into theological neutralism, which in turn aided the rise of Deism and liberalism.

14. John Murray's excellent commentary, *The Epistle to the Romans* (Grand Rapids, Michigan: Eerdmans, 1965), contains an extensive analysis of Romans 11, the section dealing with the future conversion of the Jews. Murray stresses that God's regrafting in of Israel leads to covenantal blessings unparalleled in human history. But the Israel referred to in Romans 11, argues Murray, is not national or political Israel, but the natural seed of Abraham. This seems to mean genetic Israel.

A major historical problem appears at this point. There is some evidence (though not conclusive) that the bulk of those known today as Askenazi Jews are the heirs of a converted tribe of Turkish people, the Khazars. It is well-known among European history scholars that such a conversion took place around 740 A.D. The Eastern European and Russian Jews may have come from this stock. They have married other Jews, however: the Sephardic or diaspora Jews who fled primarily to western Europe. The Yemenite Jews, who stayed in the land of Palestine, also are descendants of Abraham. The counter-evidence against this thesis of the Khazars as modern Jews is primarily linguistic: Yiddish does not bear traces of any Turkic language. On the

ings do not necessarily include universal regeneration. The blessings only require the extension of Christian culture. For the long-term progress of culture, of course, this increase of common grace (or reduction of the common curse) must be reinforced (rejuvenated and renewed) by special grace — conversions. But the blessings can remain for a generation or more after special grace has been removed, and as far as the external benefits can be measured, it will not be possible to tell whether the blessings are part of the *positive feedback program* (Deut. 8:18) or a *prelude to God's judgment* (Deut. 8:19-20). God respects His conditional, external covenants. External conformity to His law gains external blessings. These, in the last analysis (and at the last judgment), produce coals for unregenerate heads.

Universal Regeneration?

The postmillennial system requires a doctrine of common grace and common curse. It does not require a doctrine of universal regeneration during the period of millennial blessings. In fact, no postmillennial Calvinist can afford to be without a doctrine of common grace — one which links *external* blessings to the fulfillment of *external* covenants. There has to be a period of external blessings during the final generation. Something must hold that culture together so that Satan can once again go forth and deceive the nations. The Calvinist denies that men can "lose their salvation," meaning their regenerate status. The rebels are not "formerly regenerate" men. But they are men with power, or at least the trappings of power. They are powerful enough to delude themselves that they can destroy the people of God. And power, as I have tried to emphasize throughout this essay, is not the product of antinomian or chaos-oriented philosophy. The very existence of a military chain of command demands a concept of law and order. Satan commands an army on that final day.

The postmillennial vision of the future paints a picture of historically incomparable blessings. It also tells of a final rebellion that leads to God's total and final judgment. Like the long-lived men in the days of Methuselah, judgment comes upon them in the midst of power, prosperity, and external blessings. God has been gracious to them all to the utmost of His common grace. He has been gracious in response to their covenantal faithfulness to His *civil* law-order, and He has been

---

kingdom of the Khazars, see Arthur Koestler, *The Thirteenth Tribe: The Khazar Empire and Its Heritage* (New York: Random House, 1976).

If the Israel referred to in Romans 11 is primarily genetic, then it may not be necessary that all Jews be converted. What, then, is the Jew in Romans 11? Covenantal? I wrote to Murray in the late 1960s to get his opinion on the implications of the Khazars for his exegesis of Romans 11, but he did not respond.

gracious in order to pile the maximum possible pile of coals on their heads. In contrast to Van Til's amillennialist vision of the future, we must say: *When common grace is extended to its maximum limits possible in history, then the crack of doom has come—doom for the rebels.*

Epistemological Self-Consciousness and Cooperation

Van Til writes: "But when all the reprobate are epistemologically self-conscious, the crack of doom has come. The fully self-conscious reprobate will do all he can in every dimension to destroy the people of God." Yet Van Til has written in another place that the rebel against God is like a little child who has to sit on his father's lap in order to slap his face. What, then, can be meant by the concept of increasing epistemological self-consciousness?

As the wheat and tares grow to maturity, the amillennialist argues, the tares become stronger and stronger culturally, while the wheat becomes weaker and weaker. Consider what is being said. As Christians work out their own salvation with fear and trembling, improving their creeds, improving their cooperation with each other on the basis of agreement about the creeds, as they learn about the law of God as it applies in their own era, as they become skilled in applying the law of God that they have learned about, they become culturally impotent. They become infertile, also, it would seem. They do not become fruitful and multiply. Or if they do their best to follow this commandment, they are left without the blessing of God—a blessing which He has promised to those who follow the laws He has established. In short, the increase of epistemological self-consciousness on the part of Christians leads to cultural impotence.

I am faced with an unpleasant conclusion: *the amillennialist version of the common grace doctrine is inescapably antinomian.* It argues that God no longer respects His covenantal law-order, that Deuteronomy's teaching about covenantal law is invalid in New Testament times. The only way for the amillennialist to avoid the charge of antinomianism is for him to abandon the concept of increasing epistemological self-consciousness. He must face the fact that to achieve cultural impotence, Christians therefore must not increase in knowledge and covenantal faithfulness. (Admittedly, the condition of twentieth-century Christianity does appear to enforce this attitude about epistemological self-consciousness among Christians.)

Consider the other half of Van Til's dictum. As the epistemological self-consciousness of the unregenerate increases, and they adhere more and more to their epistemological premises of the origins of matter out of chaos, and the ultimate return of all matter into pure randomness, this chaos philosophy makes them confident. The Christian is humble before God, but confident before the creation which he is to subdue. This confidence leads the Christian into defeat and ultimate disaster, say amillennialists, who believe in increasing epistemological self-consciousness. On the other hand, the rebel is arrogant before God and claims that all nature is ruled by the meaningless laws of probability—ultimate chaos. By immersing themselves in the philosophy of chaos, the unbelievers are able to emerge totally victorious across the whole face of the earth, says the amillennialist, a victory which is called to a halt only by the physical intervention of Jesus Christ at the final judgment. A commitment to lawlessness, in the amillennial version of common grace, leads to external victory. How can these things be?

Amillennialism Has Things Backwards

It should be clear by now that the amillennialist version of the relationship between biblical law and the creation is completely backwards. No doubt Satan wishes it were a true version. He wants his followers to believe it. But how can a consistent Christian believe it? How can a Christian believe that adherence to biblical law produces cultural impotence, while commitment to philosophical chaos—the religion of satanic revolution—leads to cultural victory? There is no doubt in my mind that the amillennialists do not want to teach such a doctrine, yet that is where their amillennial pessimism inevitably leads. Dutch Calvinists preach the cultural mandate (dominion covenant), but they simultaneously preach that it cannot be fulfilled. But biblical law is basic to the fulfillment of the cultural mandate. Therefore, the amillennialist who preaches the obligation of trying to fulfil the cultural mandate without biblical law thereby plunges himself either into the camp of the chaos cults (mystics, revolutionaries) or into the camp of the natural-law, common-ground philosophers. There are only four possibilities: revealed law, natural law, chaos, or a mixture.

This leads me to my next point. It is somewhat speculative and may not be completely accurate. It is an idea which ought to be pursued, however, to see if it is accurate. I think that the reason why the philosophy of Herman Dooyeweerd, the Dutch philosopher of law, had some temporary impact in Dutch Calvinist intellectual circles in the late 1960s and early 1970s is that Dooyeweerd's theory of sphere sovereignty—sphere laws that are *not* to be filled in by means of revealed, Old Testament law—is consistent with the amillennial (Dutch) version of the cultural mandate. Dooyeweerd's system and Dutch amillennialism are essentially antinomian. This is why I wrote my 1967 essay, "Social Antinomianism," in response to the Dooyeweerdian

652

professor at the Free University of Amsterdam, A. Troost.[15]

Either the Dooyeweerdians wind up as mystics, or else they try to create a new kind of "common-ground philosophy" to link believers and unbelievers. It is Dooyeweerd's outspoken resistance to Old Testament and New Testament authority over the *content* of his hypothesized sphere laws that has led his increasingly radical, increasingly antinomian followers into anti-Christian paths. You cannot preach the dominion covenant and then turn around and deny the efficacy of biblical law in culture. Yet this is what all the Dutch adherents to common grace have done. They deny the cultural efficacy of biblical law, by necessity, because their eschatological interpretations have led them to conclude that there can be no external, cultural victory in time and on earth by faithful Christians. Epistemological self-consciousness will increase, but things only get worse over time.

If you preach that biblical law produces "positive feedback," both personally and culturally—that God rewards covenant-keepers and punishes covenant-breakers in time and on earth—then you are preaching a system of positive growth. You are preaching the dominion covenant. Only if you deny that there is any relationship between covenant-keeping and external success in life—a denial made explicit by Meredith G. Kline[16]—can you escape from the postmillennial implications of biblical law. This is why it is odd that Greg Bahnsen insists—perhaps for tactical reasons—on presenting his defense of biblical law apart from his well-known postmillennialism.[17] Kline attacked

---

15. Gary North, *The Sinai Strategy: Economics and the Ten Commandments* (Tyler, Texas: Institute for Christian Economics, 1986), Appendix C: "Social Antinomianism."

16. Kline says that any connection between blessings and covenant-keeping is, humanly speaking, random. "And meanwhile it [the common grace order] must run its course within the uncertainties of the mutually conditioning principles of common grace and common curse, prosperity and adversity being experienced in a manner largely unpredictable because of the inscrutable sovereignty of the divine will that dispenses them in mysterious ways." Kline, *op. cit.*, p. 184. Dr. Kline has obviously never considered just why it is that life insurance premiums and health insurance premiums are cheaper in Christian-influenced societies than in pagan societies. Apparently, the blessings of long life that are promised in the Bible are sufficiently non-random and "scrutable" that statisticians who advise insurance companies can detect statistically relevant differences between societies.

17. "What these studies present is a position in Christian (normative) *ethics*. They do *not* logically commit those who agree with them to any particular school of *eschatological* interpretation." Greg L. Bahnsen, *By This Standard: The Authority of God's Law Today* (Tyler, Texas: Institute for Christian Economics, 1985), p. 8. He is correct: *logically*, there is no connection. *Covenantally*, the two doctrines are inescapable: when the law is preached, there are blessings; blessings lead inescapably to victory.

both of Bahnsen's doctrines in his critique of *Theonomy*,[18] and Bahnsen in his rebuttal essay did respond to Kline's criticisms of his postmillennial eschatology, but he again denies that eschatology has anything logically to do with biblical ethics.[19] But Kline was correct: there is unquestionably a necessary connection between a *covenantal* concept of biblical law and eschatology. Kline rejects the idea of a New Testament covenantal law-order, and he also rejects postmillennialism.

Amillennial Calvinists will continue to be plagued by Dooyeweerdians, mystics, natural-law compromisers, and antinomians of all sorts until they finally abandon their amillennial eschatology. Furthermore, biblical law must be preached. It must be seen as the tool of cultural reconstruction. It must be seen as operating *now*, in New Testament times. It must be seen that there is a relationship between covenantal faithfulness and obedience to law — that without obedience there is no faithfulness, no matter how emotional believers may become, or how sweet the gospel tastes (for a while). And there are blessings that follow obedience to God's law-order. Amillennialists, by preaching eschatological impotence culturally, thereby immerse themselves in quicksand — the quicksand of antinomianism. Some sands are quicker than others. Eventually, they swallow up anyone so foolish as to try to walk through them. Antinomianism leads into the pits of impotence and retreat.

Epistemological Self-Consciousness

What is meant by epistemological self-consciousness? It means a greater understanding over time of what one's presuppositions are, and a greater willingness to put these presuppositions into action. It affects both wheat and tares.

In what ways does the wheat resemble the tares? In what ways are they different? The angels saw the differences immediately. God therefore restrained them from ripping up the tares. He wanted to preserve the soil — the historical process. Therefore, the full development of both wheat and tares is permitted by God.

What must be understood here is that *the doctrine of special grace in history necessarily involves the doctrine of common grace*. As the Christians develop to maturity, they become more powerful. This is not a straight-line development. There are times of locusts and blight and drought, both for Christians and for satanists (humanists). There

---

18. Kline, *op. cit.*

19. Greg L. Bahnsen, "M. G. Kline on Theonomic Politics: An Evaluation of His Reply," *Journal of Christian Reconstruction*, VI (Winter, 1979-80), No. 2, especially p. 215.

is ebb and flow, but always there is direction to the movement. There is maturity. The creeds are improved. This, in turn, gives Christians cultural power. Is it any wonder that the Westminster Confession of Faith was drawn up at the high point of the Puritans' control of England? Are improvements in the creeds useless culturally? Do improvements in creeds and theological understanding necessarily lead to impotence culturally? Nonsense! It was the Reformation that made possible modern science and technology.

On the other side of the field—indeed, right next to the wheat—self-awareness by unbelievers also increases. But they do not always become more convinced of their roots in chaos. The Renaissance was successful in swallowing up the fruits of the Reformation only to the extent that it was a pale reflection of the Reformation. The Renaissance leaders rapidly abandoned the magic-charged, demonically inspired magicians like Giordano Bruno.[20] They may have kept the humanism of a Bruno, but after 1600, the open commitment to the demonic receded. In its place came rationalism, Deism, and the logic of an orderly world. They used stolen premises and gained power. So compelling was this vision of mathematically autonomous reality that Christians like Cotton Mather hailed the new science of Newtonian mechanics as essentially Christian. It was so close to Christian views of God's orderly being and the creation's reflection of His orderliness, that the Christians unhesitatingly embraced the new science.

What we see, then, is that the Christians were not fully self-conscious epistemologically, and neither were the pagans. In the time of the apostles, there was greater epistemological awareness among the leaders of both sides. The church was persecuted, and it won. Then there was a lapse into muddled thinking on both sides. The attempt, for example, of Julian the Apostate to revive paganism late in the fourth century was ludicrous—it was half-hearted paganism, at best. Two centuries earlier, Marcus Aurelius, a true philosopher-king in the tradition of Plato, had been a major persecutor of Christians; Justin Martyr died under his years as emperor. But his debauched son, Commodus, was too busy with his 300 female concubines and 300 males[21] to bother about systematic persecutions. Who was more self-conscious, epistemologically speaking? Aurelius still had the light of reason before him; his son was immersed in the religion of revolution —culturally impotent. He was more willing than his philosopher-persecutor father to follow the logic of his satanic faith. He preferred

---

20. On the magic of the early Renaissance, see Frances Yates, *Giordano Bruno and the Hermetic Tradition* (New York: Vintage, [1964] 1969).

21. Edward Gibbon, *The History of the Decline and Fall of the Roman Empire*, Milman edition, 5 Vols. (Philadelphia: Porter & Coates, [1776]), I, p. 144.

655

debauchery to power. Commodus was assassinated 13 years after he became Emperor. The Senate resolved that his name be execrated.[22]

If a modern investigator would like to see as fully consistent a pagan culture as one might imagine, he could visit the African tribe, the Ik. Colin Turnbull did, and his book, *The Mountain People* (1973), is a classic. He found almost total rebellion against law — family law, civic law, all law. Yet he also found a totally impotent, beaten people who were rapidly becoming extinct. They were harmless to the West because they were more self-consistent than the West's satanists.

The Marxist Challenge

Marxists, on the other hand, *are* a threat. They believe in linear history (officially, anyway — their system is at bottom cyclical, however).[23] They believe in law. They believe in destiny. They believe in historical meaning. They believe in historical stages, though not ethically determined stages such as we find in Deuteronomy. They believe in science. They believe in literature, propaganda, and the power of the written word. They believe in higher education. In short, they have a philosophy which is a kind of perverse mirror image of Christian orthodoxy. They are dangerous, not because they are acting consistently with their ultimate philosophy of chaos, but because they limit the function of chaos to one area alone: the revolutionary transformation of bourgeois culture. (I am speaking here primarily of Soviet Marxists.) And where are they winning converts? In the increasingly impotent, increasingly existentialist, increasingly antinomian West. Until the West abandoned its remnant of Christian culture, Marxism could flourish only in the underdeveloped, basically pagan areas of the world. An essentially Western philosophy of optimism found converts among the intellectuals of the Far East, Africa, and Latin America, who saw the fruitlessness of Confucian stagnation and relativism, the impotence of demonic ritual, or the dead-end nature of demon worship. Marxism is powerful only to the extent that it has the trappings of Augustinianism, coupled with subsidies, especially technological subsidies and long-term credit, from Western industry.

There is irony here. Marx believed that "scientific socialism" would triumph only in those nations that had experienced the full development of capitalism. He believed that in most cases (possibly excepting Russia), rural areas had to abandon feudalism and develop a fully

---

22. Ethelbert Stauffer, *Christ and the Caesars* (Philadelphia: Westminster Press, 1955), p. 223.

23. Gary North, *Marx's Religion of Revolution: The Doctrine of Creative Destruction* (Nutley, New Jersey: Craig Press, 1968), pp. 100-1.

COMMON GRACE, ESCHATOLOGY, AND BIBLICAL LAW

capitalist culture before the socialist revolution would be successful. Yet it was primarily in the rural regions of the world that Marxist ideas and groups were first successful. The industrialized West was still too Christian or too pragmatic (recognizing that "honesty is the best policy") to capitulate to the Marxists, except immediately following a lost war.

Marxists have long dominated the faculties of Latin American universities, but not U.S. universities. In 1964, for example, there were not half a dozen outspoken Marxist economists teaching in American universities (and possibly as few as one, Stanford's Paul Baran). Since 1965, however, New Left scholars of a Marxist persuasion have become a force to be reckoned with in all the social sciences, including economics.[24] The skepticism, pessimism, relativism, and irrelevance of modern "neutral" education have left faculties without an adequate defense against confident, shrill, vociferous Marxists, primarily young Marxists, who began to appear on the campuses after 1964. Epistemological rot has left the establishment campus liberals with little more than tenure to protect them.[25]

Since 1965, however, Marxism has made more inroads among the young intellectuals of the industrialized West than at any time since the 1930s—an earlier era of pessimism and skepticism about established values and traditions. Marxists are successful among savages, whether in Africa or at Harvard—epistemological savages. Marxism offers an alternative to despair. It has the trappings of optimism. It has the trappings of Christianity. It is still a nineteenth-century system, drawing on the intellectual capital of a more Christian intellectual universe. These trappings of Christian order are the source of Marxism's influence in an increasingly relativistic world.

Satan's Final Rebellion

In the last days of this final era in human history, the satanists will still have the trappings of Christian order about them. Satan has to sit on God's lap, so to speak, in order to slap His face—or try to. Satan cannot be consistent to his own philosophy of autonomous order and still be a threat to God. An autonomous order leads to chaos and impotence. He knows that there is no neutral ground in philosophy. He knew Adam and Eve would die spiritually on the day that they ate the fruit. He is a good enough theologian to know that there is one God,

---

24. Martin Bronfenbrenner, "Radical Economics in America: A 1970 Survey," *Journal of Economic Literature*, VIII (Sept. 1970).

25. Gary North, "The Epistemological Crisis of American Universities," in Gary North (ed.), *Foundations of Christian Scholarship: Essays in the Van Til Perspective* (Vallecito, California: Ross House Books, 1976).

and he and his host tremble at the thought (James 2:19). When demonic men take seriously his lies about the nature of reality, they become impotent, sliding off (or nearly off) God's lap. It is when satanists realize that Satan's official philosophy of chaos and antinomian lawlessness is a *lie* that they become dangerous. (Marxists, once again, are more dangerous to America than are the Ik.) They learn more of the truth, but they pervert it and try to use it against God's people.

Thus, the biblical meaning of epistemological self-consciousness is not that the satanist becomes consistent with Satan's official philosophy (chaos), but rather that Satan's host becomes consistent with what Satan really believes: that order, law, power are the product of God's hated order. They learn to use law and order to build an army of conquest. In short, *they use common grace—knowledge of the truth—to pervert the truth and to attack God's people.* They turn from a false knowledge offered to them by Satan, and they adopt a perverted form of truth to use in their rebellious plans. They *mature*, in other words. Or, as C. S. Lewis has put into the mouth of his fictitious character, the senior devil Screwtape, when materialists finally believe in Satan but not in God, then the war is over.[26] Not quite; when they believe in God, know He is going to win, and nevertheless strike out in fury— not blind fury, but *fully self-conscious fury*—at the works of God, *then* the war is over.

Cooperation

How, then, can we cooperate with such men? Simply on the basis of common grace. *Common grace has not yet fully developed.* But this cooperation must be in the interests of God's kingdom. Whether or not a particular *ad hoc* association is beneficial must be made in terms of standards set forth in biblical law. Common grace is not common ground; there is no common ground uniting men except for the image of God in every man.

Because external conformity to the terms of biblical law does produce visibly good results—contrary to Prof. Kline's theory of God's mysterious will in history—unbelievers for a time are willing to adopt these principles, since they seek the fruits of Christian culture. In short, some ethical satanists respond to the knowledge of God's law written in their hearts. They have a large degree of knowledge about God's creation, but they are not yet willing to attack that world. They have knowledge through common grace, but they do not yet see what

---

26. C. S. Lewis, *The Screwtape Letters* (New York: Macmillan, 1969), Letter 7.

658

this means for their own actions. (To some extent, the Communists see, but they have not yet followed through; they have not launched a final assault against the West.)

The essence of Adam's rebellion was not intellectual; it was *ethical*. No one has argued this more forcefully than Van Til. The mere addition of knowledge to or by the unregenerate man does not alter the essence of his status before God. He is still a rebel, but he may possess knowledge. Knowledge can be applied to God's creation and produce beneficial results. Knowledge can also produce a holocaust. The issue is ethics, not knowledge. Thus, men can cooperate in terms of mutually shared knowledge; ultimately, they cannot cooperate in terms of a mutually shared ethics.

What of the *special curse*? What is the ethical rebel's ethical relation to God? Common grace increases the unregenerate man's special curse. When common grace increases to its maximum, the special curse of God is revealed: total rebellion of man against the *truth* of God and *in terms of the common grace*—knowledge, power, wealth, prestige, etc.—of God, leading to final judgment. God does remove part of His restraint at the very end: the restraint on suicidal destruction. He allows them to achieve that death which they love (Prov. 8:36b). But they still have power and wealth, as in the Babylonian Empire the night it fell.

Pagans can teach us about physics, mathematics, chemistry, and many other topics. How is this possible? Because common grace has increased. They had several centuries of leadership from Christians, as well as Enlightenment figures who adopted a philosophy of coherence that at least resembled the Christian doctrine of providence. They cannot hold the culture together in terms of their philosophy of chaos—Satan's official viewpoint—but they still can make important discoveries. They use stolen capital, in every sense.

Christians Must Lead

When there is Christian revival and the preaching and application of the whole counsel of God, then Christians can once again take the position of real leadership. The unbelievers also can make contributions to the subduing of the earth because they will be called back to the work of the law written in their hearts. Common grace will increase throughout the world. But Christians must be extremely careful to watch for signs of ethical deviation from those who seemingly are useful co-workers in the kingdom. There can be cooperation for external goals—the fulfilling of the dominion covenant which was given to all men—but not in the realm of ethics. We must watch the Soviets to see how *not* to build a society. We must construct countermeasures to their military offenses. We must not adopt their view of proletarian ethics, even though their chess players or mathematicians may show us a great deal. The law of God as revealed in the Bible must be dominant, not the work of the law written in the hearts of the unrighteous. The way to cooperate is on the basis of biblical law. The law tells us of the limitations on man. It keeps us humble before God and dominant over nature. We shall determine the accuracy and usefulness of the works of unregenerate men who are exercising their God-given talents, working out their damnation with fear and trembling.

Strangers within the gates were given many of the benefits of common grace — God's response to the conversion of the Hebrews. They received full legal protection in Hebrew courts (Ex. 22:21; 23:9; Deut. 24:17). They were not permitted to eat special holy foods (Ex. 29:33; Lev. 22:10), thereby sealing them off from the religious celebrations of the temple. But they were part of the feast of the tithe, a celebration before the Lord (Deut. 14:22-29). Thus, they were beneficiaries of the civil order that God established for His people. They also could produce goods and services in confidence that the fruits of their labor would not be confiscated from them by a lawless civil government. This made everyone richer, for all men in the community could work out the terms of the dominion covenant.

We are told that the natural man does not receive the things of the Spirit (I Cor. 2:14-16). We are told that God's wisdom is seen as foolishness by the unregenerate (I Cor. 1:18-21). We are told to beware, "lest any man spoil you through philosophy and vain deceit, after the tradition of men, after the rudiments of the world, and not after Christ" (Col. 2:8). There is an unbridgeable separation philosophically between unbelievers and believers. They begin with different starting points: chaos vs. creation, God vs. man. Only common grace can reduce the conflict *in application* between pagan and Christian philosophy. The ethical rebellion of the unregenerate lies beneath the surface, smoldering, ready to flare up in wrath, but he is restrained by God and God's law. He needs the power that law provides. Therefore, he assents to some of the principles of applied biblical law and conforms himself to part of the work of the law that is written on his heart. But on first principles, he cannot agree. And even near the end, when men may confess the existence of one God and tremble at the thought, they will not submit their egos to that God. They will fight to the death — to the second death — to deny the claims that the God of the Bible has over every part of their being.

Thus, there can be cooperation in the subduing of the earth. But Christians must set forth the strategy and the tactics. The unregenerate man will be like a paid consultant; he will provide his talents, but the Lord will build the culture.

Common Grace vs. Common Ground

We must not argue from common grace to common ground. We cannot do so because with the increase of common grace we come closer to that final rebellion in all its satanic might. Common grace combines the efforts of men in the subduing of the earth, but Christians work for the glory of God openly, while the unregenerate work (officially) for the glory of man or the glory of Satan. They do, in fact, work to the glory of God, for on that last day every knee shall bow to Him (Phil. 2:10). The wealth of the wicked is laid up for the just (Prov. 13:22). So there are no common facts, ethically speaking.

At that final day, when their rebellion begins, all of Satan's host will know about the facts of God's world, for common grace will be at its peak. Nevertheless, they turn their backs on God and rebel. All facts are interpreted facts, and the *interpretation*, not the facts as such — there are no "facts as such" — is what separates the lost from the elect. Inevitably, the natural man holds *back* (actively suppresses) the truth in unrighteousness (Rom. 1:18).[27] No philosophical "proofs" of God (other than a proof which begins by assuming the existence of the God revealed in the Bible) are valid, and even the assumption of the existence of the God of the Bible is not sufficient to save a man's soul.[28] Only God can do that (John 6:44). There is no common ground philosophically, only metaphysically. We are made in God's image by a common Creator (Acts 17:24-31). Every man knows this. We can, as men, only remind all men of what they know. God uses that knowledge to redeem men.

The unbeliever uses *stolen intellectual capital* to reason correctly — correctly in the sense of being able to use that knowledge as a tool to subdue the earth, not in the sense of knowing God as an adopted son knows Him. His conclusions can correspond to external reality sufficiently to allow him to work out his rebellious faith to even greater destruction than if he had not had accurate knowledge (Luke 12:47-48). He "knows" somehow that "2 plus 2 equals 4," and also that this fact of mental symmetry can be used to cause desired effects in the external realm of nature. Why this mental symmetry should exist, and why it should bear any relation to the external realm of nature, is unexplainable by the knowledge of natural man, a fact admitted by

---

27. Murray, *Romans*, commenting on Romans 1:18.

28. Van Til, *The Defense of the Faith* (Philadelphia: Presbyterian and Reformed, 1963), attacks the traditional Roman Catholic and Arminian proofs of God. They do not prove the God of the Bible, he argues, only a finite god of the human mind.

661

Nobel prize-winning physicist, Eugene Wigner.[29]

Christians, because they have a proper doctrine of creation, can explain both. So the unbeliever uses borrowed intellectual capital at every step. Christians can use some of his work (by checking his findings against the revelation in the Bible), and the unbeliever can use the work of Christians. The earth will be subdued. The closer the unbeliever's presuppositions are to those revealed in the Bible (such as the conservative economist's assumption of the fact of economic scarcity, corresponding to Gen. 3:17-19), the more likely that the discoveries made in terms of that assumption will be useful. By useful, I mean useful in the common task of all men, subduing the earth. Thus, there can be cooperation between Christians and non-Christians.

Conclusion

Unbelievers appear to be culturally dominant today. Believers have retreated into antinomian pietism and pessimism, for they have abandoned faith in the two features of Christian social philosophy that make progress possible: 1) the dynamic of *eschatological optimism*, and 2) the tool of the dominion covenant, *biblical law*. We should conclude, then, that either the dissolution of culture is at hand (for the common grace of the unregenerate cannot long be sustained without leadership in the realm of culture from the regenerate), or else the regenerate must regain sight of their lost truths: postmillennialism and biblical law. For common grace to continue, and for external cooperation between believers and unbelievers to be fruitful or even possible, Christians must call the external culture's guidelines back to God's law. They must regain the leadership they forfeited to the speculations of self-proclaimed "reasonable" apostates. If this is not done, then we will slide back once more, until the unbelievers resemble the Ik and the Christians can begin the process of cultural domination once more. For common grace to continue to increase, it must be sustained by special grace. Either unbelievers will be converted, or leadership will flow back toward the Christians. If neither happens, we will return eventually to barbarism.

Understandably, I pray for the regeneration of the ungodly *and* the rediscovery of biblical law and accurate biblical eschatology on the part of present Christians and future converts. Whether we will see such a revival in our day is unknown to me. There are reasons to be-

---

29. Eugene Wigner, "The Unreasonable Effectiveness of Mathematics in the Natural Sciences," *Communications on Pure and Applied Mathematics* XIII (1960), pp. 1-14. See also Vern Poythress, "A Biblical View of Mathematics," in Gary North (ed.), *Foundations of Christian Scholarship, op. cit.,* ch. 9. See also his essay in *The Journal of Christian Reconstruction*, I (Summer 1974).

lieve that it can and will happen. There are also reasons to doubt such optimism. The Lord knows.

We must abandon antinomianism and eschatologies that are inherently antinomian. We must call men back to faith in the God of the whole Bible. We must affirm that in the plan of God there will come a day of increased self-awareness, when men will call churls churlish and liberal men gracious (Isa. 32). This will be a day of great external blessings—the greatest in history. Long ages of such self-awareness unfold before us. And at the end of time comes a generation of rebels who know churls from liberals and strike out against the godly. They will lose the war.

Therefore, *common grace* is essentially *future grace*. There is an ebb and flow throughout history, but essentially it is future grace. It must not be seen as essentially prior or earlier grace. Only amillennialists can hold to such a position—antinomian amillennialists at that. The final judgment appears at the end of time against the backdrop of common grace. The *common curse* will be at its *lowest* point, the prelude to *special cursing* of eternal duration. The final judgment comes, just as the great flood came, against a background of God's external benefits to mankind in general. The iniquity of the Amorites will at last be full.

Does the postmillennialist believe that there will be faith in general on the earth when Christ appears? Not if he understands the implications of the doctrine of common grace. Does he expect the whole earth to be destroyed by the unbelieving rebels before Christ strikes them dead—doubly dead? No. The judgment comes before they can do their work. Common grace is extended to allow unbelievers to fill up their cup of wrath. They are vessels of wrath. Therefore, the fulfilling of the terms of the dominion covenant through common grace is the final step in the process of filling up these vessels of wrath. The vessels of grace, believers, will also be filled. Everything is full. Will God destroy His preliminary down payment on the New Heavens and the New Earth? Will God erase the sign that His word has been obeyed, that the dominion covenant has been fulfilled? Will Satan, that great destroyer, have the joy of seeing God's word thwarted, his handiwork torn down by Satan's very hordes? The amillennialist answers yes. The postmillennialist must deny it with all his strength.

There is continuity in life, despite discontinuities. The wealth of the sinner is laid up for the just. Satan would like to burn up God's field, but he cannot. The tares and wheat grow to maturity, and then the reapers go out to harvest the wheat, cutting away the chaff and tossing chaff into the fire. Satan would like to turn back the crack of doom, return to ground zero, return to the garden of Eden, when the dominion covenant was first given. The fulfillment of the dominion covenant is the final act of Satan that is positive—an extension of common grace. After that, common grace becomes malevolent—absolutely malevolent—as Satan uses the last of his time and the last of his power to strike out against God's people. When he uses his gifts to become finally, totally destructive, he is cut down from above. *This final culmination of common grace is Satan's crack of doom.*

And the meek—meek before God, active toward His creation—shall at last inherit the earth. A renewed earth and renewed heaven is the final payment by God the Father to His Son and to those He has given to His Son. This is the postmillennial hope.

Postscript

By now, I have alienated every known Christian group. I have alienated the remaining Christian Reformed Church members who are orthodox by siding with the Protestant Reformed Church against Point 1 of the 1924 Synod. There is no favor in God's common grace. I have alienated the Protestant Reformed Church by arguing for postmillennialism. I have alienated the premillennialists by arguing that the separation between wheat and tares must come at the end of history, not a thousand years before the end (or, in the dispensational, pretribulational premillennial framework, 1007 years before). I have alienated postmillennial pietists who read and delight in the works of Jonathan Edwards by arguing that Edwards' tradition was destructive to biblical law in 1740 and still is. It leads nowhere unless it matures and adopts the concept of biblical law as a tool of victory. I have alienated the Bible Presbyterian Church, since its leaders deny the dominion covenant. Have I missed anyone? Oh, yes, I have alienated postmillennial Arminians ("positive confession" charismatics) by arguing that the rebels in the last day are not backslidden Christians.

Having accomplished this, I hope that others will follow through on the outline I have sketched relating common grace, eschatology, and biblical law. Let those few who take this essay seriously avoid the theological land mines that still clutter up the landscape. There are refinements that must be made, implications that must be discovered and then worked out. I hope that my contribution will make other men's tasks that much easier.

SELECT BIBLIOGRAPHY

SELECT
BIBLIOGRAPHY

Studies in Revelation

Barclay, William. *The Revelation of John*. 2 vols. Philadelphia: The Westminster Press, revised ed., 1960.

Beasley-Murray, G. R. *The Book of Revelation*. Grand Rapids: William B. Eerdmans Publishing Co., [1974] 1981.

Beckwith, Isbon T. *The Apocalypse of John: Studies in Introduction with a Critical and Exegetical Commentary*. Grand Rapids: Baker Book House, [1919] 1979.

Caird, G. B. *The Revelation of St. John the Divine*. New York: Harper and Row, Publishers, 1966.

Carrington, Philip. *The Meaning of the Revelation*. London: SPCK, 1931.

Charles, R. H. *A Critical and Exegetical Commentary on the Revelation of St. John*. 2 vols. Edinburgh: T. and T. Clark, 1920.

Corsini, Eugenio. *The Apocalypse: The Perennial Revelation of Jesus Christ*. Translated by Francis J. Moloney, S.D.B. Wilmington, DE: Michael Glazier, 1983.

Farrar, F. W. *The Early Days of Christianity*. Chicago: Belford, Clarke and Co., 1882.

Farrer, Austin. *A Rebirth of Images: The Making of St. John's Apocalypse*. London: Dacre Press, 1949; Gloucester, MA: Peter Smith, 1970.

_____. *The Revelation of St. John the Divine*. Oxford: At the Clarendon Press, 1964.

667

Ford, J. Massyngberde. *Revelation: Introduction, Translation, and Commentary.* Garden City, NY: Doubleday and Co., 1975.

Goldsworthy, Graeme. *The Lamb and the Lion: The Gospel in Revelation.* Nashville: Thomas Nelson Publishers, 1984.

Goulder, M. D. "The Apocalypse as an Annual Cycle of Prophecies," *New Testament Studies* 27, No. 3 (April 1981), pp. 342-67.

Hendriksen, William. *More Than Conquerors: An Interpretation of the Book of Revelation.* Grand Rapids: Baker Book House, 1939.

Hengstenberg, E. W. *The Revelation of St. John.* 2 vols. Translated by Patrick Fairbairn. Cherry Hill, NJ: Mack Publishing Co., [1851] 1972.

Hughes, Philip Edgcumbe. "The First Resurrection: Another Interpretation." *Westminster Theological Journal* 39 (Spring 1977) 2, pp. 315-18.

Jenkins, Ferrell. *The Old Testament in the Book of Revelation.* Grand Rapids: Baker Book House, [1972] 1976.

Johnson, Alan. *Revelation.* In Vol. 12 of *The Expositor's Bible Commentary,* edited by Frank E. Gaebelein. Grand Rapids: Zondervan Publishing House, 1981.

Kallas, James. *Revelation: God and Satan in the Apocalypse.* Minneapolis: Augsburg Publishing House, 1973.

King, Max. *The Spirit of Prophecy.* Warren, OH: Max King, 1971.

Leithart, Peter J. "Biblical-Theological Paper: Revelation 19:17-18." Westminster Theological Seminary, 1985.

Lenski, R. C. H. *The Interpretation of St. John's Revelation.* Minneapolis: Augsburg Publishing House, 1943, 1963.

Lindsey, Hal. *There's a New World Coming: A Prophetic Odyssey.* Eugene, OR: Harvest House Publishers, 1973.

MacDonald, James M. *The Life and Writings of St. John.* London: Hodder and Stoughton, 1877.

MacKnight, William J. *The Apocalypse: A Reappearance.* Boston: Hamilton Brothers, Publishers, 1927.

Makrakis, Apostolos. *Interpretation of the Book of Revelation.* Translated by A. G. Alexander. Chicago: The Orthodox Christian Educational Society, [1948] 1972.

Morris, Henry M. *The Revelation Record: A Scientific and Devotional Commentary on the Book of Revelation.* Wheaton: Tyndale House Publishers, 1983.

Morris, Leon. *The Revelation of St. John.* Grand Rapids: William B. Eerdmans Publishing Co., 1969.

Mounce, Robert H. *The Book of Revelation.* Grand Rapids: William B. Eerdmans Publishing Co., 1977.

Plummer, A. *The Revelation of St. John the Divine*. London: Funk and Wagnalls Co., n.d.

Ramsey, James B. *The Book of Revelation: An Exposition of the First Eleven Chapters*. Edinburgh: The Banner of Truth Trust, [1873] 1977.

Rudwick, M. J. S., and Green, E. M. B. "The Laodicean Lukewarmness," *Expository Times* 69 (1957-58).

Rushdoony, Rousas John. *Thy Kingdom Come: Studies in Daniel and Revelation*. Tyler, TX: Thoburn Press, [1970] 1978.

Russell, J. Stuart. *The Parousia: A Critical Inquiry into the New Testament Doctrine of Our Lord's Second Coming*. Grand Rapids: Baker Book House, [1887] 1983.

Shepherd, Massey H. Jr. *The Paschal Liturgy and the Apocalypse*. Richmond: John Knox Press, 1960.

Shepherd, Norman. "The Resurrections of Revelation 20." *Westminster Theological Journal* 37 (Fall 1974) 1, pp. 34-43.

Stonehouse, Ned B. *Paul Before the Areopagus, and other New Testament Studies*. Grand Rapids: William B. Eerdmans Publishing Co., 1957.

Stuart, Moses. *Commentary on the Apocalypse*. 2 vols. Andover: Allen, Morrill and Wardwell, 1845.

Sweet, J. P. M. *Revelation*. Philadelphia: The Westminster Press, 1979.

Swete, Henry Barclay. *Commentary on Revelation*. Grand Rapids: Kregel Publications, [1911] 1977.

Tenney, Merrill C. *Interpreting Revelation*. Grand Rapids: William B. Eerdmans Publishing Co., 1957.

Terry, Milton S. *Biblical Apocalyptics: A Study of the Most Notable Revelations of God and of Christ in the Canonical Scriptures*. New York: Eaton and Mains, 1898.

Vanderwaal, Cornelis. *Search the Scriptures*. 10 vols. St. Catherines, Ont.: Paideia Press, 1979.

Vanhoye, Albert. "L'utilisation du Livre d'Ezechiel dans l'Apocalypse," *Biblica* 43 (1962), pp. 436-76.

Victorinus. *Commentary on the Apocalypse of the Blessed John*. Translated by Robert Ernest Wallis. Alexander Roberts and James Donaldson, eds., *The Ante-Nicene Fathers*. Grand Rapids: William B. Eerdmans Publishing Co., 1970. Vol. VII, pp. 344-60.

Wallace, Foy E. Jr. *The Book of Revelation*. Fort Worth: Foy E. Wallace Jr. Publications, 1966.

Wilcock, Michael. *I Saw Heaven Opened: The Message of Revelation*. Downers Grove, IL: Inter-Varsity Press, 1975.

Related Studies

Adams, Jay. *The Time Is at Hand.* Nutley, NJ: The Presbyterian and Reformed Publishing Co., [1966] 1970.

Allen, Richard Hinckley. *Star Names: Their Lore and Meaning.* New York: Dover Publications, [1899] 1963.

Allis, Oswald T. *Prophecy and the Church.* Grand Rapids: Baker Book House, [1945] 1947.

Ambrose. *On the Mysteries.*

Athanasius. *On the Incarnation of the Word of God.*

_____. *Orations Against the Arians.*

Augustine, Aurelius. *Anti-Pelagian Works.* Translated by Peter Holmes and Robert Ernest Wallis. Grand Rapids: William B. Eerdmans Publishing Co., 1971.

_____. *The City of God.*

_____. *On the Trinity.*

Bahnsen, Greg L. *Theonomy in Christian Ethics.* Phillipsburg, NJ: The Presbyterian and Reformed Publishing Co., [1977] 1984.

_____. "The Person, Work, and Present Status of Satan." *The Journal of Christian Reconstruction*, edited by Gary North. Vol. 1, No. 2 (Winter, 1974).

_____. "The *Prima Facie* Acceptability of Postmillennialism." *The Journal of Christian Reconstruction*, Vol. 3, No. 2 (Winter, 1976-77).

Baldwin, Joyce G. *Haggai, Zechariah, Malachi: An Introduction and Commentary.* Downers Grove, IL: Inter-Varsity Press, 1972.

Barr, James. *Biblical Words for Time.* Naperville, IL: Alec R. Allenson Inc. Revised ed., 1969.

Bavinck, Herman. *The Doctrine of God.* Translated by William Hendriksen. Edinburgh: The Banner of Truth Trust, [1951] 1977.

Berkhof, Louis. *The History of Christian Doctrines.* Edinburgh: The Banner of Truth Trust, [1937] 1969.

_____. *Systematic Theology.* Grand Rapids: William B. Eerdmans Publishing Co., fourth revised ed., 1949.

Bettenson, Henry, ed. *Documents of the Christian Church.* Oxford: Oxford University Press, second ed., 1963.

_____. *The Early Christian Fathers: A Selection from the Writings of the Fathers from St. Clement of Rome to St. Athanasius.* Oxford: Oxford University Press, 1956.

_____. *The Later Christian Fathers: A Selection from the Writings of the Fathers from St. Cyril of Jerusalem to St. Leo the Great.* Oxford: Oxford University Press, [1970] 1977.

Boettner, Loraine. *The Millennium.* Philadelphia: The Presbyterian and Reformed Publishing Co., 1957; revised, 1984.

Boersma, T. *Is the Bible a Jigsaw Puzzle? An Evaluation of Hal Lindsey's Writings.* St. Catherines, Ont.: Paideia Press, 1978.

Bouyer, Louis. *Eucharist: Theology and Spirituality of the Eucharistic Prayer.* Notre Dame: University of Notre Dame Press, 1968.

_____. *Liturgical Piety.* Notre Dame: University of Notre Dame Press, 1955.

_____. *The Spirituality of the New Testament and the Fathers.* Minneapolis: The Seabury Press, 1963.

Brandon, S. G. F. *The Fall of Jerusalem and the Christian Church: A Study of the Effects of the Jewish Overthrow of A.D. 70 on Christianity.* London: SPCK, 1968.

Bray, Gerald. *Creeds, Councils, and Christ.* Downers Grove. IL: Inter-Varsity Press, 1984.

Brinsmead, Robert D. *The Pattern of Redemptive History.* Fallbrook, CA: Verdict Publications, 1979.

Brown, David. *Christ's Second Coming: Will It Be Premillennial?* Grand Rapids: Baker Book House, [1876] 1983.

Brown, John. *Expository Discourses on 1 Peter.* 2 vols. Edinburgh: The Banner of Truth Trust, [1848] 1975.

Bruce, F. F. *Commentary on the Epistle to the Colossians.* Grand Rapids: William B. Eerdmans Publishing Co., 1957.

Calvin, John. *Commentaries.* 45 vols. Grand Rapids: Baker Book House, 1979.

_____. *The Institutes of the Christian Religion.* Translated by Ford Lewis Battles. 2 vols. Philadelphia: The Westminster Press, 1960.

_____. *Selected Works: Tracts and Letters.* 7 vols. Edited by Henry Beveridge and Jules Bonnet. Grand Rapids: Baker Book House, 1983.

Campbell, Roderick. *Israel and the New Covenant.* Tyler, TX: Geneva Ministries, [1954] 1983.

Chilton, David. *Paradise Restored: A Biblical Theology of Dominion.* Ft. Worth, TX: Dominion Press, 1985.

Chrysostom, John. *Homilies on St. John.*

Clark, Gordon H. *Biblical Predestination.* Nutley, NJ: The Presbyterian and Reformed Publishing Co., 1969.

Cochrane, Charles Norris. *Christianity and Classical Culture: A Study of Thought and Action from Augustus to Augustine.* London: Oxford University Press, [1940, 1944] 1957.

Cronk, George. *The Message of the Bible: An Orthodox Christian Perspective.* Crestwood, NY: St. Vladimir's Seminary Press, 1982.

Cyprian. *On the Unity of the Church.*

The Didache (*The Teaching of the Twelve Apostles*).

Dix, Gregory. *The Shape of the Liturgy.* New York: The Seabury Press, [1945] 1983.

Douglas, Mary. *Implicit Meanings: Essays in Anthropology.* London: Routledge and Kegan Paul, 1975.

671

_____. *Purity and Danger: An Analysis of the Concepts of Pollution and Taboo.* London: Routledge and Kegan Paul, [1966] 1969.

Edersheim, Alfred. *The Life and Times of Jesus the Messiah.* 2 vols. McLean, VA: MacDonald Publishing Co., n.d.

_____. *The Temple: Its Ministry and Services as They Were at the Time of Christ.* Grand Rapids: William B. Eerdmans Publishing Co., 1980.

Eliade, Mircea. *The Myth of the Eternal Return: or, Cosmos and History.* Princeton: Princeton University Press, [1954] 1971.

Eusebius. *Ecclesiastical History.*

Fairbairn, Patrick. *The Interpretation of Prophecy.* Edinburgh: The Banner of Truth Trust, [1865] 1964.

Frend, W. H. C. *The Rise of Christianity.* Philadelphia: Fortress Press, 1984.

Gaston, Lloyd. *No Stone on Another: The Fall of Jerusalem in the Synoptic Gospels.* Leiden: E. J. Brill, 1970.

Goulder, M. D. *The Evangelists' Calendar: A Lectionary Explanation of the Development of Scripture.* London: SPCK, 1978.

Grant, Michael. *The Twelve Caesars.* New York: Charles Scribner's Sons, 1975.

Harnack, Adolf. *The Mission and Expansion of Christianity in the First Three Centuries.* Translated by James Moffat. Gloucester, MA: Peter Smith, [1908] 1972.

Harrison, R. K., ed. *Major Cities of the Biblical World.* Nashville: Thomas Nelson Publishers, 1985.

Irenaeus. *Against Heresies.*

Jordan, James B. "Christian Piety: Deformed and Reformed." *Geneva Papers* (New Series), No. 1 (September 1985).

_____. *Judges: God's War Against Humanism.* Tyler, TX: Geneva Ministries, 1985.

_____. *The Law of the Covenant: An Exposition of Exodus 21-23.* Tyler, TX: Institute for Christian Economics, 1984.

_____. "Rebellion, Tyranny, and Dominion in the Book of Genesis." In *Tactics of Christian Resistance,* Christianity and Civilization No. 3. Edited by Gary North. Tyler, TX: Geneva Ministries, 1983.

_____. *Sabbath-Breaking and the Death Penalty: A Theological Investigation.* Tyler, TX: Geneva Ministries, 1986.

_____. *The Sociology of the Church.* Tyler, TX: Geneva Ministries, 1986.

_____, ed. *The Failure of the American Baptist Culture* (Christianity and Civilization 1). Tyler, TX: Geneva Ministries, 1982.

_____, ed. *The Reconstruction of the Church* (Christianity and Civilization 4). Tyler, TX: Geneva Ministries, 1985.

Josephus, Flavius. *The Jewish War.* Edited by Gaalya Cornfeld. Grand Rapids: Zondervan Publishing House, 1982.

_____. *Works.* Translated by William Whiston. Four vols. Grand Rapids: Baker Book House, 1974.

Jungmann, Josef A., S.J. *The Early Liturgy to the Time of Gregory the Great.* Translated by Francis A. Brunner, C.SS.R. Notre Dame: University of Notre Dame Press, 1959.

Justin Martyr. *The First Apology.*

Kaiser, Walter C. Jr. "The Blessing of David: The Charter for Humanity." In *The Law and the Prophets: Old Testament Studies Prepared in Honor of Oswald Thompson Allis,* edited by John H. Skilton. Philadelphia: The Presbyterian and Reformed Publishing Co., 1974.

Kik, J. Marcellus. *An Eschatology of Victory.* Nutley, NJ: The Presbyterian and Reformed Publishing Co., 1971.

Kline, Meredith G. *By Oath Consigned: A Reinterpretation of the Covenant Signs of Circumcision and Baptism.* Grand Rapids: William B. Eerdmans Publishing Co., 1968.

_____. *Images of the Spirit.* Grand Rapids: Baker Book House, 1980.

_____. *Kingdom Prologue,* two vols. Privately published, 1981, 1983.

_____. *The Structure of Biblical Authority.* Grand Rapids: William B. Eerdmans Publishing Co., second ed., 1975.

_____. *Treaty of the Great King: The Covenant Structure of Deuteronomy.* Grand Rapids: William B. Eerdmans Publishing Co., 1963.

Kuyper, Abraham. *Lectures on Calvinism.* Grand Rapids: William B. Eerdmans Publishing Co., 1931.

Lecerf, Auguste. *An Introduction to Reformed Dogmatics.* Translated by André Schlemmer. Grand Rapids: Baker Book House, [1949] 1981.

Lee, Francis Nigel. *The Central Significance of Culture.* Nutley, NJ: The Presbyterian and Reformed Publishing Co., 1976.

Lewis, C. S. *The Weight of Glory: And Other Addresses.* New York: Macmillan Publishing Co., revised ed., 1980.

Lightfoot, J. B. *The Christian Ministry.* Edited by Philip Edgcumbe Hughes. Wilton, CT: Morehouse-Barlow Co., 1983.

Lindsey, Hal. *The Late Great Planet Earth.* Grand Rapids: Zondervan Publishing House, 1970.

MacGregor, Geddes. *Corpus Christi: The Nature of the Church According to the Reformed Tradition.* Philadelphia: The Westminster Press, 1958.

Mantzaridis, Georgios I. *The Deification of Man.* Translated by Liadain Sherrard. Crestwood, NY: St. Vladimir's Seminary Press, 1984.

Martin, Ernest L. *The Birth of Christ Recalculated.* Pasadena: Foundation for Biblical Research, 1980.

_____. *The Original Bible Restored.* Pasadena: Foundation for Biblical Research, 1984.

_____. *The Place of Christ's Crucifixion: Its Discovery and Significance.* Pasadena: Foundation for Biblical Research, 1984.

McGuiggan, Jim, and King, Max. *The McGuiggan-King Debate.* Warren, OH: Parkman Road Church of Christ, n.d.

McKelvey, R. J. "Temple." In J. D. Douglas, ed. *The New Bible Dictionary.* Grand Rapids: William B. Eerdmans Publishing Co., [1962] 1965, pp. 1242-50.

Minear, Paul. *Images of the Church in the New Testament.* Philadelphia: The Westminster Press, 1960.

Moore, Thomas V. *A Commentary on Haggai, Zechariah, and Malachi.* Edinburgh: The Banner of Truth Trust, [1856] 1968.

Morris, Leon. *Apocalyptic.* Grand Rapids: William B. Eerdmans Publishing Co., 1972.

_____. *The Apostolic Preaching of the Cross.* Grand Rapids: William B. Eerdmans Publishing Co., 1955.

Murray, Iain. *The Puritan Hope: A Study in Revival and the Interpretation of Prophecy.* Edinburgh: The Banner of Truth Trust, 1971.

Murray, John. *Collected Writings.* 4 vols. Edinburgh: The Banner of Truth Trust, 1976-82.

_____. *The Epistle to the Romans.* 2 vols. Grand Rapids: William B. Eerdmans Publishing Co., 1968.

_____. *The Imputation of Adam's Sin.* Nutley, NJ: The Presbyterian and Reformed Publishing Co., [1959] 1977.

_____. *Redemption: Accomplished and Applied.* Grand Rapids: William B. Eerdmans Publishing Co., 1955.

Negev, Avraham, ed. *The Archaeological Encyclopedia of the Holy Land.* Nashville: Thomas Nelson Publishers, revised ed., 1986.

Nisbet, Robert. *History of the Idea of Progress.* New York: Basic Books, 1980.

North, Gary. *Backward, Christian Soldiers? An Action Manual for Christian Reconstruction.* Tyler, TX: Institute for Christian Economics, 1984.

_____. *Conspiracy: A Biblical View.* Fort Worth: Dominion Press, 1986.

_____. *The Dominion Covenant: Genesis.* Tyler, TX: Institute for Christian Economics, 1982.

_____. *Moses and Pharaoh: Dominion Religion Versus Power Religion*. Tyler, TX: Institute for Christian Economics, 1985.

_____. *The Sinai Strategy: Economics and the Ten Commandments*. Tyler, TX: Institute for Christian Economics, 1986.

_____. *Unconditional Surrender: God's Program for Victory*. Tyler, TX: Geneva Ministries, 1983.

_____. *Unholy Spirits: Occultism and New Age Humanism*. Fort Worth: Dominion Press, 1986.

_____, ed. *Foundations of Christian Scholarship: Essays in the Van Til Perspective*. Vallecito, CA: Ross House Books, 1976.

_____, ed. Symposium on the Millennium. *The Journal of Christian Reconstruction*, Vol. III, No. 2 (Winter, 1976-77).

Owen, John. *An Exposition of the Epistle to the Hebrews*. 7 vols. Edited by W. H. Goold. Grand Rapids: Baker Book House, [1855] 1980.

_____. *Works*. 16 vols. Edited by W. H. Goold. London: The Banner of Truth Trust, [1850-53] 1965-68.

Paher, Stanley W. *If Thou Hadst Known*. Las Vegas: Nevada Publications, 1978.

Paquier, Richard. *Dynamics of Worship: Foundations and Uses of Liturgy*. Philadelphia: Fortress Press, 1967.

Pfeiffer, Charles F., and Vos, Howard F. *The Wycliffe Historical Geography of Bible Lands*. Chicago: Moody Press, 1967.

Plumptre, E. H. *Ezekiel*. London: Funk and Wagnalls Co., n.d.

Ridderbos, Herman. *The Coming of the Kingdom*. St. Catherines, Ont.: Paideia Press, [1962] 1978.

Roberts, Alexander, and Donaldson, James, eds. *The Ante-Nicene Fathers*. 10 vols. Grand Rapids: William B. Eerdmans Publishing Co., 1970.

Robinson, John A. T. *Redating the New Testament*. Philadelphia: The Westminster Press, 1976.

Rushdoony, Rousas John. *The Biblical Philosophy of History*. Nutley, NJ: The Craig Press, 1969.

_____. *The Foundations of Social Order: Studies in the Creeds and Councils of the Early Church*. Tyler, TX: Thoburn Press, [1968] 1978.

_____. *The Institutes of Biblical Law*. Nutley, NJ: The Craig Press, 1973.

_____. *The Mythology of Science*. Nutley, NJ: The Presbyterian and Reformed Publishing Co., 1967.

_____. *The One and the Many: Studies in the Philosophy of Order and Ultimacy*. Tyler, TX: Thoburn Press, [1971] 1978.

_____. *Salvation and Godly Rule*. Vallecito, CA: Ross House Books, 1983.

675

Ryken, Leland. *How to Read the Bible as Literature.* Grand Rapids: Zondervan, 1984.

Santillana, Giorgio de, and Dechend, Hertha von. *Hamlet's Mill: An Essay on Myth and the Frame of Time.* Ipswich: Gambit, 1969.

Schaeffer, Francis A. *The Church Before the Watching World.* Downers Grove, IL: InterVarsity Press, 1971.

Schaff, Philip. *The Principle of Protestantism.* Translated by John W. Nevin. Philadelphia: United Church Press, [1845] 1964.

Schaff, Philip, ed. *A Select Library of the Nicene and Post-Nicene Fathers of the Christian Church.* 14 vols. Grand Rapids: William B. Eerdmans Publishing Co., 1969.

Schaff, Philip, and Wace, Henry, eds. *A Select Library of Nicene and Post-Nicene Fathers of the Christian Church: Second Series.* 14 vols. Grand Rapids: William B. Eerdmans Publishing Co., 1971.

Schlossberg, Herbert. *Idols for Destruction: Christian Faith and Its Confrontation with American Society.* Nashville: Thomas Nelson Publishers, 1983.

Schmemann, Alexander. *Church, World, Mission: Reflections on Orthodoxy in the West.* Crestwood, NY: St. Vladimir's Seminary Press, 1979.

_____. *For the Life of the World: Sacraments and Orthodoxy.* Crestwood, NY: St. Vladimir's Seminary Press, revised ed., 1979.

_____. *Introduction to Liturgical Theology.* Crestwood, NY: St. Vladimir's Seminary Press, 1966.

Seiss, Joseph A. *The Gospel in the Stars.* Grand Rapids: Kregel Publications, [1882] 1972.

Severus, Sulpitius. *Sacred History.*

Stauffer, Ethelbert. *Christ and the Caesars.* Philadelphia: The Westminster Press, 1955.

Suetonius. *The Twelve Caesars.*

Sutton, Ray R. *That You May Prosper: Dominion By Covenant.* Tyler, TX: Institute for Christian Economics, 1987.

Symington, William. *Messiah the Prince: or, The Mediatorial Dominion of Jesus Christ.* Philadelphia: The Christian Statesman Publishing Co., [1839] 1884.

Tacitus, Cornelius. *The Annals of Imperial Rome.*

_____. *The Histories.*

Telford, William. *The Barren Temple and the Withered Tree.* Sheffield: Department of Biblical Studies, University of Sheffield, 1980.

Terry, Milton S. *Biblical Hermeneutics: A Treatise on the Interpretation of the Old and New Testaments.* Grand Rapids: Zondervan Publishing House, 1974.

Tertullian. *Against Marcion.*

_____. *The Apology.*

Thurian, Max. *The Mystery of the Eucharist: An Ecumenical Approach.* Grand Rapids: William B. Eerdmans Publishing Co., 1984.

Toon, Peter. *The Ascension of Our Lord.* Nashville: Thomas Nelson Publishers, 1984.

_____. *Heaven and Hell: A Biblical and Theological Overview.* Nashville: Thomas Nelson Publishers, 1986.

Torrance, T. F. *Royal Priesthood.* Edinburgh: Oliver and Boyd Ltd., 1955.

Vandervelde, George, "The Gift of Prophecy and the Prophetic Church." Toronto: Institute for Christian Studies, 1984.

Vanderwaal, Cornelis. *Hal Lindsey and Bible Prophecy.* St. Catherines, Ont.: Paideia Press, 1978.

VanGemeren, Willem A. "Israel as the Hermeneutical Crux in the Interpretation of Prophecy." *The Westminster Theological Journal,* 45 (1983), pp. 132-44; 46 (1984), pp. 254-97.

Van Til, Cornelius. *Apologetics.* Philadelphia: Westmister Theological Seminary class syllabus, 1959.

_____. *Common Grace and the Gospel.* Nutley, NJ: The Presbyterian and Reformed Publishing Co., 1972.

_____. *The Defense of the Faith.* Philadelphia: The Presbyterian and Reformed Publishing Co., third revised ed., 1967.

_____. *Introduction to Systematic Theology.* Philadelphia: The Presbyterian and Reformed Publishing Co., 1974.

Vos, Geerhardus. *Biblical Theology: Old and New Testaments.* Grand Rapids: William B. Eerdmans Publishing Co., 1948.

_____. *The Pauline Eschatology.* Grand Rapids: Baker Book House, [1930] 1979.

_____. *Redemptive History and Biblical Interpretation: The Shorter Writings of Geerhardus Vos.* Edited by Richard B. Gaffin Jr. Phillipsburg, NJ: Presbyterian and Reformed Publishing Co., 1980.

Wallace, Ronald S. *Calvin's Doctrine of the Christian Life.* Tyler, TX: Geneva Ministries, [1959] 1982.

_____. *Calvin's Doctrine of the Word and Sacrament.* Tyler, TX: Geneva Ministries, [1953] 1982.

Warfield, Benjamin B. *Biblical Doctrines.* New York: Oxford University Press, 1929.

_____. *Biblical and Theological Studies.* Philadelphia: The Presbyterian and Reformed Publishing Co., 1968.

_____. *The Plan of Salvation.* Grand Rapids: William B. Eerdmans Publishing Co., 1984.

_____. *Selected Shorter Writings.* 2 vols. Edited by John E. Meeter. Nutley, NJ: The Presbyterian and Reformed Publishing Co., 1973.

Webber, Robert E. *Worship: Old and New.* Grand Rapids: Zondervan Publishing House, 1982.

Weeks, Noel. "Admonition and Error in Hebrews." *The Westminster Theological Journal* 39 (Fall 1976) 1, pp. 72-80.

Wenham, Gordon J. *The Book of Leviticus.* Grand Rapids: William B. Eerdmans Publishing Co., 1979.

_____. *Numbers: An Introduction and Commentary.* Downers Grove, IL: Inter-Varsity Press, 1981.

Woodrow, Ralph. *His Truth Is Marching On: Advanced Studies on Prophecy in the Light of History.* Riverside, CA: Ralph Woodrow Evangelistic Association, 1977.

SCRIPTURE INDEX

OLD TESTAMENT

(Boldface entries indicate that a passage has been quoted or discussed at length)

Genesis	
1	16, 173, 273, 305, 361, 478
1:1	306n
1:1-5	288, 289
1:2	222, 244, 320, 327
1:4	173
1:5	573
1:7	197n
1:8	573
1:10	173
1:12	173
1:13	573
1:14	197, 553
1:16	197, 489, 553
1:18	173
1:19	573
1:20-25	306
1:21	173, 304
1:23	573
1:24-31	345
1:25	173
1:26	327
1:26-28	306, 510
1:27	306n
1:27-28	543
1:28	370, 625, 635, 647
1:29	288
1:31	173, 304, 347n, 573
2	361
2:2-3	70
2:6	566
2:7	283, 344
2:7-8	341
2:9	288
2:10	16
2:10-12	557
2:10-14	566
2:11-12	429
2:12	110, 556
2:15	78n, 86, 576
2:16-17	288
2:17	115
2:19-20	341
3:1-5	69n, 304
3:1-6	337
3:1-15	314

Genesis	
3:5	451
3:6	432
3:7	136
3:8	**71, 86, 198**
3:13	337
3:13-15	304
3:14	307
3:15	29, 38, 298, 307, 330
3:17-18	446
3:17-19	**633, 662**
3:19	31, 131, 279
3:21	136, 279
3:22-24	126
3:24	86, 555, 576
4:1	483
4:3-8	282
4:10	194
4:15	632
4:25	307
5:5	514
5:25	514n, 644n
5:27	644n
5:28	514n
5:28-29	644n
6:1-8	514n
6:1-10	307
7:1	514n
7:6	514n, 644n
7:11	244
7:22	157
8:1	203
8:2	244
8:13	288
8:20-21	186
8:22	157
9:1-7	635, 647
9:13-16	167
9:13-17	186
9:27	514
11:1-9	431
11:9	422
12:10-20	307
14:14	613
14:22	264
15	489n
15:5	214, 215
15:9-12	241
15:11	489

Genesis	
15:16	195, 631
15:17	64
15:18	250
17:7-8	549
17:10-14	613
18	645
18:2	479
19	645
19:1	479
19:13	449
19:21-22	646
19:24-25	365, 525, 529
19:24-28	395
19:26	645
19:28	232, 365, 453, 472, 529
19:30-38	198, 645
20:1-18	307
21	373
21:8-14	131
21:9	87
22:1-14	87
22:2	354
22:6	232
22:16	264
22:17	525
22:17-18	215
23	282
23:7	479
23:12	479
25:22-23	307
26:1-11	307
26:5	489n
27	307
27:29	479
27:37	614
28:10-12	422
28:12	260
29:31-30:24	211
31:45	264
31:52	264
32:12	525
33:3	479
33:6-7	479
35:16-18	211
37:5-11	296
37:7	479
37:9	81, 159, 301
37:9-10	479

NEW TESTAMENT

694

SCRIPTURE INDEX

Revelation

2:18	90, **112**
2:18-29	46, **87-88, 90,** **111-18**
2:19	69, 550
2:19-20	**112-14**
2:20	97n, 258, 439, 499, 550
2:20-22	356, 550
2:20-23	431
2:20-24	471
2:21	258
2:21-23	**114-15**
2:23	533, 577
2:24	499
2:24-25	**115-16**
2:25	410
2:26	187
2:26-27	117n, 151, 514, 518, 579
2:26-28	488
2:26-29	85, **116-18**
2:27	1n
2:28	579
3	**119-39**
3:1	90, **119-20,** 343
3:1-6	46, **88, 119-25**
3:2	410
3:2-3	**120-21**
3:3	96, 410, 542
3:4	1n
3:4-5	195, 410
3:5	85, 187, 339, 488, 533
3:6	122
3:7	90, **126-27**
3:7-13	46, **88, 125-32**
3:8-9	**127-28**
3:9	151, 256, 332, 479, 499, 550, 578
3:10	69, 109, 129, 219, 361, 405, 428
3:10-11	**128-30**
3:11	96, 151, 187n, 282, 410, 509, 575
3:12	85, 187, 272, 342, 355, 389, 430, 488, 545, 546, 561, 570, 578, 599
3:12-13	**130-32**
3:14	91, **132-33,** 264, 475, 481, 482, 574, 580
3:14-22	46, 56, **88-89,** **132-39,** 482
3:15-16	**134-35**
3:16	322n
3:17	482
3:18	122, 410, 482
3:19-20	**136-39**

Revelation

3:20	**24,** 153, 482
3:20-21	579
3:21	85, 151, **187,** 488, 321
3:21-22	**139**
4	21, **145-64,** 168, 594, 596, 597, 610
4-7	17, 20, 46, **89,** 158
4:1	**146-49,** 284, 326, 507, 611
4:1-11	46, **145-64**
4:2	148, 552
4:2-3	149-51, 529, 554
4:3	186, 260, 557
4:3-4	429
4:4	122, **151-54,** 152, 177, 187n, 350, 475, **508,** 509, 510n, 518
4:4-6	611
4:4-11	318, 472
4:5	58n, 78, 91, 184, 276, 574
4:5-8	**154-60,** 204n
4:6	156, 384, 392
4:6-8	429
4:7	156, 241, 301n, 389
4:8	221, 366, 611
4:9-11	**160-64**
4:10	152, 187n, 339, 510n, 611
5	21, 143, 165-80, 594, 597, 605, 610
5:1	529
5:1-4	**166-69,** 181
5:1-5	46
5:2	460
5:5	152, **187,** 262n, 504, 510n, 578
5:5-6	72, 147, 213
5:5-7	**169-74**
5:6	1n, 58n, 78, 152, 155, 183, 354, 510n, **598,** 611
5:6-11	359-60
5:6-14	46
5:7	152, 510n, 529
5:8	78, 230, 231, 273, 339, 390, 518, 550, 611
5:8-10	**174-79**
5:8-14	318
5:9	151, 153n, 356, 401, 605
5:9-10	64
5:10	273, 509, 514, 518

Revelation

5:11	152, 507, 510n
5:11-14	178, **179-80**
5:14	152, 510n, 611
6	143, **181-99,** 610
6:1	481, 521n, 579
6:1-2	182, **185-88**
6:1-8	21, 46, 183, 213
6:2	184, 185, **187,** 529
6:3	579
6:3-4	182, **188-89**
6:4	185
6:4-5	185
6:5	579
6:5-6	182, **189-91**
6:7	579
6:7-8	182, **191-92**
6:8	184, 185, 534
6:9	41, 62, 389, **512,** 598
6:9-10	**193-95,** 273
6:9-11	21, 46, 182, 197n, 239, 402, 469
6:9-17	192-93
6:10	129, 185n, 201, 300n
6:11	122, 185, **195-96**
6:12	285, 413
6:12-13	184
6:12-14	**196-97**
6:12-17	21, 46, 182, 347n
6:14	184, 541
6:15	185
6:15-17	**197-99**
6:16	246, 417
7	21, 30, 143, **201-24,** 218, 381, 559, 610
7:1	183, 197
7:1-3	**203-6**
7:1-8	46, 201, **202-12,** 273
7:2	185, 300n
7:2-4	342
7:2-8	355
7:3	181, 191, 236, 355, 430, 570
7:4-8	**206-13,** 246, 296, 355, 507
7:5	559
7:5-8	555
7:9	122, **213-18,** 270, 339, 475, 611
7:9-17	46, 201, **212-24,** 318
7:10	**218-19,** 300n, 611
7:11	152, 339, 510n
7:11-12	**219**
7:13	122, 152, 510n

697

THE DAYS OF VENGEANCE

700

AUTHOR INDEX

701

AUTHOR INDEX

703

SUBJECT INDEX

as Beginning of Creation, 133
birth of, 298-300, 308-9
body of. *See* Bride of Christ; Church
Bow of, 186-87
as Branch. See Branch, Christ as
as Bridegroom, 45, 381-82. *See also* Bride of
    Christ
Caesar vs., 8-9. *See also* Beast; Nero;
    Roman Empire; Rome
coming of, 64-67, 109, 121, 130, 410, 575,
    577. *See also* First Coming of Christ
commandments of. *See* Law of God
as Conqueror, 169-70, 180, 188, 224, 315-17.
    See also Jesus Christ, victory of
deity of, 77
as First and Last. *See* First and Last
as Firstborn from dead, 61, 62, 63
as High Priest. *See* High Priest(s), Christ as
as Judge, 192, 529-31
kingdom of, 10, 43, 117, 494, 508-19, 545
as King of Kings, 62-64, 117, 192, 246,
    354-55, 488-89
as Lamb, 18, 29, 171-73. *See also* Lamb of
    God
as Lampstand, 72
as Lion, 29, 169-70
lordship of, 9-10, 39-40, 43-44, 50, 60,
    105-6, 290
mediatorial reign of, 493-94. *See also*
    Ascension; Millennium
as Michael, 311-18. *See also* Michael
as Prophet, *See* Prophet, Christ as
redemptive work of, 50
reigning with, 508-19
as Root of David, 170-71, 578-79
time of birth of, 301-3
victory of, 215-16, 223, 459
voice of, 75, 146, 154, 262
warfare of, 481-92
as Witness, 61-62, 133, 481
Jewish War, The (Josephus), 225, 246
Jews, 100, 265. *See also* Israel; Jerusalem;
    Judaism
apostate, 126, 253. *See also* Satan,
    synagogue of
carnage of, 439-40
church at enmity with, 103, 106. *See also*
    Church, Israel's enmity toward
condemnation of, 128
demons as scourge of, 245
demons worshiped by, 256. *See also*
    Jerusalem, demons in
hardness of, 255, 257
identity of modern, 613-14
influence of, 438-39
leaders of, as beast, 337-38
orthodox, 102

Palestine and, 613
synagogues of, 341, 344, 438-39
true vs. false, 101-3, 127-28
Jezebel, 87, 88, 90, 101, 379, 439, 471
Job, 103, 342
Jochebed, 299
John, Apostle
    background of, 2-3
    in the Spirit, 70-71
    style of, 26
    worldview of, 26, 67-69
John the Baptizer, 276, 277-78, 361, 375, 512
Jonah, 11, 244
Jordan River, 407
Joseph, 87, 212, 479
Joshua (priest), 276, 314
Joshua (son of Nun), 217, 278, 380, 411, 524
Josiah, 411
Judah, 212
    Christ as lion of, 169-70
    house of, 308
    Lion of, 158, 159
Judaism, 585
    apostate, 106, 336-38
    Christian Zionism and messianic, 612-19
    messianic, 619-21
    Pharisaical, 88
    reprobate, 448-49
    Talmud and, 618
Judas, 123
Judas Maccabaeus, 217
Judgment(s), 64-66, 115. *See also* Jerusalem,
    destruction of
    on Christians, 236-37. *See also* Suffering
    common grace and final, 646-48
    day of, 408, 409, 540. *See also* Last Day
    in Eden, 71
    on Jews, 128, 184-85, 189-92, 373-74. *See
        also* Land, the
    Last, 495, 504, 529-34
    nature of, 268-69, 285, 373
    praise and, 470
    prayer for, 194-95, 239, 249-50, 374,
        459
    seven, of sixth seal, 196-97
    signs of, 253-55
Julian the Apostate, 655
Julius Caesar. *See* Caesar, Julius
Jupiter, Temple of, 406
Justification, 122, 136
    faith and, 533
    works and, 533

Key(s)
    of David, 90, 126
    of Death and Hades, 77-78, 90, 499
Khazars, 613-14

713